ALAN ROGERS'
GOOD CAMPS GUIDE

FRANCE
2001

Quality Camping and Caravanning Sites

THE ALAN ROGERS'

Good camps guide

Compiled by: Deneway Guides & Travel Ltd

Cover design: Design Section, Frome

Cover photography: 'Field of Sunflowers', Telegraph Colour Library

Maps created by Customised Mapping (01985 844092)
and containing background data provided by Gis DATA Ltd.
Maps are © Customised Mapping and GisDATA Ltd 2000

Clive Edwards, Lois Edwards & Sue Smart have asserted
their rights to be identified as the authors of this work.

First published in this format 2000

© Haynes Publishing & Deneway Guides & Travel Ltd 2000

Published by: Haynes Publishing, Sparkford, Nr Yeovil, Somerset BA22 7JJ
in association with
Deneway Guides & Travel Ltd, West Bexington, Dorchester, Dorset DT2 9DG

British Library Cataloguing-in-Publication Data:
A catalogue record for this book is available from the British Library.

ISBN: 0 901586 77 3

Printed in Great Britain by J H Haynes & Co Ltd

Contents

Introduction

The new Millennium started sadly for us when we heard that our founder, Alan Rogers, had died. Alan was 81 years of age when he died in January, and although he had no day-to-day involvement with the Guides for many years, we had remained friends, and he could always be relied upon to provide wise counsel when needed for advice as an 'eminence grise'.

Alan published the first of the Guides that still bear his name back in 1968, introducing it with the words "I would like to stress that the camps which are included in this book have been chosen entirely on merit, and no payment of any sort is made by them for their inclusion".

As campers and caravanners ourselves it was this objective approach that attracted us to become regular readers of his Guides, and which eventually lead to our taking over the editing and publishing of the Guides when Alan retired in 1986. Whilst the content and scope of the Guides have expanded considerably in the fourteen years since we took over, mainly due to the huge growth in the number of campsites throughout the UK and Europe during those years, our selection of sites to be featured still employs exactly the same philosophy as Alan defined almost thirty years ago.

We would like to take this opportunity to pay tribute to Alan, and to thank him for providing us with the opportunity to enjoy what must be one of the most interesting jobs in Tourism.

The Alan Rogers' Approach to Selecting Sites

There are over 9,000 officially recognised campsites in France, plus a further 2,000 or so farm sites, etc, so to an extent the camper or caravanner in France is spoiled for choice. In fact the huge number of sites from which to choose is actually a serious problem as the facilities available, and more importantly the quality of those thousands of campsites varies from the excellent to the downright poor, so any campsite guide that lists all these sites is less than really helpful.

By including only a select number of sites, all of which have been inspected by our own team of professional Inspectors, the Alan Rogers' Guide is specifically designed to help you to choose sites which meet you and your family's needs. Our selection of sites includes not just the most expensive ones, but a range of sites designed to cater for a wide variety of preferences, from those seeking a small peaceful campsite in the heart of the French countryside, to those looking for an 'all singing, all dancing' site in a popular seaside resort, and for those with more specific needs such as sports facilities, cultural or historical attractions, even sites for naturists.

The criteria which we use when selecting sites are rigorous, but the most important by far is the question of 'quality' – whatever the size of the site, whether it's part of a campsite chain, or even a municipal site makes no difference in terms of it being required to meet our exacting standards in terms of its quality – in other words, irrespective of the size of the site or the number of facilities offered, the essentials (the welcome, the pitches, the sanitary facilities and the maintenance) must all be of a good standard.

Since none of the campsites have to pay to be featured in our guides, we are free to select exactly those which we think our readers will enjoy, to reject any that don't meet our standards and to write our own honest descriptions. This is an on-going process and depends on sites not only meeting our standards when they're initially selected, but also on their continuing to do so year after year. Looking back over our guides for the past thirty years provides an illuminating insight into just how much standards have changed. Many sites that were able to meet our standards in years past are no longer able to do so now and have therefore been 'dropped' in favour of better ones - one very good reason, amongst several, for making sure you have the latest edition of the Guide rather than an out-of-date one!

As you will see, and hopefully appreciate, unlike most other guides we don't rely on 'icons' or symbols to describe the sites featured in our Guides – partly because we prefer to write our descriptions in plain English, and partly because it is virtually impossible to express an opinion about the quality, or the ambience, for example by means of symbols. Those candid descriptions and opinions are what makes the Alan Rogers Guides unique. We also aim to provide a geographical spread that is as wide as possible within the confines of our selection process. We do find that at sites in very popular tourist destinations or city locations and those with direct access to a beach, standards can sometimes be a little variable due to the heavy demands on them. We have to balance the need for a site in that area with the maintenance of standards.

This year our team of assessors have been very busy in France and achieved a record number of visits. We have also been out and about ourselves, but our thanks are due to them for the many miles they travel, their patience with our detailed site reports and their commitment to the philosophy of the guides.

4

Hints on using the Alan Rogers Guides

Being written in plain English, our guides are exceptionally easy to use, but a few words of explanation regarding the layout, etc. may be helpful.

Regular readers will see that this year our Site Reports are grouped into sixteen 'tourist regions' and then by the various départements in each of these regions in numerical order.

Regions and départements

For administrative purposes France is actually divided into 23 official Regions, but these do not always coincide with the needs of tourists (for example the area we think of as 'The Dordogne' is split between two of the official Regions. We have, therefore, opted to feature our campsites within unofficial 'tourist regions' although we have of course subdivided these into the official French 'départements', each of which has an official number. For example, the département of Manche is number 50. We have used these département numbers as the first two digits of our campsite numbers, so any campsite in the Manche département will start with the number 50.

On pages 302-304 you will find maps that show the official regions and the départements, with the number of each département, along with a map showing the Tourist Regions that we have used in this guide and the départements in each.

Indexes

Not one, but three: On pages 290-292 you will find an index of towns where the campsites are situated.
On pages 293-296 you will find each campsite indexed by its Number.
On pages 297-301 you will find each campsite indexed by its Region.

Campsite Maps

The maps that appear on pages 306-320 relate to the Tourist Regions that we have used. The approximate position of each campsite is indicated on the map by a circle, next to which is the site number. The maps are intended to help you find the approximate location of campsites, not to navigate by. Each Site Report includes succinct directions for finding the site, based on the assumption that you will be using a proper road map, such as a Michelin or Collins atlas. All distances are shown in kilometres and metres.

The Site Reports

These are really self-explanatory, but please remember that all prices shown are per night, and all telephone numbers assume that you are 'phoning from within France. If you need to telephone France from outside that country you will need to prefix the number shown with the relevant International Code (00 33) and to drop the first 0, shown as (0) in the telephone numbers indicated in the guide.

Example of an entry:

---

number site name, nearest village, town

These details should identify the site's location to within a mile or so on any medium scale map - finer details are given in the directions section at the foot of the main report.

summary line

main text

A description of the site in which we try to give an idea of its general features - its size, its situation, its strengths and weaknesses, the quality and adequacy of the toilet block, special amenities and any special local attractions. Some things may be assumed unless the report states otherwise: that the toilet block has free hot showers, hot water in washbasins, mirrors, some razor points and chemical toilet disposal, and that dogs are accepted on leads. Throughout the reports the word 'site' is used in the sense of the campsite itself, not your individual place on the site, which we have called a 'pitch'. Practically all our sites now have electrical connections to some pitches and we include details of the amperage available. We try to tell you if the site does not take any particular type of normal touring unit - caravans, motorcaravans and tents - however, if you have an unusual unit (e.g. American motorhome or commercial vehicle) it is advisable to check with the site first to make sure that there are no special restrictions.

Directions:

Separated from the main text in order that they may be read and assimilated more easily by a navigator en route. Bear in mind that road improvement schemes can result in some road numbers being altered.

Charges

Open

Address

Tel
Fax
E-mail
(if available)

Reservations
General administrative detail is given in the right hand column.

Reservations

Except during the high season (roughly mid-July to mid-August) and in very popular tourist areas, whether to book your campsite in advance or not is very much a question of personal preference. If you do decide to book in advance there are several alternative methods.

In 2000 we introduced our own Alan Rogers Travel Service (see below and advertisement opposite page 64, or our web site at **www.alanrogers.com**) whereby you can book at more than 150 of the sites featured in this guide, each marked with the logo shown below. If you book your ferry and pitch at the same time you can be confident of saving both time and trouble by using our Travel Service. Alternatively you could decide to book a package through one of the Clubs or tour operators who advertise in our guides, and with whom our readers have been very satisfied for many years.

On the other hand you could go to the other extreme, be wholly independent, and contact the campsite(s) of your choice direct, using the telephone, fax or e-mail numbers shown in the site reports, but please bear in mind that many sites are closed throughout the winter.

Insurance

An important and quite complicated subject which is described in detail on page 271. An application form for our special Insure4Europe arrangements for readers is between pages 256/257.

Points to bear in mind

Our experiences when travelling early or late in the season have made us realise that some French site owners are very laid back when it comes to opening and closing dates. They may not be fully ready by their opening date – grass and hedges may not all be cut and perhaps only limited sanitary facilities open. At the end of the season they also tend to close down part of the facilities and generally wind down prior to the closing date (they are wanting to depart for their own holiday). This is worth bearing in mind if you are travelling early or late in the season.

The new 'Camping Cheque' system has gone some way to addressing this situation as it requires those campsites participating in the system to guarantee to have all facilities open and functioning by the opening date and to remain fully operational until the closing date. Further details are to be found in the colour advert opposite page 160 and sites participating are identified in the site reports.

Another area which has caused readers problems is the regulations which exist in some regions whereby Bermuda shorts may not be worn in swimming pools (for health reasons). It is worth ensuring the you do take 'proper' swimming trunks with you.

In 2000 we started our own escorted holidays for caravanners and, in association with the Motor Caravanners' Club, for motorcaravanners too (ideal for first-timers). Run by the Alan Rogers Travel Service in association with Four Seasons Touring, you are escorted throughout by experienced caravan journalists Dave and Liz King. Not only are these holidays escorted, but they also offer you the chance to experience a number of 'Flavour of France' optional excursions as well!

Whether you're an 'old hand' in terms of camping or caravanning in France, or contemplating your first caravanning holiday abroad, a regular reader of our Guides or a new reader, we hope that you will find this latest edition has plenty to interest you and to help you to make the most appropriate choices for your holiday in 2001.

Bonnes Vacances!

Lois Edwards MAEd, FTS
Clive Edwards BEd, FTS
Sue Smart   Directors

THE ALAN ROGERS'
travel service

THE ALAN ROGERS TRAVEL SERVICE

This unique service enables our readers to book stays at over 150 of the best sites in this guide (as well as many other sites throughout Europe) along with channel crossings and comprehensive insurance cover at extremely competitive rates. One simple call to our Travel Service on 01892 55 98 98 is all that is needed to make all the arrangements. Why not take advantage of our years of experience of camping and caravanning in France. We would be delighted to discuss your holiday plans with you, and offer advice and recommendations.

All the sites included in the special Travel Service programme have been carefully selected and we believe that we are able to offer the widest selection of sites in France, ranging from the most sophisticated 'Castels et Camping' sites to delightful, rural municipal sites. In establishing our programme, we have ensured a selection of sites in every corner of France, and, as well as offering sites in well known areas and well established resorts, we have also sought to include some superb sites in little known areas.

In brief, on the following page, is a summary by region of what we are able to offer for 2001:

The Alan Rogers' Travel Service

Brittany
30 sites in five Breton départements. Many are close to charming resorts, ideal for taking advantage of super sandy beaches, others offer the opportunity to discover the wooded valleys and villages of the less known hinterland.

Normandy
6 excellent sites ranging from the superb beaches of the Cotentin peninsula to the stylish resorts of the Côte Fleurie, as well as sites surrounded by the cider and calvados producing orchards for which the region is famous.

Northern France
4 sites in a relatively little known region embracing the sandy beaches of Picardy and the often-overlooked Pas-de-Calais which, as well as being very close to the UK has much else of interest.

Paris / Ile de France
Paris needs no introduction but there is much else to discover in the Ile de France - magnificent chateaux and hidden valleys and recently, the late 20th century monuments of Disneyland Paris and Parc Asterix. 3 sites.

Eastern France
3 sites in another often overlooked region. Why not visit the great champagne vineyards around Reims or the wooded valleys and rolling hills further east, rising up to the Vosges mountains and the border with Germany.

Vendée Charente
19 sites in one of France's best loved holiday regions. It's hard to beat the fine sandy beaches of this region, often backed by fragrant pines and lively resorts. Inland, world-class vineyards extend to the horizon.

Loire Valley
Just a few hours' drive from many of the channel ports. But this region, bisected by the great River Loire, boasts some of France's finest mediaeval towns and chateaux, most picturesque villages and elegant cities. 10 sites

Burgundy
This region claims to be the heartland of France. Best known for some of the world's finest wines, it also boasts an array of magnificent architecture and evocative mediaeval towns. 4 sites.

Jura / Alpes
This region stretches from the dense forests and rolling hills of the Jura to the Savoy - Dauphiny, one of the world's foremost winter sports areas, but also with much to offer in summer and major spa towns like Annecy and Aix-les-Bains on hand for relaxation. 10 sites

Atlantic Coast
A good choice of 11 sites in a vast region of endless sandy beaches, backed by one of Europe's largest forests, and with the Pyrénées rising spectacularly to the south.

Dordogne / Aveyron
17 sites nestling within the beautiful valleys and honey-coloured villages of the Dordogne and Vezere, and descending to the spectacular gorges of the Tarn and Truyère.

Limousin / Auvergne
3 sites in this thinly populated rural region which has much the same appeal as the Dordogne but with much still to be discovered, including awe-inspiring extinct volcanoes, lakes, rivers and forests.

Rhône Valley
One of France's most varied regions; from the dramatic gorges of the Ardèche and the mountains of the Vercors, to the Beaujolais vineyards by way of Lyon, the nation's second city. 4 sites.

Provence
4 sites in a magnificent region of lavender fields and dramatic mountains. Set back from the coast, there are sleepy villages and ancient remains to discover, such as the Roman amphitheatres of Arles and Orange.

Midi-Pyrénées
5 sites in one of France's largest regions. Many of the sleepy villages seem unchanged from the Middle Ages, but the region also boasts great cities, such as Toulouse, as well as Lourdes, the world's most visited pilgrimage site, with the Pyrénées rising to the south.

Mediterranean
Superb coastline from the Spanish border, by way of the vineyards of Corbieres and the mountains of the Cevennes, to the glittering coastline of the Cote d'Azur. Better known as the French Riviera, this last stretch of coastline stretches to the Italian border and boasts world-class resorts such as Cannes, Monte Carlo and Nice. 19 sites.

THE ALAN ROGERS'
travel service

Share our experience and let us help to ensure that your holiday will be a complete success.

The Alan Rogers Travel Service
Tel: 01892 55 98 98

BRITTANY

Major cities: Rennes, Brest
Départements: 22 Côtes d'Armor, 29 Finistère
35 Ille-et-Vilaine, 56 Morbihan, 44 Loire Atlantique

Strong Celtic roots provide this region with its own distinctive traditions, evident in the local Breton costume and music, the religious festivals and the cuisine, featuring crêpes and cider. Brittany offers 800 miles of rocky coastline with numerous bays, busy little fishing villages and broad sandy beaches dotted with charming seaside resorts. Inland you find wooded valleys, rolling fields, moors and giant granite boulders, but most impressive is the wealth of prehistoric sites, notably the Carnac standing stones. Many castles and manor houses, countless chapels and old villages provide evidence of Brittany's eventful history and wealth of traditions. The Bretons are proud of their culture, very different from the rest of France, and are determined to keep it so. If you are able to attend a 'Pardon' (a religious procession), you will understand some of the Breton history and piety, and see some beautiful traditional costumes. Brittany is a popular destination for families with young children or for those visiting France for the first time.

Note: the site reports are laid out by département, in numerical order. *See map on page 305.*

Cuisine of the region

Fish and shellfish are commonplace – lobsters, huitres, langoustes, various sorts of crabs, moules, prawns, shrimps, coquilles St Jacques, for example

Traditional 'crêperies' abound and welcome visitors with a cup of local cider

Other specialties are wafer biscuits and butter biscuits

Agneau de pré-salé – leg of lamb from animals pastured in the salt marshes and meadows

Beurre blanc – sauce for fish dishes made fron a reduction of shallots, wine vinegar and the finest butter (sometimes with dry white wine)

Cotriade – fish soup with potatoes, onions, garlic and butter

Crêpes Bretonnes – the thinnest of pancakes with a variety of sweet fillings

Galette – can be a biscuit, cake or pancake; the latter usually with fillings of mushrooms or ham or cheese or seafood, and called a Galette de blé noir (buckwheat flour)

Gâteau Breton – rich cake with butter, egg yolks and sugar

Poulet blanc Breton – free-range, fine quality, white Breton chicken

Wine

This is cider country! Crêperies serve cider in pottery type cups

Places of interest

Cancale – small fishing port famous for oysters

Carnac – 3,000 standing stones (menhirs), the last erected in 2,000 BC

Concarneau – fishing port, old walled town surrounded by ramparts

Dinan – historical walled town high above the River Rance

La Baule – resort with lovely, sandy bay and beach

Le Croisic – fishing port, Naval museum

Guérande – historic walled town

Perros-Guirec – leading resort of the 'Pink Granite Coast'

Quiberon – boat service to three islands: Belle Ile (largest of the Breton islands), Houat, Hoedic

Rennes – capital of Brittany, medieval streets, half timbered houses; Brittany Museum

St Malo – historical walled city, fishing port and yachting harbour

Tréguier – former Episcopal city, 13th-19th centuary St Tugdual cathedral

www.campingplus.fr

PIBS-C.P.26
56038 VANNES
Cedex-France
Tél 02 97 42 59 90
Fax 02 97 47 50 72

CAMPING PLUS
— B R E T A G N E —

THE BEST OF BRITTANY

2201 Camping Les Capucines, Trédrez, nr Lannion

Family run site, 1 km. from the beach and in good central location for touring Brittany.

A wam welcome awaits at Les Capucines which is quietly situated 1 km. from the village of St Michel with its good, sandy beach and also very near Locquémeau, a pretty fishing village. This attractive site has 100 pitches on flat or slightly sloping ground. All are well marked out by hedges, with mature trees and with more recently planted. There are 70 with electricity, water and drain, including 10 new ones for larger units. Two modern toilet blocks give a good supply, with British WCs, washbasins set in flat surfaces with free hot water and mainly in private cabins, controllable free hot showers, facilities for babies and disabled people, a washing machine and chemical disposal. There is a swimming pool (14 x 6 m; no bermuda style shorts) with a small children's pool, solar heated and open from May. There is a small shop for essentials (fresh bread to order), a takeaway, bar with TV, and a general room with table tennis and table football. On site are a children's playground, tennis, minigolf and bicycle hire. Fishing 1 km, riding 2 km, golf 15 km. A good value restaurant/crêperie is at Trédrez, others at St Michel. Mobile homes (2) and chalets (5) for hire. No dogs are accepted. A Sites et Paysages member.

Directions: Turn off main D786 road northeast of St Michel where signed and 1 km. to site.

Charges 2001:
-- Per person Ffr. 22.00 - 30.00; child under 2 yrs free - 14.00, 2-7 yrs free - 20.00; tent 35.00 - 50.00, caravan with water and drainage 47.00 - 67.00; electricity 4A 15.00, 7A 20.00; local tax (over 18, July/Aug) 1.00.
-- Credit cards accepted.
Open:
6 May - 10 September.
Address:
Kervourdon, 22300 Trédrez-Locquémeau.
Tel:
(0)2.96.35.72.28.
FAX: (0)2.96.35.78.98.
E-mail: les.capucines @wanadoo.fr.
Reservations:
Any length with deposit (Ffr. 400) and fee (50).

**Book this site
01892 559898**

THE ALAN ROGERS'
travel service

2214 Camping de Port La Chaîne, Pleubian

Pretty family site with pool and direct access to the sea.

The Palvadeau family have recently taken over Camping de Port La Chaîne and are working hard to establish it as a comfortable, quiet, family site in a beautiful location on the 'Untamed Peninsula' between Paimpol and Perros Guirec. The trees and shrubs provide a balance of sun and shade and are attractive, edging the central roadway and grassy bays or fields which branch off on its gradual decline towards the bay and the sea (a sandy bay with rocks). To the right are mostly French mobile homes, quite discreet, with the left side for independent units. Most of the bays have a slight slope so those with motorcaravans will need to choose their pitch carefully. More open, level pitches nearer the sea are useful for tents. In all there are 200 pitches with 6A electricity said to be available everywhere (a long lead may be useful). Two traditional style toilet blocks, although a little old fashioned, are comfortable with good hot water, mirrors, shelves, etc. You will find some Turkish style toilets, a washing machine, dryer and plentiful washing up sinks with hot and cold water. Laundry sinks have cold water only. The owners have built a nice heated pool (2/6-15/9) which is overlooked by a bar and terrace (25/6-1/9), also a play area and petanque pitch. Essentially a quiet site for families, a children's animator is provided in August. There are good opportunities for walking and cycling and a way-marked footpath runs along the coast to the Sillon du Talbert that juts out into the sea opposite the Island of Bréhat. Good fishing and diving. Village 2 km for tennis, market, shops and restaurants.

Directions: Leave D786 between Lézardrieux and Tréguier to go north to the village of Pleubian (approx. 8 km). Continue on D20 towards Larmor Pleubian and site signed on left, approx. 2 km. from Pleubian.

Charges 2001:
-- Per person Ffr. 30.00; child (under 7 yrs) 20.00; pitch 50.00; electricity 20.00; dog 6.00; extra car 20.00.
-- Less 10-20% in low seasons.
-- Credit cards accepted.
Open:
1 May - 15 September.
Address:
22610 Pleubian.
Tel:
(0)2.96.22 92 38.
FAX: (0)2.96.22.87.92.
E-mail: ptchaine @club-internet.fr.
Reservations:
Contact site.

**Book this site
01892 559898**

THE ALAN ROGERS'
travel service

2220M Camping Municipal Le Bocage, Jugon-les-Lacs

This well kept, spacious municipal is on the edge of the village beside a lake, 25 km. from the sea. It offers 180 good size pitches, all with electrical connections, set on gently sloping grass and divided by shrubs and bushes, with mature trees providing shade. Some 40 wooden chalets and mobile homes are intermingled with the touring pitches. Two main sanitary blocks serving campers' needs have now been fully refurbished. They now have facilities for disabled visitors, British and Turkish style WCs, some washbasins in private cabins and showers, all with free hot water. A smaller, very old block in the pool complex is open to the public, has only Turkish toilets and is in need of extensive refurbishment - it is not recommended for campers' use. On-site facilities include the medium sized pool (15/6-10/9) with children's section and sunbathing patio, also open to the public, a small shop (1/7-10/9) and a bar (1/7-31/8). Table tennis, tennis court, football pitch and children's play area. Washing machine. Animation and activity programmes in July/Aug. Fishing and bicycle hire on site. There is a small supermarket in the village (1 km). Chalets (42) for hire.

Directions: From the N176 (E401) Lamballe - Dinan road, approx. 15 km. from Lamballe take turning for Jugon-les-Lacs. Site is signed shortly after.

Charges 2000:
-- Per adult Ffr. 20.00; child (under 10 yrs) 12.00; pitch 32.00; dog 7.00; electricity 17.00.
-- Less 15-20% in low seasons.
-- Credit cards accepted.
Open:
1 May - 30 September.
Address:
22270 Jugon les Lacs.
Tel: (0)2.96.31.60.16.
E-mail: camping-le-bocage@wanadoo.fr.
Reservations:
Contact site or the Office de Tourisme. Tel: (0)2.96.31.70.75. Fax: (0)2.96.31.69.08.

2209 Castel Camping Château de Galinée, St Cast le Guildo

Well kept family run site a few kilometres back from St Cast.

Owned and managed by the Vervel family, Galinée is in a parkland setting on level grass with numerous and varied mature trees. It has 273 pitches, all with electricity (6A), water and drainage and separated by many mature shrubs and bushes. The top section is mostly for mobile homes which are for hire. The main tiled, modern sanitary block has free hot water to the pre-set showers and the washbasins in private cabins, British WCs, facilities for babies and a good unit for disabled people. Dishwashing is under cover and there is a laundry room and chemical disposal. Near the bar is an attractive, heated pool complex (26/5-2/9) with swimming and paddling pools, a sun terrace and two new pools with water slide and 'magic stream'. There is an excellent takeaway menu and a shop for basics (both 1/7-2/9). Further facilities include three tennis courts, bicycle hire, fishing, a children's play area and field for ball games. Entertainment is organised during peak season featuring traditional Breton music at times or weekly discos. Riding 6 km, golf 3.5 km. Gate is locked 23.00-07.00 hrs. Site owned mobile homes (45), chalets (5) and tents to rent. Used by tour operators (30 pitches).

Directions: From D168 Ploubalay-Plancoet road turn on D786 towards Matignon and St Cast. Site is very well signed 1 km. after leaving Notre Dame de Guildo.

Book this site
01892 559898
THE ALAN ROGERS'
travel service

Charges 2001:
-- Per pitch incl. water and drainage Ffr. 55.00 - 85.00; adult 25.00 - 33.00; child (under 7 yrs) 15.00 - 22.00; extra vehicle 25.00; extra tent 12.00; animal 18.00; electricity (10A) 26.00; local tax July/Aug. 2.00.
-- Credit cards accepted.
Open:
28 April - 15 September.
Address:
22380 St Cast le Guildo.
Tel:
(0)2.96.41.10.56.
FAX: (0)2.96.41.03.72.
E-mail: chateauga-linee@wanadoo.fr.
Reservations:
Made with deposit (Ffr. 200) and fee (100); min. 1 week July/Aug.
`Camping Cheque'

2212 Camping Le Cap Horn, Port-Lazo, Plouézec

Quiet site with marvellous views and satisfactory facilities.

In two distinct sections, Le Cap Horn provides some sheltered pitches in a small valley facing the sea with shade and mature trees, with newer ones on the hill top with marvellous views of the islands out to sea. These pitches are semi-terraced and newly hedged, but possibly somewhat exposed. This area now has its own modern toilet block with all facilities and new tarmac access roads. Many steps lead down to the bar, TV and games room and older, but modernised, toilet facilities in the valley. The blocks have free hot water, hairdryers, washbasins in cabins, facilities for babies and disabled people, washing machines and dryers and chemical disposal. Of the 149 pitches, 100 have electricity (6A). Amenities include a small shop for essentials, bar, swimming pool and paddling pool (all from 15/6), half-court, volleyball, table tennis and a simple children's play area. There is direct access to the secluded, quiet beach. Fishing and boat launching 1 km, bicycle hire or riding 5 km. Mobile homes (16) to hire.

Directions: Follow D786 southeast and at Plouézec turn on D77 towards Port-Lazo; watch for site signs.

Charges 2000:
-- Per pitch incl. car Ffr. 42.00; person 27.00; child (1-7 yrs) 15.00; dog 8.00; electricity 19.00.
-- Credit cards accepted.
Open:
1 April - 30 September.
Address:
Port-Lazo, 22470 Plouézec.
Tel:
(0)2.96.20.64.28.
FAX: (0)2.96.20.63.88.
E-mail: lecaphorn @hotmail.com.
Reservations:
Contact site.

2200 Camping des Vallées, Saint Brieuc

Neat attractive site, conveniently situated in wooded valley in the town of St Brieuc.

Previously run by the municipality, this site is now privately managed. Neat and tidy, it has 106 good size pitches, 70 with electrical connections (10A), set mainly on flat terraced grass and separated by shrubs and bushes. There are 14 pitches with hardstanding and electricity, water and sewage connections. Mature trees are plentiful, providing shade if required, and a small stream winds through the middle of the site. Two main sanitary blocks provide pre-set showers, some wash-basins in private cabins and British type WCs. Facilities are provided for disabled people, there is a well equipped baby room, laundry with machines and dryer, chemical disposal and motorcaravan services. Two further smaller blocks are at the bottom of the site. A lane leads to a large, outdoor public swimming pool (50 x 20 m.) with children's pool and water slide, minigolf, football pitch, tennis courts, all free of charge to campers except tennis, and open in July and August. A compact bar with snacks is on site (1/7-26/8) and a shop with basic provisions. Animation is organised in peak season, also weekly pony days for children. Children's play area, volley and basketball, arcade games and bicycle hire. A key system operates the access gate (closed 22.30-07.00 hrs). The site is only 800 m. from Saint Brieuc, but still manages to create a quiet, peaceful atmosphere. Saint Brieuc's pedestrianised centre is filled with small shops and boutiques and several speciality food emporia. The old quarter of the town and the excellent street markets on Wednesday and Saturday mornings are worth a visit. The beach at Les Rosaires is 10 km. Mobile homes (6) and chalets (3) for hire. No tour operators.

Charges 2001:
-- Per pitch incl. car and 1 adult Ffr. 45.00 - 56.00; extra adult 17.00 - 22.00; child (under 7 yrs) 12.00 - 15.00; extra car 12.00 - 15.00; animal 10.00 - 15.00; water and drainage 31.00 - 39.00; electricity (10A) 21.00.
-- Credit cards accepted.
Open:
Easter - 15 October (but contact site at other times).
Address:
Parc de Brézillet, Rue Paul Doumer, 22000 Saint Brieuc.
Tel:
(0)2.96.94.05.05.
FAX: as phone.
Reservations:
Made with deposit (Ffr. 250) and fee (90).

Directions: From the east, on entering St Brieuc, look for the sign to the railway station and from there, signs for site.

2205 Camping Le Vieux Moulin, Erquy, nr St Brieuc

Family run site with individual pitches and reasonable prices, 1 km. from sea.

About 1 km. from a beach of sand and shingle, this site is probably the best along this stretch of coast. It has 173 pitches, of which 150 have electricity and 87 have electricity, water, waste water, plus a few with satellite TV connection. All pitches are of good size in square boxes, with trees giving shade in many places and the newer pitches arranged around a pond. There are two sanitary blocks of good quality with mostly British toilets and plenty of individual basins (pre-set warm water and some in private cabins), free hot, pre-set showers and free hairdryers. Facilities are provided for disabled people and for babies and a further small block provides toilets and dish-washing only. There is a smart pizzeria and takeaway (15/5-1/9) and an attractive bar and terrace overlook the heated swimming pool, children's pool and water slides. Other activities include free tennis, free gym, two playgrounds, carousel roundabout, shop (15/5-1/9), TV room (with satellite) and games room with table tennis. Bicycle hire 1 km, fishing 1.2 km, riding 9 km, golf 7 km. Discos are arranged in high season (until midnight). Washing machines and dryer, chemical disposal and motorcaravan service point. The site is fully operational from 15/5 and it is full and busy in July/Aug. Used by tour operators.

Charges 2001:
-- Per pitch Ffr. 62.00; car 24.00; person 30.00; child (under 7) 24.00; electricity 3A 20.00; dog 16.00; local tax (July/Aug) 2.50.
-- No credit cards.
Open:
15 May - 15 September.
Address:
14 rue des Moulins, 22430 Erquy.
Tel:
(0)2.96.72.34.23 (winter) (0)2.96.72.12.50).
FAX: (0)2.96.72.36.63.
E-mail: camp.vieux.
moulin@wanadoo.fr.
Reservations:
Made for 1 week min.

Directions: Site is 2 km. east of Erquy. Take minor road towards Les Hôpitaux and site is signed from junction of D786 and D34 roads.

2202M Camping Municipal, Saint-Efflam, Plestin les Grèves

This is a purpose built, modern municipal site, 100 m. from a sandy beach in the village of Saint-Efflam on the north Brittany coast. It provides 190 level pitches, some of which are terraced with views of the sea. There is little shade at present as the shrubs and bushes need to grow. Three good toilet blocks have free hot water and facilities for disabled people, dishwashing, a washing machine and dryer and chemical disposal. Some sanitary facilities are closed in low season. Basic provisions (bread and milk) and a small bar are available in July/Aug. with a restaurant, etc. in the village. Children's play area. Fishing or sailing school 100 m. Mobile homes and chalets for hire.

Charges 2000:
-- Per pitch Ffr. 21.00; adult 16.00; child (0-10 yrs) 9.00; dog 6.00; electricity 14.00.
-- Credit cards accepted.
Open:
1 April - 30 September.
Address:
Rue Lan Carré, St Efflam 22310 Plestin les Grèves.
Tel: (0)2.96.35.62.15.
FAX: (0)2.96.35.09.75.
Reservations:
Contact site.

Directions: Take D786 Lannion road from the Morlaix bypass and, after Plestin les Grèves, watch for Saint-Efflam and camp site signs on the right.

11

2204 Camping Le Châtelet, St Cast le Guildo, nr St Malo

Pleasant site with views over the bay and steep path down to beach.
Carefully developed over the years from a former quarry, Le Châtelet is pleasantly and quietly situated with views over the estuary from many pitches. It is well laid out, mainly in terraces, with 219 individual pitches of good size marked out by hedge separators; all have electricity and 30 water and drainage also. A 'green' walking area is a nice feature around the lower edge of the site. The narrow gravel access roads can make life awkward for larger units and make the site dusty in breezy weather. The two toilet blocks, one above the other but with access at different levels, have mainly British style WCs, plentiful washbasins in private cabins and pre-set free hot water in both these and the showers. There are small toilets and showers for children. Small units for night use are at the extremities of the site. However, parts of the sanitary blocks may be closed outside July/ Aug. Chemical disposal and motorcaravan services. A little lake (unfenced) with some pitches around it can be used for fishing. An attractive, landscaped pool area has a heated swimming pool and children's pool. Small children's play area. Shop for basics, takeaway service, bar lounge and general room with satellite TV, pool table; dancing weekly in June, July and Aug. Organised games and activities for all the family in season. Games room with table tennis, amusement machines. A path leads from the site directly down to a beach (about 150 m. but including steps). St Cast, 1 km. away to the centre, has a very long beach with many opportunities for sail-boarding and other watersports. Bicycle hire, riding and golf within 1.5 km. Used by tour operators (109 pitches). Mobile homes for hire.

Charges guide:
-- Per person Ffr 25.00 - 30.00; child (under 7) 15.00 - 20.00; pitch 70.00 - 90.00, large pitch 77.00 - 103.00; electricity 6A 20.00, 10A 23.00; local tax 2.00 (high season only).
-- Credit cards accepted.

Open:
22 April - 10 September.

Address:
Rue des Nouettes, 22380 St Cast le Guildo.

Tel:
(0)2.96.41.96.33.

FAX: (0)2.96.41.97.99.

E-mail: chateletcp @aol.com.

Reservations:
Necessary for July/Aug. and made (min. 1 week) with deposit (Ffr. 250) and booking fee (130).

Directions: Best approach is to turn off D786 at Matignon towards St Cast. Just inside St Cast limits left at sign for 'campings' and follow camp signs on C90.

LE CHATELET
CAMPING-CARAVANING ★★★★

22380 Saint-Cast-Le-Guildo
Tel: 02.96.41.96.33
Fax: 02.96.41.97.99

COTE D'EMERAUDE

2206M Camping International La Hallerais, Taden, nr Dinan

As well as being an attractive old medieval town, Dinan is quite a short run from the resorts of the Côte d'Armor. This useful municipal site, open for a long season, is just outside Dinan, beyond and above the little harbour on the Rance estuary. There is a pleasant riverside walk where the site slopes down towards the Rance. The 223 pitches, all with electricity (5/6A) and most with water and drainaway, are mainly on level, shallow terraces connected by tarmac roads, with trees and hedges giving a park-like atmosphere. The three traditional toilet blocks are of good quality and heated in cool seasons, with some private cabins with shower and washbasin. Good hot water is free everywhere and there is a unit for disabled people plus a laundry room. Amenities include a useful shop, an attractive, enlarged bar and restaurant with outside terrace and takeaway (all open all season). Activities include a small swimming pool and children's pool (20/5- 15/9), tennis courts, minigolf, fishing and games room with table tennis and TV room, plus a children's playground. Mobile homes to let, 10 by tour operators, 7 by the Mairie. An efficiently run and well organised site.

Charges guide:
-- Per person over 7 yrs Ffr. 19.00 - 23.00; child (under 7 yrs) 8.00 - 10.00; caravan or motor-caravan incl. electricity 55.00 - 70.00; tent 42.00 - 52.00; local tax (May-Sept, over 12 yrs) 2.00.

Open:
15 March - 31 October.

Address:
Taden, 22100 Dinan.

Tel:
(0)2.96.39.15.93.
FAX: (0)2.96.39.94.64.
(Outside 1/3-15/11 contact the Mairie. Tel: (0)2.96.87.63.50. FAX: (0)2.96.39.86.77).

Reservations:
Made for high season only (min. 1 week) with deposit of Ffr 150.

Directions: Taden is northeast of Dinan; on leaving Dinan on D766, turn right to Taden and site before reaching large bridge and N176 junction. From N176 take Taden/Dinan exit and follow Taden signs to pick up signs for site.

2210 Camping L'Abri Côtier, Etables-sur-Mer

Small, tranquil, family run site 500 m. from sandy beach.

This is a lovely, well cared for site arranged in two sections separated by a lane. The pitches are marked out on part level, part sloping grass, divided by mature trees and shrubs with some in a charming walled area with a quaint, old-world atmosphere. The second section has an orchard type setting. Tim Lee and his French wife are busy with ideas to improve this very popular and friendly site. In total there are 130 pitches, all with electrical connections (6/10A, long lead useful) and 35 fully serviced. Excellent sanitary facilities, in good modern blocks which are heated in low season, were spotlessly clean when we visited. They include British style WCs, free controllable hot showers, washbasins, both open and in private cabins, dishwashing under cover, chemical disposal, laundry room, two units for disabled visitors with shower, washbasin and toilet and a baby bath and shower. The site boasts a sheltered, heated swimming pool with children's pool and outdoor jacuzzi. An attractive bar (with TV) and outdoor terrace area and a new children's playground adjacent to the pool are nice features. There is a well stocked shop, a set menu and a simple takeaway service. Other facilities include a games room with billiards, darts, pinball and table tennis, with entertainment organised during peak season. The beach is within walking distance (500 m.) and there are restaurants in the village. Fishing 2 km, bicycle hire 1 km, riding 3 km, golf 5 km. Barbecues are permitted. Motorcaravan service point. Mobile homes and a chalet for rent. No tour operators. Gates locked at 11 pm.

Directions: From N12 after St Brieuc take D786; site is well signed before St Quay Portrieux.

Charges guide:
-- Per person Ffr. 28.00 - 30.00; child (1-7 yrs) 18.00 - 20.00; pitch 42.00 - 46.00; serviced pitch 55.00 - 60.00; electricity 6A 20.00, 10A 32.00; extra car, boat or small tent 10.00.
-- Credit cards accepted (2% fee).

Open:
6 May - 20 September.

Address:
Ville Rouxel,
22680 Etables-sur-Mer.

Tel:
(0)2.96.70.61.57.
FAX: (0)2.96.70.65.23.
E-mail: tim.lee
@wanadoo.fr.

Reservations:
Advised in season; made with deposit (Ffr 250, sterling cheque acceptable £25).

2213 Camping de Port L'Epine, Trélévern, nr Perros Guirec

Small, friendly site on pretty promontory with pool and beach access.

Port L'Epine is a pretty little site in a unique situation on a promontory. There is therefore access to the sea on the south side of the site with views across to Perros Guirec and just outside the entrance on the north side is a further sandy bay with little boats moored and facing out to an archipelago of seven small islands. It is charming - you can sail or swim from both sides. However, in spite of this, the site has its own small heated pool and children's paddling pool. The area covered by the site is not large but there are 160 grass pitches divided by pretty hedging and trees, some of which are used for mobile homes. Access is a little tight in parts. Electricity (4/10A) is available but a long lead may be useful. The original toilet block is well equipped and the second has been refurbished in a modern style (the showers lack hooks) and it includes facilities for disabled visitors and chemical disposal. Here the dishwashing sinks are in the open air on stone units – quite attractive. A fenced children's play area is beside exit roadway (no gate) and table tennis and video games are provided. There is a bar/restaurant with takeaway facility and a shop (both 1/7-31/8). A useful small supermarket is up-hill from the site. The site's own beach has rock pools, a jetty and a slipway for small boats or fishing. There are many coastal paths to enjoy. Bicycle hire 5 km, riding or golf 15 km. Used by tour operators (29 pitches). Mobile homes to rent (12)

Directions: From roundabout south of Perros Guirec take D6 towards Tréguier. After passing through Louannec, take right turn at cross-roads for Trélévern. Go through village following camp signs - Port L'Epine is clearly marked as distinct from the municipal site.

Charges 2001:
-- Per pitch incl. 2 persons Ffr. 80.00 - 110.00; extra person 32.00; extra child (under 7 yrs) 16.00; extra vehicle 15.00; animal 15.00; electricity 20.00; serviced pitch 35.00; local tax (over 18) 1/6-30/9 1.00.
-- Credit cards accepted.

Open:
1 May - 15 October.

Address:
10 Venelle de Pors Garo,
22660 Trélévern.

Tel:
(0)2.96.23.71.94.
FAX: (0)2.96.23.77.83.

Reservations:
Made with deposit (Ffr. 600, or 300 for stay of less than 3 nights) and fee (100).

Book this site
01892 559898

THE ALAN ROGERS'
travel service

THE ALAN ROGERS'
travel service

Book your site with the experts
Call for an instant quote
01892 55 98 98

Low cost ferries
guaranteed!

2900 Camping Les Mouettes, Carantec, nr Roscoff

Sheltered site in attractive bay, near to Roscoff ferry port.

Les Mouettes is less than 15 km. from the ferry port so is well situated when heading to or from home but has many facilities for a longer stay. The area has plenty to offer for those who do not wish to drive far, with beautiful bays and many places of interest within easy reach. The site is comfortable and peaceful in a wooded setting with many attractive trees and shrubs, and there is access to the sea at the front of the site. The 273 pitches, mostly of good size, are arranged in named groups, with electrical connections throughout (6A). The three modern sanitary blocks (unisex) are clean with free hot water to all facilities, offering washbasins in cabins, mainly British toilets and a good supply of showers with hooks and shelves, all arranged in long rows. There are baby bathrooms, facilities for disabled people and laundry facilities. Chemical disposal and motorcaravan services. The centrally located bar (19/5-13/9) has a terrace overlooking a very impressive heated swimming pool complex which includes a water slide pool and three water slides, 'tropical river', swimming pool and children's pool and jacuzzi. Discos and other entertainment are organised in the main season. Takeaway meals are served and there is a shop (23/5-13/9, limited hours outside the main season). On site are volleyball, two half-courts for tennis, minigolf and archery (July/Aug), table tennis, games and TV rooms, children's play area and a small fenced fishing lake. Bicycle hire 500 m. riding 6 km. and golf 2 km. Bureau de change. Site owned mobile homes (60) are located together at the top of the site. Tour operators take 140 pitches.

Directions: From D58 Roscoff - Morlaix road, turn to Carantec. Site is approx. 6 km. from here (about 1 km. before the town itself), signed to the left at roundabout immediately after passing supermarket on right.

see colour advert between pages 160/161

Charges 2001:
-- Per pitch Ffr. 62.00 - 96.00; person 22.00 - 34.00; child (under 7 yrs) 14.00 - 21.00; dog 11.00 - 18.00; electricity 20.00; water/drainage 5.00 - 10.00; local tax 1.00.
-- Credit cards accepted.
Open:
29 May - 15 September.
Address:
La Grande Grève, 29660 Carantec.
Tel:
(0)2.98.67.02.46.
FAX: (0)2.98.78.31.46.
E-mail: camping.les.mouettes@wanadoo.fr.
Reservations:
Write to site with deposit (Ffr. 300) and fee (120).
`Camping Cheque'

Book this site
01892 559898
THE ALAN ROGERS'
travel service

2913 Camping des Abers, Landéda, nr Lannilis

Attractively situated, family run site in tranquil western Brittany.

This delightful 12 acre site is beautifully situated almost at the tip of the Ste Marguerite peninsula on the western shores of Brittany in a wide bay formed between the mouths (abers) of two rivers, L'Aber Wrac'h and L'Aber Benoit. With soft, white sandy beaches, and rocky outcrops and islands at high tide, the setting is ideal for those with younger children and the quiet, rural area provides a beautiful, tranquil escape from the busier areas of France, even in high season. Camping des Abers is set just back from the beach, the lower pitches sheltered from the wind by high hedges or with panoramic views of the bay from the higher places. There are 180 pitches in distinct areas, partly shaded and sheltered by mature hedges, trees and shrubs, all planted and carefully tended over 30 years by the Le Cuff family. These areas have been landscaped and terraced where appropriate on different levels to avoid any regimentation or crowding. Easily accessed by good internal roads, electricity is available to all (5A, long leads may be needed). Three toilet blocks (one part of the reception building and all recently refurbished) are kept very clean, providing washbasins in cubicles, British style WCs and roomy showers on payment (Ffr. 5 token). Each has dishwashing sinks and chemical disposal facilities. Simple facilities for disabled visitors and for babies have been added at the reception block and a fully equipped laundry and a motorcaravan service point are also here. A mini-market stocks essentials, a van with organic vegetables calls daily and simple takeaway dishes are available (all 1/5-15/9). A pizzeria and a restaurant are next door, plus excellent restaurants nearby at the town of L'Aber Wrac'h, a well known yachting centre. The splendid beach reached direct from the site has good bathing (best at high tide), fishing, windsurfing and other watersports with miles of superb coastal walks. Covered table tennis, good children's play area (on sand) and indoor TV and games room. Live music, Breton dancing and Breton cooking classes, and guided walks may be arranged in high season. Tennis and riding close. Mobile homes (20) for rent. Gates locked 22.30 - 07.00 hrs. Torch useful. The family, who own and run the site with `TLC', make you very welcome, speaking several languages.

Directions: From Roscoff (D10, then D13), cross river bridge (L'Aber Wrac'h) to Lannilis. Go through town taking road to Landéda and from there signs for Dunes de Ste Marguerite, 'camping' and des Abers.

Charges 2001:
-- Per person Ffr. 19.00; child (1-7 yrs) 10.00; pitch 29.00; car 8.00; electricity 14.00; dog 8.00.
-- Less 20% until 15 June and Sept.
-- Credit cards accepted.
Open:
14 April - 22 September.
Address:
Dunes de Ste Marguerite, 29870 Landéda.
Tel:
(0)2.98.04.93.35.
FAX: (0)2.98.04.84.35.
Reservations:
Write to site.
`Camping Cheque'

Book this site
01892 559898
THE ALAN ROGERS'
travel service

see colour advert between pages 160/161

2930 Camping Le Grand Large, Lambézan, Camaret-sur-Mer

Attractive, family run site in beautiful area at tip of the Armorique National Park.

This is a good quality site catering for families. The very friendly owners, M. Senechal and his family give everyone a great welcome. The site is close to the popular seaside resort of Camaret-sur-Mer (2 km) and a rural footpath leads down to the local beach (450 m). There are 123 large, partly shaded pitches (100 for touring units) and most are separated by hedges, some having wonderful sea views. They are easily accessible for all types of unit. All pitches have electricity (5/10A), water and drainage close by and there is a service point for motorcaravans and chemical disposal points. The sanitary facilities, well maintained and very clean, are in two blocks, one quite new and with only one open in low season. Most washbasins are in cabins, many of the push-button showers are controllable and the WCs are mainly British style. There are two baby rooms (only available on request in low season) and good facilities for disabled visitors. There are ample facilities for washing clothes and dishes and the laundry room next to reception has a washing machine, tumble dryer and an ironing board (free iron). The heated swimming pool (no bermuda style shorts) and surrounding terrace are attractively situated close to the bar with good sea views. Other amenities include a small shop. bar, takeaway (all June - Sept), children's play area, table tennis and a pool table. There are plenty of restaurants, activities, etc. close by in Camaret and the surrounding district and this is a good walking and cycling area.

Charges 2000:
-- Per pitch incl. 2 persons Ffr. 75.00 - 120.00; child (under 7 yrs) 18.00; dog 12.00; electricity (5A) 18.00; local tax 1.50 (7-18 yrs 0.75).
-- Credit cards accepted.

Open:
1 April - 30 September.

Address:
Lambézan,
29570 Camaret-sur-Mer.

Tel:
(0)2.98.27.91.41.
FAX: (0)2.98.27.93.72.
E-mail: lglca@
clubinternet.fr.

Reservations:
Made for min. 15 days with deposit (Ffr. 250) and fee (100).

Directions: On entering Camaret-sur-Mer turn right at roundabout onto D355 signed Pointe des Espagnols. Site is well signed and is just over 2 km.

2908 Camping Le Panoramic, Telgruc-sur-Mer

Family site in west Brittany near Châteaulin, quite close to a good beach.

This medium sized, 10 acre site is situated on quite a steep hillside, with fine views along the coast. It is well tended and personally run by M. Jacq and his family who all speak good English. The site is in two parts, divided by a fairly quiet road to the beach. The main upper site is where most of the facilities are located. The lower pitches across the road are only used in July/August, but the heated pool, children's pool and jacuzzi (all 15/5-7/9) and a playground are here. Some up-and-down walking is therefore necessary (a small price to pay for such pleasant surroundings). The 220 pitches are on flat, shady terraces, mostly in small groups with hedges and shrubs. A good sandy beach is around 700 m. downhill by road, a bit less on foot. The main site has two well kept toilet blocks with another very good block opened for the main season across the road. The three blocks have British and Turkish style WCs, washbasins in cubicles and free hot showers. Facilities for disabled people, baby baths, dishwashing, plus washing machines and dryers, chemical disposal and motorcaravan services. Small shop (15/6-7/9) and bar/restaurant with good value takeaway (1/7-31/8). There are games and TV rooms and a children's club in season. Sports ground with tennis, volleyball, bicycle hire. Barbecue area. Fishing 700 m, riding 6 km, golf 14 km. A sailing school is nearby and lovely coastal footpaths. Gites, houses and mobile homes for hire. Used by tour operators (20 pitches). A `Sites et Paysages' member.

Charges 2001:
-- Per person Ffr.30.00; child (under 7) 20.00; pitch 50.00; motorcaravan 10.00; electricity 6A 20.00, 10A 28.00; water and drainage 15.00; dog 10.00; local tax (over 10 yrs) 2.00.
-- Less 20% outside July/Aug.
-- No credit cards.

Open:
15 May - 15 September.

Address:
Route de la Plage,
29560 Telgruc-sur-Mer.

Tel:
(0)2.98.27.78.41.
FAX: (0)2.98.27.36.10.

Reservations:
Any period with deposit.

Directions: Site is just south of Telgruc-sur-Mer. On D887 pass through Ste Marie du Ménez Horn. In 11 km. turn left on D208 signed Telgruc-sur-Mer. Continue straight on through the town and site is on right within 1 km.

Book this site
01892 559898
THE ALAN ROGERS'
Travel service

Camping LE PANORAMIC ★★★★

BRITTANY

On the Crozon penninsular and the Bay of Douarnenez, this is a family campsite bordering the sea, where english is spoken and everything is well-maintened. There are many holiday activities available, including a swimming pool, childrens play area, tennis, bathing, sailing, mountain biking etc., and a further choice of cultural activities in the Armorique Regional Park - the coast, the local ports, museums and of course the richness of the Breton culture itself.

Mr et Mme JACQ - 29560 Telgruc-sur-Mer - France
Tel. 0033 298 27 78 41 - Fax: 0033 298 27 36 10

2928 La Pointe Superbe Camping, St Coulitz, Châteaulin

English owned site near bustling market town.

La Pointe, just outside Châteaulin, has been lovingly and impressively brought back to life by its delightful English owners Colin Grewer and Sue Dodds. Châteaulin is a bustling market town, 15 km. from the beach at Pentrez and within easy reach of Quimper, mediaeval Locronan and the Crozon peninsula. Although not endowed with a great deal in terms of amenities, this very tranquil site does boast particularly large, grassy pitches in a quiet valley leading down to the River Aulne, which makes up part of the Nantes - Brest canal. The 60 pitches all have electricity (6/10A) with water close by. There is a first-class toilet block, kept very clean at all times and with plenty of hot water. Toilets are British style and many washbasins are in cubicles. Showers cubicles are rather small but have adjustable taps. A large room has facilities for disabled visitors, there are chemical disposal facilities and a motorcaravan service point. There is no shop on site, but Châteaulin has a wide range of shops (700 m.), as well as plenty of restaurants and bars. Other amenities include a children's play area, table tennis, volleyball and a large activity room with basketball, badminton and a children's corner. There are woodland walks and fishing is possible in the Aulne (permit needed). Riding and tennis near. This small site, well situated for touring the area, is suited to those who like peace and quiet, with not too many amenities on site.

Directions: Site is just southeast of Châteaulin. From town centre follow D770 signed Quimper. Shortly turn left signed St Coulitz. Site is clearly signed at this point and is a further 100 m. on the right.

Charges 2001:
-- Per pitch Ffr. 30.00 - 45.00; adult 12.00 - 17.00, child (under 7 yrs) 7.00 - 10.00; animal 5.00 - 7.00; electricity (10A) 13.00 - 18.00.
-- First night pitch fee for motorhomes is higher.
-- No credit cards.

Open:
15 March - 15 October.

Address:
Route de St Coulitz, 29150 Châteaulin.

Tel/Fax:
(0)2.98.86.51.53.

Reservations:
Advised for high season and made with deposit (Ffr. 100).

Book this site
01892 559898
THE ALAN ROGERS'
travel service

2906 Camping Caravaning Le Pil Koad, Poullan-sur-Mer

Family run, attractive site just back from the sea near Douarnenez.

Pil Koad has 110 pitches on fairly flat ground, marked out by separating hedges and of quite good, though varying, size and shape. Nearly all have electrical connections (10A) and original trees provide shade in some areas. There are two main toilet blocks in modern style with mainly British style WCs, washbasins mostly in private cabins with pre-set hot water and free, pre-set hot showers. There are laundry facilities and chemical disposal, plus a motorcaravan service point and gas supplies. The heated swimming pool and paddling pool (no bermuda-style shorts) have an attractive sunbathing patio and there is a tennis court. A large room, the 'Woodpecker Bar', is used for entertainment with discos and cabaret in July/Aug. There is a small shop for basics (bread can be ordered all season) and a takeaway (both 17/6-2/9). There are restaurants in the village. Activities include table tennis, minigolf, volleyball and fishing, there is a children's playground and weekly outings and clubs for children are arranged in season (30/6-30/8) with a charge included in the tariff. Bicycle hire or riding 4 km. Privately owned units or site owned mobile homes and chalets to rent occupy 39 pitches. Gates closed 10.30 - 07.00 hrs. The site is 6 km. from Douarnenez, 4 km. from the nearest sandy beach, with a variety of others within easy reach, and 500 m. from the attractive village, with the coast offering some wonderful scenery and good for walking.

Directions: Site is 500 m. east of centre of Poullan on D7 towards Douarnenez. From Douarnenez take bypass route towards Audierne; if you see Poullan sign at roundabout, take it, otherwise camping sign at Poullan turn from D765.

Charges 2000:
-- Per pitch Ffr. 37.00 - 79.00, person 20.00 - 29.00; child (under 7 yrs) 10.00 - 15.00; electricity (10A) 22.00; local tax 1.00; dog 8.00 - 15.00.
-- Credit cards accepted.

Open:
1 May - 15 September

Address:
29100 Poullan-sur-Mer.

Tel:
(0)2.98.74.26.39.
FAX: (0)2.98.74.55.97.
E-mail: camping.pil.koad @wanadoo.fr.

Reservations:
Min. 1 week with 25% deposit and Ffr. 120 fee.
`Camping Cheque'

Book this site
01892 559898
THE ALAN ROGERS'
travel service

see colour advert between pages 160/161

2923M Camping de Mariano, Plonéour-Lanvern

This is a neat and tidy municipal site, situated 20 minutes back from the beach. Lying on the outskirts of the small town, it has some views of the surrounding countryside from its semi-terraced pitches. There are 59 pitches, all with electrical connections and most attractively hedged, although some newer pitches are rather more open. Two toilet blocks, one new, have all facilities, including a washing machine. There is a children's play area and table tennis, with a municipal tennis court adjacent.

Directions: Plonéour-Lanvern is northwest of Pont-L'Abbé. Turn by church in the town square and follow `tennis-camping' signs (north of town).

Charges guide:
-- Per unit incl. 2 adults Ffr. 55.00; electricity 15.00; dog 7.50.

Open:
15 June - 15 September.

Address:
29720 Plonéour-Lanvern.

Tel:
(0)2.98.87.74.80.
FAX: (0)2.98.87.66.09.

Reservations:
Advised - contact site.

2911 Grand Camping de la Plage, Le Guilvinec, nr Pont l'Abbé

Friendly site, ideal for family holidays, with access to good sandy beach.

Grand Camping is located on the edge of a long sandy beach between the fishing town of Le Guilvinec and the watersports beaches of Penmarc'h on the southwest tip of Brittany. This spacious site is surrounded by tall trees, which provide shelter, and is made up of several flat, sandy meadows. The 410 pitches (296 for touring units) are arranged on either side of sandy access roads, mostly not separated but all numbered. There is less shade in the newer areas. Electricity is available on most pitches (2, 6 or 10A) and there is a motorcaravan service point opposite the entrance to the site. The five sanitary blocks are of differing designs, but all provide modern, bright facilities including large, free, controllable hot showers (cubicles a little tight), washbasins in cabins, British style WCs, good facilities for children, a toilet for disabled people and chemical disposal. Like all beach-side sites, all facilities receive heavy usage, As well as the obvious attractions of the beach, the site offers a heated swimming pool with child's pool and water slide, tennis courts and many other leisure facilities including volleyball, basketball, minigolf, badminton, petanque, table tennis, giant chess/draughts, a sauna and bicycle hire. There is a play area and a TV room. The bar is bright, airy and well furnished and a crêperie and takeaway have a terrace over-looking the pool. Other amenities include a shop, laundry facilities, gas supplies and exchange facilities. Entertainment is organised all season for adults and children. Fishing and watersports near, riding 5 km, golf 20 km. Barbecues are permitted. There is plenty to occupy one at this friendly site but the bustling fishing harbour at Le Guilvinec and the watersports of Penmarc'h and Pointe de la Torche are within easy travelling distance. Gates locked 23.00 - 06.30 hrs. Used by tour operators (65 pitches). Mobile homes to rent (54). A 'Yelloh Village' member.

Directions: Site is west of Guilvinec. From Pont l'Abbé, take D785 road towards Penmarc'h. In Plomeur, turn left on D57 signed Guilvinec. On entering Guilvinec fork right signed Port and camping. Follow road along coast to site on left.

Charges 2001:
-- Per person 20.00 - 30.00; child (under 7 yrs) 10.00 - 15.00; pitch incl. car 50.00 - 99.00; electricity 2A 10.00, 5A 16.00, 10A 20.00; extra car 10.00; dog 12.00; local tax (over 16 yrs) 1.00.
-- Special rate 28/4-30/6 2 adults, pitch and electricity Ffr. 90.00.
-- Credit cards accepted.

Open:
1 May - 8 September.

Address:
Rue de Men-Meur, 29730 Le Guilvinec.

Tel:
(0)2.98.58.61.90.
FAX: (0)2.98.58.89.06.
E-mail: gcp@club-internet.fr.

Reservations:
Advised and accepted until 15/6 with deposit (Ffr. 300) and fee (120).

Book this site
01892 559898
THE ALAN ROGERS'
travel service

2929 Camping Village Le Grand Large, Mousterlin, Fouesnant

Family site with pool adjacent to sandy beach.

This is a good site on the Pointe de Mousterlin for those searching for a beach situation in natural surroundings. The site is separated from the beach by the road that follows the coast around the point. It is also protected from the wind by an earth bank with trees and a fence. The beach itself looks over the bay towards the Isles de Glénan. There are 300 level, grass pitches of average size and rather sandy in places with some shrubs and mature trees. Tour operators take 44 places and the site itself has 59 tents and mobile homes to rent. Electricity (2, 6 or 10A) is available everywhere (long leads useful) and some pitches have drainage. Two new, neat sanitary blocks provide plenty of washbasins in cabins (cold water only) and modern pre-set showers. There are two baby baths in the larger block with children's shower and toilet and facilities for disabled people in both blocks, three chemical disposal points, two washing machines, two dryers and plenty of laundry and washing up sinks with cold water. A small river runs through the site but it is fenced. Activities include a swimming pool, paddling pool and water slides in a separate pool, tennis court and an unusual multi-sport court for 5-a-side football, badminton, volleyball, handball or basketball. Small children's play area, TV room and games room with table tennis, and billiards. The bar overlooks the sea with attractive terrace and a crêperie/grill restaurant that also provides takeaways (all limited hours outside the main season). Benodet (7 km) and Fouesnant (5 km) are near in different directions and the sandy beach is just up the steps and across the road; swimming is possible. In season this is a bustling family site with plenty going on, but it would also suit walkers and nature lovers in the low seasons as it is adjacent to a large tract of protected land, Marais de Mousterlin, ideal for walking, cycling and birdwatching.

Directions: Site is 7 km. south of Fouesnant. Turn off N165 expressway at Coat Conq, signed Cincarneau and Fouesnant. At Fouesnant take A45 signed Beg Meil, then signs to Mousterlin. In Mousterlin turn left and follow camping signs.

Charges 2001:
-- Per person 20.00 - 30.00; child (under 7 yrs) 10.00 - 15.00; pitch incl. car 50.00 - 99.00; electricity 2A 10.00, 5A 16.00, 10A 20.00; extra car 10.00; dog 12.00; local tax (over 16 yrs) 1.00.
-- Special rate 28/4-30/6 2 adults, pitch and electricity Ffr. 90.00.
-- Credit cards accepted.

Open:
28 April - 9 September.

Address:
48 route du Grand Large, Mousterlin, 29170 Fouesnant.

Tel:
(0)2.98.56.04.06.
FAX: (0)2.98.56.58.26.
E-mail: gcp@club-internet.fr.

Reservations:
Made with deposit (Ffr. 300) and fee (120).

`Camping Cheque'

Book this site
01892 559898
THE ALAN ROGERS'
travel service

BRITTANY - 29 Finistère

2912 Camping Village Le Manoir de Kerlut, Plobannalec

Comfortable site near Pont l'Abbé in grounds of manor house on river estuary.
This site, opened in '89, has neat, modern buildings and is laid out on flat grass in the grounds of the old 'manoir' (not open to the public, but used occasionally for weddings and private functions). It provides 240 pitches, of which 165 are available for touring units. All have electrical connections (5, 6 or 10A), many have water and drainage also and hardstanding is available on around ten pitches. One area is rather open with separating hedges planted, the other part being amongst mature bushes and some trees which provide shade. Sanitary facilities are in two good blocks, each with several rooms (not all open outside July/Aug). There are controllable hot showers, washbasins all in cabins, British style WCs and chemical disposal, facilities for babies and disabled people and hot water throughout is free. Site amenities are of good quality, with a large modern bar with TV (satellite) and entertainment all season, two heated swimming pools with a children's pool and water slide, small shop, takeaway (both from 15/5), sauna, solarium and small gym. Tennis, badminton, volleyball, petanque, a children's play area, games room and bicycle hire. Fishing 2 km, riding 5 km, golf 15 km. Exchange facilities. Laundry. Gates closed 22.30 - 7.30 hrs. Mobile homes (55) and bungalows (21) to rent. Used by tour operators (12 pitches). A 'Yelloh Village' member.

Directions: From Pont l'Abbé, on D785, take D102 road towards Lesconil. Site is signed on the left, shortly after the village of Plobannalec.

Charges 2001:
-- Per person 20.00 - 30.00; child (under 7 yrs) 10.00 - 15.00; pitch incl. car 50.00 - 93.00; dog 12.00; electricity 2A 10.00, 5A 16.00, 10A 20.00; local tax (over 16 yrs) 1.00.
-- Credit cards accepted.
Open:
1 May - 9 September.
Address:
29740 Plobannalec-Lesconil.
Tel:
(0)2.98.82.23.89
FAX: (0)2.98.82.26.49.
E-mail: gcp@club-internet.fr.
Reservations:
Write to site with deposit (Ffr. 300) and fee (120).
`Camping Cheque'

**Book this site
01892 559898**
THE ALAN ROGERS'
travel service

2905 Castel Camping L'Orangerie de Lanniron, Quimper

Beautiful, quiet site in mature grounds of riverside estate, 15 km. from the sea.
This is a peaceful, family site in 10 acres of a XVIIth century, 42 acre country estate on the banks of the Odet river. It is just to the south of Quimper and about 15 km. from the sea and beaches at Bénodet. The family have a five year programme to restore and rehabilitate the park, the original canal, fountains, ornamental Lake of Neptune, the boat-house and the gardens and avenues. The original outbuildings have been attractively converted around a walled courtyard that includes a heated swimming pool (144 sq.m.) with children's pool and a small play area. A new pool is planned for 2001. The site has 200 grassy pitches, 149 for touring units, of three types (varying in size and services) on fairly flat ground laid out in rows alongside access roads. Most have electricity and 32 have all three services, with shrubs and bushes providing pleasant pitches. The main, heated sanitary block, along one side of the courtyard, has been totally refurbished and is excellent, with free hot water in all services. A second modern block serves the newer pitches at the top of the site. They have British style toilets, washbasins in cabins, adjustable showers and facilities for disabled people and babies. There is a shop (all season), bar, snacks and takeaway, plus a restaurant in the beautiful XVIIth century Orangerie with very attractive views across the gardens (open daily to the public from 20/5, reasonably priced and with children's menu). The Gardens are also open to the public and in Spring the rhododendrons and azaleas are magnificent, with lovely walks within the grounds. Activities include tennis, minigolf, attractively set among mature trees, table tennis, fishing, archery and bicycle hire. Animation is provided including outdoor activities and with a large room for indoor activities. General reading, games and billiards rooms. TV/video room (cable and satellite). Karaoke. Washing machines and dryers, gas supplies, motorcaravan service point and chemical disposal. The historic town of Quimper, which has some attractive old areas and a cathedral, is under 3 km. and two hypermarkets are 1 km. Used by tour operators (45 pitches). Mobile homes (9) for hire and five cottages in the park to let. All facilities are available when the site is open.

Directions: From Quimper follow 'Quimper Sud' signs, then 'Toutes Directions' and general camping signs, finally signs for Lanniron.

Charges 2001:
-- Per pitch incl. 2 persons: normal pitch (100 sq.m.) 137.00, with electricity (10A) and water 176.00, special pitch 120/150 sq.m. with water and electricity 186.00; animal 22.00.
-- Less 10% outside July/Aug.
-- Credit cards accepted.
Open:
15 May - 15 September.
Address:
Château de Lanniron, 29336 Quimper Cedex.
Tel:
(0)2.98.90.62.02.
FAX: (0)2.98.52.15.56.
E-mail: camping@lanniron.com.
Reservations:
Made with deposit (Ffr. 400) and fee (100).

**Book this site
01892 559898**
THE ALAN ROGERS'
travel service

*see colour advert
between pages 32/33*

18

2927 Camping des Dunes, Lesconil

Open site with direct beach access, near unspoiled fishing port.

Les Dunes is one of few sites in the 'pays Bigouden' with the great advantage of direct access (across the dunes) to an excellent sandy beach. The 120 pitches have little shade but are quite spacious, and all have electricity (6A). There are two unisex toilet blocks adjacent to each other, the most recent designed to a very high standard, even incorporating a central leisure area. The second block, although older is kept very clean. Toilets are mainly British style with washbasins either in cubicles or open areas. Free hot showers are pre-set. Two cabins for disabled people have shower, WC and washbasin (designed by a disabled customer of the site). Washing machines and dryers (lines not permitted) and two chemical disposal points. Although there is no shop, a baker's van visits every morning in high season, and other provisions are available in the village (800 m). Lesconil, a delightfully unspoiled fishing port where you can still see the little fishing fleet return each day and it offers a good choice of restaurants and cafes. On site leisure facilities include trampolines (free), a small bowling alley, table tennis, volleyball court, two children's play areas and a games room. Watersports are possible at the 'Centre nautique' in the village where there are also tennis courts.

Directions: From Pont l'Abbé and Plobannalec, take Dl02 to Lesconil. Turn right on entering village following signs to site (next to Camping La Grande Plage).

Charges 2000:
-- Per pitch Ffr. 48.50; adult 24.90; child (under 7 yrs) 13.30; extra car 9.10; electricity 17.90; local tax 1.00 (over 16 yrs only).
-- Credit cards accepted.
Open:
24 May - 15 September.
Address:
67 rue Paul Langevin, 29740 Lesconil.
Tel:
(0)2.98.87.81.78.
FAX: (0)2.98.82.27.05.
Reservations:
Essential for high season and made with deposit (Ffr. 400).

2924 Camping de Keranterec, La Forêt Fouesnant

Well established family site with access to small beach and the coastal footpath.

The area around La Forêt Fouesnant is very much picture postcard Brittany – plenty of enticing crêperies or seafood restaurants, delightful mediaeval villages and towns, such as Concarneau, and mile after mile of soft, sandy beaches. For these and many other reasons, there are plenty of campsites to choose in this area. Keranterec is amongst these, and is worth considering. A well established family site with a very French ambience (unlike some neighbours which have a much higher UK presence), Keranterec has 265 grassy pitches in two distinct areas. The upper part of the site is relatively new and has little shade – it is also largely taken up by private mobile homes. The lower and more mature area is predominantly for tourers with shaded, terraced pitches in a former orchard, some with views of the little cove at the rear of the site. The spacious, hedged pitches have electricity and most also offer water and drainage. The two toilet blocks are of modern design and kept in very good order. They include facilities for disabled people and babies. The heated pool (no bermuda style shorts) is at the front of the site and has a good-sized terrace and a children's pool adjacent. There is table tennis, a tennis court (free) and a sports area, as well as a children's playground. At the back of the site a gate leads to a small beach and the coastal footpath (Concarneau 8 km). Just 10 minutes' walk, there is an attractive sandy beach (Kerleven). Golf 1 km, riding 3 km. Animation is organised in high season. Takeaway (1/7-31/8). We recommend the site's cider produced from its own apples ....

Directions: Site is 2 km. southeast of La Forêt Fouesnant. Leave N165 at Coat Conq signed Concarneau. At roundabout right on D44 signed Forêt Fouesnant. In 2.5 km. at T-junction turn right on D783 (Quimper, Forêt Fouesnant). On entering La Forêt Fouesnant turn left signed Beg Meil following camping signs to site.

Charges 2000:
-- Per pitch Ffr. 46.00; adult 34.00; child (under 7 years) 17.00; electricity 18.00; dog 10.00.
-- Less 25% outside July/Aug.
-- Credit cards accepted.
Open:
1 April - 30 September.
Address:
Route de Port la Forêt, 29940 La Forêt Fouesnant.
Tel:
(0)2.98.56.98.11.
FAX: (0)2.98.56.81.73.
Reservations:
Advised in high season and made with deposit (Ffr 500) and fee (120).

Book this site
01892 559898
THE ALAN ROGERS'
travel service

Camping de
KÉRANTEREC
★★★

SOUTH BRITTANY

Bordering a small beach, and only 400 m from the main beach, we can assure you of a pleasant stay in a calm and pretty environment.
Facilities include organised activities, bar, childrens play area, free tennis, heated swimming pool, TV and table tennis rooms. Volleyball and basketball pitches, laundry and baby baths.

29940 LA FORÊT-FOUESNANT
Tel. 0033 298 56 98 11 - Fax: 0033 298 56 81 73
www.camping-keranterec.com
E-mail: info@camping-keranterec.com

BRITTANY - 29 Finistère

2903 Camping du Letty, Bénodet

Excellent, family run site with high quality amenities and access to small beach.

Du Letty is personally run by the owner and is a select site built around a former farm, with excellent facilities and an attractive floral entrance. On the edge of the popular resort of Bénodet, it is not far on foot to the main beaches, but there is direct access from the site to an attractive small, sandy beach at the mouth of the river (safe bathing depends on the tides). There are 493 pitches here in 22 acres, although the site does not appear large as they are arranged in small groups enclosed by neat, high hedges and trees. There is plenty of well kept, grassy space and almost all pitches have electricity (5/10A), water and drainage. Sanitary facilities in seven blocks around the site are of very good quality with modern fittings. They offer mixed style WCs, washbasins in large cabins, controllable hot showers (Ffr. 4 charge) and bathrooms (also on payment). Baby rooms (3) and chemical disposal are provided and in one block, facilities for disabled visitors. There is no swimming pool here, but the site does provide an extensively equipped fitness room, saunas, solarium, table tennis, squash and tennis courts. An attractively furnished library/reading room, a hairdressing room, small launderette, games lounge with billiards and card tables and an entertainment room with satellite TV are also located in the converted farm buildings. A modern, purpose built, concrete entertainment hall with a bar is adjacent to the site entrance. There is an extensive snack bar and takeaway (July/Aug) and a shop. Activities and entertainment are organised in high season. Bicycle hire 50 m, riding 500 m, golf 2 km. Motorcaravan service point. Reservations are not accepted but there is usually space, although the site is only open over a short season.

Directions: From D44 Bénodet - Fouesnant road, follow signs to Fouesnant, then `Toutes Directions' sign - site sign follows very soon afterwards.

Charges 2001:
-- Per adult Ffr. 28.00; child (under 7 yrs) 14.00; pitch 40.00; car 11.00; m/cycle 8.00; electricity (1, 2, 5 or 10A) 10.00 - 26.00; water connection 5.00; local tax 2.00.
-- Credit cards accepted.

Open:
15 June - 6 September.

Address:
29950 Bénodet.

Tel:
(0)2.98.57.04.69.
FAX: (0)2.98.66.22.56.
E-mail: reception@ campingduletty.com.

Reservations:
Not made.

2902 Camping Club du Saint-Laurent, La Forêt-Fouesnant

Shady, attractively situated seaside site with a range of activities.

Saint-Laurent is a well established site, by the sea on a sheltered wooded slope at the mouth of an estuary with attractive views. There is direct, ungated access to two small strips of beach, but at low tide the sea recedes from the estuary. The 260 pitches are on levelled terraces, under tall trees. They are divided into individual numbered pitches, most of around 100 sq.m, but some do vary in size and shape. Pitches adjacent to the estuary lead onto steep, poorly fenced cliffs which could be dangerous. Access roads are fairly narrow and some pitches with the best views, those on corners or those with awkwardly placed trees, can be more difficult to get on to. However, the site management will assist with caravans. All have electrical connections (6A). The two sanitary blocks are of differing age. Both blocks have spacious new free hot shower and washbasin suites, hairdryers, British style WCs, plus further washbasins in cabins of acceptable standard. There are facilities for disabled people and babies, laundry and a motorcaravan service point. Interesting sea water pools (good for crabbing!) have been supplemented by a conventional swimming pool and children's pool, terraced and overlooked by the bar club, gym and sauna. There is a small shop for essentials, a bar and snack bar with takeaway (12/5-10/9). Activities include a sports area with volleyball, basketball, a good, small children's playground, two tennis courts, two half-courts and table tennis. Golf or riding 2 km, bicycle hire 1 km. The coastal footpath from Kerleven to Concarneau passes through the site. Around 50% of the pitches are occupied by tour operators or site owned mobile homes to rent.

Directions: Approach from Quimperlé either via N783 and Concarneau or via Rosporden and D70; from Quimper via N783. Follow signs for Fouesnant but turn left to Kerleven, Pont La Forêt and site at roundabout on outskirts of the town.

Charges 2000:
-- Ffr. Per unit incl. 1 or 2 persons, electricity and water Ffr. 100.00 - 155.00; extra person over 7 yrs 15.00 - 28.00, 2-7 yrs 10.00 - 20.00; extra car 10.00 - 20.00; dog free - 12.00.
-- Euro: Per unit incl. 1 or 2 persons, electricity and water 15.24 - 23.63; extra person over 7 yrs 2.29 - 4.27, 2-7 yrs 1.52 - 3.05; extra car 1.52 - 3.05; dog free - 1.83.
-- Credit cards accepted.

Open:
12 May - 15 September.

Address:
Kerleven, 29940 La Forêt-Fouesnant.

Tel:
(02) 98.56.97.65.
FAX: (02) 98.56.92.51.

Reservations:
Advised for July/Aug. and made with deposit (Ffr. 500) and fee (150).

see colour advert between pages 32/33

20

2917 Camping-Caravaning de la Piscine, Beg-Meil, Fouesnant

Attractive site with relaxed atmosphere and a warm welcome.

There are many campsites in this area but La Piscine is notable for the loving care and attention to detail which contributes to the well-being of its guests. Created by the Caradec family from an orchard, the 185 level pitches are of generous size and separated by a variety of hedges and trees. Water, waste water and electricity points (6/10A) are provided. Three refurbished sanitary units are of varying size and design, the largest centrally located, with two small units serving the pool area and the furthest end of the site respectively. These provide British and Turkish style toilets, washbasins in cabins, pre-set showers, dishwashing and laundry sinks all with hot water, washing machines and dryers, and facilities for disabled people. There are plenty of amenities – a swimming pool with separate flume (from 1/6, no bermuda style shorts), BMX track, football pitch, volleyball, half-court tennis, table tennis, a TV room, sauna and solarium, and a children's play area. Entertainment is organised in high season. The site shop is well stocked with basic provisions (1/6-15/9, times vary). Takeaway in high season – there is no bar or restaurant. The site is within easy reach of the sea (a 15 minute walk) and the nearby towns of Beg-Meil and Fouesnant, and (a little further) Quimper, are well worth a visit. Bicycle hire, fishing, riding within 4 km, golf 7 km. Motorcaravan service point. Caravan storage. Used by tour operators (16 pitches). Mobile homes to rent (15). A quieter site, set back from the sea, La Piscine will appeal to families looking for good quality without too many on site activities.

Charges 2001:
-- Per person Ffr. 19.50 - 27.50; child (under 7 yrs) 10.00 - 14.00; pitch incl. vehicle 38.50 - 55.00; dog 10.00; electricity 3A 16.00, 6A 19.00, 10A 25.00; local tax 2.00 (child 0-16 yrs 1.00).
-- Credit cards accepted.

Open:
15 May - 15 September.

Address:
Kerleya,
Beg-Meil BP 12,
29170 Fouesnant.

Tel:
(0)2.98.56.56.06.
FAX: (0)2.98.56.57.64.
E-mail: campingde-lapiscine@altica.com.

Reservations:
Contact site.

Directions: Site is 5 km. south of Fouesnant. Turn off N165 at Coat Conq signed Concarnau and Fouesnant. At Fouesnant join D45 signed Beg Meil and shortly turn left on D145 signed Mousterlin. In 1 km. turn left and follow signs to site.

2919 Les Prés Verts, Kernous-Plage, nr Concarneau

Popular family site, with stylish pool complex, near small, fine sandy beach.

What sets this site apart from the many others in this region are its more unusual features - the Romanesque style columns, statues, plants and flower tubs around the pool, the excellent and colourful playground for small children, plus the most unusual `big kids' play-frame with an upper age limit of 19 years. The 150 pitches are mostly arranged on long open grassy areas either side of access roads with specimen trees, shrubs or hedges to divide the site into smaller areas. There are a few individual pitches and an area where pitches have sea views towards the rear of the site. The sanitary facilities are housed in two modern units which provide unisex WCs, but separate washing facilities for ladies and men. Washbasins are in cabins for ladies, and pre-set hot showers are free (08.00-21.00 only). In addition there are sinks for dishwashing and laundry, a washing machine and dryer, child size toilets, and chemical disposal points. At present there are no dedicated facilities for disabled people. The swimming pool (1/6-31/8) is around 18 x 11 m. and there is also a children's pool and minigolf. Other site amenities include a small shop (1/7-25/8), bar (evenings only) and a pizza service on Tuesday and Saturdays (18.00-21.00). There is a path to the beach from the site (300 m). Concarneau is just 2.5 km. and there are numerous marked coastal walks to enjoy, plus watersports or boat and fishing trips available nearby. Riding 1 km, bicycle hire 3 km, golf 5 km. Mobile homes for rent (8). A Sites et Paysages member.

Charges 2001:
-- Per pitch incl. 2 adults Ffr. 130.00; extra adult 38.00; child (2-7 yrs) 25.00; extra car 12.00; dog 9.50; electricity 2A 19.00, 3A 21.00, 4A 25.00, 5A 26.00, 6A 29.00; local tax (June-Sept) over 18 yrs 1.50.
-- Low seasons less 20%.
-- Credit cards accepted.

Open:
1 May - 22 September.

Address:
Kernous-Plage,
29900 Concarneau.

Tel:
(0)2.98.97.09.74.
FAX: (0)2.98.97.32.06.
E-mail: pres-verts-camp@wanadoo.fr.

Reservations:
Contact site for details.

Directions: Turn off C7 road, 2.5 km. north of Concarneau, where site is signed.

2926 Camping La Plage, Bénodet

Surprisingly green and tranquil town-centre campsite in popular seaside resort.
Considering its position within easy walking distance of the town centre and beach, this is a surprisingly pretty site, catering equally in two fairly distinct parts for clients in mobile homes and independent campers and caravanners. From our point of view rather disappointingly, the quite large pool complex is closer to the mobile homes than it is to the touring pitches. However, this does at least result in the touring pitches being more peaceful, without the shrieks of delight from youngsters! The 150 touring pitches are on fairly flat grass, pleasantly arranged among trees and bushes along several avenues. Electricity is available on virtually all. A good range of facilities are housed in some quite attractive buildings close to the entrance. These include a large bar, takeaway, play area, games room, two billiards/pool tables and the pools with the inevitable toboggan. The somewhat traditional sanitary facilities in three blocks are adequate, if unremarkable, and include hot showers, washbasins with hot water, both British and Turkish style WCs, and dishwashing and laundry facilities. Maintenance seemed acceptable when we visited in late June, but the site was by no means full so we reserve judgement as to the high season. The main attraction of this site must be its close proximity to a popular and quite stylish resort, and the fact that one could combine this with staying in fairly tranquil surroundings. Mobile homes and chalets to rent.

Charges guide:
-- Per pitch Ffr. 36.00; adult 31.00; child (under 7 yrs) 16.00; car 14.00; electricity 6A 19.00, 10A 25.00; dog 6.00; local tax (July/Aug) 1.00, 10-16 yrs 0.50.
-- Low season less 10%.
Open:
1 June - 30 September.
Address:
Kérambechennec, 29950 Bénodet.
Tel:
(0)2.98.57.00.55.
FAX: (0)2.98.57.12.60.
Reservations:
Advised for July/Aug and made with 25% deposit and Ffr. 100 booking fee.

Directions: From Bénodet Plage follow signs to site.

2910 Camping du Manoir de Pen-ar-Steir, La Forêt-Fouesnant

Useful small site open all year, with few amenities but within village limits.
Manoir de Pen-ar-Steir will appeal to those who prefer a quiet place to stay out of season without lots of amenities and entertainment on the site. It is arranged on terraces up the steep sides of a valley in the grounds of an old Breton house and has a picturesque, garden-like quality, with well tended trees and flowers, a pond and stream and an attractive floral entrance. There are some steep slopes to reach many of the 105 pitches, but they are on flat, grassy, terraces with hedges around them. They are of reasonable size and all have electricity, water and drainage. The two sanitary blocks, both refurbished to high standards, have mixed British and Turkish style toilets and cabins with washbasin and shower, plus washbasins in rows. There are also good, heated facilities for winter use, including facilities for disabled people and babies, in a small block which is part of the farm-house, that also houses washing machines and dryers. There is a tennis court, minigolf and a playground but no bar, restaurant or shop (baker 50 m.), however the facilities of the town are easily reached by foot. Some site owned mobile homes to rent.

Charges 2000:
-- Per adult Ffr. 28.00; child (under 7 yrs) 17.00; pitch 47.00; electricity 3A 14.00, 6A 18.00, 10A 20.00; dog 10.00; local tax 2.10 (10-16 yrs 1.00).
-- No credit cards.
Open:
All year.
Address:
29940 Forêt-Fouesnant.
Tel:
(0)2.98.56.97.75.
FAX: (0)2.98.56.80.49.
E-mail: camping-pen-ar-steir@wanadoo.fr.
Reservations:
Write for details.

Directions: Site signed off roundabout at northeast edge of La Forêt-Fouesnant.

2916 Camping Les Genets d'Or, Bannalec

Small, rural site in the heart of Finistère with English owners.
A jewel of a small site, Les Genets d'Or is situated in a tiny country hamlet at the end of a road from Bannalec, 12 km. from Pont-Aven. The spacious surroundings offer a safe haven for children and a rural, tranquil environment for adults. The gently sloping, grassy site is edged with mature trees and divided into hedged glades with the odd apple tree providing shade. There are only 52 pitches (46 for touring units), all of a good size - some of over 100 sq.m. - and most pitches have electricity (6A), each glade having a water point. A toilet block of good quality provides the necessary amenities with British style toilets, free, controllable hot showers and washing facilities. There is a small bar and bread is delivered in season. Reception has a small library, an indoor room provides snooker and table tennis, and bicycle hire is available. Riding 3 km, golf 20 km. Alan and Judy, the English owners, ensure a warm friendly welcome and are justifiably proud of their site which they have improved over the last few years and keep in pristine condition. There are plans for a play area. A flat (2 bed), a cottage (4 bed) and a mobile home are for rent. Caravan storage. The village is 15 minutes walk.

Charges 2001:
-- Per person Ffr. 14.00; child (under 6 yrs) 9.00; pitch 20.00; vehicle 9.00; m/cycle 5.00; dog 6.00; electricity (6A) 16.00.
-- Less 15-20% outside July/Aug..
-- No credit cards.
Open:
Easter/1 April - 30 September.
Address:
Kermerour, Pont Kereon, 29380 Bannalec.
Tel/Fax:
(0)2.98.39.54.35.
E-mail: enquiries@holidaybrittany.com.
Reservations:
Contact site.

Directions: Take exit D4 from N165 towards Bannalec. In Bannalec turn right into Rue Lorec (signed Quimperlé) and follow camp signs for 1 km.

Book this site
01892 559898
THE ALAN ROGERS'
travel service

2914 Domaine de Kerlann, Land Rosted, Pont-Aven

Haven Europe owned holiday park with pleasant touring section, with super complex of indoor and outdoor pools and a range of entertainment and activities.

Starting with a small original site, Haven Europe have invested imaginatively with much care for the existing environment and thoughtful planning on the infrastructure side. The result is that a large number of mobile homes blend into the new landscaping and the many carefully retained original trees. The remaining 20% of 150-odd touring pitches (some 80 sq.m, some 120 sq.m) have been left in a more natural situation on rough grass with a small stream flowing through and with some of the mature trees providing shade. Electricity is available to all pitches. Land drainage may be poor due to the park being situated on low lying ground. The main large toilet block is on the edge of the mobile home area and offers a good provision with pre-set showers, washbasins in cubicles, outside dishwashing and laundry sinks (H&C) and good laundry facilities. A second block in the touring section is opened in high season. The 'piece de resistance' is the amazing pool complex comprising three outdoor pools with separate toboggan, attractively landscaped with sunbathing terraces, and an indoor tropical style complex complete with jacuzzi and its own toboggan. Lifeguards are very much in evidence. Further plus factors are the bar area with separate French style restaurant, snack restaurant and takeaway, shop and a large terrace with a raised stage overlooking the pool complex, where much of the evening, holiday camp style entertainment with a French flavour takes place. Three children's clubs for different age groups organise activities and a number of well equipped play areas, an all weather multi-sports court, tennis courts, minigolf , video games room, pool tables and satellite TV in the bar are provided. If you tire of activity on site, the nearby town of Pont-Aven with its Gauguin connection, art galleries and museums is well worth visiting or there is a range of safe beaches and small ports and villages to enjoy. Gas barbecues are not permitted.

Directions: From Tregunc - Pont-Aven road, turn south towards Névez and site is on right.

Charges 2001:
-- Per pitch incl. up to 2 persons with electricity Ffr. 70.00 - 199.00; extra person 15.00 - 35.00; extra vehicle 10.00 - 20.00.
-- Credit cards accepted.
Open:
7 April - 26 October.
Address:
Land Rosted,
29930 Pont-Aven.
Tel:
(0)2.98.06.01.77.
FAX: (0)2.98.06.18.50.
Reservations:
Accepted at any time for min. 4 days; no booking fee. Contact site or Haven Europe in the UK on 0870 242 7777 for information or reservation quoting FAR01.

see colour advert opposite page 256

2909 Camping Le Raguenès Plage, Névez, nr Pont-Aven

Well regulated, attractive site in small seaside village, with beach access.

Personally run by the owner and her family who take great pride in the site, there are many attractive shrubs and trees and it is kept very clean and neat. A sandy beach can be reached by footpath (300 m.) and there is a sailing school and small fishing port adjacent to the site. The 287 pitches all have electrical connections and are of good size, on flat grass, arranged in rows on either side of asphalt access roads, separated by hedges and trees. It could be said that this site's best features are not discovered until you get past reception and the sanitary block nearest the entrance; indeed the furthest sanitary unit is the most modern and the quietest pitches are to the rear of the site. The sanitary facilities are in three well maintained blocks of different size, design and age. They provide British WCs, pre-set hot showers, washbasins in private cabins, plus free hairdryers and include good baby bathrooms, excellent facilities for disabled people and chemical disposal. Hot water is free throughout. Amenities include a sauna and an attractive heated swimming pool with terrace (from 1/5). Table tennis, volleyball, games room, good play areas and animation are offered for children. A small bar and restaurant (from 1/6) have an outside terrace with lots of flowers; breakfast is served here. Takeaway. Small shop (from 15/5, supermarket 3 km.). Reading, TV rooms and films. Laundry. Exchange facilities. Fishing and watersports 300 m, riding 4 km. Bicycle hire can be arranged, with delivery. Motorcaravan service point. Used by tour operators (105 pitches). Mobile homes for hire (27).

Directions: From D783 Concarneau - Pont-Aven road go south to Névez. Site is signed from there, 5 km. on the Raguenès-Plage road.

Charges 2001:
-- Per unit incl. 2 persons Ffr. 84.00 - 140.00; extra person 22.40 - 32.00; child (under 7 yrs) 12.60 - 18.00; electricity 2A 15.00, 6A 20.00; dog 8.00; local tax (over 18 yrs) 2.00.
-- No credit cards.
Open:
13 April - 30 September.
Address:
19 Rue des Iles,
29920 Névez.
Tel:
(0)2.98.06.80.69.
FAX: (0)2.98.06.89.05.
Reservations:
Recommended in high season, min. 7 days preferred for July/Aug. Write with deposit (Ffr. 500).

Book this site
01892 559898

THE ALAN ROGERS'
travel service

23

2918 Camping Les Embruns, Le Pouldu, nr Clohars-Carnoët

Attractively landscaped family site, with excellent facilities and own pool.
This site is unusual in that it is located in the heart of a village, yet only 250 m. from a sandy cove, and also close to beautiful countryside and the Carnoët Forest. The entrance to the site, with its card operated barrier and superb floral displays, is the first indication that this is a well tended and well organised campsite. The 180 pitches (80 occupied by site rental or privately owned units) are separated by trees, shrubs and bushes, and most are fully serviced with electricity (3/5A), water and waste water facilities. The two modern sanitary blocks (mostly unisex) provide British style WCs, washbasins in cubicles, controllable hot showers, facilities for babies and disabled people, dishwashing sinks, and a laundry with washing machines and dryers. The floral nature of the site even extends inside these units with plants and silk flower displays. The bar (1/7-31/8) with a small terrace overlooks the heated swimming pool (15.5 x 7.5 m; open 1/6-10/9) and circular paddling pool, making it a pleasant place to rest, whilst keeping an eye on the children. The site has a small shop, although it is only a short walk to the village centre with all its attractions and services. Other amenities on site include a games hall with table tennis, children's playground and a play field for ball games, and minigolf. Motorcaravan service point. Nearby there is both sea and river fishing and watersports. Bicycle hire 50 m, riding 2 km. and there is good cycling in the surrounding countryside. Chalets, mobile homes and caravans for rent.

Directions: Take D24 from Clohars-Carnoët or D49 from Quimperlé. Both join at the village of Le Pouldu where the site is signed.

Charges 2000:
-- Per adult Ffr. 25.00;
child (under 7 yrs) 16.00;
pitch 41.00; fully
serviced pitch (incl. 5A
electricity) 69.00;
electricity other pitches
3A 17.00, 5A 20.00;
animal 4.00; local tax
(Jun-Sept) 2.00.
-- Use of motorcaravan
services Ffr. 12.00.
-- Less in low seasons.
-- Credit cards accepted.

Open:
1 April - 15 September.

Address:
Le Pouldu, 29360
Clohars-Carnoët.

Tel:
(0)2.98.39.91.07.
FAX: (0)2.98.39.97.87.
E-mail: camping-les-embruns@wanadoo.fr.

Reservations:
Advised for high season,
contact site.

2920M Camping Forestier du Bois de Pleuven, St-Yvi, nr Rosporden

Set in 17 ha. of forest surroundings, this very large municipal site has 280 pitches of varying size, most with electricity (5A). They are very spacious and some provide a good degree of privacy. The two sanitary blocks are rather elderly and basic, with showers, some washbasins in cabins and British and Turkish style WCs, but hot water is free throughout. Leisure facilities on the site include a swimming pool complex with one large pool, two smaller ones and two new water slides, bicycle hire, tennis courts and minigolf (open to the public but with reduced charges for campers). There is also a football pitch, two children's play areas, a TV room with satellite, bar and takeaway (20/6-31/8) and washing machines. Fishing 7 km, riding 1 km, golf 4 km. Telephones. Torches are useful. Mobile homes for hire (20). The site is between Concarneau and Quimper, within an easy drive of the coast.

Directions: From Quimper on D783 Quimper - Concarneau road, take left turn signed Pleuven (approx. 13 km. from Quimper). Continue along this road to camp site sign (note: there is a convalescent home with the same name, approx. 50 m. along from the site). From N165 take exit for Troyalac'h towards St Yvi.

Charges guide:
-- Per pitch Ffr. 22.00;
adult 15.00; child (under
7 yrs) 8.50; car 7.00;
m/cycle 3.20; electricity
15.00 - 18.00; local tax
(over 18 yrs, 1/6-30/9)
1.50.
-- Small charges for
amenities (closed winter).
-- No credit cards.

Open:
All year.

Address:
Saint-Yvi,
29140 Rosporden.

Tel:
(0)2.98.94.70.47.
FAX: (0)2.98.94.78.99.

Reservations:
Contact site.

2901 Castel Camping Ty Nadan, Arzano, nr Quimperlé

Well organised country site beside the River Ellé, with swimming pools.

Ty Nadan is set deep in the countryside in the grounds of a country house some 18 km. from the sea. It has 220 individual pitches, 160 with 10A electricity, of good size on fairly flat grass, some on the banks of the river with some shade. The two toilet blocks are of an unusual design with access from different levels and are of fair quality. The blocks have British style WCs, free hot water in washbasins (in cabins), sinks and showers (push-button, pre-set temperature), and baby rooms. Access for disabled people may be a little difficult although there are facilities in one block. Dishwashing facilities are in two attractive gazebo style units and there is a laundry room with washing machines and dryers. There are plenty of activities for young people here, including a heated pool (17 x 8 m.), a pool with water slides and a paddling pool, a small beach on the river (unfenced), tennis courts, table tennis, pool tables, archery and trampolines. A new adventure play park has been added. Riding is offered, bicycles, skateboards, roller skates and boats may be hired and there are facilities for fishing and a small roller skating rink. Many activities are organised all season (30/6-1/9), particularly sports, exercises, excursions, etc. and guided mountain bike tours. Canoeing trips may include some white water stretches more suitable for the experienced (arranged daily in season to Quimperlé, return by bus). Restaurant, takeaway, bar and shop (all open all season). Across the road, by the attractive house and garden in converted Breton outbuildings, are a delightful crêperie and a disco. Tents, mobile homes and chalets for rent. Used by a tour operator (60 pitches).

Charges 2001:
-- Per person Ffr. 35.00; child (under 7) 22.00; pitch 75.00; electricity 28.00; water/drainage 35.00; dog 18.00.
-- Less outside July/Aug.
-- Credit cards accepted.
Open:
19 May - 8 September.
Address:
Route d'Arzano, 29310 Locunolé.
Tel:
(0)2.98.71.75.47.
FAX: (0)2.98.71.77.31.
E-mail: TY-NADAN@ wanadoo.fr.
Reservations:
Exact dates with deposit (Ffr. 300) and fee (150).

Book this site
01892 559898

THE ALAN ROGERS'
travel service

see colour advert between pages 32/33

Directions: Make for Arzano which is northeast of Quimperlé on the Pontivy road and turn off D22 just west of village at camp sign. Site is approx. 3 km.

2925 Camping Bois des Écureuils, Guilligomarc'h

'An old-fashioned campsite that does things well.'

Seldom do we use a proprietor's own words to describe a campsite, but on this occasion his remarks were so appropriate we couldn't resist the temptation to quote them. This delightful little site offers an attractive alternative to the more luxurious ones in the area and is well situated for exploring the lovely countryside hereabouts, or for walking, cycling, canoeing or fishing; it is also within easy reach of the beaches of southern and western Brittany. The British owners, David and Barbara Reed are knowledgeable about the area and can provide a wealth of advice on places to visit and things to do. The site itself, with only some 40 fairly level, grassy pitches in 2.5 ha. of unspoiled lightly wooded countryside, provides a choice of shade or sun. Although not all are officially provided with electricity, the owners say electricity is possible everywhere. There is a small, well equipped and immaculately clean sanitary block with controllable hot showers, washbasins (H&C), British and Turkish style WCs, dishwashing and laundry sinks. Small play area, plus an activity area including petanque, table tennis, badminton and a TV tent. Bicycle hire and a reception/ shop for basics and tourist information complete the on-site amenities, but frankly it is the tranquillity and friendly reception that makes this a little gem of a site for those seeking peace and quiet without too many distractions.

Charges 2001:
-- Per pitch Ffr. 15.00; person 15.00; child (under 7 yrs) 8.00; car 9.00; electricity (5A) 14.00; animal 6.00.
-- No credit cards.
Open:
15 May - 15 September.
Address:
29300 Guilligomarc'h.
Tel:
(0)2.98.71.70.98.
FAX: as phone.
E-mail: david.reed1@ libertysurf.fr.
Reservations:
Made with deposit (Ffr. 100, 15.24 or £10); contact site.

Directions: From Arzano follow D222 to Guilligomarc'h, from where site is signed (via the C2).

2921M Camping Municipal Bois de la Palud, Plougoulm, nr Roscoff

This delightful, small municipal site is on the edge of the little village of Plougoulm, to the southwest of Roscoff. It sits on the brow of a hill with lovely views across the Guillec valley and the sandy bay and estuary to which there is access by footpath. There are 34 reasonably level, numbered pitches grouped in small hedged bays and most have access to 6A electricity (although long leads may be necessary). A small central building with all the necessary sanitary facilities also houses reception. Children's play area. Fishing, bicycle hire, riding and golf, all within 4 km. The season is short - only 15 June - 15 Sept.

Charges guide:
-- Per adult Ffr. 18.00; child 12.00; pitch 22.00; electricity 17.00.
-- No credit cards.
Open:
15 June - 15 September.
Address:
29250 Plougoulm.
Tel: (0)2.98.49.81.82, or (0)2.98.29.90.76.
Reservations:
Advised in high season.

Directions: On leaving Roscoff, follow signs for Morlaix. After 6 km. take D10 (west) signed Plouescat and after 3 km. watch for camp signs in Plougoulm.

2922M Camping Municipal de Kerisole, Scaër, nr Rosporden

Camping Kerisole is a pleasant municipal site in a park-like situation on the northeast edge of the town of Scaër. On neatly kept grass, the 80 mostly level pitches (some on a slight slope) are not hedged but are marked and numbered. Most have electrical connections (10A). Modern sanitary facilities are in three central buildings - one for ladies, one for men and the other for dishwashing, washing machines and facilities for disabled people. Although facilities are clean, maintenance can be slow. Public phone. River nearby.

Directions: Site is clearly marked on the eastern edge of Scaër, in the direction of Faouet.

Charges guide:
-- Per pitch Ffr. 13.00; car 7.50; m/cycle 6.00; motorcaravan 20.00; adult 11.50; child (under 7) 7.50; electricity 13.00.

Open:
15 June - 15 September.

Address:
29390 Scaër.

Tel:
(0)2.98.57.60.91 when open or otherwise the Mairie: (0)2.98.59.42.10. FAX: (0)2.98.57.66.89.

Reservations:
Advised - contact site.

3504 Camping Le P'tit Bois, St Jouan des Guérêts, nr St Malo

Busy, well kept site near ferry port and yachting centre of St Malo.
On the outskirts of St Malo, this neat, family oriented site is very popular with British visitors, being ideal for one night stops or for longer stays in this interesting area. Le P'tit Bois provides 294 large level pitches (approx. 140 for touring units) which are divided into groups by mature hedges and trees, separated by shrubs and flowers and with access from tarmac roads. Nearly all have electrical hook-ups (6A) and over half also have water taps. There are two sanitary blocks, one in the newer area across the lane, with British style WCs, washbasins in cabins, free, pre-set showers, chemical disposal facilities in the men's sections and laundry facilities and baby baths in the ladies'. Simple facilities for disabled people are provided. Behind reception, an attractive, sheltered terraced area around the pools provides a focus for the site, containing a bright snack bar with takeaway food, small bar, TV room (large screen for sports events) and games rooms and outdoor chess. The swimming pool complex includes a standard pool, two paddling pools and two water slides (from 15/5). At the far end are a tennis court, minigolf and table tennis. To one side of the site is a children's playground (on hard sand) and multi-sports court. Small shop (from 15/5). At the entrance, opposite reception, is a bar where entertainment and discos are organised. Motorcaravan service point. Charcoal barbecues are not permitted. Card operated security gates (Ffr 100 deposit). Fishing 1.5 km, bicycle hire or riding 5 km, golf 7 km. There are many British tour operators (25%) and site-owned mobile homes and chalets to rent, but this does mean that the facilities are open over a long season (possibly for limited hours).

Directions: St Jouan is west off the St Malo - Rennes road (N137) just outside St Malo. Site is signed from the N137 (exit St Jouan or Quelmer).

Charges 2001:
-- Per person Ffr. 32.00; child (under 7 yrs) 20.00; pitch and car 60.00 - 92.00; extra car 20.00; dog 25.00; electricity (6A) 25.00; water and drainage 15.00.
-- Credit cards accepted.

Open:
28 April - 8 September.

Address:
St Jouan-des-Guérêts, 35430 St Malo.

Tel:
(0)2.99.21.14.30. FAX: (0)2.99.81.74.14. E-mail: camping.ptitbois @wanadoo.fr.

Reservations:
Made on receipt of 25% of total cost, plus fee (120) for July/Aug.

Book this site
01892 559898

THE ALAN ROGERS'
travel service

3500 Camping Le Vieux Chêne, Dol-de-Bretagne

Attractive, family owned farm site between St Malo and Mont St Michel for families.
This site has been developed in the grounds of a farmhouse dating from 1638, with its lakes. It offers 200 good sized pitches, most with electricity, water tap and light, in spacious rural surroundings on gently sloping grass. They are separated by bushes and flowers, with mature trees for shade. A very attractive tenting area (without electricity) is located in the orchard. Three very good, unisex sanitary blocks have British style toilets, pre-set showers, washbasins in private cabins, a baby room and facilities for disabled people. Two blocks have recently been refurbished, the third nearest reception is older but still in very good order. Other facilities include a small laundry with washing machine, dryer and iron, chemical disposal and motorcaravan services. Centrally situated leisure facilities include an attractive pool complex (18/5-15/9) with a medium sized, heated swimming pool, children's pool, toboggans, slides, jacuzzi, etc. with a lifeguard during July/Aug. (traditional swimming trunks, no shorts). Added in 2000 were a new TV room (satellite) and a games room. Other free facilities include a tennis court, trampolines (no safety matting), minigolf, giant chess and a children's play area. Riding in July/Aug. Bicycle hire. Open all season are a bar, a café with terrace overlooking the pools, takeaway and a new shop. Supermarket in Dol (3 km). Fishing is possible in two of the three lakes. Some entertainment is provided in high season, free for children. Golf 12 km. Wooden chalets, mobile homes and gites for hire. Used by a Dutch tour operator (10 pitches).

Charges 2001:
-- Per unit Ffr. 40.00 - 83.00; adult 30.00; child (under 7 yrs) 15.00; electricity (5A) 22.00.
-- Credit cards accepted.

Open:
1 April - 1 October.

Address:
Baguer-Pican, 35120 Dol-de-Bretagne

Tel:
(0)2.99.48.09.55.
FAX: (0)2.99.48.13.37.
E-mail: vieux.chene @wanadoo.fr.

Reservations:
Made with deposit (Ffr. 200 or 30,49) and fee (Ffr. 120 or 18,29); contact site.

Directions: Site is by the D576 Dol-de-Bretagne - Pontorson road, just east of Baguer-Pican. It can be reached from the N176 road taking exit for Baguer-Pican and Dol-Est.

3507 Camping-Caravaning de Bel Event, St Père, nr Châteauneuf

Friendly site convenient for St Malo.
This English owned site is just 13 km. south of St Malo and is ideal for en-route stops to or from the port. It is also a good base for visiting Mont St Michel, Dinan and Rennes. Bel Event is a friendly, if unsophisticated, site with 96 grassy pitches, although some expansion is planned. Pitches are clustered in little groups and are flat with varying degrees of shade. All have electricity (6/10A). Road noise from the D74 is audible in certain areas. The central toilet block is modern with British style WCs and washbasins in cubicles. Shower cubicles are large with pre-set water temperature. The block is heated early and late in the season and there are facilities for disabled people. The site offers a good range of leisure facilities, including a heated swimming pool (June-Sept) and a separate children's pool, bicycle hire, basketball court, minigolf, table tennis and a number of bouncy castles! The modern bar overlooks the pool and is lively in high season, the same building also housing a games area and TV area. There is a well stocked shop (from Easter) with other shops in St Père or Châteauneuf, and hypermarkets in St Malo. Golf and tennis nearby. Mobile homes to hire.

Charges guide:
-- Per pitch incl. 2 adults Ffr. 80.00; electricity 20.00; extra adult 22.00; child (under 10 yrs) 15.00; extra car 10.00; extra tent 10.00.
-- Less 10% outside July/Aug.

Open:
1 March - 30 November.

Address:
St Père, 35430 Châteauneuf.

Tel:
(0)2.99.58.83.79.
FAX: (0)2.99.58.82.24.

Reservations:
Advised in high season and made with deposit (Ffr. 100 p/week).

Directions: Leave N137 St Malo - Rennes dual-carriageway at Châteauneuf exit and take D74 signed St Père and Cancale. Site is approx. 1.5 km on the left, before reaching St Père.

3502 Castel Camping Domaine des Ormes, Epiniac, Dol-de-Bretagne

Impressive site on an estate of wooded parkland and lakes, with 18 hole golf course.
This site is in the northern part of Brittany, about 30 km. from the old town of St Malo, in the grounds of the Château des Ormes. It has a pleasant atmosphere, busy in high season, almost a holiday village, but peaceful at other times, with a wide range of facilities. The 700 pitches, of which only 150 are available for touring units, are divided into a series of different sections, each with its own distinctive character, offering a choice of terrain - flat or gently sloping, wooded or open - and mixed with the range of tour operator units. There are electrical connections (3/6A) on 200 pitches. A marvellous 'Aqua Park' with pink stone and palms and a variety of pools, toboggans, waterfalls and jacuzzi (free) is situated just above the small lake with pedaloes and canoes for hire. A pleasant bar and terrace overlooks the pools and a grass sunbathing area surrounds them - almost a touch of the Caribbean! The other, original, traditional pools (heated) are sheltered by the restaurant building, parts of which are developed from the original, 600 year old water-mill. Amenities include a shop, takeaway, games room and a bar and disco, recently refurbished. A particular feature is an 18 hole golf course; also a golf practice range and a beginners 5 hole course. Other activities include minigolf, bicycle hire, two tennis courts, new sports ground with volleyball, etc, fishing, paintball, archery, horse riding on site and a cricket club. Sanitary installations are of a fair standard, providing British style WCs, washbasins in private cubicles, pre-set hot water in showers and sinks, at no charge, ample facilities for disabled people, chemical disposal and motorcaravan services. A new hotel with pool and restaurant is now part of the complex. A popular site with British visitors, with some 80% of the pitches occupied by tour operators and seasonal units and consequently very busy with much organised entertainment.

Directions: Site access road leads off main D795 about 7 km. south of Dol-de-Bretagne, north of Combourg.

Charges 2001:
--- Per person Ffr. 35.00; child (under 7) 20.00; pitch incl. vehicle 120.00; animal 7.00; electricity 3A 20.00, 6A 23.00; water and drainage 7.00; local tax (over 10 yrs) 0.50.
-- Less 10% outside July/Aug.
--- Credit cards accepted.
Open:
15 May - 10 September.
Address:
35120 Dol-de-Bretagne.
Tel:
(0)2.99.73.53.00. FAX: (0)2. 99.73.53.55.
E-mail: info@lesormes.com.
Reservations:
Made for min. 3 nights; details from site.
`Camping Cheque'

 Book this site 01892 559898

3506 Camping La Touesse, St Lunaire, Dinard

Family campsite close to Dinard and only 300 metres from the beach.
La Touesse has been purpose built and developed since 1987 by Alain Clement, who is keen to welcome more British visitors. Set just back from the coast road in a semi-residential area, it is, nevertheless, an attractive sheltered site with a range of trees and shrubs. The 142 level, grass pitches in bays (95 for touring units) have 5/10A electricity and are accessed by circular tarmac roads. A centrally situated toilet block, heated in low season, provides all modern facilities and is well maintained with free hot water everywhere. However, part of the block may not be open outside July/Aug. There are washbasins in cabins with warm water, showers with dividers, chemical disposal, a baby bath and a toilet for disabled people. Dishwashing and laundry sinks, plus two washing machines and a dryer. Motorcaravan service point. A pleasant bar restaurant, or 'club house' as it is called, operates with TV and a shop for basics (1/5-15/9). However, many amenities are nearby. Volleyball, table tennis and video games for children. Bicycle hire 1 km, Fishing 300 m, riding 500 m, golf 2 km. Mobile homes (27), chalets (10) and apartments to rent. Winter caravan storage. The plus factor of this site, besides its proximity to Dinard, is the fine sandy beach which is sheltered, so useful in early season, safe for children and just a short walk (5 minutes). The owners speak English.

Directions: From Dinard take the D786 coast road towards St Lunaire; watch for site signs to the left.

Charges 2001:
-- Per pitch Ffr. 25.00 - 36.00; adult 20.00 - 28.00; child (under 7 yrs) 12.00 - 16.00; car 14.00 - 19.00; electricity 5A 17.00 - 18.00, 10A 20.00; water 6.00; dog 5.00 - 6.00; local tax 1.50 (4-10 yrs 0.50).
-- No credit cards.
Open:
1 April - 30 September.
Address:
35800 Dinard-St Lunaire.
Tel:
(0)2.99.46.61.13. FAX: (0)2.99.16.02.58.
E-mail: camping.la.touesse@wanadoo.fr.
Reservations:
Made with deposit (Ffr. 300) and fee (100); contact site.

THE ALAN ROGERS' travel service

Book your site with the experts Call for an instant quote 01892 55 98 98

Low cost ferries guaranteed!

28

3508 Camping Le Balcon de la Baie, Saint Marcan

Peaceful, wooded site with views over the 'Baie de Mont Saint-Michel'.

Located at the top of the hill, in a preservation area, this site has superb views over the bay, with the ruins of an old mill at the back of the site. Unfortunately the Mont is just hidden from view. There are 66 pitches, of which 60 are for tourists, with 35 electric hook-ups (10A). Some pitches are in a more shady wooded area, others are around the sides of an open meadow and have a better view of the bay. The sanitary facilities are in a recently extended wooden chalet style block, with British style WCs, some washbasins in cubicles, spacious modern push-button showers, laundry and dishwashing sinks, and excellent facilities for disabled people. On-site facilities are few, a small children's playground, a 'salle' (with TV) open on demand, and a pétanque court. Soft drinks and ices are available, with bread to order. Torches could be useful, there is little site lighting.

Directions: From Pontorson take D797 for 10 km. approx, turning left on D89 after leaving La Poultière (site is signed), continue up hill through village, site is signed to left at far end.

Charges 2000:
-- Per adult Ffr. 22.00; child (under 7 yrs) 16.00; pitch 27.00; animal 10.00; electricity 16.00.
-- Credit cards accepted.
Open:
1 April - 31 October.
Address:
Saint Marcan, 35120 Dol de Bretagne.
Tel:
(0)2.99.80.22.95.
FAX: as phone.
Reservations:
Contact site for details.

4404 Castel Camping Parc Sainte-Brigitte, La Turballe, nr La Baule

Well established site in the grounds of a manor house, 3 km. from beaches.

A mature and spacious site, Sainte Brigitte has 150 pitches, 106 with electricity (6A) and 25 with water and waste water also. Some are in a circular, park-like setting near the entrance, more are in the wooded areas under tall trees and others are on more open grass in an unmarked area near the pool. One can walk around many of the areas of the estate not used for camping, there are farm animals to see and a fishing lake is very popular. The main sanitary block has free hot water in all facilities and is of fair quality, supplemented by a second block next to it. They offer British style toilets, washbasins in private cabins, with bidets for women, fully controllable, well equipped showers, two bathrooms and sinks. Water taps around. Washing machines and dryer (no washing to be hung out on pitches, lines are provided), chemical disposal and motorcaravan services are provided. Amenities include a children's playground, bicycle hire, boules, volleyball, pool and 'baby-foot' and table tennis room. A TV room and traditional 'salle de reunion' are in renovated outbuildings of the manor house. A heated swimming pool and a children's pool are open all season, there is a small shop for basics and a nice little restaurant/bar with takeaway (both 15/5-15/9). Bread is available (baker calls). A quiet place to stay outside the main season, with few facilities open; in high season, however, it is mainly used by families with its full share of British visitors and it can become very busy. Inland from the main road, it is a little under 3 km. from the nearest beach, with a variety of sandy ones near with safe bathing. Riding 2 km, golf 15 km. Used by a tour operator (20 pitches).

Directions: Entrance is off the busy La Turballe-Guérande D99 road, 3 km. east of La Turballe. A one-way system operates - in one lane, out via another.

Charges 2001:
-- Per person Ffr 30.50 plus 1.00 tax; child (under 7) 20.00; pitch 31.50, with water and electricity 69.50; car 16.50; dog 9.50.
-- No credit cards.
Open:
1 April - 1 October.
Address:
44420 La Turballe.
Tel:
(0)2.40.24.88.91.
FAX: (0)2.40.23.30.42.
Reservations:
Made for any length with exact dates and recommended for July/Aug, with deposit (Ffr. 500) plus fee (100).

Book this site
01892 559898

THE ALAN ROGERS'
travel service

PARC SAINTE-BRIGITTE

★ ★ ★ ★ N.N.
De Luxe Camping Site

HEATED SWIMMING POOL
Covered pool planned for 2001

Close to the fishing village of La Turballe and neighbouring beaches. 10 km. from the well-known resort of La Baule. The charm of the countryside with the pleasures of the seaside. Sanitary facilities as in a first class hotel.

BRITTANY - 44 Loire-Atlantique

4403 Castel Camping Le Pré du Château de Careil, Guérande

Select, small, 'tranquil haven' for all units, near La Baule.

This site is totally different from the more usual Castel sites. It is the smallest site in the group and has few of the facilities or activities usually associated with such sites. It has a quiet atmosphere and is very popular with couples, retired people and those with young children. In the grounds of the Château de Careil, a building dating from the 14th century, this small site, shaded by mature trees, contains just 50 good sized pitches. All are equipped with electricity (6/10A) and water, some with drainage. There is a small pool (11 x 5 m. open 15/6-5/9). In season some emergency provisions are kept and bread can be ordered; a supermarket is near. Children's playground, TV room, volleyball and table tennis. Sanitary facilities provide British style WCs with washbasins in cubicles, and are in the same building as reception. Four unisex shower and washbasin rooms have been added, the old external WCs have been re-tiled and there is free hot water. En-suite facilities for disabled people, a baby room and a washing machine are provided. A mobile pizzeria/crêperie visits in high season. Fishing or golf 10 km, bicycle hire 2 km, riding 5 km. In July/Aug, tours of the Château are possible (Ffr. 25), also by candlelight (Ffr. 30). Archery is offered occasionally in the Château courtyard.

Directions: Take D92 from Guérande to La Baule and turn east to Careil before the town. From D99 Guérande - St Nazaire road, turn on D92, following signs for Château de Careil. Entrance gate is fairly narrow and is between two bends.

Charges 2001:
-- Per unit incl. 2 persons and 6A electricity Ffr. 110.00 - 129.00; extra person 26.00; extra child (under 10 yrs) 16.00; 10A electricity 10.00; local tax 3.00 (4-10 yrs 1.50).
-- No credit cards.

Open:
1 May - 24 September.

Address:
Château de Careil, 44350 Guérande.

Tel:
(0)2.40.60.22.99.
FAX: as phone.

Reservations:
Possible with deposit (Ffr 400) and booking fee (100).

4411 Airotel La Roseraie, La Baule

Modern site close to holiday resort of La Baule and beaches.

A useful base, being only 1 km. from the town and 2 km. from the beach, this site has its own swimming pool and reasonably modern facilities. The 224 mostly individual pitches are on grass with some quite tall dividing hedges. Around 175 are for tourists, the remainder occupied by site owned rental or privately owned units. All pitches have electricity (3, 6 or 10A), and many are fully serviced with water and waste water drain. The two sanitary units have British style WCs, washbasins (some in private cabins), and controllable free hot showers. There are good facilities for babies and disabled people, plus dishwashing sinks and a well equipped laundry. Grouped around the entrance and open in high season are the shop, bar and restaurant (1/7-31/8), and swimming pool (21 x 10 m) with water slide and children's pool. Other amenities include a playground, tennis and half-courts, a fitness room, TV room and table tennis. Security is good with a card operated barrier by day, gates locked from 23.00-07.00 and a night security guard. However, the site is adjacent to N171 which lies in a cutting, and there may be some road noise at times. Golf 2 km, riding 1 km. There is a daily market, casino, night clubs and a cinema in town. Used minimally by tour operators (10 pitches). Mobile homes (42) and chalets (11) to rent.

Directions: Site is 2.5 km. north of the town centre towards the golf course, close to the N171/D99, and is well signed in the town.

> **Book this site**
> **01892 559898**
> THE ALAN ROGERS'
> travel service

Charges 2000:
-- Per pitch Ffr. 50.00 - 65.00, with electricity (3A) 70.00 - 85.00; adult 25.00 - 35.00; child (1-5 yrs) 16.00 - 20.00; dog 12.00 - 15.00; water and drainage 12.00 - 15.00; local tax July/Aug. 2.00.
-- Credit cards accepted.

Open:
April - September.

Address:
20 avenue Jean Sohier, Route du Golf, 44500 La Baule.

Tel:
(0)2.40.60.46.66.
FAX: (0)2.40.60.11.84.
E-mail: roserie@ post.club.internet.fr.

Reservations:
Made with deposit (Ffr 600, Euro 91.46), fee (100, 15.24) and insurance (50, 7.62).

4402M Camping Municipal Le Moulin, Clisson

This good value, small site is conveniently located on one of the main north - south routes on the edge of the interesting old town of Clisson. The site has 47 good sized, marked and level pitches with electricity (6A) and divided by hedges and trees; also an unmarked area for small tents. The single unisex toilet block has British style WCs, washbasins, some in cabins and others in a separate large room, with hot and cold water. Hot and cold showers are roomy and there is a unit for disabled people, dishwashing and laundry sinks and chemical disposal. Cleaning can be a bit haphazard at times. A barbecue area is to the rear of the site above the river where one can fish or canoe (via a steep path). Table tennis, volleyball, and small children's playground. The warden lives on site in high season. The town is within walking distance, a supermarket is across the road, and bread is delivered daily. No double axle or commercial vehicles accepted.

Directions: Entering Clisson from the north on N149 (Nantes - Poitiers) road, turn right at roundabout after supermarket on left. Access is directly off roundabout.

Charges 2001:
-- Per pitch 13.00; adult 15.00; child (0-7 yrs) 10.00; car or m/cycle 9.00; electricity 15.00.

Open:
1 April - 31 October.

Address:
Route de Nantes, 44190 Clisson.

Tel:
(0)2.40.54.44.48.
FAX: (0)2.40.80.17.66 (Office du Tourisme).

Reservations:
Contact site.

4409 Castel Camping Château du Deffay, Pontchâteau

Relaxed, family managed site, near Côte d'Amour and Brière Regional National Park.

Château de Deffay is a refreshing departure from the usual Castel formula in that it is not over organised or supervised and has no tour operator units. The landscape is natural right down to the molehills, and the site blends well with the rural environment of the estate, lake and farmland which surround it. For these reasons it is enjoyed by many. However, with the temptation of free pedaloes and the fairly deep, unfenced lake, parents should ensure that children are supervised. The 120 good sized, fairly level pitches have pleasant views and either on open grass, shallow terraces divided by hedges, or informally arranged in a central, semi-sloping wooded area. Most have 6A electricity. The main sanitary unit, housed in a converted barn, is well equipped with modern free controllable hot showers, British type toilets, washbasins in cabins with hooks and shelves. Provision for disabled people and a baby bathroom have been added and there are washing machines, a dryer and chemical disposal. Maintenance can be variable and, with the boiler located at one end of the block, hot water can take time to reach the other in low season. Motorcaravan services. Extra facilities are available in the old courtyard area of the smaller château (which dates from before 1400) which is also where the bar and small restaurant with takeaway, well stocked shop and the solar heated swimming pool and paddling pool are located (all 15/5-15/9). The larger château (built 1880) and another lake stand away from this area providing pleasant walking. The reception has been built separately to contain the camping area. There is a play area on grass, a TV in the bar, a separate room for table tennis and English language animation in season including a children's mini-club. Activities include tennis and swimming, pedaloes and fishing in the lake, all free, plus riding and bicycle hire. The Guérande Peninsula, La Baule Bay and the natural wilderness of the Grande Brière are near. Golf 5 km. Alpine type chalets (23) to let overlook the lake and fit well with the environment. Torch useful.

Directions: Site is signed from the D33 Pontchâteau - Herbignac road near Ste. Reine. Also signed from the D773 and N165.

Charges 2001:
-- Per pitch Ffr. 39.00 - 59.00, with electricity (4A) 60.00 - 80.00; with 3 services 69.00 - 90.00; per adult 16.00 - 26.00; child (2-12 yrs) 11.00 - 17.00.
-- Credit cards accepted.

Open:
5 May - 22 September.

Address:
BP 18, Sainte Reine, 44160 Pontchâteau.

Tel:
(0)2.40.88.00.57.
FAX: (0)2.40.01.66.55.

Reservations:
Accepted for a min. period of 6 nights with deposit (Ffr. 60 per day) and fee (100).

`Camping Cheque'

Book this site
01892 559898

THE ALAN ROGERS'
travel service

see colour advert between pages 160/161

4412 Parc de Léveno, Guérande

Holiday-style site on outskirts of historic walled town.

The historic walled town of Guérande is delightful, albeit too crowded for comfort in the high season, but Parc de Léveno could offer a degree of tranquillity for those looking to explore this area and visit Guérande and La Baule. In fact Parc de Léveno seems to be something of an enigma. Built as a holiday-style site with lots of facilities and lots of mobile homes, by contrast its 200 or so touring pitches are amongst the nicest we have seen, with ample space, good shade and very attractive surroundings. The sanitary facilities on the other hand are something of a disappointment - adequate, relatively modern, but generally tired looking and in need of some TLC. As to maintenance, we reserve judgement as (in late June) the site was less than half full when we visited. The pitches themselves deserve more description - not only are they all quite large, on mainly flat grass, but they are situated amongst a variety of mature trees and bushes which makes the touring area a very attractive one. The majority have older style French electrical connections, all are said to have water on tap, and many also have drainage connections. The site has a large swimming pool, children's pool and a toboggan which empties into a small separate pool, fair sized sunbathing area, two tennis courts, children's play area (unfenced, but not too close to traffic) and minigolf. Catering facilities include a takeaway, cafeteria style restaurant with terrace, and a shop, but what attracted us to this site was the pitches and touring area which offers the possibility of peace and quiet, yet within the confines of a busy, holiday style site. Mobile homes and tents to rent.

Directions: Site is actually about 5 km. north of La Baule and east of Guérande and is signed from the Guérande bypass, past the new Leclerc.

Charges guide:
-- Per pitch Ffr. 64.00, with 6A electricity 81.00, with water and drainage 92.00; adult 25.00; child (under 7 yrs) 13.00; extra car 10.00; animal 10.00; 10A electricity plus 5.00; local tax June-Sept 3.00 (4-10 yrs 1.50).
-- Per pitch 9.85, with 6A electricity 12.46, with water and drainage 14.15; adult 3.85; child (under 7 yrs) 2.00; extra car 1.54; animal 1.54; 10A electricity plus 0.77.
-- Less 30% outside July/Aug.

Open:
1 May - 25 September.

Address:
44350 Guérande.

Tel:
(0)2.40.24.79.30 or
(0)2.40.24.79.50.
FAX: (0)2.40.62.01.23.

Reservations:
Made with 30% deposit; contact site.

4410 Camping Caravaning International Le Patisseau, Pornic

Friendly, busy site with its own pool, near fishing port of Pornic.

Le Patisseau is rurally situated 2.5 km. from the sea. It is quite a relaxed site which can be very busy and even a little noisy in high season due to its popularity with young families and teenagers. The older part of the site has an attractive woodland setting, although the pitches are slightly smaller than in the newer 'field' section, but most have water and electricity (4, 6 or 10A). Hedges are growing well in the newer section marking individual pitches. A railway line runs along the bottom half of the site with trains two or three times a day, but they do finish at 10.30 pm. and the noise is minimal. The site's restaurant and bar (1/4-30/8) were rebuilt for 2000 overlooking a new indoor pool (with sauna, jacuzzi and spa). Outside are two water slides, a medium sized open air pool (from 1/5-30/8), a games area with volleyball and table tennis and play areas. Three sanitary blocks with the one behind reception most recently refurbished. The other two date from the late '80s and are beginning to show their age. These include free hot showers, washbasins in private cabins, British style WCs, child-size toilets, baby baths, fully equipped laundry rooms and dishwashing. Chemical disposal. Shop (all season). Bicycle hire. Fishing 1.5 km, golf 5 km. This a happy, busy site and the Morice family work hard to maintain a friendly atmosphere, but don't expect it to be too neat and tidy with everything run like clockwork - they want people to enjoy themselves. Pornic itself is a delightful fishing village and the coastline is interesting with secluded sandy coves and inlets. Chalets and mobile homes for hire.

Directions: Site signed at roundabout junction of D751 (Pornic - Nantes) road, and from the town centre.

Charges 2001:
-- Per unit incl. 2 persons Ffr. 90.00 - 148.00; extra adult 33.00; child (1-7 yrs) 22.00; dog 25.00; electricity 25.00 - 35.00; local tax 1.70.
-- Credit cards accepted.
Open:
1 April - 15 September.
Address:
29 Rue du Patisseau, 44210 Pornic.
Tel:
(0)2.40.82.10.39.
FAX: (0)2.40.82.22.81.
E-mail: contact@ lepatisseau.com.
Reservations:
Made with deposit (Ffr. 300) and fee (Ffr. 100).

Book this site
01892 559898

THE ALAN ROGERS'
travel service

see colour advert between pages 64/65

4413 Camping L'Hermitage, Guémené-Penfao

Neat ex-municipal site with pool, for en-route or longer stops.

The helpful staff, even though their English is a little limited, provide a warm welcome and maintain this ex-municipal to high standards. The smallish pool and accompanying paddling pool is nicely maintained with a few sun loungers and all carefully fenced. There are 110 pitches including around 20 with site owned Trigano tents (some to hire). Half the rest of the touring pitches are level and `semi-delimité' with various bushes and trees, while the other half are more natural and less formally arranged amongst light woodland. Electricity (6A) is available to all (a long lead may be useful). The central, fairly typical municipal-type toilet block has pre-set roomy showers and some washbasins in cabins, others vanity style, with warm water. Laundry and dishwashing sinks are under cover and have cold water, but a hot tap is provided and a washing machine. During July/Aug. snacks, drinks, etc. are available, but the centre of the village is only 1 km. for all facilities. On site amenities include a small children's play area, table tennis, petanque and 'salle de jeune' with baby foot and video games. A leisure complex is next to the site and there are many walking trails. Fishing 500 m. Riding 2 km. This is a useful, reasonably priced site.

Directions: Exit N137 at Derval (signed Châteaubriant) but take D775 for Redon. Guémené-Penfao is approx. 13 km. Watch for site signs before village centre. Site is in the outskirts in a semi-residential area to the northeast.

Charges guide:
-- Per unit incl. 2 adults Ffr. 45.00 - 52.00; extra adult 15.00; child (under 10 yrs) 8.00; electricity 13.00; dog 3.00.
-- Credit cards accepted.
Open:
1 April - 15 October.
Address:
36 avenue du Paradis, 44290 Guémené-Penfao.
Tel:
(0)2.40.79.23.48.
FAX: (0)2.40.51.11.87.
Reservations:
Contact site.

Book this site
01892 559898

THE ALAN ROGERS'
travel service

4414M Camping Municipal Henri Dubourg, Nozay

This good, small site is ideal for short stays or as an overnight stop, being situated in the northern outskirts of Nozay with easy access from the N137 Rennes - Nantes road. The neat, modern toilet block has plenty of hot water, roomy showers and includes an odd Turkish style toilet. A washing up area is under cover behind the block and laundry sinks are inside. There are 25 well hedged, level, grassy pitches with electricity (6A) and a more open area at the rear of the site. Tourist information and an ice pack service are available at reception, there is a barbecue area and a baker calls each morning. Nozay has two supermarkets. A small lake with a playground and minigolf are a five minute walk and a pool is nearby. Fishing or golf 400 m. Reception opens 07.30-09.00 and 18.00-20.30 hrs.

Directions: From N137 take N171 Chateaubriant exit, then take first right D121 for Nozay. Site is on right after the lake (approx. 1 km).

Charges 2000:
-- Per pitch Ffr. 12.00; car 10.00; adult 12.00; child (under 7 yrs) 6.00; animal 6.00; electricity 12.00.
Open:
15 May - 15 September.
Address:
Route de Rennes, 44170 Nozay.
Tel:
(0)2.40.87.94.33.
Mairie: (0)2.40.79.79.79.
Reservations:
Contact the site.

For everything about caravanning,
motor caravanning and camping, go to
www.oakwood-village.com

Camping**** du Petit Port
NANTES
21, Bd du Petit Port - 44300 Nantes
Tél. 33 (0)2 40 74 47 94 - Fax : 33 (0)2 40 74 23 06 - E-Mail : nge@nge-nantes.fr

Camping du Petit Port

North ring road :
Exit **Porte de La Chapelle**
Direction :
Petit Port / Université

A11

A821

N 160
Angers
le Mans
Paris

Pont
de la jonelière

RN 165

Saint-Nazaire
Vannes
Lorient
Brest

RD 201

NANTES

Pont de Bellevue

N 249
Poitiers
Cholet

Porte de
La Chapelle

Porte
de
Rennes

Hippodrome

Tramway n°2

CAMPING

P Université

Pont de Chevire

RN 149
Poitiers
Cholet

CENTRE
DE LOISIRS
du PETIT PORT

P

Rond-point
de Rennes

RD 751
Pornic
Saint-Brévin

A 801
La Roche-sur-Yon
La Rochelle
Niort
Bordeaux

Nantes
centre

NANTES

NGE
GESTION
EQUIPEMENTS

Mobile-homes for rent

La Grande Métairie
★★★★

LES CASTELS

CAMPING PLUS
BRETAGNE

" EXCEPTIONAL HOLIDAYS! "

Route des Alignements de Kermario
B.P. 85 - 56342 CARNAC Cedex
Bretagne-Sud - France
Tél. 33 (0)2 97 52 24 01 - Fax. 33 (0)2 97 52 83 58
e-mail : grande.metairie@wanadoo.fr

4401M Camping du Petit Port, Nantes

This modern site, which is within the town limits, is well maintained and of good quality in a park-like area with mature trees. It has 120 flat good-sized, hedged hardstandings for caravans, all with electricity (10A), water and drainaway (awning pegs possibly a problem). From Easter - 30 Sept. it also takes about 80 tents on separate grass areas. At certain times the caravan pitches become full with those working in the town or visiting for commercial reasons; however, in the holiday season, it is said that about half are available for tourists and one should usually find a space. The four sanitary blocks are good and unusually have code-controlled access. They can be heated and provide British style toilets, individual washbasins in cubicles (a little cramped), free hot water throughout including the showers and facilities for disabled people. Motorcaravan service point open to all (free for those staying on the site, otherwise Ffr. 18). Amenities on site include a shop for basics (1/6-30/8), launderette, TV room, bicycle hire and a children's play area. Telephones. A heated swimming pool (free for campers), ice rink (discount), bowling alley and café are very close, a bakery 100 m. and an English-owned restaurant is opposite. A golf course is easily accessible via the new tramway and the site offers an all-inclusive golfing package. The tramway system within the town is cheap and reliable (tickets available from reception) and the site is easily reached by bus or tram from the railway station. Mobile homes for hire (23). Winter caravan storage.

Directions: Site is on the northern edge of the town on Bvd. Petit Port, near the university (ring road east). From express road use exit signed Porte de la Châpelle and follow signs for Petit Port and university. Alternatively follow signs 'Porte de Rennes'.

Charges 2000:
-- Per caravan incl. car or motorcaravan Ffr. 39.20 - 49.00; tent plus car 29.60 - 37.00, without car 20.80 - 26.00; person 14.40 - 18.00; child (under 10 yrs) 9.60 - 12.00; electricity (10A) 18.00; double axle caravans 73.60 - 92.00; local tax 1.00.
-- Less 20% for stays over 3 days.
-- Special golf packages.
-- Credit cards accepted.

Open:
All year.

Address:
21 Bvd. du Petit Port, 44300 Nantes.

Tel:
(0)2.40.74.47.94.
FAX: (0)2.40.74.23.06.
E-mail: nge@nge-nantes.fr.

Reservations:
Not made, but you could phone the previous day.

see colour advert opposite

5601 Castel Camping La Grande Métairie, Carnac

Good quality site in southern Brittany with many facilities.

La Grande Métairie is quietly situated, a little back from the sea, close to some impressive rows of the famous 'menhirs' (giant prehistoric standing stones). It has much to offer on site and is lively and busy over a long season. There is a feeling of spaciousness with a wide entrance and access road, with 574 individual pitches (180 for touring units), surrounded by hedges and trees. All have electricity (30 m. cables are needed in parts). Paddocks with ponds are home for ducks, goats and ponies to watch and feed and there is a large playing field with football posts. New in 2000 was a swimming pool complex comprising heated pools, water slides and toboggans, flowing river, jacuzzi and a covered pool, in addition to the original pool. The new complex has a poolside bar and terrace. An entertainment area includes an outside amphitheatre developed for musical evenings and barbecues. Events are organised daytime and evening. The three large toilet blocks are good and well maintained, with free hot water, British toilets, washbasins in private cabins, free pre-set showers, hairdryers, and facilities for babies and disabled people, chemical disposal, and each with a laundry room. Other amenities include a shop, boutique, restaurant, good takeaway, bar lounge and terrace, and adjoining TV and games rooms. Occasional dances are arranged (pitches near these facilities may be noisy late at night – the bar closes at midnight). Activities include pony rides around the site, two tennis courts, volleyball and basketball, minigolf, two children's playgrounds, a BMX track, bicycle hire, table tennis and fishing (on permit). Riding 1 km, golf 12 km. Motorcaravan service points. Mobile homes for hire (63). The nearest beach is about 3 km. by road. Local market at Carnac on Wednesdays and Sundays. The site, although large and not cheap, is well known and popular. Services are limited before late May. American motorhomes accepted up to 30 ft. Dogs and other pets are only accepted by arrangement. It has a large British contingent with 310 pitches taken by several tour operators, plus the site-owned mobile homes to rent and many British touring caravanners and campers.

Directions: From N165 take Quiberon/Carnac exit onto the D768. After 5 km. turn left on D119 towards Carnac and after 4 km. turn left at traffic lights onto D196 to the site.

Charges 2001:
-- Per person Ffr. 35.00; child (under 7 yrs) 25.00; pitch incl. car 140.00, with electricity (6A) 160.00 local tax (over 15) 2.20.
-- Less 20% 26/5-29/6 and after 25/8, 40% before 26/5.
-- Credit cards accepted.

Open:
31 March - 15 September (all services from 26/5).

Address:
B.P. 85,
56342 Carnac-Cedex.

Tel:
(0)2.97.52.24.01.
FAX: (0)2.97.52.83.58.
E-mail: grande.metairie@wanadoo.fr.

Reservations:
Made (min. 1 week) with deposit (Ffr. 20 per person, per day, no fee). English is spoken - office open from 2 Jan.

see colour advert opposite

5605 Camping Kervilor, La Trinité-sur-Mer, nr Carnac

Quieter, more spacious site, slightly inland from busy resort.

Kervilor may be a good alternative for those who find the beach-side sites in La Trinité too busy and lively. In a village on the outskirts of the town, it has 200 pitches on flat grass and is attractively landscaped with trees (silver birches) and flowers. The pitches, 180 with electricity (3/6A), are in groups divided by hedges, and are separated by shrubs and trees. There is a feeling of spaciousness. Sanitary facilities are in two modern blocks of good standard with further facilities in an older block by the entrance (all very clean when seen). They offer pre-set, free hot showers, washbasins, many in cabins, free hairdryers, British style WCs, chemical disposal and facilities for disabled people and babies. Dishwashing is under cover and there is a small laundry. Centrally placed is a bar with terrace (20/5-9/9), a medium sized swimming pool, children's pool, water slide pool and sunbathing area. A new pool complex is planned. At one end of the site is a play area with children's play equipment on sand and with minigolf, pétanque, tennis, volleyball and table tennis outside and under cover. Bicycle hire. Fishing or riding 2 km, golf 12 km. The site has a small shop for basics and takeaway food in season, but the facilities of the town are not far away by car (1.5 km). The sandy beach is 2 km. Mobile homes for hire (21). Used by tour operators (22).

Directions: Site is north of La Trinité-sur-Mer and is signed in the town centre. From Auray take D186 Quiberon road; turn left at camp sign at Kergrioux on D186 to La Trinité-sur-Mer, and left again at outskirts of town.

Charges 2001:
-- Per person Ffr. 25.00; child (under 7 yrs) 16.00; local tax (over 10 yrs) 2.00; pitch 64.00; car 15.00; m/cycle 10.00; electricity 3A 13.00, 6A 16.00.
-- Low season less 25%.
-- 7 days for the price of 6 outside July/Aug.
-- No credit cards.
Open:
15 May - 15 September.
Address:
56470
La Trinité-sur-Mer.
Tel:
(0)2.97.55.76.75.
FAX: (0)2.97.55.87.26.
Reservations:
Made with deposit (Ffr. 300) and fee (120).

5609 Camping Le Moulin de Kermaux, Carnac

Family run, compact site close to the Carnac megaliths.

Only 100 m. from the famous Carnac megaliths, Le Moulin de Kermaux is an excellent venue from which these ancient stones can be seen, as they portray their ever changing mood, colour and profile. The family run site has 150 pitches (120 with 6-10A electricity) and its compact nature offers a safe environment for parents and children alike. A well stocked shop caters for daily needs (20/5-7/9) with large supermarkets for serious shopping 3 km. away. The 70 pitches for touring units are mostly separated by hedges and numerous mature trees offer welcome shade. All amenities in the sanitary block are under cover, and are of a high standard of cleanliness. Toilets are a mixture of (mainly) British and (a few) Turkish types. Showers, individual washrooms, laundry, washing up facilities and special baby bath have hot water. Washing machine and dryer – a large washing line can be found behind the shop. Alongside the bar the conservatory overlooks the children's paddling pool, which is adjacent to the main pool. Sun-loungers are provided in the adequate surrounding area. Sauna and jacuzzi nearby. The bar is open evenings in low season (20/5-7/9), all day in high season. Children are well catered for with a challenging adventure playground, volley and basketball courts, minigolf and table tennis. During high season, a resident 'animateur' organises a variety of competitions during the day and a weekly disco and karaoke in the evening. Fishing, bicycle hire and riding within 2 km. Keen distance walkers, and families with young children alike, will enjoy the numerous footpaths in the area which provide a refuge from the busy highways. Sandy beaches and rocky coves are within 3 km. Carnac town provides an assortment of boutiques, crêperies, restaurants and night clubs. Motorcaravan service point. Mobile homes (20) for rent. Used by tour operators (25 pitches).

Directions: From N165 take Quiberon/Carnac exit onto D768. After 5 km. turn left on D781 to Carnac and following camp signs, turn left at traffic lights to site.

Charges 2001:
-- Per person Ffr. 24.00; child (under 7 yrs) 17.00; pitch and car 74.00; dog 10.00; electricity 3A 16.00, 6A 18.00; local tax 2.20.
-- Less 10-40% outside high season.
-- Credit cards accepted.
Open:
3 April - 15 September.
Address:
56340 Carnac.
Tel:
(0)2.97.52.15.90.
FAX: (0)2.97.52.83.85.
Reservations:
Contact site.

5610 Camping du Moulin Neuf, Rochefort en Terre

Quiet family site in wooded countryside, 600 m. from small medieval town.

Ian and Norma Hetherington have worked hard over the last few years to develop Moulin Neuf into a neat, tidy and comfortable site and provide a warm welcome. The site has 60 pitches (44 with 10A electrical connections) of good size (120 sq.m.) on neat grass, and is laid out on two levels. The top level, with a limited number of electrical hook-ups, is flat and pitches are divided by young shrubs. The entrance to the site is here and reception is just beyond the security gate. The lower level is partly sloping but offers mature trees, shade and electricity on all the pitches. The modern heated sanitary block, although on the bottom half, is convenient for both levels. Facilities are kept very clean and include large, comfortable showers, cabins with washbasins, mirrors, hooks, shaver points, etc. and British and Turkish style WCs. There is provision for disabled people, a baby changing room, dishwashing area and laundry room with sinks, washing machine and dryer, also washing lines and chemical disposal. For leisure there is a heated swimming pool, tennis court, table tennis, basketball, football area and two boules pitches, also an attractive bar with pool table. Children enjoy two play areas and riding and golf are available locally. A lake is within 500 m. of the site with water-sports possibilities. The beach is a 30 minute drive to Vannes and the Golfe du Morbihan. Basic foodstuffs are available on site and bread is delivered each morning. Weekly barbecues are organised in season. Rochefort en Terre itself is a marvellous medieval town, beautifully preserved and only ten minutes walk from the site, with a wealth of art and craft workshops, antique shops and art galleries.

Charges guide:
-- Per pitch Ffr. 42.00 - 50.00; adult 18.00 - 21.00; child (under 8 yrs) 12.00 - 14.00; electricity 25.00; local tax 1.00 - 2.00.

Open:
1 April - 30 September.

Address:
56220 Rochefort en Terre.

Tel:
(0)2.97.43.37.52. FAX: (0)2.97.43.35.45.

Reservations:
Made with deposit (Ffr. 250) and fee (50); contact site for booking form.

Directions: From Redon take D775 Vannes road west for 25 km. Branch north on D774 signed Rochefort en Terre. Follow road past the lake on left, in 800 m. Turn left and follow sign to site.

5611 Camping du Moustoir, Carnac

Developing site, with good pool complex and relaxed atmosphere.

Du Moustoir is a family run site which is within easy reach of Carnac (2 km), the beach and the 'menhirs' – the standing stones for which the area is renowned. The 103 marked and numbered tourist pitches, most with electricity (6A), are on slightly sloping ground, some amongst pine trees and some more open but divided by very new plantings of shrubs. In addition there are a further 62 pitches occupied by tour operators or site owned units to rent. The substantial, traditional sanitary unit is central and is divided into four separate rooms, giving two complete sets of facilities for both ladies and men (but outside peak times one set may be closed). These provide British style WCs (with bidets for ladies), washbasins and pre-set free hot showers. Chemical disposal and motorcaravan service facilities. The showers were refitted for the '98 season, and the site has an ongoing programme of refurbishment planned for the rest of the facilities over the next few years. Behind reception is the heated swimming pool (21 x 8 m) with water slides and landing pool, and a children's pool with mushroom (from 15/5). Other amenities include a small shop, bar and takeaway (all from 20/5, hours vary), a small adventure style children's playground, games room, an area for ball games including volleyball, football and basketball, plus boules and tennis courts. A 'Kids Club' (10.30-12.00 daily) and other family entertainment are organised in high season. Fishing, bicycle hire or riding 2 km, golf 5 km. An attractive, good value Auberge is within walking distance.

turn left (oblique turning) after a hotel, and site is 500 m. on your left.

Charges 2001:
-- Per pitch Ffr. 39.00 - 70.00; adult 17.00 - 26.00; child (under 7 yrs) 10.00 - 17.00; extra car 10.00 - 20.00; electricity 12.00 - 19.00; water and drainage 17.00 - 26.00; local tax (over 15 yrs) 2.20.
-- No credit cards.

Open:
1 May - 9 September.

Address:
56340 Carnac.

Tel:
(0)2.97.52.16.18. FAX: (0)2.97.52.88.37.

Book this site
01892 559898

THE ALAN ROGERS'
travel service

Directions: From the N165, take exit to D768 (Carnac and Quiberon), at second crossroads after 5 km. take left hand junction (D119) towards Carnac. After 3 km.

5604 Camping de Penboch, Arradon, nr Vannes

Quietly situated site with good facilities on the Golfe du Morbihan.

Penboch is 200 m. by footpath from the shores of the Golfe du Morbihan with its many islands, where there is plenty to do including watersports, fishing and boat trips. There are also old towns with weekly markets near and it is 30 minutes walk to Arradon which has a good range of shops and restaurants. The site is in a peaceful, rural area and is divided into two parts - one in woodland with lots of shade and used mainly for mobile homes and youth groups (which can be very noisy at times) and the other main part, across a minor road on more open ground with hedges and young trees. Penboch offers 175 pitches on flat grass, mostly divided into groups; electricity is available on most pitches (6/10A) and there are plenty of water points. The three sanitary blocks, two on the main part of the site and one on the annex, provide showers with free hot water, washbasins in cabins and British style WCs. These blocks come under considerable pressure in peak season. There are washing machines and dryers, chemical disposal and a motorcaravan service point. There is a friendly bar with satellite TV, snacks and take-away, where basic food supplies are also kept (all 24/5-9/9) and a further TV room. A heated swimming pool with water slide, a toboggan and a children's pool with mushroom fountain (1/5-15/9) are in the centre of the site and a good playground, visible from reception, is provided with interesting play equipment. Games room. Fishing 200 m, bicycle hire 6 km, golf or riding 6 km. Sailing and windsurfing 2 km. Barbecues are allowed. American motorhomes accepted in low season. Caravan storage. Site owned mobile homes and bungalows for rent (20). Popular with British tour operators (40 pitches). A 'Sites et Paysages' member.

Charges 2001:
-- Per person Ffr. 20.00 - 28.00; child (under 7 yrs) 10.00 - 20.00; pitch incl. car 25.00 - 95.00; electricity 6A 18.00, 10A 25.00; water/drainage 20.00; extra car 15.00; dog free - 10.00; local tax (over 18 yrs) 3.00.
-- Credit cards accepted.

Open:
7 April - 23 September.

Address:
9 Chemin de Penboch, 56610 Arradon.

Tel:
(0)2.97.44.71.29.
FAX: (0)2.97.44.79.10.
E-mail: camping.penboch @wanadoo.fr.

Reservations:
Advised for high season (min. 7 days 10/7-18/8).

Directions: From N165 at Auray or Vannes, take D101 along northern shores of the Golfe du Morbihan; or leave N165 at D127 signed Ploeren and Arradon. Take turn to Arradon and site is signed.

Book this site
01892 559898
THE ALAN ROGERS'
travel service

CAMPING DE PENBOCH ★★★★
F 56610 ARRADON

SITES & PAYSAGES DE FRANCE

At the heart of the picturesque region of Southern Brittany, 200 m from the Gulf of Morbihan, and 5 km from Vannes (excursions to the islands, fishing, sailing ...)
On the camp site there is:
♦ Heated swimming pool with water toboggan.
♦ Children's playground - Minigolf - Bar - Young people's room - Service area for motorhomes.
♦ Caravans and Bungalows for hire.
Tel: 02 97 44 71 29   Fax: 02 97 44 79 10
email: camping.penboch@wanadoo.fr

5608M Camping Municipal du Pâtis, La Roche Bernard

This is another of those excellent municipal sites one comes across in France. Situated beside the River Vilaine, just below the very attractive old town of La Roche Bernard and beside the port and marina, it provides 60 level grass, part-hedged pitches, with 10A electricity and water, in bays of 4. Two sanitary blocks, one new and very modern, the other fully refurbished, provide excellent showers, washbasins in cabins, all with hot water, and British style WCs. A new laundry room behind reception houses a washing machine and dryer. Small children's play area. Public telephone. Next door is a sailing school, boats to hire, fishing, tennis, archery, etc. Bicycle hire 500 m, riding 5 km, golf 15 km. A restaurant and bar are on the quay-side, with others uphill in the town.

Directions: Go into town centre and follow signs for the Port around a one-way system and then a sharp turn down hill.

Charges guide:
-- Per pitch Ffr. 20.00; adult 16.00; child (under 9 yrs) 8.00; vehicle 7.00; electricity 14.00.
-- No credit cards.

Open:
Easter/April - 30 Sept.

Address:
3 Chemin de Pâtis, 56130 La Roche Bernard.

Tel:
(0)2.99.90.60.13 or (0)2.99.90.60.51 (Mairie). FAX: (0)2.99.90.88.28.

Reservations:
Contact site.

5613 Camping Mané Guernehué, Baden

Pleasant family site, between sea and countryside.

Located close to the Morbihan gulf, Mané Guernehué is a smart, modern site offering a variety of pitches. Some are terraced beneath pine trees, others in a former orchard with delightful views of the surrounding countryside. The site has plenty of excellent amenities, notably a heated swimming pool and waterslide, jacuzzi and gym. There is also a special teenagers' room with table tennis, pool, billiards and TV. A varied entertainment programme is on offer in high season, based around a large purpose built hall. A fitness track runs through the site, and on the edge you will find a well stocked fishing lake. The 200 pitches are generally large, 70 being occupied by mobile homes and chalets which are available to rent. All pitches have electricity and a few are also equipped with water and drainage. Many are level but others, particularly those in the centre of the site, slope to varying degrees. The three toilet blocks are modern with British type toilets, washbasins in cabins and free hot showers. In high season, the maintenance of the blocks seems to be under some pressure. There are washing machines and dryers, chemical disposal and facilities for disabled visitors. A small shop, bar and takeaway are beside reception. The beach is 3 km. Golf 3 km. Used by tour operators (around 37 pitches).

Directions: From Auray or Vannes use D101 to Baden and watch for signs to site.

Charges 2001:
-- Per pitch and car Ffr. 63.00 - 87.00; adult 18.00 - 31.00; child (2-7 years) 12.00 - 22.00; dog 8.00 - 15.00; electricity 6A 19.00, 10A 25.00.
-- Credit cards accepted.
Open:
Easter - 30 September.
Address:
56870 Baden.
Tel:
(0)2.97.57.02.06.
FAX: (0)2.97.57.15.43.
E-mail: mane.guernehue @wanadoo.fr.
Reservations:
Advised for high season and made with deposit (Ffr. 400) and fee (130).
`Camping Cheque'

Book this site
01892 559898
THE ALAN ROGERS'
travel service

5612 Camping Des Iles, La Pointe du Bile, nr Pénestin

Friendly. family run site with direct access to beach.

You are assured of a warm and friendly welcome at this family run campsite where the owners, M. & Mme. Communal, encourage everyone to make the most of this beautiful region. The 124 pitches are mostly of a reasonable size (although larger caravans and American motorhomes are advised to book) and all have electricity (6A). The large central sanitary block has mostly British style WCs, washbasins in cabins (with hairdryers for ladies), pre-set push-button showers, dishwashing and laundry sinks, plus facilities for disabled people and two baby baths. All facilities have hot and cold water. A motorcaravan service point is across the road at 'Parc des Iles', the mobile home section of the site. Adjacent to the reception area is a shop selling groceries and other goods, and a bar with takeaway that has a terrace overlooking the swimming and paddling pools (14/5-16/9). Across the road a multi-sports pitch provides football, basketball, volleyball and tennis. Other facilities include bicycle hire and riding, whilst in July/Aug. a full range of activities and entertainment for adults and children is provided. Services are fully open 14/5-16/9, with a limited service at other times. Local activities include windsurfing (500 m.) with a sailing school 3 km. There is direct access to cliff-top walks and local beaches (you can even walk to small off-shore islands at low tide). Used by a tour operator (20 pitches). Mobile homes to rent.

Directions: From Pénestin take D201 south, taking a right fork to Pointe du Bile after 2 km. Turn right at crossroads just before beach and site is on left. The barrier is close to the entrance, but there is some parking along the road outside.

Charges 2000:
-- Per unit incl. 2 adults Ffr. 79.50 - 168.00; extra adult 14.00 - 19.00; child (under 7 yrs) 8.00 - 11.00; animal 5.50 - 10.00; electricity (6A) 16.00.
-- Credit cards accepted.
Open:
1 April - 30 September.
Address:
La Pointe du Bile, 56760 Pénestin.
Tel:
(0)2.99.90.30.24.
FAX: (0)2.99.90.44.55.
E-mail: accueil@ camping-des-iles.com.
Reservations:
Made with deposit (Ffr 600) and fee (120).

Book this site
01892 559898
THE ALAN ROGERS'
travel service

5614M Camping Municipal du Bas de la Lande, Guégon-Josselin

Bas de la Lande is a top quality municipal site, ideally located for overnight stops (it is close to the N24, a busy dual-carriageway and road noise can be audible in all parts of the site) or for discovering the delights of inland Brittany, not least Josselin with its superb fortified 15th century château. Attractive discounts are offered for longer stays. The Oust river, which makes up part of the Nantes - Brest canal, runs opposite the site and provides good fishing opportunities (permit needed). Bas de la Lande has 60 pitches, 49 of which have electricity. Pitches are on a number of flat terraces and are large, grassy and lightly shaded. The principal toilet block is just behind reception and is of a very high standard, with all British type toilets, washbasins in cabins and large showers with pre-set temperature, plus a washing machine and dryer and chemical disposal. Unit for disabled people (with shower, washbasin and toilet). A second, much older block is only used at peak periods. Nearest shops are in Josselin (2 km), where there is also bicycle hire and tennis. Table tennis, minigolf (opposite site - free to campers). A bar/crêperie is adjacent to the site entrance (open 1/7-31/8).

Directions: Leave N24 Rennes - Lorient road to west of Josselin following signs to Guégon, then Josselin. Site is clearly signed from this point.

Charges 2001:
-- Per pitch Ffr. 12.00 - 18.00; adult 15.00 - 20.00; child (under 7 years) 9.00 - 10.00; car or motorcaravan 10.00 - 13.00; m/cycle 5.00 - 6.00; electricity (5A) 20.00.
-- Less 10% for stays of 3-5 nights, 20% for stays of 6 or more.
-- No credit cards.

Open:
1 May - 30 September

Address:
56120 Guégon-Josselin.

Tel:
(0)2.97.22.22.20.
FAX: (0)2.97.73.93.85.

Reservations:
Unlikely to be needed but can be made; contact the numbers above.

Book this site
01892 559898

THE ALAN ROGERS'
travel service

5616 Camping La Vallée de Ninian, Taupont, Ploërmel

Peaceful, rural site in central Brittany.

M. & Mme. Joubaud developed this family run site from a farm area in 1988 and take care to ensure that everyone has an enjoyable holiday. The level site falls into the three areas - the orchard with 32 large, hedged pitches with electricity, the wood with about 13 pitches more suited to tents, and the meadow by the river providing a further 35 pitches delineated by small trees and shrubs, some with electricity. The central building houses unisex sanitary facilities with British style WCs, pre-set showers and washbasins in cubicles, and a laundry area with washing machines, a dryer and an ironing board. There is a large cubicle with facilities for disabled visitors. At the side of the building there is a covered dish-washing area with hot water and a separate chemical disposal point. The shop sells basic provisions and has, as a centre-piece, a working cider press with which M. Joubaud makes his own 'potion magique'. The adjoining covered bar area is the venue for song and dance evenings with a Breton flavour and occasional camp fire sing songs are organised. There is a small (7 x 12 m) heated swimming pool and, in addition to swings and slides, a large trampoline, popular with children. There are a few site-owned caravans and mobile homes for rent. Activities include fishing, swimming and sailing at nearby Lac du Duc (4 km), a nine hole golf course at Ploërmel (7 km) and restaurants and bars at Josselin.

Directions: From Ploërmel centre follow signs to Taupont north on the N8. Continue through the village of Taupont and turn left (east) signed Vallée du Ninian and follow road until 1 km. before Hellean. From Josselin follow signs for Hellean. Go through village and turn sharp right after the bridge over the river Ninian. Site is 400 m. on the right.

Charges 2001:
-- Per pitch incl. vehicle Ffr. 30.00; adult 25.00; child (under 7 yrs) 15.00; electricity 3A 10.00, 6A 20.00; local tax 1.00.

Open:
May - September.

Address:
56800 Taupont.

Tel:
(0)2.97.93.53.01.
FAX: (0)2.97.93.57.27.

Reservations:
Contact site.

NORMANDY

Major cities: Caen, Rouen
Départements: 14 Calvados, 27 Eure, 50 Manche
61 Orme, 76 Seine Maritime

Normandy is a pastoral region – or, in fact, the dairy of France providing rich cream, butter, and fine cheeses such as Camembert and 'Pont l'Evêque'. Contented cows graze the apple orchards – the apples are used in producing cider and the well known 'Calvados', Normandy's apple brandy. Normandy also has a superb coast line including the Cotentin Peninsula, the cliffs of the Côte d'Albâtre and the fine beaches and fashionable resorts of the Côte Fleurie.

The history of Normandy is closely linked with our own as in 1066 the Norman Duke William defeated the Saxon King Harold in the battle of Hastings and was crowned King of England, his exploits well chronicled on the famous Bayeux Tapestry. In more recent times, June 1944, the Allied Forces landed on the Normandy coast. Many museums, exhibitions, sites and monuments, including the Caen Memorial Museum, commemorate operations that took place between 6 June and August of 1944.

Note: the site reports are laid out by département in numerical order not by region.
See map on page 306.

Cuisine of the region

Andouillette de Vire – small chitterling (tripe) sausage

Barbue au cidre – brill cooked in cider and Calvados

Douillons de pommes à la Normande – baked apples in pastry

Escalope (Vallée d'Auge) – veal sautéed and flamed in Calvados and served with cream and apples

Ficelle Normande – pancake with ham, mushrooms and cheese

Marnite Dieppoisse – fish soup with some or all of the following: sole, turbot, rouget, moules, crevettes, onions, white wine, butter and cream

Poulet (Vallée d'Auge) – chicken cooked in the same way as Escalope Vallée d'Auge

Tripes à la Mode de Caen – stewed beef tripe with onions, carrots, leeks, garlic, cider and Calvados

Wine

Cider usually accompanies a meal

Trou Normand Calvados – a 'dram' drunk in one gulp, between courses; claimed to restore the appetite

Places of interest

Alençon – famous for lace, fine art museum, birthplace of Ste Thérèse

Bagnoles-de-l'Orne – spa resort and casino, guided tours of Arthurian land of Lancelot

Bayeux – home to the famous tapestry; 15th-18th century houses, cathedral, museums

Caen – feudal castle, Museum of Normandy, Museum for Peace

Omaha Beach – D-Day beaches, Landing site monuments commemorating the Allied Forces, American Cemetery

Deauville – internationally famous seaside resort and horse racing centre

Giverny – home of impressionist painter Claude Monet, Monet Museum

Honfleur – picturesque port city with old town and bridge

Lisieux – pilgrimage site, shrine of Ste Thérèse, Basilic and Carmelite convent

Mont St Michel – world famous abbey on island which becomes isolated by incoming tide

Rouen – Joan of Arc Museum; Gothic churches, cathedrals, abbey, clock tower

1408 Camping Le Puits, St Martin des Besaces, nr Caen

Traditional village site in the heart of historic Normandy.

This little site on the edge of the village has only 30 pitches in two areas, either individual ones divided by flowers and shrubs, or on an open grassy field (these mainly used for short stays). All have electricity (6/10A) and are slightly sloping. The Ashworth family are gradually upgrading the simple, basic sanitary facilities on what was originally an 'a la ferme' site. At the rear of the farmhouse, these can be heated and provide three unisex British style WCs, plus two open washbasins and one controllable shower per sex. There are sinks for dishwashing and laundry, plus a washing machine and dryer. Behind the building are chemical disposal and motorcaravan services. Several touring caravans are for hire and the farmhouse has four rooms to let. In renovated barns are a small shop and a bar with a snack bar and a traditional, café style eating area outside. Bread, croissants or breakfast can be ordered daily. Another barn provides a function room and a 'salle de jour'. Activities include minigolf, table tennis, billiards, volleyball and fishing in the pond. Tyres, logs and planks provide children with a DIY play park. Activities are organised in season - barbecues, murder mysteries, quizzes and visits to local cider makers (even bungee jumping). Bicycle hire 5 km, riding 10 km. The site has its own newsletter and comprehensive tourist information in reception. A museum with a difference is nearby featuring a unique account of the Battle of Normandy with displays, sound and light presentations and personal memorabilia. St Martin des Besaces market is on Saturday. Winter caravan storage.

Charges 2000:
-- Per caravan or tent Ffr. 30.00; hiker's tent 20.00; adult 15.00; child (3-9 yrs) 10.00; electricity (6A) 15.00; extra car 20.00.
-- Credit cards accepted.
Open:
1 February - 31 October.
Address:
La Groudière, 14350 St Martin des Besaces.
Tel:
(0)2.31.67.80.02.
FAX: as phone.
E-mail: camping.le.puits @wanadoo.fr.
Reservations:
Advised in season and made with deposit of 1 nights fees.

Directions: From Caen take A84 at Porte de Bretagne towards Avranches to St Martin des Besaces (exit 41). Follow signs to village on D53. At lights turn right on N175 and site is signed to left at far end of village. From Cherbourg follow N13 and after Carentan (c. 50 km) take N174 signed St Lô. In St Lô follow signs for Vire, then Torigni-sur-Vire. After Torigni in 9 km. take N175 (not A84) turn left towards St Martin des Besaces and site is signed to right at entrance to village.

1409 Castel Camping Le Brèvedent, Pont L'Evêque

Well established traditional site, with own swimming pool and fishing lake.

Le Brèvedent's 140 pitches (96 for tourists) are set in the grounds of an elegant 18th century hunting pavilion. Level pitches are around the fishing lake or in the lower gardens, others now levelled are in the old orchard. All have electricity (10A). Three sanitary units of varying ages including a new one, are well tiled and clean, with British WCs, washbasins in cubicles, pre-set warm showers, laundry and dishwashing sinks, with free hot water throughout and facilities for babies and disabled people. There is a good drive-over motorcaravan service point and laundries with washing machines and dryers, plus a clubroom with TV and library. The shop is well stocked and the baker calls each morning. Takeaway service (all season) and a family meal on Sundays at 7 pm. Other on-site amenities include a snack bar (high season only), rowing boats (with lifejackets) and bicycle and buggy hire, a large children's playground in the old walled garden, with table tennis tables in the open fronted barns alongside, minigolf, boules, volleyball, games room with games machines, and a pool table. The swimming pool and children's pool (unsupervised) are heated and in separate enclosures each with paved sun terrace. The small site bar is located in the hunting lodge itself and is open each evening. Reception provides a vast amount of tourist information, with organised tours in the main season to Paris, Disney, a cider farm and a local distillery. Activities for children are organised daily in high season (10/7-20/8) including pony lessons. Fishing is free (but put the fish back). Nearby St Julien golf club offers 20% discount for campers, and tennis is available on the local court (on payment, keys from reception). Riding 1 km. Attractions in the area include cheese factories, Pont L'Evêque (14 km.) has a market (Sun. and Mon.) and the Château de Betteville with its motor museum. Market days in Cormeilles (Fri), Lisieux and Honfleur (Thurs). No dogs are accepted. Local church bells ring each morning at 7 am. Used by a tour operator (43 pitches). This is an excellent holiday site within easy reach of the Channel ports. It is a peaceful environment for mature campers or families with younger children (but the lake is unfenced).

Charges 2001:
-- Per unit Ffr. 50.00; adult 30.00; child (under 7 yrs) 18.00; electricity 18.00.
-- Less 10% in low season (excl. electricity).
-- Credit cards accepted.
Open:
12 May - 20 September.
Address:
14130 Pont L'Evêque
Tel:
(0)2.31.64.72.88.
FAX: (0)2.31.64.33.41.
Reservations:
Recommended for main season.

Book this site
01892 559898
THE ALAN ROGERS'
travel service

Directions: From Pont L'Evêque take D579 toward Lisieux for 4 km. then D51 towards Moyaux. At Blangy le Château turn right (still on D51) to Le Brèvedent.

1403 Castel Camping de Martragny, Martragny, nr Bayeux

Attractive site in parkland setting adjoining château and close to D-Day beaches.

Martragny is a particularly convenient location for both the ports of Caen and Cherbourg, and has the facilities and charm to encourage both long stays and stop-overs. The pleasant lawns surrounding and approaching the château take 160 units, with electricity connections for 140. The majority of the pitches are divided by either a small hedge or a couple of trees, and only a few are not marked out. There are two sanitary blocks, the one in the woodland area having been fully refurbished in '99. The other is in the main complex. Both have British style WCs, washbasins in private cabins, good showers and sinks for dishes and clothes, all with ample, free hot water. Disabled people are well catered for and there are two baby baths, a good laundry with washing machine and dryer and chemical disposal facilities. The free swimming pool (20 x 6 m.) and children's paddling pool are heated when the weather is inclement. The pool, well stocked shop and takeaway food bar are all open 15/5-15/9. Other amenities include play areas, minigolf, a bar with large terrace, games and TV room, table tennis and billiards. Fishing and bicycle hire on site, riding 1 km, golf 20 km. Bed and breakfast (en-suite) are available in the château all year (reservation essential). Madame de Chassey takes great pride in the site and takes care that the peace and quiet is preserved. A perfect place for a quiet relaxing holiday, yet only 12 km. from the sea, the Landing Beaches and the excellent museum at Arromanche. Also within easy reach is the Bayeux tapestry and there is also the Calvados 'Cider Route'.

Directions: Site is off N13, 8 km. southeast of Bayeux. Take Martragny exit from dual-carriageway.

Charges 2000:
-- Per person Ffr. 29.00; child (under 7) 17.00; simple pitch 58.00, pitch for caravan or motor-caravan 63.00; extra car 10.00; electricity (6A) 18.00; local tax 1.00.
-- Low season less 15%.
-- Credit cards accepted.

Open:
1 May - 15 September.

Address:
14740 Martragny.

Tel:
(0)2.31.80.21.40.
FAX: (0)2.31.08.14.91.
E-mail: chateau.
martragny@wanadoo.fr.

Reservations:
Min. 3 nights; deposit and small fee required.

`Camping Cheque'

**Book this site
01892 559898**

THE ALAN ROGERS'
travel service

1402M Camping Municipal, Bayeux

Whether or not you want to see the tapestry, this site makes a very useful night stop on the way to or from Cherbourg, and in addition it is only a few kilometres from the coast and the landing beaches. Pleasantly laid out with grassy lawns and bushes, its neat, cared for appearance make a good impression. The 140 pitches are in two areas. In the main area 27 new hardstanding pitches have been created, with the remaining pitches well marked, generally of good size and with electricity. The two toilet blocks are of good quality and have British style WCs, washbasins in cabins in the main block, free, roomy hot showers and units for disabled people. A large public indoor swimming pool adjoins the site with children's pool and jacuzzi. Takeaway food and snacks. A large supermarket is very close (closes 8 pm). Two children's playgrounds. Reading room with TV. Games room. Laundry room. Bicycle hire 1 km, riding 5 km, golf or fishing 8 km. The site is busy over a long season - early arrival is advised as reservations are not taken. There is a full time site warden from 15/6-15/9, otherwise reception is only open for one hour in the morning and two in the evening.

Directions: Site is on the south side of northern ring road to town.

Charges 2001:
-- Per person Ffr. 18.30; child (under 7) 9.80; pitch and car 22.60; electricity 18.60.
-- Less 10% for stays over 5 days.
-- Credit cards accepted.

Open:
1 May - 30 September.

Address:
Bvd. Eindhoven, 14400 Bayeux.

Tel:
(0)2.31.92.08.43.
FAX: as phone.

Reservations:
Not made.

1410M Camping Municipal du Château, Falaise

The location of this site is really quite spectacular, lying in the shadow of the Château Falaise, in the old part of the town, in the 'coeur de Normandie'. The site itself is small, with only 66 pitches (all with 5A electricity). It has a rather intimate `up-market' feel about it, rather different from the average municipal site. With good shade, tarmac roads and easy access, it was well recommended by the British campers we met there. The sanitary facilities could be insufficient in terms of quantity when the site is full - perhaps it never is and campers we met felt they were adequate. The quality is good, with free hot showers and British style WCs, and they are clean. A unit for disabled visitors provides a shower room and separate WC. Access to the showers, laundry and dishwashing closed 22.00-07.30. Whatever this site lacks in size and facilities it makes up for in its situation, close to the town centre, the swimming pool and tennis club and near to the river for fishing. The charges are reasonable and the reception friendly.

Directions: Site is on western side of town. From N158 heading south take first roundabout into Falaise (site signed).

Charges 1999:
-- Per pitch Ffr. 15.00; adult 17.00; child (under 10 yrs) 12.00; dog 8.00; electricity 14.00.

Open:
Easter - 30 September.

Address:
3 rue du Val d'Ante, 14700 Falaise.

Tel:
(0)2.31.90.16.55.

Reservations:
Advised for July/Aug; contact site.

NORMANDY - 14 Calvados

1407 Camping de la Vallée, Houlgate

Fresh, well kept site, close to lively little resort of Houlgate.

Camping de la Vallée is an attractive site with good, well maintained facilities. Situated on a grassy hillside overlooking Houlgate, the 278 pitches (180 for touring units) are large and open, with hedging planted and all have electricity. Part of the site is sloping, the rest level, with gravel or tarmac roads. An old farmhouse has been converted to house a new bar and comfortable TV lounge and billiards room. Amenities include a heated swimming pool (from 15/5), shop (from 1/5) and a small snack-bar with takeaway in season (from 15/5). A large grassy area has a children's playground, volleyball and a football field. There is tennis, bicycle hire, petanque and organised entertainment in Jul/Aug. Three toilet blocks of a good standard have free hot water in controllable, well fitted showers; washbasins in cabins; mainly British style toilets, facilities for disabled people and a baby bathroom. Dishwashing, laundry with machines, dryers and ironing boards (no washing lines allowed), chemical disposal and motorcaravan services. The beach is 1 km, the town 900 m. Fishing 1 km, riding 500 m. Championship golf course 2 km. English is spoken in season. Mobile homes to rent (12). Used by tour operators (55 pitches). Very busy in high season, maintenance and cleaning could be variable at that time.

Directions: Site is 1 km. from Houlgate, along D24A (route de Lisieux). Turn right on D24, rue de la Vallée and look for site sign.

Charges 2001:
-- Per person Ffr. 35.00; child (under 7) 20.00; pitch 50.00, with services 60.00; dog 20.00; electricity 4A 20.00, 6A 25.00; local tax 2.00.
-- Credit cards accepted (min. Ffr. 500).

Open: 1 April - 30 September.

Address: Rue de la Vallée, 14510 Houlgate.

Tel: (0)2.31.24.40.69. FAX: (0)2.31.28.08.29. E-mail: camping.lavallee @wanadoo.fr.

Reservations: Made with deposit (Ffr. 400) and fee (100).

CAMPING CARAVANING

☐ SHOP ☐ BAR
☐ GAMES ROOM ☐ TENNIS
☐ HEATED SWIMMING POOL
☐ CHILDREN'S POOL
☐ ENTERTAINMENT

★★★★ LA VALLÉE

88, Rue de la Vallée - 14510 Houlgate
Tel: 02.31.24.40.69   Fax: 02.31.28.08.29

1401 Camping de la Côte de Nacre, St Aubin sur Mer, nr Caen

Large site just back from the sea, with swimming pool.

This stretch of the Normandy coast comprises a long series of towns which tend to run together. Nonetheless, the beaches and bathing are good and they are within walking distance of the site. There are some standard sized, disc marked pitches here, laid out adjacent to semi-circular gravelled access roads; 200 have electricity (4, 6 or 10A). Some 100 holiday statics are placed around the perimeter of the flat, open site. Because it is fairly new, the trees and shrubs planted have not yet had much time to grow so there is little to separate pitches or to give shade and shelter, with a somewhat bare appearance at present. The two sanitary blocks are of modern construction and style. Washbasins are in cabins and all hot water is free. On site activities are not extensive although there is a small pool (no shorts) with a paddling pool, a children's playground, boules, table tennis and bicycle hire. Some animation and excursions are organised in season. The reception complex houses a restaurant/bar (open all season), TV and games room and a small shop. Used by tour operators.

Directions: Site is on southern side of the town centre relief road and well signed from the approach roads to St Aubin, but make sure you leave the adjacent towns first.

Charges guide:
-- Per pitch Ffr. 32.00 - 40.00; adult 25.00 - 28.00; child (under 7 yrs) 15.00 - 18.00; electricity 18.00 - 32.00, acc. to amps (4, 6 or 10); extra car or tent 12.00 - 15.00; animal 12.00 - 15.00; local tax 1.60.

Open: 1 April - 30 September.

Address: BP 18, 14750 St Aubin sur Mer.

Tel: (0)2.31.97.14.45. FAX: (0)2.31.97.22.11.

Reservations: Advised for July/Aug. and made with deposit (Ffr. 400) and fee (100).

1405 Castel Château-Camping Le Colombier, Moyaux, nr Lisieux

Quality Normandy site with the aspect of a spacious country estate.

Le Colombier is a quality site in an attractive landscaped setting of formal French gardens, between the manor house and the 'Colombier' (a circular building housing the bar and library). Reception is in a newly restored building and the staff are efficient and friendly. The site has 180 large pitches, all with electricity (12A), marked out by trees at the corners, but with no dividing hedges. There is a free heated swimming pool (25 x 12 m). The two toilet blocks are of good quality, with private cabins, roomy controllable showers, British style WCs, and a good unit for visitors with disabilities. There are chemical disposal facilities, a motor-caravan service point, washing machine and dryer. The bar, shop, crêperie and takeaway are open all season. Special dinners (limited numbers) are served some days in the château. A baby sitting is available for the château diners. A large general room provides for reading, cards, etc. with TV. Activities include a tennis court, bicycle hire, minigolf, volleyball and free fishing on a nearby lake. You do pay for the quality here, and there are no off-peak reductions, but the site's main amenities are open all season and the château and its surroundings do have a certain elegance. Riding 8 km, golf 20 km. Lisieux is 16 km. and places on the coast such as Deauville and Honfleur 30 to 40 km. Used by a tour operator (18 pitches). No mobile homes or bungalows.

Directions: Site is 3 km. northeast of Moyaux on the D143, well signed from the Cormeilles - Lisieux road.

Charges 2001:
-- Per person Ffr. 35.00; child (under 7) 15.00; pitch 70.00; electricity (12A) 15.00.
-- Credit cards accepted.

Open:
1 May - 15 September, with all services.

Address:
Le Val Sery, 14590 Moyaux.

Tel:
(0)2.31.63.63.08.
FAX: (0)2.31.63.15.97.
E-mail:
chateau@camping-lecolombier.com.

Reservations:
Advised for main season and made for min. 3 days with deposit and fee (Ffr. 100).

see colour advert between pages 32/33

1406 Camping-Caravaning Les Hautes Coutures, Benouville

Neat, tidy site near Caen-Portsmouth ferry terminal, for overnight or longer stays.

Les Hautes Coutures is situated beside the Caen ship canal, 2 km. from the sea (and ferry port) and 10 km. from Caen - the site gates are opened at 6.30 am. for early ferries. There are 152 well drained, grass pitches of 100 sq.m, clearly marked by mature hedges formed from flowering shrubs, with tarmac roads. All pitches have electrical connections. An area close to the canal is being developed to provide further pitches. There is a small heated swimming pool (from May) on site and two tennis courts near the bar/reception area with a small lounge/TV area and games room. A small shop keeps basic items as the town is close. Takeaway food is provided in season. Volleyball. Children's play area on sand. Minigolf. Two sanitary blocks (the more open one is closed outside main season) have free hot water in the showers and washbasins in cabins (no cold tap). Dishwashing and laundry facilities, with washing machine and dryer. Used by a tour operator. The site is within walking distance of Quistreham along the canal (fishing free), and the Pegasus Bridge Airborne Division Museum.

Directions: Site is just off D514, north of Benouville. From Caen, follow Ouistreham car ferry signs and take first exit from D514 after Benouville.

Charges 2000:
-- Per person Ffr. 33.00; child (under 7) 21.00; pitch with car and tent/caravan 35.00; electricity 2A 20.00, 4A 25.00, 6A 32.00.

Open:
15 March - 15 October.

Address:
Route de Ouistreham, 14970 Benouville.

Tel:
(0)2.31.44.73.08.
FAX: (0)2.31.95.30.80.
E-mail: camping-hautes-coutures@wanadoo.fr.

Reservations:
Write to site.

1411 Camping du Traspy, Thury-Harcourt

Attractive former municipal site near lake and leisure park.

Somewhat akin to a tiny nature park, close to a lake (reputedly excellent for fishing) and with a small stream running through it, this secluded, former municipal site is resplendent with mature tall trees. The 92 pitches are on two levels, both flat, with a choice of 6 or 10A electrical connections. Sanitary facilities include both British and Turkish type WCs, free hot showers and some washbasins in private cabins. External dishwashing facilities and a laundry room. There is no on-site restaurant or shop, but the village facilities are only about 500 m. away. A useful site for night stops, or for longer stays for keen anglers! The popular leisure park of the Valley of Traspy is only 200 m. from the site.

Directions: Site is signed in the town of Thury-Harcourt on D562 Caen - Vire road, 26 km. from Caen.

Charges guide:
-- Per pitch Ffr. 23.00; adult 23.00; child (under 16 yrs) 15.00; dog 7.00; electricity 6A 18.00, 10A 21.00.

Open:
30 April - 12 September.

Address:
Rue du Pont Benoit, 14220 Thury-Harcourt

Tel:
(0)2.31.79.61.80.
FAX: (0)2.31.84.76.19.

Reservations:
Advised July/Aug; made with deposit (Ffr 120).

5000 Camping L'Etang des Haizes, La Haye-du-Puits

Friendly, attractive and informal site with new pool complex and pretty lake.

This already appealing site has added a new swimming pool complex with four lane slides, jacuzzi and a paddling pool (20/5-10/9). L'Etang des Haizes also offers 98 good size pitches, of which 58 are for touring units, on fairly level ground and all with electricity (6/10A). They are set in a mixture of conifers, orchard and shrubbery, with some very attractive slightly smaller pitches overlooking the lake and 40 mobile homes inconspicuously sited. The two sanitary blocks are of modern construction, open plan and unisex, and are kept very clean. They have British WCs, free controllable showers, washbasins in private cabins and units for disabled people. Dishwashing under cover, a small laundry with two washing machines and a dryer, chemical disposal and motorcaravan services are provided. The lake offers good coarse fishing for huge carp (we are told!), pedaloes, a small beach, ducks and, believe it or not, a turtle can sometimes be seen on a fine day! Other facilities include an attractive bar with TV and a terrace overlooking the lake and pool (both 20/5-10/9), two children's play areas, bicycle hire, table tennis, pool table, petanque and volleyball. Activities and entertainment are organised for all ages, including treasure hunts, archery and food tasting. Only milk, bread and takeaway snacks are available on site (no gas available), but La Haye-du-Puits (1 km) has two supermarkets, good restaurants and a market on Wednesdays. Gate locked 22.00 - 07.00. The site is 8 km. from a good, sandy beach and a 25 km. drive from the Normandy Landing Beaches. Mobile homes (18) and chalets to rent.

Directions: From Cherbourg follow N13 (Mont St Michel) as far as Valognes, then the D2 to St Sauveur-le-Vicomte. Continue on the D900 for La Haye-du-Puits, go straight on at new roundabout on the outskirts of town and site is signed almost immediately on the right.

Charges 2001:
-- Per unit incl. 2 adults Ffr. 73.00 - 120.00; extra person (over 3 yrs) 15.00 - 25.00; electricity 6A 10.00, 10A 35.00; dog 12.00.
-- Credit cards accepted (after 15/5).

Open:
1 April - 15 October.

Address:
50250 St Symphorien-le-Valois.

Tel:
(0)2.33.46.01.16. FAX: (0)2.33.47.23.80.

Reservations:
Made with 25% deposit. For reservations from Ireland contact G & R Boyce, 6 Lynda Crescent, Jordanstown, Co.Antrim BT37 ONS: Tel/Fax 02890 867988.

'Camping Cheque'

Book this site
01892 559898

THE ALAN ROGERS' travel service

see colour advert between pages 160/161

5006 Camping Le Grand Large, Les Pieux, nr Cherbourg

Established family site with direct access to a long sandy beach.

This good quality site is within a 20 km. drive of Cherbourg. It is a mature site with both touring and mobile home pitches discreetly divided and separated by hedging, which gives an orderly well laid out appearance. At the entrance, alongside the security barrier, stands the modern reception area. Decorating the forecourt are low brick walls with sunken flower beds and behind reception is a swimming pool, new heated children's pool and a sunbathing terrace overlooked by the bar/café (snacks from 24/5). There are two sanitary blocks, the main one being modern with ornate outside brick, stone and woodwork. The interior has a similar theme and many flower troughs add colour. The facilities are decorated in bright colours and are well maintained, including washbasins in cubicles, plus an open wash area with hairdryer, hand dryer, mirrors, etc. Showers are well equipped with seat, hooks and divider. WCs are mostly to the outside of the building. Other facilities include good provision for people with disabilities, baby bathroom, dishwashing sinks, laundry area, chemical disposal and motorcaravan service point. There is a shop for basic groceries and a takeaway service. To the rear of the site and laid out in the sand-hills is an excellent play area for children, with swings, slides and climbing frame. Leisure facilities include tennis, table tennis volleyball, boules, animation in July/Aug. with the sandy beach a big attraction. Bicycle hire or riding 5 km, golf 15 km. Roads around the site are tarmac and there are pleasant views across the bay to the tip of the Cherbourg peninsula. A 'Sites et Paysages' member.

Directions: From Cherbourg port take N13 south for approx. 2 km. Branch right on D904 signed Cartaret. Continue for 18 km to Les Pieux and follow camp signs via D117/517.

Charges 2001:
-- Per unit incl. 2 persons Ffr. 130.00; extra person 28.00; under 7 years 18.00; electricity (6A) 20.00.
-- Low seasons less 20%.
-- Motorcaravan services Ffr. 40.00 - 50.00 (free to guests).
-- Credit cards accepted.

Open:
7 April - 16 September.

Address:
50340 Les Pieux.

Tel:
(0)2.33.52.40.75. FAX: (0)2.33.52.58.20. E-mail: le-grand-large @wanadoo.fr.

Reservations:
Made with Ffr 500 deposit.

Book this site
01892 559898

THE ALAN ROGERS' travel service

5005 Camping Le Cormoran, Ravenoville-Plage, nr Ste-Mère-Eglise

Neat, seaside site on eastern Cotentin coast, 5 km. north of Utah Beach.

Set in a flat and open landscape and only separated from the beach by the coast road, Le Cormoran is ideal for a holiday or short break quite near to Cherbourg (33 km), with the Landing Beaches close by. Holiday mobile homes, many privately owned, take 130 places but the remaining 80 are comfortable touring pitches sheltered from the wind by neat hedges and with 6A electricity available. With a narrow frontage, decorated with flags and a fountain, it is a fairly long site with most of the amenities at the entrance. These include reception (in front of the owner's home), a small shop, bar with snacks (all season) and takeaway, with an entertainment and games room opposite. Swimming pool with paved surrounds (heated 1/6-15/9, unsupervised), tennis court, boules pitch and three small children's play areas on sand. Adjacent to the site are a sports field and storage for up to 60 boats. Entertainment and activities such as archery are organised and day trips to the Channel Islands or horse riding can be arranged. Golf 5 km. Bicycle and shrimp net hire. A hairdresser calls twice weekly (resident on site July/Aug). Communal barbecue. Sanitary facilities are in four blocks of varying styles, but all clean and tidy. Improvements continue including extra cabins with shower, WC and washbasin. Hot water is free in the controllable showers, the washbasins in cabins and the dishwashing sinks. A washing machine and dryer are in three blocks. The smallest block is of the mobile type and serves 15 extra large pitches (150 sq.m.) at the back of the site. This is a well run, family managed site with many regular visitors. A 'Sites et Paysages' member.

Directions: From N13 take Ste Mère Eglise exit and in centre of town take road to Ravenoville (6 km), then Ravenoville-Plage (3 km). Just before beach turn right and site is 500 m.

Charges 2001:
-- Per unit incl. 2 persons Ffr. 93.00 - 120.00; extra person 25.00 - 32.00; child (under 7 yrs) 10.00 - 13.00; dog 12.00 - 16.00; electricity (6A) 23.00; local tax (July/Aug) 1.00.
-- Low season overnight rate for motorcaravans Ffr. 70.00.
-- Credit cards accepted.

Open:
6 April - 30 September.

Address:
Ravenoville-Plage, 50480 Ste Mère Eglise.

Tel:
(0)2.33.41.33.94. FAX: (0)2.33.95.16.08. E-mail: lecormoran @wanadoo.fr.

Reservations:
Advised for July/Aug. and made with 25% deposit; contact site.

**Book this site
01892 559898**

THE ALAN ROGERS'
travel service

5003 Castel Camping Lez Eaux, Granville

Family site with swimming pools just back from sea on Cotentin coast.

Set in the spacious grounds of a château, Lez Eaux lies in a rural situation just off the main route south, under 2 hours from Cherbourg. The nearest beach is 3 km, St Pair is 4 km. and Granville 7, and it is a very pleasant situation from which to explore this corner of the Cotentin peninsula. However, because of its location, Lez Eaux receives much en-route trade, both from tour operator clients and independent campers on their way further south and at times this can put heavy pressure on the facilities (it is a good idea to book for peak season visits, or for single nights arrive early). There are 229 pitches, nearly 50% taken by British and some Dutch tour operators with special places provided for late arrivals and early departures. Most pitches are of a very good size, semi-separated by trees and shrubs on either flat or very slightly sloping, grassy ground overlooking Normandy farmland and on either side of a small lake (with carp and other fish). All pitches have electrical connections (5/10A) and some have drainage. Two modern toilet blocks have British WCs, washbasins in cabins, showers with free hot water and full provision for disabled people. They are cleaned three times daily. There is a small heated swimming pool (12 x 6 m.) and an attractive fun pool with slide and water slide that for 2001 will have a glass roof (from 15/5, no T-shirts or Bermuda style shorts). Shop, small bar and snacks and takeaway with set meal each night to order in advance (all from 15/5). Activities include an adventure play area, good tennis court (Ffr. 40 per hour in high season), games room with table tennis, jacuzzi, bicycle hire, lake fishing and a TV room. Riding 5 km, golf 7 km. Torches required at night. Only one animal per pitch is accepted. Note: facilities not fully open until 15/5.

Directions: Site access is signed west about 7 km. southeast of Granville on main D973 road to Avranches.

Charges 2001:
-- Ffrancs: per pitch incl. 2 persons Ffr. 110.00 - 140.00, with 5A electricity 130.00 - 170.00, 10A electricity 140.00 - 180.00, with all services 140.00 - 195.00; extra person 32.00 - 43.00; child (under 7 yrs) 20.00 - 30.00.
-- Credit cards accepted.

Open:
1 May - 15 September.

Address:
50380 Saint Pair-sur-Mer.

Tel:
(0)2.33.51.66.09. FAX: (0)2.33.51.92.02. E-mail: lez.eaux@wanadoo.fr.

Reservations:
Advisable for high season and made for min. 5 days with deposit (Ffr. 200) and fee (100).

**Book this site
01892 559898**

THE ALAN ROGERS'
travel service

*see colour advert
between pages 64/65*

5004M Camping Municipal Sainte Mère Eglise

This is a typically unpretentious, basic municipal site providing 69 pitches set on level grass amongst apple trees with hard access roads. All pitches have electricity (8A). The site is next to tennis courts and a sports centre. Sanitary facilities are utilitarian but adequate, providing hot showers, British style WCs (plus one for disabled people) and some washbasins in cabins. Maintenance and cleaning may suffer in high season. Chemical disposal. Games room and small children's play area. Bread may be ordered and ice creams are sold at reception. The site is ideally situated within about 5 minutes level walking distance of the centre of this historic little town (the first town in France to be liberated by the Allies), with its war museum and strategic position near to the Normandy landing beaches. Look for the parachutist hanging from the 13th century church. Reception is open limited hours (8.00-10.00, 12.00-14.00 and 17.00-22.00 hrs).

Directions: Site is signed from the centre of the town, by the church.

Charges guide:
-- Per person Ffr. 9.50 - 11.50; child (under 7 yrs) 4.00 - 5.00; tent/caravan + car or motorcaravan 14.00 - 17.00; small tent 10.00; extra vehicle 5.00; pet 12.00; electricity 10.50 - 13.50.
Open:
All year.
Address:
50480 Ste. Mère Église.
Tel:
(0)2.33.41.35.22 or the Mairie: (0)2.33.41.79.15.
Reservations:
Not normally necessary.

5002M Camping Pré de la Rose J-L Bougourd, Villedieu-les-Poëles

Villedieu is 28 km. inland on a route followed by many who use the port of Cherbourg, and to a lesser extent Le Havre. The Pré de la Rose, also known as Camping Jean-Louis Bougourd is a small, well kept site taking some 100 units on individual pitches; these are of good size, marked out and separated by low hedges. A small river, La Sienne, runs alongside the site (fenced off) with fishing. Electricity is available in all parts from very modern connection points. One good sized toilet block with Turkish style WCs for men and British for women (plus bidets), and a smaller one with British WCs for all, make up a good provision. A few washbasins are in private cabins with free hot water, the others are not enclosed and with cold. Free hot showers pre-set and chain-operated. Like the site itself, the blocks have a cared for look. Amenities include a TV room, children's playground on sand, table tennis and volleyball, with tennis adjacent. Shops are 400 m. in town centre, with a market on Tuesdays. It becomes full in main season but there are departures each day providing places for early arrivals.

Directions: Site is an easy walk from the town centre; entrance past market place car park.

Charges 2000:
-- Per adult Ffr 15.50; child 8.00; pitch 15.50; car 4.50; electricity 16.00.
-- No credit cards.
Open:
Easter - 30 September.
Address:
50800 Villedieu.
Tel:
(0)2.33.61.02.44.
FAX: (0)2.33.61.18.58 (Mairie).
Reservations:
Made for about a week or more without deposit.

5008M Camping Municipal Les Rives du Couesnon, Pontorson

A fairly typical municipal site but it is very close to the Mont St Michel. There are 110 pitches all for tourists, 55 with electricity (6A), plus a separate area for tents. The single sanitary unit provides British and Turkish style WCs, washbasins in cubicles, push-button showers, dishwashing and laundry sinks, and limited facilities for disabled people. All was acceptably clean when we visited in high season. There is a small children's playground, and free fishing in the River Couesnon. Organised trips to Mont St Michel run from campsite 21.00 - midnight (mid-July to mid-August).

Directions: Site is 300 m. from the town centre, west of D976, alongside the river, and is well signed from the town.

Charges 2000:
-- Per adult Ffr. 10.00 - 15.00; child (under 7 yrs) 7.50 - 8.00; pitch 10.00 - 15.00; dog 2.50 - 3.50; electricity 13.00 - 15.00.
Open:
1 April - 31 October.
Address:
50170 Pontorson.
Tel:
(0)2.33.68.11.59.
FAX: as phone.
E-mail: camping-monto @ville-pontorson.fr
Reservations:
Contact site for details.

5007 Camp L'Anse du Brick, Maupertus-sur-Mer, nr Cherbourg

Friendly, family run coastal site 8 km. east of Cherbourg Port.

Overlooking a picturesque bay on the northern tip of the Contentin Peninsula, this quality site makes a pleasant night halt, or an ideal long stay destination for those not wishing to travel too far. Its pleasing location offers access to a small sandy beach, also a woodland walk, where only the noise of a cascading stream disturbs the peace. Beyond the site lies miles of walking tracks through the gorse-covered hills which, together with a stark rock face cluster around the site, make it a sheltered sun-trap. This is a mature, terraced site with magnificent sea and hill views from certain pitches. Tarmac roads climb gradually to the pitches which are level, separated and mostly well shaded by the many trees, bushes and shrubs. The two sanitary blocks, although not ultra-modern, are kept spotlessly clean by an ongoing cleaning programme and are maintained to a satisfactory standard. Facilities include pre-set showers with adequate space, seats and hooks, provision for disabled visitors, a motorcaravan service point, plus laundry and dishwashing areas. A feature is the swimming pool complex that is overlooked by the popular bar/pizzeria with its extensive menu. There is also a restaurant before the site entrance. On site is a tennis court, children's play area, organised entertainment in season, also bicycle and kayak hire. Mobile homes and chalets for hire.

Directions: From Cherbourg port turn left at crossroads (where site is signed) onto D116 coast road. Continue for 8 km. and site is signed on right.

Charges 2000:
-- Per unit incl. 2 persons Ffr. 77.00 - 110.00 (incl. tourist tax); extra person 21.00 - 30.00; child (3-10 yrs) 12.00 - 16.00; dog 8.00 - 10.00; electricity (10A) 15.00 - 22.00.
-- Credit cards accepted.
Open:
1 April - 15 September.
Address:
Route du Val de Saire, 50330 Maupertus-s-Mer.
Tel:
(0)2.33.54.33.57.
FAX: (0)2.33.54.49.66.
E-mail: anse-du-brick@ cherbourg-channel.tm.fr.
Reservations:
Advised for July/Aug; contact site.
`Camping Cheque'

6101M Camping La Campière, Vimoutiers

This small, well kept site is situated in a valley to the north of the town, which is on both the Normandy Cheese and Cider routes. Indeed the town is famous for its cheese and has a Camembert Museum, five minutes walk away in the town centre. The 40 pitches here are flat and grassy, separated by laurel hedging and laid out amongst attractive and well maintained flower and shrub beds. There is some shade around the perimeter and all pitches have electricity (6/10A). The single central, clean sanitary block provides British style WCs, push-button showers, open washbasins, a separate bathroom for disabled visitors, chemical disposal and dishwashing and laundry facilities under cover. The site is open all year so heating is provided. No shop but a large supermarket is 300 m. Tennis courts and a park are adjacent. Water sports facilities or riding 2 km., also a ski slope.

Directions: Site is on northern edge of town, signed from main Lisieux-Argentan road next to large sports complex.

Charges 2001:
-- Per person Ffr. 14.70 - 16.20; child (under 10 yrs) 7.40 - 8.10; pitch 9.20 - 11.40; car 7.40 - 9.20; animal 5.60; electricity 11.10 (17.90 in winter).
-- Reductions for 7th and subsequent days.
-- Credit cards accepted.
Open:
All year.
Address:
Bvd. du Docteur Dentu, 61120 Vimoutiers.
Tel:
(0)2.33.39.18.86.
FAX (Mairie):
(0)2.33.36.51.43.
E-mail: mairie.vimoutiers @wanadoo.fr.
Reservations:
Not normally necessary.

6104M Camping Municipal du Champ Passais, Domfront

Situated on the edge of this lovely old town, this small site has 34 individual pitches on a series of level terraces, a separate open grassy area for tents with a boules court and a small children's playground. Pitches on the top terrace nearest the entrance are mostly on hardstanding each with 10A electricity and a small lawn (much favoured by motorcaravanners). Pitches on lower levels are grassy and divided by well tended shrubs and hedges. Electricity (5A), water and waste water points are available to most. There are no other on-site facilities, but a supermarket, with cheap fuel is 800 m. Excellent sanitary facilities are housed in a modern building, with British style WCs, some washbasins in cubicles, controllable showers with dividers, facilities for disabled people, dishwashing and laundry sinks plus a washing machine. Hot water is free throughout. Tennis available, fishing 1 km. The town has all the shops and services that one might require and the site fees are very reasonable. The site has a card operated barrier (card deposit Ffr. 100). Double axle caravans are not accepted.

Directions: Site is well signed from the town.

Charges 2000:
-- Per unit incl. 1 adult Ffr. 24.00; adult 12.00; child (under 10 yrs) 7.00; electricity 5A 12.00, 10A 20.00; tent incl. 1 person 13.00; dog 4.00.
-- Low season less 20%.
-- No credit cards.
Open:
1 April - 15 October.
Address:
61700 Domfront.
Tel:
(0)2.33.37.37.66.
Reservations:
Not normally necessary.

7609M Camping Municipal d'Etennemare, Saint-Valery-en-Caux

This comfortable, neat municipal site is 2 km. from the harbour and town, 30 km. west of Dieppe. Quietly located, it has 116 pitches of which 50% are available for touring units. The grassy pitches are all on a slight slope, all with electricity (6A), but there is very little shade. The two clean and well maintained sanitary buildings are located side by side - both of which can be heated in winter, one containing showers with dividers, shelves and hooks and the other recently refitted and with British style WCs, both open and cubicled washbasins, shaving or hairdressing area and facilities for disabled people. There are also dishwashing and laundry sinks, and washing machines. Hot water is free throughout. Also on site is a small shop (only July/Aug), a children's playground and table tennis. Reception is open daily from June - mid-Sept. but is closed on Wednesdays in low season and there is now a card operated security barrier. The site is close to the municipal sports complex with tennis and football field, and there are shops and restaurants in the town. Wooden chalets to rent (10).

Directions: Site is southwest of town centre and is signed from D925 (Fécamp) road, just west of the railway station. Follow signs to site or 'terrain de sports'.

Charges 2001:
-- Per unit incl. 2 adults and electricity Ffr. 78.00; extra adult 16.00; extra child (under 10) 10.00.
-- Credit cards accepted.
Open:
All year.
Address:
Hameau d'Etenemare, 76460 St-Valery-en-Caux.
Tel:
(0)2.35.97.15.79.
FAX: (0)2.35.97.15.79.
Reservations:
Essential for July/Aug; contact site.

7604 Camping La Source, Petit Appeville, Hautot sur Mer

Flat, shady site, convenient for Newhaven - Dieppe ferries.

This friendly, attractive, site is just 4 km. from Dieppe and is useful for those using the Newhaven - Dieppe ferry crossing. The 120 pitches are flat and shady, and the site is quietly located in a valley with the only disturbance the occasional passing train. A shallow stream flows along one border (not protected for young children), with opportunities for eel fishing, rowing or canoeing. There are hardstandings for motorcaravans and electricity is available (3, 6, 10A). The single toilet block (men to the left, ladies to the right) is good and kept clean, providing washbasins in cubicles, pre-set showers with dividers and mixed British and Turkish style WCs (less in number). Chemical disposal, dishwashing under cover (H&C) and laundry with washing machine, dryer and ironing. A well equipped unit for disabled people has a toilet, shower and washbasin, but the unmade gravel roads may cause problems. The site is well lit and, with an arrangement with Stena Line, stays open for late night ferries (so there could be some noise late at night). A small bar and terrace, recently attractively renovated, also provides snack meals and is open for late ferries. Small play field for children. TV room, and room for young people with table tennis and amusement machines. The latest addition is a small gym with modern fitness machines, free for campers. Fishing on site, riding 2 km, bicycle hire 1 km, golf 4 km. Caravan storage.

Directions: On leaving dock, follow one way system bearing left at Canadian War memorial, below castle. Follow signs to Paris and Rouen. After long hill, at large roundabout, take first exit to right on D925, Av. St Jaures. After 2 km. turn left at traffic lights on D153 (Pourville sur Mer to right). Just past railway station turn left under bridge (3.10 m.) into narrow road with stream on right. Site is a short distance on the left.

Charges 2000:
-- Per caravan Ffr. 42.00; motorcaravan 48.00; tent 30.00; person 23.00; child (under 7 yrs) 14.00; car 6.00; dog 6.00; electricity 16.00.
-- Credit cards accepted.
Open:
15 March - 15 October.
Address:
Petit Appeville, 76550 Hautot sur Mer.
Tel:
(0)2.35.84.27.04.
Reservations:
Write to site.

7605M Camping Municipal Parc du Château, Eu

Situated in the grounds of the Château d'Eu, the setting for this site is quite lovely, even with the main town of Eu only minutes away. On entering the site, there is a long woodland area and park providing excellent picnic opportunities with lots of shade. The main building, on a bank to one side of the site, houses reception, recreation rooms and the sanitary unit including laundry and dishwashing facilities. This unit is fairly elderly, but can be heated and offers free hot water and British style WCs, with some facilities shared by both sexes. The showers are of good quality with an adequate provision for the size of the site which is quite small despite its initial appearance. Of the 75 pitches, around 55 are available for touring units and there is an area of hardstanding for inclement weather. Most of the pitches are on grass under tall trees and all have access to electricity (6A). Also on site are a children's playground, volleyball, basketball and boules courts. Previously the property of the Princes of Orleans, the Château houses the Town Hall and a museum, and some of the rooms and the gardens are open to the public. The park gates are closed 10 pm. - 7 am. Mobile homes to rent.

Directions: Take the D925 from Le Tréport into the town centre from which the Château and site are signed.

Charges 2000:
-- Per person Ffr. 11.20; child (2-10 yrs) 5.70; tent or caravan 11.20; car or m/cycle 11.20; motor-caravan 15.20; electricity (6A) 19.50.
Open:
1 April - 31 October.
Address:
76260 Eu.
Tel:
(0)2.35.86.20.04.
Reservations:
Contact site.

7608M Camping Municipal du Colombier, Offranville

Approaching through the town, the work of the parks department is immediately evident with many floral displays, and this dedication extends to the site itself, where the 103 pitches are all individual, divided by hedges and shrubs with well tended grass, and hardstanding for vehicles. Many are taken by seasonal units, with only 33 for tourers. Electricity is available to all pitches (6/10A) and the site is well lit. From reception one passes through the barrier, and down an attractive drive through a park to the site. The single, modern and spotlessly clean sanitary building provides single sex facilities with both British and Turkish style WCs, open and cubicled washbasins, roomy showers with dividers and seats, good facilities for disabled people and chemical disposal. Hot water is free throughout. Under cover at the end of the building are dishwashing and laundry sinks. In the park adjacent to the site there is minigolf, tennis, children's playgrounds, horse and pony riding lessons and lovely gardens. The park also has a beautifully restored building 'La Maison du Parc' with a tea-room and bar on the ground floor and a museum above. The town with its shops and restaurants is an easy walk. A swimming pool is in nearby Dieppe. Golf 8 km, fishing 10 km. Five chalets for hire. Caravan storage.

Directions: Site is well signed from all major roads into the town.

Charges 2000:
-- Per pitch Ffr 19.50; person 18.00; child (under 7 yrs) 11.00; vehicle 11.00; electricity 6A 12.50, 10A 15.50.
-- No credit cards
Open:
1 April - 15 October.
Address:
76550 Offranville.
Tel:
(0)2.35.85.21.14.
Reservations:
Recommended for high season.

7610M Camping Municipal, Cany-Barville

This good quality site first opened in 1997, adjacent to the municipal sports stadium, has a floral entrance and tarmac roads. Of the 100 individual hedged pitches around 74 are available for tourists. There are around 40 concrete hardstandings and the remainder are on grass, all are fully serviced with water, drain and electric hook-ups (10A). As yet, there is not very much shade from newly planted specimen trees. The modern, centrally located, sanitary unit can be heated, and has British style WCs, washbasins in cubicles, good hot showers, dishwashing and laundry sinks, and separate suites for disabled people. A drive-over motorcaravan service point with a chemical disposal facility and rubbish bins is at one side of the site. Cany-Barville is a bustling small town with a market on Monday morning, and an annual Antiques Fair in mid-August. There is a Château and an Eco-museum (1/4-30/10), and the Durdent valley has numerous other châteaux, mills, churches and 'colombiers'.

Directions: From traffic lights on eastern side of town turn off D925 on to D268 towards Yvetot. Go under railway arch and continue straight on. Site is 600 m. from town centre adjacent to sports field.

Charges 2000:
-- Per adult Ffr. 13.00; child (under 7 yrs) 6.00; caravan 15.00; tent 10.00; vehicle 7.00; animal 5.00; electricity 15.00.
Open:
All year.
Address:
76450 Cany-Barville.
Tel:
(0)2.35.97.70.37.
Reservations:
Advised for July/Aug; contact site.

NORTHERN FRANCE

The area we have defined as Northern France combines two of the official French Regions:

NORD/PAS DE CALAIS

Major City: Lille
Ports: Calais and Boulogne
Departements: 59 Nord
62 Pas-de-Calais

PICARDY

Major City: Amiens
Departements: 02 Aisne,
60 Oise, 80 Somme

This is an area where centuries of invaders from the north as well as Britain have left their mark. Evidence of this is visible in the 17th century defensive citadels designed by Vauban at the end of a long period of conquests by English kings and Burgundian dukes; and from a more recent age the area around Flanders and the Somme is imprinted with the battles of two Great Wars with acres of immaculately tended war graves. At Vimy Ridge near Arras, First World War trenches have been preserved intact, a most poignant sight: while almost every village between Arras and Amiens has its memorial. On the other hand, it is the birthplace of Gothic architecture with six cathedrals, Amiens, Laon, and Beauvais the better known and Amiens arguably the grandest in France.

The area is however predominately rural with forests of mature beech and oak, though in Maritime Flanders the landscape is of polders and copses, a contrast to the industrial cities such as Lille now sporting a futuristic image with the development of Eurolille. The coastline has sandy beaches, dunes and ports. Le Touquet combines the modernity of its sports facilities with an old world charm. Boulogne and its ramparts is home to Nausicaa, the world's largest sea-life centre and from Cap Griz-Nez you may be able to see the White Cliffs of Dover. Perhaps though for some of us it is the huge hypermarkets which have grown up in this area that interest us as we stock up with wine, beer and cheese, etc. on our way home via ferry or the Tunnel.

Note: the site reports are laid out by département in numerical order not by region.
See map on page 307.

Cuisine of the region

Carbonnade de Boeuf à la Flamande – braised beef with beer, onions and bacon
Caudière (Chaudière, Caudrée) – versions of fish and potato soup
Ficelles Picardes – ham pancakes with mushroom sauce
Flamiche aux poireaux – puff pastry tart with cream and leeks
Hochepot – a thick Flemish soup with virtually everything in it but the kitchen sink
Soupe courquignoise – soup with white wine, fish, moules, leeks and Gruyère cheese
Tarte aux Maroilles – a hot creamy tart based on Maroilles cheese
Waterzooï – a cross between soup and stew, usually of fish or chicken

Places of Interest

Amiens – Notre Dame cathedral, impressive for its size and the richly sculpted facade and the wood and stone carvings of the choir; monument to 1918 Battle of the Somme, also known for its remarkable 'hortillonnages' (water gardens) and interlinking canals
Chantilly – the Château of Chantilly now houses the Musée Condé with impressive Baroque gardens to walk around, as well as a 17th century stable with a 'live' Horse museum *(for discount voucher offer see advertisement between pages 256/257)*
Compiègne – Seven miles east of the town is Clairière de l'Armistice. The railway coach here is a replica of the one in which the 1918 Armistice was signed and in which Hitler received the French surrender in 1942
Laon – 12th century cathedral, WW1 trenches, Vauclair Abbey
Marquesterre – at the mouth of the Somme, one of Europe's most important bird sanctuaries

0206M Camping Municipal, Guignicourt

This very pleasant little municipal site has 100 pitches, 50 for long stay units and 50 for tourists. The manager takes great pride in his site, which is clean and tidy with many floral displays. Pitches are generally large and level, although you might need an extra long lead for some, but there are few dividing hedges. Pitches along the river bank have most shade, with a few specimen trees providing a little shade to some of the more open pitches. The modern sanitary unit has British and Turkish style WCs, washbasins (cold only except for the one in a cubicle), push-button hot showers, dishwashing and laundry sinks. Also on site is a children's playground, tennis and boules courts, and fishing. Golf is nearby. The town is quite attractive and is worthy of an evening stroll, it has all services including a supermarket, bank, etc. You may notice a low level hum from the nearby Generale Sucrière factory, a major industry of the town. At the junction of the N44 and D925, 7 km. west of the town, is the Chemin des Dames, Monument des Chars d'Assaut - a memorial to the WW1 tank campaign at Berry-au-Bac, with two remarkably well preserved tanks. Further to the west is the Caverne du Dragon, a former stone quarry which sheltered troops during the 1914-18 conflict, which is now a museum depicting everyday life on the front line.

Charges 2000:
-- Per adult Ffr.11.00 ;
child (2-10 yrs) 6.50;
pitch 12.00; animal 7.00;
extra car 7.0; electricity
18.00 (6A), 30.00 (10A).

Open:
1 April - 30 September.

Address:
02190 Guignicourt.

Tel:
(0)3.23.79.74.58.

Reservations:
Contact site for details.

Directions: Guignicourt is about 20 km. north of Reims, just east of the A26, junction 14. The site is well signed from D925 in the village.

0200 Camping Caravaning Vivier aux Carpes, Seraucourt-le-Grand

Small, quiet site, close to A26, two hours from Calais, ideal for overnight or longer stay.

This neat, purpose designed site is imaginatively set out taking full benefit of large ponds which are well stocked for fishing (Ffr. 35 p/day). There is also abundant wild life. The 60 well spaced pitches, are at least 100 sq.m. on flat grass with dividing hedges. The 45 for touring units all have electricity (6A), some water points also and there are special pitches for motorcaravans. The site has a comfortable feel, close to the village centre (with post office, doctor, chemist and small supermarket), but it is quiet. The spacious, clean sanitary block with British style WCs has separate, heated facilities for disabled visitors, which are also available to other campers in the winter months. Laundry facilities. Upstairs in a large TV/games room with table tennis and snooker. Small children's play area, bicycle hire and a petanque court. Riding 4 km, golf 12 km. There is plenty to see in the area, with the cathedral cities of St Quentin, Reims, Amiens and Laon close, Disneyland is just over an hour away, Compiegne and the WW1 battlefields are near and Paris easily reachable by train (1¼ hrs from St Quentin). The enthusiastic owners and the manager speak excellent English and are keen to welcome British visitors. Although there is no restaurant on site, good and reasonable hotels are close. We were impressed by the ambience created and would recommend this site to those seeking tranquillity in an attractive setting. Gates close 10 pm, office open 09.00-21.30. Motorcaravan service point (for large vans fresh water is Ffr. 10). Caravan storage (indoor or out). Rallies welcome.

Charges 2001:
-- Per unit incl. 2 persons
and electricity Ffr. 90.00;
extra person 15.00; child
(under 10 yrs) 10.00; pet
5.00.
-- Monthly, weekly or
weekend rates available.
-- Discounts for students
with tents.
-- No credit cards.

Open:
All year
except Xmas - New Year.

Address:
10 Rue Charles Voyeux,
02790
Seraucourt-le-Grand.

Tel:
(0)3.23.60.50.10.
FAX: (0)3.23.60.51.69.
E-mail: camping.du.
vivier@wanadoo.fr.

Reservations:
Recommended for peak
season.

Directions: Leave A26 (Calais - Reims) at exit 11 then D1 left towards Soissons. Take D8 and on entering Essigny-la-Grand (4 km.) turn sharp right on D72 signed Seraucourt-le-Grand (5 km). Site is clearly signed - in centre of village.

NORTH - 59 Nord

5907 Camping Domaine de la Sablière, Mont-Noir

Good quality, mature site convenient for the channel ports.

Whether en-route to or from the channel ports or wanting to spend time visiting the WW1 cemeteries, this site offers spacious pitches and modern clean sanitary facilities. Mont-Noir, which straddles the France/Belgium border, enjoys an elevated, rural situation approximately 40 km. southeast of Dunkirk and 25 km. northwest of Lille. Entry to the site is on the brow of a hill, but not difficult. From the security gate and reception area the site, which is terraced, is laid out in avenues shaded by mature trees and shrubs. The 100 pitches are level and separated by hedging with water, drainage and electricity (6A). There are many seasonal caravans but 10 pitches are allocated for touring units. The warden is helpful and escorts you to your pitch, care is needed for larger units negotiating sharp bends and a steep descent if sited at lower levels. One way traffic operates. The central sanitary block is of a modern design, clean and attractively sited on a high level amid the foliage and surrounded by a wooden fence. It is approached by a paved walkway and tiled forecourt. Facilities include WCs, washbasins, mirrors, electric points, washbasins in private cabins and showers. On a lower level a sanitary block of older construction houses additional WCs, washbasins and showers. Also dishwashing sinks, laundry facilities and chemical disposal unit. A bar, café and games room are on site, a baker calls each morning and, across the road, a restaurant offers excellent value snacks and meals.

Directions: Leave A25 Lille - Dunkerque autoroute at Bailleul (exit 10) on D10. Continue through Bailleul and follow camp signs to St-Jans-Cappel - through village and turn right at crossroads to Mont-Noir. Site is on right at top of hill opposite restaurant.

Charges 2000:
-- Per adult Ffr. 15.00; child (under 7 yrs) 7.50; pitch 15.00; car 12.00; dog free; electricity 15.00.

Open:
1 April - 31 October.

Address:
Mont-Noir,
59270 Saint-Jans-Cappel.

Tel:
(0)3.28.49.46.34.

Reservations:
Contact site.

5905M Camping Municipal de Maubeuge, Maubeuge

This is an attractive site convenient for a night-stop or for longer stays close to the RN2 road. It is one of those neat and tidy municipal sites and has 92 marked pitches of fair size. They are on mainly level ground and are separated by trim hedges. Most have electricity (3, 6 or 10A) and some have hardstanding. A variety of broadleaf trees provides shade when needed. Two circular sanitary blocks provide good modern facilities, with British style WCs, hot showers with dividers, hooks and mats, washbasins with warm water, undercover dishwashing sinks and washing machines. The block used in winter can be heated. There are four pitches with private facilities (WC and washbasin) for a small supplement. When inspected, reception staff were friendly and helpful. There is a small adventure-style playground for children. Although there are few amenities on the site, the interesting town centre of Maubeuge itself is only about 1 km

Directions: Site is on the RN2 road (known as the N6 in Belgium) north of the town, on the right going towards Mons.

Charges 2000:
-- Per pitch Ffr. 20.00; person 20.00; child (4-7 yrs) 11.00; dog free; electricity 3A 17.00, 6A 27.00, 10A 33.00; pitch with private sanitary facilities 27.00.

Open
All year.

Address:
Route de Mons,
59600 Maubeuge.

Tel:
(0)3.27.62.25.48.

Reservations:
Not normally made or necessary, but if in doubt telephone site.

5906M Camping Municipal de la Plage, Grand Fort Philippe

This useful municipal site is midway between Calais and Dunkerque and is therefore an ideal night stop. It has the good, modern sanitary block typical of municipal sites with British style toilets, push-button showers, some washbasins in private cabins and chemical disposal. There are also facilities for disabled people. The block was clean when we visited but maintenance is variable. The site is quite open, flat and grassy with 84 tourist pitches, some with electricity and water connections. Bread is delivered at breakfast time and there are restaurants and bars nearby in the town of Gravelines (2 km). A swimming pool and sports complex are 5 km. Fishing, bicycle hire, riding and golf within 5 km. Regular public transport to the town operates from nearby. In July and August there is a boat service to Gravelines twice a day.

Directions: From main N1/E40 Calais - Dunkerque road, turn in Gravelines where camping signs are shown. The site is some distance - follow road through port area, bearing left. Alternatively, D119 from Calais passing through Oye-Plage, turn to site in 2 km.

Charges 2000:
-- Per pitch Ffr. 18.40; car 9.20; adult 23.40; child (under 7 yrs) 10.20; dog free; electricity 17.90.
-- Credit cards accepted.

Open:
1 April - 31 October.

Address:
Rue Marechal Foch,
59153 Grand Fort Philippe.

Tel:
(0)3.28.65.31.95 (or low season (0)3.28.65.40.00).

Reservations:
Contact site.

6001 Camping Campix, St Leu-d'Esserent, nr Chantilly

Unusual, peaceful, modern site in old sandstone quarry.

Opened in 1991, this informal site has been unusually developed in what used to be a sandstone quarry on the outskirts of the small town. The quarry walls provide very different boundaries to most of the site, giving a sheltered, peaceful environment. Trees have been grown to soften the slopes. Not a neat, manicured site, the 160 pitches are arranged in small groups on the different levels with stone and gravel access roads (some fairly steep and possibly muddy in poor weather). Electricity (6A) is available to approximately 150 pitches. There are very many secluded corners mostly for smaller units and tents. Torches are advised. There is plenty of space for children to explore (parents must supervise - some areas, although fenced, could be dangerous). A footpath leads from the site to the town where there are shops, restaurants and an outdoor pool (in season). At the entrance to the site, a large building houses reception and two clean, heated sanitary units - one for tourers, the other usually reserved for groups. These have pre-mixed hot showers with dividers and seats, washbasins in rows with hooks and mirrors, some British style WCs, two suites for disabled people which double as baby rooms and laundry facilities with washing machine and dryer. Hot water is free throughout. At quieter times only one unit is opened. Facilities may be congested at peak times. In high season (July/Aug) bread and milk are delivered daily and a basic snack bar operates from a mobile unit. Chemical disposal and motorcaravan service facilities. Bottle bank. Fishing 1 or 5 km, riding or golf 5 km. This site is best suited to those wanting to get away from it all, those not needing sophisticated on-site facilities, or for visiting local places of interest. The friendly, English speaking owner will advise on these places of interest, which include Chantilly (see advert between pages 256/7) 5 km, the Asterix Park and the Mer de Sable, a Western theme amusements park, both 20 km. Disneyland is 70 km. It is possible to visit Paris by train and reception will advise on the easiest route.

Directions: St Leu d'Esserent is 11 km. west of Senlis, 5 km. west of Chantilly. From the north on the A1 autoroute take the Senlis exit, from Paris the Chantilly exit. Site is signed north of town off the D12 towards Cramoisy or in the village.

Charges 2001:
-- Ffrancs: per unit Ffr. 20.00 - 30.00; small tent 5.00 - 25.00, acc. to location; person 15.00 - 25.00; child (under 10 yrs) 10.00 - 15.00; dog 5.00 - 10.00; electricity 15.00 - 20.00. '
-- Euro: per unit 3.00 - 5.00; small tent 1.00 - 4.00, acc. to location; person 3.00 - 4.50; child (under 10 yrs) 2.00 - 3.00; dog 1.00 - 2.00; electricity 2.50 - 3.50.
-- Credit cards accepted.
Open:
1 March - 30 November.
Address:
BP 37, 60340
St Leu-d'Esserent.
Tel:
(0)3.44.56.08.48 or
(0)3.44.56.28.75.
FAX: (0)3.44.56.28.75.
E-mail: campixfr
@aol.com.
Reservations:
Advisable for July/Aug.
Write for details.

6205 Camping Caravaning St Louis, Autingues

Peaceful little site, convenient for the ferry port at Calais.

This site has 84 pitches with many privately owned holiday homes, but there are around 25 pitches for tourists. They are individual, grassy with some shade and are in a garden-like setting, with 4A electric hook-ups. The sanitary facilities are clean and tidy, with British style WCs, showers on payment (Ffr. 8), and washbasins in cubicles. There are also dishwashing and laundry sinks, a washing machine, facilities for disabled people and a baby room. Also on-site is a children's playground, a games room with table football, table tennis, etc, and a restaurant which opens for July/Aug. Near the entrance is a good motorcaravan service point, free to campers (Ffr. 25.00 for non-residents). Two mobile homes for rent.

Directions: From Calais take N43 towards St Omer for 15 km, and just east of Ardres, turn south on D224, where site is signed.

Charges guide:
-- Per adult Ffr. 15.00;
child (2-7 yrs) 7.00; pitch 20.00; electricity 10.00.
Open:
31 March - 31 October.
Address:
Rue Leulène, 62610
Autingues par Ardres.
Tel:
(0)3.21.35.46.83.
FAX: (0)3.21.00.19.78.
Reservations:
Advised for high season; contact site.

NORTH - 62 Pas de Calais

6201 Castel Camping Caravaning La Bien-Assise, Guînes, nr Calais

Mature, quality site with pools, close to cross channel links.

The chequered history of La Bien-Assise goes back to the 1500s, but today the Château, farm and mill are all in the hands of the Boutoille family and they can provide you with a fascinating brief history. However, now the farm buildings house the shop, bar/grill, TV room and takeaway (all from 1/5). The entrance to a more formal restaurant, 'La Ferme Gourmande' (open all year, closed Mondays) is in the mellow farmyard opposite the dovecote with the Auberge du Colombier next door. The pool complex (10/5-10/9) utilises a barn area to provide a partly covered, sheltered and heated pool (16 x 6 m.) and fun pool with toboggan and paddling pool with mushroom fountain. A small sanitary block has been added for these facilities. There are 180 grass pitches mainly set among mature trees, apart from one new field. Of good size and connected by gravel roads, shrubs and bushes make them 'semi-delimité'. Three good, well equipped toilet blocks are ample with free, controllable showers, many washbasins in cabins, mostly British style WCs and provision for babies, clothes and dishwashing, and chemical disposal. Play areas, minigolf and a tennis court are sheltered by a mature garden wall, which together with the Château itself, combine to give a comfortable, mature feel. Bicycle hire on site, fishing 8 km, riding 10 km. There is a local market and walks from the site. Its position 15 minutes from Calais, the Channel Tunnel exit 6 km. and Boulogne 20 minutes, make it a popular venue en-route north or south, but it is well worth a longer stay. Reception opens long hours to meet the needs of those crossing the Channel and the site can have heavy usage at times (when maintenance can be variable). Used by tour operators (50 pitches).

Directions: From ferry terminal follow A16 south (Boulogne) for junction 15, turning towards St Pierre de Calais to immediately pick up Guînes signs before going under autoroute following the D127. Continue beside canal to Guînes. Site is just southwest of village on D231 Marquise road. From Tunnel also follow A16 south (Boulogne) to immediately pick up Guînes signs at junction 11 and following D215 past St Tricat to Guînes. From south on autoroute A26, use exit 2 (Ardres, Guînes) onto N43 and D231 (15 km).

Charges 2000:
-- Per unit Ffr. 62.00; adult 26.00; child (under 8 yrs) 20.00; electricity (6A) 20.00.
-- Low seasons less 10%.
-- Credit cards accepted.

Open:
25 April - 20 September, (full facilities: 6/5-16/9).

Address:
62340 Guînes:

Tel:
(0)3.21.35.20.77.
FAX: (0)3.21.36.79.20.
E-mail: castel@
bien-assise.com.

Reservations:
Advised for July/Aug; made with deposit (Ffr 250) and fee (50) for stays 5 days or more.

Book this site
01892 559898

THE ALAN ROGERS'
travel service

see colour advert between pages 64/65

6203 Camping Château du Gandspette, Eperlecques, nr St Omer

Friendly, comfortable, family run site with swimming pools in grounds of château.

Conveniently situated for the channel ports and tunnel, this family run site provides useful overnight accommodation and has a range of facilities for a longer stay. It has the benefit of two swimming pools, one large and one smaller, with paved sheltered sunbathing area (15/5-30/9). There is also an attractive bar, grill restaurant and takeaway (all 15/5-15/9) situated in the 17th century building adjacent to the château. A gravel site road gives access to three different camping areas and a central open space. There are 170 pitches (100 or 150 sq.m), of which 55 are taken by semi-permanent French holiday caravans which intermix with some of the touring pitches giving a real French ambience. All pitches have electricity (6/10A) and are delineated by trees and some hedging. Mature trees form the perimeter of the site, through which there is access to woodland walks and a playing field. A new adventure style children's playground has rubber safety bases. The partially renovated sanitary block provides satisfactory facilities with British style WCs, a mixture of open and cubicled washbasins, and push-button hot showers housed in tiled cubicles with separators. There are covered sinks for dishwashing with hot water, washing machines and dryers, chemical disposal and a good, new motorcaravan service point. A new sanitary unit should be ready for the 2001 season. Activities on site include tennis, petanque, children's room with table tennis and electronic games. Entertainment is organised in season. Riding 3 km, fishing 3 km, golf 10 km. Small supermarket in village 1 km. Rooms in the château (B&B). Used by tour operators (8 pitches). Market at Watten (Friday) and St Omer (Saturday). A 'Sites et Paysages' member.

Directions: From Calais follow N43 towards St Omer for 25 km. Southeast of Nordausques take D221 (east) and follow camp signs for 5-6 km. From St Omer follow N43 to roundabout at junction with D600. Turn right onto D600 towards Dunkirk and after 5 km. turn left on D221. Site is 1.5 km. on right.

Charges 2000:
-- Per unit incl. 2 persons Ffr. 100.00; extra person (over 4 yrs) 25.00, under 4 free; dog free; extra car 10.00; electricity (6A) 20.00; local tax 2.00 (child 4-10 yrs 1.00).
-- Credit cards accepted.

Open:
1 April - 30 September.

Address:
62910 Eperlecques.

Tel:
(0)3.21.93.43.93.
FAX: (0)3.21.95.74.98.

Reservations:
Necessary for July/Aug - write to site.

`Camping Cheque'

Book this site
01892 559898

THE ALAN ROGERS'
travel service

see colour advert between pages 160/161

6204 Caravaning du Château, Condette, nr Boulogne

Useful small site on the coast, south of Boulogne.

Within about 15 minutes drive of Boulogne and only 5 minutes by car from the long sandy beach at Hardelot, this is a particularly conveniently situated site for those using the Seacat services. This modern site has 70 pitches with around 50 available for touring units, the rest occupied by long stay or units to rent. Pitches are of varying size on level grass, all with access to electricity (6A). Hedging plants between the pitches are maturing well and there is shade from mature trees around the site. No frills sanitary facilities include large hot showers with dividers (poor water flow), washbasins (H&C), British style WCs and a baby bath are in two recently constructed units, one with heating. Dishwashing sinks (H&C), laundry facilities (washing machine and dryer), chemical disposal and motor-caravan services. A fitness room has been added and the site has an excellent children's playgound and entertainment for them in season, but there are few other on-site facilities. However, a pub/restaurant is within walking distance, run by an Englishman! With friendly and accommodating owners, this site provides a useful overnight stop. Fishing 800 m, riding 1 km, bicycle hire or golf 3 km.

Charges 2000:
-- Per unit incl. 2 persons Ffr. 75.00 - 92.00; extra person 22.00 - 27.00; child (under 7 yrs) 13.00 - 17.00; extra car 12.00 - 17.00; dog free; electricity (6A) 20.00.
-- No credit cards.

Open:
1 April - 31 October.

Address:
21 Rue Nouvelle, 62360 Condette.

Tel:
(0)3.21.87.59.59 (in season) or (0)3.21.31.74.01.

Reservations:
Advised - contact site.

Directions: South of Boulogne, take N1 Amien (Paris) road, then on the outskirts take the right fork for Touquet-Paris Plage (D940). Pass Elf garage and signs for Condette and turn right at new roundabout. Continue to next roundabout and turn right again. Site entrance (narrow) is on the right after a short distance.

8004 Caravaning du Royon, Fort-Mahon-Plage

Busy holiday site with pleasant atmosphere and good range of activities.

This family run site, some 2 km. from the sea, has 280 pitches of which 120 are available to touring units. Of either 95 or 120 sq.m, the marked and numbered pitches are divided by hedges and arranged either side of access roads. Electricity (6A) and water points are available to all. The site is well lit, fenced and guarded at night (Ffr. 200 deposit for barrier card). The four sanitary buildings provide mostly unisex facilities with British or Turkish style WCs, both open and cubicled washbasins, showers with dividers and seats, units for disabled people, baby baths and covered dishwashing and laundry sinks. Hot water is free throughout. There is an excellent friendly clubroom and bar which serves all types of drinks and ices, sells bread and newspapers and has the usual games machines. A mobile take-away calls each evening in July/Aug with a good selection of dishes. Also on site are a small shop (open July/Aug), table tennis, new multi-court, tennis court, bicycle hire, boules, a children's playground, plus an attractive swimming pool (16 x 8 m; 1/5-15/9) with children's pool and a sunbathing terrace (Ffr. 50 deposit for pool bracelet). Entertainment is organised for adults and children in July/Aug. Opportunities for fishing, riding or golf within 1 km. and for windsurfing, sailing, sand yachting, canoeing, swimming, climbing, and shooting nearby. The site is close to a cinema, disco and casino and the Baie de L'Authie which is an area noted for migrating birds. Chalets and mobile homes to rent.

Charges 2000:
-- Per pitch (95 sq.m.) incl. caravan, car, water tap, electricity (6A), and 3 persons Ffr. 110.00 - 131.00; pitch (120 sq.m), as above 125.00 - 147.00; extra adult 34.00; child (1-7 yrs) 4.00; extra car 22.00; dog 10.00; local tax (over 10 yrs) 1.00.
-- Credit cards accepted.

Open:
13 March - 31 October.

Address:
1271 Route du Quend, 80120 Fort-Mahon-Plage.

Tel:
(0)3.22.23.40.30.
FAX: (0)3.22.23.65.15.

Reservations:
Essential for July/Aug; made with deposit (Ffr 200).

Directions: Site is on outskirts of Fort Mahon Plage, on D32 towards Quend.

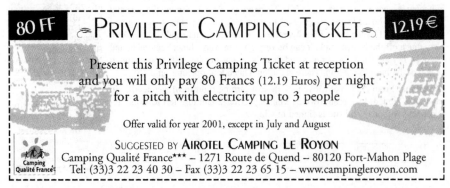

8001 Castel Camping Domaine de Drancourt, St Valéry-sur-Somme

Popular site with pools and other amenities, between Boulogne and Dieppe.

A popular, lively holiday site within easy distance of Channel ports, Drancourt is in four sections. The original section has 100 marked and numbered grassy pitches of good size with good shade. An extension taking some 90 units is in light woodland and two newer touring sections are on flat or gently sloping meadow, with little shade as yet. It can be dusty around reception buildings and château in dry weather. There are 326 pitches, of which 120 are occupied by several tour operators. Electricity (6A) is available in all areas. Sanitary facilities consist of three modern, well equipped blocks. All have British style WCs, washbasins in cubicles, roomy showers, and free pre-set hot water, some new family bathrooms and facilities for disabled visitors, plus laundry and dish-washing sinks, washing machines and dryers. However, drainage difficulties can still cause occasional problems. Amenities include three free heated swimming pools (from 1/5), one inside and two open air, one with water slide. Two are 17 x 6 m. but of different depths, the third is 45 cm. deep for children. Shop (from 1/5), takeaway and pizzeria (July/Aug) open until late and restaurant closing at 9 pm. There is a bar in the château, a new large first floor bar and a pool-side bar with karaoke in season. There are three TV rooms, one for children, a disco (free entry) and a games room with table tennis. Activities include a tennis court, golf practise range and minigolf in an enclosed setting, bicycle hire, pony riding in season (stables 15 km), free fishing and bicycle hire. Activities and weekly excursions to Paris (June-Aug) are organised. Bureau de change. The pools and sanitary instal-lations can become busy at times in peak season. Stony beach at Cayeux 8 km, or sandy beach 25 km. English is spoken and the site is run personally by the energetic owner and his staff.

Charges 2000:
-- Per person Ffr. 33.00 + local tax (over 10 yrs) 2.00; child (under 5 yrs) 25.00; pitch for caravan or tent 52.00; car 16.00; pitch for motorcaravan 70.00; dog free; electricity (6A) 18.00.
-- Credit cards accepted.

Open:
Easter - 15 September.

Address:
BP 22, 80230 Saint-Valery-sur-Somme.

Tel:
(0)3.22.26.93.45.
FAX: (0)3.22.26.85.87.

Reservations:
Advised for the main season and made for any length, with deposit for longer stays.

Directions: Site is 2.5 km. south of St Valéry, near Estreboeuf, and is signed from the St Valéry road N40.

Book this site
01892 559898

THE ALAN ROGERS'
travel service

8006 Camping Le Val de Trie, Bouillancourt, Moyenneville

Natural countryside touring site, in a woodland location, near small village.

Le Val de Trie is maturing into a well managed site with modern facilities. The 100 numbered pitches are grassy and of a good size, divided by hedges and shrubs with mature trees providing good shade in most areas. Electricity (6A) and water are available to all pitches. Access roads are of gravel (the site is possibly not suitable for the largest motorcaravans). The original sanitary building was extended in '97 doubling its size and a second unit was opened for the 2000 season including a washing machine and dryer. These provide British style WCs, showers with divider and seat, washbasins in cubicles, units for disabled people, babies and children, plus laundry and dishwashing facilities, with free hot water throughout. The small swimming pool (6 x 12 m. open 1/5-15/9) is pleasant, with a fenced enclosure, paved surround and a new paddling pool for children. Other facilities include table tennis, boules and volleyball courts, fishing lake (free), bicycle hire, children's play areas and a small animal enclosure. Riding 5 km, golf 6 km. A small shop (from 1/5) provides basic necessities, farm produce and wine, bread can be ordered each evening and a butcher visits twice weekly in season, and there is a bar and terrace (1/5-15/9). There are good walks around the area and the site notice board keeps campers up to date with local market, shopping and activity news. The site has a friendly, relaxed atmosphere and English is spoken. Very much off the beaten track, it can be very quiet in April, June, September and October. If you visit at these times and there is no-one on site, just choose a pitch or call at the farm to book in. There are a few Dutch tour operator tents (5).

Charges 2000:
-- Per unit incl. 2 persons without electricity Ffr. 65.00 - 98.00, with electricity 80.00 - 98.00; extra person 19.00 - 23.00; child (under 7 yrs) 12.00 - 14.00; extra vehicle 10.00 - 12.00; dog 5.00.
-- No credit cards.

Open:
1 April - 1 November.

Address:
Bouillancourt-sous-Miannay, 80870 Moyenneville.

Tel:
(0)3.22.31.48.88.
FAX: (0)3.22.31.35.33.
E-mail: raphael@ camping-levaldetrie.fr.

Reservations:
Made with dates, plus deposit (Ffr. 200; no fee for AR readers).

Directions: From A28 take Moyenneville exit turning right to Moyenneville. In town (site signed) take road towards Miannay. After 2 km. turn left to Bouillan-court sous Miannay and site is signed in village.

Book this site
01892 559898

THE ALAN ROGERS'
travel service

*see colour advert
between pages 64/65*

8007   Caravaning La Ferme des Aulnes,   Fresne, Nampont St Martin

Countryside site on a restored 17th century farm in village location.
This peaceful site has been developed on the grassy meadows of a small farm on
the edge of the village, with the reception and facilities being housed in the
restored outbuildings, arranged around a central courtyard which houses a fine
heated swimming pool (16 x 9 m; July/Aug), together with a fitness room.
Sanitary fittings are smart, modern and well maintained, comprising British style
WCs, washbasins in cubicles and excellent showers with divider, but no seat. A
large cubicle is available for disabled people. Dishwashing and laundry sinks
complete the fittings, and hot water is free throughout. Of the 105 pitches, 50 are
available for touring units, with most of the remainder occupied by or for sale to
private owners for holiday mobile homes. Around 25 tourist pitches have
electricity (6A) and are level, individual and divided by shrubs and young trees.
The remainder (without electricity) are on an open, slightly sloping, grassy area.
Other amenities include the small bar, a shop for necessities (high season only),
TV, playground for small children and archery. Site owned mobile homes to rent.
Fishing is available in the river 200 m. from the site and a golf course is 3 km.

Charges guide:
-- Per unit incl. 2 adults
and 1 child (under 7 yrs)
Ffr. 100.00; extra adult
30.00; extra child (under
7 yrs) 15.00; extra tent
38.00; electricity (6A)
28.00.
Open:
Easter - 1 November.
Address:
Fresne, 80120 Nampont
Saint Martin.
Tel:
(0)3.22.29.22.69 or
(0)3.22.29.97.08.
FAX: as phone.
Reservations:
Contact site for details.

Directions: At Nampont St Martin, turn off the N1 on to the D85E (site is signed),
towards Fresne, site is on right after about 3 km.

8008M   Camping Municipal Le Bois des Pecheurs,   Poix-de-Picardie

In an area where good municipal sites are hard to find, the municipal site at Poix-
de-Picardie is excellent for a one night stop, or even a few days to explore the
region. The 135 pitches are on level, neatly mown grass, either individual or in
hedged bays of four. Half the pitches at one end are reserved for long stay or
holiday groups, leaving the other half for tourists, with electricity (10A) on most.
The well maintained, central sanitary unit provides British style WCs, washbasins
(some in cubicles) and showers, with free hot water throughout. Two rooms
provide ample dishwashing and laundry sinks and there is a washing machine and
dryer. Other amenities include a small children's playground, volleyball and table
tennis. Fishing 1 km. There is no shop on site but camping gaz is stocked. Shops
and services are in Poix de Picardie which is approx. 1.5 km. The city of Amiens
(28 km.) is worth visiting for its famous cathedral and quayside market (Thursday
and Saturday) in the old, restored St Leu quarter. Caravan storage.

Charges 2000:
-- Per unit incl. 2 adults
FFr. 60.00; child 8.00;
dog 8.00; electricity
22.00.
-- No credit cards.
Open:
1 April - 30 September
Address:
Rte de Forges Les Eaux,
80290 Poix-de-Picardie.
Tel:
(0)3.22.90.11.71.
Reservations:
Write for details.

Directions: Site is southwest of the town on the D919 road, and is signed from the
D901 Grandvilliers road.

8009   Camping Caravaning Le Val d'Authie, Villers-sur-Authie

Very well run family owned site with heated outdoor pool.
In a village location, this well organised site is fairly close to several beaches, but
also has its own excellent pool complex, small restaurant and bar. The owners
have carefully controlled the size of the site, leaving space for a leisure area at the
end of the site, which has a multi-court and tennis court, fitness trail and running
track, mountain bike circuit, with plenty of good paths for an evening stroll. There
are 158 pitches, but with 100 holiday homes and 13 rental chalets, there are only
45 tourist pitches. These are on grass, some are divided by small hedges, with 3
or 6A electricity and 15 have full services. Excellent modern sanitary facilities
have push-button hot showers (some shower/washbasin units), washbasins in
cubicles, and facilities for disabled people and babies. The heated swimming pool
with a small jacuzzi and paddling pool is open April to mid-September, with
surveillance in July/August. There is a well stocked shop by reception, and a
bar/restaurant which serves excellent value meals, with a choice of 17 ice-cream
flavours (opening hours vary according to season). There is a good playground for
small children, a club room with TV, and weekend entertainment in season.
Freezer pack service. Quality mobile homes for rent. Ideas for excursions include
the 15-16th century chapel and Hospice, belfry and Aviation Museum at Rue, a
pottery at nearby Roussent, a flour mill at Maintenay, and the steam railway which
runs from Le Crotoy to Cayeux-sur-Mer around the Baie de Somme.

Charges 2000:
-- Per adult Ffr. 32.00;
child (under 7 yrs) 16.00;
pitch 28.00; extra vehicle
12.00; animal 7.00;
electricity 15.00 (3A),
extra amps 5.00.
-- Min. per pitch
July/Aug. Ffr. 124.00.
-- Credit cards accepted.
Open:
1 April - 31 October.
Address:
20 Route de Vercourt,
80120 Villers-sur-Authie.
Tel:
(0)3.22.29.92.47.
FAX: (0)3.22.29.94.05.
Reservations:
Advisable for high
season, peak weekends
and B.Hs; contact site for
details.

Directions: Villers-sur-Authie is 25 km. NNW of Abbeville. From A16 junction
24 take N1 to Vron, then left on D175 to Villers-sur-Authie. Alternatively use D85
from Rue, or D485 from Nampont-St-Martin. Site is at southern end of village.

`'Camping Cheque'`

57

PARIS / ILE DE FRANCE

Major cities: Paris, Versailles, Ivry, Melun, Nanterre,
Bobigny, Creteil, Pontoise

Départements: 75 Paris, 77 Seine-et-Marne, 78 Yvelines, 91 Essone,
92 Hauts-de-Seine, 93 Seine-St-Denis, 94 Val de Marne, 95 Val d'Oise

How many millions of words have been written about Paris? Quite
simply, it is a marvellous place of infinite variety - the list of things to
do is virtually endless and could easily fill many holidays -
window shopping, the Eiffel Tower, Montmartre, the
Louvre, trips on the Seine, pavement cafés, the
Moulin Rouge, etc, etc! Both the bus and Metro
systems are excellent, efficient and reasonably
priced, so there is no need to take your car into
the centre. The history, customs and language of
the Ile-de-France region have merged with those of
Paris, and spread throughout the whole country. The
destiny of France was played out in the Ile-de-France, in
the magnificent castles of Fontainebleau, Compiègne,
Provins, Saint-Germain and Versailles. This `garden of
kings' is in fact made up of many smaller regions whose
names - Valois, Beauvaisis, Vexin, Brie, Gatinais,
Hurepoix - irresistibly evoke royal banners and the
pageantry of past years. Square bell towers in gentle valleys, white silos on endless plains of
wheat: subtle and harmonious landscapes painted and praised by Racine, La Fontaine, Corot
and all the landscape painters. Paris is surrounded by forests: Fontainebleau, Compiègne,
Saint-Germain-en-Laye, which attract Parisians in their thousands every weekend.
Note: site reports are laid out by département in numerical order. *See map on page 307.*

Cuisine of the region

Although without a specific cuisine of its own, Paris and Ile de France offer a wide selection of
dishes from all the regions of France. Paris also has a wide choice of foreign restaurants,
such as Vietnamese and North African.

Places of interest

Paris – the list of places to visit is too extensive to include here – the city is the subject of
innumerable guide books!
Auvers-sur-Oise – Van Gogh museum
Fontainebleau – château and national museum, history of Napoléon from 1804-1815
Malmaison – château and museum devoted to the story of Napoléon and Joséphine
Meaux – agricultural centre, Gothic cathedral, chapter house and palace
Rambouillet – château and park with national sheep farm and Queen's Dairy
St Denis – basilica, Funeral Art museum, tombs of the Kings of France
St Germain-en-Laye – château, Gallo-roman and Merovingian archeological museum.
Sèvres – ceramics museum, history of fine china and pottery
Versailles – the most famous Royal Castle in the world, Royal Apartments, Hall of Mirrors,
Chapel, Royal Opera and French History Museum. Park with statues, fountains, the Grand
Trianon, the Petit Trianon, the Temple of Love
Vincennes – château (fortified castle) and museum

Leisure Parks

Parc Astérix (April-October) – Discover the world of the Gauls with Astérix and Obélix.
Disneyland Paris – the 'magic kingdom'. Discover the Mysteries of the Nautilus, experience
Space Mountain, and much more
France Miniature (April-October) 150 historic monuments, 20 typical villages, countryside,
scenes from everyday life.
Mer de Sable (April-September) – a page out of the history of the American West.
Saint-Vrain (April-October) – A prehistoric world with wild animals. Boat-safari.
Thoiry – château and Parc Zoologique, 450-hectare park with gardens and African reserve
containing 800 animals

7502 Camping du Bois de Boulogne, Paris

Conveniently situated campsite beside the Seine and close to the city limits.

This busy site is the nearest one to the city, set in a wooded area between the Seine and the Bois de Boulogne. One can reach the Champs Elysees in 10-15 minutes by car or, from April to Oct, a shuttle bus runs from the site to the Metro station. The site is quite extensive but nevertheless becomes very full with many international visitors of all ages. There are 510 pitches of which 280 are marked, with electricity (10A), water, drainage and TV aerial connections. At the entrance is a functional, modern reception building (open 24 hrs) with a card operated barrier system and a new mini-market. The site has undergone a huge improvement and redevelopment programme including the replacement of all toilet blocks. These have British and Turkish style WCs, washbasins in cubicles and showers with divider and seat. All hot water is free. All these facilities suffer from heavy use in season. Bar and snack bar (1/4-15/10). The bar is open 8 am. - midnight at most times and until 3 am. in peak season. Washing machines and dryers. Motorcaravan service point. Bureau de change. Ticket sales for Disneyland, Asterix Parc, etc. Children's playground. Organised excursions (July/Aug). Fishing 1 km, bicycle hire 2 km. Mobile homes (57) and chalets (4) to rent. Reservations are now made for the pitches, if not booked, early arrival (in the morning) in season is necessary. Note: you are in a major city environment - take care of valuables.

Directions: Site is on east side of Seine between the river and the Bois de Boulogne, just north of the Pont de Suresnes. Easiest approach is from Port Maillot, watch for traffic lights at site entrance. Follow signs closely and use a good map.

Charges guide:
-- Per caravan, car, 2 persons, 10A electricity, water and drainage Ffr. 127.00 - 149.00; without services 96.00 - 133.00; tent incl. 2 persons 65.00 - 84.00; extra adult 24.00 - 31.00; child (under 7 yrs) 12.00 - 15.00; dog 10.00 - 12.00; local tax 1.00.
-- Credit cards accepted.

Open:
All year.

Address:
Allee du bord de l'eau, 75016 Paris.

Tel:
(0)1.45.24.30.00.
FAX: (0)1.42.24.42.95.

Reservations:
Contact site.

7703M Camping de la Base de Loisirs, Jablines

Newly developed site 9 km. from Disneyland, boasting a range of leisure activities.

Redesigned in 1996, Jablines replaces an older site in an upmarket, modern style which, with the accompanying leisure facilities of the adjacent 'Espace Loisirs', provides an interesting, if a little impersonal alternative to other sites in the region. The whole complex close to the Marne has been developed around old gravel workings. The man-made lakes of the leisure complex, complete with beach, provide marvellous water activities - dinghy sailing, wind-surfing, canoeing, fishing and supervised bathing. There is also a large equestrian centre. In season the activities at the leisure complex are supplemented by a bar/ restaurant and a range of very French style group activities. The 'Great Lake' is said to have the largest beach on the Ile-de-France! Whilst staying on the camp-site, admission to the leisure complex is free. The site itself provides 150 pitches, all of a good size with gravel hardstanding and grass, accessed by tarmac roads and clearly marked by fencing panels and newly planted shrubs. All have 10A electricity, nearly half with water and waste connections also. The two identical toilet blocks, which can be heated in cool weather, are solidly built and well equipped. They provide large, pre-set showers, washbasins (all with H&C, some in cubicles) and British style WCs, indoor dishwashing and laundry facilities with washing machine and dryer, and chemical disposal. Motorcaravan service point (Ffr. 10 gives 1 hour electricity or 100 litres of water). A central, modern reception provides a shop in high season only. Children's play area. Disneyland is 15 minutes drive (9 km. with a map provided at reception), Paris is 30 km. Some of the pitches are used by construction workers.

Directions: From A4 Paris - Reims autoroute take A104 north before Disneyland. From the A1 going south, follow signs for Disneyland immediately after Charles de Gaulle airport using the A104. Take exit 8 off the A104 and follow D404 and signs to Base de Loisirs Jablines (8 km). At park entry péage go to campsite lane.

Charges 2001:
-- Per standard pitch incl. 10A electricity Ffr. 50.00 - 60.00; luxury pitch incl. water and waste 55.00 - 65.00; person 27.00 - 30.00; child (under 12 yrs) 17.00 - 20.00; dog 5.00; extra vehicle 15.00.
-- Credit cards accepted.

Open:
1 April - 31 October.

Address:
77450 Jablines.

Tel:
(0)1.60.26.09.37.
FAX: (0)1.60.26.52.43.
E-mail: mairie.jablines@wanadoo.fr.

Reservations:
Essential for July/Aug. and made with booking form from site and 20% deposit.

7701 The Davy Crockett Ranch, Disneyland Paris, Marne-la-Vallée

The Disney campsite with excellent indoor pool, close to Disneyland.
Most sectors of Disney's site contain log cabins (498) which are well equipped and quite attractively priced, but one sector, the Moccasin Trail, provides 97 numbered touring pitches. Each consists of a long, narrow hardstanding with a roughly 25 sq.m. sand-topped tent area at the far end (awnings are not therefore possible). Each pitch is separated from the next by an area of small trees and shrubs and the whole site is well endowed with tall trees for shade. Each place has an individual electric point, water supply and drain, a large picnic table and a robust iron barbecue. At the centre of the oval Trail is a modern, heated toilet block of ample proportions and containing every facility, including washing machines and dryers (free). Maintenance can be variable.

The touring sector is furthest away from the main complex (styled like a Western movie set!), but a 400 m. walk or trip on the small 'train' is well rewarded. The shop provides a rather wider choice of Disney souvenirs than food, but all the basic requirements can be obtained, and there are a number of supermarkets within a short drive. However, most campers will be tempted into using the self-service restaurant, which offers both French and American style food. A major attraction is the large leisure pool, with flume and jacuzzis (closed 15/5-19/5). It is inside a huge log cabin which opens out onto a terrace with chairs and sunbeds. The terrace overlooks Indian Meadows, a large field, with adventure play equipment, archery, beach volleyball and basketball. There are small animal enclosures and pony rides. Bicycle hire on a daily or hourly basis and a good covered tennis court and a half court.

Connection with the Magic Kingdom is via the autoroute taking 10 minutes (free car parking at Disneyland for campers). There may be cheaper sites within range of Disneyland, but this one may offer you the Disney magic throughout your stay, although it can be somewhat impersonal with a heavy turnover of staff. The site is also eminently suitable for visits to that other magic city, Paris, only 35 km. away by autoroute or train. However, in the main season the campsite will be busy and the toilet block may be under pressure with queuing, for example in the early mornings when everyone is eager to start the day. The site may be noisy with cars and motorcaravans returning from late evening shows (possibly also some noise from aircraft or the autoroute). In high season you must reserve well in advance and be prepared for queues in reception. A member of 'Les Castels' group.

Directions: From Paris take A4 eastwards, following signs for Metz/Nancy. For Disneyland itself take exit 14, but for the Davy Crockett Ranch, turn right at exit 13. From Calais, follow Paris signs until just before Charles de Gaulle airport, then follow signs to Marne la Vallée - eventually you should join the A4.

Charges 2000:
-- Per pitch, all incl. Ffr. 300.00 - 400.00; local tax 1.50 (child 0.75).
-- Credit cards accepted.

Open:
1 March - 31 October, plus 20 Dec. - 5 Jan. (log cabins all year).

Address:
Disneyland Paris, BP 117, 77777 Marne la Vallée cedex 4.

Tel:
(0)1.60.30.60.30. FAX: (0)1.60.45.69.33.

Reservations:
For information and reservations phone 0990 030303 (UK).

7708M Camping Municipal Les Prés, Grez sur Loing

A typical municipal site, this has 136 grassy pitches and a fair number of long stay units. However, there are usually around 35 pitches available for tourists, all with 5A electric hook-ups. A two storey building has separate male and female facilities on the upper level, and unisex facilities at ground level. They provide both British and Turkish style WCs, washbasins and push-button showers, dishwashing and laundry facilities, with an excellent suite for disabled people in a separate new building. The town of Grez sur Loing dates back to medieval times and is well worth investigating. The site makes an ideal base for fishing, cycling (the warden can provide a booklet with five suggested routes - in French, of course), walking and rock climbing in Fontainebleau.

Directions: Grez sur Loing is northwest of Nemours, and south of Fontainebleau. From N7 north of town, turn at new roundabout on to D40^D towards Montcourt, cross river bridge and almost immediately turn right (signed). The site access road is one-way.

Charges 2000:
-- Per adult Ffr. 15.00; child (3-11 yrs) 11.00; car 10.00; commercial vehicles 12.00; motor-caravan 26.00 - 35.00, acc. to length; caravan or tent incl. 3 persons 15.00; tent incl. 2 persons 12.00; m/cycle 8.00; animal 5.00; electricity 15.00.

Open:
15 March - 11 November.

Address:
77880 Grez sur Loing.

Tel:
(0)1.64.45.72.75.

Reservations:
Advised for July/Aug; contact site.

7706 Camping Parc de la Colline, Torcy

Large site with easy access to Paris and Disneyland.
Situated in the heart of Marne-la-Vallée, a relatively green area on the outskirts of Paris, this site has 271 terraced pitches. Some are quite secluded, most have shade from mature trees and about one third have hardstandings. Some traffic noise is possible on the lower pitches. The site is on a fairly steep slope, necessitating some up and down walking. The two original (and fairly elderly) sanitary units are functional not luxurious, and provide British and Turkish style WCs, washbasins and push-button showers, a laundry with washing machines and dryers and facilities for disabled people. Amenities include several play areas, minigolf, basketball, table tennis, a shop that is open all year, and a snack bar in July/Aug, with ice boxes for rent. The site operates a minibus service to the metro station at Torcy (every 15 minutes between 0800-1200, one at 1300, and every 15 minutes between 1400-2400) for Paris or Disneyland, plus trips to Parc Asterix, and group visits to central Paris (Eiffel Tower). Campers receive a comprehensive information package on booking-in, and reception will advise on the best value travel cards (travel cards and tickets for Disneyland or Parc Asterix can be purchased from reception). Reception staff speak good English. In a corner of the car parking area is a motorcaravan service point. The site also has chalets, mobile homes and bedrooms for rent. NB. You are in a major city environment - crime can be a problem so take care of valuables; the site does have safety deposit boxes.

Directions: From A104 (la Francilienne) take exit 10, turn left (westwards), and site entrance is approx. 1 km.

Charges guide:
-- Per pitch incl. 2A electricity Ffr. 57.00, pitch incl. 6A electricity 77.00; adult 30.00; child (under 7 yrs) 18.00.
Open:
All year.
Address:
Route de Lagny, 77200 Torcy.
Tel:
(0)1.60.05.42.32.
FAX: (0)1.64.80.05.17.
Reservations:
Advised for high season; contact site.

7704 Caravaning des 4 Vents, Crevecœur-en-Brie

Peaceful site in countryside location, within easy reach of Disneyland.
This very pleasant site has been owned and run by the same family for 35 years. There are around 200 pitches, with many permanent or seasonal units; however, there are about 100 spacious grassy pitches for tourists, well separated by good hedges and all with 6A electricity. The three sanitary units are modern and provide a good number of British style WCs and push-button hot showers but rather fewer washbasins. There are also facilities for disabled people, a washing machine and dryer and a good motorcaravan service point by the main gates. Children are well provided for with an excellent playground, a large games room with table tennis and table football, volleyball court, a billiard hall and a boules court. The well fenced, circular swimming pool (16 m. diameter) is open 09.00-21.00 hrs. June to Sept. In high season (July/Aug) a mobile snack bar and pizzeria visit, and a baker calls in the mornings, while nearby La Houssaye (1 km) has a grocer, bakery and post office. Fontenay (5 km) has a supermarket and all other services. Crevecœur celebrates the 'feast of small villages' on 21/22 June each year. Disneyland is an easy run up the D231 and then one intersection on the A4 (less than 16 km). Central Paris is just a 40 minute train ride from the nearest railway station (8 km) and there are trains to Disneyland.

Directions: From A4 exit 13, take D231 towards Provins for about 12 km. After passing a large obelisk turn right at signs to Crevecœur and follow signs to site. Site is on western side of village.

Charges 2001:
-- Per unit incl. 2 adults and electricity Ffr. 120.00; extra person 25.00; child (under 5 yrs) free; animal 12.00.
-- Credit cards accepted.
Open:
1 March - 1 December.
Address:
77610 Crevecœur-en-Brie.
Tel:
(0)1.64.07.41.11.
FAX: (0)1.64.07.45.07.
Reservations:
Essential for July/Aug; contact site.

Book this site
01892 559898

THE ALAN ROGERS'
travel service

7705M Camping Municipal La Grange aux Dîmes, Samoreau

A small site with a charm of its own, 56 large pitches (with 4A electricity) and adequate, but basic toilet facilities (little else, it must be said), it is on one of the prettiest stretches of the river Seine. It is close to commuter lines to Paris, good for visiting Fontainebleau (7 km), the château and the forest, and within range of Disneyland (Paris 60 km). The pitches are partly delineated on gently sloping grass. There is a small café beside the river in high season and all facilities of the village (300 m).

Directions: The scenic route is by the D39 south from Melun. Follow the river for about 20 km. to Samoreau. Site is through the village behind the beautifully restored barn, La Grange aux Dîmes (dating from the 16th century).

Charges 2000:
-- Per adult Ffr 13.45; child (under 10 yrs) 7.30; caravan 25.00; tent 17.00; motorcaravan 41.20; car 10.10; electricity incl.
Open:
15 March - 30 September.
Address:
77210 Samoreau
Tel:
(0)1.64.23.72.25.
Reservations:
Not usually needed.

PARIS / ILE DE FRANCE - 78 Yvelines

7801 Camping Caravaning International, Maisons-Laffitte, Paris

Busy all year site on the banks of the Seine convenient for central Paris.

Maisons-Laffitte is a pleasant suburb which has a château, a racecourse and some large training stables. There is also a good train service, including an express service, to the Gare St Lazare (the station is a ten minute walk from the site). Trains run every ten minutes, journey time 15-30 minutes, returning until 12.30 am. The site has multilingual and friendly reception staff and occupies a grassy, tree covered area bordering the river. There are 350 pitches, 50 occupied by mobile homes for hire and 71 used by tour operators, plus two areas dedicated to tents. Most pitches are separated by hedging, are of a good size with some over-looking the Seine (unfenced access), and 220 have electric hook-ups (6/10A). There are three sanitary blocks, two insulated for winter use. The third, more open in style, is used only in July and August. These were clean when we stayed but, because of the volume of campers, need constant supervision. Facilities include free hot showers, provision for people with disabilities, laundry and dishwashing areas, chemical disposal and a motorcaravan service point. There is a self-service shop for summer months, a restaurant/bar with takeaway food and a pizzeria. Also on site are a TV room, table tennis, billiards and a football area. A sports complex adjoins the site. Being close to Paris this site is consistently busy. There is direct rail access to Disneyland (55 minutes). Train noise can be expected.

Directions: Site is best approached from A13 or A15 autoroute. From A13 take Poissy exit and follow signs to Maisons-Laffitte, then site signs before town centre. From A15 take N184 exit to St Germain, for 300 m. After crossing large steel bridge turn left at traffic lights to Maisons-Laffitte and follow camp signs.

Charges 2001:
-- Per unit incl. 2 persons Ffr. 89.00 - 135.00, with electricity 105.00 - 146.00; tent plus 2 persons 53.00 - 82.00; extra adult 26.00 - 33.00; child (5-10 yrs) 13.00 - 16.00; extra tent 10.00 - 15.00; animal 15.00; local tax 3.00.

Open:
All year
from 1 March 2001.

Address:
1 Rue Johnson,
78600 Maisons-Laffitte.

Tel:
(0)1.39.12.21.91.
FAX: (0)1.34.93.02.60.

Reservations:
Advisable for July/Aug. and made with deposit (Ffr. 65).

`Camping Cheque'

Book this site
01892 559898

THE ALAN ROGERS'
travel service

7803 Domaine d'Inchelin, St Illiers la Ville, nr Bréval

Quiet, family run site in the Seine valley within 60 km. of Paris.

Domaine d'Inchelin is in a village location, set in rolling countryside within easy reach of Paris and Versailles. It is an attractive site which has been developed around charming old farm buildings. The 150 pitches (50 for tourers) are large (250 sq.m.) and arranged amongst ornamental trees and shrubs, with well kept hedges providing privacy and shelter. All have electricity (4/6A) and most have water points nearby. An aviary with peacocks (rather noisy in spring!) is by reception, and other tame birds parade the site and roost in the trees. There are two children's playground areas, one located in the woodland. Tennis and riding are available nearby. Neatly arranged in the timbered buildings surrounding three sides of the old farm yard, are a small shop, bar (both May - Sept), and a covered play area. An attractive, sheltered swimming pool lies in the centre. The main sanitary facilities are split into two areas on opposite sides of the courtyard - one room with toilets (British style), the other with spacious showers, washbasins in cabins, dishwashing and laundry facilities. Also a separate unit for disabled visitors. Hot water is free throughout and facilities are well kept and clean. An additional modern block at the rear of the site is open mid-June until September. Chemical disposal. The Daniel family provide a friendly welcome and will advise on what to see in the area and how to reach the attractions of Paris, Versailles and Giverny. Fishing or golf 10 km, riding 2 km. Used by tour operators (50 pitches). A 'Sites et Paysages' member.

Directions: From A13 autoroute take Chaufour exit (15) onto N13. Turn off within 1 km. and left at traffic lights into centre of Chaufour. Take D52 to Lommoye, through village then fork left via D89 to St Illiers le Ville. Take Bréval road and site entrance is almost immediately on the left.

Charges 2001:
-- Including car, unit and pitch: per adult Ffr. 85.00; child (4-12 yrs) 40.00, under 4 yrs free; dog 10.00; electricity 4A 30.00, 6A 45.00.
-- No credit cards.

Open:
1 April - 15 October.

Address:
St Illiers la Ville,
78980 Bréval.

Tel:
(0)1.34.76.10.11.

Reservations:
Write to site for details.

62

7804M Camping Municipal de l'Etang d'Or, Rambouillet

A pleasant site in a peaceful forest location, with good tarmac access roads, site lighting and 220 pitches. Some of the individual pitches are divided by hedges, others are more open and sunny. All have electricity (6/10A), 83 also have water and drainage, with a few hardstandings. There are two heated sanitary buildings providing British and Turkish style WCs, washbasins (a few in cubicles), push-button showers, dishwashing and laundry sinks, plus facilities for baby changing and for disabled persons. One of these blocks is closed in the winter months. Other facilities include a café/bar and a small shop (1/4-30/9), washing machine and dryer and a good children's playground. Campers get a discount brochure for local sites or activities (e.g. the municipal swimming pool, animal park, bowling and billiards, bicycle hire), and a special permit for the fishing lake. Motorcaravan service point on site (Ffr. 10). There are many good cycle and footpaths in the area. There is a very large supermarket at the southern end of the town, and it is possible to visit Paris by rail, the Mobilis 'transport package' ticket is available from the railway station.

Charges 2000:
-- Per adult Ffr. 22.00; child (2-10 yrs) 15.00; pitch 26.00; dog 6.00; electricity 18.00 (6A), 23.00 (10A).
-- Credit cards accepted.

Open:
All year.

Address:
Route du Château d'Eau, 78120 Rambouillet.

Tel:
(0)1.30.41.07.34.

Reservations:
Contact site for details.

Directions: Rambouillet is 52 km. southwest of Paris, midway between Versailles and Chartres. Site is southeast of town, from N10 southbound take Rambouillet / Les Eveuses exit, northbound take Rambouillet centre exit, loop round and rejoin N10 southbound, taking next exit, where site is signed.

9100 Camping-Caravaning La Bois du Justice, Monnerville

Conveniently located site close to Paris and Versailles.

The site is situated in a wood in the middle of farmland and has a rough, pot-holed 1.2 km. approach road. The 150 pitches, of which 50 are for touring units, are laid out among the trees, well shaded but sloping (12 are in a new, open area). Electricity is available throughout. The one large toilet block can be heated, is very well appointed with British style WCs, and clean, although it is some way from the furthest pitches. A medium sized pool (approx. 1/6-15/9), children's playground, open air table tennis and a volleyball court provide sporting diversions and a bar with snacks is open during the day and early evening in July/Aug. There is no shop, but a bread and provisions van calls morning and evening. Shops and restaurants are to be found in the village (3 km), or a little further in Etampes. Riding 1.5 km, fishing 7 km. The site is acceptable as an overnight stop for touring the area southwest of Paris - Chartres; Fontainbleau and Versailles are within easy range. Paris is only an hours drive, Disneyland not much more.

Charges 2000:
-- Per caravan, or large tent 20.00 - 30.00; 2 person tent 10.00 - 15.00; adult 20.00 - 30.00; child (2-17 yrs) 10.00 - 20.00; car 10.00 - 15.00; electricity (6A) 15.00.
-- No credit cards.

Open:
1 March - 30 November.

Address:
91930 Monnerville.

Tel:
(0)1.64.95.05.34.
FAX: (0)1.64.95.17.31.

Reservations:
Contact site.

Directions: Going south on the N20 (Paris-Orléans), take exit for Monnerville. Keep right over N20 into village, straight over crossroads and site is well signed.

THE ALAN ROGERS'
travel service

Book your site with the experts
Call for an instant quote
01892 55 98 98

Low cost ferries
guaranteed!

PARIS / ILE DE FRANCE - 95 Val d'Oise

9500 Parc de Sejour de L'Etang, Nesles-la-Vallée, nr L' Isle Adam

Small, informal site in pretty valley 33 km. northwest of Paris.

This family run site is on the southern outskirts of the village of Nesles-la-Vallée in a pretty, tree lined river valley not far from L'Isle-Adam, which is a popular destination for Parisiens at weekends. Many of the 165 pitches are occupied by seasonal caravans but there are 65 pitches available for touring units. The site is informally arranged around a duck pond with many trees to provide shelter and shade and semi-tame rabbits competing with the ducks for food and attention. Pitches are large and flat and electricity (3/9A) is available. The main, central sanitary block (which can be heated in cooler weather) is a plain but substantial building providing showers in modern cubicles with dividers and seats, wash-basins in rather small cubicles and, in separate rooms, rather older style British and Turkish WCs. In addition there are covered dishwashing and laundry sinks, plus a washing machine. Hot water to all facilities is free. A smaller, much older unit including facilities for disabled people is near the sports field. Other facilities include a good playground, volleyball and basketball areas, an under cover play barn with table tennis tables. There are no other on-site facilities but the village and a restaurant are within walking distance. Fishing permits for the river are available in the village. Riding 500 m, golf 7 km. Chantilly (see advertisement between pages 256/7), Parc Asterix and Disneyland are easily reached by car. By far the best way to visit Paris is by train from Valmondois, five minutes away via the D15 road (trains every half hour, journey time about 50 minutes).

Directions: From A15 exit 10 take D915 to Pontoise, then D27 to Beauais which joins the D927 and then D79 to Nesles-la-Vallée. From N1 or A16 (exit 11) take the N332 southwest towards L'isle Adam, and then D64 northwest to Nesles-la-Vallée. Site is on the right as you enter the village.

Charges 2001:
-- Per pitch Ffr. 17.50 - 25.00; person 17.50 - 25.00; child (under 7 yrs) 9.00 - 12.50; electricity 3A 18.00, 9A 22.00.
-- No credit cards.

Open:
1 March - 15 November.

Address:
10 Chemin des Bellevues, 95690 Nesles-la-Vallée.

Tel:
(0)1.34.70.62.89.
FAX: as phone.
E-mail: patrickbrehinier @hotmail.com.

Reservations:
Contact site.

Book this site
01892 559898

THE ALAN ROGERS'
travel service

THE ALAN ROGERS'
travel service

Book your site with the experts
Call for an instant quote
01892 55 98 98

Low cost ferries
guaranteed!

Camping le Val de Trie ***

Moyenneville
tel. 00 33 3 22 31 48 88
fax. 00 33 3 22 31 35 33
www.camping-levaldetrie.fr

Situated at only 1 hour from Calais (A16)
Ideal spot for first or last night of your holiday or longer stay.
Quiet and relaxing, swimming pools and fishing pond.

LES CASTELS

CASTEL – Camping

LA BIEN – ASSISE

Crossroads of Europe
Calais-Ferries (Channel) Tunnel

Hotel** open all the year

Tel: 03 21 35 20 77
Fax: 03 21 36 79 20

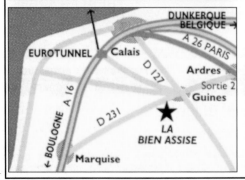

Domaine Le Pas Opton

★ ★ ★ ★

offers you comfort, cleanliness and installations of high quality, with the peacefulness of the countryside only a few minutes from the sea

Large pitches with separators • First-class toilet blocks with free hot water, kept very clean
Hot takeaway food • Friendly bar with regular music or dancing in season • Free swimming
pool and children's paddling pool • Large river adjoining camp • Boats and Pedalos for hire
Fishing possible • Large children's playground • Volley-ball • Recommended camp for
families with children

**For reservations write to: S.A.R.L. Domaine Le Pas Opton,
85800 Le Fenouiller – St. Giles Croix de Vie, France
or telephone 02 51 55 11 98, fax 02 51 55 44 94**

Le Pas Opton

A top quality camp with luxurious installations. Large pitches with connections for electricity, water, drainaway. Most comfortable toilet blocks with cleanliness of the utmost importance. Comprehensive bar and restaurant in Spanish style, with take-away food. Swimming pool of over 200 sq. m. and children's pool, both heated. Tennis court, Volley Ball, Table Tennis, etc. . . Wooden chalets for 5/6 persons for hire.

Daily recreational programme in main season, with sporting competitions, evening events until midnight, organised excursions, etc. . .

HOTELLERIE
DE PLEIN AIR
LA PUERTA DEL SOL
★★★★
'great comfort'

**LES BORDERIES, 85270 ST. HILAIRE DE RIEZ, VENDÉE.
Tel: 02 51 49 10 10   Fax: 02 51 49 84 84**

Selected by 'Le Caravanier' Magazine for review as one of the
30 BEST CAMP SITES IN EUROPE

RESERVATIONS TAKEN FROM JANUARY
ONWARDS FOR ANY LENGTH OF STAY

LES CASTELS

CAMPING & CARAVANING

A DIFFERENT FRANCE

There are 50 4-star Castels caravan
and camp sites dotted round the
most beautiful regions of France.
Many are set in the grounds of
chateaux or manor houses and offer:

- *amenities of the highest standards,*
- *activities and entertainment for
  the young and not so young,*
- *a broad choice of pitches and
  different types of very comfortable
  accommodation.*

*100 F a night for a pitch for 2 people,
with electricity, whatever the site and length of stay
when you present your Privilege Card*.*

To find out more, contact us and

- receive our brochure-road map free of charge
- book your Privilege Card for the year 2001 (50 FF)
- order the presentation guidebook for our 50 Castels camp sites
  (contribution to expenses: 50 FF)

*offer valid at most camp sites from opening up until 30/06 and from 1/09 until the closing of the comp sites
for anyone who has ordered the Privilege Card from our secretary.

e mail: mail@les-castels.com - Fax: + 33 (0)2 97 47 50 72
Address: Secrétariat LES CASTELS - PIBS - C.P. 26 - 56038 VANNES Cedex - Frai
Internet sites: www.les-castels.com- www.castels-campings.com
Tel : + 33 (0)2 97 42 57 12

Un Air de Vacances. RC Bayonne 99 B 416.

EASTERN FRANCE

The area we have defined as Eastern France combines three of the official French Regions:

CHAMPAGNE-ARDENNE	LORRAINE VOSGES	ALSACE
Major City: Reims	Major Cities: Nancy, Metz	Major City: Strasbourg
Départements: 08 Ardennes, 51 Marne, 10 Aube, 52 Haute-Marne	Départements: 54 Meurth-et-Moselle, 55 Meuse, 57Moselle, 88 Vosges	Départements: 67 Bas, 68 Haut Rhin

This north-eastern area of France has seen many European Battles. In 1871 Alsace and a large part of Lorraine were acquired by Germany under the Treaty of Frankfurt and were only restored to France in 1919; to again be back in German hands in 1940, then to be liberated for the second time five years later at the end of World War Two. Today there are many poignant reminders and a noticeable German influence in, for example, architecture, cuisine and language.

Champagne is home to the most northerly vineyards in France where special processing turns the light, dry wine into 'le Champagne' and names such as 'Moet et Chandon' and 'Veuve Clicquot' spring to mind. Nowhere else in France, or even the rest of the world, are you allowed to make champagne or, more correctly you can make bubbly wine but you cannot call it champagne. The area is also known for the spa towns such as Vittel, Bains-les-Bains and Plombières and the birth place of St Joan of Arc at Domrémy. The Vosges crests formed part of the World War One battle front and military requirements dictated the building of the road now known as the Route des Cretes which links these natural ramparts, taking in the major peaks of Hohneck and Grand Ballon. Today you can descend from the mountains into the Alsace vineyards and fairy tale wine villages. The 'Route des Vins' follows the vineyards along the Rhine valley from Mulhouse to Colmar and north almost to Strasbourg.

Note: the site reports are laid out by département in numerical order not by region.

See map on page 308.

Cuisine of the region

Quiche Lorraine – made only in the classical manner with cream, eggs and bacon.
Potage Lorraine – potato. leek and onion soup
Tart (aux mirabelles) – golden plum tart. Also made with other fruits
Tarte a l' oignon Alsacienne – onion and cream tart

Places of Interest

Épernay – the real capital of champagne – the drink. Here 72 miles of underground galleries in the chalk beneath the city store the wine for the delicate operations required to make the champagne. It was near by in the Abbey of Hautvillers that the blind Dom Perignon discovered how to put the bubbles into Champagne and keep them there

Le Linge – a football pitch-sized hilltop where in 1915, 17,000 French and German soldiers lost their lives. The opposing trenches including rusty barbed wire have been left as they were – a poignant reminder of the pain and futility of war

Reims – in 496, Clovis, the first king of France, was baptised in the cathedral and the Kings of France from Louis VII to Charles X were crowned in the city. The 13th century Gothic cathedral is a masterpiece; the west front facade is among the world's greatest man-made creations. The Pommery château to the south-east, one of the great Champagne houses built above a network of underground chalk galleries and 'pyramids' is well worth a visit

Riquewihr – almost untouched since the 18th century, whilst virtually every other village was decimated by war; 13/14th century fortifications and many medieval houses and courtyards

Verdun – some of the most savage fighting of World War 1 took place north of Verdun and the town is a centre for touring the battlefields and hill forts such as Fort de Vaux and Fort de Douaumont. There is also a large military cemetery at Douaumont

EAST - 08 Ardennes

0801M Camping Municipal du Mont Olympe, Charleville-Mézières

Attractively situated alongside the Meuse River, within easy walking distance across a footbridge to the centre of the pleasant large town, this site provides some 100 numbered pitches. Of irregular size and shape on mainly level grass and among a variety of trees which provide ample shade, most have the possibility of electrical connection. The municipal indoor pool is adjacent and boat trips operate on the river virtually from the site. The sanitary facilities have been of a poorer standard than we usually require, but with the rebuilding of one block and plans to renew another, they are much improved. Generally this is a very attractive site, unusually quiet and secure for a town centre location and conveniently situated for exploring the town and surrounding area.

Directions: Site is north of Charleville on the island of Montcy St Pierre and is signed from the city centre `Mont Olympe'. From north D988/D1 follow the river, over the bridge, then immediately left. From the southeast (A203/N51/N43) take 'centre' exit, head for `Gare' then follow Avenue Forest north and over bridge.

Charges guide:
-- Per person Ffr. 12.00; child (2-7 yrs) 6.00; pitch 7.00; vehicle 7.00; supplement for mobile home or caravan over 5 m. 4.00; electricity (10A) 14.00.

Open:
Easter - 15 October.

Address:
Rue des Paquis, 08000 Charleville-Mézières.

Tel:
(0)3.24.33.23.60 or (0)3.24.32.44.80.

Reservations:
Contact site.

0802M Camping du Lac des Vieilles-Forges, Les Mazures, Revin

An attractive lakeside site with a large range of facilities and activities, du Lac provides 300 large pitches (260 for tourers), all with electricity (3-10A). They are mainly on individual, gravel hardstandings, arranged on several terraces, but easily accessible via tarmac approach roads. The attractively arranged pitches offer ample shade from a variety of trees and shrubs. It is situated only 100 metres or so back from the large lake which offers a large variety of watersports, and its somewhat remote location is approached by a road which forms part of the Route des Fortifications. The purpose built sanitary blocks provide modern facilities with pushbutton pre-set showers, WCs, washbasins in private cabins, washing machines and dryers, etc. Activities such as tennis, bicycle hire, table tennis, fishing, swimming, sailing, windsurfing, and canoeing are just some of the reasons this is a popular site.

Directions: From N43, 11 km. northwest of Charleville-Mézières, take the D40 north in the direction of Revin for approx. 8 km. The lake is signed on the left - follow the lakeside road to the site; a one way system operates in high season.

Charges guide:
-- Per person Ffr. 17.20; child (under 7 yrs) 8.60; pitch 9.50; supplement for large vehicle 8.50; electricity 3A 11.50, 5A 14.80, 10A (not July/Aug) 24.60; dog 5.40.
-- Credit cards accepted.

Open:
All year.

Address:
08500 Les Mazures.

Tel:
(0)3.24.40.17.31.

Reservations:
Not normally made or necessary, but if in doubt telephone.

0803M Camping Départemental du Lac de Bairon, Le Chesne

This modern rural campsite is located in the heart of the French Ardennes, an area with relatively few good quality sites. This lakeside site is set on two terraces, with four modern sanitary units, one heated for use in the winter months. It has 172 pitches which are generally arranged in bays for about six units, with waste bins and water taps by each area. All pitches have electric hook-ups (3.5, 6, 10A), and around 83 have gravel hardstanding. The sanitary facilities include British style WCs, washbasins in cubicles, pre-set hot showers, dishwashing and laundry facilities, with washing machines and dryers, plus facilities for disabled people at two of the units. Other on-site amenities include a small children's playground with two adventure style units for 3-6 yrs and 4-12 yrs, plus tennis, table tennis, volleyball and a boules court. Canoes, kayaks and bicycles can be hired. Fishing is also available. The site can be very busy in main season, at weekends, and on public holidays. There is no restaurant or shop on site, but Le Chesne is only about 3 km. and has a good parking area by the side of the Canal des Ardennes.

Directions: Le Chesne is 25 km. due south of Charleville-Mezières. From Le Chesne take D991 north for approx. 500 m, then turn right on to D212. Follow signs to site. Note: a bridge on the access road has a weight limit of 3500 kg.

Charges 2000:
-- Per adult Ffr. 15.50 ; child (under 7 yrs) 7.75; pitch 8.20; vehicle (+125 cm3) 8.20; animal 5.50; electricity 11.70 (3.5A), 15.00 (6A), 25.00 (10A).
-- Credit cards accepted (Ffr. 100 min).

Open:
All year.

Address:
08390 Le Chesne.

Tel:
(0)3.24.30.11.66.

Reservations:
Advisable for high season, contact site for details.

1001 Camping du Tertre, Dienville

Pleasant, privately run site, ideal for watersports enthusiasts.
This is a modern (1989) campsite which is situated opposite a major watersports centre on Lac du Temple, and also within easy distance of Lac d'Orient, the former for motorboats and waterskiing, the latter for sailing, windsurfing, etc. The site provides 156 large pitches, 113 for touring units and all with electrical connections (4A). They are on mainly level grass, separated by hedges and with some young trees which, as yet, do not provide much shade. The modern sanitary blocks, all to a good standard, provide hot showers, with dividers and hooks, some washbasins in private cabins, British type WCs, dishwashing facilities and a washing machine. There are chemical disposal and motorcaravan service facilities. A bar and snack bar are open in July/Aug. when there is also some entertainment. A heated swimming pool (8 x 16 m; 1/5-30/9) and children's pool were added in 2000. Bicycle hire on site, fishing 200 m, riding 3 km. Caravan storage. A baker calls daily; there is a variety of restaurants, shops, etc. at the watersports centre opposite and the village is about 5 minutes walk away.

Charges 2001:
-- Per pitch Ffr. 32.00 - 40.00; person 17.60 - 22.00; child (4-10 yrs) 12.50 - 16.00; animal 3.20 - 4.00; electricity (4A) 12.80 - 16.00.
-- Less for longer stays.
-- Credit cards accepted.
Open:
30 March - 15 October.
Address:
10500 Dienville.
Tel/Fax:
(0)3.25.92.26.50.
E-mail: michel.peillard@wanadoo.fr.
Reservations:
Made for min. 7 nights with deposit (Ffr. 400) and fee (70).

Directions: Dienville is 5-6 km. south of Brienne le Château (with its Napoleon connections) and the site is opposite the port. From A5 autoroute take exit for Vendeuvre sur Barse and follow D443 north for approx. 23 km. Otherwise, site is well signed in Dienville.

1005M Camping Municipal de Troyes, Troyes

A typical town site, completely renovated in '93, this is close to the River Seine, but separated by allotments. The 100 or so grassy pitches, all with electricity (6A), are of reasonable size, on fairly level ground and are situated around the large central facilities buildings. These include the sanitary block, table tennis area, meeting room, etc. The pitches are numbered and separated by young, small hedging plants and there is some shade from mature trees. Sanitary facilities are modern and include hot showers with dividers, hooks, etc., washbasins in private cabins, British type WCs, undercover dishwashing sinks and laundry sinks - all of a very high standard and with free hot water. There are few other facilities, apart from a games room and small children's play area, but bread is delivered to order and there is a restaurant and a supermarket nearby. The town, famous for its knitwear, is about 20 minutes walk away (3 km) or there is a bus stop 50 m. from the entrance. Possibly some road noise. Card operated barrier (deposit Ffr. 100).

Charges guide:
-- Per unit Ffr. 30.00; adult 25.00; child (under 7 yrs) 10.00; car and caravan 25.00; car and tent 10.00, with m/cycle 9.00; motorcaravan 36.00; animal 4.00; electricity 17.00.
Open:
1 April - 15 October.
Address:
7 Rue Roger-Salengro, 10150 Pont-Sainte-Marie.
Tel:
(0)3.25.81.02.64.
Tourist office:
(0)3.25.73.00.36.
Reservations:
Probably unnecessary, but if in doubt 'phone.

Directions: From town centre take Chalons sur Marne direction (2 km). Site is on northeast outskirts of the town in the Pont-Sainte-Marie area. The easy way is from the A26 (exit for Troyes) and follow direction of Pont-Sainte-Marie – watch for site signs. Site is well signed from the south.

5102M Camping Municipal, Châlons-en-Champagne

The location of Châlons, south of Reims and near both the A4 and A26, about 200 miles from Calais and Boulogne, make this an ideal stopover when travelling from the French coast to Switzerland, Germany or the south of France. It is also ideal for exploring this famous region in the plain of the River Marne. This campsite is on the southwest edge of town. The wide entrance with its well tended appearance of neatly mown grass and flower beds set the tone that extends across the site. About half of the 135 pitches, accessed from hard roads, are on a gravel base with the others on grass. Some 70 have electricity (6A), most are separated by hedges and are of a generous size. Trees abound though there is no shade in some parts. There are two sanitary blocks, one behind reception and the other at the far end of the site. Sections of these facilities are of varying standards due to an ongoing programme of refurbishment. The washbasins (some in cabins), showers and sinks all have hot and cold water and WCs are British style. Facilities for visitors with disabilities are provided, plus a washing machine and dryer. The snack bar offers simple meals, takeaway, bread and ice cream in high season. Camping gas available. Games and TV rooms. Children's playground, tennis, table tennis, volleyball, boules. Fishing (free for campers) is nearby.

Charges 2000:
-- Per person Ffr 26.00; child (under 7) 10.00; pitch 24.00; vehicle 17.00; electricity 18.00; local tax 2.00.
Open:
1 May - 31 October.
Address:
Ave des Allies, 51000 Châlons-en-Champagne.
Tel:
(0)3.26.68.38.00.
Reservations:
Write to site.

Directions: From A4, take La Veuve exit and go south on N44 which by-passes the town. Although it is a tortuous route, the camp is signed. From the A26, take exit 28, head towards town and keep a sharp look-out for site signs.

EAST - 52 Haute-Marne

5201M Camping de la Presqu'ile de Champaubert, Braucourt

This is one of those 'magnificent municipals' at which the French seem to excel. It is situated beside what we believe to be the largest man-made inland lake in Europe (4,800 ha.), the Lac du Der Chantecoq. This provides superb facilities for windsurfing, sailing, etc. and even for swimming from a 100 m. beach alongside the site (lifeguard in main season). The site itself is situated on the shores of the lake, with 195 fairly level grassy pitches of a good size, mostly with electrical connections (10A). They are separated by hedges and trees that also provide a fair amount of shade. The general appearance and the views across the lake are very attractive. The sanitary facilities, in two modern blocks, are of a good standard with individual small buildings for WCs (British type), hot showers with dividers, hooks, etc, and washbasins in private cabins, plus washing-up and laundry facilities and a new motorcaravan service point. There is a small shop for essentials in the reception area and a bar/fast-food service during the main season.

Directions: From St Dizier, take the D384 past Eclaron to Braucourt and follow camp signs on to the site (3 km).

Charges 2000:
-- Per unit incl. 2 persons Ffr. 99.00; extra person 27.00; child (under 7 yrs) 14.00; electricity 23.00; dog 5.00; plus local tax.

Open:
15 April - 30 September.

Address:
52290 Eclaron-Braucourt.

Tel:
(0)3.25.04.13.20.
FAX: (0)3.25.94.33.51.
E-mail (Office de Tourisme): lac-du-der@wanadoo.fr.

Reservations:
Required for high season - write to site with Ffr. 350 deposit.

5202 Castel Camping La Forge de Ste Marie, Thonnance-les-Moulins

Attractive site with indoor pool, popular with tour operators, in pleasant country.

Attractive site with indoor pool, popular with tour operators, in pleasant country. The département of Haute-Marne is situated between the better known areas of Champagne and the Vosges. It is a sleepy land of rolling hills, forests and farmland. In the heart of this lies Thonnance-les-Moulins, 12 km. east of Joinville and the north - south N67 main road between St Dizier and Chaumont. In 1994 the dilapidated old forge buildings and the surrounding 40,000 sq.m. were transformed into a most attractive campsite. As soon as one enters through the arched gateway, one is impressed by the setting. The main building houses reception, shop and an excellent restaurant (all 15/5-15/9) which, with its terrace overlooks a small lake in the river which drifts through the site. A picturesque bridge links the upper part of the site with a lower road going to the section near the river. Opposite reception, another old building has been skilfully converted into apartments for renting. Grass pitches, 115 for touring units, are of a generous size on terraces amongst the trees or in more open areas, with electricity (6A) and water. Two modern sanitary blocks have British style WCs and free hot water in washbasins, sinks and showers (pre-mixed from single taps). The enthusiastic British and Dutch managers are determined to make a success of the site and have much activity planned for high season – games, etc. for children and a varied programme for adults including a farm visit by tractor with a barbecue, music, dancing and excursions. Four play areas are imaginatively placed around the site, and there is a level open grass area for football and volleyball, plus bicycle hire and free fishing. Golf 35 km, riding 20 km. However, the crowning glory of the site must be the splendid heated indoor pool with a smaller one for children. A games room occupies a gallery in the main building where youngsters may gather. There is much of interest in the area, Joan d'Arc and General de Gaulle lived near and it is not too far to the Champagne vineyards and cellars at Reims. Nigloland for the children is within range and Joinville is worth exploring. It is also possible to visit the largest man-made lake in Europe at Giffaumont- Champaubert. The site has a high proportion of mobile homes and tour operators use the site. Maintenance may not be so good in early or late season.

Directions: Site is about 12 km. southeast of Joinville between Poissons and Germay on road D427 - well signed.

Charges 2001:
-- Per person Ffr. 40.00; child (0-6 yrs) 20.00; pitch 65.00; pitch with electricity 80.00; local tax 1.00.
-- Less 20% outside July/Aug.
-- Credit cards accepted.

Open:
24 April - 29 September.

Address:
52230 Thonnance-les-Moulins.

Tel:
(0)3.25.94.42.00.
FAX: (0)3.25.94.41.43.
E-mail: la.forge.de.sainte.marie@wanadoo.fr.

Reservations:
Contact site for details.

Book this site
01892 559898

THE ALAN ROGERS'
travel service

5400 Camping Le Brabois, Nancy

Good quality campsite within city boundary.

This former municipal site, within the city boundary and 5 km. from the town centre, was taken over by the Campeole group in 1998. Situated within a forest area, there is shade on most parts and although the site is on a slight slope, the 190 good-sized, numbered and separated pitches are level. Of these, 160 pitches have electrical connections (5/15A) and 30 also have water and drainage. Six sanitary blocks are spread around the site and have a mix of British and Turkish style WCs and free hot water in washbasins (some in cubicles), showers (pre-set, pushbuttons) and sinks. One block can be heated in cool weather and there are two units for disabled visitors. A small shop is open all season, and a bar and snack bar in July/Aug. Restaurants and shops are about 1 km. from site. There is a playground for young children, an area for ball games and table tennis under cover. Occasional music evenings in are held high season. Being on one of the main routes from Luxembourg to the south of France, Le Brabois makes a good night stop but Nancy is a delightful city in the heart of Lorraine and well worth a longer stay, not only for the interesting 18th century Place Stanislas and 11th century city centre, but for the many attractions of the area. The British manager has a wide range of tourist literature and is pleased to help plan visits and day trips. Horse racing takes place every two weeks at the Nancy race track next to the campsite, there are some excellent walks and cycle rides and good wine is produced nearby.

Directions: Take exit 2b 'Brabois' from autoroute A33, continue for about 500 m. to 'Quick' restaurant on left. Turn left here, pass the racetrack to T-junction, turn right and after about 400 m. turn right on to site entrance road.

Charges 2001:
-- Per unit incl. two persons Ffr. 58.00 - 63.00; hiker 35.00 - 40.00; extra adult 20.00; child (2-7 yrs) 10.00; dog 10.00; electricity 18.00.
-- Credit cards accepted.
Open:
1 April - 15 October.
Address:
Avenue Paul Muller, 54600 Villers les Nancy.
Tel:
(0)3.83.27.18.28.
FAX: (0)3.83.40.06.43.
Reservations:
Advised for July but site say no-one is turned away.

5501 Hotel de Plein Air Les Breuils, Verdun

Pretty site beside small fishing lake, close to famous town.

The defence of Verdun during the First World War cost half a million French casualties and the city is justly proud of its determined resistance. Les Breuils is close to the Citadel and provides 162 flat pitches on two levels (144 for touring units). Separated by hedges, they are beside a small fishing lake and most offer the possibility of electricity connection (5A). The overall appearance is attractive. The site has a new outdoor swimming pool (200 sq.m.) and children's pool (1/6-31/8). A little shop doubles as reception, selling essentials with various local guide books (1/5-31/8). Snacks are provided in the main season (1/5-20/8). Sanitary facilities, in two blocks, are a mixture of old and new, the newer parts being of a very high standard with roomy hot showers, including dividers and hooks, washbasins in private cabins, British type WCs, washing machines and dryers. The other, older facilities upstairs are adequate. An unusual feature is a number of groups of four washing up sinks, under attractive pitched roofs, conveniently sited among the pitches. Attractive play area. Bicycle hire 1 km., riding 5 km. The town centre is 1 km.

Directions: The RN3 forms a sort of ring road round the north of the town. Site is signed from this on the west side of the town (500 m. to site).

Charges 2000:
-- Per person Ffr. 23.00; child (under 10 yrs) 10.00; caravan or motor-caravan 20.00; double axle caravan 50.00; tent 15.00; animal 7.00; electricity (5A) 19.00.
-- Discounts for low season and longer stays.
-- Credit cards accepted.
Open:
1 April - 15 October.
Address:
55100 Verdun.
Tel/Fax:
(0)3.29.86.15.31.
E-mail: camping.
lesbreuils@wanadoo.fr.
Reservations:
Recommended for high season - contact site.

5705M Terrain de Camping Municipal de Metz-Plage, Metz

As this site is just a short way from the autoroute exit and within easy walking distance for the city centre, it could make a useful night stop if travelling from Luxembourg to Nancy or for a longer stay if exploring the area. By the Moselle river, the 145 pitches are on level grass, most are under shade from tall trees and 80 have electricity (10A) and water connections. Tent pitches have a separate place on the river banks. The two sanitary blocks, one newer than the other, have free hot water in washbasins and showers and British style WCs. These facilities are acceptable if not luxurious.

Directions: Take the Metz-Nord exit from the autoroute, follow `Autres Directions' sign back over the motorway and follow camp signs.

Charges guide:
-- Per pitch incl. electricity Ffr. 35.00 - 40.00; tent and vehicle 20.00; person 15.00; child (2-7 yrs) 7.00; pet 10.00.
Open:
2 May - 30 September.
Address:
57000 Metz.
Tel:
(0)3.87.32.05.58.
Reservations:
Not possible.

EAST - 67 Bas-Rhin / 68 Haut-Rhin

6701M Camping Eichelgarten, Oberbronn, nr Niederbronn

This is an attractive, inexpensive and well run site, set amidst the mountains and forests of northern Alsace, not far from the German border. There are good views over the valley to one side with trees sheltering the other. The circular internal road has pitches around the outside, some on terraces (100 are for touring units, 50 for seasonal units), as well as space in the centre where there is also a children's playground. Two well appointed sanitary blocks, one heated in cool weather, have British type WCs, washbasins (some private cabins for ladies), good free showers, washing machines and dryers, a baby room and facilities for disabled people. The solar-heated swimming pool (open July/Aug) and children's pool are of excellent quality and a general purpose room provides billiards, table tennis and table football. Minigolf and two hard tennis courts on site, fitness circuit in the nearby forest, riding 700 m, fishing 3 km. The site has a small shop with a supermarket in the village (1 km). Chalets (11) to let.

Directions: Travel northwest from Haguenau on N62 for approx. 20 km. Near Niederbronn turn left onto D28 for Oberbronn-Zinswiller - site signed from here.

Charges 2001:
-- Per person Ffr. 19.00; child (under 7) 11.40; pitch 12.40; vehicle 9.00; electricity per amp 4.80; dog 9.00; local tax 1.00. -- Less 5% outside 1/7-31/8 or 10% for stays over 15 days.
-- No credit cards.

Open:
13 March - 2 November.

Address:
67110 Oberbronn.

Tel:
(0)3.88.09.71.96.
FAX: (0)3.88.09.65.12.

Reservations:
Advised for high season. Write with precise dates; no deposit required.

6702M Camping Municipal du Herrenhaus, Le Hohwald

This municipal site is in a scenic, remote situation, high up in the hills of Alsace. It is quite a tortuous drive whichever road is taken - narrow and slow rather than steep. The 100 pitches, many with good shade, are either on four small terraces or in individual, levelled places. Around 30 of the places are taken by seasonal units but you should find space. The one, central, heated sanitary block is of average standard with the usual provision including British and Turkish style WCs, but might be hard pressed if the site was full. Chemical disposal and motorcaravan service points. There is an excellent community room with a kitchen. Two restaurants are very near the site entrance, with others in the village a short distance away. Fishing 500 m, bicycle hire 1 km.

Directions: Site is at the southwest end of the village on D425 road.

Charges 2000:
-- Per person Ffr. 17.00 - 19.00; child (under 7 yrs) 9.50; vehicle 9.00; pitch 11.00; dog 9.00; electricity (1-10A) 5.00 - 32.40; local tax (over 10 yrs) 3.00.
-- No credit cards.

Open:
All year.

Address:
28 rue de Herrenhaus, 67140 Le Hohwald.

Tel:
(0)3.88.08.30.90.
FAX: (0)3.88.08.30.25.

Reservations:
Contact site.

6803M Camping Municipal Masevaux, Masevaux

Masevaux is a pleasant little town in the Haut-Rhin département of Alsace, just to the north of the A36 Belfort - Mulhouse motorway in the Des Ballons region. The municipal camping site is situated in a quiet edge of town next to the sporting complex which has a good indoor swimming pool and other sporting opportunities. As one approaches, the pretty flower decked appearance promises a neat, excellent site and one is not disappointed. This must rank as one of the best municipals, having recently been judged the best municipal campsite of the 30 in the region. The neatly mown 120 pitches available for tourists are on level grass, of reasonable size, numbered, marked by trees and hedges, and all have electrical connections (3/6A). Most are well shaded by a variety of trees and have good views of the surrounding hills. The modern, well designed and well equipped sanitary block has British style WCs and free hot water in all washbasins (most in private cabins), showers and sinks. There is a baby room, laundry and covered washing-up area. There is no shop, but a supermarket and restaurants are near with ice-creams and soft drinks available at reception. A baker calls in high season when the pleasant and helpful Gardien, who takes great pride in the site, welcomes visitors on Sundays with a glass of local wine. Tennis courts and minigolf (extra charge) and a children's play area are on site, with fishing nearby. The attractive town is a short walk away. This is a good choice for one night or a longer stay to explore the delights of this interesting region.

Directions: Site is well signed all around the town as 'Camping Complexe Sportif'.

Charges 2000:
-- Per pitch Ffr. 15.50; person 15.50; child (under 7 yrs) 7.50; local tax 1.00; dog 4.00; electricity 3A 15.50, 6A 29.00; extra car 7.50.
-- No credit cards.

Open:
Easter – 30 September.

Address:
Rue du Stade, 68290 Masevaux.

Tel:
(0)3.89.82.42.29.
FAX: as phone.

Reservations:
Made with Ffr. 200 deposit; contact site.

70

6801M   Camping de l'Ile du Rhin, Biesheim, nr Colmar

In a pleasant island situation between the Rhine and the Canal d'Alsace with views across the river to Breisach in Germany, this site is well situated to explore the Vosges or the Black Forest. A well kept site, it has 253 hedged pitches, many occupied by seasonal static caravans, but providing 60 touring pitches. Some vary in size but all have electrical connections and are on flat grass with good shade. The three sanitary blocks (one heated) are very well kept and have been refurbished to a high standard with free hot showers, washbasins in cabins and a good supply of hooks, mirrors and electric points. The provision also includes a laundry and washing up sinks (H&C), a washing machine and dryer, plus chemical disposal facilities. Activities include table tennis, boules and a children's playground. There is a bar, shop and takeaway (15/6-15/9, weekends only after 15/5 and until 30/9). A restaurant, heated pool (free entry for campers), sports ground and marina are 200 m. Fishing 100 m, riding 1.5 km. Caravan storage.

Directions: Site is reached from the bridge into Germany using the N415 Colmar - Freiburg road, signed beside the frontier post. Proceed under bridge northwards and site is to left past the restaurant.

Charges 2000:
-- Per unit incl. 1 person Ffr. 43.00, 2 persons 75.50; extra person 23.00; child (under 7) 11.50; electricity 4A 19.20, 6A 26.60, 10A 36.80; local tax 2.00.
-- No credit cards.
Open:
All year except Christmas and New Year.
Address:
Zone Touristique, 68600 Biesheim.
Tel:
(0)3.89.72.57.95.
FAX: (0)3.89.72.14.21.
Reservations:
Only made for longer stays.

6804M   Camping Municipal Les Trois Châteaux, Eguisheim

The village of Eguisheim is on the Alsace 'Rue du Vin' to the west of Colmar. The three châteaux from which the site gets its name are clearly visible on the distant hills above the site and add to the interesting surroundings. About 400 m. from the village, Les Trois Châteaux is a good example of the best type of municipal site and it is busy and popular. Flowers, shrubs and a variety of trees, along with the well tended grass areas make this a very pleasant place. The 125 pitches are either on a slight slope or a terrace. All have electricity (4/6A), are marked and numbered and most have good shade. Caravans over 7 m. and/or 1 ton in weight are not accepted. A single sanitary block in the centre of the site has British (seatless) style WCs, hot showers but cold water elsewhere. There is a children's playground. Fishing 3 km. The facilities of the fascinating village of Eguisheim are close and the site is well located for exploring this delightful part of Alsace. Information on the local tourist attractions is available at reception.

Directions: Eguisheim is just off the N83 and site is well signed in the village.

Charges 2000:
-- Per person Ffr. 19.00; child (under 7) 9.00; pitch 20.00, extra tent or car 8.00; dog 5.00; local tax 2.00; electricity 4A 16.00, 6A 21.00; unit over 5.5m. long +8.00.
-- No credit cards.
Open:
Easter - 15 October.
Address:
10 rue du Bassin, 68420 Eguisheim.
Tel:
(0)3.89.23.19.39.
FAX: (0)3.89.24.10.19.
Reservations:
Only made for July/Aug, write to site.

6808   Clair Vacances Camping, Ste Croix-en-Plaine, nr Colmar

Delightful small campsite, 1 km. from exit of A35.

Alsace is not only a popular and picturesque area of lovely villages, large vineyards, mountains and forests, but the route taken by many heading for Switzerland or Italy. Clair Vacances, opened in '97, is one of those little gems which we might prefer to keep to ourselves. The very neat, tidy and pretty site has an abundance of trees, shrubs and plants and just 60 level pitches of generous size which are numbered and separated by trees and shrubs. All have electricity connections (4-13A) and 10 are fully serviced with water and drainage connections. The site has been imaginatively laid out with pitches from hard access roads grouped around the excellent sanitary block which has British style WCs and free hot water in all washbasins (in cabins), sinks and showers. There is a well equipped baby room and good facilities for disabled visitors. A swimming pool is under construction and there is a small children's playground, a community room and archery in high season. This is, above all, a quiet family site where you are requested not to play music. The shop has limited supplies but Colmar with restaurants and shops is not far away. Although this makes an excellent night stop when en-route to the south, you may well be tempted to stay longer and use this peaceful base for exploring the region. The friendly couple who own and run the site have a good selection of tourist information and will be pleased to advise on the attractions of the area. Dogs are not accepted in July/Aug.

Directions: Site is signed from exit 27 of the A35 south of Colmar on the Herrlisheim road (D1).

Charges 2000:
-- Per unit incl. 2 adults Ffr. 72.00 - 95.00; extra adult 21.00 - 33.00; child (under 7 yrs) 10.00 - 20.00; electricity 4A 13.00, 8A 19.00, 13A 29.00.
-- Credit cards accepted.
Open:
Week before Easter - 27 October.
Address:
68127 Ste Croix-en-Plaine.
Tel:
(0)3.89.49.27.28.
FAX: (0)3.89.49.21.55.
E-mail: clairvacances @wanadoo.fr.
Reservations:
Made with deposit (Ffr. 100); contact site.

EAST - 68 Haut-Rhin

6807 Camping Les Sources, Wattwiller, nr Thann

Hillside site in quiet wooded location, with pools.

Wattwiller is just off the N83 Alsace 'Rue du Vin', tucked away in the forest hills beyond the vineyards, but not far from them, in the popular region of the Vosges. Camping Les Sources occupies a fairly steep slope above the village under a covering of tall trees. The 160 tourist pitches, all with electricity (5A) are mainly single ones in clearings on scant grass. The trees mean that the site is very shady so it can be rather gloomy in overcast or wet weather. A narrow hard road meanders between pitches and is steep in places making it difficult for large units, although staff will assist with a tractor if required. Three sanitary blocks are spread around the site and, although old, were clean at the time of our visit. They have British style WCs and free pre-mixed, warm water from push-button taps in washbasins and showers. There is no provision for disabled visitors who, in any case, would find the steep roads difficult. This site would suit those who wish to enjoy the quiet, secluded location and although activities were not up and running during our early season visit, there would appear to be plenty on offer during high season. There is an arena for horse riding activities, a tennis court, table tennis, bicycle hire, two swimming pools, one outdoor (15/4-30/9) and another heated and covered (all season), an entertainment area, playground, table tennis, mini-golf, volleyball and an organised programme with walking, games and creative activities. Also a games room. Shop and good restaurant (open lunch-times and then from 6 pm - midnight). There are washing machines and dryers, chemical disposal points and a motorcaravan service point. The site issues a map for walking in the area and a sheet in English with places to visit. Staff will be pleased to give further information. A Sites et Paysages member.

Directions: From N66 Thann - Mulhouse road, go north to Cernay and continue through Uffholtz to Wattwiller. Turn left after village sign and follow camp signs. From the north leave N83 for Berrwiller and go south on D5 to Wattwiller.

Charges 2001:
-- Ffr: per person Ffr. 34.00; child (1-7 yrs) 21.00; pitch 47.00; electricity (5A) 20.00; animal 7.00; local tax 1.00 (1-7 yrs 0.50).
-- Euro: per person 5,18; child (1-7 yrs) 3,20; pitch 7,17; electricity (5A) 3,05; animal 1,07; plus local tax.
-- Less 15-20% in low seasons.
-- Credit cards accepted.

Open:
1 April - 15 October.

Address:
68700 Wattwiller.

Tel:
(0)3.89.75.44.94.
FAX: (0)3.89.75.71.98.

E-mail:
camping.les.sources
@wanadoo.fr.

Reservations:
Made with deposit (Ffr 300-500) and fee (50); contact site.

Book this site
01892 559898

THE ALAN ROGERS'
travel service

6806 Camping Intercommunal, Riquewihr

Friendly, well run site on the Alsace wine route.

Surrounded by vineyards and minutes from the delightful village of Riquewihr, this site has earned its reputation not only from the quality of its facilities, but also from the welcome reception accorded to campers by the couple who manage the site. Situated in the heart of the wine region the site covers three hectares with views across the open countryside. Immediately to the right of the security barrier stands a modern, part-timbered building which houses reception and information area. Close by is a small summer house and both are heavily garlanded with flowers. The 150 spacious grass pitches, many with shade and divided by hedging, have electrical connections (6A). The tent area is separate and also offers individual pitches. There are three sanitary blocks which are kept clean, one is of a more modern design. Facilities include British style WCs, washbasins, mirrors, electric points, private cabins with basins, showers with hooks and mat, baby room and excellent facilities for disabled people. There are also dishwashing and laundry areas, chemical disposal, motorcaravan service point, good night lighting and campers have the use of a room with tables and chairs. A new shop provides basic necessities, drinks and papers (from 1/5). A sand based children's play area and sports field are adjacent. Fishing 3 km, bicycle hire 5 km. A novelty is two visiting storks who arrive at 7 pm. each evening to be fed by the Madame.

Directions: Travelling south on N83 Sélestat - Colmar road turn west onto D106 to Ribeauvillé. At roundabout turn left onto D1B Riquewihr (do not enter village). Site is on left approx. 800 m. past junction with D3 to Riquewihr. Travelling north on N83, go northwest on N415 at Ingersheim (west of Colmar) and then north on D10 to Riquewihr; site is signed at roundabout.

Charges 2000:
-- Per person Ffr. 23.00; child (under 7 yrs) 10.00; pitch 26.00; electricity 25.00; dog 5.00; local tax 2.00; use of motorcaravan services 30.00.
-- Credit cards accepted.

Open:
Easter - 31 October.

Address:
Route du Vins, 68340 Riquewihr.

Tel:
(0)3.89.47.90.08.
FAX: (0)3.89.49.05.63.

Reservations:
Not accepted

8807 Camping-Caravaning Domaine des Messires, Herpelmont

Rural lakeside camp in the heart of the Vosges.

Domaine des Messires nestles under a cover of tall trees by a landscaped lake on the edge of the small village of Herpelmont. It is well situated for exploring the rural countryside of the Vosges, the lakes and mountains of the region and the interesting towns of St Dié, Colmar and Épinal. The 125 good sized pitches are on grass over stones, with some by the lakeside. Each has a water tap, drain and electricity hook-up (4A) and most have good shade cover, except for those at the end of the site which are in the open. The modern sanitary block in the centre of the site has British style WCs and hot water to washbasins (all in cabins), showers (pre-mixed, push-button taps) and sinks. There is provision for disabled visitors (key from reception) and a baby room. The modern, refurbished reception building just inside the entrance also houses a small shop (from 16/5), games and TV room, and a restaurant overlooking the lake (also 16/5). There are two small children's play areas and a programme of activities is offered for children and adults in high season. The lake is available for non-powered boats and there are sections for both swimming and fishing. Weekly markets are held in nearby Bruyères, Corcieux and St Dié. If you write to reserve a pitch, ask for their very comprehensive route from Calais to the site.

Directions: From Épinal, exit N57 on N420 for St Dié and follow signs until you pick up signs for Bruyères. Lac du Messires is signed as you leave Bruyères on D423, at Laveline go south to Herpelmont and site.

Charges 2001:
-- Per person Ffr. 26.00 - 30.00; child (0-6 yrs) 13.00 - 16.00; pitch incl. 3 services 66.00 - 78.00; local tax 1.10.
-- In low season stay 7 days, pay for 6.
-- Credit cards accepted.
Open:
28 April - 15 September.
Address:
88600 Herpelmont.
Tel:
(0)3.29.58.56.29.
FAX: as phone.
(when closed tel/fax: 031.321.33.1456).
Reservations:
Made with 25% deposit and Ffr 75 fee; contact site for details.

Camping-Caravaning Domaine des Messires

Quiet 4 star campsite in the middle of nature
Private lake for fishing, boating & swimming
Ideal for discovering the Vosges & Alsace
English spoken

Campsite tel/fax: 0033 329 58 56 29
When closed tel/fax: 0031 321 33 14 56
88600 Herpelmont, Vosges France

8805 Camping Parc du Château d'Épinal, Épinal

Newly privatised site in pleasant surroundings.

A municipal site until recently, the sanitary accommodation was rather basic. The new owner is promising to upgrade the amenities and to add new facilities (for example, a pool, shop, restaurant and new reception building). Being about 2 km. from the centre of Épinal, it makes a good overnight stop between Nancy and Basel or for a longer stay to explore the Vosges. The 92 pitches, some on sloping ground, some on levelled places on grass, are divided by short, low fences which carry pitch numbers, most with electricity (6A). Although there are a number of large and decorative trees, shade is scarce at certain times of the day. There is also an area of tarmac which can be used for one night stops. A small shop and snack bar operate in high season, with restaurants in the town. Bicycle hire on site, golf 1 km, riding 3 km. Caravan storage.

Directions: Site is in the southeast outskirts of the town on the D11 road to Gerardmer. Watch carefully for signs.

Charges guide:
-- Per unit incl. 2 persons Ffr. 60.00 - 90.00; extra person 15.00 - 30.00; child (2-7 yrs) 10.00 - 18.00; dog 5.00 - 10.00; electricity (6A) 20.00, extra amp 2.00.
-- Credit cards accepted.
Open:
All year.
Address:
Chemin de Chaperon Rouge, 88000 Epinal.
Tel:
(0)3.29.34.43.65.
FAX: (0)3.29.64.28.03.
Reservations:
Made with deposit (Ffr 30 per day) and fee (100).

EAST - 88 Vosges

8804 Camping-Club Lac de Bouzey, Sanchey, nr Épinal

Pleasant all year site with heated pool, overlooking the lake.

Camping-Club Lac de Bouzey is some 8 km. west of Épinal at the beginning of
the Vosges Massif and is well placed for exploring the hills, valleys, lakes and
waterfalls of the south of Alsace Lorraine. The word 'Club' has recently been
added to the name of the site to indicate the large number of activities organised
by the management during high season (July/Aug). The 160 good sized, level,
back-to-back grass pitches are arranged on either side of tarmac access roads with
electricity connections (4-12A). They are on a gentle slope, divided by beech
hedging, under a cover of tall, silver birch trees and overlooking the 130 ha. lake.
The lake has a number of sandy beaches, trees and a back-cloth of wooded hills
and a number of watersports may be enjoyed, from pedaloes to canoes, windsurfing and sailing. In high season an animation team offer a full daily programme
of activities for all ages, including excursions and visits, sports, entertainment and
a mini-club for young children. The heated swimming pool is of an original shape
and is backed by two sunbathing terraces with sun-beds (1/4-30/9). Below
ground, under the restaurant, is a sound-proof room for cinema shows and discos
for those staying on site only. Site staff escort young people back to their pitch at
the end of the evening. The large, imposing building at the entrance to the site
houses reception, a well stocked shop and an excellent restaurant and bar with
both open and covered terraces overlooking the lake, where a good menu includes
a range of dishes. The central sanitary block, partly below ground level is being
refurbished. It includes a baby room and one for disabled people (although there
is up and down hill walking on the site). During the winter a small, heated section
in the main building with toilet, washbasin and shower is used. English is spoken
and the very pleasant owners would like to welcome more British visitors to their
site. Two bars by the lake would indicate that the lake-side is popular with the
public during the summer but the camping area is quiet, separated by a road and
well back and above the main entrance. Fishing, riding and bicycle hire on site,
golf 8 km. Barbecues are not permitted. Caravan storage available. This is a site
with good provision for families with lots going on for teenagers. A 'Sites et
Paysages' member.

Directions: Site is 8 km. west of Épinal on D460 and is signed from some parts
of Épinal. Follow signs for Lac de Bouzey and Sanchey.

Charges guide:
-- Per unit incl. 2 adults
Ffr. 85.00 - 110.00; extra
person 20.00 - 40.00;
child (2-7 yrs) 16.00 -
20.00; extra small tent
free - 30.00; electricity
4A 20.00, each extra amp
2.00; dog 5.00 - 10.00.
-- Credit cards accepted.

Open:
All year.

Address:
19 Rue du Lac,
88390 Sanchey.

Tel:
(0)3.29.82.49.41.
FAX: (0)3.29.64.28.03.
E-mail: camping.lac.de.
bouzey@wanadoo.fr.

Reservations:
Made with deposit (Ffr
40 per day) and fee (100).

`Camping Cheque'

*see colour advert
between pages 160/161*

8801 Camping Les Deux Ballons, St Maurice-sur-Moselle

Good mountain site on road to Col de Bussang.

St Maurice-sur-Moselle is in a narrow valley 7 km. from the source of the River
Moselle in the massif of Haute-Vosges on the main N66 which leads to the Col de
Bussang. This is a pleasant leafy area for winter skiing and summer outdoor activities. Les Deux Ballons lies in a small valley surrounded by mountains, with a
stream running through the site and with a cover of trees which give shade in most
parts. The 180 pitches are on stony ground under the firs or on two terraces, and
all have electrical connections (4A). There are four good sanitary blocks, one new
and the others recently renovated, spread around the site. They provide a baby
room, washing machines and dryers and chemical disposal. Motorcaravan service
point and gas supplies. A bar with terrace (30/6-25/8) has pizzas to take away. The
large swimming pool (30 x 20 m.) with water slide and a smaller pool for children,
are open in high season (15/6-31/8) when there are also organised walks, fishing,
bowls, riding and summer sledging. There is a TV room, a tennis court, table
tennis, volleyball and basketball. Fishing on site, bicycle hire 5 km, riding 3 km.
Chalets (5) for hire. English is spoken.

Directions: Site is on main N66 Le Thillot - Bussang road on northern edge of St
Maurice near Ners filling station (entrance partly obscured - keep a look out).

Charges 2001:
-- Per caravan or tent
incl. 1 or 2 persons Ffr.
102.00; (low season
24.00 per person, pitch
27.00); extra person
24.00 - 25.00; child 2-7
yrs 17.00 - 18.00, 0-2 yrs
free - 18.00; electricity
4A 24.00, 15A 31.00;
dog 10.50 - 11.50; local
tax 2.00 (child 1.00).
-- Less in low seasons.
-- No credit cards.

Open:
15 April - 30 September.

Address:
17 Rue du Stade, 88560
St Maurice-sur-Moselle.

Tel:
(0)3.29.25.17.14.
FAX: (0)3.29.25.27.51.
E-mail: verocamp
@aol.com.

Reservations:
Write with deposit (25%)
and booking fee (Ffr. 80).

8802 Camping de Belle-Hutte, La Bresse, nr Gérardmer

Pleasant mountain site for summer and winter sports.

La Bresse, in the heart of the Vosges mountains, makes a good base for winter skiing and summer walking and although a little off the beaten track, is on one of the southern routes to the Col de la Schlucht. Camping de Belle Hutte, although surrounded by mountains and trees, occupies an open hill slope (900 m. above sea level) with 100 numbered grass pitches on six terraces. Places of about 90 sq.m. are divided by hedges and all have electrical connections. The reception office at the entrance carries basic food supplies with larger shops and restaurants in the village about 400 m. away. The well built, brick sanitary block is centrally placed, of excellent quality and heated in cool weather, with facilities for disabled people and babies, plus chemical disposal. Here also is a laundry room with washing machines and dryers, a drying room, a play room with table tennis, rest room with open fire and TV and a ski storage room. A small swimming pool (10 x 4 m; no Bermuda shorts) for children is open for July/Aug. Children's playground. Fishing on site or 4 km, riding 10 km. Motorcaravan service point. Two chalets to rent. Caravan storage. To reach the site you would have to depart from the usual main through routes but it is a good site in pleasant surroundings.

Directions: Site is about 9 km. from La Bresse on the D34 road towards the Col de la Schlucht.

Charges 2001:
-- Per person Ffr. 14.00 - 25.00; child (under 7 yrs) 10.00 - 16.00; car 8.00 - 10.00; caravan 9.00 - 13.00; tent 8.00 - 11.00; motorcaravan 25.00 - 36.00 (less for stays over 1 night); dog 8.00- 10.00; electricity 2A 8.00 - 11.00, 10A 32.00 - 41.00; local tax 2.00.
-- Higher prices are for winter.
-- Credit cards accepted.

Open:
All year excl. 1-14 April.

Address:
88250 La Bresse.

Tel:
(0)3.29.25.49.75 or (0)3.29.25.47.49.
FAX: (0)3.29.25.52.63.
E-mail: camping-belle-hutte@wanadoo.fr.

Reservations:
Necessary in winter (not summer). Write for booking form and return with Ffr. 150 deposit.

8808 Castel Camping Domaine des Bans, Corcieux, nr St Dié

Large, well equipped site with heated swimming pool, in the Vosges.

Corcieux is in the heart of the Vosges mountains, near the lakeside resort of Gerardmer, Alsace 'Route de Vin' and on the edge of the Ballons des Vosges National Park. Domaine des Bans is a large, very well organised campsite in a country setting. Although there is a high percentage of static and tour operator units, there are said to be 400 tourist places. Pitches (all with electricity, water and drainage), numbered and separated by hedges, vary in size with some on low terraces from tarmac access roads. Some of these are tucked away in quiet areas with others nearer to where activities take place. Most of the site is under cover of tall trees with a few areas in the open. Six well built, modern sanitary blocks of excellent quality are spread around the site with British style WCs and free hot water in washbasins (some in private cabins), showers and sinks. The centre-piece of the site is the large, heated swimming pool (1/6-10/9), part of which is covered and surrounded by a sun terrace with snack bar. Next to the pool are a children's playground and an open area for ball games. With tennis courts, table tennis, badminton, minigolf, volleyball, lakes for fishing and boating, riding, archery and bicycle hire, there are plenty of opportunities to be active. A golf driving range is under construction. In high season the entertainment programme includes discos (sound-proof underground room), performances in the splendid theatre and other live music. Tucked away in one corner of the site is 'Goats Castle', where about two dozen goats with their own chalet provide extra interest for children. There is a well stocked shop (15/6-31/8), bar, takeaway and splendid restaurant (all 1/6-10/9) with another smaller one just outside the site boundary and others a short distance away in the village. Domaine des Bans really is a campsite for all ages, for those who want sport and entertainment and those who enjoy a quiet peaceful holiday. Not really a site for short stays but excellent for enjoying what is on offer, as well as being a base for exploring the varied and interesting countryside, Haut Koenigsbourg Castle with Colmar, Épinal and Strasbourg within range for day trips.

Directions: From D8 St Die – Gerardmer road, turn west on D60 just north of Gerbepal to Corcieux.

Charges 2001:
-- Per person Ffr. 40.00; child (under 6 yrs) 20.00; pitch 80.00; local tax 2.20.

Open:
1 May to 1 October.

Address:
88430 Corcieux.

Tel:
(03).29.51.64.67.
FAX: (0)3.29.51.64.65.

Reservations:
Advised in high season and made with deposit (Ffr. 75).

Book this site
01892 559898

THE ALAN ROGERS'
travel service

VENDÉE CHARENTE

We have exercised a little license with this area taking one département from the official **WESTERN LOIRE** region, namely number **85 Vendée**, and one from the Poitou-Charentes region, number **17 Charente-Maritime** .

The Vendée along with the coastal area stretching down from La Rochelle past Rochefort to Royan, ie. Charente-Maritime, has become well known as a tourist destination. It is popular with British visitors because of its micro climate and marvellous sandy beaches yet within a fairly easy drive from the Normandy or Brittany ferry ports.

The Vendée was the centre of the counter-revolutionary movement between 1793 and 1799 and a two hour 'son et lumiere' extravaganza held at the Chateau Puy-du-Fou from mid June to end of August (Fri and Sat) tells the whole story with the aid of ultra-modern technology. On the Ile de Noirmoutier, mimosa blooms in February, so mild is its climate. Les Sables d'Olonne is its main resort renowned for its excellent sandy beach and it also has a thriving sardine fishing industry.

The area between the Vendée and Charentes, the Marais Poitevin, is one of the most unusual in France - a vast tract of marshland with a thousand or more tree-lined canals and streams where everything is moved by punt, including the animals. Further south the port of La Rochelle, once a Protestant stronghold, with massive medieval towers, buzzes with life. The islands of Ré (toll bridge), a haven for cyclists, and Oléron (free toll bridge 2 miles long) are popular with those seeking beaches and small, quiet ports. Royan is the leading seaside resort at the confluence of the Gironde estuary and the Atlantic ocean and is said to have launched the fashion for sea bathing in the 19th century. La Palmyre, where pine forests planted to stabilise the dunes flank the beaches, is popular with the British .

Note: the site reports are laid out by département in numerical order.
See map on page 309.

Cuisine of the region

Fish predominates, both fresh water (eel, trout, pike), and sea water (shrimps, mussels etc), and *'huitres'* – oysters!

Cagouilles – snails from Charentes

Chaudrée – ragout of fish cooked in white wine, shallots and butter

Chevrettes – local name for crevettes (shrimps)

Mouclade – mussels cooked in wine, egg yolks and cream, served with Pineau des Charentes

Soupe de moules à la Rochelaise – soup of various fish, mussels, saffron, garlic, tomatoes, onions and red wine

Sourdons – cockles from the Charentes

Wine

Light fruity wines from Haut-Poitou, Deux-Sèvres and Charente

Very popular – Cognac and Pineau des Charentes (an aperitif of grape juice and Cognac)

Places of interest

Marais Poitevin – marshes known as the 'Green Venice'

Angoulême – Hill-top town surrouded by ramparts; cathedral, Renaissance château

La Rochelle – port, Porte de la Grosse Horloge (clock gate), Museum of the New World

Le Puy-du-Fou – 15th-16th century castle, sound and light show involving over 700 participants

Les Sables d'Olonne – fishing port and seaside resort

Noirmoutier – linked to the mainland by a 3 mile bridge

Saint Savin – 17th century abbey, mural painting

1702 Airotel Le Puits de l'Auture, St Palais sur Mer, nr Royan

Seaside site on La Grande Côte, to west of Royan and St Palais.

This popular region has a very sunny climate and this site is well situated with the sea outside the gates, just across the road, with a long sandy beach starting 400 m. away. As soon as you enter this site there is a feeling that it is well cared for, with an abundance of flower beds at the entrance. All 400 numbered pitches are level and have electricity connections (6A), some are separated by bushes and there are some trees to give welcome shade. Water and drainage is provided on 200 pitches. The sanitary blocks were very clean when we visited (late July) and were more than adequate for the number of visitors. Most WCs are British type and all wash-basins are in cabins; showers are adjustable and hot water is free and plentiful. Baby baths and showers, and full facilities for disabled people are near reception. There are washing machines and ample sinks for dishwashing and laundry. The shop is well stocked, and there is takeaway food and a bar (all 10/6-25/9). At the rear of the site are three swimming pools with sunbathing areas which are most attractive with banana plants making a backdrop with a difference. Volleyball, bicycle hire, table tennis, games room and play area on site. Riding and golf 800 m. A doctor visits. Several restaurants are nearby specialising in sea food. Barbecues are only allowed in a special area. No dogs are accepted. Used by a tour operator (13%). Mobile homes to rent (60). Considering its close proximity to the beach and its popularity, there is a remarkably calm and relaxed atmosphere and it is well worth considering.

Directions: Site is on coast, 2 km. from St Palais and 8 km. from Royan. From Royan take D25 past St Palais following signs for La Palmyre. At two lane junction system turn back left signed Grande Côte and St Palais and site is 800 m..

Charges 2000:
-- Per unit incl. up to 3 persons Ffr. 115.00 - 175.00, with electricity 6A 145.00 - 195.00, 10A 160.00 - 210.00, with water and drainage also 200.00 - 225.00; extra person (over 3 yrs) 29.00 - 39.00; extra vehicle 18.00 - 27.00; plus local tax.
-- Credit cards accepted.

Open:
1 May - 30 September.

Address:
La Grande Côte, 17420 St Palais sur Mer.

Tel:
(0)5.46.23.20.31.
FAX: (0)5.46.23.26.38.
E-mail: camping-lauture @wanadoo.fr.

Reservations:
Made for min. 5 days with exact dates; deposit and fee required.

1704 Camping International Bonne Anse Plage, La Palmyre

Spacious, well organised, family run site amongst shady pine trees with large pool.

On the edge of the Forêt de la Coubre, just beyond the popular resort of La Palmyre, Bonne Anse has a lovely setting amongst pine trees, just a short stroll from the sweeping sands that almost surround an inlet from the sea (now very tidal). It is a gently undulating site, carefully designed to provide 865 level, marked pitches, of which 600 have electricity (6/8A). Most are shaded by the pines, those nearer the sea less so (and rather more sandy). The site's amenities are centred around the entrance and reception building and include a restaurant (from 20/6) and bar with a spacious outdoor terrace which forms the social focus of the site and overlooks the boules area. Opposite is a splendid, lively swimming pool complex with a heated pool (35 x 25 m), three water toboggans and a splash pool with water slide. A shopping centre (open all season) includes a supermarket, excellent delicatessen and takeaway, crêperie, shops for bread and pastries, holiday goods and papers, and a launderette, plus visiting traders' stalls (wines, seafood, etc) in high season. Children have a good playground, large video games room, TV (satellite), minigolf and table tennis. A new, enclosed area with an all-weather surface has been added for football, volleyball or basketball. Entertain-ment and dancing are arranged in the season. Fishing or riding 1 km, golf 5 km, plus facilities for watersports and tennis nearby. The site has direct access to cycle tracks (bicycle hire available) which avoid the main road and there are many supervised, safe beaches close by, also a fitness track. Seven sanitary blocks (including two new ones and with further replacements planned) provide free hot water, washbasins in cabins, British style toilets with a few Turkish, hot (control-lable in the new blocks) and cold showers and facilities for disabled visitors and babies. Washing up and laundry sinks are under cover. English is spoken and rallies welcomed with visit programmes organised. Motorcaravan service point. Exchange facilities. No dogs are accepted. Only gas barbecues are permitted. Mobile homes for rent (14) and used by tour operators (150 pitches). With plenty to do for the active, the site is perhaps a little impersonal.

Directions: Leave A10 autoroute at Saintes and head for Royan (N150). In Royan take signs for La Palmyre (D25). At La Palmyre roundabout follow signs for Ronce-les-Bains and site is 1 km. on the left.

Charges 2001:
-- Ffr: per unit incl. 3 persons Ffr. 176.00, 1 or 2 persons 147.00; extra person (over 1 yr) 42.00; extra car 17.00; electricity (6A) 26.00; local tax 2.00 (4-10 yrs 1.00).
-- Euro: per unit incl. 3 persons 26,83, 1 or 2 persons 22,41; extra person (over 1 yr) 6,40; extra car 2,59; electricity (6A) 4,27.
-- Discounts for reservation.
-- Credit cards accepted.

Open:
23 May - 9 September.

Address:
17570 La Palmyre.

Tel:
(0)5.46.22.40.90.
FAX: (0)5.46.22.42.30.
E-mail: Bonne.Anse@wanadoo.fr.

Reservations:
Min. 5 days - phone, fax or write for details.

see colour advert between pages 64/65

VENDÉE CHARENTE - 17 Charente-Maritime

1701 Camping Bois Soleil, St Georges-de-Didonne, nr Royan

Large site with various amenities, by sea south of Royan.

Close to the sea and the resort of St Georges, Bois Soleil is a fairly large site in three separate parts with 225 pitches for touring caravans and 19 for tents. The main part, 'Les Pins', is mature and attractive with ornamental trees and shrubs providing shade. Opposite is 'La Mer' which has direct access to the beach and is used only in the main season. It has some areas with rather less shade and a raised central area for tents. The sandy beach here is a wide public one, sheltered from the Atlantic breakers although the sea goes out some way at low tide. The third and largest part of the site, 'La Forêt', is mainly for static holiday homes (many privately owned), although there are some touring pitches here for both tents and caravans. A little swimming pool has been added in this area for small children. The site has an hotel-type reservation system for each caravan pitch and can be full mid-June - late August. The areas are well tended with the named pitches (not numbered) cleared and raked between clients and with an all-in charge including electricity and water. The sanitary facilities have been completely rebuilt. Each area of the site is served by one large block which is supplemented by smaller blocks providing toilets only, and there is a heated block near reception. The well designed buildings have fittings of very good quality which are cleaned twice daily and include good, controllable, free hot showers, washbasins in cubicles, facilities for disabled people (WC, basin and shower) and for babies, chemical disposal. A busy little shopping area beside reception (in Les Pins) provides an upstairs restaurant and bar with terrace, an excellent takeaway (from April), supermarket, bakery (July/Aug), beach shop, launderette, TV room, library, a very comprehensive tourist information and entertainment office and a little nursery for babies. Over the road is a 'Parc des Jeux' with tennis, table tennis, minigolf, boules, bicycle hire and a children's playground. Fishing or riding within 500 m, golf 2 km. Safe deposit. Doctor visits daily. No charcoal barbecues but gas ones can be hired by the evening. No dogs or other animals are accepted. Caravan storage. This lively site offers something for everyone, whether they like a beach-side spot or a traditional pitch, plenty of activities or the quiet life - it is best to book for the area you prefer.

Directions: From Royan centre take coast road (D25) along the sea-front of St Georges-de-Didonne towards Meschers. Site is signed at roundabout at end of the main beach.

Charges 2000:
-- Per unit with 3 persons: tent with 2A electricity Ffr. 135.00, with 6A electricity, water and drainage 155.00; extra person 29.00; child (3-7 yrs) 18.00; 10A electricity 25.00; extra car 26.00; local tax 1.50.
-- Less 20% outside July/Aug.
-- Credit cards accepted.

Open:
1 April - 30 September.

Address:
2 Ave. de Suzac, 17110 St Georges-de-Didonne.

Tel:
(0)5.46.05.05.94.
FAX: (0)5.46.06.27.43.
E-mail: camping.
bois.soleil@wanadoo.fr.

Reservations:
Made with no min. stay with deposit (Ffr. 450) and fee (150).

`Camping Cheque'

*see colour advert
between pages 160/161*

1711 Camping-Caravaning Monplaisir, Les Mathes

Small, quiet site with a garden atmosphere, close to town.

Monplaisir provides a small, quiet haven in an area with some very hectic campsites, and is ideal for couples or families with young children. The site is set back from the road and the entrance leads through an avenue of trees, past the owners home, to a well kept, garden-like site with many varieties of trees and shrubs. There are only 114 level, marked pitches and all but 9 have electricity (6A). The sanitary block provides good facilities with some washbasins in cabins, pre-set showers, British style WCs, chemical disposal and excellent facilities for disabled people. Laundry and dishwashing sinks are outside, but under cover and a washing machine and dryer are near reception, as are a TV and games room. There is no shop, bar or restaurant but bread is delivered daily and a supermarket is a short walk. On five days a week takeaways are available from reception. There is a small play area, bicycle hire and minigolf is adjacent (owned by the site). The swimming pool and paddling pool have a paved sunbathing area (15/5-15/9). Ice pack service and gas supplies in reception, with tourist information and library. Fishing 500 m, riding 1 km, golf 5 km. There are no tour operators. Apartments (5) to let. Winter caravan storage. A happy, friendly site with visitors who return year after year.

Directions: Follow the D25 to La Palmyre and, in the town, turn north to Les Mathes. At roundabout turn right to town centre and site is on left. From north on D14 La Tremblade road turn to Les Mathes at Arvert. Site is in western outskirts of the town on the D141 La Palmyre road.

Charges 2001:
-- Per pitch incl. 2 persons Ffr. 92.00, 3 persons 106.00; extra person 25.00, baby under 2 yrs 12.00; local tax 2.00, 14 yrs 1.00; electricity 19.00.
-- Less 20% outside July/Aug.
-- No credit cards (planned for 2001).

Open:
1 April - 1 October.

Address:
Route de La Palmyre, 17570 Les Mathes-La Palmyre.

Tel:
(0)5.46.22.50.31.
FAX: as phone.

Reservations:
Contact site for details; made with deposit (Ffr. 200) and fee (100), min. stay 4 nights.

78

1703 Camping L'Estanquet, La Palmyre

Pleasant modern site, a short drive from seaside town of La Palmyre.

L'Estanquet is a large and well-established site, very close to L'Orée du Bois (1705), and just 10 minutes drive from the superb sandy beaches of La Palmyre. It is set in the pine forest of La Coubre and its 320 pitches are large with dappled shade from the towering pines above (watch out for pine cones). Touring units are taken on 150 pitches, the rest taken up for the most part by private mobile homes or chalets. Despite its size, only around 20 pitches are given over to tour operators. Unlike some sites in the area, this ensures that the ambience remains predominantly French. All pitches have electricity (6A). L'Estanquet's focal point is its magnificent solar heated pool, one of the largest in the area, and large water slide. There are two tennis courts (free in low season), minigolf and volleyball area. Plenty of animation is offered in high season, when the site becomes very lively. A cluster of shops is at the site entrance, including a boulangerie (from 1/6). A bar and snack bar overlook the pool. Four toilet blocks are all of modern design with British style toilets, washbasins in cabins, pre-set showers and washing machines. Charcoal barbecues are allowed in specially designated areas.

Directions: From the north follow D14 La Tremblade road. At Arvert turn onto D141 to Les Mathes and turn east, signed La Palmyre, to second roundabout where site signed. From the south, at Royan take D25 towards La Palmyre, then towards Les Mathes to roundabout where site is signed. No. 1705 is next door.

Charges guide:
-- Per pitch incl. 2 adults Ffr. 95.00 - 130.00; extra person 26.00; child (under 4 yrs) 16.00; electricity 26.00; extra car 26.00.

Open:
15 May - 15 September.

Address:
La Fouasse, 17570 Les Mathes - La Palmyre.

Tel:
(0)5.46.22.47.32.
FAX: (0)5.46.22.51.46.

Reservations:
Essential for high season with booking fee (Ffr. 120.00) and deposit.

1716 Camping Le Clos Fleuri, Médis, nr Royan

Pretty, family site with friendly atmosphere.

Clos Fleuri is a delightful family site with a friendly, laid back atmosphere, which is in marked contrast to some of the busy sites on the coast. Yet it is located just 5 km. from the sandy beaches at Royan and St Georges de Didonne. The Devais family have developed their site around an old Charentais farmhouse, beyond which are located the 140 large, grassy pitches. The camping area is very pretty and Mme Devais is justifiably proud of its floral appearance. Most pitches are reasonably shaded with around 10% in full sun, and 100 have electrical connections. There is a small pool and separate children's paddling pool, with a good sunbathing terrace. The site shop stocks basic provisions (from 1/7, but bread is delivered in June) with other shops close by in Médis (500 m). The bar is very much the focal point of the site and it is here that most of the animation takes place – in high season there are two 'soirées' weekly. Boules competitions are popular too, as well as archery, which is organised throughout the high season. Other leisure facilities include a sauna, an imaginative minigolf course, table tennis and a small football pitch. There are two toilet blocks, one of modern construction and one part of the old farm buildings. Both are maintained to a high standard with British style toilets, washbasins in cubicles, pre-set showers and baby baths, plus washing machines and dryers. Chalets to let.

Directions: Medis is around 5 km. north of Royan on the road to Saintes (N150). The site is well signed from the N150.

Charges 2001:
-- Per pitch incl. 2 adults Ffr. 130.00; extra person 24.00; child under 2 yrs free; electricity 5A 25.00, 10A 30.00.
-- Less 20% in June and Sept.
-- Credit cards accepted.

Open:
1 June - 15 September.

Address:
8 impasse du Clos Fleuri, 17600 Médis.

Tel:
(0)5.46.05.62.17.
FAX: (0)5.46.06.75.61.
E-mail: clos-fleuri@ wanadoo.fr.

Reservations:
Essential for high season and made with deposit.

Book this site
01892 559898

THE ALAN ROGERS'
travel service

VENDÉE CHARENTE - 17 Charente-Maritime

1705 Camping L'Orée du Bois, La Fouasse, Les Mathes

Large, attractive site amidst beautiful pines and oaks of the Forêt de la Coubre.

L'Orée du Bois has 388 pitches of about 100 sq.m. in a very spacious, pinewood setting with 150 for touring units. These include 40 large pitches with hardstanding and individual sanitary facilities (built in small, neat blocks of four and containing your own shower, toilet, washbasin and washing up sink). Pitches are on flat, fairly sandy ground, separated by trees, shrubs and growing hedges and all have electrical connections (6A). The forest pines offer some shade. The four main sanitary blocks are attractively designed with good fittings, providing British style WCs and free hot water to controllable showers and the washbasins (in private cabins). Three blocks have a laundry room, washing up under cover and fully equipped units for disabled people. The excellent bar, restaurant and crêperie have terraces overlooking the large swimming pools,which include a water toboggan, and children's paddling pool (proper swimming trunks, not shorts). Takeaway service and well stocked shop. Other activities include a tennis court, boules, games room, TV lounge (with satellite), bicycle hire, two sand based children's play areas, volleyball, table tennis and new football and basketball areas. Twice weekly discos and free, all day children's entertainment are organised in July/Aug. Exchange facilities. Fairly near are sandy beaches (with lifeguards in season), plus plenty of opportunities for walking, riding or cycling in the 10,000 hectare forest. Fishing 4 km, riding 300 m, golf 20 km. Site rules are specific about total silence 23.30 and 07.00 (except when entertainment is organised). Barbecues are allowed in special areas. Caravans and mobile homes (60) for hire. Used by several tour operators. A lively site in high season, suitable for all age groups, it is tranquil in low season with large, spacious pitches.

Directions: From north follow D14 La Tremblade road. At Arvert turn on D141 to Les Mathes and turn east, signed La Palmyre, to second roundabout where site signed. From the south, at Royan take D25 towards La Palmyre, then towards Les Mathes to roundabout where site is signed. Note: there is now a new roundabout with a boat on it - follow sign for La Tremblade. Site is signed from this road, and this way is said to be quicker.

Charges 2001:
-- Per unit incl. 2 persons Ffr. 95.00 - 170.00, with private sanitary facilities 135.00 - 220.00; extra person (over 3 yrs) 27.00; local tax 2.00 (child 4-10 yrs 1.00); animal 12.00.
-- Min. 7 days in high season.
-- Credit cards accepted.

Open:
12 May - 8 September.

Address:
225 Rte. de la Bouverie, La Fouasse, 17570 Les Mathes.

Tel:
(0)5.46.22.42.43. FAX: (0)5.46.22.54.76. E-mail: contact@camping-oree-du-bois.com.

Reservations:
Made with 30% deposit plus fee (Ffr 135); min. 7 days in high season.

see colour advert between pages 64/65

1710 Les Charmettes, Les Mathes

Haven Europe holiday park with small touring area and plenty of lively amenities.

A long straight drive leads to this open, modern, Haven Europe-owned park on the outskirts of Les Mathes. The site is very popular with British holiday makers, with many of the 950 caravan holiday homes privately owned, the remainder for hire, and the professional reception staff are multi-lingual. Once through the entrance barrier (security code required), the holiday homes are neatly arranged in mainly circular groups on either side of tarmac roads. At the far end of the long site (1 km!) are just 10 or so neat touring pitches in three groups near the tennis courts. Sheltered by hedges and low fencing, they are a good size (120 sq.m.) and all have electricity. They are served by a single, modern unisex toilet block with facilities opening off a central area or from the outside. It provides British style WCs, washbasins in cubicles and pre-set showers with divider, seat and hooks. As one would expect, there are plenty of lively amenities, mostly arranged around the new indoor entertainment centre and next to a complex of swimming pools, water slides and paddling pools. Facilities include shops, the Restaurant L'Atlantique, fast food outlets and a bar, plus a launderette. Activities include tennis, minigolf, table tennis, pool, large screen TV, games rooms and bicycle hire (very useful), all available over a long season. There is also plenty of organised entertainment, plus children's clubs for 1-14 year olds with daytime and evening games and activities. Reception will advise on the attractions of the area and provides an excellent information booklet, safety deposit boxes and exchange facilities. This well run, predominantly British site would perhaps suit those with teenage children or young families.

Directions: Follow D25 to La Palmyre and, in the town, turn north to Les Mathes. At roundabout turn right to town centre and site is on left. From north on D14 La Tremblade road turn to Les Mathes at Arvert. Site is in western outskirts of the town on the D141 La Palmyre road.

Charges 2001:
-- Per pitch incl. up to 2 persons and electricity Ffr. 139.00 - 259.00; extra person 25.00 - 40.00; extra vehicle 10.00 - 25.00.

Open:
7 April - 28 September.

Address:
Avenue de La Palmyre, 17570 Les Mathes-La Palmyre.

Tel:
(0)5.46.22.50.96. FAX: (0)5.46.23.69.70.

Reservations:
Accepted at any time for min. 4 days; no booking fee. Contact site or Haven Europe in the UK on 0870 242 7777 for information or reservation quoting FAR01.

see colour advert opposite page 256

1712 Camping-Caravaning International Rex, St Georges d'Oléron

Relaxed, informal holiday site right beside the beach on the Ile d'Oléron.

International Rex is situated towards the western tip of the Ile d'Oléron. Well away from any main roads and with direct access to two sandy beaches, it is just the place for beach lovers. Covering a large area on hilly, sandy ground amongst pine trees, the site has 400 touring pitches, all with electricity connections (3, 6 or 10A). A terraced site with some superb sea views, not all the pitches are suitable for caravans, although 8 pitches have concrete bases for motorcaravans. Tent pitches are perched in groups on ledges on the hillside. An unusual site with character, it is dissected by two small roads and has two reception areas. The main reception also has the majority of the site amenities centred around it. These include a bar with takeaway, shop (from 1/6), games room, laundry and a well stocked, multi-lingual library. Opposite is a large outdoor pool (proper trunks, no shorts) with paved sunbathing area and paddling pool, tennis court and archery area. There are communal barbecue areas (charcoal barbecues are not permitted), children's play equipment and minigolf. The three main sanitary blocks are modern, providing all the usual services, including British style WCs, showers, washbasins in cubicles and laundry and dishwashing sinks. These blocks are supplemented by five smaller blocks containing WCs, washbasins in cubicles, chemical disposal and laundry and dishwashing sinks, so no-one has too far to walk. When visited in August they were very clean and well maintained. Disabled people are also well catered for. Daytime entertainment is organised in July/Aug. but the nights are quiet with security guards to ensure this. Entrance to the site is by card. Free car wash. This is a very relaxing and informal site to suit families with teenagers seeking sun and sand. Mobile homes to hire (10).

Directions: From N734 main island road, go past St Pierre and turn left in Chéray to Domino. Site is 2 km. and very well signed.

Charges 2000:
-- Per pitch incl. 2 persons Ffr. 100.00 - 125.00; extra person 28.00 - 33.00; child (under 7 yrs) 20.00 - 22.00; electricity 3A 18.00 (each extra amp 2.00).
-- Credit cards accepted.

Open:
1 May - 15 September.

Address:
Domino, 17190 St Georges d'Oléron.

Tel:
(0)5.46.76.55.97. FAX: (0)5.46.76.67.88.

Reservations:
Necessary for July/Aug; contact site for details.

1706 Airotel Domaine de Montravail, Le Château, Ile d'Oléron

Attractive, traditional site on the Ile d'Oléron with pool and riding stables.

The Ile d'Oléron's western coast has wide sandy beaches, the eastern coast is a tidal estuary with safe sandy beaches at high tide and mud flats at low tide. Montravail, on the east coast, is a mature, traditional type of site with 260 well shaded pitches of average to large size amongst an attractive mix of mature trees and ornamental shrubs. It will be heaven on earth for horse enthusiasts as there are riding stables at the entrance (hats can be supplied, but probably best to bring your own). The stable yard gives the site an `olde world' atmosphere and there are birds in pens and peacocks which wander freely. The pitches all have shade and are level, with electricity. The two toilet blocks are in the traditional French style but have mainly British WCs. Some washbasins are in cabins and showers are free, some pre-set with the old style chain to pull, others adjustable but with no divider. There are washing machines plus laundry and dishwashing sinks at each block. We found the blocks functional rather than luxurious but when we visited they were clean, although maintenance can be variable. The swimming and paddling pools have sunbathing areas and are overlooked by a bar and restaurant (15/6-15/9), plus a TV and games room. The shop is quite well stocked. Two tennis courts, table tennis and a play area, also a lake for canoeing. The site is used by French tour operators. There is a little organised entertainment, but on the whole this is a quiet site, worth considering if the beach is not your main requirement.

Directions: Immediately after the viaduct turn right to Le Château and follow camp signs at junctions.

Charges guide:
-- Per unit incl. 2 persons Ffr. 60.00 - 95.00; extra person (over 3 yrs) 20.00 - 33.00; local tax in July/Aug. 1.00; extra car 10.00 - 15.00; dog 10.00 - 15.00; electricity (8A) 15.00 - 25.00.
-- Credit cards accepted.

Open:
Easter - 15 October.

Address:
17480 Le Château, Ile d'Oléron.

Tel:
(0)5.46.47.61.82. FAX: (0)5.46.47.79.67.

Reservations:
Made for exact dates (min. about one week in Aug.) with deposit (Ffr. 470) and fee (130).

For a list of sites which are open all year - see page 262

VENDÉE CHARENTE - 17 Charente-Maritime

1717 Camping Les Charmilles, Fouras

Site in quieter resort, for touring units and mobile homes.

Fouras is a relatively little known resort situated between La Rochelle and Rochefort and which retains much of the charm missing from some of the larger, more heavily commercialised resorts in the area. Les Charmilles is a member of the Chadotel group and is located about a mile from the town centre. It is very easily accessed from the main La Rochelle – Rochefort road (N137). There are 270 large pitches, all of which have electricity (6A) and many have water and drainage. Roughly a third are well shaded, with the remainder having a sunnier, more open setting. The latter area also has the advantage of being well away from the busy road which runs past the front of the site. Around 100 pitches are taken up with the site's own mobile homes or chalets. The five toilet blocks are modern and kept clean and well maintained. Toilets are British style and washbasins are nearly all in cubicles with pre-set hot water. Facilities are provided for babies and disabled people and there are washing machines and dryers. The bar and snack bar (15/5-15/9) are adjacent to reception, along with the small shop (1/6-15/9). Opposite are the heated swimming pool and water slide (15/5-15/9), surrounded by a large sunbathing terrace. Other leisure facilities include minigolf, table tennis, bicycle hire, a concrete basketball court and a good children's playground. There is a minibus service to the beach in July/Aug. Charcoal barbecues are not permitted.

Directions: Leave N137 at exit for Fouras and St Laurent de la Prée, joining D937 towards Fouras. Site is on left in about 800 m.

Charges 2001:
-- Per pitch incl. 2 adults Ffr. 75.00 - 128.00, with electricity 95.00 - 148.00; extra adult 33.00; child (under 5 yrs) 21.00; animal 16.00.
-- Credit cards accepted.
Open:
1 April - 25 September.
Address:
St Laurent de la Prée, 17450 Fouras.
Tel:
(0)2.51.33.94.89.
FAX: (0)2.51.33.94.04.
Reservations:
Necessary for high season with deposit (Ffr. 250) and fee (150). Central reservations: Siege Social - Centrale de Reservation, BP 12, 85520 Jard sur Mer. Tel: (0)2.51.33.05.05. FAX: (0)2.51.33.94.04. E-mail: chadotel@wanadoo.fr.

**Book this site
01892 559898**

THE ALAN ROGERS'
travel service

1713 Camping-Caravaning L'Ile Blanche, La Flotte, Ile de Ré

Good quality wooded site with covered pool.

In a popular holiday area and used by families, L'Ile Blanche is a good quality site. It provides 40 spacious touring pitches (120 sq.m.) all fully equipped with 10A electricity, water and drainage, together with 120 mobile homes (all but 12 privately owned). Arranged under medium sized, mixed trees, it is a shady and pleasant environment with hard access roads. Two sanitary blocks, well designed and maintained, provide good, clean facilities with free hot showers and wash-basins mostly in private cabins. Dishwashing and laundry sinks, plus washing machines in each block. Chemical disposal and motorcaravan service facilities. Smart, modern buildings by the entrance provide reception and a large restaurant and bar which is open all season and also provides snacks and takeaway. The restaurant overlooks the swimming pool, which is cleverly protected in poor weather by a sliding glass cover, and a children's pool, both with paved surrounds, plus a large, sandy children's play area. On site are a tennis court, volleyball, basketball and picnic areas. Entertainment is organised in season. Fishing, bicycle hire, riding within 1.5 km, golf 10 km. The beaches and holiday villages of the Ile de Ré are within easy driving distance and there is a good network of cycle paths in the area. Barbecues are not permitted. English is spoken.

Directions: Cross bridge to Ile de Ré (toll, Ffr. 110 for car) and follow La Flotte bypass on D735 signed St Martin de Ré. Site is approx. 1 km. after roundabout. Turning (to left) is quite narrow and sharp.

Charges 2000:
-- Per pitch Ffr. 40.00 - 55.00; extra adult 27.00 - 30.00; child (under 16 yrs) 17.00 - 20.00; pet 10.00; electricity 22.00.
-- Credit cards accepted.
Open:
1 April - 11 November.
Address:
Déviation de La Flotte, 17630 La Flotte de Ré.
Tel:
(0)5.46.09.52.43.
FAX: (0)5.46.09.36.94.
E-mail: camping.ile.
blanche@wanadoo.fr.
Reservations:
Contact site for details.

**Book this site
01892 559898**

THE ALAN ROGERS'
travel service

L'île BLANCHE Camping Caravaning ★★★★

ILE DE RE

**Déviation de la Flotte, 17630 LA FLOTTE EN RÉ
Tel: (0)5.46.09.52.43   Fax: (0)5.46.09.36.94**

1714 Castel Camping Séquoia Parc, Saint Just-Luzac

see colour advert between pages 160/161

Top class site in the grounds of a château, with pool complex.

Approached by an impressive avenue of flowers, shrubs and trees, Séquoia Parc is set in the grounds of La Josephtrie, a striking château with beautifully restored outbuildings and a spacious courtyard. The site itself is designed to a high specification with reception in a large, light and airy room retaining its original beams and leading to the courtyard area where you find a shop, restaurant/bar (from 15/5) and takeaway service. The pitches are 140 sq.m. in size with 6A electricity connections and separated by young shrubs. Although mostly unshaded, some pitches are to be found amongst mature trees which, with woodland, surround the site. The three luxurious sanitary blocks are maintained to a high standard, with decorative indoor plants and subtle colour schemes. These provide units with washbasin and shower, a laundry, dishwashing sinks, facilities for disabled visitors, baby baths and chemical disposal. The swimming pool complex is impressive with a paddling pool and sunbathing terrace, shrubs and flower beds. There is tennis, volleyball, a football field, games and TV room, bicycle hire and pony trekking, plus organised entertainment in July/Aug. Motor-caravan service point and gas supplies. Mobile homes (100) and (40) chalets to rent. Used by tour operators (125 pitches). A popular site, reservation is necessary in high season.

Directions: Site is 2.5 km. southeast of Marennes. From Rochefort take D733 south for 12 km. Turn west on D123 to Ile d'Oléron. Continue for 12 km. and turn southeast on D728 towards Saintes. Site clearly signed, in 1 km. on the left.

Charges 2000:
-- Per unit incl. 2 persons and electricity Ffr.95.00 - 165.00; extra person 24.00 - 31.00; child under 3 yrs free, 3-7 yrs 16.00 - 21.00; dog 15.00; local tax 2.00.
-- Credit cards accepted.
Open:
28 April - 9 September.
Address:
17320 Saint Just-Luzac.
Tel:
(0)5.46.85.55.55.
FAX: (0)5.46.85.55.56.
E-mail: sequoia.parc @wanadoo.fr.
Reservations:
Made to site with 30% deposit and Ffr. 130 booking fee. For reservations from Ireland contact G & R Boyce, 6 Lynda Crescent, Jordanstown, Co.Antrim BT37 ONS: Tel/Fax 02890 867988.

'Camping Cheque'

Book this site
01892 559898
THE ALAN ROGERS'
travel service

1709M Camping Municipal du Soleil, La Rochelle

Le Soleil has been neatly and attractively landscaped and has 156 level pitches amongst trees and shrubs. Numbered and marked with low wooden fences, many have electricity (10A). Those in a circular, central area are designed for motor-caravans with part gravel hardstanding. Two toilet blocks provide British and Turkish style toilets, pre-set hot water, some washbasins in cabins and 12 hot and 2 cold showers, all opening from the outside. Facilities for disabled visitors are provided and there is hot water for clothes and dishwashing sinks. There may be some noise from the road and an industrial area nearby, but accessibility to the amenities of the town balance this to a degree (5 minutes to grassy picnic areas by the harbour and 20 minutes to the town centre shops, restaurants and bars or to the beach). Delivery vans call with bread, milk, etc. and a launderette is near. There are table tennis tables, boules and barbecue areas, plus an area for dogs. A half hourly bus service to town runs from outside the site and a ferry service across the harbour to town. Very busy in high season, reservation is advised. Maintenance can be variable.

Directions: From ring road (peripherique), follow signs for Gare or Centre-Ville and from either of these follow signs to Vieux Port Sud, Aquarium or Port les Minimes. From there follow small signs to site.

Charges 2000:
-- Per unit incl. 1 person Ffr. 42.00; extra person 19.00; child (under 10 yrs) 13.00; electricity 19.00; animal 13.00; local tax (1/4-30/9) 1.00.
-- Less in low season.
Open:
15 May - 15 September.
Address:
Ave. Michel Crépeau, 17000 La Rochelle.
Tel:
(0)5.46.44.42.53.
Reservations:
Min. 5 days. Contact: Mairie de La Rochelle, Service de Campings, B.P. 1541, 17086 La Rochelle Cedex 02. Tel: (0)5.46.51.51.25.

1715M Camping Municipal du Château, Benon

Benon was once the capital of this area (its castle was built in 1096) and had strong English connections but now, all that remains is a single round tower. However the mayor and villagers are still anxious to welcome English visitors. The municipal campsite is beautifully kept, with open and shady areas and is ideal for a peaceful stay, and to stroll or cycle through the fields and woods which surround Benon. There are 70 pitches on neat grass, 60 with 10A electricity, with a reasonably modern toilet block, fully equipped with hot water always available, facilities for disabled visitors and chemical disposal. Motorcaravan service point. Small children's play area and tennis court. High season entertainment includes dances and organised dinners. Fishing or bicycle hire 7 km, riding 5 km, golf 13 km. An auberge, general shop and post office are near and La Rochelle is within easy reach (25 minutes). A pretty, quiet site where visitors are made welcome.

Directions: Benon is 28 km. east of La Rochelle on the N11. Turn south at 'Relais de Benon', Benon 2 km. and site in centre of village.

Charges guide:
-- Per pitch Ffr. 13.00; adult 13.00; child 8.00; electricity 13.00.
-- Reductions for longer stays.
-- No credit cards.
Open:
1 May - 30 September.
Address:
17170 Benon.
Tel:
(0)5.46.01.61.48 (Mairie).
FAX: (0)5.46.68.22.01.
Reservations:
Advised for 14 July - 15 Aug; contact the Mairie.

VENDÉE CHARENTE - 85 Vendée

8502 Camping du Jard, La Tranche-sur-Mer

Well maintained, welcoming site, between La Rochelle and Les Sables d'Olonne.

First impressions on booking in at du Jard are good, with a friendly welcome from Mr and Mme Besnard, and each new arrival being personally shown to their pitch. The 350 pitches are level and grassy, hedged on two sides by bushes. The smallest are 100 sq.m. (the majority larger) and most are equipped with electricity, half with water and drainage. It is a comparatively new site, but the large variety of trees are beginning to provide a little shade. The site is 700 m. from a sandy beach but it also has its own heated swimming pool with toboggan, paddling pool and lifeguard, plus a good heated indoor pool with jacuzzi (no bermuda-style shorts in the pools). Other activities include a tennis court, minigolf, table tennis, bicycle hire, a play area, games room and TV room, also a sauna, solarium and fitness room with instructors. The three toilet blocks are well designed and maintained, light and airy, with excellent facilities for babies and disabled people. There is ample free hot water, mostly British style WCs, washbasins (most in cabins) and chemical disposal. In the same blocks are washing machines and dryers, plus dishwashing and laundry sinks. There is a bar with terrace (25/5-10/9), a restaurant and a small shop for basics (both 1/6-10/9), with many shops and restaurants near. Exchange facilities. Car wash. American motorhomes are not accepted. Card operated barrier with outside parking. Mobile homes to rent. Used by British tour operators (100 pitches). Dogs are not accepted.

Directions: Site is east of La Tranche-sur-Mer, 3 km. from D747/D46 roundabout, on the D46. From new bypass southeast of La Tranche, take exit for La Grière and then turn east to site.

Charges 2000:
-- Per standard pitch incl. 2 persons Ffr. 125.50, with electricity (6 or 10A) 144.50 - 156.00, with electricity, water and drainage 159.00 - 170.00; extra person (over 5 yrs) 29.00; extra child (under 5 yrs) 20.00; extra small tent 21.00; plus local tax.
-- Less 25% outside 1/7-25/8.
-- Credit cards accepted.

Open:
25 May - 15 September.

Address:
123, Route de la Faute, 85360 La Tranche-s-Mer.

Tel:
(0)2.51 27 43 79.
FAX: (0)2.51.27.42.92.

Reservations:
Advisable for July/Aug. (min. 1 week, Sat.- Sat.) with deposit (Ffr. 650).

Book this site
01892 559898

THE ALAN ROGERS'
travel service

8503 Camping La Loubine, Olonne-sur-Mer

Attractive, lively family site with friendly atmosphere and good facilities for teenagers.

La Loubine has 368 level and grassy pitches of which some 180 are available for touring units. All have electricity (6A), and some with water and drainage are available at a small extra cost. The original part of the site has shady pitches, elsewhere they are more open. The buildings around a pleasant courtyard over-looking the pool have been tastefully converted to provide an attractive bar, takeaway and shop (15/5-15/9). It is here that evening entertainment takes place (of the disco/karaoke variety). The restaurant is near reception (also 15/5-15/9). The impressive swimming pool complex includes an indoor pool with jacuzzi, sauna and fitness room (free), as well as outdoor facilities (from 1/5; no bermuda style shorts) consisting of two heated outdoor pools with a total of five water slides, a children's pool and plenty of sunbathing space. The four modern toilet blocks are tiled throughout, with mainly British style WCs, washbasins in cabins and free, pre-set showers. Babies and disabled people are well catered for, there are washing machines, dryers, washing lines and irons, an ample supply of dish-washing and laundry sinks (all with free hot water), chemical disposal and motor-caravan services. Activities and sports are organised with a daily club for children in July/Aug. Tennis (free in low season), table tennis, minigolf, badminton, bicycle hire and a large children's play area (on grass and sand) are other activities. Riding 200 m, golf 3 km, fishing 3 km. The beach at Sauveterre is 1.8 km, Les Sables d'Olonne 5 km. No dogs are accepted. There is a night security barrier. Used by tour operators (70 pitches). Site owned mobile homes and chalets to hire. This is a busy site, popular with families with children and teenagers.

Directions: Site is west of Olonne beside the D80 road. Turn towards the coast at traffic lights, signed La Forêt d'Olonne and site (75 m).

Charges 2000:
-- Per pitch incl. 2 persons, with tent/caravan and car, without electricity Ffr. 124.00, with electricity (6A) 139.00, with all services 149.00; extra adult 25.00; extra child (under 7) 15.00; extra car 10.00.
-- Less 30% outside 2/7-25/8.
-- Credit cards accepted.

Open:
1 April - 30 September. (full facilities from 15/5).

Address:
1 Route de la Mer, 85340 Olonne-sur-Mer.

Tel:
(0)2.51.33.12.92.
FAX: (0)2.51.33.12.71.
E-mail: camping.la. loubine@wanadoo.fr.

Reservations:
Made with deposit and Ffr 120 fee (min. 7 days in Jul/Aug.)

see colour advert between pages 64/65

84

VENDÉE CHARENTE - 85 Vendée

camping du Jard ★★★★ NN
GRAND CONFORT

- Open 25 May – 15 September
- Free heated swimming pool
- 350 flat grassy pitches
- 700 yds from beach

123, Route de la Faute
85360 La Tranche-Sur-Mer
Tel: 02.51.27.43.79 Fax: 02.51.27.42.92

8521 Camping Les Ecureuils, Jard-sur-Mer

see colour advert between pages 64/65

Attractive, wooded site in quieter part of southern Vendée.

Les Ecureuils is undoubtedly one of the prettiest sites on this stretch of coast, with an elegant reception area, attractive vegetation and large pitches separated by low hedges and with plenty of shade. Of the 261 pitches, some 120 are for touring units, each with water and drainage as well as easy access to 10A electricity. The good sized, L-shaped swimming pool and separate paddling pool are surrounded by a terrace, overlooked by the friendly bar. Snacks and ice-creams are available from the bar, there is a small shop and a takeaway (pre-order). All facilities are open throughout the season. The two toilet blocks are well equipped and kept very clean. They include baby baths, laundry rooms and chemical disposal. Amenities include a modern children's play area, minigolf, table tennis and a pool table. A club for children (5-10 yrs) takes place daily in July/Aug. Jard is rated among the most pleasant and least hectic of Vendée towns. The nearest beach is just 400 m, with other good beaches a short distance. The harbour is home to some fishing boats and rather more pleasure craft, and has a public slipway for those bringing their own boats. There is a range of places to eat at the nearby marina or in the town which has a good supermarket and a weekly market. Fishing and bicycle hire 400 m. Dogs are not permitted. Only gas barbecues are allowed. Mobile homes to rent (21). The site is very popular with tour operators (126 pitches). And in case you are curious, yes there are squirrels on site, including red ones!

Directions: Jard sur Mer is on the D21 road between Talmot St Hilaire and Longeville sur Mer. Site is well signed from the main road - caravanners will need to follow these signs to avoid tight bends and narrow roads.

Charges 2001:
-- Per pitch Ffr. 70.00, with electricity (10A) 90.00; person over 10 yrs 32.00; child 0-4 yrs 12.00, 5-9 yrs 24.00; local tax July/Aug. (over 10) 3.30.
-- Less 10% outside 30/6-1/9.
-- Credit cards accepted.

Open:
24 May - 10 September.

Address:
85520 Jard sur Mer.

Tel:
(0)2.51.33.42.74.
FAX: (0)2.51.33.91.14.
E-mail: camping-ecureuils@wanadoo.fr.

Reservations:
Advised for July/Aug.

Book this site
01892 559898
THE ALAN ROGERS'
travel service

8527 Camping L'Océano d'Or, Jard-sur-Mer

Busy holiday site with many facilities, 900 metres from beach.

This site should appeal to families with children of all ages. It is very lively in high season, but appears to be well managed, with a full programme of activities in high season (July/Aug). There are 431 flat, grassy/sandy pitches of which 40% are occupied by tour operators and mobile homes. The 200 for touring units (all with 10A electricity) are all quite large (about 100 sq.m.). Some are separated by high hedges, others are more open with low bushes between them. Sanitary facilities in four blocks are modern and unisex, with all washbasins in private cabins, free hot showers (push-button) and plenty of dishwashing and laundry sinks plus washing machines and dryers. Chemical disposal. There is a small shop on site (1/6-15/9) and a modern complex at the entrance with a bar and snack bar (both 15/6-15/9, but limited hours outside high season). The swimming pool (15/5-15/9) with its water slide, children's pool and large terrace is very popular and there is a walled (three sides) play area with lots of recently refurbished equipment on sand for children. Tennis, table tennis, volleyball, pétanque and minigolf are also available. Golf, riding, karting and numerous other activities are to be found within 15 km. Above all, of course, the excellent beach is within walking distance, as are the shops, bars and restaurants, and weekly market of this pleasant little town.

Directions: Site is on the D21 Talmont St Hilaire - Longeville sur Mer road, just east of the turning to the town centre.

Charges 2001:
-- Per pitch incl. 2 adults Ffr. 75.00 - 128.00, with electricity 95.00 - 148.00; extra adult 33.00; child (under 5 yrs) 21.00
-- Credit cards accepted.

Open:
1 April - 25 September.

Address:
Rue Georges Clemenceau 85520 Jard-sur-Mer.

Tel:
(0)2.51.33.05.05.
FAX: (0)2.51.33.94.04.

Reservations:
Necessary for high season with deposit (Ffr. 250) and fee (150). Central reservations: Siege Social - Centrale de Reservation, BP 12, 85520 Jard sur Mer. Tel: (0)2.51.33.05.05. FAX: (0)2.51.33.94.04. E-mail: chadotel@wanadoo.fr.

Book this site
01892 559898

THE ALAN ROGERS'
travel service

85

VENDÉE CHARENTE - 85 Vendée

8524M Camping Jarny Océan, Le Bouil, Longeville-sur-Mer

Jarny Ocean is the sort of the site the French love - wooded and with many pitches separated by thick hedges. There are other areas, however, that are more open and with plenty of sun. There are 303 large, grassy pitches on level ground, 250 for tourers. All have electricity (6/10A), about 15 with water and drainaway also. The five sanitary blocks are of differing ages and have a mixture of British and Turkish style WCs. Showers are quite roomy with free hot water. There is a large central play area on sand and grass, table tennis, tennis (free in low season) including short court tennis, bicycle hire, volleyball and basketball. The small heated swimming pool with sunbathing area (1/5-15/9) would be hard pressed if the site was full. Overlooking the pool is the bar and terrace (weekends in low season, 11.00 - 01.00 hrs in July/Aug). All this is well away from the nearest pitches. Behind reception (English is spoken) is a small shop selling basics in July/Aug, but bread, etc. can be ordered all season. A takeaway is in the Centre de Vacances that shares the site. Bars, restaurants and minigolf are a short walk. A beach is within easy walking distance (800 m) or a beach with lifeguards (and parking) is a short 4 km. drive. Riding or fishing 4 km. Some mobile homes to rent.

Charges 2000:
-- Per unit incl. 2 adults Ffr. 55.00 - 117.00, with 6A electricity 65.00 - 145.00; extra adult 13.00 - 20.00; child (3-10 yrs) 8.00 - 15.00; dog 5.00 - 10.00; local tax 2.20.
-- Credit cards accepted.
Open:
1 May - 30 September.
Address:
Le Bouil, 85560 Longeville-sur-Mer.
Tel:
(0)2.51.33.58.19.
FAX: (0)2.51.33.95.37.
Reservations:
Made with deposit (Ffr. 300) and fee (100).

Directions: From D21 Talmont - Longeville road, soon after Jard, pass through St Vincent and very shortly the site is signed towards the coast (before Longeville). Turn left in village of Le Bouil (site signed) and site is on left in 800 m.

Book this site
01892 559898

THE ALAN ROGERS'
travel service

8537 Camping Les Mancellières, Avrillé

Pleasant, traditional campsite, just 5 km. from the sea.

This is a family run site on the edge of the small town of Avrillé, on the road between La Rochelle and Noirmoutiers, yet only a short drive from some of the delightful beaches of the southern Vendée. It is a simple, well-established site with 130 pitches (82 touring pitches), most with a mixture of sun and shade, but some very shaded. It has a swimming pool and water slide (until 15/9), a children's play area and a good sized sports area. There are two games rooms. A small shop and adjacent snack bar are open in July/Aug; the fact that this is not licensed might appeal to those who prefer a simple life! However, there is a weekly outdoor disco and other activities including pétanque, volleyball, water polo and table tennis competitions, and a France v. The Rest football match (all July/Aug). There are two sanitary blocks that are kept clean, with mainly British style WCs (albeit seatless), washbasins (some cubicles), pre-set hot showers, a baby bath in the ladies' wash rooms, a unit for disabled visitors (toilet, shower and washbasin), and sinks for dishwashing and laundry (H&C) and a washing machine. Tennis (800 m) riding (7 km), golf (10 km). Some caravans and mobile homes for rent.

Charges 2000:
Per unit incl. 2 persons Ffr. 89.00; extra person 18.00; child (under 7 yrs) 15.00; dog 9.00; extra vehicle 11.00; electricity (6A) 18.00; local tax (over 10 yrs) 1.10.
Open:
1 May - 30 September.
Address:
Rte de Longeville-sur-Mer, 85440 Avrillé.
Tel:
(0)2.51.90.35.97.
FAX: (0)2.51.90.39.31.
Reservations:
Advised for high season; contact site.

Directions: Avrillé is on D949 (Les Sables d'Olonne - Luçon), 23 km. from Les Sables. Site is about 1 km. south of the town, on D105 to Longeville-sur-Mer.

8539 Camping des Batardières, St Hilaire-la-Forêt

'Haven of tranquillity' on the edge of unspoilt village, yet just 5 km. from the sea.

This is an attractive, unsophisticated little site, lovingly maintained by its owners for the past 23 years. Many guests return year after year, and it was one of these who described it as a 'haven of tranquillity'. There are 75 good-sized pitches (a few up to 130 sq.m.) and all are for touring units (no mobile homes and no tour operators!) All have easy access to water and electricity (6A, or 2A for tents). The central sanitary block is kept very clean and visitors are encouraged to keep it that way (no shoes in shower cubicles, for instance) - it seems to work. Hot water is free, with some washbasins in cubicles for ladies, showers have push-buttons and WCs are British style. Chemical disposal, dishwashing and a washing machine and dryer. There are no special facilities for children or disabled customers. Amenities include a TV room, table tennis, tennis (free), a play area and a field for games, kite-flying and the like. No shop or takeaway, but the village shop is only a short walk (200 m). There is also a bar and restaurant open to all on the village's other campsite. In nearby Jard-sur-Mer (5 km) you will find a good supermarket, shops, bars, restaurants, a weekly market and, of course, the sea.

Charges 2000:
-- Per unit inc. 2 persons Ffr. 89.00, with electricity 109.00; extra person 18.00; child (under 7 yrs) 12.00; dog 8.00.
Open:
27 June - 5 September.
Address:
85440 St Hilaire-la-Forêt.
Tel:
(0)2.51.33.33.85.
Reservations:
Contact site.

Directions: Site is on edge of St Hilaire-la-Forêt. From Les Sables d'Olonne take D949 towards Talmont St Hilaire and Luçon. 7 km. after Talmont turn right on D70 to St Hilaire-la-Forêt and site is signed to right as you approach village.

8513 Camping Pong, Landevieille

Pleasant, traditional site, just 5 km. from the coast at Brétignolles.

In a rural situation on the edge of a neat village, 12 km. southeast of St Gilles-Croix-de-Vie, this is a comfortable, family run site in its second year under new management. It has 185 pitches, all with electricity (4/6A). They are all of a good size with some larger ones (up to 180 sq.m.) costing a little more. The original part of the site around the small, lightly fenced fishing lake (parents need to watch children) has a mixture of mature trees, whereas, in the newer, terraced area, the trees and bushes are less developed. Three modern, unisex sanitary blocks provide toilets of mixed styles, free hot water for showers (push-button) and washbasins (some open plan, some in private cabins), facilities for disabled people, a separate baby room, washing up under cover, laundry room and chemical disposal. Maintenance can be variable. A heated semi-oval pool with jacuzzi, combine with the original pool and toboggan, a delightful new paddling pool (with many fascinating features for children) and a patio area with palms and sun-loungers, to provide an attractive leisure area (from 15/5). A small shop also offers takeaway meals and there is a bar with terrace overlooking the pool (both 15/6-15/9). Other facilities include a small gym, TV lounge, games room, bicycle hire and an exciting new fenced, sand based children's play area. There is a regular children's club. Tennis 200 m. Golf or riding 5 km. The site is 2.5 km. from the large Lac du Jaunay (canoeing and pedaloes), 14 km. from Lac d'Apremont and its XVl century château and only 6 km. from the nearest beach. Markets and vineyards are near. No tour operators. Mobile homes, chalets and caravans for hire.

Directions: Site is on edge of Landevieille, signed from both D32 (Challons - Les Sables d'Olonne) and D12 (La Mothe Achard - St Gilles Croix de Vie) roads.

Charges 2000:
-- Per unit incl. 2 persons Ffr 75.00 - 99.00, supplement for larger pitches 15.00 - 35.00; extra person 24.00; child (under 5 yrs) 16.00; electricity 4A 18.00, 6A 23.00; water and drainage 5.00; dog 13.00; local tax 1.65 (over 10 yrs).
-- Less 25% in low season.
-- Credit cards accepted.

Open:
Easter - 30 September.

Address:
Rue du Stade, 85220 Landevieille.

Tel:
(0)2.51.22.92.63.
FAX: (0)2.51.22.99.25.

Reservations:
Made with dates of arrival and departure, plus deposit and fee.

**Book this site
01892 559898**

THE ALAN ROGERS'
travel service

8538M Camping Municipal Orée de l'Océan, Landevieille

Landevieille is rightly proud of this charming site, described as being 'near the beaches, yet far away from the bustle'. The smart reception building with its friendly, welcoming staff sets the tone that is maintained throughout the site. The 140 pitches (128 for touring units) are well laid out, separated by trees and bushes. Most are level, some have shade and all have electricity (10A) with water nearby. Access might be a problem for some twin-axle units or large motorhomes. The two sanitary blocks are well maintained with mainly British style WCs, washbasins mainly in cubicles, push-button showers and sinks for dishwashing and laundry. Hot water is free throughout. There is one washing machine, a dedicated unit for disabled visitors and for babies and chemical disposal points. The site has its own small, but neat and very clean, heated pool with a separate children's pool (14/7-15/8) and a good play area for children of varying ages with equipment clearly marked accordingly. The site is next to the village's 'Salle de Fetes' where there is a TV room and where children's activities are organised twice a week. Each week there is a family evening with karaoke, moules-frites, dancing, etc (all activities mid July - late Aug). In the Espace de Loisirs (300 m) there are tennis courts, fishing, boules pitches, etc. Nearby (5 km) is the extensive Lac du Jaunay with fishing, sailing and 13 km. of tracks for walking or cycling (the area has a further 240 km. of signposted routes awaiting the enthusiastic cyclist!) Just outside the site is the village bakery and round the corner are a small store, café-tabac, bicycle hire and wine cellars, whilst nearby Brétignolles-sur-Mer (5 km.) has a good supermarket, plenty of shops, bars and restaurants and a bustling twice-weekly market. The nearest of the varied beaches of the southern Vendée is just 6 km.

Directions: Landevieille is on the D32 Challans - Les Sables d'Olonne road, just south of LA Chaize Giraud. Site is near the centre of the village on the minor road to Brétignolles-sur-Mer and is signed.

Charges 2000:
-- Per unit incl. 2 persons Ffr. 68.00; extra person 15.00; child (under 10 yrs) 8.00; animal 8.00; electricity 17.00; local tax (over 10 yrs) 1.10.

Open:
15 June - 15 September.

Address:
Rue de Mazenod, 85220 Landevieille.

Tel:
(0)2.51.22.96.36.
FAX: (0)2.51.22.91.12.

Reservations:
Advised for high season; contact site.

VENDÉE CHARENTE - 85 Vendée

8504 Castel Camping La Garangeoire, St Julien-des-Landes

Rurally situated site in grounds of château, 15 km. from the Atlantic coast.

La Garangeoire is one of a relatively small number of seriously good sites in the Vendée. Situated some 15 km. inland, near the village of St Julien des Landes. One of its more memorable qualities is the view of the château through the gates as you drive in. Imaginative use has been made of the old `main road' to Noirmoutiers central to the site which now forms a delightful, quaint thoroughfare, nicknamed the Champs Elysée. It is busy at most times with the facilities opening directly off it and providing a village like atmosphere. The site is set in the 200 ha. of parkland which surrounds La Garangeoire, the small château. The peaceful fields and woods, where campers may walk, include three lakes, one of which may be used for fishing and boating (life jackets supplied from reception). The site has a spacious, relaxed atmosphere and many use it as a quiet base. There is a new swimming pool complex with water slides, fountains and a children's pool. The main camping areas are arranged on either side of the old road, edged with mature trees. The 320 pitches, each with a name not a number and individually hedged, are especially large (most 150-200 sq.m.) and are well spaced. Most have electricity (6A), some have water and drainage. The ample sanitary facilities are of a good standard and well situated for all areas. One excellent block has facilities for babies and disabled people. All have British style toilets, washbasins in cabins and free controllable hot water. Good laundry facilities. There is a full restaurant, takeaway and a separate crêperie with bars and attractive courtyard terrace. A large playing field with new play equipment is provided for children's activities, whether organised or not, plus a games room, two tennis courts, bicycle hire, table tennis, crazy golf, archery and volleyball. Riding in July/Aug. Good shop, exchange facilities, motorcaravan service point. The site is popular with British tour operators (144 pitches) and has mobile homes and chalets to rent.

Directions: Site is signed from St Julien; the entrance is to the north off the D21.

Charges 2001:
-- Per unit incl. 2 persons Ffr. 90.00 - 135.00, with electricity 110.00 - 160.00, with services 120.00 - 175.00; extra person 22.00 - 35.00; child (under 7) 11.00 - 16.00; dog 11.00 - 15.00.
-- Credit cards accepted.

Open:
15 May - 15 September.

Address:
St Julien-des-Landes, 85150 La Mothe-Achard.

Tel:
(0)2.51.46.65.39. FAX: (0)2.51.46.69.85. E-mail: garangeoire @wanadoo.fr.

Reservations:
Made for min. 7 days with deposit (Ffr. 400) and fee (150).

`Camping Cheque'

Book this site
01892 559898

THE ALAN ROGERS'
travel service

*see colour advert
between pages 160/161*

8531 Camping La Trévillière, Bretignolles sur Mer

Relaxed site with good range of activities and amenities.

A member of the Chadotel group, La Trévillière has a pleasant semi-rural setting on the edge of the little resort town of Bretignolles. Although just 2 km. from the nearest beach and less than 5 km, from the Plage des Dunes (one of southern Vendée's best beaches), La Trévillière has a more 'laid-back' feel than many other sites in the area, particularly in low season. The 180 pitches are grassy and either level or on a slight slope; almost all have easy access to electricity (6/10A) and water. They are separated by hedges or low bushes, and there is a mixture of shady or more open positions. There are around 50 mobile homes and chalets on site, many available to rent, and the site is used by three small tour operators, but it remains very much a camping and caravanning site. The three toilet blocks are all modern and kept very clean providing British style toilets, washbasins in cubicles, pre-set hot showers and chemical disposal. Washing machines and dryers are in one block, another has a unit for disabled people and a baby room with bath, shower and toilet. There is a heated swimming pool (20/5-15/9) with water slide, a small paddling pool and a large sunbathing terrace with plenty of loungers. Overlooking the pool is the building housing the bar and reception. There is a small independently operated shop and snack bar with takeaway (20/6-15/9). Early in the season the site is very quiet; in July/Aug. it becomes much livelier with a good range of morning activities for children, afternoon events for families and evening entertainment for all. Also on site are minigolf, table tennis and a children's play area. There is a sports complex just around the corner providing tennis courts. Golf, riding, karting, water sports and water parks are all within easy reach, as are museums, châteaux and numerous other days out.

Directions: Bretignolles is on the D38 coast road (Noirmoutiers - Les Sables d'Olonne). From north, after St Gilles go through Bretignolles-La Sauzaie (take left fork) and before reaching Bretignolles itself turn left (sign for site) on sharp right hand bend, heading for water tower. Site is on right in 800 m. From south, after centre of Bretignolles, turn right (sign 'Ecoles') and then left (signs for sports centre and sit). Site is signed to left after stadium.

Charges 2001:
-- Per pitch incl. 2 adults Ffr. 75.00 - 128.00, with electricity 95.00 - 148.00; extra adult 33.00; child (under 5 yrs) 21.00; animal 16.00; extra car 15.00.
-- Credit cards accepted.

Open:
1 April - 25 September.

Address:
Route de Bellevue, 85470 Bretignolles sur Mer.

Tel:
(0)2.51.33.94.04. FAX: (0)2.51.33.94.04.

Reservations:
Necessary for high season with deposit (Ffr. 250) and fee (150). Central reservations: Siege Social - Centrale de Reservation, BP 12, 85520 Jard sur Mer. Tel: (0)2.51.33.05.05. FAX: (0)2.51.33.94.04. E-mail: chadotel@wanadoo.fr.

Book this site
01892 559898

THE ALAN ROGERS'
travel service

8506 Airotel Domaine Le Pas Opton, Le Fenouiller, nr St Gilles-Croix

Well established site with good installations and swimming pool, 6 km. from sea.

Le Pas Opton is family managed and run and much work has been carried out to make it worth considering for a stay in this popular region. It is 6 km. back from the sea at St Gilles Croix de Vie and quietly situated. With a well established atmosphere, it is a select type of site but at the same time, offers on-site amenities such as a heated swimming pool (20/5-10/9) with water slide and children's pools and an attractive bar with a pleasant terrace looking across to the pool. There are 200 pitches, most with electricity and some with hardstanding, water and drainage. Those pitches in the original part are well shaded by mature trees and tall hedges. The newer areas have less shade but are developing well with a more spacious feel. The four toilet blocks are of good quality and are kept very clean and in good order. They have free hot water in all facilities, British style WCs, showers and individual washbasins, mainly in cabins for women, partly for men. A unit for disabled people, laundry facilities, chemical disposal and a motor-caravan service point are provided. Other amenities include a shop (30/6-1/9), bar, café and takeaway (all 1/7-31/8), volleyball, basketball, table tennis, a children's playground and a car wash area. Entertainment and some dancing is organised in season. The river Vie runs past the rear of the site (fishing possible, licences available in the village) and it is fenced and gated. Non-powered boats can be put on the river, but there can be a current at times. Riding, golf, bicycle hire within 7 km, sailing centre and windsurfing 2 km. and markets at St Gilles-Croix two or three times weekly. Chalet and large caravans for hire.

Charges 2001:
-- Per unit incl. 2 persons Ffr. 76.00 - 115.00, with electricity (6A) 101.00 - 140.00, with water and drainage 117.00 - 156.00; extra adult 28.00; child (under 7) 16.00; dog (small only) 12.00; local tax 2.20 in July/Aug.
-- Credit cards accepted.
Open:
20 May - 15 September.
Address:
Le Fenouiller, 85800 St Gilles Croix de Vie.
Tel:
(0)2.51.55.11.98.
FAX: (0)2.51.55.44.94.
E-mail: lepasopton@free.fr.
Reservations:
Made from Jan. with deposit and fee.

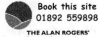

Book this site
01892 559898

THE ALAN ROGERS' travel service

see colour advert between pages 64/65

Directions: Site is northeast of St Gilles, on the D754 past Le Fenouiller towards the junction with D32.

8526 Village de La Guyonnière, St Julien-des-Landes

Spacious, rural site, away from the hectic coast - unsophisticated except for smart pool.

La Guyonnière is a popular site for many reasons, the main ones being the free and easy atmosphere and its reasonable pricing. Dutch owned, the majority of its customers are Dutch, but English is spoken and British visitors are made very welcome. It is a farm type site with four different fields, each being reasonably level and each having a toilet block. The 181 pitches are sunny and very large (the few smaller ones are cheaper) and are separated by a tree and a few bushes. All have access to electricity (6A) although long leads may be required. The toilet blocks are modern, functional and central for each area. Most of the cubicles are quite small but they serve their purpose and were very clean when we visited; however, the number may be inadequate in high season. Hot water is free, washbasins are in cubicles, showers pre-set and the WCs are British style. There is provision for babies and disabled visitors, and dishwashing and laundry sinks at each block. A small shop (1/5-30/9) sells bread daily, or it can be ordered from reception outside these dates. The bar has TV, a pool table, plus tables outside. Off the bar is a pleasant restaurant (1/5-30/9). These are housed in the original farm buildings attractively converted. Entertainment is provided in the bar on high season evenings. A perfect place for families, there are large play areas on sand and grass, table tennis, a sand pit and paddling pond with shower, volleyball and football fields. The original swimming pool is small and very plain, but the new heated pool with jacuzzi and slide is very attractive and can be covered in cool weather. There is a paddling pool and sunbathing terrace. Being so far out in the country (although only 10 km. from the nearest beach), this is a haven for cyclists and walkers, with many signed routes (bicycle hire available). A pleasant 500 m. walk takes you to the Jaunay lake where fishing is possible (permits from the village), canoeing (lifejackets from reception) and pedaloes to hire. Riding 3 km, golf 8 km, beaches 10 km. A few mobile homes, bungalow tents and wooden chalets (two equipped for disabled visitors) are for rent, as well as stone chalets in a separate field. No tour operators and, needless to say, no road noise.

Charges 2001:
-- Per unit incl. 2 persons Ffr. 132.00; extra person 29.00; child (under 10 yrs) 18.00; electricity 18.00, animal 15.00; local tax (10 yrs and over) 2.20.
-- Less 10-20% outside high season.
-- Credit cards accepted.
Open:
1 April - 30 October.
Address:
85150 St Julien-des-Landes.
Tel:
(0)2.51.46.62.59.
FAX: (0)2.51.46.62.89.
E-mail: pierre.jaspers @wanadoo.fr.
Reservations:
Made with 25% deposit; contact site.

Book this site
01892 559898

THE ALAN ROGERS' travel service

see colour advert between pages 64/65

Directions: Site is off the D12 (La Mothe Achard - St Gilles Croix de Vie), 4 km. west of St Julien-des-Landes. It is signed about 1 km. from the main road.

VENDÉE CHARENTE - 85 Vendée

8532 Camping-Caravaning Val de Vie, Maché

Small new site in rural village back from the coast.

Opened in 1999, Val de Vie is a small, quality site run with enthusiasm and dedication by its English owners. There are currently 52 pitches for touring units (34 with electricity; 4, 6 or 10A) that vary in size from 80-137 sq.m. on mostly level grass with newly planted hedging. The ground can become very hard so steel pegs are advised. The pitches are arranged in circular fashion around the toilet block which provides excellent, modern facilities including pre-set hot showers, washbasins (some in cabins), a baby bath, facilities for disabled people, washing up and laundry sinks, washing machines and a chemical disposal point. All facilities have hot and cold water. Both the toilet block and reception are built in local style with attractive, red tiled roofs. Next to reception is a small play area for young children and a swimming pool (open from May). Bicycle hire is available. Across the road is a heated outdoor municipal pool and tennis courts. The site is within the village confines, so shops, bar, tabac, etc. are all within walking distance, with a good restaurant 2 km. away. The Lac d'Apremont is 300 m. walk with a 'Centre d'Loisirs' which has a café, picnic tables and canoe hire. The town of Apremont is just 4 km. with its Renaissance château. The owners, the McClearns, want you to experience real French village life and culture and encourage you to enjoy the local surroundings but, if you are looking for a beach, the Vendée coast are 25 km. away. Mobile homes to rent.

Directions: From D948 at Aizenay take D107 northwest to Maché (6 km). Site signed in the village.

Charges 2001:
-- Per unit incl. 2 persons Ffr. 76.00; extra person 20.00; child (under 10 yrs) 16.00; electricity 4A 15.00, 6A 18.00, 10A 20.00; dog 10.00; local tax (July/Aug) 1.10, child 0.55.
-- Less 25% in low season, excl. electricity.
-- No credit cards.
Open:
Easter - 30 September.
Address:
Rue du Stade,
85190 Maché.
Tel:
(0)2.51.60.21.02.
FAX: as phone.
E-mail:
campingvaldevie@
aol.com.
Reservations:
Contact site.

8519 Camping-Caravaning Le Marais Braud, St Hilaire de Riez

Unsophisticated site with swimming pool, near the sea.

Le Marais Braud occupies a peaceful wooded setting, slightly inland from the busy coastal areas of the Vendée, but only 7 km. from sandy beaches. There are 150 pitches, of which 109 are available for touring units. The spacious pitches are level, sandy with some grass, shaded and some divided by low hedges. Electricity is available within 30 m. of every pitch (although this may sometimes require that cables cross the road). There are two toilet blocks (one smaller and newer than the other), both providing mostly British style toilets, washbasins (some in cabins), pre-set hot showers, dishwashing and laundry sinks with hot water, chemical disposal and a washing machine. Facilities for disabled visitors are provided. The site has a small heated swimming pool with water slide and a children's pool (from 1/6; no bermuda style shorts), a tennis court, boules area and children's play areas. At the far end of the site is a small lake for fishing, which is also home to white and black swans, and geese. The friendly bar and crêperie (with takeaway) incorporates a games area with a skittle alley and there is a little shop for basics (all 1/7-31/8). Bicycle hire 6 km, riding 7 km. Chalets and mobile homes for rent. Caravan storage. No tour operators. Although the site is only open for a short season, the owners, M. & Mme Besseau, ensure that it provides a welcoming, family atmosphere, ideal for families or couples looking for a budget holiday.

Directions: From Le Pissot roundabout (north of St Hilaire de Riez), take D59 signed Le Perrier. Site is well signed about 3 km. along this road on the right.

Charges 2000:
-- Per unit incl. 2 persons Ffr. 70.00 - 90.00, with electricity (6A) 84.00 - 106.00, with water also 96.00 - 122.00; extra person 17.00 - 22.00; child (under 7 yrs) 11.00 - 14.00; dog 7.00 - 10.00; local tax July/Aug. (over 10 yrs) 1.90.
-- Credit cards accepted.
Open:
1 June - 15 September.
Address:
298 Route du Perrier,
85270 St Hilaire de Riez.
Tel:
(0)2.51.68.33.71.
FAX: (0)2.51.35.25.32.
Reservations:
Advised in high season and made with deposit (Ffr. 450) and fee (100).

90

8508 Hotel de Plein Air La Puerta del Sol, St Hilaire de Riez

Good quality site a short distance away from the busy coast.

La Puerta del Sol is a good quality campsite suitable not only for families with teenage children to entertain, but also for those seeking a more peaceful and relaxing holiday. There are 216 pitches, of which 158 are available for touring units. Pitches are level with dividing hedges and many receive shade from the mature trees on the site. Each pitch is fully serviced with water, waste water point and electricity. The three toilet blocks are of identical design with a mix of Turkish and British style WCs, washbasins in cabins and roomy adjustable showers, as well as baby baths, dishwashing and laundry sinks, a laundry with washing machines and irons and fully equipped rooms for disabled visitors. All sinks have hot and cold water, and everything is kept very clean and well maintained. The bar (15/5-15/9) and self-service restaurant and takeaway (1/7-31/8) provide reasonably priced food and the bar terrace overlooks the swimming and paddling pools (15/5-15/9; no bermuda style shorts). There is a small shop (1/7-31/8). In July/Aug. a range of activities is provided for adults and children, including a children's club, aqua aerobics, swimming lessons, tournaments and games, with evening entertainment in the bar. There is a children's play area on sand, tennis court, bicycle hire, volleyball, table tennis and video games. Riding, fishing and golf within 5 km. The nearest sandy beach is 5 km. and St Jean de Monts, 7 km. American motorhomes are accepted in limited numbers with reservation. Chalets (30), mobile homes (5) and caravans (3) for hire. There is one small French tour operator on site (20 pitches).

Directions: From Le Pissot (7 km. north of St Gilles Croix-de-Vie on D38) take the D59 towards Le Perrier. The site is 2 km. along this road on the right side down a short side road. There is a large sign for the site 200 m. before the turning and another sign on the left directly opposite the turning.

Charges 2001:
-- Per unit incl. up to 2 persons and services Ffr. 95.00 - 180.00, 3 persons 105.00 - 200.00; extra person 28.00 - 38.00; child (under 7) 14.00 - 19.00; extra tent 20.00 - 30.00; animal 10.00; local tax (July/Aug) 2.20.
-- Credit cards accepted.

Open:
1 May - 15 September.

Address:
Les Borderies, 85270 St Hilaire de Riez.

Tel:
(0)2.51.49.10.10.
FAX: (0)2.51.49.84.84.
E-mail: puerta-del-sol@wanadoo.fr.

Reservations:
Advised for high season and made for any period with deposit (Ffr. 900) and fee (200).

**Book this site
01892 559898**

THE ALAN ROGERS'
Travel service

*see colour advert
between pages 64/65*

8523 Camping Les Ecureuils, St Hilaire de Riez

Attractive site close to the beach with a friendly, family atmosphere.

Of the numerous sea-side sites on the Vendée, Les Ecureuils has to be one of the best, run by a friendly and most helpful family whose aim is for everyone to be 'très content'. Set just 300 m. from a superb beach, the site is ideally situated for exploring from Les Sables d'Olonne to Noirmoutier. Developed on what was originally the family farm, there are 230 pitches (79 for touring units) of sandy grass, all with electricity (6A), water and drainage. The well kept hedges and mature trees give shade and privacy, although for sun lovers some more open pitches are also available. The two main sanitary blocks are spacious, modern and tiled, with adjustable hot showers, washbasins in cubicles, British style toilets and facilities for babies and disabled people. Laundry and dishwashing sinks are provided with hot water. A separate building near the front of the site houses washing machines, a tumble dryer, iron and board. Chemical disposal facilities. The large, airy bar with a screened terrace is adjacent to the swimming pool complex which includes a pool for small children with its own 'mini aqua park', a large heated swimming pool and an adult-sized water slide with separate splash pool. The surrounding paved sunbathing area has chairs and loungers. In addition to these facilities, a brand new indoor pool, paddling pool and jacuzzi are planned for 2001. Everything on Les Ecureuils is spotless and well maintained with an abundance of flowers and shrubs planted throughout the site giving a very attractive appearance. Adjacent to the front gate are a small shop (25/5-6/9) and a restaurant (all season), but there are supermarkets, bars and restaurants all within 500 m. Bicycle hire 200 m, fishing 4 km, riding 5 km, golf 6 km. Popular with British tour operators (60%). Mobile homes and two apartments for hire.

Directions: Driving south on D38 St Jean-de-Monts - St Gilles road, turn right at L'Oasis hotel/restaurant in Orouet (6 km. outside St Jean de Monts), signed Les Mouettes. After 1.5 km. at roundabout turn left signed St Hilaire de Riez and site is 500 m. on the left.

Charges 2000:
-- Per unit incl. 2 persons and 3 services Ffr. 118.00 - 162.00; extra person 22.00 - 28.00; child (under 5 yrs) 12.00 - 17.00; dog 11.00 - 16.00; local tax 2.40 (July/Aug, under 10 yrs).
-- No credit cards.

Open:
15 May - 15 September.

Address:
100 Avenue de la Pège, 85270 St Hilaire de Riez.

Tel:
(0)2.51.54.33.71.
FAX: (0)2.51.55.69.08.
E-mail: info@camping-aux-ecureuils.com.

Reservations:
Advised for July/Aug; contact site.

VENDÉE CHARENTE - 85 Vendée

8516 Camping-Caravaning Sol a Gogo, St Hilaire de Riez

Popular site with direct access to the beach and an attractive pool complex.

Situated right beside the sea, Sol a Gogo has 196 level, sandy pitches, of which 78 are available for touring units. Each pitch has electricity, water and drainage, and the pitches are clearly marked by bushes. These are growing slowly and do not provide a great deal of shade or privacy so the site is rather open, although reed type fencing has been used effectively in some areas. The two toilet blocks are clean and well designed, with free hot water throughout, adjustable showers with taps in one block, pre-set pushbuttons in the other and British style toilets throughout. Washbasins are in cabins, with laundry and dishwashing facilities on the outside of each block (but covered) and washing machines and dryers are provided. Although there is a private path from the campsite to the sandy beach (guarded in high season), the well designed pool complex is also very popular. Both the main pool, with central water fountain, and smaller children's pool are heated, there is a water slide and areas around the pool for sunbathing (free loungers provided). A covered pool, new slide and a jacuzzi have been added recently. The bar and restaurant (1/6-10/9) has a terrace which overlooks the pool area, and provides good quality food at reasonable prices and takeaway meals. Other facilities on site include tennis (one full, one half court), table tennis, pétanque and a play area for children. A small supermarket is 200 m. along the main road. Bicycle hire 200 m, riding 3 km, golf 6 km. Very popular with tour operators (around 50% of the pitches).

Charges 2000:
-- Per pitch with all facilities, 3 persons and car Ffr. 190.00; extra person 30.00; child (under 5) 20.00; extra car 8.00; dog 8.00; local tax (over 10 yrs) 2.40.
-- Less 20% outside July/Aug.
-- No credit cards.

Open:
15 May - 15 September.

Address:
61 Avenue de la Pège, 85270 St Hilaire-de-Riez.

Tel:
(0)2.51.54.29.00.
FAX: (0)2.51.54.88.74.
E-mail: arondeau@free.fr.

Reservations:
Possible except in high season.

Directions: Driving south on D38 St Jean de Monts - St Gilles road, turn right at L'Oasis hotel/restaurant in Orouet (6 km. outside St Jean de Monts), signposted to Les Mouettes. After 1.5 km. you come to a roundabout. Turn left here signed to St Hilaire de Riez and site is 1.5 km.

8517 Camping Caravaning Le Bois Tordu, St Hilaire-de-Riez

Small but friendly site, only 300 m. from the beach.

Set in a popular holiday area, with a full range of amenities close to hand, Le Bois Tordu is a small but busy site, well suited for motorcaravanners and motorcyclists. The site itself has 110 pitches, of which 47 are available for touring caravans and tents. Pitches are grassy and sandy, and most have some shade, although there are 20 newer pitches near the front of the site which are as yet unshaded. All pitches have electricity (6A), water and drainage, and are divided by low hedging. The sanitary block is situated near the front of the site, and provides unisex facilities. Showers are adjustable with push-buttons, and the cubicles are spacious. Washbasins are both open plan and in cubicles, and toilets are all British style. Facilities for disabled visitors and a baby bath are also available. Dishwashing and laundry sinks are within the block, and all installations have both hot and cold water. A washing machine, tumble dryer and ironing board are provided. A children's play area has slides, a roundabout and see-saws and there is a covered ping pong table. Although it is close to a large and inviting beach, the site also has its own swimming pool, paddling pool and splash pool for the water slide, with free loungers and chairs. At the front entrance of the site there is a `Relais Marche' supermarket, bar, snack bar, bakery , newsagents, currency exchange and bicycle hire. These provide a full range of facilities without the need to leave the site, and are open all season. Mobile homes to let. The site is under the same ownership as Sol a Gogo (above).

Charges 2000:
-- Per pitch incl. 3 persons, water, electricity and drainage Ffr. 173.00; extra person over 5 yrs 29.00; extra child under 5 yrs 18.00; extra car 8.00; dog 8.00; local tax (over 10 yrs, July/Aug. only) 2.40.
-- Less 20% in May, June and Sept.
-- No credit cards.

Open:
1 April - 15 October.

Address:
Route de La Pège, 85270, St Hilaire de Riez.

Tel:
(0)2.51.54.33.78.
FAX: (0)2.51.54.08.29.

Reservations:
Not accepted in high season.

Directions: Driving south on D38 St Jean de Monts - St Gilles road, turn right at L'Oasis hotel/restaurant in Orouet (6 km. outside St Jean de Monts), signposted to Les Mouettes. After 1.5 km. you come to a roundabout. Turn left here signed to St Hilaire de Riez and site is 1.5 km. on the left.

8522 Camping Acapulco, St Jean de Monts

Friendly site, ideal for family holidays.

Situated mid-way between St Jean de Monts and St Hilaire de Riez, and 600 m. from the beach, Acapulco is ideal for family holidays. The site currently has 410 pitches (40 for touring units), but an extension of a further 130 pitches (of which 80 will be for tourers) is proposed for 2001. These new pitches will be larger than average (around 130 sq.m). All pitches have water and electricity, but few have any shade. The three main sanitary blocks boast clean, modern facilities with British style toilets, washbasins in cabins, showers, baby baths and facilities for disabled visitors. There are laundry and dishwashing sinks, washing machines in each block and motorcaravan services. In the centre of the site are a large bar, snack bar, games room and well stocked shop (all season) overlook the interestingly shaped, heated pool with slide and paddling pool. An indoor pool and a sports pitch are planned for 2001. Lively entertainment and activities for all ages in high season. Shops, bars and restaurants are within 1 km. Golf 10 km, bicycle hire 200 m, riding 2 km. Popular with tour operators (50%). Mobile homes to let.

Directions: Driving south on D38 St Jean de Monts - St Gilles road, turn right at L'Oasis bar/restaurant in Orouet, signed Les Mouettes. Site is on left after 1 km.

Charges 2000:
-- Per unit incl. 3 persons and electricity Ffr. 168.00; extra person (over 5 yrs) 30.00; child (under 5 yrs) 16.00; local tax (July/Aug) 2.20.
-- Low season less 20%.
-- Credit cards accepted.

Open:
15 May - 15 September.

Address:
Avenue des Epines, 85160 St Jean de Monts.

Tel:
(0)2.51.59.20.64.
FAX: (0)2.51.59.53.12.

Reservations:
Necessary in July/Aug.

8507 Camping Les Biches, St Hilaire de Riez, nr St Gilles-Croix

Popular, quality site in a pinewood with swimming pools, 4 km. from the sea.

Les Biches is covered by a pinewood, so nearly everywhere has shade. There are almost 400 pitches, with around 90 for touring units. They are large and spacious, mostly hedged and on fairly sandy ground. All pitches have electricity, water and drainage. The majority of the pitches for tents and caravans are in the far area behind the tennis courts, although a few are scattered through the rest of the site. The four sanitary blocks are clean and well maintained, with very spacious cubicles for the pre-set showers. Toilets are British style, washbasins (H&C) are either in rows or in cabins with a bidet alongside. All blocks have laundry and dishwashing facilities with hot water. Washing machines and dryers are provided, and facilities for disabled visitors. There is a very attractive pool complex near the site entrance, comprising two heated swimming pools (unsupervised), a children's pool, water slide, jacuzzi and an indoor pool for cooler days. Other amenities include a large bar (all season), restaurant and crèperie (1/6-9/9) with a terrace overlooking the pools, a takeaway (20/5-16/9) and shop (all season) with ice service. Activities include tennis, volleyball, table tennis, a games room, a disco, large adventure type children's playground, minigolf, bicycle hire and a TV room with satellite TV. An internet terminal is in reception. Various activities, such as boules tournaments and sporting events are organised by the site during high season. A private fishing lake is 2.5 km, riding 4.5 km. and golf 6 km. The site is very popular with British tour operators (65%), so tends to be busy and active all season. Mobile homes and studios to let.

Directions: Site is about 2 km. north of St Hilaire, close to and well signed from the main D38 road.

Charges 2001:
-- Per pitch incl. 3 persons and car Ffr. 195.00, with electricity (10A) 220.00; extra person 40.00; child (under 7) 20.00; extra car or dog 10.00; local tax (over 10 yrs, July/Aug) 2.40.
-- Less 30% May, June and Sept.
-- No credit cards

Open:
15 May - 15 September.

Address:
85270 St Hilaire-de-Riez.

Tel:
(0)2.51.54.38.82.
FAX: (0)2.51.54.30.74.
E-mail:
campingdesbiches
@wanadoo.fr.

Reservations:
Required for high season and made with deposit (Ffr. 400) and fee (100).

VENDÉE CHARENTE - 85 Vendée

8535 Camping-Caravaning La Ningle, St Hilaire de Riez

Well established, family run campsite in a popular tourist area.

Camping La Ningle is well situated to explore the beautiful port of St Gilles Croix de Vie, with its abundance of restaurants and pedestrianised shopping area with a variety of individual boutiques. You will receive a warm welcome from M. & Mme. Guibert, who have created a very pleasant campsite with a friendly, family atmosphere. There are 150 pitches, of which 85 are for touring units. All pitches have electricity (6A) and a limited number are fully serviced (electricity, water and drainage). Pitches are spacious, with dividing hedges and all have some shade. Two regularly cleaned sanitary blocks provide British style WCs, washbasins (some in cubicles), pre-set showers, laundry and dishwashing facilities. All facilities have hot and cold water. The main block has a well equipped toilet/shower room for disabled people and a large family shower room. Washing machines and a dryer are provided. The nearest beach is a 500 m. walk through a pine forest, but there are also three small swimming pools on site - a paddling pool for toddlers, a larger children's pool and a main pool. Sun loungers are provided around the pool area. The bar has a small terrace overlooking the pools and, in high season, has entertainment twice a week. Children's activities are offered four mornings each week in July/August, and petanque and tennis competitions are arranged. Although there is no restaurant on site, takeaway dishes are available three evenings per week. At the far end of the site is a small lake that can be used for fishing (free), a tennis court and a games field with a volleyball net and table tennis table. A games room is near reception, along with a small fitness suite with a range of equipment (no instructor, but free). Bread and croissants are available on site each morning, with a small supermarket and takeaway only 200 m. from the site. Mobile homes for rent.

Charges 2000:
-- Per pitch incl. 3 persons Ffr. 90.00 - 117.00, with electricity (6A) 105.00 - 132.00; supplement for 10A electricity 7.00; extra person 19.00 - 22.00; child (under 7 yrs) 10.00 - 13.00; dog 12.00; extra car 12.00; local tax (over 10 yrs, July/Aug) 2.20.
-- Credit cards accepted.

Open:
15 May - 15 September.

Address:
Chemin des Roselières, 85270 St Hilaire de Riez.

Tel:
(0)2.51.54.07.11. FAX: (0)2.51.54.99.39.

Reservations:
Made with deposit (Ffr. 400) and fee (100).

Directions: Driving south on D38 St Jean de Monts - St Gilles road, turn right at L'Oasis hotel/restaurant in Orouet (6 km. outside St Jean de Monts), signed Les Mouettes. After 1.5 km. you come to a roundabout. Turn left here signed St Hilaire de Riez. After passing two campsites (Bois Tordu and Les Ecureuils) take next left turn, signed La Ningle. Site is approx. 150 m. on the left.

8536 Camping La Forêt, St Jean de Monts

Small, well run and attractive site with a friendly, family atmosphere.

Camping La Forêt has recently been taken over by M. and Mme. Jolivet, who work hard to provide a small, quality site. There are 65 pitches in total, with 45 available for touring units. Pitches of 100 sq.m. are surrounded by mature hedges and have water and electricity. Over 50 species of trees are planted on the site, providing shade to every pitch, and the Jolivets have provided an information panel by the reception to help you identify the various types. There is one sanitary block in the centre of the site, which is kept scrupulously clean, with hot showers, washbasins in cubicles, laundry and dishwashing sinks, a baby bath and British style toilets. All sinks have both hot and cold water. A washing machine is available, and although clothes lines are prohibited, the owner will lend you free-standing clothes airers for drying. Facilities for disabled people are also available. There is a chemical disposal point outside the block, and facilities for emptying motorcaravan waste tanks upon request. Individual charcoal barbecues are not permitted, but a communal barbecue area is provided in the centre of the site. The swimming pool is small but inviting, with a sun terrace (free loungers provided), and is open from the end of May until September. There is a children's play area and table tennis table, and bicycles can be hired. A range of basic provisions are sold in season, including fresh bread each morning, and the takeaway offers good food at excellent prices all season. The local beach is only 400 m. away, along a forest path, and a network of cycle paths runs through the forest and local marshland. Although there is one tour operator on the site (16 pitches), their presence is in no way intrusive, and the site has a quiet and relaxed atmosphere, ideal for couples or families with young children.

Charges 2000:
- Per pitch including 2 persons Ffr. 100.00 - 130.00; electricity (6A) 20.00; extra person 20.00 - 25.00; extra child (under 7) 15.00; extra car 10.00; dog 10.00.

Open:
15 April - 30 September.

Address:
190 Chemin de La Rive, 85160 St Jean de Monts.

Tel:
(0)2.51.58.84.63. FAX: (0)2.51.58.84.63.

Reservations:
Advised, particularly for high season and made with Ffr. 200 deposit; min. 15 nights 2/7-19/8.

Directions: Site is 5.5 km. from town centre, just off the D38. Follow D38 out of St Jean de Monts, towards Notre Dame de Monts. After 4.5 km. go straight over roundabout, and in 1 km. turn left at sign for site and 'Plage de Pont d'Yeu'. Follow road as it almost doubles back on itself. Site is on left in about 100 m.

8533N Camping Naturiste Cap Natur, St Hilaire-de-Riez

Very welcoming campsite for naturists, on the Vendée coast.

Situated on the northern outskirts of the busy resort of St Hilaire-de-Riez, and only about 1 km. from the nearest beach (6 km. from the nearest naturist beach beside the Plage des 60 Bornes) this is a recently created campsite in an area of undulating sand dunes and pine trees. The 120 touring pitches nestle among the dunes and trees and offer a wide choice to suit most tastes, including the possibility of electrical connections (4/10A), although in some cases long leads are needed. Despite the undulating terrain, some pitches are quite level and thus suitable for motorcaravans, and some are newly hedged for those preferring a degree of privacy. The modern facilities are excellent and include both open air and indoor pools, and a jacuzzi. Around the pool is an ample paved sunbathing area with free sun-loungers. Adjacent to the pool area is a good sized bar, with TV, comfortable, light and airy restaurant, with a reasonably extensive menu (including some local specialities), a pool table and various indoor table games (not of the irritating electronic variety!) There is a volleyball court and archery, plus a children's play area on soft sand. In season a regular Saturday evening 'soirée' is held with a set Vendéen meal, wine and entertainment. The sanitary facilities are basic but clean, consisting of one indoor and one outdoor (but roofed) block. Both blocks have open plan hot showers, British style WCs, washbasins and dishwashing sinks. In addition the indoor block has showers in cubicles, laundry sinks, baby baths and children's toilets. All sinks and basins have both hot and cold water. There is an air of peace and quiet about this site which contrasts with the somewhat frenzied activity which pervades many of the resorts in this popular tourist area of the Vendée, with a friendly and warm welcome from the family that run it. Apartments, tents and mobile homes for rent.

Directions: Site is on north side of St Hilaire-de-Riez. From Le Pissot roundabout go south on D38, follow signs for St Hilaire at first roundabout you come to (first exit off roundabout), then at second roundabout (more oblong than round!) turn right signed 'Terre Fort'. At third Y-shaped junction turn right again signed 'Parée Prèneau'. The site is about 2 km. along this road on the left.

Charges 2000:
-- Per unit incl. 2 adults Ffr. 82.00 - 137.00; extra person 15.00 - 31.00; child (under 8 yrs) 10.00 - 20.00; extra vehicle 7.00 - 17.00; animal 10.00 - 17.00; electricity (10A) 28.00; plus local tax.

Open:
1 April - 31 October.

Address:
151 Avenue de la Faye, 85270 St Hilaire-de-Riez.

Tel:
(0)2.51.60.11.66.
FAX: (0)2.51.60.17.48.
E-mail: info@ cap-natur.com.

Reservations:
Made with 25% deposit and Ffr. 180 booking fee; contact site for details.

**Book this site
01892 559898**
THE ALAN ROGERS'
travel service

8515 Camping La Yole, Orouet, St Jean de Monts

Attractive, popular, well run site, 1 km. from sandy beach.

La Yole offers 278 pitches, the majority under trees with ample shade and separated by bushes and the trees. All have electricity (6A), water and drainage and are of 100 sq.m. or more. Two of the sanitary blocks are of an older design but one has been refurbished and they are tiled, with British style WCs. There is free hot water to pre-set showers, washbasins in cabins, units for disabled people and new baby baths, all kept very clean. The third block is in the newer part of the site and is very modern. It includes a hair care room and a baby room. There is also a laundry with washing machine, dryer and iron, and chemical disposal. The swimming pool is also quite new with a water slide, large pool, paddling pool, plus an indoor heated pool with jacuzzi. They are surrounded by a paved sunbathing area and overlooked by the new bar (all season) and restaurant (from 15/5) with a large terrace. There is also a takeaway and a well stocked shop. Children have exceptional space with a play area on sand, a large field for ball games and picnics and a club room. Tennis, table tennis, pool and video games plus organised entertainment in high season. A pleasant walk through pine woods then by road leads to two sandy beaches. Fishing, golf and watersports are 6 km. at St Jean. The security barrier is closed at night. No dogs are accepted. Only gas barbecues are permitted. Used by tour operators (45%). A Sites et Paysages member. This a friendly, popular site with welcoming owners.

Directions: Signed off the D38, 6 km. south of St Jean de Monts in the village of Orouet.

see colour advert between pages 160/161

Charges 2000:
-- Per tent incl. 2 persons, electricity and water Ffr 90.00 - 135.00, or for caravan incl. drainage also 98.00 - 148.00; extra person 23.00 - 30.00; extra child (under 5) 13.00 - 19.00; local tax 2.20 (July/Aug. over 10 yrs).
-- Credit cards accepted.

Open:
1 May - 15 September.

Address:
Chemin des Bosses, Orouet, 85160 St Jean de Monts.

Tel:
(0)2.51.58.67.17.
FAX: (0)2.51.59.05.35.
E-mail: camping-layole @wanadoo.fr.

Reservations:
Advised, particularly for July/Aug.

`Camping Cheque'

**Book this site
01892 559898**
THE ALAN ROGERS'
travel service

VENDÉE CHARENTE - 85 Vendée

8509 Camping L'Abri des Pins, St Jean-de-Monts, nr Challans

Family run, well equipped site with pool on outskirts of popular resort.

L'Abri des Pins is situated on the outskirts of the pleasant, modern resort of St Jean-de-Monts and is separated from the sea and long sandy beach by a strip of pinewood. From the back entrance of the site it is a pleasant 10 minute walk to the beach. Bathing is said to be safer here than on most of the beaches on this coast, but is nevertheless supervised in July/August. The site has 216 pitches, of which 30 are 'luxury' pitches - larger than average, with electricity, water and drainage. Electricity is also available to the other pitches which are around 100 sq.m, fully marked out with dividing hedges and quite shady. Many of the pitches are occupied by privately owned mobile homes, but there are no tour operators on the site. The two sanitary blocks have been modernised and provide mainly British style toilets, washbasins in cabins, laundry and dishwashing sinks and free, fully controllable showers, plus chemical disposal. There are two heated swimming pools and a water slide, plus a small pool for children, with a paved sunbathing area where loungers are supplied free of charge (1/6-15/9; no bermuda style shorts). A new pool complex is planned for 2001. The bar/restaurant on the far side of the site provides good quality, value for money meals, both to eat in and take away, and next to the bar is a good small shop (all 1/7-31/8). In high season there is a daily children's club, as well as a range of free activities for adults (football, petanque, aqua aerobics). Throughout the season visitors may use the facilities at Les Places Dorées (under the same family ownership) across the road. Mobile homes and chalets for hire.

Directions: Site is 4 km. from the town centre on St Jean-de-Monts - Notre Dame-de Monts/Noirmoutiers road (D38), on left heading north, just after Camping les Amiaux.

Charges 2000:
-- Per unit incl. 3 persons and electricity Ffr. 116.00 - 167.00, with electricity, water and drain 121.00 - 172.00; extra adult 18.00 - 26.00; child (under 5) 11.00 - 16.00; pet free - 16.00; local tax (over 10 yrs, July/Aug) 2.20.
-- Deposit required (Ffr. 20 p/person) for armband for access to pool and site (high season only).
-- Credit cards accepted.

Open:
1 June - 17 September.

Address:
Rte. de Notre Dame de Monts,
85160 St Jean-de-Monts.

Tel:
(0)2.51.58.83.86 (winter: (0)2.40.73.09.70).
FAX: (0)2.51.59.30.47.

Reservations:
Advised for high season; min. stay 12 nights between 14/7-15/8. Contact site for details.

Book this site
01892 559898
THE ALAN ROGERS' travel service

8528 Camping Les Places Dorées, St Jean de Monts

Modern site with good pool complex.

Although there are many top quality sites in this area, many are dominated by British tour operators and it is always refreshing to find one which is not. Les Places Dorées is owned by the same family as L'Abri des Pins (8509) which is just across the road. It is a much newer site, but maturing trees are gradually beginning to offer some shade. The site has excellent facilities, notably a new (2000) swimming pool complex, complete with water slides, jacuzzi area and a waterfall (no bermuda style shorts), and free sun-loungers are provided around the pool area. One of the main reasons for visiting the Vendée is for its beaches and the closest beach to Les Places Dorées is a pleasant ten minute walk away (through L'Abri des Pins and then alongside the pine forest and sand dunes). The site's 245 pitches are large and grassy, the quietest being towards the back of the site, and each is separated. All have electrical connections (6A) and some are also equipped with water and drainage. The three toilet blocks are modern and kept very clean, providing British style toilets, washbasins in cubicles and powerful showers, as well as facilities for disabled visitors. Each block has laundry and dishwashing sinks with hot water, and chemical disposal points, with washing machines and dryers available on site. In high season the site becomes quite lively with plenty of organised entertainment, most based around the bar/restaurant area. In July/August a daily children's club is available at L'Abri des Pins, as well as organised activities for adults (football, petanque tournaments, aqua aerobics, etc). Throughout the season, campers are able to use the facilities at L'Abri des Pins, which include a tennis court, fitness room, a well stocked shop, swimming pools and a games room. There is one small British tour operator on site (15 pitches).

Directions: Site is 4 km. north of St Jean de Monts on D38 St Jean de Monts - Notre Dames de Monts road on right hand side, almost opposite L'Abri des Pins.

Charges 2000:
-- Per pitch incl. 3 persons and electricity Ffr. 162.00; extra person 26.00; child 16.00; local tax (over 10 yrs) 2.20.
-- Less in low season.
-- Deposit required (Ffr. 20 p/person) for armband for access to pool and site (high season only).

Open:
16 June - 10 September.

Address:
Route de Notre Dame de Monts,
85160 St Jean de Monts.

Tel:
(0)2.51.59.02.93 (winter: (0)2.51.58.83.86).
FAX: (0)2.51.59.30.47.

Reservations:
Advised for high season; min. stay 12 nights between 14/7-15/8. Contact site for details.

Book this site
01892 559898
THE ALAN ROGERS' travel service

Book your camping accommodation

ON INTERNET

www.mistercamp.com

Weekends and holidays

choose between :

More than 5 000 offers

of mobile homes, chalets or bungalows in ★★★ and ★★★★ campsites

More than 100 destinations

in France and Europe

Take also advantage

of our weekend getaways, special deals and last minute offers...

On line booking

we guarantee
- a constant update of our offers
- 100 % secure payment.

www.
mistercamp.com

Book your camping accommodation on line

MISTERCAMP S.A. - Travel agency licence nr LI 04400 00062, rue Robert Schuman - 44400 REZÉ FRANCE

VENDÉE CHARENTE - 85 Vendée

8510 Le Bois Dormant, St Jean-de-Monts

Haven Europe owned family holiday park with good facilities near popular resort.

Le Bois Dormant is on the outskirts of the pleasant, modern resort of St Jean de Monts, 3 km. from the beach. The site has 565 pitches, most of which are occupied by tour operators or privately owned mobile homes, with 30-odd pitches available throughout the site for touring units. Pitches are sandy, separated by hedges and all with electricity and water. The bar/restaurant, which also serves takeaway snacks, has a terrace overlooking the pool complex which has a large (200 sq.m.) swimming pool, paddling pool and water slides (no bermuda style shorts). There is a games room here, plus minigolf, table tennis and a multi-sport sports pitch with track. Tennis courts are near the entrance. The four sanitary blocks are well designed and offer good facilities including showers, washbasins in cabins, British style WCs, baby baths and toilets, facilities for disabled people, as well as sinks for laundry and dishwashing, washing machines and dryers. All facilities have free hot water. Only gas barbecues are permitted. There is a small shop at the entrance to the site, but campers may also use the restaurant, entertainment facilities, indoor pool and supermarket at the larger, busier sister site Le Bois Masson, which is 100 m. across the road and also owned by Haven. The site can be expected to be very busy for most of the season, with many organised activities for children of all ages. Mobile homes, apartments and chalets for rent.

Directions: Site is well signed from roundabout at southeast end of the St Jean de Monts bypass (CD38). Follow signs off the roundabout to 'centre ville' and site is about 500 m. on the left.

Charges 2001:
-- Per pitch incl. up to 2 persons and electricity Ffr. 70.00 - 209.00; extra person 15.00 - 300.00; extra vehicle 10.00 - 20.00.
-- Credit cards accepted.

Open:
7 April - 14September (campers may use the facilities at Le Bois Masson until 28 April when all facilities a Le Bois Dormant open).

Address:
Rue des Sables, 85160 St Jean-de-Monts.

Tel:
(0)2.51.58.01.30.
FAX: (0)2.51.59.35.30.

Reservations:
Accepted at any time for min. 4 days; no booking fee. Contact site or Haven Europe in the UK on 0870 242 7777 for information or reservation quoting FAR01.

see colour advert opposite page 256

8530 Camping La Grand' Métairie, St Hilaire la Forêt

Busy, well run site in small village in popular holiday area.

Just 5 km. from the super sandy beach at Jard sur Mer, La Grand' Métairie offers many of the amenities of its seaside counterparts, but with the important advantage of being on the edge of a delightful, sleepy village, otherwise untouched by tourism. The central leisure area has an attractive, kidney-shaped heated pool with a jacuzzi and paddling pool to one side, and a large sunbathing terrace. The pool is overlooked by the smart bar/restaurant (all 15/5-15/9) which is the focal point for the site's lively entertainment programme in high season. A new covered pool is planned for 2001. The site has 172 pitches (72 for touring units), all with electricity (6A), water and drainage. The pitches as yet have little shade but are all separated by small trees and bushes and are generous in size. The two toilet blocks are modern and kept very clean, with British style toilets, washbasins mainly in private cabins and adjustable hot showers. There are washing machines and dryers, chemical disposal points and units for disabled people. Fridges may be hired. Basic provisions are available on site, with a useful village store just 100 m. from the gate. In high season, a regular free minibus service runs to the beach and to a number of local markets. Other amenities include tennis, minigolf (both free in low season) and a visiting hairdressing salon! Riding and fishing within 5 km. Mobile homes and chalets to rent.

Directions: Site is in centre of St Hilaire la Forêt. From Les Sables d'Olonne take D949 (La Rochelle) towards Talmont St Hilaire and Luçon. 7 km. after Talmont turn right on D70 to St Hilaire la Forêt. Site is on the left before village centre.

Charges 2000:
-- Per unit incl. 2 persons and electricity (6A) Ffr. 85.00 - 120.00; extra person 22.00 - 30.00; child (under 5 yrs) 14.00 - 20.00; dog 15.00.
-- Credit cards accepted.

Open:
1 April - 30 September.

Address:
8 rue de la Vineuse en Plaine, 85440 St Hilaire la Forêt.

Tel:
(0)2.51.33.32.38.
FAX: (0)2.51.33.25.69.
E-mail: grandmetairie @wanadoo.fr.

Reservations:
Advised for high season with 25% deposit and fee (Ffr. 120).

Book this site
01892 559898

THE ALAN ROGERS'
travel service

VENDÉE CHARENTE - 85 Vendée

8534M Camping du Bois du Bouquet, Moutiers Les Mauxfaits

This is a fairly traditional municipal site with none of the bells and whistles of its coastal counterparts. It offers excellent value with its attractive, well maintained camping area, high quality toilet block and friendly ambience - you are quite likely to meet the Mayor who takes a personal interest in the site. Just a short walk from the centre of the pleasant little market town of Moutiers les Mauxfaits, the site has 70 large, marked pitches, most with electricity (6A), in a mixture of sunny and shady locations. There is also an open area without electricity. Built on the town's former football field, the old toilet block used to be the changing rooms. The men's half is unaltered, but the ladies' has been refitted (the men are to be similarly treated for 2001!) The new block is first-class, with large washing and shower cubicles, British style toilets and excellent facilities for disabled visitors. There are plenty of sinks for dishwashing and laundry and a washing machine. The site has a barrier to control the arrival and departure of over-height vehicles (caravans, motorcaravans, etc.) operated by the warden. After his departure at 8 pm, any such vehicle would be unable to drive on to or off the site. Shops and restaurants are in the town and the nearest beaches are a 20 minute drive away.

Charges 2000:
-- Per pitch incl. 2 adults Ffr. 43.00; extra person 12.00; child (under 7 yrs) 5.00; electricity 10.00; extra vehicle 8.00.

Open:
15 June - 1 September.

Address:
85540 Moutiers les Mauxfaits.

Tel:
(0)2.51.98.96.41 or (0)2.51.98.91.39 (Mairie).

Reservations:
Unlikely to be necessary.

Directions: Site is on D747 (La Roche sur Yonne - La Tranche sur Mer), just south of Moutiers, and is well signed.

8520M Camping Municipal La Petite Boulogne, St Etienne-du-Bois

Set in countryside 24 km. northwest of La Roche sur Yonne, St Etienne is a quiet village, well away from the bustle of the big Vendée resorts. The campsite has 35 grassy pitches (slightly sloping), all with electricity (6A), water and drainage. Pitches are marked by low hedging giving the site an open and sunny aspect. The modern, heated sanitary block has free pre-set showers, washbasins (some in cabins) British style WCs, laundry and dishwashing sinks, a room for disabled people with toilet and shower and a washing machine and dryer. A small unheated pool is open June - Aug. with an open-air, heated pool nearby. Other facilities on site include a TV room, table tennis, a small children's play area, two free tennis courts and bicycle hire. The reception sells bread and a few other essentials, with a supermarket 8 km at Legé. A bar and restaurant are a few minutes walk away in St Etienne village. Fishing is possible in the nearby river and volleyball and petanque at the local sports centre (300 m). Daily events in the area are listed in reception and occasional animation in high season introduces the region and its produce. It is only 20 km. to the coast, but there are many places to visit inland. This good value municipal provides a great base from which to explore the region.

Charges 2000:
-- Per unit incl. 2 persons Ffr. 60.00; extra person 10.00; child (under 7 yrs) 5.00; dog 5.00; electricity (6A) 10.00.
-- No credit cards.

Open:
1 May - 31 October.

Address:
12 Rue du Stade. 85670 St Etienne-du-Bois.

Tel:
(0)2.51.34.54.51.
Low season: Mairie: (0)2.51.34.52.11.
FAX: (0)2.51.34.54.10.

Reservations:
Made with deposit.

Directions: From Legé take D978 south towards Palluau for 7 km. then left on D94 towards St Etienne-du-Bois. Go straight through village and, as you come out the other side, cross a small bridge over the river. Site is 50 m. further on.

Book this site
01892 559898

THE ALAN ROGERS'
travel service

N8514 Camping Naturiste Le Colombier, St Martin-Lars

Countryside site in 125 acres in a valley for naturists, near La Roche sur Yon.
Almost akin to 'Camping a la Ferme', but with the benefit of good facilities, this site provides around 160 pitches in seven very natural fields linked by informal grass tracks. There are level, terraced areas for caravans and a lovely feeling of spaciousness with unmarked pitches around the edges of fields, with electricity (up to 16A) at various strategic points. A bar/restaurant (order before 10 am), home baked bread and pizzas, is in an old, attractive converted barn, where there is also local tourist information, table tennis, etc. A grocer/baker calls daily (shop 1 km.). There is fishing, bicycle hire, volleyball and boules, and a playground. A new swimming pool, added for 2000, is overlooked by a café area. In high season there are pony and trap rides and weekly, children can make their own bread. The site's 125 acres provide many walks in the wooded valley and around the lake. The sanitary facilities in modern blocks are good, with hot showers in cubicles, British style WCs, dishwashing and chemical disposal. Volunteers help out around the site and there is lots going on for children (ghost tours in the woods, sledging down the artificial ski slope, etc). Motorcaravan services. Caravan storage. Mobile homes and chalet tents to rent. Naturist licences required.

Charges 2000:
-- Per person Ffr. 40.00; child 4-9 yrs 18.00, 10-16 yrs 25.00; electricity 15.00.
-- No pitch fee.
-- Credit cards accepted.

Open:
1 April - 30 October.

Address:
Le Colombier - Centre de Vacances Naturiste, 85210 St. Martin-Lars en Ste Hermine.

Tel:
(0)2.51.27.83.84.
FAX: (0)2.51.27.87.29.
E-mail:
lecolombier-nat@free.fr.

Reservations:
Not considered necessary.

Directions: From N148, La Roche sur Yon - Niort road, at St Hermine, turn on D8 east for 4 km. Turn left on D10 to St Martin-Lars where there are signs to site.

LOIRE VALLEY

We have taken the liberty of enlarging the official Loire Valley region to make a more easily identifiable tourist region which the British understand. The area includes all the Loire Valley.

LOIRE VALLEY	WESTERN LOIRE	POITOU-CHARENTES
Major cities: Orleans, Tours	From this offical region we include the following départements:	From this offical region we include the following départements:
Departements: 18 Cher, 28 Eure-et-Loir, 36 Indre, 37 Indre-et-Loire, 41 Loir-et-Cher, 45 Loiret	49 Maine-et-Loire, 53 Mayenne, 72 Sarthe	79 Deux Sevres, 86 Vienne

For centuries the Loire Valley was frequented by French royalty and the great River Loire winds its way past some of France's most magnificent châteaux. Known as the Garden of France, it is a most productive and lush area with large farms and a mild climate making it a favourite with visitors. Well known for its wines, over 100 different ones are produced from vineyards stretching along the 1,000 km (620 mile) course of the River Loire. Imposing abbeys, troglodyte caves, tiny Romanesque churches, woodlands such as the Sologne and sleepy, picturesque villages reward exploration. Cities like Blois and Tours are elegant with fine architecture and museums and Paris is only one hour by the TGV. Today Poitiers is home to Futuroscope, the 'museum of the moving image' (see colour advertisement opposite page 289).

Note: The site reports are laid out by département in numerical order not by region.

See maps on pages 310-311.

Cuisine of the region

Wild duck, pheasant, hare, deer, and quail are classics and fresh water fish such as salmon, perch and trout are favourite. A tasty '*beurre blanc*' is the usual sauce with fish.

This is the home of *Tarte Tatin* – upside down tart of caramelised apples and pastry

Tarte a la citrouille – pumpkin tart

Bourdaines – apples stuffed with jam and baked

Such specialties as rillettes, andouillettes, tripes, mushrooms and the regional cheeses of Trappiste d' Entrammes and Cremet d' Angers, Petit Sable and Ardoises d'Angers cookies.

Places of interest

Amboise – château by the river, Clos Lucé and Leonardo da Vinci museum with scale models of his inventions

Azay-le-Rideau – Renaissance château

Beauregard – château near Chambord, famous for its Delft tiled floors and timbered ceilings

Blois – château with architecture from Middle Ages to Neo-Classical periods

Chambord – Renaissance château, park and terraces, grandiose creation of François I

Chartres – cathedral with famous stained glass windows

Chenonçeau – château with great gallery and bridge

Cheverny – delightful privately owned château

Chinon – old town, Pavillon de l'Horloge, Joan of Arc museum

Langeais – château and tapestry collection

Loches – old town, château and its fortifications

Orléans – Holy Cross cathedral, house of Joan of Arc

Tours – Renaissance and Neo-Classical mansions, cathedral of St Gatien, museums of archeology and modern art

Vendôme – Tour St Martin, La Trinité

Villandry – famous renaissance gardens

LOIRE VALLEY - 18 Cher / 28 Eure-et-Loir

1801M Camping Municipal de Bellon, Vierzon

This is a useful, if average, site en-route to Clermont-Ferrand (10 minutes form the A20) in the town of Vierzon on the Cher river, a tributary of the Loire. It has 95 pitches separated by low hedges, some with shade and 44 with water and electricity connections (some require a long lead). Two fabricated sanitary blocks have washbasins in cubicles, showers, British and Turkish style WCs (take your own toilet paper), plus a shower and toilet for disabled visitors. There are stainless steel dishwashing and laundry sinks with hot water, also a chemical disposal unit and a motorcaravan service point. The nearest shop is 500 m. Boules area, table tennis. Sand based play house and slide for children. Access is possible to the River Cher for canoeing or enjoying the park area with its picnic tables. Close by are opportunities for walking or cycling in the forest areas or on quiet roads. The lady 'Guardienne' who manages this site does so single-handedly and it is very much used as an overnight stop-over. Care and maintenance can be lacking at times.

Charges 2000:
-- Per person Ffr. 17.00; pitch 23.70; electricity 14.60.

Open:
1 May - 30 September.

Address:
Rte. de Bellon,
18100 Vierzon.

Tel:
(0)2.48.75.49.10 (low season: (0)2.48.52.65.24).
FAX: (0)2.48.71.62.21.

Reservations:
Contact site.

Directions: Site is signed from Vierzon on old N20 towards Châteauroux. From Vierzon centre take D918 towards Issoudun. Turn left onto D27 and second left off D27 at Intermarché supermarket sign.

2810M Camping Municipal de Mont Jouvin, Illiers-Combray

This well kept site is very green and offers 89 grass pitches on a slope in most areas, with electricity connections (5A). Tall trees surround the camping areas and there is plenty of shade, peace and quiet. The two large sanitary blocks are fully tiled, with British style WCs and showers with free hot water and dressing areas, some washbasins in cabins and the usual under cover laundry and dishwashing sinks. There are good facilities for disabled people including telephone booths and, although the site is on a slope, it could possibly be acceptable for wheel chairs. All restaurant, shop and bar amenities are to be found in the town itself (2 km). A new municipal swimming pool alongside the site should now be open. There are boules pitches, bicycle hire, two children's playgrounds and table tennis on site, but no other sporting facilities or other organised activities. This is a site really for those who want peace and quiet or a convenient overnight stop.

Charges guide:
- - Per pitch Ffr. 17.00; adult 12.50; child (under 7 yrs) 6.25; electricity 14.00.

Open:
1 April - 31 October.

Address:
Rte. de Brou,
28120 Illiers-Combray.

Tel:
(0)2.37.24.03.04 (site)
(0)2.37.24.00.05 (Mairie).

Reservations:
Contact site.

Directions: Site is on D921 Illiers-Combray to Le Mans road.

2811M Camping Municipal de Bonneval, Bonneval, nr Chartres

On the outskirts of Bonneval and within walking distance of the centre, this municipal site offers good facilities in peaceful surroundings. The site has thick cover from trees in most parts with some pitches entirely hidden for those who like lots of privacy. Otherwise, pitches are marked out on grass in clearings, some on a slope, but the majority fairly flat. All 130 have 6A electricity, some hardstanding. Sanitary facilities consist of one large block and three smaller units with toilets, washbasins, laundry and dishwashing sinks plus chemical disposal only. Motorcaravan service point. The large block has chain operated hot showers, all the WCs are British style, some washbasins in cubicles, and facilities for disabled people. Laundry room with washing machine and ironing facilities, large TV/games room and a children's playground. Fishing and bicycle hire on site. No bar, restaurant or shop, but all in Bonneval itself or, when open, in the municipal swimming pool and tennis complex adjacent (reduced rates for campers). No double axles or units over 5.6 m. accepted. Caravan storage.

Charges guide:
-- Per pitch incl. 1 person Ffr. 31.00; with electricity 44.00; 2 persons 43.00 or 56.00; 4 persons 67.00 or 80.00.
-- No credit cards.

Open:
1 March - 30 November.

Address:
4 Bois de Chièvre,
28800 Bonneval.

Tel:
(0)2.37.47.54.01.
FAX: (0)2.37.96.26.79.

Reservations:
Contact site.

Directions: Site signed from Bonneval town centre on N10 from Châteaudun to Chartres (on Rte de Vouvray).

3603M Camping Municipal Le Val Vert, La Châtre, nr Châteauroux

In a peaceful rural location, 3 km. from the town, this neatly presented small touring site has 77 grassy pitches all with electricity connections. Some pitches are individual, others are in small bays for two or three units, with low dividing hedges. The modern, clean sanitary building, which has an unusual louvered front wall (ensuring a well ventilated atmosphere), provides both British and Turkish WCs, some washbasins in cubicles, push-button showers, covered dishwashing and laundry sinks, baby bathroom, chemical disposal point and a WC for disabled people. Motorcaravan service point. The only other on-site facilities are table tennis, two children's playgrounds, and a covered terrace with picnic tables and benches. Reception is open 09.00-12.30 and 15.00-19.30. Barrier closed 22.00-07.00. La Châtre is chiefly known for its connections to George Sand (pseudonym of the writer Armandine Lucie Dupin). Nearby, and also worth a visit, is the distinctive Château de Sarzay.

Directions: From La Châtre take D943 towards Montluçon, then, just outside the town fork right on D83A towards Briantes. Site is 3 km from town.

Charges 2000:
-- Per unit incl. 2 persons Ffr. 50.00; extra adult 15.00; child (3-7 yrs) 7.00; 'grand confort' pitch 15.00; electricity 15.00; local tax (per person) 1.00.
Open:
1 June - 30 September.
Address:
36400 La Châtre.
Tel:
(0)2.54.48.32.42.
FAX: (0)2.54.48.32.87.
Reservations:
May be necessary for 1-17 July only; contact site.

3605M Camping Municipal Les Vieux Chênes, Chaillac

A delightful site on the outskirts of an attractive village, this is another little gem - a small site within walking distance of the centre, where there are shops, bars, cafés, restaurants, etc. The 34 grass pitches, all with electricity (15A), are very generous in size, slightly sloping, with hedging and some mature trees. The well manicured appearance and relaxed atmosphere add to the attraction of this peaceful environment. The heated sanitary facilities are insulated for winter use and include hot showers with dividers and hooks, washbasins in private cabins, British style WCs and chemical disposal. Bicycle hire on site. The adjacent lake is for fishing only, although there is access to a larger lake just 1 km. away where varied watersports - swimming, windsurfing, canoeing and pedaloes - can be enjoyed. The small water toboggan is free of charge. In high season it is possible some noise may carry from this area to the site. Chalets to rent (3). Winter caravan storage.

Directions: From the north leave A20, south of Argenton sur Creuse, take D1 to St Benoit (16 km.) and then west to Chaillac on D36 (8.5 km). From the south leave A20 at exit 21, take D10 to St Benoit, then D36 as before. Go through the village and turn left by the Mairie.

Charges 2000:
-- Per person (over 14 yrs) Ffr. 10.00; child free; pitch 10.00 - 15.00; electricity 10.00.
Open:
All year.
Address:
36310 Chaillac.
Tel:
(0)2.54.25.61.39.
FAX: (0)2.54.25.65.41.
Reservations:
Not made.

3607M Camping Municipal Les Chênes, Valençay

Les Chênes is directly off the D960, within walking distance of the town of Valençay, which lies in a green belt and is noted for its fine château. This is an excellent municipal site, with flags flying to herald an easily negotiable entrance, modern reception area and broad parking space. Behind reception is the town swimming pool (July/Aug) on payment and a small fishing lake that is overlooked by several pitches. Large oaks dominate the entrance, beyond which are the 50 spacious, level, grass pitches, divided by hedges. A forest borders the site to the left and many trees on site give shade. The sanitary block, beside which is a covered wet weather area for campers, is centrally positioned and of modern design, fronted by a pebbled forecourt. Facilities are of a high standard and kept very clean, with washbasins in cubicles, showers, children's sinks, British style WCs, facilities for disabled people, dishwashing and laundry sinks with very hot water and a washing machine. Table tennis, bicycle hire, children's play field and three adjacent tennis courts. Shop (July/Aug). An excellent base for exploring the countryside around the Indre which is one of the two départements making up the Berry region of central France.

Directions: Site is 800 m. west of Valençay on the D960.

Charges guide:
- - Per pitch (acc. to facilities) Ffr. 18.00 - 30.00; adult 17.00; child (2-10 yrs) 9.00; electricity 4A 10.00, 6A 15.00, 10A 20.00.
-- Less 10% for stays of 8 days or more (excl. electricity)
Open:
1 May - 30 September.
Address:
Complexe de Sports et de Loisirs,
Rte. de Loches,
36600 Valençay.
Tel:
(0)2.54.00.03.92.
Reservations:
Contact site.

3701 Camping de la Mignardière, Ballan-Miré, nr Tours

Pleasant little site quietly situated just southwest of Tours.

The situation of this site may appeal - only 8 km. from the centre of the city of Tours, yet within easy reach of several of the Loire châteaux, notably Azay-le-Rideau, and with various sports amenities on or very close to the site. There are now 177 numbered pitches of which around 135 are for touring units, all with electricity (6A) and 100 with drainage and water. They are on rather uneven grass but are of good size. Four rather ordinary sanitary blocks have British WCs, washbasins (in private cabins) and sinks, and premixed warm water in the showers. There is a unit for disabled people, a baby bath in the heated block near to reception, chemical disposal and laundry facilities. Amenities on the site include a shop, two heated, large swimming pools (15/5-15/9) with sunbathing terrace, a good tennis court, table tennis and bicycle hire. A bar, restaurant and crêperie (all 10/5-30/9) with takeaway in high season are nearby. Just outside the site is a small 'parc de loisirs' with pony rides, minigolf, small cars, playground and some other amusements. An attractive lake catering particularly for wind-surfing is 300 m. (boards can be hired or use your own) and there is a family fitness run. Fishing 500 m, riding 1 km, golf 2 km. Barrier gates with card (100 Ffr. deposit), closed 22.30 - 07.30 hrs. Motorcaravan service point. Mobile homes and chalets for hire. Reservation is essential for most of July/Aug.

Directions: From A10 autoroute take exit 24 and D751 towards Chinon. Turn right after 5 km. at Campanile Hotel following signs to site. From Tours take D751 towards Chinon.

Charges 2001:
-- Pper unit incl. 2 persons Ffr. 86.00 - 112.00, with electricity, water and drainage 120.00 - 150.00; extra person 24.00 - 30.00; child (2-10 yrs) 16.00 - 18.00; electricity 18.00.
-- Credit cards accepted.

Open:
10 April - 30 September.

Address:
Ave des Aubépines, 37510 Ballan-Miré.

Tel:
(0)2.47.73.31.00.
FAX: (0)2.47.73.31.01.
E-mail: info@mignardiere.com.

Reservations:
Made for any length with 30% deposit and fee (90).

Book this site
01892 559898

THE ALAN ROGERS'
travel service

Camping ★★★★
DE LA MIGNARDIERE

37510 Ballan-Miré

Tel: 02 47 73 31 00 Fax: 02 47 73 31 01

All the comforts of a 4 star camp with a wide range of activities for enjoyment and relaxation of adults and children; heated swimming pool and tennis on site, water sports lake, ponies and minigolf very close, the Loire châteaux and all the attractions of Tours.

Mobile Homes and Chalets for hire

www.mignardiere.com

3703 Camping Le Moulin Fort, Chenonceaux

Small riverside site close to Château.

The 137 pitches on this tranquil site are enhanced by an interesting variety of shrubs and trees. Electricity (6A) is available to all of the pitches with water points nearby. Two toilet blocks have all the usual amenities which are of a good standard (no toilet paper). They include private washbasins, hair dryers, baby baths and chemical disposal. The site has unusual features, not least the River Cher flowing near the restored old mill building. There is access to the swimming pool (1/6-30/9) over the mill race by a wooden walkway from the terraced restaurant. This serves breakfasts, good value evening meals and takeaway meals three nights a week. Bicycles and canoes are available to rent. Also on site are minigolf, a games room, TV and other activities including a children's mini-club and campfire evenings. Although not visually intrusive, there is some noise from the nearby railway line - a few trains run at night. The campsite is just under 2 km. from Chenonceaux, where a 'Son et Lumière' spectacle is held every evening in high season.

Directions: Take D40 Tours - Chenonceaux road, go through the village and after 2 km. turn right on D80 to cross river at Chisseaux. Site is on left just after bridge.

Charges 2001:
-- Per pitch incl. 2 persons Ffr. 110.00; extra adult 28.00; child (under 12 yrs) 20.00; dog 10.00; electricity (6A) 23.00.
-- Low season less 10%.
-- Credit cards accepted.

Open:
1 April - 30 September.

Address:
37150 Francueil-Chenonceaux

Tel:
(0)2.47.23.86.22.
FAX: (0)2.47.23.80.93.

Reservations:
Write to site.

Book this site
01892 559898

THE ALAN ROGERS'
travel service

see colour advert
between pages 96/97

3711M Camping Municipal Au Bord du Cher, Veretz, nr Tours

Managed by the Barot family who provide a warm welcome and, in season, live on the site in their caravan, this is an inexpensive, well laid out site on the banks of the River Cher, with views through tall elm trees to the Château of Veretz. With 58 pitches, most divided by small hedges and all with at least 6A electricity, the site is just outside the town of Veretz where shops, restaurants, bars, etc. can be found. Baker 700 m. Outdoor swimming pool (July/Aug) 5 km. The large, modern, basic sanitary block includes free hot showers, British and Turkish style WCs, dishwashing under cover, chemical disposal, laundry and washing machine. Motorcaravan service point. Children's playground and table tennis. Fishing. Bicycle hire 12 km, riding 3 km. A new wooden chalet houses reception and plenty of tourist information, with notice boards giving weather forecasts, etc. Of particular interest is information for railway enthusiasts, there are restored steam trains and track in the area. River trips are possible in the replica of a sail boat used to carry goods (mainly wine) on the river until the '20s. Bus service from Tours station to Bleré passes site entrance. English spoken.

Directions: Site is at Veretz, via the N76 road, 10 km. southeast of Tours (much better than the municipal at St Avertin en-route).

Charges guide:
-- Per pitch Ffr. 10.00; adult 12.00; child (under 7 yrs) 5.00; vehicle 12.00; electricity (6A) 15.00.
-- No credit cards.

Open:
22 May - 26 September.

Address:
37270 Veretz.

Tel:
(0)2.47.50.50.48.
FAX: (0)2.47.50.33.22 (Mairie).
E-mail: mairie.veretz @wanadoo.fr.

Reservations:
Contact site.

4104 Camping Château des Marais, Muides sur Loire, nr Chambord

Impressive site with excellent facilities, near famous royal château.

The château at Chambord, with its park, is certainly impressive and well worth a visit. The nearby Château des Marais campsite is also well situated to visit other châteaux in the 'Vallée des Rois'. The recently designed site, providing 230 large pitches, all with electricity (6/10A), water and drainage and with ample shade, is situated in the oak and hornbeam woods of its own small château (in which there are rooms to let). It boasts a heated swimming pool and water slide with its own pool, with a new pool complex planned for 2001. There is a pleasant bar/restaurant with a large terrace, bicycle hire and a fishing lake. Excursions by coach to Paris, an entertainment programme and canoe trips are organised in high season. Riding 4 km, golf 12 km. The village of Muides sur Loire, with a variety of small shops, etc. is five minutes walk. Four modern, purpose built sanitary blocks have good facilities including some large showers and washbasins en-suite, British style WCs, chemical disposal, washing machine, etc. with hot water throughout. Motorcaravan service point. English is spoken and the reception from the enthusiastic owners and the staff is very welcoming. Used by tour operators (90 pitches). Bungalows and mobile homes to let, as well as the rooms in the château (breakfast included) - useful out of season. A 'Sites et Paysages' member.

Directions: From A10 autoroute take exit 16 to Mer, then cross the Loire to join the D951 and follow signs. Site is signed off D103 to southwest of village. 600 m. from junction with the D112.

Charges 2001:
-- Per pitch incl. vehicle and 2 persons Ffr. 160.00; extra person 35.00; child (under 5 yrs) 20.00; dog 20.00; electricity 6A 22.00, 10A 35.00; local tax (over 16 yrs) 2.00.
-- Credit cards accepted (for amounts over Ffr. 500).

Open:
19 May - 9 September.

Address:
41500 Muides sur Loire.

Tel:
(0)2.54.87.05.42.
FAX: (0)2.54.87.05.43.
E-mail: chateau.des. marais@wanadoo.fr.

Reservations:
Advised July/Aug. and made with 30% deposit.

Book this site
01892 559898
THE ALAN ROGERS'
travel service

LOIRE VALLEY - 41 Loir-et-Cher

4101 Le Parc du Val de Loire, Mesland, nr Blois

Family owned site with swimming pools, situated between Blois and Tours.

This site is quietly situated away from the main roads and towns, but is nevertheless centrally placed for visits to the châteaux; Chaumont, Amboise and Blois (21 km.) are the nearest in that order. There are 300 pitches of reasonable size, either in light woodland marked by trees or on open meadow with separators. Some 142 pitches have electricity (6A), water and drainage. The two original toilet blocks are of varying standards with British style WCs (external entry), washbasins in cabins, free pre-set hot showers. A third block has more modern facilities. There are units for disabled visitors, baby bathrooms, laundry facilities, chemical disposal and a motorcaravan service point. Three swimming pools are on site, the newest (200 sq.m.) with sunbathing area, and heated all season, plus a smaller pool with a very popular water slide, and a small children's pool. Other activities include a tennis court with floodlighting, good children's playgrounds with skate board facilities, bicycle hire, table tennis, minigolf, BMX track, tennis training wall, football pitch, volleyball, badminton and basketball. Pony rides and some sports and competitions are organised in July/Aug.when there is a weekly disco and a dance for adults. Barbecue area. There is a large shop with bakery, a bar adjacent to the pools, with restaurant, snack service, pizzeria and takeaway, TV room and large, recreation room. Wine tasting opportunities each Friday and a coach to Paris one day each week. Local walks on marked footpaths (maps Ffr.2). Fishing 2 km, riding 10 km, golf 9 km. Mobile homes (16) and chalets (10) for hire. Used by tour operators (100 pitches).

Charges 2001:
-- Per unit incl. 2 persons: standard pitch (100 sq.m.) Ffr. 105.00 - 150.00, large pitch (150 sq.m.) with water and drainage 115.00 - 160.00; extra person 25.00 - 36.00; child (2-7 yrs) 12.00 - 20.00; electricity (6A) 18.00 - 22.00; animal 12.00.
-- Credit cards accepted.

Open:
15 April - 17 September.

Address:
Route de Fleuray, 41150 Mesland.

Tel:
(0)2.54.70.27.18.
FAX: (0)2.54.70.21.71.

Reservations:
Made for min. 4 days with deposit (Ffr 500) and fee (130).

Directions: The village of Mesland is 5 km. northwest of Onzain, accessible from the Château-Renault/Amboise exit of A10 autoroute via D31 to Autrèche, continue 5 km. then left at La Hargardière at camp sign and 8 km. to site.

Le Parc du Val de Loire ★★★★

41150 MESLAND - Tel. 0033 254 70 27 18 - Fax: 0033 254 70 21 71

"In the heart of Loire Chateaux country and the vineyards of Touraine"

CHALETS AND MOBILE HOMES TO LET

- Swimming pool complex with 3 pools, 2 of which are heated and a water slide.
- Tennis, mini-golf, football pitch, volleyball, basketball and boules (pétanque).
- Childrens play area and BMX track, bicycle hire.
- Electronic games, children entertainment and sports tournament during July and August.
- Self-service, bar, restaurant, take-away and TV room.

Open from 28 April to 15 September 2001

4102 Castel Camping Château de la Grenouillère, Suevres

Comfortable site with good amenities, on the N152 midway between Orléans and Tours.

This site is well situated for visiting many of the Loire châteaux and makes a good stopover, but there are also enough attractions on site and locally to make it suitable for a longer stay. It is set in a 28 acre park and the 250 pitches are in three distinct areas. The majority are in a well wooded area, with about 60 in the old orchard and the remainder in open meadow, although all pitches are separated by hedges; 200 of the pitches have electricity (5A) and there is one water point for every 4 pitches. Additionally, there are 15 'grand confort' pitches with a separate luxury sanitary block in the outbuildings of the château itself. The three other sanitary blocks, one for each area, are modern and well appointed. All the toilets are British style with hand-washing facilities nearby. Other washbasins are in private cabins with hot water, mirror and shelf. Some showers are pre-set, some controllable and all have dressing area, hooks and shelf. Razor points in the men's and hair dryers are provided. Washing machines and dryers. Site facilities include a shop, a well appointed bar, a swimming pool complex of four outdoor pools including a water slide, tennis, squash, minigolf, table tennis, pool, baby foot and video games. Bikes and canoes may be hired in July/Aug. and guided tours are organised once a week. The site is popular with tour operators.

Charges guide:
-- Per unit incl. 2 persons, simple pitch Ffr. 90.00, with 5A electricity 110.00, luxury pitch 160.00; extra person 35.00; child (under 7 yrs) 25.00.
-- Less 10-30% in low seasons.

Open:
13 May - 10 September.

Address:
41500 Suevres.

Tel:
(0)2.54.87.80.37.
FAX: (0)2.54.87.84.21.

Reservations:
Made for min. 5 days with Ffr. 500 deposit.

Directions: Site is between Suevres and Mer on north side of N152; well signed.

4103 Sologne Parc des Alicourts, Pierrefitte sur Sauldre

Secluded 21 hectare site in the heart of the forest, with many sporting facilities.

This site is situated in a very secluded, forested area midway between Orléans and Bourges, about 20 km. to the east of the A10. There are 300 pitches, all with electricity (4/6A) and good provision for water. Most pitches are 150 sq.m. (min. 100) and vary from wooded to more open areas, thus giving a choice of amount of shade. There are three modern sanitary blocks with washbasins (open and in private cabins), razor points, hair dryers, controllable hot showers and five baby bathrooms. Also provided are washing machines and drying facilities, chemical disposal and motorcaravan services. There is a restaurant using fresh produce and traditional cuisine plus a takeaway service in a pleasant bar with terrace. The shop has a good range of produce in addition to the basics (the nearest good sized town is some distance). All facilities are open all season. Leisure amenities are exceptional: an inviting swimming pool complex (all season) with three pools (two heated), a spa and three water slides, a 7 hectare lake with fishing, bathing, canoes, pedaloes and children's play area, 5 hole golf course (very popular), football pitch, volleyball, tennis, minigolf, table tennis, boules, bicycle hire with cyclo-cross and mountain bikes and a way-marked path for walking and cycling. New for 2000 was a roller skating area. Competitions are organised for adults as well as children and, in high season, a club for children with an entertainer twice a day, a disco once a week and a dance for adults. Used by tour operators (120 pitches). Mobile homes (22) and chalets (22) to rent.

Directions: From A71 take Lamotte-Beuvron exit 3, on D923 towards Aubigny. After 14 km. turn right at camp sign onto D24E. Site is clearly signed in 4 km.

Charges 2001:
-- Per unit incl. 2 persons Ffr. 130.00 - 180.00, with water/drainage 150.00 - 210.00; extra person over 18 yrs 40.00 - 50.00, 7-17 yrs 26.00 - 36.00, 1-6 yrs 21.00 - 27.00; electricity (6A) 32.00; dog 32.00; local tax (1/6-13/9) 1.50.
-- Reductions for low season longer stays.
-- Credit cards accepted.

Open:
18 May - 10 September.

Address:
Domaine des Alicourts, 41300 Pierrefitte sur Sauldre.

Tel:
(0)2.54.88.63.34. FAX: (0)2.54.88.58.40. E-mail: parcdesalicourts@wanadoo.fr.

Reservations:
Min. 7 days for July/Aug. only, with 25% deposit and Ffr 100 fee.

Large family campsite near the famous 'Chateaux de la Loire', with a beautiful lake and private beach, a golf course, a large playground for children, two swimming pools with two water slides and every facility.

★★★★

Sologne Parc Des Alicourts

Chalets and mobile homes for hire

Sologne Parc Des Alicourts
Domaine des Alicourts
41300 Pierrefitte sur Sauldre
Tel: 0254 886334
Fax: 0254 885840

4106 Camping de Dugny, Onzain, nr Blois

All year round site in wonderfully quiet rural location.

This well organised campsite started life as an 'a la ferme' back in 1976. Since then it has grown into a nine hectare camping site surrounded by many acres of farmland under the same ownership. The are 226 pitches, with some mobile homes (privately owned and to rent) leaving 182 tourist pitches. Of a generous size, they are partially separated, some with shade and others on a newer more open area. All have electricity (10A), and 55 are fully serviced. Two new and one refitted sanitary units have both open and cubicled washbasins, push-button hot showers, dishwashing and laundry sinks, and provision for disabled people. On-site facilities include an outdoor swimming pool (15 x 7 m), a children's pool and two small playgrounds for 4-12 year olds. This is not a site for teenagers, unless they are interested in country life. Sports facilities include minigolf, table tennis, volleyball, basketball and a pétanque court. There is a small restaurant and takeaway, and barbecues are organised on the terrace. Although there is no shop, bread, ices and soft drinks, etc. are available and gas is stocked. A little train takes guests to a nearby wine cave, and a local farm that produces goats cheese. The site has a varied activity programme that includes a children's disco, boules and table tennis tournaments, and campfire evenings. Adjacent to the site is an official light aircraft landing strip, which is used annually for a 'rally' by microlight enthu-siasts, and can be used by visiting guests. Local markets are in Onzain (Thurs. pm), Montrichard (Fri. am), Blois (Sat. am), Amboise (Sun. am). Golf 2 km.

Charges 2000:
-- Per adult Ffr. 30.00 - 45.00; child (5-14 yrs) 24.00 - 30.00; confort pitch 12.00; grand confort pitch 20.00; animal 10.00; electricity 20.00.
-- Credit cards accepted.
Open:
All year.
Address:
41150 Onzain.
Tel:
(0)2.54.20.70.66.
FAX: (0)2.54.33.71.69.
E-mail: info@ camping-de-dugny.fr.
Reservations:
Not normally required. Ask site for details.

Directions: From N152 (north bank of River Loire between Tours and Blois) turn north on D1 at Le Moulin-à-Vent. Turn right in Onzain on D58 and then left on to D45 where site is signed. Site is 4 km. north of town (15 km. southwest of Blois).

4510M Camping Municipal du Château, La Chapelle St Mesmin

Within an hour's walk, along a footpath beside the Loire, of the centre of Orléans, this is a really delightful little site, ideal for visiting Orléans and/or this stretch of the Loire Valley. The site itself is small with 90 marked and separated pitches for caravans, all with electricity (6A), plus an area for 30 tents. These are attractively arranged alongside the river, beside which runs a footpath to the nearby village (a must!) and on to Orléans - the opposite way leads to a forest leisure park. There are two sanitary blocks, one central, the other at the extremity of the site, which provide good controllable hot showers of a reasonable size, washbasins (H&C) and mainly Turkish type WCs, apart from two British, officially designated for disabled people. Overall, it is a reasonable, if not particularly luxurious, provision. For a site close to a large city, it is not only remarkably pretty, but security seems to be good too, despite the adjacent riverside footpath. Apart from a small play area and a telephone, the site has no amenities (bread to order), but shops, restau-rants, etc. are within reasonable walking distance. Motorcaravan service point.

Charges 2000:
-- Per person Ffr. 20.05; child (under 7 yrs) 11.75; pitch 21.55; electricity 24.10.
Open:
1 April - 31 October.
Address:
45380
La Chapelle St Mesmin.
Tel:
(0)2.38.43.30.31.
(Mairie:
(0)2.38.43.60.46).
FAX: (0)2.38.88.23.76.
Reservations:
Policy unclear - suggest phone for high season to confirm availability.

Directions: Site is at Chapelle St Mesmin, 7 km. southwest of the city, from the N152, signed `Camping'. From the A10 autoroute, use exit for Orléans in the direction of Blois on the N152 - watch carefully for camping signs (easy to miss).

4105 Camping des Grands Prés, Vendôme

Well situated site for visiting lovely town on the Loir.

Vendôme is a fascinating and beautiful old town situated on, and criss-crossed by tributaries of the River Loir (not to be confused with the Loire). It is well worth a visit and is only 42 minutes from Paris on the TGV. Camping des Grands Prés is conveniently situated beside the river, only a 250 m. level walk from the town centre and next door to the swimming pool (free to campers), canoeing centre, etc. The 200 pitches, 150 with electricity (4/6A), are on mainly flat grass, clearly marked, but not actually separated. There is variable shade from a variety of trees. It has a very modern, purpose built sanitary block which is well equipped with all British style WCs. This site is busy over an extended season and, although the sanitary units are regularly cleaned throughout the day, the toilets adjacent to entry doors remain a problem, mainly due to use by unsupervised children and lazy adults. Some traffic noise from the N10 that passes the rear of the site.

Charges 2001:
-- Per unit incl. 2 persons Ffr. 45.00; extra adult 13.00; child (5-15 yrs) 9.00; electricity 17.00 - 25.00; local tax 2.00.
Open:
1 April - 30 September.
Address:
Rue Geoffrey-Mantell, 41100 Vendôme.
Tel:
(0)2.54.77.00.27 (low season: (0)2.54.89.43.51).
FAX: (0)2.54.89.43.58.
Reservations:
Advised in main season.

Directions: Site is signed from the N10 through the town.

4501 Les Bois du Bardelet, Gien

Attractive, lively family run site with lake and pool complex, in eastern Loire.

This site, in a rural setting, is well situated for exploring the less well known eastern part of the Loire Valley. A lake and pools have been attractively landscaped in 20 acres of former farmland, blending old and new with natural wooded areas and more open field areas with rural views. Bois du Bardelet provides 260 pitches with around 160 for touring units. All are larger than 100 sq.m. and all have electrical connections (10A) with some fully serviced (electricity, water and waste water). The communal areas are based on attractively converted former farm buildings and include two sanitary blocks (only one open outside 15/6-31/8). They have controllable hot showers, washbasins in cabins, British style toilets, facilities for people with disabilities and for babies, free hairdryers and washing machines. The range of leisure facilities includes three pools, one for serious swimmers, one with a child's pool, both free, and the other indoor, heated and charged for. There are facilities for archery, a lake for canoeing and fishing, tennis, minigolf, boules, table tennis and bicycle hire (some activities high season only). A playground for the under-eights has been added. A family club card can be purchased to make use of these activities on a daily basis. Shop for basics only (supermarket 5 km). Snack bar, takeaway and restaurant (1/4-15/9), pizzeria, plus a pleasant terraced bar. Various activities and excursions are organised, the most popular being to Paris on Wednesdays, which can be pre-booked. Walking and cycling routes of different lengths are available at reception. Chalets and mobile homes to rent.

Directions: From Gien take D940 road towards Bourges. After 5 km. turn right (signed) and right again to cross the road and follow signs to site. From Argens sur Sauldre take D940 towards Gien and site is signed to right after approx. 15 km. It is a narrow road.

Charges 2000:
-- Per unit incl. 2 persons Ffr. 129.00, with electricity 155.00; extra person (over 2 yrs) 31.00; animal 11.00.
-- Family club card Ffr. 280 in July/Aug, 220 other times; valid for 7 days.
-- Low season less 15-25% (40% for over 60s).
-- Credit cards accepted (amounts over Ffr 150).

Open:
1 April - 30 September.

Address:
Rte. de Bourges, Poilly, 45500 Gien.

Tel:
(0)2.38.67.47.39.
FAX: (0)2.38.38.27.16.
E-mail: contact@bardelet.com.

Reservations:
Made with deposit (Ffr. 350) and fee (100) - contact site for details.

`Camping Cheque'

Book this site
01892 559898

THE ALAN ROGERS'
Travel service

LOIRE VALLEY - 49 Maine-et-Loire

4901 Castel Camping L'Etang de la Brèche, Varennes-sur-Loire

Peaceful, spacious family site with swimming pool, adjacent to the Loire.

The Saint Cast family have developed L'Etang de la Brèche with loving care and attention over 25 years on a 25 ha. estate 4 km. southeast of Saumur on the edge of the Loire behind the dykes. It is a lovely base from which to explore the châteaux for which the region is famous and also its abbeys, wine cellars, mushroom caves and Troglodyte villages. It provides 200 large, level pitches with shade from mixed tall trees and bushes, facing central grass areas used for recreation and less shaded with a nice spacious feel. There are electrical connections to most pitches, water and drainaway on some. The three toilet blocks have been modernised to a high standard, providing showers with washbasins, hooks, mirrors, and dividers, separate British WCs. Good hot water supply to washing up sinks, laundry, baby facilities and two units for disabled people. Chemical disposal and motorcaravan services. The good restaurant, also open to the public, blends well with the existing architecture and, together with the bar area and terrace, provides a social base and is probably one of the reasons why the site is popular with British visitors. The site includes a small lake (used for fishing) and wooded area ensuring a quiet, relaxed and rural atmosphere. The enlarged pool complex provides three heated pools, a water slide and jacuzzi, for youngsters of all ages and a lovely pool for little ones with safe, miniature equipment (a prototype for the future?) Well organised, varied sporting and entertainment programme (10/7-25/8) including pony rides. There is a new terrace restaurant, plus a shop, epicerie, takeaway, pizzeria, general room, games and TV rooms. Tennis, basketball, minigolf, a field for football and bicycle hire. Child minding is arranged in the afternoons. In the low season excursions 'Getting to know the Area' and wine tastings are organised, plus French conversation groups. Riding 2 km, golf 8 km. Torches required at night. Used by tour operators (85 pitches). This is a comfortable holiday base for couples and families.

Directions: Site is 100 m. north off the main N152, about 4 km. southeast of Saumur on the north bank of the Loire.

Charges 2001:
-- Per unit incl. 2 persons Ffr. 89.00 - 140.00, 3 persons 110.00 - 157.00; extra adult 22.00 - 30.00; extra child (2-7 yrs) 12.00 - 17.00; dog free; electricity (10A) free - 18.00; water and drainage 14.00; extra car 22.00.
-- 7th night free in low season.
-- Credit cards accepted.

Open:
15 May - 10 September.

Address:
49730 Varennes-sur-Loire.

Tel:
(0)2.41.51.22.92. FAX: (0)2.41.51.27.24. E-mail: etang.breche@ wanadoo.fr.

Reservations:
Made for min. 7 days in high season (3 days in low seasons) with deposit and fee.

Book this site
01892 559898

THE ALAN ROGERS'
travel service

see colour advert between pages 96/97

4902 Camping de Chantepie, St Hilaire-St Florent, Saumur

Pleasant site with swimming pools, close to Saumur with lovely views over the Loire.

Your drive along the winding road bordered by apple orchards and vineyards is well rewarded on arriving at the floral entrance to Camping de Chantepie. The reception and well stocked shop are housed in the tastefully restored ancient farmhouse. The 150 grass pitches are level and spacious, most with electrical connections (5A), and separated by low hedges of flowers and trees which offer some shade. They are linked by gravel paths. The panoramic views over the Loire from the pitches on the terraced perimeter of the meadow are stunning. There is, from here, a footpath leading to the river valley. The sanitary block is very clean and the provision of facilities is adequate. There is hot water to all the private washbasins and showers, which are of the pre-set, push-button variety. In a separate section of the building, the WCs are British style and there are facilities for visitors with disabilities. Two paddling pools and two heated swimming pools are surrounded by an attractive sunbathing area, protected from the wind by a stone wall. Bar and terraced restaurant with a comprehensive choice of menus and separate takeaway (from 15/5). For those wanting to do their own cuisine, a well stocked herb garden is at their disposal. Leisure activities for all ages are catered for in July/Aug. by the 'Chantepie Club'. Bicycle and mountain bike hire (maps from reception) are provided and there is a terraced minigolf course. A children's play area has a wide variety of apparatus. Volleyball, TV, video games and table tennis. Fishing 200 m, riding 6 km, golf 2 km. Wine tasting evenings, excursions and canoeing expeditions are organised in high season. Mobile homes (12) and Trigano tents (11) for hire.

Directions: Take D751 signed Gennes from Saumur. Turn left in Mimerolle as signed and continue 4 km. to site.

Charges 2001:
-- Per adult Ffr. 22.80 - 28.50; child (2-9 yrs) 12.40 - 15.50; pitch incl. car 53.00 - 66.10; electricity 14.80 - 18.50; local tax 2.00 (child 1.00).
-- Credit cards accepted.

Open:
29 April - 16 September.

Address:
St Hilaire-St Florent, 49400 Saumur.

Tel:
(0)2.41.67.95.34. FAX: (0)2.41.67.95.85. E-mail: camping. chantepie@wanadoo.fr.

Reservations:
Contact site for details.

`Camping Cheque'

see colour advert between pages 160/161

4906 Camping L'Européen de Montsabert, Coutures

Peaceful, spacious site, ideal for exploring the Saumur and Angers area.

Under management for the Commune of Gennes, this extensive campsite has a rural atmosphere in the shadow of Montsabert château, from where visiting peacocks happily roam in the spacious surroundings. The 158 large pitches (some are enormous) are mostly divided by hedges and provided with shade by abundant mature trees. The 107 pitches for touring units all have water, waste water point and electricity (5A) and there are a few with hardstanding. The main central toilet block can be heated and has push-button showers, washbasins and bidets in cabins, British style toilets, outside dishwashing and laundry facilities, and a washing machine and dryer. A second block serves the pool and another unit provides more WCs. Leisure facilities are generous and include a large sports hall, minigolf, volley and basketball, table tennis, tennis and a large 25 m. heated pool (1/6-15/9; no bermuda style shorts). Picnic tables are provided in the shade near the entrance and there is a communal barbecue area. There is a restaurant and takeaway (both 15/6-15/9) and a bar (1/6-15/9). Activities such as windsurfing, canoeing and sailing are near. Fishing 5 km, golf or riding 8 km. This partially wooded site, fringed with impressive redwood trees offers the peace of the countryside and yet easy access to Saumur and Angers. It is an ideal base for exploring, whether by foot, bicycle or car. Mobile homes and bungalows to rent (23). Used by tour operators (16 pitches). Torches are necessary at night.

Directions: From Saumur take D952 Angers road to Les Rosiers-sur-Loire, cross the river Loire to Gennes and take D751 signed Coutures. Follow camp signs in Coutures.

Charges 2001:
-- Per unit incl. 2 persons Ffr. 80.00 - 105.00; extra person 28.00; electricity (5A) 18.00.
-- Credit cards accepted.

Open:
15 May - 15 September.

Address:
Montsabert, 49320 Coutures.

Tel:
(0)2.41.57.91.63.
FAX: (0)2.41.57.90.02.
E-mail: anjoucamp@
wanadoo.fr.

Reservations:
Made with 30% deposit and fee (Ffr. 50 or 7,62); contact site.

Book this site
01892 559898

THE ALAN ROGERS'
travel service

4907 Camping La Vallée des Vignes, Concourson-sur-Layon

New, modern site beside the Layon river.

The young English/French owners at La Vallée des Vignes have made an energetic start in landscaping their new 8.5-hectare site. Many young trees and shrubs have been planted to add to the existing mature trees that surround the site. Bordering the river Layon, all 52 touring pitches are a good size, fully serviced (10A electricity) and reasonably level. There are five pitches with hardstanding. The sanitary block is extremely comfortable and well appointed. There is hot water throughout, spacious showers, private washbasins, British style WCs and chemical disposal. Dishwashing and laundry facilities are at either end of the building under cover. A generously sized sun terrace surrounds the swimming and paddling pools (15/5-15/9). Nearby there is a bar (all season) and a restaurant (1/6-30/9) serving refreshments, snacks and a takeaway service. Attractions include minigolf, a fitness trail, children's playground and games area, small football pitch, volleyball, basketball, table-tennis, bicycle hire and fishing on the site's own stretch of river. Mobile homes to rent. The site is well placed for visiting the zoo and rose gardens of Doué-la-Fontaine, châteaux of the Loire valley, and the caves and vineyards of the area.

Directions: Site signed off D960 Doué - Vihiers road, just west of Concourson-sur-Layon.

Charges guide:
-- Per unit incl. 2 persons Ffr. 85.00 - 110.00; extra adult 20.00 - 25.00; child (2-10 yrs) 12.00 - 15.00; electricity (10A) 28.00; animal 10.00; local tax 2.00.
-- Special offers available.
-- Credit cards accepted.

Open:
Easter - 30 September.

Address:
49700 Concourson-sur-Layon.

Tel:
(0)2.41.59.86.35.
E-mail: campingvdv @aol.com.

Reservations:
Contact site.

LOIRE VALLEY - 49 Maine-et-Loire / 53 Mayenne

4904 Camping de l'Étang, Brissac

Rural campsite with own vineyard.

Originally the farm of the ancient Château de Brissac, the tasteful conversion has retained the tranquillity and ambience of bye-gone days and added the necessary comforts expected by today's campers. The adapted farmhouse houses the office, a small shop, a bar, restaurant and takeaway (15/5-15/9), and a laundry room with washing machine, dryer and sinks for hand washing. The 52 generously sized, level touring pitches, are all separated and numbered and have a little shade. All have electricity (6A), with water and drainage nearby. Well maintained sanitary blocks have hot water and all the usual facilities. The second larger block was nearing completion during our visit and both are of a high standard. Separate chemical disposal point. Surrounding the swimming pool (15 x 7 m) there is a sun terrace with relaxing views across the countryside. A small bridge crosses the river Aubance which runs through the site and there is a lake here where fishermen can enjoy themselves. The adjacent Parc de Loisirs is a paradise for young children with many activities including boating, pedaloes, pony rides, miniature train, water slide, bouncy castle and swings (entry discounts for campers). Wine is produced and sold on the campsite (6 bottles £10!) Many other activities are organised during high season. Bicycle hire. Golf or riding 10 km. Mobile homes and tents for rent. The maintenance of the campsite, vineyards and park offer, under guidance, employment to mentally handicapped personnel. A reader was disturbed by noisy frogs in June!

Charges 2001:
-- Per adult Ffr. 22.80 - 28.50; child (2-9 yrs) 12.40 - 15.50; pitch incl. car 53.00 - 66.10; electricity 14.80 - 18.50; local tax 2.00 (child 1.00).
-- Credit cards accepted.

Open:
27 April - 16 September.

Address:
St Sarturnin sur Loire, 49320 Brissac.

Tel:
(0)2.41.91.70.61.
FAX: (0)2.41.91.72.65.
E-mail: camping.etang @wanadoo.fr.

Reservations:
Contact site.

Directions: Take D748 south from Angers. Follow signs to Brissac-Quincé but do not enter the town, proceed to site on D55 (well signed) towards St Mathurin.

4900M Camping du Lac de Maine, Angers

The Parc de Loisirs du Lac de Maine lies to the southwest of the city, and is a leisure area with all sorts of activities. The campsite is located at the southern end of the Parc towards Bouchmaine, with 150 individual pitches for tourists. There are also 15 bungalow tents for rent. The site is level, and rather open with very little shade. Most pitches are part grass with a gravel hardstanding, although some are totally gravel, all have water, drain and electricity hook-up (6A). The sanitary facilities are in two units, one of which can be heated. They provide British style WCs, some washbasins in cubicles, and controllable hot showers, with facilities for babies and disabled people. In addition there are dishwashing and laundry facilities and a drive-over motorcaravan service point. There is a heated L-shaped swimming pool, a restaurant/bar, volleyball and pétanque courts, bicycle hire and a children's playground. Activities are organised for children in peak season. The adjacent 100 acre lake has a sandy beach, windsurfing, sailing and pedaloes available, and the parkland provides tennis courts and a nature reserve. Reception stocks Campingaz. Barrier card deposit Ffr. 100. The site entrance has a height restriction of 3.2 metres (there is an alternative entrance).

Charges 2000:
-- Per unit incl. 2 persons Ffr. 61.00 - 80.00; extra adult 12.50; child (under 7 yrs) 8.00; extra vehicle 15.00; animal 7.50; electricity 18.50.

Open:
25 March - 10 October.

Address:
Avenue du Lac de Maine, 49000 Angers.

Tel:
(0)2.41.73.05.03.
FAX: (0)2.41.73.02.20.
E-mail: angers.lac@ wanadoo.fr

Reservations:
Advised for July/Aug; contact site.

Directions: Site is signed from centre of Angers (5 km.), and also from N23 towards Nantes.

5301M Camping Parc des Loisirs de Vaux, Ambrières-les-Vallées

This very pleasant municipal site is adjacent to a sports complex that provides an open air, heated swimming pool, canoe and kayak rental, tennis and badminton courts, archery, horse riding, minigolf, pétanque, cycle hire and a playground for youngsters. There are 61 tourist pitches, all on grass, all with electricity available (10A), although some long leads may be necessary. The sanitary facilities are in two units, one close to the entrance, and a smaller one at the far end of the site. Both are fairly modern and well cared for, with British style WCs, push-button hot showers, open and cubicle washbasins, and a new laundry building which will be ready for the 2001 season. Six mobile homes for rent. The latest additions to the site are 12 new Canadian manufactured chalets. Heated and double glazed, one is adapted for handicapped people, and they will be available for all year use.

Charges 2000:
-- Per adult Ffr. 12.00 - 15.00; child (under 10 yrs) 6.00 - 7.00; pitch 48.00 - 60.00; animal free; electricity 14.00.
-- Reductions for longer stays.

Open:
1 April - 22 September.

Address:
BP 27, 53300 Ambrières-les-Vallées.

Tel:
(0)2.43.04.00.67.
FAX: (0)2.43.08.93.28.

Reservations:
Contact site for details.

Directions: Ambrières-les-Vallées is 12 km. north of Mayenne. Site is well signed from D23, 1.5 km. south of town centre.

7203 Castel Camping Le Château de Chanteloup, Savigne l'Evèque

Peaceful, pleasant site 15 km. from Le Mans, from which to explore La Sarthe.

Situated in the park of an old château in the heart of the Sarthe countryside, this site has a certain rural charm. There are 100 pitches, some well wooded, many on the lawn and completely open, plus a few overlooking the lake, so the degree of shade varies. Apart from those in the wood, the pitches are open and about 70% have electricity (6A, long leads may be necessary). This lack of regimentation enhances the atmosphere and feeling of spaciousness in the grounds surrounding the 19th century château. Sanitary facilities are in the château outbuildings, so are a long way from some pitches. All toilets are British style, washbasins are in cabins. Some showers are push-button, some operate by chain and all have dressing areas with hooks and shelf. Dishwashing sinks are under cover and there is a washing machine. There is a small shop and a pleasant bar with a terrace in the château with breakfast, lunch and dinner served (all 6/6-25/8). Leisure facilities include a swimming pool, children's play area, a room for teenagers, tennis, volleyball, table tennis and mountain bike hire. Tours of the grounds and the village by pony and cart can be arranged and there are organised activities in high season. Golf 14 km, riding 7 km. Free use of tennis club in Le Mans (tennis, squash and badminton). Rooms and gites to let. Torches are useful.

Directions: Site is 15 km. northeast of Le Mans. From autoroute take exit for Le Mans Est, then follow D301 for Yvré l'Evèque, Savigne l'Evèque and Bonnétable. Site is halfway between these last two villages.

Charges 2001:
-- Per pitch Ffr. 55.00; adult 35.00; child (under 8 yrs) 20.00; electricity 20.00.
-- Credit cards accepted.
Open:
1 June - 8 September.
Address:
Sillé-le-Philippe, 72460 Savigne l'Evèque.
Tel:
(0)2.43.27.51.07.
FAX: (0)2.43.89.05.05.
Reservations:
No min. length - contact site.

**Book this site
01892 559898**

THE ALAN ROGERS'
travel service

7201M Camping de la Route d'Or, La Flèche

This is a useful site to know as La Flèche lies at the junction of the Le Mans-Angers and Laval-Saumur roads, along which Britons frequently travel. Set in quiet, park-like surroundings on the south bank of the River Loir (not to be confused with the Loire a few miles to the south), the site is only a pleasant stroll from the town centre where there are plenty of shops and restaurants (neither on site). There are 250 marked pitches on flat grass, many over 100 sq.m. and some with dividing hedges. Some pitches are in the open park, others are shaded by tall trees. Electricity (6/10A) is available in all areas (but long leads may be needed) and there are 30 shady pitches with water and drainaway. The two original sanitary blocks are of the older style but the rather cramped showers are free and WCs are British and Turkish style. The new central block (open from 1/6), has more modern equipment including a second unit for disabled visitors. All the facilities were very clean when we visited. An additional separate block for disabled visitors can be heated in cool weather (used by other campers in winter) and also houses two washing machines and dryers. Good motorcaravan service point (drive-over) with overnight hardstanding possible for larger units. On site are tennis, boules, a playground, swimming and paddling pool (indoor pool in La Flèche), fishing (permit available locally), pedaloes and canoes for hire on the river and bicycle hire (routes in English from reception).

Directions: Site is in southwest outskirts of town just off D938 road to Saumur and is signed from a junction on the bypass.

Charges 2000:
-- Per person Ffr. 17.60; child (under 7) 8.80; car 4.60; tent 5.00; caravan 7.60; motorcaravan 17.60; electricity 6A 8.20 (winter 16.70), 10A 19.30 (winter 38.60); local tax 1.00.
Open:
1 March - 31 October.
Address:
Allée de la Providence, 72200 La Flèche.
Tel:
(0)2.43.94.55.90 or the Office de Tourisme: (0)2.43.94.02.53.
Reservations:
Made without deposit for min. 7 days, but space is usually available.

7206M Camping Municipal du Val de Sarthe, Beaumont-sur-Sarthe

This riverside site is conveniently located just 250 m. walk from this pretty little town and its shops and services. The 73 level, grassy individual pitches are large, divided by growing hedges and all have electricity (5A). At first sight, the exterior of the sanitary unit with its long access ramp is rather bleak. However, inside it has the most modern fittings with British style WCs, some washbasins in cubicles, a good number of semi-open washbasins, but rather few hot showers. The latter are, however, controllable and have dividers. In addition there are facilities for people with disabilities, dishwashing and laundry sinks and a washing machine. Hot water is free. A small children's playground, boules, fishing in the river, shop (1/6-31/8) and a 'salle' complete the on-site facilities. A returnable deposit of Ffr. 200 is required for the entrance barrier card, but the site fees are inexpensive. No double axle caravans are accepted. Motorcaravan service point. Reception opens 08.00-22.00 daily.

Directions: Site is well signed from approach roads and from the town centre.

Charges 2000:
-- Per unit Ffr. 13.10; adult 9.20; child (under 8 yrs) 4.60; electricity 12.10.
-- Credit cards accepted.
Open:
1 May - 30 September.
Address:
Rue de l'Abreuvoir, 72120 Beaumont-sur-Sarthe.
Tel:
02.43.97.01.93.
FAX: (0)2.43.97.02.21.
Reservations:
Not normally necessary.

LOIRE VALLEY - 72 Sarthe / 79 Deux-Sèvres / 86 Vienne

7202M Camping Municipal du Lac, St Calais

St Calais is a small town some 37 km. east of Le Mans. Camping du Lac has some 60 marked pitches, all with electricity (3/6A), water and drain, and is close to a lake and river. It offers very good value in terms of price. There is a swimming pool adjacent and the site is within walking distance of the town and restaurants. Two sanitary blocks provide British style WCs, large hot showers with dividers and some washbasins in private cabins. There are few on-site facilities, but being so close to the town centre this hardly matters. Reception is very welcoming, the value is excellent and this would make a good night stop or base for visiting the Le Mans 24 hour race. Some road noise.

Directions: Well signed from N157, site is by lake north of town, near station.

Charges guide:
-- Per pitch Ffr. 12.20; adult 13.50; child (0-10 yrs) 7.00; electricity 3A 8.70, 6A 15.00.

Open:
1 April - 15 October.

Address:
72120 St Calais.

Tel:
(0)2.43.35.04.81.

Reservations:
Made with Ffr. 100 deposit; contact site.

7901M Camping Municipal de Noron, Niort

A good example of the better type of municipal, this well kept site should be highly satisfactory for overnight or a bit longer. On flat ground, in a quiet setting beside the River Sèvre (fenced, with gate) with mature trees and next to exhibition grounds, it has 168 individual pitches with good shade and a general meadow with play area. Electricity is available (3, 8 or 13A). The sanitary block is of a very fair standard, with British style toilets, many washbasins, some in cabins, plentiful free showers with pre-set hot water, and chemical disposal. Washing machine and ironing board. Children's playground, bicycle hire and fishing on site, riding or golf 5 km. When we visited a mobile snack bar and takeaway service was working well (open 1/6-30/9). A shopping centre is close. The barrier is closed 22.00-07.00 hrs. There is road noise on many pitches. Winter caravan storage.

Directions: Site is west of the town, well signed and adjacent to the ring road running between the N148 and N11 roads.

Charges 2000:
-- Per person Ffr. 17.00; child (under 7 yrs) 10.00; pitch 7.00; pitch 14.00 - 18.00; electricity 15.00.
-- Credit cards accepted.

Open:
1 April - 30 September.

Address:
21 Bd. Salvador Allende, 79000 Niort.

Tel/Fax:
(0)5.49.79.05.06.

Reservations:
Contact site or Tourist office - (0)5.49.24.18.79.

7902 Camping de Courte Vallée, Airvault

Small, attractive, British-run family site on the Route d'Or.

Within minutes of arriving at Courte Vallée, situated in the river valley on the outskirts of Airvault, one is made to feel completely at home, such is the warmth of the welcome. All needs are catered for with vigilance, but yet in a very relaxed manner by Richard and Wendy Curtis, the owners. There are 41 pitches on gently sloping grass, all with electricity (8A). Small trees and shrubs provide some shade and separation. The single, unisex sanitary building, bedecked with flowers, is of a very high standard. Dishwashing and laundry sinks are under cover and there is a free spin dryer. The owners will deal with larger loads of laundry (small charge) in their own washing machine. Like the rest of the site, the swimming pool with surrounding small sunbathing area is well maintained. Essentials, snacks and gas can be purchased from reception, but the historic town of Airvault is only 10-15 minutes walk. Fishing 300 m, riding 8 km. Accompanied visits can be arranged to vineyards, restaurants and châteaux. Futuroscope, Puy de Fou, Fontevrand and Saumur are a reasonable distance. Mobile homes for rent (2). Caravan storage.

Directions: Site is 50 km. south of Saumur, signed off D938 road to Airvault. Watch for signs to Airvault and Courte Vallée with logo.

Charges 2001:
-- Per person Ffr 21.00; child (under 7) 10.00; pitch and vehicle 41.00; animal 10.00; electricity (8A) 15.00.
-- No credit cards.

Open:
1 May - 30 September.

Address:
79600 Airvault.

Tel:
(0)5.49.64.70.65.

FAX: as phone.

E-mail: Ccv79@aol.com.

Reservations:
Contact site for details.

8605M Camping Municipal Le Riveau, La Roche-Posay

This 200 pitch site is in two parts, one new (flatter and more open), the other more mature on something of a slope but with the benefit of shade from tall trees. Each section has some electrical connections (16A). The two sections are divided by a small stream with access to the river Creuse, on which boating and fishing are allowed. The two good sanitary blocks, one in each section, offer free hot showers, British style WCs and facilities for washing, dishwashing, etc. in clean, modern surroundings, with excellent facilities for visitors with disabilities. There are few other facilities, apart from a children's play area, but the town is only about 1.5 km. away. A pleasant, well run site, satisfactory enough and useful for a night-stop or as a base to tour the area.

Directions: Site is signed from the D725 town bypass, turning north at roundabout onto D5 towards Lesigny. Site is 50 m. on right.

Charges 2000:
-- Pitch incl. 1 person Ffr. 31.00; adult 21.00; child 9.00; electricity 15.00.

Open:
1 March - 31 October.

Address:
86270 La Roche-Posay.

Tel:
(0)5.49.86.21.23 or (0)5.49.86.20.59.

Reservations:
Not made and said not to be necessary.

8603 Camping Le Relais du Miel, Châtellerault

New site being developed in the grounds of country house, close to A10 autoroute.

With very easy access from the A10 and N10 roads, in the northern outskirts of Châtellerault, this family owned site is of very promising quality. The site is being developed in the 10 acre grounds of a rather grand house dating from Napoleonic times, beside the River Vienne and surrounded by majestic old trees. Twin barns form two sides of a courtyard behind the house, one of which has already been converted very stylishly into reception and a high ceilinged function and games room, plus a bar and restaurant which serves good value meals. Beyond are an orchard and stone gateposts leading onto ground, previously the home farm, that now forms 80 large, flat pitches. The grass is gradually growing and over 1,000 trees and bushes have been planted, some now providing a little shade. All the 100-200 sq.m. pitches have electricity and water, 20 with drainage connections also. Sanitary facilities of first class quality have been created from three sets of outbuildings with free controllable showers, washbasins in cabins, British style WCs, facilities for disabled people, chemical disposal, dishwashing sinks and a washing machine and dryer in one block. A swimming pool (15 x 7 m; not open all season) with paved surrounds is beside a small snack bar with outdoor tables sheltered by a canopy and which is open in the evenings in season. You are welcome to stroll in the gardens and there is a gate in the walled grounds to the river bank where you may fish. Children's playground, bicycle hire, boules and games room with electronic games, pool and table tennis. Riding 5 km, golf 11 km. Basic essentials and gas are kept, supermarket 400 m. Takeaway. Futuroscope (see advertisement opposite page 289) is 16 km. Caravan storage. The outer gates are closed at 10 pm. and you need a code to get in after this time. Torches are necessary.

Charges 2000:
-- Per pitch incl. 2 persons, electricity and water Ffr. 130.00; extra person over 5 yrs 20.00; extra tent 20.00; dog 10.00.
-- Less 15% for 1 week, 20% for 2 weeks.
-- Credit cards accepted.

Open:
1 May - 30 September.

Address:
Route d'Antran, 86160 Châtellerault.

Tel:
(0)5.49.02.06.27.
FAX: (0)5.49.93.25.76.
E-mail: camping@ lerelaisdumiel.com.

Reservations:
Contact site for details.

Book this site
01892 559898

THE ALAN ROGERS'
travel service

Directions: Take exit 26 from A10 autoroute (Châtellerault-Nord); site is signed just off the roundabout. From N10 follow signs for Antran north of the town.

8606M Camping Municipal de Bonnes, Bonnes

Bordering the Vienne river (unfenced) this tranquil, well managed site enjoys attractive views of the river and surrounding countryside. The 60 numbered, but not separated grassy, level pitches all have electricity (15A) and water connections. The unisex sanitary block is modern and well maintained, with showers, toilets (some British style), dishwashing and laundry facilities. There are no on-site catering facilities but the small village only 100 m. away will satisfy basic needs. River fishing is permitted from the river bank. Canoe hire. In high season there are guided local walks and archery once a week. A large tent accommodates further activities. Bungalows to rent.

Charges guide:
-- Per adult Ffr. 17.00; child (under 7 yrs) 8.00; vehicle 6.00; pitch 11.00; dog 7.00; electricity 15.00.

Open:
1 May - 30 September.

Address:
Rue de la Varenne, 86300 Bonnes.

Tel:
(0)5.49.56.44.34 or the Mairie (0)5.49.56.40.17.
FAX: (0)5.49.56.48.51.

Reservations:
Contact site.

Directions: Site is just south of the village of Bonnes, 5 km. from N151 road, 22 km. from Poitiers and 5 km. from Chauvigny.

LOIRE VALLEY - 86 Vienne

8601 Castel Camping Le Petit Trianon de St Ustre, Ingrandes

Good family run site close to main N10 between Tours, Poitiers and Futuroscope.

Le Petit Trianon has been a popular overnight stop close to the N10, one of the main routes to the southwest, for a good number of years. The site consists of a slightly sloping meadow surrounded by trees in front of the château, a newer, large, more open field to one side, with a woodland area between. The 95 spacious, open but marked pitches are arranged to leave plenty of free space and there is shade in parts. Over 70 have electricity (6/10A) and 5 are fully serviced. Reception is housed in the château and this and the old traditional outbuildings contain many of the main facilities, including the original sanitary unit which is beginning to look a little dated and in need of refurbishment, but a few rooms can be heated in cool weather. Besides the usual showers, washbasins in cabins and British style WCs, other rooms contain washbasin and shower combination units, baby bathrooms, a laundry with washing machines and sinks for dishwashing. The newer and smaller blocks have been added to serve the newer parts of the site and one contains facilities for disabled people. Notices on these blocks say which pitch numbers should use which facilities. The heated swimming and paddling pools (open at set hours) are on the sunny side of a rather picturesque castled facade in which is a large, cool reading room. There is a restaurant 50 m. away with the menu displayed on the site. Shop with essentials and drinks (open certain hours). Takeaway. Activities include a children's playground, minigolf, table tennis, badminton, croquet, volleyball and boules. TV room with satellite, books and games. Bicycle hire and organised VTT rides, plus other excursions. Fishing 3 km. Some self-catering accommodation, chalets and gite to let. Chemical disposal and motorcaravan service point. Caravan storage. Futuroscope at Poitiers is well worth at least a day's visit (if you stay for the after dusk laser, firework and fountain show, remember your late night entry code for the site gate).

Charges 2001:
-- Per person Ffr. 38.00; child 3-6 yrs 19.00, 0-2 yrs 6.00; vehicle 22.00; pitch 23.00; electricity 5A 23.00, 10A 25.00; local tax (over 3 yrs) 1.00.
-- Less 10-20% for longer stays.
-- Credit cards accepted.

Open:
15 May - 20 September.

Address:
86220 Ingrandes-sur-Vienne.

Tel:
(0)5.49.02.61.47. FAX: (0)5.49.02.68.81. E-mail: chateau@petit-trianon.fr.

Reservations:
Made with 25% deposit and fee (Ffr. 80); min. 5 days in July/Aug.

Directions: Ingrandes is signed from the N10 north of the town, which is between Dangé and Châtellerault. From autoroute A10 take exit 26 for Châtellerault-Nord and at roundabout follow signs for Tours to Ingrandes where site is signed.

8604 Camping Le Futuriste, St Georges-Baillargeaux, nr Poitiers

Purpose built site on a hill overlooking Futuroscope, open all year.

On raised ground with panoramic views over the strikingly modern buildings and night-time bright lights that comprise the popular attraction of Futuroscope, Le Futuriste is a neat, modern site. It is ideal for a short stay to visit the park which is only 1.5 km. away (tickets can be bought at the site) but it is equally good for longer stays to see the region. With a busy atmosphere, there are early departures and late arrivals. Reception is open 08.00-22.00 hrs. There are 112 individual, flat, grassy pitches, all divided by young trees and shrubs which are beginning to provide some shelter for this elevated and otherwise rather open site (possibly windy). There are 28 pitches without electricity for tents, 22 with electricity (16A) and a further 62 with electricity, water, waste water and sewage connections. All are accessed via neat, level and firmly rolled gravel roads. Excellent, very clean sanitary facilities are housed in two modern, insulated blocks which can be heated in cool weather. In the newest block the facilities are unisex. There are roomy, controllable showers, washbasins in cabins and British style WCs and facilities for disabled people. In separate rooms are dishwashing and laundry sinks, plus a washing machine and dryer. If you have time to spend on the site, there are two outdoor pools, one with a slide, with paved surrounds (1/5-30/9), a children's play area and TV/games room. A snack bar/takeaway is open mornings, lunchtimes and evenings until 10 pm. and a small shop (all 1/5-30/9) provides essentials (order bread the night before); there are plenty of supermarkets near. Free fishing on site. Bicycle hire 500 m, golf 5 km. Of course, the area has other attractions and details are available from the enthusiastic young couple who run the site. New heated chalets to rent (6). It is best to see the first evening show at Futuroscope (see opposite page 289) otherwise you will find youself locked out of the site - the gates are closed at 23.30 hrs.

Charges 2000:
-- Per pitch incl. 1-3 persons Ffr. 75.00 - 102.00; extra person 8.00 - 13.00; local tax 1.00, under 10 yrs 0.50; dog 9.00 (1/7-31/8 only); electricity 13.00 -18.00.
-- Credit cards accepted (not Amex).

Open:
All year.

Address:
86130 St Georges Les Baillargeaux.

Tel:
(0)5.49.52.47.52. FAX: as phone. E-mail: d.Radet@libertysurf.fr.

Reservations:
Phone bookings accepted for min. 2 nights.

Camping Cheques

**Book this site
01892 559898**

THE ALAN ROGERS'
travel service

*see colour advert
between pages 160/161*

Directions: From A10 autoroute or the N10, take Futurosope exit. Site is east of both roads, off the D20 to St Georges-Les-Baillargeaux. From all directions follow signs to St Georges. Site is on hill; turn by water tower to site on left.

BURGUNDY

Major city: Dijon

Départements: 21 Côte d'Or, 58 Nièvre, 71 Saône-et-Loire, 89 Yonne

Burgundy (Bourgogne), in the rich heartland of France, is an historic region, once a powerful independent state and important religious centre. Its golden age is reflected in the area's magnificent art and architecture – the grand palaces and art collections of Dijon, the great pilgrimage church of Vézelay, the Cistercian Abbaye de Fontenay and the evocative abbey remains at Cluny, once the most powerful monastery in Europe. However Burgundy is best known for its wine including some of the world's finest, produced from the great vineyards of the Côte d'Or and Chablis, and perhaps for its rich cuisine including such dishes as 'Boeuf Bourguignon'. No-one can visit Burgundy without going to the 15th century Hotel Dieu at Beaune. It is both an attractive home for the elderly and where the annual Burgundy wine auctions are held. Once inside, take the conducted tour and you will see the wonderful patterned tile roofs and even the old hospital wards where patients were laid two to a bed. The area is criss-crossed by navigable waterways and also includes the 'Parc Régional du Morvan' good walking country. It is interesting to note that Dijon itself is only an hour and a half from Paris on the TGV.

Note: the site reports are laid out by département in numerical order. **See map on page 312.**

Cuisine of the region

Many dishes are wine based, eg. *'Coq au Chambertin'* and *'Poulet au Meursault'*
Dijon is known for its spiced honey-cake (*pain d'épice*) and spicy mustard
Boeuf Bourguignon – braised beef simmered in a red wine-based sauce
Charolais (Pièce de) – steak from the excellent Charolais cattle
Garbure – heavy soup, a mixture of pork, cabbage, beans and sausages
Gougère – cheese pastry based on Gruyère
Jambon persillé – parsley-flavoured ham, served cold in jelly
Matelote – fresh-water fish soup, usually based on a red wine sauce
Meurette – red wine-based sauce with small onions, used with fish or poached egg dishes

Wine

Burgundy is produced mainly from vineyards in the sheltered valleys that stretch south from Dijon to Lyon. The region is further subdivided into five main areas (north to south): Chablis, Côte d'Or, Côte Chalonnaise, Mâconais and Beaujolais. It is the Côte d'Or region centred around Beaune that produces the great wines on which Burgundy's reputation depends

Places of interest

Autun – 12th century St Lazare cathedral.
Beaune – medieval town; its Hospices are a masterpiece of Flemish-Burgundian architecture; Museum of Burgundy Wine
Cluny – Europe's largest Benedictine abbey
Dijon – Palace of the Dukes, Fine Arts Museum, Burgundian Folklore Museum. Unfortunately development has ruined much of the original medieval city centre
Fontenay – Fontenay Abbey and Cloister
Joigny – medieval town
Mâcon – Maison des Vins (wine centre)
Paray-le-Monial – Romanesque basilica, pilgrimage centre
Sens – historic buildings, museum with fine Gallo-Roman collections
Vézelay – fortified medieval hillside, Magdalene Basilica

2104M Camping Municipal de Fouché, Arnay le Duc

Useful as an overnight stop en-route to or from the Mediterranean or indeed for longer stays, this quite large but peaceful, lakeside site has good facilities and the added advantage of being open all year. It can be very busy during the school holidays, and is probably better visited outside the main season. There are 190 good sized pitches, on fairly level grass and all with 10A electricity (some with water). This part of Burgundy is popular and Arnay le Duc is an attractive little town with an interesting history and renowned for its gastronomy, with many hotels and restaurants. The site is within walking distance of the town centre, where there are also an indoor pool, tennis courts, etc. In season there is a shop on site (with bread) and snacks and drinks are served. Amenities include a TV/games room, boules pitch, table tennis and a children's playground. The pitches, many of which are hedged, offer a choice of shade or more open aspect. Two of the four sanitary blocks are reasonably modern, well maintained with modern fittings and include free hot showers, some British style WCs, washbasins in cabins, facilities for disabled visitors, washing machines and dishwashing facilities under cover.

Directions: Site is on east side of town (well signed), 15 km. from A6 autoroute (exit at péage de Puilly en Auxois).

Charges 2001:
-- Per unit incl. 2 persons Ffr. 50.00 - 60.00; extra person 14.00 - 17.00; child (under 7 yrs) 7.00 - 8.50; electricity 15.00 - 18.00; animal 5.00 - 6.00; local tax 1/4-30/9 (over 16 yrs) 2.00.
-- Credit cards accepted.

Open:
All year.

Address:
Rue de 8 mai 1945, 21230 Arnay-le-Duc.

Tel:
(0)3.80.90.02.23.
FAX: (0)3.80.90.11.91.

Reservations:
Advised; contact site.

CAMPING OF FOUCHÉ*** In the heart of Burgundy

The campsite*** enjoys a family atmosphere and has 190 pitches, in a calm and shaded environment. Medieval town. Open all year.
Beside a lake - Fishing - Supervised beach Aquatic toboggan - Paddleboats - Children s playground - Playroom - TV - Footpath - Mountain bike amenities.

21230 ARNAY-LE-DUC
Tel: 33 (0)380 90 02 23
Fax: 33 (0)380 90 11 91
www.arnay-le-duc.com

NEW : HUTS ON HIRE

2102M Camping Municipal Les Cent Vignes, Beaune

This well kept, 2 ha. site has 116 individual pitches of good size, separated from each other by neat beech hedges high enough to keep a fair amount of privacy. Rather over half of the pitches are on grass, ostensibly for tents, the remainder on hardstandings with electricity for caravans. The two modern sanitary blocks, one heated, provide British style toilets, washbasins (nearly all in cabins), free hot pre-set showers and sinks. Washing machines. Shop, restaurant with takeaway (all 1/4-15/10). Children's playground, sports area with tennis, basketball, volleyball, boules, table tennis and a barbecue area. Fishing or golf 4 km, bicycle hire 1 km. A popular site, within walking distance of the town centre, Les Cent Vignes becomes full mid-June to early Sept. Beaune, of course, is in the Burgundy wine producing area, and several 'caves' in the town can be visited.

Directions: From autoroute exit 24 (new) follow signs for Beaune centre on the D2 road, camping signs to site in approx. 1 km. Well signed from other routes.

Charges 2000:
-- Per person Ffr. 18.00; child (2-7 yrs) 9.00; pitch 25.00; electricity (6A) 20.00; local tax 2.00.
-- Credit cards accepted.

Open:
15 March - 31 October.

Address:
10 Rue Auguste Dubois, 21200 Beaune.

Tel:
(0)3.80.22.03.91.

Reservations:
Made before 30 May without deposit.

2103M Camping Municipal Les Premiers Pres, Savigny-lès-Beaune

This popular site is ideally located for visiting the Burgundy vineyards, for use as a transit site or spending time in the town of Beaune. It offers an alternative to our already popular site (no. 2102M). In high season it is full every evening, so arrive by 4 pm. The 90 level pitches are marked and numbered, with electric hook-ups and room for an awning. If reception is closed when you arrive, find a pitch and report later, otherwise `Madame' will allocate a place. Sanitary facilities, kept very clean and renovated and extended, are housed in a modern building behind reception. Hot water is free. Additional WCs and water points are towards the middle of the site and there is a motorcaravan service point. Torches useful at night. The bureau staff are pleasant and a bottle of local wine, soft drinks and ice may be purchased.

Directions: From A6 autoroute take exit 24 signed Beaune, Savigny-lès-Beaune on D2. Turn right towards Savigny-lès-Beaune (3 km) and follow signs to site.

Charges guide:
-- Per person Ffr. 10.00; child (under 7 yrs) 5.00; vehicle 5.00; pitch 16.00; electricity 19.00.

Open:
1 May - 30 September.

Address:
21420 Savigny-lès-Beaune.

Tel:
(0)3.80.26.15.06 or (0)3.80.21.51.21.
FAX: (0)3.80.21.56.63.

Reservations:
Not accepted.

2101M Camping Municipal Louis Rigoly, Châtillon-sur-Seine

This well kept, small, hillside municipal site has 54 pitches, mainly individual and separated on fairly flat grass, 48 with electricity (4A). Mature trees provide shelter. The main toilet block at the lower end of the site is satisfactory with washbasins in open cubicles with hot water and pre-set, free showers. A smaller heated unit behind reception contains facilities for babies, plus a washing machine and dryer. Chemical disposal. Facilities for disabled visitors are provided in a separate block. Adjoining the site is the municipal swimming pool complex with both indoor and outdoor pools (on payment), and minigolf. Snack bar July/Aug. Children's play area. No shop, but town is close. Fishing or bicycle hire 1 km, riding 4 km. The site, which has much transit trade, can become full by evening in season.

Directions: On northeast outskirts of town; site is signed from centre (steep hills approaching site, narrow roads).

Charges 2001:
-- Per person Ffr. 17.00; child (under 7) 8.00; vehicle 8.00; m/cycle 5.00; pitch 13.00; electricity 12.00 - 24.00.
-- No credit cards.

Open:
1 April - 30 September.

Address:
Esplanade Saint-Vorles, 21400 Châtillon-s-Seine.

Tel:
(0)3.80.91.03.05.
FAX: (0)3.80.91.21.46.
E-mail: tourism.chatillon-sur-seine@wanadoo.fr.

Reservations:
Not officially made, but if you write they will reserve until 7 p.m.

2100 Camping Lac de Panthier, Vandenesse en Auxois

Attractively situated lakeside site in Burgundy countryside.

Spread over what was formerly two campsites, the owners of Lac de Panthier have now successfully created two distinctively different locations within one campsite - one where the site activities take place and the other where the reception, shop, bar and restaurant can be found, the latter offering a quieter and more attractive setting. There are four good quality sanitary blocks, one ultra modern. Facilities include provision for babies and people with disabilities. There are 200 pitches, all with electricity connections (6A), mostly on level grass, although in parts there are shallow terraces. A swimming pool complex offers an adults' pool, children's pool and water-slide, but the most obvious attraction is their proximity to the lake with its many watersports facilities. This site is in beautiful countryside within 2 km. of the lovely Canal de Bourgogne, which links the Seine and the Saône rivers. Boat excursions are available from Pouilly en Auxois which is about 8 km. Dijon, Autun and Beaune are also within easy reach. A 'Sites et Paysages' member.

Directions: From the A6 use exit 24 (where the A6 joins the A38). Take the N81 towards Arnay Le Duc (back over the A6), then almost immediately turn left on D977 for 5 km. Fork left again for Vandenesse en Auxois. Continue through village on D977 for 2.5 km, turn left again and site is on left.

Charges guide:
-- Per unit incl. 2 adults Ffr. 104.00; child under 7 years 16.00; electricity 20.00.

Open:
1 May - 30 September.

Address:
21320 Vandenesse en Auxois.

Tel:
(0)3.80.49.21.94.
FAX: (0)3.80.49.25.80.

Reservations:
Contact site for details.

`Camping Cheque'

5806M Camping Municipal Les Pres de la Ville, Premery

Quietly located on the edge of this attractive small town and close to the river and lake, this small site is a useful, budget-priced, all weather option. There is a pleasant walk around the lake and into the town. The 32 caravan and motor-caravan pitches are grouped into small bays surrounded by tall laurel hedges, there is a tree to shade each unit, and electricity is available to all (5A). All these pitches are on gravel hardstanding, but a grassy area is provided for tents. The neat little unisex sanitary unit, despite its rather bare concrete floor in the main areas, provides two very large, well tiled, controllable hot showers, each with a plastic stool and hooks but no divider. In addition there are British and Turkish style WCs and six washbasins (two in cubicles), plus shaver or hairdryer sockets. Dishwashing and laundry sinks, plus chemical disposal. Hot water is free throughout and there is a WC and shower for disabled people. Reception opens 08.30-09.30, 19.00-20.00, from 1/5-29/6 and 08.00-22.30 in high season. A baker calls daily in season. Fishing, boating and swimming is possible in the lake. Golf 10 km, bicycle hire 300 m. Six chalets for rent.

Directions: Site off the D977 on the eastern outskirts of the town and is well signed.

Charges 2000:
-- Per unit incl. 2 adults Ffr. 45.00; extra adult 18.00; child (under 12 yrs) 11.00; small tent with bicycle or m/cycle 21.00; electricity 6.00 - 10.00.
-- No credit cards.

Open:
1 May - 15 September.

Address:
58700 Premery.

Tel:
(0)3.86.68.12.40.

Reservations:
Not normally necessary.

BURGUNDY - 58 Nièvre

5801 Camping-Caravaning Les Bains, St Honoré-les-Bains

Attractive family run site with pool, close to small spa-town.

With 130 large, separated pitches (100 sq.m. and all with 6A electricity) and many trees, this is an attractive site, owned and run by the Luneau family who are keen to welcome British visitors. It is well situated for exploring the Morvan area. However, the site is low-lying, pitches can be rather soft in wet weather and it can also be quite cold at night in early or late season. The site has its own small swimming pool (12 x 12 m) with a separate aqua slide (15/6-15/9), an excellent new children's play area, and two small streams for children to fish in, one of which is warm from the thermal springs. The actual thermal park is next door with added attractions for children. A traditional family bar (1/6-30/9) also provides food and a takeaway service (1/6-15/9). Table tennis, minigolf and entertainment weekly for children in July/Aug. The two main sanitary units have mostly British WCs, washbasins in separate cabins and ample hot showers. A new block has been added in '99. There are dishwashing sinks (with hot water), a baby bath, facilities for disabled people, chemical disposal and laundry facilities. There are opportunities locally for 'taking the waters' which, combined with the clean, pollution free environment, are said to be very good for asthma sufferers ('cures' run for three week periods). A canal-side cycle route runs for 50 km. from Vandenesse (6 km). Bicycle hire or riding 500 m, fishing 5 km. Modern gîtes for hire all year. Winter caravan storage. A Sites et Paysages member.

Charges 2001:
-- Per unit incl. 2 persons Ffr. 93.00; extra person 25.00; child (under 7 yrs) 15.00; dog 6.00; local tax 2.00 (child 1.00); electricity (6A) 18.00.
-- Less 20-30% outside 1/7-29/8.
-- Credit cards accepted.

Open:
1 May - 30 September.

Address:
BP 17, 15 Av. Jean Mermoz, 58360 St Honoré-les-Bains.

Tel:
(0)3.86.30.73.44. FAX: (0)3.86.30.61.88.

Reservations:
Write to site with deposit (Ffr. 420) and fee (80).

Directions: From the north approach via D985 from Auxerre, through Clamecy and Corbigny to St Honoré-les-Bains, from where site signed 'Village des Bains'.

Book this site
01892 559898

THE ALAN ROGERS'
travel service

5803 Castel Camping Manoir de Bezolle, St Péreuse-en-Morvan

Well situated site for exploring the Morvan Natural Park and the Nivernais area.

This site has been attractively landscaped to provide a number of different areas and terraces, giving some pleasant views over the surrounding countryside. Clearly separated pitches are on level grass with some terracing and a choice of shade or otherwise. The majority have electricity (6A or more) and some are large (150 sq.m). Several features are worthy of special mention including a large swimming pool (1/6-15/9) and children's pool with terrace, a good restaurant with a varied menu (15/5-15/9), pizza and takeaway service (main season only), two small lakes one of which is used for fishing, and a Red Indian village with ponies for children. Animation is organised in season. Sanitary facilities are in four units – a small older style unit by the pool and restaurant complex, and a new fibreglass unit containing two tiny family WC/basin/shower suites available for rent. Two large, more central units of different ages provide the main services. Facilities include baths, pre-set showers, basins in private cabins (many with cold water), mostly British WCs, provision for disabled people and a baby bath. Laundry, chemical disposal and motorcaravan service facilities. Some sanitary facilities may be closed at the beginning and end of the season. Shop (15/5-15/9). Activities on site include horse riding (June-Sept), minigolf, a games room, bicycle hire for children (otherwise 8 km). table tennis and fishing. Mobile homes for rent. Used by British tour operators. Caravan storage available.

Charges 2000:
-- Per unit incl. 2 persons Ffr. 80.00 - 120.00; extra person 20.00 - 30.00; child (under 7 yrs) 15.00 - 20.00; electricity 6A 25.00, extra 4A 12.00; water and drainage connection 14.00; animal 10.00; extra car 10.00 - 12.00; local taxes 3.00.
-- Credit cards accepted.

Open:
15 April - 30 September.

Address:
58110 Saint Péreuse en Morvan.

Tel:
(0)3.86.84.42.55. FAX: (0)3.86.84.43.77.
E-mail:
info@bezolle.com.

Reservations:
Made with deposit (Ffr. 300) and fee (100); contact site.

Directions: Site is mid-way between Châtillon-en-Bazois and Château-Chinon, just north of the D978 by the small village of St Péreuse-en-Morvan.

Book this site
01892 559898

THE ALAN ROGERS'
travel service

see colour advert
between pages 96/97

Camping
des Bains
★ ★ ★

Burgundy — Morvan
at the spa & tourist resort of
SAINT-HONORE-LES-BAINS

☆ Peaceful family holiday, individual shaded pitches in hedged bays
☆ 300 metres from the Thermal Park ☆ On the edge of the MORVAN
REGIONAL NATURE PARK with abundant flora and fauna for the rambler to
see, whether on foot, bicycle or even horse-back ☆ 65 km from the vineyards
of BOURGOGNE and VÉZELAY Basilica ☆ Swimming pool, Paddling pool,
waterchute, volley ball, table tennis, pony-riding, children's playground
☆ Crazy golf ☆ Snack-pizza ☆ RESERVATION ADVISED

CAMPING LES BAINS, Route de VANDENESSE,
58360 ST-HONORE-LES-BAINS Tel. 03 86 30 73 44

7102M Le Village des Meuniers, Dompierre-les-Ormes, nr Mâcon

In a tranquil setting, with panoramic views, the neat appearance of the reception building, that also houses a café, bar, shop and takeaway, sets the tone for the rest of this attractive site. It is an excellent example of current trends in French tourism development. The 113 terraced, grassy pitches, some with hardstanding, are all fairly level, each with electricity (15A) and ample water points. They all enjoy stunning views of the surrounding countryside – the Beaujolais, the Maconnais, the Charollais and the Clunysois. The site is 500 m. from Dompierre-les-Ormes, a small village of 850 people, offering all services (banks and some shops, closed Sun/Mon). Sanitary facilities are mainly in an unusual, purpose designed hexagonal block, with modern fittings, all of a very high standard with British style WCs. A smaller unit is in the lower area of the site, plus further WCs in the main reception building. A motorcaravan service point is in the site car park. An extensive sunbathing area surrounds the attractively designed swimming pool complex (three heated pools and a toboggan run; 1/6-30/9). This is a superior municipal site, tastefully landscaped, with a high standard of cleanliness in all areas. As the hedges and trees mature they will offer more shade. Fishing 1.5 km, riding 10 km. Children's activities are organised in high season. Adjacent to the main site is an overflow field with electricity, water and a small toilet block, offering two star accommodation in high season. The site has a complex of high quality wooden gites operated by Gites de France (all year), plus 8 of their own small chalets. This is an area well worth visiting, with attractive scenery, interesting history, excellent wines and good food. Used by tour operators (28%).

Directions: Town is 35 km. west of Macon. Follow N79/E62 (Charolles/Paray/Digoin) road and turn south onto D41 to Dompierre-les-Ormes (3 km). Site is clearly signed through village.

Charges 2001:
-- Per person Ffr. 25.00 - 35.00; child (under 7 yrs) 12.00 - 17.00; pitch 30.00 - 40.00; electricity 15.00; family rate (2+ children) 110.00 - 150.00.
-- Credit cards accepted.

Open:
28 April - 30 September.

Address:
71520 Dompierre-les-Ormes.

Tel:
(0033) (0)3.85.50.36.60. FAX: as phone in season (winter): (0033) (0)3.85.50.36.61). E-mail: levillagedesmeuniers @wanadoo.fr.

Reservations:
Advised for July/Aug; contact site.

**Book this site
01892 559898**

THE ALAN ROGERS'
travel service

*see colour advert
between pages 96/97*

7101M Camping Municipal, Mâcon

Always useful and well cared for, this site has been greatly improved in recent years. For a large site near a big town and close to a main route south, it has a neat, well cared for appearance, with 275 good sized pitches, all with 5A electricity, plus a number of 'super' pitches. They are on mown, flat grass, accessed by tarmac roads, with a generally bright and cheerful ambience. The sanitary facilities are in three modernised, well maintained units with British and Turkish style WCs, washbasins in cubicles, and pre-set hot showers with dividers and shelves. A fourth modern block is adjacent to the new unheated swimming and paddling pools (built for the use of campers only). There are facilities for disabled visitors, dishwashing and laundry sinks, plus a washing machine and dryer. Some sanitary facilities are closed out of peak season. Other amenities include a shop/tabac, bar, takeaway, a restaurant (le Tipi) open midday and evenings, a good TV lounge and a children's playground. Gates closed 10.00-06.30 hrs. Swimming pool, sports stadium and supermarket nearby. Excellent motorcaravan service point (with Fiamma sewage couplings), but large units note - the security barrier has a 3 m. height restriction so watch those top boxes and air-conditioners! This is a conveniently located transit site.

Directions: Site is on northern outskirts of Mâcon on main N6, 3 km. from the town centre (just south of A40 autoroute junction).

Charges 2000:
- - Per tent incl. 2 adults Ffr. 60.00, with electricity (5A) 75.00; caravan or motorcaravan incl. 2 adults 71.00, with electricity (5A), water and drain 86.00; extra adult 19.00; child (under 7 yrs) 10.00; dog 4.50; electricity (10A) 17.00.
-- Credit cards accepted.

Open:
15 March - 31 October.

Address:
71000 Mâcon.

Tel:
(0)3.85.38.16.22 or (0)3.85.38.54.05. FAX: (0)3.85.39.71.24

Reservations:
Not normally required.

BURGUNDY - 71 Saône-et-Loire

7107 Camping-Caravaning Château de l'Epervière, Gigny-sur-Saône

Enthusiastically run rural site in the grounds of a château.

Peacefully situated on the edge of the little village of Gigny-sur-Saône, yet within easy distance of the A6 autoroute, this site nestles in a natural woodland area near the Saône river. With 135 pitches, nearly all with 6A electricity, the site is in two fairly distinct areas - the original with semi-hedged pitches on part-level ground with plenty of shade from mature trees, close to the château and fishing lake. The centre of the second area has a more open aspect, with large hedged pitches and mature trees offering shade around the periphery and central open grass area. There is an unheated swimming pool (1/5-30/9), partly enclosed by old stone walls protecting it from the wind, plus a smaller indoor heated pool with jacuzzi and sauna, a children's play area and paddling pool, and bicycle hire. The tastefully refurbished restaurant in the château has a distinctly French menu (1/4-30/9). There is also a second with a more basic menu and a takeaway service. A converted barn houses an attractive bar, TV and games room. The shop provides bread and basic provisions (1/5-30/9). There are two sanitary blocks, one beside the château and a newer one on the lower section, both providing modern facilities, including free hot showers, washbasins in cabins and British type WCs (some 'state of the art' in the newer block). Chemical disposal. Dishwashing and laundry areas are under cover. A washing machine and dryer are in an upper room off the courtyard. Chrisophe Gay, the owner, and his team enthusiastically organise a range of activities for visitors that include wine tastings in the cellars of the château and a Kids' Club in July/Aug. Christophe is the founder and driving force behind 'Camping Cheques', the low season 'Go as you please' package that gives flexibility to visit Camping Cheque sites in Europe (see colour advertisement opposite page 160). Riding 15 km, golf 20 km. Used by tour operators (60 pitches). Apartments to let in the château. A member of 'Les Castels' group.

Directions: From N6 between Châlon-sur-Saône and Tournus, turn east on D18 (just north of Sennecey-le-Grand) and follow site signs for 6.5 km. From A6, exit Châlon-Sud from the north, or Tournus from the south.

Charges 2001:
-- Per adult Ffr. 29.00 - 37.00; child (under 7 yrs) 20.00 - 24.00; pitch 41.00 - 56.00; dog 11.00 - 12.00; electricity 20.00 - 24.00.
-- Credit cards accepted.
Open:
1 April - 15 October.
Address:
71240 Gigny-sur-Saône.
Tel:
(0)3.85.94.16.90.
FAX: (0)3.85.94.16.93.
E-mail:
FFH@wanadoo.fr.
Reservations:
Contact site.
`Camping Cheque'

Book this site
01892 559898
THE ALAN ROGERS'
travel service

see colour advert
between pages 160/161

7106 Camping du Château de Montrouant, Gibles

Pretty rural site open for a short season (popular for fishing).

This small pretty site is in a steep valley in the rolling Charollais hills, beside a small lake in the grounds of an imposing château (access road is poor). There is ample shade from the many mature trees and the 45 pitches are on reasonably flat grassy terraces, mainly separated by small hedges, all having electrical connections (min. 6A), but probably best for smaller units as access is difficult and roadways poor. The whole appearance is attractive with some pitches overlooking the lake, some next to the field where ponies graze. A swimming pool, with secluded sunbathing area, has been sympathetically landscaped. There is also a very small open-air bar/restaurant for evening barbecues (only open certain evenings), half-court tennis and pony riding. The enthusiastic owner is quite laid-back, but organises several unusual and interesting activities during the main season, including stone masonry, model boat building, walks, wine tours, etc. Good fishing is possible in the site's lakes and is a feature of the site. Essentials are available from reception but the village of Gibles, with shops, restaurant, etc. is only 2 km. The sanitary facilities, not too well designed and with maintenance that can be variable, are housed in a part of the château. They include washbasins in cabins, hot showers with dividers, dishwashing sinks, British style WCs, washing machine, dryer, etc. A torch is useful. Regrettably the season here is short and the site becomes quickly full mid-July - mid-Aug. and is very popular with the Dutch. The best times could be from late June - mid July or the second half of August. Used by a Dutch tour operator. A Sites et Paysages member.

Directions: Site is to the west of Mâcon and can be reached from the A6 via the N79 to Charolles (approx. 55 km). Take the D985 road south from Charolles for 19 km. to La Clayette, then follow signs for Gibles and site (approx. 7 km). Alternatively the site can be reached from the D982 Roanne - Digoin road. Exit for Pouilly, pass through Charlieu and Châteauneuf to La Clayette.

Charges guide:
-- Per person Ffr. 24.50; child (under 7) 15.50; pitch 22.00; vehicle 22.00; electricity (6A) 21.00; dog 12.00.
-- Special weekly charges.
Open:
1 June - 8 September.
Address:
71800 Gibles.
Tel:
(0)3.85.84.54.30 or (0)3.85.84.51.13.
FAX: (0)3.85.84.52.80.
Reservations:
Essential for 8/7-25/8 and made with 25% deposit.
`Camping Cheque'

7103M Camping Municipal St Vital, Cluny

Close to this attractive small town (300 m. walk), and adjacent to the municipal swimming pool (free for campers), this site has 174 pitches all on gently sloping grass, with some small hedges and shade in parts. Electricity (6A) is available, but long leads may be needed. Some rail noise is noticeable during the day but we are assured that trains do not run 23.30-07.00 hrs. The two sanitary buildings provide British and Turkish style WCs, some washbasins in cubicles, controllable showers (no dividers), dishwashing and laundry sinks, a washing machine and dryer, plus a chemical disposal point. Hot water is free throughout. A rubbish recycling system operates. In high season, on Friday evenings, there is a presentation of local produce in the 'salle de reunion'. The town has the largest number of Roman houses in France, the National Stud farm, and don't miss the Cheese Tower for the best views of Cluny. In the surrounding area you will find the Grottes de Blanot (a network of grottoes and underground passages) the largest in Burgundy, and many other items of interest. Ask for a free copy of 'Cluny, town of Art and History', at reception or the tourist office. The really excellent traffic free cycle path from Cluny to Givry is highly recommended.

Charges 2001:
-- Per pitch Ffr. 11.00; adult 19.00; child (under 7 yrs) 10.00; vehicle 11.00; electricity 15.00; dog free.
-- Credit cards accepted.
Open:
15 May - 30 September.
Address:
Rue des Griottons, 71250 Cluny.
Tel:
(0)3.85.59.08.34. FAX: as phone.
Reservations:
Advised for high season; contact site.

Directions: Site is east of town, by the D15 road towards Azé and Blanot.

7104M Camping Municipal Le Val d'Arroux, Toulon-sur-Arroux

This budget priced, well managed and neatly laid out site, is located on a quieter more minor cross-country route, where good sites are not that easy to find. About 40 of its 68 pitches are available to tourists and these are level, grassy and divided into small sections by hedges and flowers, with some mature trees for shade. All have electricity (6A). The central unisex sanitary unit has British style WCs, washbasins in cubicles, hot showers, facilities for disabled people, plus chemical disposal, dishwashing and laundry sinks. Free hot water throughout. A small children's playground, floodlit minigolf, fishing in the adjacent river, a covered area, plus games machines and table tennis complete the on-site amenities. Reception is open from 07.30-12.00 and 14.00-22.00 in main season and a map of walks around the area is available for a small charge. The town with its shops and other services is within walking distance.

Charges 2000:
-- Per pitch Ffr. 7.50; adult 8.50; child (under 7 yrs) 4.40; vehicle 7.50; electricity 16.00.
Open:
Easter - 31 October.
Address:
71320 Toulon-sur-Arroux
Tel:
(0)3.85.79.51.22 (Mairie: (0)3.85.79.42.55 FAX: (0)3.85.79.52.76).
Reservations:
Not normally necessary.

Directions: Site is just off the D985 and is well signed from the town. It is on the western edge of town, on the west bank of the river.

7105 Camping Moulin de Collonge, Saint-Boil

Well run, family site in the heart of the Burgundy countryside.
This site offers an 'away from it all' situation surrounded by sloping vineyards and golden wheat fields, and has instant appeal for those seeking a quiet, relaxing environment. There are 50 pitches which are level and most have electrical hook-ups. Reception and the sanitary facilities are housed in a converted barn which is tastefully decorated and well kept. There are British style WCs, washbasins in cubicles, shaving points and showers. Sinks for dishes and laundry are outside with washing machine and dryer under cover. Hanging flower arrangements are in abundance and, like the shrubs and grounds, are constantly being attended to by the proprietor and his family (M. Gillot's other interest is the restoration of classic cars). Beyond the stream which borders the site are a swimming pool, patio and a pizzeria which is also open to the public all year. The pool is covered by a plastic dome - some of the walls can be opened in good weather. A new lake, 1.8 m. deep, has been created for leisure activities. Ices and cool drinks can be purchased but there is no food shop - baguettes and croissants arrive at 8.30 each morning. Freezer for campers' use. Other on-site activities are bicycle hire, table tennis, fishing and pony trekking. Riding 4 km. The 'Voie Vert', a 40 km. track for cycling or walking starts near the site.

Charges 2000:
-- Per unit Ffr. 35.00; adult 22.00; child (under 7 yrs) 12.00; electricity 18.00.
-- Less 20% outside July/Aug.
-- Credit cards accepted.
Open:
15 April - 15 September.
Address:
71940 Saint-Boil.
Tel:
(0)3.85.44.00.40. FAX: as phone.
Reservations:
Accepted - contact site.
`Camping Cheque'

Directions: From Chalon-sur-Saône travel 9 km. west on the N80. Turn south on D981 through Buxy (6 km). Continue south for 7 km. to Saint-Boil and site is signed at south end of the village.

8901M Camping Municipal de Sous-Rôche, Avallon

This site is in an attractive, low lying, sheltered, part wooded situation, 2 km. from the centre of Avallon. There is a choice of 109 pitches on the pleasant grassy terrain - on shady terraces, on flat open ground, or by a stream; 43 electrical connections (6, 8 or 14A). It may be very busy. The single toilet block is in need of refurbishment, but is kept clean and provides British style WCs, including one with a large cubicle for disabled visitors (no other facilities), individual wash-basins (4 private cabins), showers, traditional sinks for clothes and dishes, all with free hot water. Shop and takeaway (July/Aug). A children's playground and table tennis have been added. Fishing on site, bicycle hire 2 km, riding 4 km. Information and reading room with telephone. A very useful night stop on the way to or from Lyon and the south

Directions: From centre of Avallon take N944 to south towards Lormes. After 2 km. turn left at camp sign (a fairly steep, downhill road to site). From A6 take Avallon exit (8 km).

Charges 2000:
-- Per person Ffr 18.00; child (under 7) 9.00; car 13.00; caravan or tent 13.00; motorcaravan 23.00; electricity 18.00.
-- No credit cards.

Open:
15 March - 15 October.

Address:
Cousin La Roche, 89200 Avallon.

Tel/Fax:
(0)3.86.34.10.39.

Reservations:
Write to
Office du Tourisme,
4 rue Bocquillot,
89200 Avallon.
Tel: (0)3.86.34.14.19.
FAX: (0)3.86.34.28.29.

8901M

Sous-Rôche
Avallon

*The site's
peaceful setting*

8903M Camping Municipal Les Coullemières, Vermenton

On the banks of the River Cure, 500 m. from the N6, this small site achieves noteworthy quality at reasonable cost. A warm welcome at the flower bedecked bureau and the immediately inviting environment sets the tone for a restful stay. The 50 level pitches are of good size and separated by hedging and interspersed with mature trees. Water points are strategically placed and almost every pitch has electricity (6A). The impeccable, heated, central sanitary block has washbasins in private cubicles, roomy showers with adjustable taps and a mixture of British and Turkish style toilets. A washing machine, dryer and iron are provided, there is provision for visitors with disabilities (paths are convenient for manoeuvring wheelchairs), chemical disposal and motorcaravan services. Part of this building houses an attractive, covered community room. Bicycles, pedaloes and canoes may be hired on the site. Immediately adjacent is a landscaped leisure area, tennis courts, football pitch, table tennis, cycle track and boule court. Fishing on site, riding 8 km. Milk and very basic provisions are available at reception. There is an emergency night bell. Twin axle caravans are not accepted. There is infrequent intrusive train noise but the close proximity to the station offers the added attraction of a day excursion to Paris (2 hours). Balloon flights can be booked.

Directions: Site is well signed from the N6 in Vermenton. Proceed through town towards station and site is a little way beyond. From A6 use Nitry exit (15 km).

Charges 2001:
-- Per adult Ffr. 18.00; child (under 10 yrs) 10.00; car or m/cycle 10.00; pitch 10.00; motorcaravan 18.00; animal 6.00; electricity (6A) 15.00.
-- Credit cards accepted.

Open:
10 April - 10 October.

Address:
89270 Vermenton.

Tel:
(0)3.86.81.53.02 (or Mairie (0)3.86.81.50.01).
FAX: (0)3.86.81.63.95.

Reservations:
Contact site in season or the Mairie when site closed.

JURA / ALPES

We have taken the liberty of putting two official French regions together to form the Jura/Alpes. The Franche-Comté and Savoy/Dauphiny and, although not next to each other, they both border the Alpes.

FRANCHE-COMTÉ

Major city: Besançon

Départements: 25 Doubs, 39 Jura
79 Haute-Saône, 90 Tre. de Belfort

SAVOY/DAUPHINY

Major city: Grenoble

Départements: 38 Isère, 73 Savoie
74 Haute-Savoie

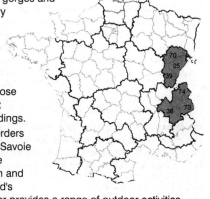

Franche-Comté is really two regions consisting of the high valley of the Saône, gently rolling country, while the Jura mountains are more rugged with dense forests, sheer cliffs, deep gorges and torrents of water. In winter this means cross-country skiing over 2,000 km. of marked trails and, in the summer, rafting along the gentle Lison and Loue rivers or the more challenging Saône or Doubs. The spa towns of Salins les Bains and Besançon offer relaxation and a chance to 'take the waters'. The region's postion, bordering Switzerland and close to Germany, is reflected in its culture and the great diversity of architectural style in the many fine buildings.

Lying between the Rhône Valley and the Alpine borders with Switzerland and Italy are the old provinces of Savoie and Dauphine. This is an area of enormous granite outcrops, deeply riven by spectacular glacier hewn and river etched valleys. It has become one of the world's leading wintersport playgrounds and in the summer provides a range of outdoor activities. Aix-les-Bains, Evian and Annecy were three major lakeside spa resorts of the Victorians; while Chamonix, under Mont Blanc, and Grenoble, attracted the more active (often British) 19th century travellers who poineered modern ski-ing and 'alpinism'.

Note: the site reports are laid out by départements in numerical order not by Region.

See map on page 313.

Cuisine of the region

Freshwater fish such as trout, grayling, pike and perch are local specialities

'*Plat gratine*' applies to a wide varity of dishes; in the Alps this means cooked in breadcrumbs; gratins of all sorts show how well milk, cream and cheese combine together.

Fondue – hot melted cheese and white wine; a classic of the region

Gratin Dauphinois – a classic potato dish with cream, cheese and garlic

Gratin Savoyard – another classic potato dish with cheese and butter

Omble chevalier – a char, it looks like a large salmon trout

Tartiflette – potato, bacon, onions and Reblochon cheese

Gougère – hot cheese pastry based on the local 'Comté' cheese

Places of interest

Aix-les-Bains – spa resort on the Lac du Bourget, boat excursions to the Royal Abbey of Hautecombe

Albertville – 1992 Winter Olympics, museum, now has an active night-life!

Annecy – canal-filled lakeside town, 12th century château, old quarter

Belfort – sandstone lion sculpted by Bartholdi; castle and Vauban fortifications; Memorial and Museum of the French Resistance

Besançon – citadel with good views over the city; cathedral is a mixture of influences ranging from a Roman altar to a 19th century astronomic clock

Chamonix – site of first Winter Olympics in 1924; world capital of mountain climbing; Mont Blanc tunnel, 11.6 km. long (for many years the longest tunnel in the world – closed at present after a disastrous fire)

Evian-les-Bains – spa and casino on Lake Geneva, home of Evian water

JURA / ALPES - 25 Doubs

2500 Castel Camping Caravaning Le Val de Bonnal, Rougemont

Well managed, attractive site in large country estate.

This is an impressive site, harmoniously designed in keeping with the surrounding countryside, well away from main roads and other intrusions. Having said that, the site itself is very busy, with a wide range of activities and amenities. The 320 pitches, all of a good size and with electricity (5A), are separated by a mixture of trees and bushes, carefully landscaped. Some of the newer pitches are less secluded, but the ambience generally is peaceful despite the size of the site (300 pitches in a large area) and its deserved popularity. The four toilet blocks, very clean when visited, provide free hot showers (some with dividers) washbasins in private cabins and British style WCs. There are separate washing up blocks, with sinks and free hot water, and washing machines, ironing boards and sinks for laundry. Amenities include a riverside restaurant, snack bar/takeaway, bar, terrace, shop (all 20/5-8/9), situated in sympathetically converted former farm buildings. A new swimming pool complex features water slides. There are well equipped children's play areas and a range of sport facilities including table tennis, boules, bicycle hire, etc. The main attraction must be the variety of watersports on the three large lakes and nearby river which include swimming, pedaloes, and fishing as well as water skiing, windsurfing and canoeing. In fact, the range of activities available at this site is almost inexhaustible, not to say exhausting. There are also 150 hectares to walk in and it is ideally placed for day trips to Switzerland. Golf 6 km. Used by tour operators (140 pitches).

Directions: From Vesoul take D9 towards Villersexel. After approx. 20 km. turn right in the village of Esprels at sign for Val de Bonnal. Follow for 3½ km. and site is on the left. From autoroute A36 take exit for Baume-les-Dames; go north on A50, then A18 to Rougemont and follow signs to site.

Charges 2000:
-- Per pitch with electricity, incl. 2 persons Ffr. 166.00, extra person 38.00; child (2-7 yrs) 15.00; local tax 2.00.
-- Less 20% outside July/Aug.
-- Credit cards accepted.

Open:
8 May - 15 September.

Address:
Bonnal,
25680 Rougemont.

Tel:
(0)3.81.86.90.87
FAX: (0)3.81.86.03.92.
E-mail: val-de-bonnal
@wanadoo.fr.

Reservations:
Only made for pitches with electricity. Contact site.

2503 Camping du Bois de Reveuge, Huanne-Montmartin

Hill-side site with summer activities.

As du Bois de Reveuge was only opened in 1992 it still has a new look about it, in as much as there is little shade yet from the young trees. Being on a hillside, the pitches are on terraces with good views across the surrounding countryside and leading down to two lakes which may be used for fishing and canoeing. The site also has private use of a 10 hectare lake set in a park 10 km. away where there is a watersport school and other boating opportunities. Tall trees have been left standing at the top of the hill where there are a few pitches, although most of these have been used for the site's mobile homes which are for hire. The 200 pitches available for tourists each have a water supply as well as electricity at 6A, and will eventually grass over. The enthusiastic owner has installed a good solar heated swimming pool (15/5-15/9) which can be covered in cool weather and another pool with four water slides. A 'Swim Master' is in attendance during the summer who, as well as acting as a lifeguard, offers swimming lessons. In season there is a kiosk for basic food supplies and a restaurant with terrace (both 1/6-3/9). Four children's play areas are still being developed. The three modern sanitary blocks are nicely spaced around the site and have British and Turkish style WCs and free hot water in the showers (pre-mix, single tap), sinks and basins which are mainly in cabins. High season 'baby club' with a large tent for wet weather, large video screen and some music and other entertainment for adults. Groups may request special activities such as orienteering. A package deal includes use of canoes, sailing boats and sailboards as well as archery, fishing and pedaloes. For an extra charge, rock climbing, potholing in nearby caves and rowing on the river Ognon can be organised, as well as bicycle hire. Mobile homes to rent (107).

Directions: Site is well signed from the D50. From A36 autoroute south of the site, take exit for Baume-les-Dames and head north on D50 towards Villersexel for about 12 km. to camp signs.

Charges 2000:
-- Per package for 2 persons Ffr. 110.00 - 160.00; extra person over 6 years 15.00 - 30.00, 2-6 yrs 10.00 - 20.00; local tax 2.00.

Open:
22 April - 30 September.

Address:
25680 Huanne-Montmartin.

Tel:
(0)3.81.84.38.60 (winter (0)3.81.84.12.42).
FAX: (0)3.81.84.44.04.

Reservations:
Made with 30% deposit and Ffr. 80 fee; contact site.

`Camping Cheque'

Book this site
01892 559898

THE ALAN ROGERS'
travel service

*see colour advert
between pages 192/193*

124

2505M Camping Municipal de Saint Point-Lac, Saint Point-Lac

A good example of a municipal campsite in which the village takes a pride, this site is on the banks of a small lake with views to the distant hills. The 84 level, numbered pitches are on grass and 60 have electricity (16A). There is a good central sanitary block with British style WCs and free hot water in washbasins, showers and sinks. Fishing is possible on site. Bicycle hire 5 km. Hot snacks and takeaway food are available in high season (July/Aug). The village shop and restaurant are an easy 200 m. walk from the site entrance. It is worth making a detour from the Pontarlier - Vallorbe road or for a longer stay.

Directions: From north, take D437 south of Pontarlier and keep on west side of the lake to the second village (Saint Point-Lac); from south exit N57 at Les Hopitaux-Neufs and turn west to lake.

Charges 2000:
-- Per unit incl. 2 persons Ffr. 48.00 - 55.00, with services 72.00 - 80.00; extra person 13.00 - 15.00; child (4-10 yrs) 6.00 - 7.50; pet 6.00; local tax (over 10) 1.50.
-- Credit cards accepted.
Open:
1 May - 30 September.
Address:
25160 Saint Point-Lac.
Tel:
Site: (0)3.81.69.61.64.
FAX: (0)3.81.69.65.74.
Reservations:
Made with deposit (Ffr. 300) and fee (50).
Contact site from 1 May, or Mairieby fax or post.

3803 Camping La Cascade, Bourg d'Oisans, nr Grenoble

Small site amongst the mountains, with heated sanitary facilities.

Although very much among the mountains, with the ski resorts of Alpe d'Huez and Les Deux Alpes close at hand, Bourg d'Oisans, which is in the Romanches valley at 725 m. above sea level, presents no access problems at all for caravanners. You simply drive from Grenoble along the wide N91 Briançon road with no passes or steep gradients. La Cascade is close to, and within sight and sound of, the waterfall from which it takes its name. It has 123 individual pitches of varying but quite adequate size on mainly flat ground and with 7/15A electricity. The two heated sanitary blocks are of top quality with mainly British toilets, washbasins in cabins with light, mirror, free hot water; good free hot showers, fully controllable. There is a good sized, heated and sheltered swimming pool (15/5-30/9) which is surrounded by a large, enclosed sunbathing area. Amenities include a bar and snack bar (1/7-31/8), children's playground, general room with TV, games room, table tennis, volleyball and boules. Evening entertainment and lots of activities are organised in season. Bicycle hire 1 km, fishing 500 m. Washing machine. Caravan storage. Chalets and caravans for hire all year.

Directions: Site is about 400 m. along the road towards Alpe d'Huez which leads off from the N91 just east of Bourg d'Oisans.

Charges 2000:
-- Per unit incl. 2 persons Ffr. 86.00 - 130.00; extra person (over 5 yrs) 22.00 - 31.00; animal free; local tax (15/6-31/8) 2.00; electricity (6A) 16.00.
-- Credit cards accepted.
Open:
1 February - 30 Sept.
Address:
Rte. de l'Alpe d'Huez, 38520 Bourg d'Oisans.
Tel:
(0)4.76.80.02.42.
FAX: (0)4.76.80.22.63.
E-mail: lacascade@ wanadoo.fr.
Reservations:
Made for any length with deposit (Ffr 400) and fee (100).

3804 Camping La Rencontre du Soleil, Bourg d'Oisans, nr Grenoble

Small, friendly site in mountain area.

Nestling between two mountain ranges, this site is situated at the foot of France's largest National Park, Le Parc des Ecrins, just 2 km. from Bourg d'Oisans which is the centre of the staging points for the Tour de France. There are 73 mainly flat pitches of varying size with mature trees offering welcome shade. Electricity is available (2, 6 or 10A). The large heated toilet block provides all the usual amenities, all of very high quality and extremely well maintained. There are also chemical disposal facilities, a washing machine and dryer, and a motorcaravan service point. The site has a restaurant and takeaway, with bread to order. There is no shop but a supermarket is 1.5 km. towards Bourg d'Oisans. There is a sitting room with TV and a children's play room adjoining, a small, sheltered swimming pool with a sunbathing area and a children's play area. A programme of activities is organised in high season including walking, mountain biking and a mini-club for children. Fishing and bicycle hire 2 km. Canoeing, rafting, riding and many other activities are possible nearby. The site is used by tour operators (30 pitches). A 'Sites et Paysages' member.

Directions: Site is almost opposite no. 3803 on the Alpe d'Huez D211 road from the N91, just east of the town. Entrance is on a sharp bend - take care.

Book this site
01892 559898
THE ALAN ROGERS'
travel service

Charges 2001:
-- Per unit incl. 2 persons Ffr. 92.00 - 140.00; extra person 31.00 - 34.00; dog 5.00; electricity 2A 18.00, 6A 23.00, 10A 24.00; local tax 2.00.
-- Credit cards accepted.
Open:
19 May - 16 September.
Address:
Rte de l'Alpe-d'Huez, 38520 Bourg d'Oisans.
Tel:
(0)4.76.79.12.22.
FAX: (0)4.76.80.26.37.
E-mail: rencontre.soleil @wanadoo.fr.
Reservations:
Made for min. 1 week with deposit and fee.
`Camping Cheque'

3808 Camping-Caravaning Au Joyeux Réveil, Autrans

Simple site set in wonderful scenery.

Autrans is set on a plateau, 1,030 m. high, in the Vecors region. Au Joyeux Réveil is ideally situated for any of the activities that this wonderful area has to offer - from walking, mountain biking and pot-holing in summer to downhill and cross-country skiing in winter, it is all there for you in magnificent scenery. The site is on the outskirts of Autrans, set below a ski jump and short lift. We visited for the first time in August and found the toilet block (with central heating) basic and functional, but the facilities were clean and well maintained. A new heated toilet block is planned , together with a new office, bar, games room and meeting room. The pitches are mainly on grass, reasonably level with a small tree to mark the corners of each. All have electricity (2/10A) and are in a sunny location with fantastic views. There is a small, kidney-shaped swimming pool with sunbathing area, a small play area on grass and games and TV rooms. A short ski-lift is near the site and a shuttle bus runs regularly the 5 km. to the longer runs. The site is only a short walk from the small town of Autrans. Fishing or riding 300 m. The D531 road and then the D106 look a little daunting on the map but they are good roads with very easy gradients. English is spoken.

Directions: Travelling south on A48 take exit for Veurey-Voroize on N532. Head south for approx. 7 km. to Sassenage, then turn on D531 to Autrans. Site is signed in Autrans (up the mountain but with easy gradient).

Charges guide:
-- Per unit incl. 1 or 2 persons Ffr. 70.00; extra person 25.00; child (under 6 yrs) 20.00; electricity 12.00 - 15.00; local tax 1.00.
-- Winter prices - apply to site.
-- Credit cards accepted.
Open:
All year excl. Oct. and Nov.
Address:
38880 Autrans.
Tel:
(0)4.76.95.33.44.
FAX: (0)4.76.95.72.98.
Reservations:
Contact site.

AU JOYEUX RÉVEIL

WINTER **SUMMER**

Camping - Caravaneige★ ★ ★

38880 AUTRANS (alt.1050 m)

Vercors - France

Tél. 04 76 95 33 44

Fax 04 76 95 72 98

camping-au-joyeux-reveil.fr

VERCORS

Situated in the splendid scenery of the quiet heart of the nature reserve of the Vercors.
On the site : *Heated swimming pool, childrens club. Luxurious sanitary buildings.*
In the neighbourhood : *Skiing, snow-shoeing, mushing, walking, cycling, fishing, horse riding, rock climbing, potholing, canyoning, heritage, historical and cultural sites...*

3805 Camping-Caravaning Le Temps Libre, Bougé Chambalud

Good value, friendly, family site, not too far from the autoroute.

Le Temps Libre offers 80 touring pitches, but with a further 72 for a variety of permanent caravans used at weekends or long stay units in a separate area. The terraced pitches are fairly small and can be difficult to acccess. Divided by hedges and trees with some shade, all have electrical hook-ups (9A). The site has a lot by way of on-site activities, including three swimming pools (from 15/5) with two water slides, three tennis courts, minigolf, trampoline, numerous boules courts, volleyball, basketball, bicycle hire, a climbing wall and a small fishing lake. There is an open air theatre for children's activities, a small bar with terrace, takeaway and snacks, and a small shop (all 1/7-31/8). The three modern toilet blocks (one recently refurbished) provide all the necessary facilities, including British style WCs and good showers. There is a motorcaravan service point plus a poorly situated chemical disposal point. Generally the site needs more 'TLC' but it would make a useful stop-over en-route or for a short stay to explore the area. Chalets (12) and mobile homes (6) to rent. English is spoken. A 'Sites et Paysages' member.

Directions: From A7 exit 12 (Chanas) or the N7, take D519 towards Grenoble for about 7 km. to Bougé Chambalud from where site is signed off to the right (sharp turn in village).

Charges 2001:
-- Per pitch and vehicle Ffr. 25.00 - 35.00; person 21.00 - 30.00; child (2-4 yrs) 10.00 - 15.00; dog free - 5.00; electricity (9A) 20.00.
-- No credit cards.
Open:
Easter - 30 September.
Address:
38150 Bougé Chambalud.
Tel:
(0)4.74.84.04.09.
FAX: (0)4.74.84.15.71.
E-mail: camping.temps-libre@libertysurf.com.
Reservations:
Made with deposit (Ffr 400) and fee (50); contact site.

Book this site
01892 559898

THE ALAN ROGERS'
travel service

3801 Le Coin Tranquille, Les Abrets

Family run site with swimming pool and restaurant, in peaceful surroundings.

Set in the Dauphiny countryside north of Grenoble, Le Coin Tranquille is truly a quiet corner, especially outside school holiday times, although it is popular with families in high season. Les Abrets is well placed for visits to the Savoy regions and the Alps. Originally a small site of 18 pitches developed by Martine's parents, who are still very active about the site, this is a family affair with Martine running the site and her husband Gilles as the restaurant chef. It has developed into a neat, tidy and well maintained site of 152 grass pitches (160 for touring units), all with electricity (2, 3 or 6A). They are separated by well maintained hedges of hydrangea, and other flowering shrubs, and walnut trees to make a lovely environment doubly enhanced by the rural aspect and marvellous views across to the mountains. Amenities include a swimming pool and paddling pool (15/5-30/9; no bermuda shorts) with sunbathing areas, a busy shop and an excellent restaurant, which is open all year (closed two days weekly in low season) and attracts a local clientele. The central large sanitary block is heated in low season, is of good quality and kept very clean. It provides private washing cabins, British style WCs, controllable roomy showers, a laundry room, and facilities for children and disabled people. Two other blocks on either edge of the site have been refurbished to a very high standard and all have dishwashing facilities. The children's play area is on grass and there is a TV/video room with balcony, games room and a quiet reading room. Supervised games for children, slide shows of the region's attractions and weekly entertainment for adults including live music (not discos) are arranged inhigh season. Bicycle hire on site, fishing 5 km. riding 6 km. Used by tour operators (14 pitches). Chalets to rent (10). This is a popular site with a warm welcome, that makes a wonderful base for exploring the area, especially in low season – the Chartreuse caves at Voiron are well worth a visit. A Sites et Paysages member.

Directions: Site is northeast of Les Abrets. From the town take N6 towards Chambery, turning left after about 2 km. where site is signed.

Charges 2001:
-- Per pitch incl. 2 persons Ffr. 82.00 - 139.00; extra adult 24.00 - 36.00; child (2-7 yrs) 14.00 - 24.00; extra vehicle 13.00 - 24.00; electricity 2A 8.00, 3A 12.00 or 6A 19.00.
-- Credit cards accepted.
Open:
1 April - 31 October.
Address:
38490 Les Abrets en Dauphine.
Tel:
(0)4.76.32.13.48.
FAX: (0)4.76.37.40.67.
E-mail: contact@ coin-tranquille.com.
Reservations:
Write with deposit (Ffr. 700) and fee (100).
`Camping Cheque'

**Book this site
01892 559898**

THE ALAN ROGERS'
travel service

3806 Camping Les Trois Lacs, Trept, nr Sablonnières

Country site on the edge of three lakes.

In flat, open country in the north of Dauphine, Trois Lacs is a pleasant relaxing base to enjoy either the countryside, the historic places of the region or the programme of leisure activities provided by the site. The land around the lakes has been well landscaped with smooth lawns and a variety of shrubs and trees. The camping area is on one side of the largest lake with tall trees on one side and views of distant mountains. The 160 good sized pitches are in pairs on either side of hard access roads separated by low hedges, but there is little shade. Good quality sanitary blocks are in the centre of the camping area with British style WCs, hot water in washbasins, sinks and showers, a laundry room and chemical disposal. The attractive bar/restaurant near reception serves drinks (all season) and simple snacks (June - Aug) and there are other snack bars around the lakes. A mobile shop calls in high season and there are other shops at Trept (2 km). Well away from the camping area is a large building, open on one side, for roller skating and entertainment which is provided in July/Aug. This includes two discos for teenagers and one for older people each week. There are two small children's playgrounds and a games area. The smallest lake is kept for fishing and the others for boating and watersports with one section for swimming having a water slide (with lifeguard July/Aug). Other activities include tennis, minigolf, beach volleyball, badminton, walking, riding (500 m) and mountain biking (hire 10 km). A 'Rabbit Club' card is required to use the site's activities (tennis, minigolf and fishing); this costs Ffr. 100 for people over 10 yrs, Ffr. 40 for under 10s. Caravan storage.

Directions: Leave N75 Grenoble - Bourg-en-Bresse road at Morestel and travel west on D517. Site is between Sablonnières and Trept.

Charges 2001:
-- Per person Ffr. 32.00, under 10 yrs 22.00; pitch 45.00; animal 10.00; electricity 18.00.
-- No credit cards.
Open:
1 May - 10 September.
Address:
38460 Trept.
Tel:
(0)4.74.92.92.06.
FAX: (0)4.74.92.93.35.
Reservations:
Made with deposit (Ffr. 450) and fee (50).

JURA / ALPES - 38 Isère / 39 Jura

3807 Camping-Caravaning La Chabannerie, St Martin-de-Clelles

Quiet, all year site in glorious countryside.

La Chabannerie is a former municipal site and its Belgian owner has been working hard to upgrade the facilities. The site is set amongst pine trees amidst glorious countryside and some pitches have marvellous views of the mountains. With only 47 pitches it is small, friendly and unsophisticated, with no organised entertainment. There is a small swimming pool (open June-Sept) and reception doubles as a shop – for such a small site they carry quite a large selection of goods and fresh bread daily, but no gas. Overlooking the pool is a small snack bar with food to either eat inside or take away. There is a family room for reading or playing board games in inclement weather, a small play area and table tennis and volleyball. The main toilet block is new and is heated in winter. The other smaller blocks are older and only opened in July and Aug. WCs are mainly British style, showers are large and washbasins are mainly in cubicles. A large unit containing WC, washbasin and shower is especially adapted for disabled people and this can also be used as a family shower room. Chemical disposal. A reader reports only one tap for drinking water. Facilities for skiing or riding are only 8 km, fishing or rafting 5 km. (this depends on the state of the river). The hills are all around for walking and there are mountain bike tracks to suit every level of ability. Sporting opportunities in the area range from rock climbing, paragliding, sailing, bungee jumping to donkey hire (for walking the mountain trails). The site is popular with amateur botanists as it is home to 38 different wild orchids. English is spoken and you can be sure of a warm welcome.

Charges 2000:
-- Per person Ffr. 24.00 - 29.00; child (2-12 yrs) 13.00 - 17.00; caravan or large tent 13.00 - 17.00; car 8.00 - 10.00; motorcaravan 21.00 - 27.00; electricity (10A) 16.00 - 18.00.
-- Less 5-18% for stays over 1 night.
-- Credit cards accepted.
Open: All year.
Address: 38930 St Martin-de-Clelles.
Tel: (0)4.76.34.00.38. FAX: (0)4.76.34.43.54. E-mail: chabanne @infonie.fr.
Reservations: Recommended in July/Aug; contact site.

Directions: Site is off the N75 south of Grenoble (approx. 48 km) and is signed approx. 16 km. south of Monastiere (east of the N75).

3901 Camping-Caravaning La Plage Blanche, Ounans

Attractive riverside site with good amenities.

Situated in open countryside, along the banks of the River Loue, this site has 220 good sized, marked pitches on level ground, all with electricity (6A). Trees provide fully shaded and semi-shaded pitches. Approximately a kilometre of riverside and beach provide the ideal setting for children to swim and play safely in the gently flowing, shallow water. Inflatables are popular and there is a canoe/kayak base. A new swimming pool and children's pool were added on the site in 2000. Modern, well kept sanitary facilities in three unusual blocks have tiled hot showers with push-button controls, separate washing cabins, British style WCs and chemical disposal. Dishwashing facilities are in blocks of 8 sinks, there is a launderette and a motorcaravan service area. Bar/restaurant with terrace (1/4-30/9), pizzeria and takeaway (all season). Activities include river fishing, table tennis, and bicycle hire. TV room. Children's play area. Riding 700 m, golf 10 km. Caravans for hire.

Charges 2001:
-- Per person Ffr. 28.00; child (1-7 yrs) 17.00; pitch 35.00; extra tent or car 12.00; dog 5.00; electricity (6A) 19.00; local tax (over 14 yrs) 2.00.
-- Less 10% outside July/Aug.
-- Credit cards accepted.
Open: 13 April - 30 September.
Address: 39380 Ounans.
Tel: (0)3.84.37.69.63. FAX: (0)3.84.37.60.21. E-mail: la-plage-blanche @wanadoo.fr.
Reservations: Made with deposit (Ffr. 200) and fee (50).

Directions: Ounans is 20 km southeast of Dole. From autoroute A39 from Dijon or autoroute 36 from Besançon, take Dole exit and then D405 to Parcey. After Parcey take N5 to Mont Sous Vaudrey (8 km) then D472 towards Pontarlier to Ounans from where site is signed.

Book this site 01892 559898
THE ALAN ROGERS' travel service

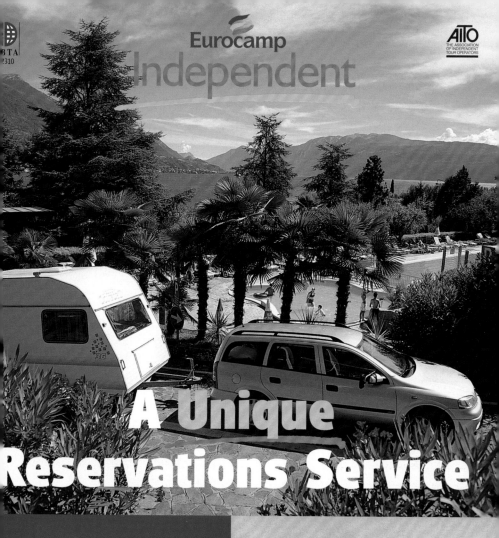

Eurocamp
Independent

A Unique
Reservations Service

s part of Eurocamp Travel ve are proud to be able to ffer a <u>unique</u> service nmatched by any other ur operator.

r people with their own nt, trailer tent, caravan or otorhome, no one se offers the ame total holiday rvice from initial nquiry to on-site rvice.

- ▲ Choose from 100 of Europe's best sites in 8 countries
- ▲ Choose any ferry route you like
- ▲ The ultimate travel pack
- ▲ Courier service on site
- ▲ Children's courier service
- ▲ Friendly and experienced reservations staff
- ▲ Tailored insurance policies
- ▲ One phone call will book your whole holiday...its so easy!

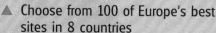

o receive your copy of the 2001 brochure call **01606 787954**

your holidays
in color

CAMPING VILLAGES
yelloh!
VILLAGE

With Yelloh! Village you
holiday will get new colours
Situated in exceptional regions
the Yelloh ! Village camping
guarantee you high quality
holidays.

- All services, entertainmen
  programmes for childre
  and adults and organise
  activities are alway
  available.

yelloh! orange

yelloh!yellow

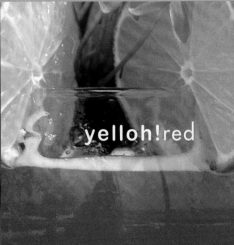

yelloh!red

yelloh!blue

- A friendly and personal welcome
- An environment of quality nature: green and well kept surroundings with water in all its forms (luxurious swimming pools, sea, ocean, rivers, lakes)
- Fully equipped pitches and an ample selection of quality accommodation to let (mobile homes, chalets…)
- Booking made easy and practical

ARDÈCHE
Soleil Vivarais ref.0703

BRETAGNE
Le Grand Camping de la Plage ref.2911
Le Grand Large
Le Manoir de Kerlut ref.2912

CHARENTE ATLANTIQUE
Sequoia Parc ref.1714

COSTA DORADA
La Torre del Sol - Spain,
Guide Europe ref.8540

GERS SUD-OUEST
Le lac des 3 vallées ref.3206

LANDES ATLANTIQUE
Panorama
La Paillotte ref.4004

MÉDITERRANÉE CAMARGUE
La Petite Camargue ref.3002
Les Petits Camarguais ref.3013

MÉDITERRANÉE CATALANE
Le Brasilia ref.6607

MÉDITERRANÉE LANGUEDOC
Club Farret

Haute Saison - AGE/SDP

information - bookings :
+33 4 66 739 739
www.yellohvillage.com

If you're interested in the

ALAN ROGERS' GOOD CAMPS GUIDE

you'll probably be interested in

THE GOOD MAGAZINE GUIDE

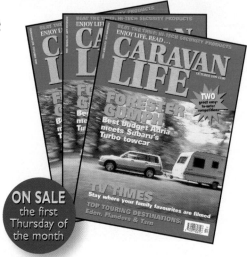

For tests and touring features 12 months of the year choose Britain's premier caravan and motorhome magazines.

On sale at most good newsagents or by subscription – telephone

01778 391134

MPINGS
SITES
&
YSAGES
ANCE

Choose the region and enjoy your holidays !

In camping-caravaning or rented accomodation, our 51 campsites are ready to welcome you anywhere in France

Paris

INFORMATION AND BOOKING CENTER
Tél : 00 33 228 114 036
Fax : 00 33 251 590 535
Campings Sites & Paysages - Orouet -
85 160 ST JEAN DE MONTS - FRANCE
Sites.et.Paysages@wanadoo.fr - http://www.sites-et-paysages.com

2000 - Conception réalisation A&V Communication : 06150 Cannes la Bocca - France - Tél 00 33 493 471 101
Crédit photos : OT Grand Bornand - DR - Narberue - Sites et Paysages.

LES CASTELS

CAMPING & CARAVANING

A DIFFERENT FRANCE

There are 50 4-star Castels caravan and camp sites dotted round the most beautiful regions of France. Many are set in the grounds of chateaux or manor houses and offer:

- amenities of the highest standards,
- activities and entertainment for the young and not so young,
- a broad choice of pitches and different types of very comfortable accommodation.

100 F a night for a pitch for 2 people, with electricity, whatever the site and length of stay when you present your *Privilege Card*.

To find out more, contact us and

- receive our brochure-road map free of charge
- book your Privilege Card for the year 2001 (50 FF)
- order the presentation guidebook for our 50 Castels camp sites (contribution to expenses: 50 FF)

*offer valid at most camp sites from opening up until 30/06 and from 1/09 until the closing of the comp sites for anyone who has ordered the Privilege Card from our secretary.

e mail: mail@les-castels.com - Fax: + 33 (0)2 97 47 50 72
Address: Secrétariat LES CASTELS - PIBS - C.P. 26 - 56038 VANNES Cedex - Fra
Internet sites: www.les-castels.com- www.castels-campings.com
Tel : + 33 (0)2 97 42 57 12

le Moulinal
CAMPING VILLAGE
DORDOGNE PERIGORD
You can feel the holiday spirit in the Dordogne region

Discover the Dordogne spirit

Old stonework and a beautiful countryside. The Moulinal offers most facilities from Easter on : bar, ice-creams, restaurant, shop.... A heated swimming pool with a paddling pool for the small ones, a lake, a club for children over 2 years old, tournaments and water games, evening entertainment for young and old. Your holiday at our camping village Le Moulinal has a lively spirit !

Le Moulinal proposes pitches where many rare flowers and plants grow. Very comfortable chalets, mobile homes and bungalows... Don't hesitate to use our special offers in low-season. At our camping-village Le Moulinal comfort is reality.

Le Moulinal. 24540 BIRON. France.
Tel. +33 (0) 5 53 40 84 60
Fax. +33 (0) 5 53 40 81 49
e.mail : lemoulinal@perigord.com
Free brochure

internet : www.lemoulinal.com

3902 Camping de Surchauffant, La Tour du Meix, nr Orgelet

Comfortable site on the shores of Lac de Vouglans.

This site is one of a group which includes site no. 3903 but it is much smaller. With only 180 pitches, it may appeal to those who prefer a more informal or intimate atmosphere. It is pleasantly situated above the beaches bordering the Lac de Vouglans, which also offers a variety of watersports activities, boat trips, etc. and is used for fishing and swimming (guarded in high season as it shelves steeply). The 152 touring pitches are of reasonable size, informally arranged, and most offer electricity; they are divided by hedges and there is some shade. The sanitary installations are adequate rather than luxurious, with British (seatless) style WCs, hot showers, some washbasins in private cabins. a laundry and chemical disposal. Amenities include a shop, snack bar (both 15/6-1/9) and a bar/ restaurant (all season); another restaurant and shops are nearby. Children's games are organised. Bicycle hire or riding 5 km. Chalets for rent. English is spoken.

Directions: From Lons le Saunier take D52 to Orgelet. Site is by the D470, at La Tour du Meix, about 4 km. east of Orgelet.

Charges 2000:
-- Per unit incl. 2 persons Ffr. 68.00 - 80.00; extra person (over 4 yrs) 18.00 - 20.00; electricity (5A) 16.00; electricity, water and drainage 22.00; dog 8.00; local tax 1.50.
-- Credit cards accepted.
Open:
1 May - 10 September.
Address:
39270 La Tour du Meix.
Tel:
(0)3.84.25.41.08.
FAX: (0)3.84.35.56.88.
E-mail: surchauffant @chalain.com.
Reservations:
Contact site for details.

3903 Le Domaine de Chalain, Doucier, nr Lons-le-Saunier

Large lakeside site with many sports and amenities available.

Doucier lies east of Lons-le-Saunier among the wooded hills of the Jura and rather away from the main routes. This large, park-like site (804 pitches) is on the edge of the Lac de Chalain surrounded on three sides by woods and some cliffs. Large areas are left for sports and recreation. The lake shelves gently at the edge but then becomes deep quite suddenly. Day visitors can be very numerous during low weekends. The site is divided into two parts, one (nearer the lake) with larger pitches (costing more). You should find room in the other part, but for July and August, it is better to reserve to make sure. There are over 200 electrical connections; little shade. The nine sanitary blocks have been improved over the years, with British style WCs, washbasins with warm water (all in private cabins) and free hot showers in separate blocks. One block can be heated and has facilities for babies and disabled people. Washing machines. Medical centre - doctor calls daily in high season. There are shops (15/5-15/9), a bar, takeaway and snacks (1/5-20/9) and a community room. Activities include tennis, table tennis, minigolf and pedaloes for hire, fishing and bicycle hire. There are animals and birds in enclosures, a cinema and organised activities, plus a disco for the young. Riding 2 km, golf 25 km. Used by tour operators (100 pitches).

Directions: Site can only be approached via Doucier: from Switzerland via N5 (from Geneva), then the N78 and D39; from other directions via Lons-le-Saunier or Champagnole.

Charges 2000:
-- Per unit incl. 3 persons Ffr. 85.00 - 145.00; electricity 16.00; electricity, water and drainage 107.00 - 167.00; extra person 30.00 - 40.00; child (4-15 yrs) 15.00 - 20.00; dog 10.00; local tax 1.50
-- Credit cards accepted.
Open:
1 May - 20 September.
Address:
Domaine de Chalain, 39130 Doucier.
Tel:
(0)3.84.24.29.00.
FAX: (0)3.84.24.94.07.
E-mail: chalain@ chalain.com.
Reservations:
Contact site for details.

3906 Camping La Marjorie, Lons-le-Saunier

Spacious site set on outskirts of spa town.

La Marjorie, a former municipal site, has 200 level pitches, mainly on hardstanding and separated by well trimmed hedges interspersed with tall trees which gives privacy plus a little shade at some part of the day. Bordering one area of the site are open fields and woodlands. All pitches have electricity (6/10A) and a few are fully serviced. The three sanitary blocks are clean and well maintained. Two are modern and can be heated, with British style WCs, cubicles with washbasins and large showers. There are baby baths, good facilities for disabled people, chemical disposal, washing and motorcaravan services (Ffr. 20 charge). At the site entrance is reception, small shop, and a small bar with reasonably priced takeaway meals (all 15/6-31/8). There is a TV room, table tennis, a small play area, boule, volleyball and a football field. Archery, canoeing or riding can be arranged (fee). The site is 2.5 km. from the spa town of Lons-le-Saunier, the capital of the Jura region. There is a bicycle path into town and a mountain bike track behind the site. The local swimming pool is 200 m. and restaurants are 500 m. Golf 5 km. Caves and waterfalls 17 km. Mobile homes and chalets for rent. English is spoken.

Directions: Site is off the N83 (Lons-le-Saunier - Besancon). From Lons on the D52 or the N78 or D471, site is signed from first roundabout on town outskirts.

Charges 2000:
-- Per unit incl. 2 persons Ffr. 63.00 - 76.00, with electricity (6A) 75.00 - 89.00; extra person 17.00 - 19.00; child (under 10) 9.00 - 11.00; dog 6.00.
-- Credit cards accepted.
Open:
1 April - 15 October.
Address:
640 Bvd. de l'Europe, 39000 Lons-le-Saunier.
Tel:
(0)3.84.24.26.94.
FAX: (0)3.84.24.08.40.
Reservations:
Made with deposit (Ffr. 250) and fee (60); contact site.

3904 Camping La Pergola, Marigny, Lac de Chalain

Neat, tidy terraced site overlooking lake.

Close to the Swiss border and overlooking the sparkling waters of Lac de Chalain, La Pergola is set amongst the rolling hills of the Jura. Awaiting discovery as it is not on the main tourist routes, La Pergola is a very well appointed site with 350 pitches, mainly on gravel and separated by small bushes. Arranged on numerous terraces, connected by steep steps, some have shade and the higher ones have good views over the lake. All have electricity, water and drainage. A tall fence protects the site from the public footpath that separates the site from the lakeside but there are frequent access gates. The entrance is very attractive and the work that Mme. Gicquaire puts into the preparation of the flower-beds is very evident. The bar/restaurant terrace is beautiful, featuring grape vines for welcome shade and a colourful array of spectacular flowers leading on to a landscaped waterfall area next to the three swimming pools and entertainment area. Two of the pools are heated. The latest sanitary block serves the lower pitches and is well appointed with private cabins. Slightly older blocks serve the other terraces. Visitors with disabilities are advised to select a lower terrace where special facilities are provided. Washing machines and dryers. There is a good children's play area and a children's club. An organised programme in high season includes cycle tours, keep fit sessions and evening entertainment with a disco twice weekly. Table tennis and volleyball. Watersports include windsurfing, pedaloes and small boats for hire. Riding 3 km. English is spoken. Mobile homes for rent (80). Used by tour operators (120 pitches).

Directions: Site is 2.5 km. north of Doucier on Lake Chalain road D27.

Charges guide:
-- Per unit incl. 2 persons, electricity and water: lake pitch Ffr. 90.00 - 228.00; standard pitch 90.00 - 198.00; extra person 28.00; child (3-6 yrs) 20.00; baby (0-2 yrs) 10.00; extra car 15.00; dog 5.00; local tax 1.50.
-- Special offers available.
-- Credit cards accepted.

Open:
13 May - 16 September.

Address:
39130 Marigny.

Tel:
(0)3.84.25.70.03.
FAX: (0)3.84.25.75.96.
E-mail:
contact@lapergola.com.

Reservations:
Made with Ffr. 800 deposit and 170 fee.

`Camping Cheque'

Book this site
01892 559898

THE ALAN ROGERS'
travel service

*see colour advert
between pages 192/193*

3905 Fayolan Eurocamping, Clairvaux-les-Lacs

Modern site in the heart of the French Jura.

This relatively new site, backed by wooded hills, is situated on the shores of Le Petit Lac about a mile from the town of Clairvaux-les-Lacs amid the lakes and forests of the Jura. Here one can relax, enjoy the peaceful countryside, explore the interesting villages, historic towns and museums of the area by car or cycle or take to the water where you can swim, windsurf and canoe. The neat, tidy site is in two parts, with pitches from 80-100 sq.m. either on terraces overlooking the lake or on the flatter area near the shore. There are electrical connections (6A) for those who want them and 200 pitches have electricity, water, drainage and sewage connections. The upper part has little shade until the young trees grow but there is some on the lower section. A pleasant area in the centre of the site is where the shop, restaurant, children's playground and pools are located. Entertainment also takes place here. Four modern sanitary units spread around the site have warm water from push-button taps in washbasins and showers and hot water in sinks. Chemical disposal. There are two good attractive swimming pools (heated from mid-May), one with a slide, a smaller one for children and a sunbathing area. It is necessary to obtain and wear a bracelet to use the pools and trunks, not shorts, must be worn. Organised activities include archery, a fitness trail, walks, games, competitions, children's club and dancing. Fishing from the site, bicycle hire 800 m, riding 4 km. Used by tour operators (130 pitches).

Directions: Clairvaux-les-Lacs is on the N78 between Lons-le-Saunier and Morez. In Clairvaux follow signs for 'Lacs Campings' and Fayolan.

Charges 2000:
-- Per unit incl. 2 persons, pitch and car Ffr 65.00 - 124.00; extra person 29.00 - 32.00; child 11-14 yrs 15.00 - 18.00, 4-10 yrs 10.00 - 13.00; extra car 13.00 - 15.00; animal 12.00; electricity 16.00 - 18.00; fully serviced pitch 25.00 - 30.00; lakeside pitch in high season plus 11.00; local tax 2.00 (under 7 yrs 1.00).

Open:
1 May - 30 September.

Address:
BP 52, 39130 Clairvaux-les-Lacs.

Tel:
(0)3.84.25.26.19.
FAX: (0)3.84.25.26.20.
E-mail: Relais.
SoleilJURA@wanadoo.fr.

Reservations:
Advised for July/Aug; write with deposit (Ffr 500) and fee (125).

7002M Camping Municipal International du Lac, Vaivre-Vesoul

This is one of the better examples of a municipal site and is part of a leisure park around a large lake. A 5 km. path has been made around the lake for jogging, walking and cycling and there is a large open space for ball games or sunbathing, along with a good children's playground and bar/restaurant. A map at the entrance shows the water areas for swimming, boating and windsurfing. Watersports are organised by the Club Nautique Haut-Saonois Vesoul and there is also tennis, table tennis, archery, basketball and night-time carp fishing. The campsite does not have direct access to the lake as it is separated by a security fence, but access is possible at the site entrance. There are 160 good sized, level, grass pitches, all with electricity at 10A. Access is from hard roads and pitches are separated by shrubs and bushes. There is a large hard area in the centre of the site brightened by flowers and young trees. Three good quality toilet blocks, one of which is heated, are well spaced around the site. They have a mix of British and Turkish style WCs and free, pre-mixed warm water from push-button taps in the washbasins and showers. Although the staff on duty did not speak English, they were friendly and helpful. Bungalows for rent.

Directions: On road D474 to west of Vesoul on route to Besançon, well signed around the town.

Charges 2001:
-- Ffrancs: per person Ffr. 19.70; child (under 7 yrs) 8.50; pitch 20.30, with electricity 33.50; dog 10.50.
-- Euro: per person 3,00; child (under 7 yrs) 1,30; pitch 3,10, with electricity 5,10; dog 1,60.
-- No credit cards.

Open:
1 March - 31 October.

Address:
70000 Vaivre-Vesoul.

Tel:
(0)3.84.96.22.86.
FAX: (0)3.84.75.74.93.

Reservations:
Contact site.

7301 Camping Le Bois Joli, La Chambre, St Martin-sur-la-Chambre

Very quiet, pleasant rural park in mountain area.

If you are looking for somewhere different, off the beaten track, or happen to be passing through on the N6 from Albertville to Modane and the Frejus tunnel to Italy, this could be a good stopping place. Le Bois Joli (roughly speaking, 'pretty woodland', which it certainly is) is in wooded country and a most peaceful situation. The numerous trees provide good shade to all pitches, although the natural layout of the site may not suit those who prefer uniformity and order. There are 116 grass pitches, all with electrical connections (2-10A), in small terraced clearings and the site is divided by a minor road. Every effort has been made to disturb the natural habitat as little as possible and, although the camping area could be increased to accommodate more people, the owners like it just as it is, and with a chorus of early morning bird-song who can blame them. The two sanitary blocks, an older one (which has been refurbished) near the heated swimming pool (free) and a newer, pre-fabricated one in the other section, are quite adequate (although the supply of hot water may be variable at peak times). They provide British and Turkish style toilets, a room for disabled people, a baby room, laundry and dishwashing sinks and chemical disposal facilities. There is a kiosk with terrace for drinks, takeaway food and basic food supplies, with a bar and rest room offering local cuisine form time to time and continental breakfasts daily (all 25/6 - 31/8). Two children's play areas, archery and table tennis. This is a delightfully rural site run by a pleasant family who are extremely helpful. The proprietor, Bernard, is also a qualified guide and twice weekly organises and leads walks in the surrounding area, all at no extra cost. The Savoie region is probably better known for its winter activities, but the beauty of the landscape and variety of plants existing beneath the winter snow means it is under valued, and well worth visiting in the summer. Mobile homes and chalets to rent.

Directions: The A43 has now been extended south towards St Jean de Maurienne, parallel with the N6. Exit for La Chambre and follow D123 and camp signs. Site is 1 km. northeast of St Avre.

Charges 2000:
-- Per unit incl. 2 persons Ffr. 75.00; extra person 20.00; child (under 7 yrs) 13.00; electricity 15.00 - 20.00, acc to amps; local tax 1.10.

Open:
1 April - 15 September.

Address:
73130
St Martin La Chambre.

Tel:
(0)4.79.59.42.30 or (0)4.79.56.21.28.
FAX: (0)4.79.56.29.95.
E-mail: camping.le. bois.joli@universal.fr

Reservations:
Write to site.

Book this site
01892 559898

THE ALAN ROGERS'
travel service

131

7302 Camping-Caravaneige Le Versoyen, Bourg-St Maurice

Good quality mountain site open all year.

Bourg-St Maurice is on a small, level plain at an altitude of 830 m. on the River Isère, surrounded by high mountains. For many years a winter ski-ing resort, it now caters for visitors all year round. The Parc National de la Vanoise is near, along with a wealth of interesting places. Le Versoyen itself attracts visitors all year round (except for a month when they close). Trees typically seen at this altitude give shade in some parts. The 200 flat, grass pitches are divided by young trees and marked by numbers on the tarmac roads. All have electrical connections (4/6A). Duckboards are provided for snow and wet weather and hardstandings for motorcaravans. The two acceptable sanitary blocks are in separate places and can be heated, although the provision may be hard pressed in high season. They have British and Turkish style WCs, laundry, chemical disposal and motorcaravan service facilities. There is a heated rest room with TV, a small bar with takeaway in summer. A new commercial centre 300 m. from the site provides a variety of shops. Fishing or bicycle hire 200 m, tennis and swimming pool 300 m, riding 1 km. A good base for winter ski-ing and summer walking, climbing, rafting or canoeing, plus car excursions.

Directions: Site is 1.5 km. east of Bourg-St Maurice on CD119 Les Arcs road.

Charges 2001:
-- Per unit incl. 1 person 51.60 - 52.60; extra person Ffr. 27.10 - 27.60; child 2-7 yrs 14.50 - 15.00, 7-12 yrs 25.55 - 26.05; electricity 4A 22.50 - 26.00, 6A 27.00 - 35.60, 10A 30.00 - 47.00; cyclist or hiker's tent incl. 1 person 43.10 - 43.60; animal 5.00; local tax 1.10.
-- Credit cards accepted.
Open:
15 Dec - 2 May
and 15 May - 6 Nov.
Address:
73700 Bourg-St Maurice.
Tel:
(0)4.79.07.03.45.
FAX: (0)4.79.07.25.41.
E-mail: leversoyen@ wanadoo.fr.
Reservations:
Write to site with deposit (Ffr. 200) and fee (60).

7405M Camping Municipal, Saint-Ferréol

This is a value for money site in a very popular area. Surrounded by glorious alpine scenery, it offers a relaxing environment away from the busy lakeside roads around Lake Annecy. Reception is located on the forecourt beside the security gate and also within this area is the St Ferréol village hall and boule club. The 114 pitches on the site are grass, numbered and have electric hook-ups. The ground is level and there is some shade from the tall fir trees in the centre. Two spotlessly clean toilet blocks are fully tiled. An electronic barrier is in operation and campers are issued with a key. Two supermarkets are a few minutes away by car at Faverges where you will also find banks, post office, etc. This is an excellent base from which to explore the high mountain passes, visit Chamonix or linger by the turquoise coloured lake. However in low season it is run with limited staff, with reception only open in the evening.

Directions: From Annecy follow N508 towards Albertville to Faverges by-pass. Leave at second roundabout on N508 towards Albertville and site is clearly signed on left in 1 km.

Charges 2000:
- Per unit incl. 2 persons for 1 night Ffr. 70.00, more than 1 night 55.00; extra person 12.00; animal 6.00; electricity 12.00.
-- No credit cards.
Open:
15 June - 15 September.
Address:
74210 Saint-Ferréol.
Tel:
(0)4.50.32.47.71
or the Mairie:
(0)4.50.44.56.36.
Reservations:
Contact site.

7401 Camping Les Deux Glaciers, Les Bossons, nr Chamonix

Well kept mountain site close to well known resort.

A pleasant little summer or winter site, Les Deux Glaciers has 135 individual pitches on terraces or single plots, levelled out of quite steeply rising ground, with electricity available in all areas. Pleasantly laid out with different trees, and floral displays in their season, it is well tended and maintained. It is quietly situated with fine views of the surrounding high mountains, but being a northern slope it loses the sun a little early. The two small sanitary blocks, both heated in cool weather, have British style toilets, at least half the washbasins in private cabins, free hot water in all basins and showers and most of the sinks, and facilities for disabled visitors. Snack restaurant (1/6-15/9). Mobile traders call in season, otherwise the village shop is 500 m. On site is a general room (for winter use only), table tennis and a washing machine and drying room. Fishing, bicycle hire or riding within 2 km, golf 4 km. With a good position and commendable amenities and welcome, the site becomes full for much of July/Aug. They are not keen on reservations but could make some for Britons, so try. In season, if not reserved, arrive early.

Directions: From west take second road leading off main N506 to right for Les Bossons, which takes you direct to site. From east turn right at sign for Les Bossons, then left at T-junction, and on to site.

Charges 2000:
-- Per unit with 2 persons Ffr. 72.00; extra person 27.00; child (under 7) 14.00; local tax 1.50; under 10s 1.00; electricity 2A 14.00, 3A 15.00 or 6A 20.00.
-- No credit cards.
Open:
All year exc 15/11-15/12.
Address:
Rte. des Tissières, 74400 Les Bossons.
Tel:
(0)4.50.53.15.84.
FAX: (0)4.50.55.90.81.
E-mail: glaciers@ clubinternet.fr.
Reservations:
See text.

7403M Camping Municipal Le Belvédère, Annecy

Hillside camp with good views over lake, in lovely area.

Annecy is an attractive town in a beautiful setting at the head of the lake of the same name. The old centre is intersected by flower decked canals and also has historical interest. There is much to see and do in this region in both summer and winter, being near Geneva and the high Alps. Le Belvédère, as its name implies, overlooks the lake and is the nearest camp to the town. It is now under private management, on lease from the authorities. There are hardstanding terraces for 80 caravans and 50 grass pitches for tents, but space may be limited if the site is busy. Electrical connections (10A) are available. One small area is reserved for groups. Tall pines and a steep hillside provide a backdrop to the site on the west and small trees provide decoration without giving much shade. Three modern sanitary blocks are situated around the site and were clean when we visited. One is heated in cold weather, and has a washroom for visitors with disabilities. There is a games room and a good children's playground. Swimming is possible in the lake. Shop (from May) and laundry facilities. A site which is ideally placed for visiting Annecy.

Directions: From town centre follow signs for Le Belvédère, Camping Municipal towards Albertville on road N508. Turn right to follow sign for `Hopital' up hill and take first left after passing this towards Semnoz and site.

Charges 2000:
-- Per unit incl. 2 persons Ffr. 90.00; tent incl. 2 persons 65.00, 1 person 45.00; extra person 25.00; child (2-11 yrs) 15.00; electricity 15.00.
-- Credit cards accepted.

Open:
February - 30 October.

Address:
8 Route de Semnoz, 74000 Annecy.

Tel:
(0)4.50.45.48.30.
FAX: (0)4.50.45.55.56.
E-mail: camping @ville-annecy.fr.

Reservations:
Necessary for July/Aug. - write to Mairie d'Annecy, BP 2305, 74011 Annecy Cedex.
Tel: (0)4.50.33.87.96.
FAX: (0)4.50.51.81.62.

7404 Camp de la Ravoire, Doussard, nr Annecy

Quality site with pool, overlooking Lake Annecy.

De la Ravoire, some 800 m. from the lake, is noted for its neat and tidy appearance and the quietness of its location in this popular tourist region. The 112 numbered pitches, on well mown grass and separated by small shrubs, have little shade, although there are trees on the lake side of the site. The 90 pitches for touring units have electricity connections (10/15A). The sanitary block in the centre of the site is very good with British WCs and hot water in washbasins (in cabins), sinks and showers. There are facilities for disabled people, chemical disposal and a laundry room with washing machines, dryers and irons. The outdoor pool, with a new water slide, is overlooked by the terrace of the snack bar where limited basic food items may be stocked. Near this building is a children's play area. Another addition is an area for sports. A good restaurant is on the lakeside where the camp road leaves the main road, with others near, plus shops in Doussard village. Those looking for a quiet, quality campsite in this most attractive region without the 'animation' programmes which so many French sites feel are necessary will find this a peaceful base, although disco noise from a site by the lake may drift across under some weather conditions. Fishing, boat launching, bicycle hire 1 km, riding 6km, golf 8 km. Used by a tour operator (18 pitches).

Directions: Site is signed from Annecy - Albertville road, just north of Bout-du-Lac (watch carefully, signs are small).

Charges 2001:
-- Per unit incl. 2 adults and electricity (5A) Ffr. 154.00, plus 1 child under 10 yrs 159.00; pitch with water and drainage 174.00 or 179.00; extra adult 34.00; child under 10 yrs 14.00, 10-15 yrs 22.00; electricity 10A 10.00, 15A 17.00; motorcaravan services 55.00; plus local tax.
-- Low season less 20%.
-- Credit cards accepted.

Open:
15 May - 15 September.

Address:
Bout du Lac, Route de la Ravoire, 74210 Doussard.

Tel:
(0)4.50.44.37.80.
FAX: (0)4.50.32.90.60.
E-mail: info@camping-la-ravoire.com.

Reservations:
Essential for July/Aug; made for min. 10 days; details from site.

Book this site
01892 559898

THE ALAN ROGERS'
travel service

JURA / ALPES - 74 Haute-Savoie

7407 Camping-Caravanning L'Escale, Le Grand-Bornand

Friendly, family site in magnificent mountain setting, open all year.

Situated at the foot of the Aravis range in the Savoy region and overlooking the ski resort of Le Grand-Bornand, L'Escale is clearly popular all year round. It comprises 149 standard pitches of 95-100 sq.m, all fairly clearly marked, level and with electricity (2-10A) on grass or gravel, with some terracing. A further 80 fully serviced grass pitches are available. The original, brick built toilet block which can be heated, is a little dark but very solid (unisex). It provides washbasins in cubicles, British style toilets, controllable hot showers and a baby bath. There is further provision in two chalet buildings and a mobile unit complete with ramped access for disabled campers. It can get very busy in the sanitary facilities during peak periods. A large drying room and laundry area is below the main building, with laundry sinks (H&C) and three washing machines. A torch is advisable late at night as the site lighting goes off completely. Activities include tennis, a children's play area, table tennis and there is a separate room for skis if holidaying in winter and a TV room. All other facilities are readily available in the town, including an excellent municipal pool complex, archery, paragliding, hang-gliding and ice hockey. Bicycle hire 200 m, riding and golf 3 km. In summer a variety of well signed footpaths provide forest or mountain walks and, in winter, the area provides superb facilities for down-hill and cross-country skiing. La Maison du Patrimoine is a must to visit. A 'Sites et Paysages' member.

Directions: Probably the best access is via Annecy following the D16 and D909 roads for La Clusaz. Follow signs for Grand Bornand (D4) at St Jean-de-Sixt and site is signed before entering the town.

Charges 2001:
-- Per unit incl. 2 persons Ffr. 73.00 - 83.00 (winter 93.00); extra person 21.00 - 24.00; animal 9.00; electricity 2A 19.00, 3A 24.00, 6A 33.00, 10A 41.00 - 49.00; local tax (over 15 yrs) 2.00.
-- Credit cards accepted.

Open:
All year except Oct. and Nov.

Address:
74450 Le Grand-Bornand.

Tel:
(0)4.50.02.20.69. FAX: (0)4.50.02.36.04. E-mail: grandboescale @aol.com.

Reservations:
Made with deposit (Ffr. 400) and fee (50).

`Camping Cheque'

Book this site 01892 559898

THE ALAN ROGERS'
travel service

see colour advert between pages 192/193

7409 Camping Le Plan du Fernuy, La Clusaz

Small compact site with good indoor pool in scenic location.

The pretty little village of La Clusaz (pop 1,800) is 32 km. east of Annecy at 1,200 m. above sea level in the heart of the Savoie Alps. Le Plan du Fernuy, 2 km. east of the village lies just to the north of the Avaris mountain range in a quiet and peaceful location. The neat, rectangular site has 53 of its 80 pitches available for tourists. Of reasonable size, all with electricity connections and 22 fully serviced, the pitches are arranged in rows on either side of hard access roads with good mountain views. Although surrounded by trees, there is little shade. The large apartment building at the entrance houses the very good sanitary provision on the ground floor and is heated in cool weather. There are British style WCs and free hot water in all washbasins (some private cabins), showers and sinks. It also has a baby room and facilities for those with disabilities. There are separate rooms for washing-up and laundry with a washing machine and dryer. The pleasant bar provides snacks and takeaway, basic food supplies (shops and restaurants in the village), video games and a TV room. The site's crowning glory is the excellent indoor heated pool around 13 x 7 m. in size with a separate paddling pool. Large windows look out on the mountains and there are sun beds by these. Reception is at the front of the pool building and, although the pool is not supervised, it can be seen from here. Site has a motorcaravan service point. This is good ski-ing (free ski bus) in winter and walking country in summer with other sporting opportunities nearby. The pleasant owners speak good English.

Directions: From Annecy take D909 to La Clusaz and turn towards Les Confins for site after 2 km. (well signed). Best to avoid using D909 from Flumat particularly with caravan or motorhome.

Charges 2000:
-- Per pitch incl. 2 persons Ffr. 80.00 - 121.00; child (2-12 yrs) 15.00; extra adult 28.00; animal 7.00; electricity 4A 19.00 - 27.00, 8A 28.00 - 37.00; local tax 2.00.
-- Higher prices are for winter.
-- Credit cards accepted.

Open:
5 June - 12 September and 20 Dec. - 25 April.

Address:
Route des Confins, 74220 La Clusaz.

Tel:
(0)4.50.02.44.75. FAX: 04.50.32.67.02. E-mail: leplan.du. fernuy@wanadoo.fr.

Reservations:
Advised for mid-July - mid-Aug. and winter.

7406 Camping La Colombière, Neydens, nr St Julien-en-Genevois

Neat and tidy small site with pool, within easy reach of Geneva.

La Colombière, on the edge of the small residential village of Neydens, is a few minutes from the A40 autoroute and only a short drive from Geneva. It is a small site with only 107 pitches, all reasonably level and separated by fruit trees and flowering bushes. There are views to the east and west of the mountain ridges. Three good sanitary blocks have British style WCs, washbasins in cubicles, good-sized showers, a baby room, facilities for disabled people and chemical disposal. One block was refurbished for the '99 season. Motorcaravan service point. The small shop at reception stocks basic necessities including bread (1/6-1/10). The terrace of the bar/restaurant overlooks the heated pool (15/5-1/10). The restaurant serves good quality, good value meals to campers and locals alike. M. Bussat owns a small vineyard close to the site, has the wine made in Switzerland and sells it by glass or bottle in the restaurant (a very nice rosé). A programme of activities includes mountain walks, guided cycle tours (bicycle hire on site), archery, volleyball and boules competitions, and French country music evenings. Fishing or riding 1 km, golf 5 km. One of France's long-distance footpaths (GR65) passes close to the site. The village of Neydens is the first stage for pilgrims from Northern Europe on the route to Santiago de Compostella on their way to cross the Pyrénées at St Pied de Port. The site has a dormitory with seven beds for pilgrims or for anyone else who may need a bed, for example, motorcyclists or a family en-route south. There are also chalets (5), caravans (4) and rooms to let. Neydens makes a good base for visiting Geneva and the Lac Leman region and is a very pleasant, friendly site where you may drop in for a night stop - and stay for several days! Low season caravan storage available. English is spoken. A 'Sites et Paysages' member.

Directions: Take exit 13 from A40 autoroute south of Geneva, and take N201 towards Annecy. Turn into village of Neydens and follow campsite signs.

Charges 2000:
-- Per unit incl. 2 persons Ffr. 87.00 - 97.00; extra person 22.00 - 25.00; child (under 7 yrs) 18.00 - 20.00; dog 9.00 - 10.00; electricity (5/6A) 20.00.
-- Credit cards accepted.
Open:
20 March - 3 November.
Address:
74160 Neydens.
Tel:
(0)4.50.35.13.14.
FAX: (0)4.50.35.13.40.
E-mail: la.colombiere @wanadoo.fr.
Reservations:
Write to site.
`Camping Cheque`

Book this site 01892 559898
THE ALAN ROGERS' travel service

see colour advert between pages 192/193

7408 Camping Les Rosières, Chamonix, Mont-Blanc

Peaceful, friendly site in glorious surroundings, 2 km. from Chamonix.

This is one of the most spectacular settings imaginable for a campsite. Here the scenic grandeur of the Alps excels, with Mont Blanc and it sister peaks towering above, providing a perfect backdrop. Within walking distance of Chamonix by way of a riverside path, this site attracts both summer and winter campers. It offers a relaxing environment in warm sunshine beneath the snow-capped peaks, or makes an ideal base for a winter skiing holiday. In keeping with the setting, a timbered chalet adorned with flowers houses reception. Adjacent, and in a central position, is the heated sanitary block. Facilities are clean, well laid out and maintained to a high standard, with attractive mosaic tiled floors, a theme which is carried around the washbasins. These are both open style and in cabins with hot water. Controllable showers are well equipped with changing space, divider, shelf, seat, hooks and soap dish. WCs are mostly British style. Provision for disabled people includes a shower, WC and washbasin and, in same unit, a baby bath and shower. A laundry room in the basement has two washing machines, two dryers, ironing board and drying lines. There is also accommodation for campers in wet weather, a dishwashing area, chemical disposal, motorcaravan service point, gas supplies and night lighting. There are 147 pitches, 102 for tourers, which are of average size, grass, level, numbered and separated by trees and shrubs. Electricity hook-ups (4/10A) are available on 60. In July/Aug. there is a small bar, snacks and takeaway. Shop (closed 22/4-2/6, otherwise 50 m.) for basics. Mobile homes (7) to rent. Swimming pool or golf 800 m, fishing or riding 2 km. In winter the bus to the ski station is free.

Directions: Enter Chamonix by Route Blanche. Continue towards town and turn right at crossroads signed Les Praz. Site on right in 2 km.

Charges 2001:
-- Per unit incl. 2 persons Ffr. 84.00 - 100.00; extra person 28.00 - 33.00; hiker and tent 13.00 - 15.00; child under 7 years 19.00; electricity 4A 17.00, 5A 19.00; local tax 1.00.
Open:
3 February - 17 October
Address:
121 Clos des Rosières, 74400 Chamonix Mont-Blanc.
Tel:
(0)4.50.53.10.42.
FAX: (0)4.50.53.29.55.
Reservations:
Contact site.

ATLANTIC COAST

We have taken the coastal departements of the official French region of Aquitaine, stretching from Bordeaux in the north to the Pyrenees and the Spanish border in the south to make our 'tourist' region.

Major city: Bordeaux
Departements: 33 Gironde, 40 Landes, 64 Pyrenees Atlantiques

The Landes stretches north from Biarritz to Arcachon. The most notable features are the uninterrupted line of sandy beaches, over 100 miles long, and the giant pine forests in the hinterland. Water also plays a feature in the many 'etangs' which lie just behind the beaches and provide and attractive situation for many campsites. Dax on the banks of the Adour is a spa town.

The département of the Gironde covers the area from the Bassin d'Arcachon, famed for its oysters, and Europe's highest sand dune to the Gironde estuary and Bordeaux. The vineyards of Bordeaux are world famous and especially well known for their Medoc, Sauternes, and St Emilion wines.

The Pays Basque area (Pyrénées Atlantiques) in the south west corner is much influenced by Spain. The most famous Basque towns are Biarritz, Bayonne and the picturesque old port of St-Jean-de-Luz. Further inland and nearer the Pyrénées is the attractive town of St-Jean-Pied-de-Port on the pilgrims' route to northern Spain and Santiago de Compostela and only 20 km from the forest of Iraty with its lakes and ski runs. Look for the high, unusually shaped walls used for the Basque game of 'pelota'; St-Jean is one of the strongest centres of the sport.

Note: the site reports are arranged by département in numerical order.
See map on page 314.

Cuisine of the region

Foie Gras – specially prepared livers of geese and ducks, seasoned and stuffed with truffles
Confits – (preserved goose and duck) are a key ingredient in a number of dishes
Fish and seafood – like carp stuffed with foie gras, mullet in red wine and besugo (sea bream)
Chorizos – spicy sausages
Jambon de Bayonne – raw ham, cured in salt and sliced paper thin
Lamproie – eel-like fish with leeks, onions and red Bordeaux wine
Gâteau Basque – shallow custard pastry, often with fruit fillings
Cèpes – fine, delicate mushrooms; sometimes dried
Chou farci – stuffed cabbage, sometimes aux marrons (with chestnuts)

Wine

Three distinctive areas: Médoc, famous for fine red wines, Graves and Sauternes left of the Garonne and Saint-Emilion and its surroundings – for Entre-Deux-Mers and Côtes de Blaye

Places of interest

Bayonne – old streets and fortifications; Basque Museum
Bordeaux – see the 14,000 piece Bohemian glass chandelier in the foyer of the Grand Theatre, and the 29 acre Esplanade des Quinconces
Pau – famous motor racing circuit on (closed) public highway; stadium for the Basque game of pelota
St Emilion – visit the castle ramparts or drink premier cru St Emilion at pavement cafés
St Jean-de-Luz – seaside resort and fishing village
St Jean-Pied-de-Port – ancient city with citadel; bright Basque houses in steep streets

3306 Camping Le Palace, Soulac-sur-Mer, nr Royan

Large, traditional site close to beach, south of Royan across the estuary.

This large, flat site has 535 good-sized individual pitches regularly laid out amongst a variety of trees including pines which provide good shade. On very sandy ground, the pitches for caravans have hardened areas with electricity. Most pitches have water taps, some also have sewage connections. There are twelve separate toilet blocks, some smaller and more simple than others. All have British style WCs and free pre-set hot showers, some opening from the outside only, washbasins in private cabins, baby bathrooms (0-24 months) in four blocks and facilities for disabled people in one. A wide, sandy beach is 400 m. from the site gates and bathing, said not to be dangerous in normal conditions, is controlled by lifeguards. However, the site has its own swimming pool (20 x 10 m), also with lifeguards, attractively set in a raised, part grass, part tiled area with its own shower facilities, etc. Arranged around a lush green roundabout with a fountain at the centre of the site are a self-service shop, butcher, fish and general shops, restaurant and bar with dancing and concerts (all mostly from 10/6). Supervised children's playground with paddling pool. Bicycle hire. Programme of sports, entertainments and excursions for adults and children in July/Aug. Tennis courts are adjacent, riding 400 m. Washing machines. Treatment room and doctor will call. Mobile homes (31) and chalets (31) for rent. Winter caravan storage. English is spoken.

Directions: Site is 1 km. south of Soulac and well signed. The shortest and simplest way is via the ferry which runs from Royan across the Gironde estuary to the Pointe de Grave, but this is quite expensive with a caravan. Alternatively make the trip via Bordeaux.

Charges 2000:
-- If reserved: per unit incl. 2 persons, 5A electricity and water Ffr. 88.00 - 119.00, plus drainage 90.00 - 121.00; tent pitch incl. 2 persons 70.00 - 96.00; extra person (over 10) 18.00 - 24.00; local tax (over 10 yrs, July/Aug) 2.00.
-- Credit cards accepted.

Open:
1 May - 15 September.

Address:
B.P. 33,
Bd. Marsan de Montbrun,
33780 Soulac-sur-Mer.

Tel:
(0)5.56.09.80.22.
FAX: (0)5.56.09.84.23.
E-mail: campingpalace
@libertysurf.fr.

Reservations:
Made with deposit;
contact site.

3320 Camping de l'Eyre, Mios

Convenient night halt 8 km. from the A63 autoroute.

A friendly welcome is guaranteed at this well kept, former municipal site which is close to Bordeaux, Arcachon and the Dune de Pilat. It has 107 pitches, 50 for touring units, and good basic facilities. Pitches are marked out, some on flat ground, others more sloping. Many are well shaded and have water and electricity connections (6A). The site abuts an extensive sports complex and it is possible to swim or fish in the Eyre river, which runs alongside the campsite. Bicycle hire is provided on site. Riding 3 km. Shops, restaurants and all services are to be found in Mios village.

Directions: From A63 south of Bordeaux take exit 22 on A660 signed Arcachon. After 5 km. at junction 1 take D216 to Mios. Mios is on the D3 and site is on the western end of the village, well signed.

Charges guide:
-- Per unit incl. 2 persons Ffr. 69.00; extra person 20.00; child (2-8 yrs) 10.00; electricity 19.00.

Open:
All year

Address:
Allée de la Plage,
33380 Mios.

Tel/Fax:
(0)5.56.26.42.04.
E-mail:
teurlaylinda@free.fr.

Reservations:
Advised for mid-July -
mid-Aug.

ATLANTIC COAST - 33 Gironde

3305 Camping Les Ourmes, Hourtin

Pleasantly and conveniently situated site close to lake, providing good value.

Located only 500 m. from the largest freshwater lake in France, only 10 minutes drive from the beach and with its own pool, this is essentially a holiday site. Pitches, marked but in most cases not actually separated, are arranged amongst tall pines and other trees which give good shade. There are 270 pitches, all with electricity. The site's amenities are arranged around a pleasant entrance courtyard and include a bar/restaurant with many outdoor tables and serving snacks and takeaway meals (1/7-31/8), a small shop (1/6-15/9), TV and games rooms and boules pitches. The medium sized swimming pool (15/6-15/9) has a paved sunbathing area and there is a separate large leisure area with a children's play area, volleyball and basketball courts and table tennis tables (under cover). Evening entertainment programme in season. Watersports and fishing are possible on the lake, with bicycle hire, tennis and riding within 500 m. The sanitary facilities are in three purpose built blocks and are of a good standard with free hot showers, some washbasins in cabins and British type WCs. There is a washing machine in each block and a dryer, with hot water taps for washing up. This site has a busy, cosmopolitan feel, with visitors of many different nationalities. Mobile homes for rent (13).

Directions: Follow Route du Port (Ave du Lac) from the town centre and site is signed.

Charges 2001:
-- Per unit incl. 2 persons Ffr. 72.00 - 95.00, with electricity 90.00 - 115.00; extra person (over 2 yrs) 12.00 - 19.00; extra car 8.00 - 10.00; dog 8.00 - 10.00; local tax (over 10 yrs) 1.10.
-- No credit cards.

Open:
1 April - 30 September.

Address:
Av. du Lac, 33990 Hourtin.

Tel:
(0)5.56.09.12.76.
FAX: (0)5.56.09.23.90.
E-mail: lesourmes @free.fr.

Reservations:
Necessary in high season - contact site.

3311 Airotel Camping de la Côte d'Argent, Hourtin-Plage

Large, family run Medoc site with walkway to the beach.

Spread over 17 hectares of undulating sand-based terrain and in the midst of a pine forest, this site is well placed and well equipped for leisurely family holidays. It also makes an ideal base for walkers and cyclists, with over 100 km. of cycle lanes leading through the Medoc countryside. Hourtin-Plage is a pleasant invigorating resort on the Atlantic coast and a popular location for watersports enthusiasts, or those who prefer spending their days on the beach. More appealing though may be to stay on site, for Côte d'Argent's top attraction is its swimming pool complex with four pools, waterslides and flumes. Wooden bridges connect the pools and islands, on which there are sunbathing patios and children's play areas. Facilities on site consist of five very clean sanitary blocks, provision for disabled visitors, plenty of laundry machines, chemical disposal, motorcaravan service points, a large supermarket, restaurant, takeaway and pizzeria bar and night lighting. There are 500 touring pitches which are not clearly defined and in the trees, some on soft sand-based ground. When we visited 48 hardstandings for motorcaravans were almost complete. Due to the work on the site the access roads are in a poor condition, but we are told will be repaired in the near future. Other on site facilities include two tennis courts, pool tables, four play areas, a mini-club and organised entertainment in season. There are mobile homes, chalets and caravans for hire.

Directions: Turn off D101 Hourtin-Soulac road 3 km. north of Hourtin. Then join D101E signed Hourtin-Plage. Site is 300 m. from the beach.

Charges 2000:
-- Per unit incl. 2 persons Ffr. 121.60 - 147.00; extra person 18.20 - 26.00; child (2-10 yrs) 12.60 - 18.00; tent incl. 2 persons 99.80 - 134.00; motorcaravan incl. 2 persons 112.40 - 152.00; electricity (6A) 25.00; dog 11.20 - 16.00; local tax over 10 yrs 3.30.

Open:
13 May - 16 September.

Address:
33990 Hourtin-Plage.

Tel:
(0)5.56.09.10.25.
FAX: (0)5.56.09.24.96.
E-mail: camping-cote-dargent @wanadoo.fr.

Reservations:
Necessary for July/August; contact site.

`Camping Cheque'

see colour advert between pages 192/193

3302 Camping de Fontaine-Vieille, Andernos-les-Bains, Arcachon

Large site on east side of Bassin d'Arcachon with pool and frontage to Bassin.

Fontaine-Vieille is a large, well-established site that recently celebrated its 50th anniversary. The site stretches along the edge of the Bassin d'Arcachon under light woodland in the residential area of the small town of Andernos. It has 800 individual pitches, some with views and 600 with electricity connections. On flat grassy ground, they are marked by stones in the ground or young trees. The seven sanitary blocks, of rather unusual design, provide an adequate number of hot showers, plus facilities for people with disabilities and children. All the blocks, open when we visited, are refurbished to a high standard and kept clean. A beach runs alongside the tidal Bassin which can be used for boating when the tide is in. When it is out, it is sand and mud but they claim that bathing in the channels is still possible. A new swimming pool complex was opened for 2000. There is also a shop (15/5-15/9), a bar with terrace and restaurant with takeaway (all season) with town shops, etc. near. Activities provided include four tennis courts, a TV room, two children's play areas for little ones, adventure area for older children and minigolf. Boats, sailboards and bicycles may be hired and sports are organised. There is a communal barbecue or your own gas barbecue may be used. Riding 5 km, golf 3 km. Caravan storage is available and mobile homes, chalets and bungalows to rent.

Directions: Turn off D3 at southern end of Andernos towards Bassin at camp sign.

Charges 2000:
-- Per unit incl. 2 persons Ffr. 65.00 - 95.00, with electricity (5A) 80.00 - 115.00; extra person 15.00 - 20.00; child (2-7 yrs) 12.00 - 15.00; local tax 1.10; animal 11.00-14.00.
-- Credit cards accepted.

Open:
1 April - 30 September.

Address:
4 Bvd. du Colonel Wurtz, 33510 Andernos-les-Bains.

Tel:
(0)5.56.82.01.67.
FAX: (0)5.56.82.09.81.

Reservations:
Made for any length with deposit (Ffr. 500) and fee (120).

CAMPING CARAVANNING
FONTAINE VIEILLE

☆ ☆ ☆

NEW Extension to pool complex

4, Boulevard du Colonel Wurtz

33510 ANDERNOS-LES-BAINS

Tel: 05 56 82 01 67 ◆ Fax: 05 56 82 09 81

On the edge of the beach, in the Arcachon Basin with the rhythm of the tides in the heart of a pine and oak forest, this is an ideal location for family holidays in peaceful and relaxing surroundings. We offer a swimming pool, supermarket, restaurant, bar, takeaway meals, cinema, television, exchange facilities

Mobile homes and chalets to rent.

For a list of sites which are open all year - see page 262

3312 Camping La Cigale, Arès

Attractive little site with charm and ambience.

The owners at La Cigale extend a very warm welcome at this delightful site. Small and beautifully maintained, it is set amid pine trees and M. Pallet's floral displays. The 95 pitches, most with electricity and of 100 sq.m. in size, are level and grassy, divided by hedges and flower borders. The majority have shade from the pine trees. There are two small swimming pools in a pleasant setting and under the ample shade of a large plane tree, drinks, meals and snacks are available on the bar terrace. The flower-bedecked and attractive toilet facilities (unisex) are centrally located and meticulously maintained. They include a family room with two showers, facilities for disabled visitors and laundry facilities with a washing machine and dryer. There are points for chemical disposal and motorcaravan services. A second block is scheduled for 2001. There is a small children's play area (soon to be redeveloped) and full-time animators are provided for children and adults in July and August. Every Sunday morning there is a special treat for children of a free donkey cart ride. The site, conveniently placed for a wide choice of beaches, is a short distance from the Bassin d'Arcachon and 10 km. from the rolling dunes and waves of the Atlantic coast. It is an exceptional area for cycling, with designated routes. Across the bay lies bustling Arcachon and the enormous Dune de Pilat, easily reached by ferry from Cap Ferret. Used by tour operators (22%).

Directions: Leave Bordeaux ring-road at exit 10 (D213) or exit 11 (D106) and continue on good roads direct to Arès. Turn into Arès following road to church square. Turn right following signs for Lège/Cap Ferret. Site is 800 m. on right.

Charges 2000:
-- Ffrancs: per unit incl. 1 or 2 persons Ffr. 90.00 - 115.00; extra person 25.00; child (under 7 yrs) 15.00; electricity (4/6A) 24.00; local tax (1/6-30/9) 1.10.
-- Euro: per unit incl. 1 or 2 persons 13,72 - 17,53; extra person 3,81; child (under 7 yrs) 2,29; electricity (4/6A) 3,66; local tax (1/6-30/9) 0,17.
-- Credit cards accepted.

Open:
15 May - 15 September.

Address:
Route de la Lège, 33740 Arès.

Tel:
(0)5.56.60.22.59.
FAX: (0)5.57.70.41.66.

Reservations:
Advised for July/Aug. and made with deposit (Ffr. 500) and fee (100).

3308 Camping Domaine de la Barbanne, St Emilion, nr Libourne

Pleasant, friendly, family-owned site in heart of celebrated wine region.

La Barbanne, with 160 pitches, has been transformed into a carefully maintained, well equipped site by its new owners. The original parts of the site bordering the lake have tarred roads, good shade and pleasant surroundings, whilst the newer area has younger trees, some shade and gravel access roads. The pitches are in the process of being re-numbered and are all large, level and grassy with dividing hedges and electricity connections. The site has two toilet blocks, the one in the original area having been fully refurbished, the other in the newer area being very modern. Both provide British style WCs, washbasins (most in private cabins) and free hot showers. Visitors with disabilities are well catered for in each block. There are good facilities for chemical disposal and a motorcaravan service point. The site has two well appointed and landscaped swimming pools, both with high quality, free sun-loungers. One pool is heated and has a cork-screw water slide. La Barbanne has an attractive entrance and reception area with ample space for parking or turning. Adjacent to reception is a small, well stocked shop, open all day. There is a bar with terrace, a takeaway and a pretty new restaurant. Sports and activities on the site, all free, include tennis, boules, volleyball, table tennis and minigolf. The lake provides superb free fishing, pedaloes, canoes and lakeside walks. Bicycle hire is provided and there is a new, fully enclosed children's play area with seats for parents and an organised children's club from 1 July. The site owners run a free minibus service three times a day to St Emilion and also organise excursions to local places of interest, including Bordeaux. Mobile homes and chalets for hire. A 'Sites et Paysages' member.

Directions: At St Emilion take D122 for 2.5 km. Turn right just before Montagne and site is on left after 400 m. Caravans and motorhomes are forbidden through the village of St Emilion. They must approach the site by taking the D243 from Libourne or from Castillon on the D936 via D130/D243.

Charges 2000:
-- Per adult Ffr. 22.00 - 30.00; child under 7 yrs 15.00 - 25.00, under 3 yrs 12.00 - 15.00; pitch 36.00 - 42.00; animal free - 7.00; electricity (6A) 18.00 - 23.00; extra tent 15.00; local tax 1.10 (child 0.55).
-- Credit cards accepted.

Open:
1 April - 30 September.

Address:
33330 St Emilion.

Tel:
(0)5.57.24.75.80.
FAX: (0)5.57.24.69.68.
E-mail:
camping.domaine.de.
la.barbanne@wanadoo.fr.

Reservations:
Made for min. 4 days.

Book this site
01892 559898

THE ALAN ROGERS'
travel service

3309 Camping Le Pressoir, Petit Palais, nr Lussac

Good quality site based on an old wine farm in rolling, wine producing countryside.

Buried in the famous wine producing countryside of the Lussac, Pomerol and St Emilion area north of Bordeaux, Le Pressoir is surrounded by fields of vines. With a manicured entrance featuring attractive trees, shrubs and flowers, together with preserved equipment from its former role, it is a neat site with good quality facilities. The 100 large pitches are arranged on either side of a gravel road leading up a slight hill and many are shaded by attractive trees. They are over 100 sq.m. and equipped with electricity (blue EC plugs) and interspersed with five Trigano type tents for hire. Very good sanitary facilities are in a purpose built block near the farmhouse which provides washbasins (oval, vanity style) in cabins, roomy controllable showers, British style WCs, hair and make-up area for ladies, facilities for disabled visitors, washing machine and chemical disposal. The old barn has been converted into a stylish bar and really charming, separate restaurant (all season). An attractive outdoor terrace has tables and a snack bar with takeaway. Near to this is a swimming pool (14 x 7 m, open 15/5-15/9, no bermuda shorts) plus facilities for petanque, volleyball and table tennis. A children's playground has timber equipment. Tennis nearby, fishing 5 km, riding 10 km. A quiet, family site, Le Pressoir provides a comfortable base for a holiday in this area famous for good food and wine. Gates locked 22.00 - 08.00 hrs.

Directions: From N89 Bordeaux - Périgueux turn at Saint Médard de Guizières towards Lussac on the D21. Site is signed here and also from Lussac.

Charges 2000:
-- Per standard pitch Ffr. 42.00, with 6A electricity 60.00; person 35.00; child (2-6 yrs) 20.00.
-- Credit cards accepted.

Open:
1 April - 3 October.

Address:
Petit Palais,
33570 Lussac.

Tel:
(0)5.57.69.73.25.
FAX: (0)5.57.69.77.36.
E-mail:
camping.le.pressoir
@wanadoo.fr.

Reservations:
Advised for July/Aug. and made with deposit and Ffr. 75 fee.

Book this site
01892 559898

3310 Camping-Caravaning La Forêt, Pyla-sur-Mer, nr Arcachon

Popular site within easy reach of many fine, sandy beaches.

Set amongst tall pine trees, La Forêt is a well established site with a sandy base at the foot of the Dune du Pilat. All the 512 touring pitches are shaded by the pines and 250 have electricity connections. The site is sloping, but most of the pitches are reasonably level. The six toilet blocks are of varying age and quality, the newest opened for '99, with another new block planned. All provide the usual amenities including British style WCs, free hot showers (some large cubicles also with washbasin), some washbasins in cubicles, others open but all with cold water only. There are dishwashing and laundry sinks (cold water), washing machines and dryers and chemical disposal facilities. Some blocks have good provision for disabled visitors. The attractive restaurant, bar and takeaway open all season. La Forêt's supermarket is very well stocked at reasonable prices. The nearest town is Arcachon, 11 km. Daily clubs, tournaments and games are organised in July/Aug. On site are a swimming pool (10 x 20 m) and small paddling pool, tennis, volleyball, table tennis and bicycle hire - the area is excellent for cycling as there are tracks through the forest. This is a busy site in high season, suitable for families. Cabins and mobile homes to rent.

Directions: From A63 heading south, take A660 westwards to La Teste, then follow signs for Dune du Pilat. Site is on right on the D218 heading south.

Charges guide:
-- Per unit incl. 2 persons Ffr. 77.00 - 135.00, with electricity 89.00 - 160.00; extra person 20.00 - 33.00; child (under 7 yrs) 12.00 - 24.00; dog 15.00; plus local tax

Open:
1 April - 1 November.

Address:
Route de Biscarrosse,
33115 Pyla-sur-Mer.

Tel:
(0)5.56.22.73.28
winter: (0)5.56.66.16.90.
FAX: (0)5.56.22.70.50
winter: (0)5.56.66.91.47.
E-mail: camping.foret
@wanadoo.fr.

Reservations:
Advised for Jul;y/Aug. and made with deposit (Ffr. 850) and fee (150).

Book your site with the experts
Call for an instant quote
01892 55 98 98

Low cost ferries guaranteed!

3301 Camping de la Dune, Pyla-sur-Mer, nr Arcachon

Busy site with pool and other amenities separated from sea by famous giant dune.

La Dune is a good example of a busy French family site. It is an informal, friendly and lively site with a comprehensive range of amenities. From its situation at the foot of the enormous dune (the highest in Europe) you can reach the beach either by climbing over the dune – a ladder goes up nearly to the top – or driving round, or you can use the free medium-size swimming pool at the far side of the site. The 325 marked pitches, some sloping, some terraced but level, vary somewhat in size but all are hedged with shade from pine trees. Nearly half are caravan pitches with electricity, water and drainaway. Some of the roads on the site are quite narrow and parts are quite sandy. There are three modern sanitary blocks including one small one, in addition to an existing one that has been refurbished to make roomy showers and washbasins en-suite and which can be heated in cool weather. They should be a good provision with WCs of British and Turkish types, individual washbasins with many in private cabins (with H&C) and a good supply of pre-set hot showers (although some blocks may be closed at night). There is a small supermarket and a pleasant little bar and restaurant, with a takeaway, that can get busy and noisy at times (opens June, all other facilities are all season). There is a purpose built barbecue (only individual gas ones are allowed) and fridges for hire. Open-air theatre and sports and tournaments are organised July -end Aug. Children's playground with mini-club. Riding 2 km, fishing 3 km, golf 10 km. Motorcaravan service point. Mobile homes and chalets for hire (39). English spoken in season. No tour operators.

Directions: The new D259 signed from the N250 to Biscarrosse and Dune du Pilat, just before La Teste, avoids Pyla-sur-Mer. At end of new road turn left at roundabout onto D218 coast road. La Dune is second site on right.

Charges 2000:
-- Per unit incl. 2 persons: with tent Ffr 70.00 - 130.00; with caravan incl. electricity and water 90.00 - 150.00; extra person 15.00 - 45.00; extra child (under 7) 10.00 - 20.00; extra car 10.00 - 30.00; dog 5.00 - 15.00; local tax 2.50 (under 10 yrs 1.25).
-- Credit cards accepted.

Open:
1 May - 30 September.

Address:
Rte. de Biscarrosse, 33115 Pyla sur Mer.

Tel:
(0)5.56.22.72.17. FAX: as phone.

Reservations:
Made for min. 1 week in high season with 25% deposit and fee (Ffr. 150) at least 1 month in advance.

SEA,
SUN,
FOREST

Unique site at the foot of the highest dune in Europe.

325 pitches 'délimité' and shaded. Chalets and Mobile homes 4 and 6 persons for rent.

Swimming pool – Tennis
All shops
Security – Animations
Aire de service Camping Car

**ROUTE DE BISCARROSSE –33115 PYLA / MER
TEL / FAX : 05.56.22.72.17**

4013 Camping-Caravaning de la Côte, Messanges, nr Vieux-Boucau

Peaceful family site near the beaches of the Landes.

This family site, surrounded by pine forests, has large, level pitches which are edged with newly planted trees and shrubs. A number of the 142 touring pitches are set among trees that provide shade, 118 have electricity connections (6/10A) and some also have water. The beach and the dunes are 20 minutes walk. Two modern toilet blocks built in the Landes style are of excellent quality and very well maintained. All the facilities are unisex, with showers (some pre-set, others adjustable) washbasins in private cabins British style WCs. There is a baby room with bath, provision for disabled people, washing machines and dryer with sinks for laundry and dishes, chemical disposal and a motorcaravan service point. Reception sells bread and milk, a few basic supplies and gas (1/7-31/8). Facilities for leisure include a games room, play area, football, volleyball, table tennis and a boules pitch. Fishing or riding within 1 km, bicycle hire 1.5 km, golf 2 km. Barbecues are only permitted at a designated area. There is a supermarket near, plus the resort of Vieux-Boucau. M. and Mme. Moresmau are very proud of their site and do their utmost to maintain a quiet family atmosphere with customers who return year after year. Mobile home, gite and two caravans to rent.

Directions: Site is signed off the D652, 1.5 km. north of Vieux-Boucau.

Charges 2001:
-- Per unit incl. 2 persons Ffr. 54.00 - 67.00; extra person 15.00 - 18.00; child (under 7 yrs) 10.00 - 13.00; electricity 6A 14.00 - 16.00, 10A 21.00 - 25.00; dog free - 7.00; local tax (June-Sept) 2.20.
-- Credit cards accepted.

Open:
1 April - 30 September.

Address:
Rte de Vieux-Boucau, 40660 Messanges.

Tel:
(0)5.58.48.94.94.
FAX: (0)5.58.48.94.44.
E-mail: lacote@ wanadoo.fr.

Reservations:
Recommended and made with deposit - contact site for details.

Book this site
01892 559898

THE ALAN ROGERS'
travel service

4020M Camping-Caravaning Municipal Le Grandjean, Linxe

This is a small, very unsophisticated site away from the hectic tourist centres of the coast. Only 1 km. from the village and 9 km. from the sea, the entrance is very attractive with well tended flower beds. There are only 100 marked and numbered pitches, all level and under pine trees, 58 with electricity and water. The two toilet blocks are of excellent quality and, when we visited, were very clean. They have British style WCs, washbasins in cabins and pre-set showers, with good facilities for disabled people and babies. There are plenty of laundry and dishwashing sinks and a washing machine. A small games room has table tennis, there is a play area on sand and boules and volleyball pitches. Barbecues are only permitted in the two barbecue areas provided. A quiet family site, Le Grandjean will appeal to families with young children who need peaceful days and nights, but with only a short ride to the beach. Golf or fishing 6 km, bicycle hire 1 km. No tour operators, one mobile home to hire.

Directions: Leave the N10 at Castets and take D42 to Linxe. Site is signed from the village and is at the extreme western end.

Charges 2000:
-- Per adult Ffr. 17.00; child (under 8 yrs) 7.00; tent 20.00; caravan or motorcaravan 34.00.
-- Credit cards accepted.

Open:
28 June - 6 September.

Address:
40260 Linxe.

Tel:
(0)5.58.42.90.00.
FAX: (0)5.58.42.94.67.

Reservations:
Can be made (in French) on 58.42.92.27 or in writing to La Mairie, 40260 Linxe.

For lists of sites that offer facilities on site for
FISHING, GOLF, HORSE RIDING or BICYCLE HIRE
see pages 263 - 265

ATLANTIC COAST - 40 Landes

4004 Camping La Paillotte, Azur, nr Soustons

Very attractive, good lakeside site with an individual atmosphere.

La Paillotte, in the Landes area of southwest France, is a site with a character of its own. The buildings (reception, shop, restaurant, even sanitary blocks) are all Tahitian in style, circular and constructed from local woods with the typical straw roof (and layer of waterproof material underneath). Some are now being replaced but still in character. It lies right by the edge of the Soustons lake, 1½ km. from Azur village, with its own sandy beach. This is very suitable for young children because the lake is shallow and slopes extremely gradually. A swimming pool complex was added for the 2000 season (from 1/5, no bermuda style shorts). For boating the site has a small private harbour where non-powered boats of shallow draught can be kept. Sailing, windsurfing (with lessons) and rowing boats and pedaloes for hire. The Atlantic beaches are 10 km. All 310 pitches at La Paillotte are marked, individual ones and are mostly shady with shrubs and trees. The 125 pitches for touring units vary in price according to size, position and whether they are equipped with electricity, water, etc. The circular rustic-style sanitary blocks are rather different from the usual amenities, but are modern and fully tiled with British style WCs and free hot showers in central enclosed positions, individual washbasins, part-enclosed with free hot water (some toilets and basins en-suite). There are separate 'mini' facilities for children, outside washing-up sinks with hot water, washing machines and dryers, chemical disposal and motorcaravan services. Amenities include a shop (1/6-6/9), good restaurant with a very pleasant terrace overlooking the lake and a bar (all 12/5-10/9) and takeaway (high season). Games and activities are organised, there is a 'mini-club' room, TV room, library and an amusement room with juke box. Activities include fishing, bicycle hire and table tennis. Riding 5 km, golf 10 km. Used by tour operators (45 pitches). Mobile homes and Polynesian style bungalows to rent. Torches useful. Dogs not accepted. Member 'Sites et Paysages', 'Camping Qualité Plus' and 'Yelloh Village'.

Directions: Coming from the north along N10, turn west on D150 at Magescq. From south go via Soustons. In Azur turn left before church (site signed).

Charges 2000:
-- Per unit incl. 2 persons: standard pitch Ffr. 85.00 - 162.00; extra person (over 3 yrs) 20.00 - 34.00; electricity (10A) 28.00; water and electricity 32.00 - 41.00; pitch by lake plus 20.00 - 41.00; local tax (over 10) in July/Aug 1.65.
-- Credit cards accepted.

Open:
1 May - 15 September.

Address:
Azur, 40140 Soustons.

Tel:
(0)5.58.48.12.12. FAX: (0)5.58.48.10.73. E-mail: la.paillotte@wanadoo.fr.

Reservations:
Advised for high season; made for Sat. to Sat. only 2/7- 27/8, with deposit (Ffr. 250 per week) and fee (160).

`Camping Cheque'

4005 Camping Le Col Vert, Vielle-Saint-Girons, nr Castets

Family holiday centre with long frontage to lake, 5 km. from Atlantic beaches.

This extensive but natural site, edging a nature reserve, stretches right along the Lac de Léon, a conservation area, for 1 km. on a narrow frontage which makes it particularly suitable for those who want to practise water sports such as sailing and windsurfing. Bathing is also possible; the lake bed shelves gently making it easy for children and the site has a supervised beach. Sail-boarding courses are arranged and there are some boats and boards for hire. There are two heated pools (all season), both supervised, an open air one with whirl pool and a covered one, with sunbathing areas. An overall charge is made for the leisure activities but this excludes certain facilities, eg. riding, bicycle hire, sauna, tennis, minigolf. The 380 pitches for touring units are flat and covered by light pinewood, most with good shade. They are of around 100 sq.m., only partly separated, some 72 with water and electricity. The four modern toilet blocks, one very large at the far end of the site, are a good provision, with excellent facilities for disabled people. They have mostly British WCs, washbasins in private cabins and free showers with pre-set hot water (a reader reports that the hot water supply can be variable). There are dishwashing sinks mainly with cold water but with hot tap to draw from, chemical disposal, washing machines, dryer and dishwasher, and a motorcaravan service point. A good terraced bar/restaurant is by the lake (open to all) and there is a simple takeaway. Two areas are provided for barbecues. Amenities include shops (15/5-15/9), a sports area with tennis and volleyball, fitness centre and a sauna and solarium. Sailing school (15/6-15/9). TV room, table tennis, amusement machines. Children's playground. Minigolf. Walking and cycle ways in the forest and two jogging tracks. Fishing (with lessons for children). Stables with riding on site. Golf 10 km. Much 'animation' is organised in season: children's games, tournaments, etc. by day and dancing or shows evenings. Safety deposit boxes. Chalets and mobile homes for hire. Used by tour operators (80 pitches).

Directions: Roads to lake and site lead off D652 St Girons - Léon road at Vielle-St-Girons, clearly signed.

Charges 2000:
-- Per unit incl. 2 persons Ffr. 49.50 - 229.00; extra person 12.00 - 26.00; child (under 7 yrs) 9.00 - 20.00; dog 6.00 - 10.00; electricity 3A 20.00, 6A 22.50, 10A 32.00; local tax 2.30, child 1.15.
-- Leisure charge: adults Ffr. 2.50 - 4.50, child (under 7 yrs) 1.50 - 3.50.
-- Many special offers.
-- Video tape available.
-- Credit cards accepted.

Open:
Easter - 30 September.

Address:
Lac de Léon, 40560 Vielle-Saint-Girons.

Tel:
(0)5.58.42.94.06. FAX: (0)5.58.42.91.88. E-mail: contact@colvert.com.

Reservations:
Any length with £42 deposit per week booked and £25 fee.

Book this site
01892 559898

THE ALAN ROGERS' travel service

N4012 Domaine Naturiste Arnaoutchot, Vielle-Saint-Girons

Large naturist site with extensive facilities and direct access to beach.

Although 'Arna' is a large site with 500 pitches, its layout in the form of a number of sections, each with its own character, makes it quite relaxing and all very natural. These sections amongst the trees and bushes of the Landes provide a variety of reasonably sized pitches, most with electricity, although the hilly terrain means that only a limited number are flat enough for motorcaravans. The sanitary facilities include not only the usual naturist site type of blocks with individual British type WCs and communal hot showers, but also a number of tiny blocks with one hot shower, WC and washbasin each in an individual cabin. All of the blocks have been upgraded to provide fully tiled, modern facilities, one heated in low season. Facilities include a laundry, chemical disposal and a motorcaravan service point. The amenities, situated centrally, are extensive and of excellent quality. They include a heated, indoor swimming pool with solarium, whirlpool and slide, outdoor pool and terraced sunbathing area, health centre with sauna, steam, whirlpool and massage treatments, a bar/restaurant, pizzeria, a large super-market and a range of other shops, mainly built of timber in an attractive style. The site has the advantage of direct access to a large, sandy naturist beach, although access from some parts of the site may involve a walk of perhaps 600-700 m. The 'Arna Club' provides more than 30 activities and workshops (in the main season) including riding, archery, golf practise, tennis, petanque, swimming, rambling, cycling, sailing school, handicrafts, excursions and special activities for children. TV, video and games rooms, cinema and library. There is a hairdresser and a chiropodist. Bicycle hire and fishing on site. Riding or golf 5 km. Chalets, mobile homes and tents for hire. English is spoken. Torch very useful. Barbecues are not permitted. Used by a tour operator (20 pitches). A 'Sites et Paysages' member.

Directions: Site is signed off D652 road at Vielle-Saint-Girons - follow D328 for 3-4 km..

Charges 2000:
-- Per unit incl. 2 persons Ffr. 80.00 - 162.00; extra person (over 3 yrs) 20.00 - 33.00; extra car 8.00 - 13.00; animal 8.00 - 13.00; leisure club 2.50 - 6.50; electricity 3A 20.00, 6A 32.00; local tax in high season 2.50 (3-7 yrs 1.25).
-- Deposit on arrival for entry pass 100.00.
-- Special offers available.
-- Credit cards accepted.
Open:
1 April - 30 September.
Address:
40560 Vielle-St-Girons.
Tel:
(0)5.58.49.11.11. FAX: (0)5.58.48.57.12. E-mail: contact@ arna.com.
Reservations:
Made with deposit (Ffr 400 or £42) and fee (Ffr 180 or £20).

Book this site
01892 559898

THE ALAN ROGERS'
travel service

4010 Camping du Domaine de la Rive, Biscarrosse

Landes site in superb beach-side location on Lac de Sanguinet.

La Rive is set in pine woods and provides mostly level, numbered and clearly defined pitches of 100 sq.m. All have electricity (6A) and there is good shade. The five modern toilet blocks are of very good quality with washbasins in cabins and mainly British style toilets. Visitors with disabilities are well catered for in three blocks and there are baby baths and chemical disposal. We found the facilities very clean. The bar, which also serves snacks and takeaway, has a games room adjoining and the restaurant provides reasonably priced family meals (1/6-15/9). The swimming pool complex is wonderful, with various pools linked by water channels and bridges, the four-slide pool having a wide staircase to the top to speed up enjoyment (15/5-15/9). There is a jacuzzi, paddling pool and two large, unusually shaped swimming pools, all surrounded by paved sunbathing areas and decorated with palm trees (the pools are supervised July/Aug). An indoor pool is planned for 2001. The beach is excellent, shelving gently to provide safe bathing for all ages. There are windsurfers and small craft can be launched from the site's slipway. Other activities include a children's play area on sand, water skiing, fishing, two tennis courts, bicycle hire, a new hand-ball or basketball court, table tennis, boules, archery and football. Watersports equipment may be hired and tournaments in various sports are arranged in July/ Aug. Discos and karaoke evenings are organised outside the bar with a stage and tiered seating, plus a mini-club for children twice daily. Riding 5 km, golf 10 km. A well stocked shop (with gas) is at the site entrance (15/5-15/9) and there is a motorcaravan service point. Charcoal barbecues are not permitted on the pitches (central area available). This is a friendly site with a good mix of nationalities. Mobile homes and cabins to hire. Caravan storage.

Directions: Take D652 from Sanguinet to Biscarrosse and site is signed on the right in about 6 km.

Charges 2000:
-- Per pitch incl. 2 persons and electricity Ffr. 165.00, with water and drainage also 185.00; extra person 27.00; child (3-10 yrs) 17.00; boat 28.00.
-- Less 30% outside July/Aug.
-- Credit cards accepted.
Open:
1 April - 30 October.
Address:
40600 Biscarrosse.
Tel:
(0)5.58.78.12.33. FAX: (0)5.58.78.12.92. E-mail: larive@ wanadoo.fr.
Reservations:
Advised for July/Aug; write or fax site.

`Camping Cheque'

Book this site
01892 559898

THE ALAN ROGERS'
travel service

see colour advert
between pages 192/193

ATLANTIC COAST - 40 Landes

4011 Camping-Caravaning Sen Yan, Mézos

Superb family site set in the Landes forest area.

This exotic site is about 12 km. from the Atlantic coast and set just outside the village. There are 310 pitches marked with hedges, 190 with electricity (6A), and with ample water points. Some mobile homes and tour operator pitches are in a separate 'village'. The three toilet blocks with good quality fittings have showers and washbasins in cabins and some British style WCs. The newest block is specially suitable for pre- and post-season visitors, with a special section for young children and babies, plus facilities for disabled people. The reception, bar and pool area is almost tropical with the luxuriant greenery of its banana trees, palm trees, tropical flowers and its straw sunshades. This attractive area has a terrace for sunbathing with swimming pools (1/6-30/9), one of which can be covered. Activities include minigolf, tennis court, petanque, archery, table tennis, children's games, mountain bike hire and a fitness centre (Fr. 170 per week per adult). Shop (from 15/6), restaurant and snacks (1/7-31/8) with animation and evening entertainment including a disco twice a week in high season. Only gas barbecues are permitted. Fishing 500 m, riding 6 km.

Directions: From N10 take exit 14 (Onesse-Laharie), then D38 Bias/Mimizan road. After 13 km. turn south to Mézos from where site is signed.

Charges 2001:
-- Per pitch incl. 2 persons Ffr. 140.00, with 6A electricity 170.00; extra person 32.00; child (under 7 yrs) 20.00; extra car 15.00; animal 15.00.
-- Credit cards accepted.

Open:
1 June - 15 September.

Address:
40170 Mézos.

Tel:
(0)5.58.42.60.05.
FAX: (0)5.58.42.64.56.
E-mail: Le.Village.
Tropical@wanadoo.fr.

Reservations:
Made with deposit (Ffr. 550) and fee (170).

`Camping Cheque'

4021M Camping Municipal L'Airal, Soustons

This site is set in typical Landes countryside near several lakes, just 2 km. from Soustons and 6 km. from the coast. There are 400 pitches, all of over 100 sq.m. Those for caravans are in a grassy area with lots of smaller trees and bushes, those for tents in open forest between large mature pines. Both areas offer adequate shade, 270 pitches have electricity (5/8A) and there are plenty of water points. The five toilet blocks (being refurbished in turn), close to the pitches, have washbasins in private cabins and showers with plenty of free hot water, and provision for disabled people. The laundry area has washing machines, dryers and irons. Additional facilities include a heated swimming pool (no Bermuda style shorts), four tennis courts, table tennis, games for children, minigolf, volleyball, basketball, boules, organised sports and swimming competitions. There is a reading/TV room, bar/café, takeaway food and a small shop. A large lake (200 m) provides fishing, canoeing and sail-boarding. English is spoken. Chalets for hire.

Directions: Leave N10 at exit 10 for Soustons (D116). From Soustons take D652 towards Vieux-Boucau. Site is well signed 2 km. west of Soustons on D652.

Charges 2000:
-- Per adult Ffr. 22.50; child (under 7 yrs) 13.30; pitch 26.70; electricity 5A 16.00, 8A 21.50; local tax 2.85.
-- Low season less 10%.

Open:
1 April - 15 October.

Address:
61 Ave de Port d'Albert, 40140 Soustons.

Tel:
(0)5.58.41.12.48.
FAX: (0)5.58.41.53.83.

Reservations:
Necessary for July/Aug and taken Jan-June with deposit and fee (Ffr. 116).

4007 Camping Lous Seurrots, Contis-Plage, nr Mimizan

Large and shady site with superb pool complex and close to beach to south of Mimizan.

Lous Seurrots is only a short 300 m. walk from the beach and parts of the site have views across the estuary. There are 610 pitches, mainly in pine woods on sandy undulating ground. They are numbered but only roughly marked out, most have good shade and over 80% have electricity. The six modern toilet blocks cope very well and were immaculate when we visited in late July, with washbasins in cabins, good pre-set showers, some also with washbasins, and British style WCs. Also provided are baby rooms, good facilities for disabled people, numerous laundry and dishwashing sinks and washing machines. The site's swimming pool complex (15/5-30/9) is in a setting of palm trees and flower beds and the paved sunbathing areas have wonderful views out to the estuary and the sea. There are four pools and a jacuzzi with keep fit classes held daily in July/Aug. Evening entertainment is held twice weekly in high season in an open-air auditorium. Large well stocked shop (1/6-15/9), and a bar, takeaway and restaurant (15/5-15/9). Sports enthusiasts have tennis, table tennis, archery, volleyball, minigolf and canoeing, with a mini-club organised for younger children. Bicycle hire and fishing on site, riding 3 km. Only gas barbecues are permitted. Motorcaravan service point. Chalets and mobile homes to rent. Used by tour operators. For all its size, Lous Seurrots is a family site with the emphasis on peace and tranquillity (no discos).

Directions: Turn off D652 on D41 (15 km. south of Mimizan) to Contis-Plage and site is on left as you reach it.

Charges 2000:
-- Per unit incl. 2 adults Ffr. 80.00 - 140.00; extra person 25.00 - 27.00; child (3-7 yrs) free - 25.00; extra car free - 13.00; electricity (6A) 21.00; animal free - 15.00; local tax 2.20.
-- Credit cards accepted.

Open:
1 April - 30 September.

Address:
Contis Plage, 40170 St. Julien en Born.

Tel:
(0)5.58.42.85.82.
FAX: (0)5.58.42.49.11.
E-mail: info@
uza.alienor.fr.

Reservations:
Made with deposit (Ffr. 300) and fee (120).

4008 Parc Saint-James Eurolac, Aureilhan, nr Mimizan

Pleasant, attractively laid out, lakeside site with large pitches and pools, 9 km. from sea.

This site is now under the ownership of the Parc Saint-James group. In a peaceful situation by a lake (with a minor road to cross), it is largely used by families but offers a choice of activities – bathing or boating in the lake (with sailing school in season), windsurfing (boards for hire), a riding school on site and organised events for young and old. The Atlantic beaches are 9 km. (for surfing) and there are two butterfly shaped swimming pools and a jacuzzi on the site (1/5-15/9). The terrain is flat, grassy and park-like, divided into 380 large, numbered touring pitches, all with electricity (long leads may be needed) and with shade from some mature trees. Six sanitary blocks give a very reasonable provision. The newest one is good with mainly British style WCs, washbasins in private cabins and pre-set showers. Hot water is free and can be drawn from a tap for washing-up. Facilities for disabled people and babies, washing machines and chemical disposal. In the main season activities and events are organised for adults and children. Amenities include a shop, bar/restaurant (both 1/5-15/9) and takeaway, a general room with TV, bar and some special evenings; dancing twice weekly in season. Activities include fishing, tennis courts, games room, table tennis, volleyball, basketball, minigolf, children's playground, mini-club and bicycle hire. Only gas barbecues are permitted. Treatment room. Chalets, caravans and bungalows to let.

Charges 2000:
-- Per unit incl. 1 or 2 persons Ffr. 55.00 - 125.00, with electricity 80.00 - 150.00; extra person 10.00 - 30.00; child (4-10 yrs) 5.00 - 15.00; extra car or tent free - 25.00; animal 25.00.
-- Credit cards accepted.
Open:
1 April - 30 September.
Address:
Aureilhan,
40200 Mimizan.
Tel:
(0)5.58.09.02.87.
FAX: (0)5.58.09.41.89.
Reservations:
Made for any period with deposit and Ffr. 115 fee.

Directions: Turn north off D626 at campsite sign 3 km. east of Mimizan-Bourg.

4015 Camping les Ecureuils, Port Navarrosse, Biscarrosse

Neat and tidy site, competitively priced and within 200 m. of Lake Sanguinet.

A pleasant entrance, new reception area and well tended flower beds at the very attractive restaurant lead into this neat, well cared for site with all its buildings in the style of alpine chalets. With only 130 touring pitches it is quite small in comparison to many sites in the area. There are a 10 mobile homes for hire and 30 privately owned (these are attractive with flowers around them). The level pitches are mostly in shade on sand or gravel ground and all are of at least 100 sq.m. and have electricity (10A - long leads may be required). The toilet blocks are of a very high quality with washbasins in cabins, roomy, pre-set showers and, apart from one Turkish style toilet in each block, British type WCs. The medium sized swimming pool (l/5-30/9) has a paved sunbathing area and paddling pool. Close to the restaurant, with a terrace overlooking the pool, is minigolf with well tended lawns and flower beds. Near the entrance, away from the pitches, is a games room. Boules, volleyball, basketball, table tennis, tennis (charged) and a play area on sand. There is no shop but bread and milk are sold at the takeaway and there is a supermarket 3 km. Bicycle hire - the area is a maze of cycle tracks. The lake is 200 m. for all types of watersports. Ony gas barbecues permitted. This is a quiet, family oriented site, well maintained and reasonably priced.

Charges 2000:
-- Per unit incl. 1 or 2 persons Ffr. 99.00 - 135.00; extra adult 22.00 - 26.00; child (under 10 yrs) 20.00 - 24.00; electricity 22.00; dog 22.00; local tax 3.30.
-- Credit cards accepted.
Open:
15 April - 30 September.
Address:
Port Navarrosse,
40600 Biscarrosse.
Tel:
(0)5.58.09.80.00.
FAX: (0)5.58.09.81.21.
E-mail: camping.les. ecureuils@wanadoo.fr.
Reservations:
Made with deposit (Ffr. 600 or 91,47) and fee (Ffr. 150 or 22,87).

Directions: Going south on D652 (Bordeaux - Biscarrosse), bear right on D305 signed Navarrosse Port & Plage'. Take second right signed Port to site on right.

4009M Camping Lou Broustaricq, Sanguinet, nr Arcachon

This is a good municipal site, if lacking a little in atmosphere, with some 555 pitches on flat ground in light woodland, partly shaded by high trees. Some pitches are separated by shrubs and trees. Caravan pitches with hardstanding are 110 sq.m. with electricity and water, pitches for tents average 100 sq.m. A path of about 200 m. leads to the lake (access for cars 2 km). There are seven unisex toilet blocks and one modern one (heated) with mainly British style WCs, washbasins in cabins, free hot water in showers and sinks, facilities for disabled people and babies and washing machines. A reliable site, there is always a chance of finding space. The pool complex has sunbathing areas and features a slide. Activities include two good tennis courts, bicycle hire, minigolf, table tennis, volleyball, basketball and three playgrounds. Tournaments are organised in season. A commercial centre by the entrance includes a supermarket and other shops, snack bar and takeaway, mostly opening mid-June and a restaurant in July/Aug. Area for barbecues. Mobile homes to rent. Used by a British tour operator.

Charges guide:
-- Per unit incl. 1 or 2 persons Ffr. 56.00 - 120.00; extra person 9.00 - 15.00; animal 9.00 - 11.00; electricity (6A) 17.00; local tax 2.20.
-- Credit cards accepted.
Open:
All year.
Address:
40460 Sanguinet.
Tel:
(0)5.58.78.62.62.
FAX: (0)5.58.82.10.74.
Reservations:
Any length with deposit (Ffr 300, 45.73) and fee (130, 19.82).

Directions: Turn northwest off D46 at site sign, 1 km. northeast of Sanguinet.

4006 Camping Eurosol, St Girons-Plage, Castets, nr Dax

Well shaded site with swimming pool, only 500 m. from sandy beach.

The sandy beach 500 m. from Eurosol has supervised bathing in high season and the site also has two swimming pools and a paddling pool, with paved sunbathing areas which are planted with palm trees giving quite a tropical feel (from 1/6). The site itself is on undulating ground amongst mature pine trees and the pitches on the slopes are mainly only suitable for tents. The 460 pitches for touring units are numbered (although with nothing to separate them, there is little privacy) and 250 have electricity with 130 fully serviced. Of the four main toilet blocks, three have been refurbished and provide good facilities with washbasins in cabins, British style WCs and free, pre-set showers. The other large block is in older style and half of the toilets are the Turkish type. Two smaller blocks have facilities for babies and disabled people. There is a bar, restaurant and takeaway (15/6-5/9) with outdoor tables on a raised deck and a stage for live shows. These are held in July/Aug. mainly finishing for midnight and the location of this area ensures that noise to the pitches is kept to a minimum. A family site with entertainers who speak many languages, games and tournaments are organised and a beach volley-ball competition is held each evening in front of the bar. The shop is well stocked (15/6-5/9). Minigolf, bicycle hire, tennis, a play area and a riding school opposite. Fishing 700 m. Motorcaravan services and chemical disposal. Fridges to rent. Charcoal barbecues are not permitted. Mobile homes to let (83).

Charges 2000:
-- Per unit incl. 2 persons Ffr. 55.00 - 114.00, with electricity 65.00 - 140.00, with water and drainage also 65.00 - 149.00; extra person (over 4 yrs) 25.00; local tax 2.50 (child 1.25); dog free.
-- Credit cards accepted.
Open:
12 May - 16 September.
Address:
40560 St Girons-Plage.
Tel:
(0)5.58.47.90.14.
FAX: (0)5.58.47.76.74.
E-mail: contact@ camping-eurosol.com.
Reservations:
Made for min. 1 week with deposit (Ffr. 600) and fee (150).

Directions: Turn off D652 at St Girons on D42 towards St Girons-Plage. Site is on left before coming to beach (4.5 km).

4014 Camping-Caravaning Lou P'tit Poun, St Martin de Seignanx

Friendly, family run site in a quiet setting with swimming pool.

The manicured grounds surrounding Lou P'tit Poun give a well kept appearance, a theme carried out throughout this very pleasing site. It is only after arriving at the car park that you feel confident it is not a private estate. Beyond this point the site unfolds to reveal an abundance of thoughtfully positioned shrubs and trees. Behind a central sloping flower bed lies the swimming pool (1/6-15/9) which fronts the open plan reception area, café and shop (both 1/7-31/8). The avenues around the site are wide and the 168 pitches are spacious. All have electricity (6/10A), 30 are fully serviced and some are separated by low hedges. Two unisex sanitary blocks, one behind reception, the other at rear of the site, are maintained to a high standard and kept clean. They include WCs (British style), washbasins in cabins, pre set showers, baby bath, provision for disabled people, dishwashing and laundry facilities with washing machine and dryer. Chemical disposal and motorcaravan services. Children's play area, games room, TV, half tennis court, table tennis and bicycle hire. The jovial owners make their guests welcome and organise weekly entertainment in high season. Despite its tranquil surroundings, the site is 6 km. from Bayonne and a 10 minute drive from the sandy beaches of the Basque coast. Fishing or riding 7 km, golf 10 km. Mobile homes and chalets for hire. Caravan storage. A 'Sites et Paysages' member.

Charges 2000:
-- Per pitch Ffr. 49.00 - 61.00, with electricty, water and drainage 76.00 - 95.00; person 25.00 - 32.00; child (under 7) 13.00 - 17.00; animal 12.00 - 16.00; electricity 4, 6 or 10A 20.00 - 30.00.
-- No credit cards.
Open:
1 June - 15 September.
Address:
Ave du Quartier Neuf, 40390 St Martin de Seignanx.
Tel:
(0)5.59.56.55.79.
FAX: (0)5.59.56.53.71.
E-mail: ptitpoun@ club-internet.fr.
Reservations:
Made with deposit (Ffr. 300) and fee (160).

Book this site
01892 559898
THE ALAN ROGERS'
travel service

Directions: At A63 exit 6 join N117 towards Pau. Site signed at Leclerc supermarket. Continue on N117 for 5.5 km. and site is then clearly signed on right.

4002 Camping Les Chênes, Dax

Established, attractive and well kept site on outskirts of busy spa town.

Dax is not a place that springs at once to mind as a holiday town but, as well as being a spa, it has a comprehensive programme of events in the summer season. Les Chênes is well situated on the edge of town amongst parkland (near the river) and close to the spa for the thermal treatments. The 183 touring pitches are of two types, some large and traditional, with hedges, water and electricity, others more informal, set amongst tall pines with electricity if required. The two toilet blocks are very different. One is new and very modern with heating, British style WCs, washbasins in cubicles, free hot showers, facilities for disabled people and a good provision for babies and young children. The other, older block has Turkish and British type toilets, washbasins in cabins and hot showers. Both have chemical disposal. A laundry room has washing machines, dryers and ironing and ample laundry and dishwashing sinks. The shop is fairly well stocked and provides takeaways (31/3-27/10). A mini-club for children is organised in July/Aug. with special evenings of meals and dancing for adults. To one side of the site is a large field for ball games, there is table tennis, bicycle hire and a boule pitch, plus a good play area on sand and swimming and paddling pools of unusual shape with an island in the middle, a wooden bridge across, a paddling area with mushroom shaped fountain and surrounded by paved sunbathing areas (28/4-15/9). Fishing 100 m, riding and golf 300 m. Beaches 28 km. A restaurant is opposite the site. Charcoal barbecues not permitted. A well run site, with a little of something for everyone, but probably mainly for adults. Mobile homes and chalets to rent.

Directions: Site is west of town on south side of river, signed after main river bridge and at many junctions in town - Bois de Boulogne (1½ km). Note: in very wet weather the access road to the site may be flooded (but not the site).

Charges 2000:
-- Per pitch incl. 1 or 2 persons and electricity (5A) Ffr. 82.00 - 96.00, pitch with water and drainage 98.00 - 112.00; extra person 19.00; child (2-7 yrs) 11.00; animal 6.00; local tax 2.00 in high season.
-- Credit cards accepted.
Open:
24 March - 3 November.
Address:
40100 Dax.
Tel:
(0)5.58.90.05.53.
FAX: (0)5.58.90.42.43.
Reservations:
Made with deposit (Ffr. 300) and fee (50).

4003 Les Pins du Soleil, St Paul lès Dax, nr Dax

Family oriented site with swimming pool close to spa town of Dax.

This site will appeal to families, particularly those with younger children who prefer to be some way back from the coast within easy reach of shops, cultural activities, etc. and well placed for touring the area. Dax is a busy spa town with many attractions - Les Pins du Soleil is actually at St Paul lès Dax, some 3 km. from Dax itself. The site has 145 good sized pitches, 99 for touring units of which 59 have electricity and drainage. Although new, the site is in light woodland so there is a fair amount of shade from the many small trees. There is an attractive, medium sized pool with surrounding sunbathing area and a café (both 2/6-15/9). Modern sanitary facilities include free hot showers, washbasins (H&C), British style WCs, facilities for babies, disabled visitors and laundry. Playground and a mini-club in high season, with volleyball, table tennis and bicycle hire on site, fishing 1 km, riding 3 km. Takeaway (from June), small supermarket and a bar, but no restaurant (many in Dax). There is a bus to the thermal baths, and excursions to St Sebastian, Lourdes, etc. English is spoken. Mobile homes and chalets to rent (one designed for disabled visitors).

Directions: Fom west on N124, avoid bypass following signs for Dax and St Paul. Turn right on D459 and follow signs. Site is a little further on left. Also signed from town centre, north of the river.

Charges 2001:
-- Per pitch incl. 2 persons Ffr. 51.00 - 100.00, with electricity, water and drainage 70.00 - 130.00; extra person 37.00; child (4-10 yrs) 22.00; animal 10.00; local tax 1.50.
-- Credit cards accepted.
Open:
7 April - 27 October.
Address:
40990 St Paul lès Dax.
Tel:
(0)5.58.91.37.91.
FAX: (0)5.58.91.00.24.
E-mail: pinsoleil @aol.com.
Reservations:
Made with deposit (Ffr. 200) and fee (35).

Book this site
01892 559898
THE ALAN ROGERS'
travel service

6423M Camping Municipal de Mosqueros, Salies de Béarn

In scenic surroundings convenient for the A64, this is a 3 star municipal site, worthy of its grading and attractively located in parkland 1 km. from the pretty little town of Salies de Béarn. It has an immaculate appearance, welcoming wardens and clean facilities. Tarmac roads lead from the barrier (locked at night), past reception to spacious, numbered pitches, most with electricity (10A), many with water and all separated by tall shrubs and hedges giving privacy. The central toilet block is maintained to a high standard. It offers adequate WCs (British type), washbasins, showers, shaver points, etc. There is also a washing up and laundry area with sinks, washing machine, dryer and iron. On site is a TV and recreation room, plus a swimming pool and tennis courts adjacent.

Directions: Site signed in town and is on D17 Bayonne road, west of the town.

Charges 2000:
-- Per person Ffr. 15.60; child 9.40; pitch 16.00 - 32.00; electricity 15.30.
Open:
15 March - 15 October.
Address:
64270 Salies de Béarn.
Tel:
(0)5.59.38.12.94 or the Mairie (0)5.59.38.00.40.
Reservations:
Advised for July/Aug.

ATLANTIC COAST - 64 Pyrénées-Atlantiques

6411 Camping du Col d'Ibardin, Urrugne

Family owned site with swimming pool at foot of Basque Pyrénées.

This is a highly recommended site which deserves praise. It is well run with emphasis on personal attention, the smiling Madame, her staff and family ensuring that all are made welcome and is attractively set in the middle of an oak wood. Behind the forecourt, with its brightly coloured shrubs and modern reception area, various roads lead to 193 individual pitches. These are spacious and enjoy the benefit of the shade (if preferred a more open aspect can be found). There are electricity hook-ups (4/10A) and adequate water points, with rubbish disposal near the entrance gate. The two toilet blocks are kept very clean and house WCs (British style), a WC for disabled people, washbasins, free pre-set hot showers and sufficient shelves, hooks, razor points, etc. The second block has been completely rebuilt to a high specification. Dishwashing facilities are in separate open areas close by and a laundry unit with washing machine and dryer is behind reception. Chemical disposal and motorcaravan service point. A small shop sells basic foodstuffs and gas, with orders for bread taken (1/5-15/9), but a large supermarket and shopping centre are 5 km. In July/Aug. there is a catering and takeaway service on site, also a bar and occasional evening entertainment which includes Flamenco dancing. Other amenities include a swimming pool and paddling pool, tennis courts, bicycle hire, boules, table tennis, video games and a children's playground and club with adult supervision. Fishing 5 km, riding 2 km, golf 7 km. From this site you can enjoy the mountain scenery, be on the beach at Socoa within minutes or cross the border into Spain approximately 14 km. down the road. Used by tour operators (20 pitches). Mobile homes to rent (16).

Directions: Leave A63 autoroute at St Jean-de-Luz sud, exit no. 2 and join the RN10 in the direction of Urrugne. Turn left at roundabout (signed Col d'Ibardin) on the D4 and site is on right after 5 km. Do not turn off to the Col itself, but carry on towards Ascain.

Charges 2000:
-- Per unit incl. 2 persons Ffr. 75.00 - 110.00; extra adult 17.00 - 26.00; child (2-7 yrs) 10.00 - 14.00; electricity 4A 16.00 - 18.00, 6A 20.00 - 22.00, 10A 30.00; animal free - 10.00; local tax 1.10 (high season).
-- No credit cards.

Open:
1 April - 30 September.

Address:
64122 Urrugne.

Tel:
(0)5.59.54.31.21.
FAX: (0)5.59.54.62.28.
E-mail: camping-ibardin @wanadoo.fr.

Reservations:
Are accepted - contact site.

Book this site
01892 559898

THE ALAN ROGERS'
travel service

see colour advert between pages 128/129

6407 Castel Camping Le Ruisseau des Pyrénées, Bidart, nr Biarritz

Pleasant, busy site with swimming pool, just back from sea, with reasonable charges.

This site, just behind the coast, is about 2 km. from Bidart and 2½ km. from a sandy beach but it does have two swimming pools on the site - one 1,100 sq.m. pool complex with slides on the main site and an indoor heated pool on the newer area opposite. There is also a little lake, where boating is possible, in the area at the bottom of the site which has a very pleasant open aspect and now includes a large play area. Pitches on the main campsite are individual, marked and of a good size, either on flat terraces or around the lake. The terrain is wooded so the great majority of them have some shade. There are 330 here with a further 110 on a second area where shade has developed and which has its own good toilet block. Electrical connections are available throughout. The sanitary facilities (unisex) consist of two main blocks and some extra smaller units. They have British style WCs, washbasins in private cabins with hot water, free hot showers, nearly all pre-set, and are regularly refurbished and maintained. Washing machines. Shop. Large self-service restaurant with takeaway and separate bar with terraces, and TV. Activities include two tennis courts (free outside July/Aug), volleyball, table tennis, fitness track, TV and games rooms, minigolf, fitness room, sauna, solarium and a large children's playground. Animation is provided in the main season, with organised day-time sports and evening entertainment nightly in season. Bicycle and surf board hire. Riding or golf 2 km. The site is popular with tour operators. Mobile homes to rent (74).

Directions: Site is east of Bidart on a minor road towards Arbonne. From autoroute take Biarritz exit, turn towards St Jean-de-Luz on N10, take first left at traffic lights and follow camp signs for 1.5 km. When travelling south on N10 the turning is the first after passing the autoroute entry point.

Charges 2000:
-- Per unit incl. 2 persons Ffr. 104.00 - 130.00; extra adult 27.00 - 34.00; child (under 7) 14.00 - 18.00; electricity 19.00 - 23.00; dog 6.00; local tax (over 10) 2.20.
-- Credit cards accepted.

Open:
19 May - 22 September, with all amenities.

Address:
64210 Bidart.

Tel:
(0)5.59.41.94.50.
FAX: (0)5.59.41.95.73.
E-mail: francoise. dumont3@wanadoo.fr.

Reservations:
Made for exact dates, for min. a week or so in main season, with deposit (Ffr 350), fee (62) and cancellation insurance (18). Total Ffr. 430.

`Camping Cheque'

Book this site
01892 559898

THE ALAN ROGERS'
travel service

6406 Camping du Pavillon Royal, Bidart, nr Biarritz

Comfortable, popular site by sandy beach, with excellent facilities and pool.

Le Pavillon Royal has an excellent situation on raised ground overlooking the sea, and with good views along the coast to the south and to the north coast of Spain beyond. Beneath the site – and only a very short walk down – stretches a wide sandy beach. This is the Atlantic with its breakers and a central marked-out section of the beach is supervised by lifeguards. There is also a section with rocks and pools. If the sea is rough, there is a large swimming pool, paddling pool and sunbathing area on site. The site is divided up into 303 marked out, level pitches, many of a good size. Connected by asphalt roads, all have electricity and some are serviced with electricity, water and drainage. Much of the campsite is in full sun, although one area is shaded. All sanitary blocks are of the highest quality with mainly British style WCs, washbasins in cabins with shelves and mirrors, free hot water in washbasins, fully controllable showers, sinks and baby baths and good units for disabled people, all thoroughly cleaned twice daily. Washing facilities are closed at night except for night units. Washing machines and dryers, chemical disposal and motorcaravan services. There is a well stocked shop (including gas) and a restaurant with takeaway service (open all season). General room, TV room, games room with table tennis, also used for films, etc. Children's playground. Fishing on site, bicycle hire 3 km, riding 1 km. Sauna. Reservation in high season is advisable. No dogs are accepted.

Directions: Don't go into Bidart as site is on Biarritz side. From north, keep on N10 bypassing Biarritz, then turn sharp back right on D911 (last possible road to Biarritz). After 600 m. left at camp sign (easy to miss). From A63 take C4 exit.

Charges guide:
-- Per unit incl. 2 persons, electricity and water Ffr. 139.00 - 189.00; tent pitch incl. 1 or 2 persons 95.00 - 139.00; extra person (over 4 yrs) 35.00; extra car 25.00.
-- Credit cards accepted.

Open:
15 May - 25 September.

Address:
Av. du Prince-de-Galles, 64210 Bidart.

Tel:
(0)5.59.23.00.54.
FAX: (0)5.59.23.44.47.

Reservations:
Made for exact dates with deposit and fee.

Le Pavillon Royal
camping caravaning **** NN

64210 BIDART   Tél: 05.59.23.00.54

- Right by a sandy beach with direct access
- On the outskirts of Biarritz
- Very peaceful situation
- Sanitary installations of really exceptional quality

6408 Camping Tamaris-Plage, St Jean-de-Luz

Pleasant, well tended site with individual pitches, close to a beach.

Well outside the town but just across the road from a sandy beach, this well kept, neat, little site has 79 numbered pitches, 60 with electricity. They are of very good size and separated by hedges, on slightly sloping ground with some shade. It becomes full for nearly all July and August with families on long stays, so reservation then is advisable. The single toilet block is of superb quality and unusual design and should be an ample provision for the site. It has free hot water in washbasins and showers (some in private cabins), mainly British style WCs, dishwashing sinks with hot and cold water, facilities for disabled people and a washing machine. Amenities include a general room with TV, minigolf and a children's playground. Fishing 30 m, bicycle hire or golf 4 km, riding 7 km. Mobile homes (20) and bungalows (10) to let.

Directions: Proceed south on N10 and 1.5 km. after Guethary take first road on right (before access to motorway and Mammoth centre commercial) and follow camp signs.

Charges 2000:
-- Per unit (100 sq.m. pitch) incl. 2 persons and electricity (5A) Ffr. 135.00 - 180.00; tent pitch (80 sq.m.) incl. 2 persons 107.00 - 150.00; extra person (over 2 yrs) 23.00 - 32.00; local tax 2.20 (4-10 yrs 1.10).
-- Credit cards accepted.

Open:
1 April - 30 September.

Address:
Acotz,
64500 St Jean-de-Luz.

Tel:
(0)5.59.26.55.90.
FAX: (0)5.59.47.70.15.
E-mail: tamaris1@ clubinternet.fr.

Reservations:
Made with 20% deposit, fee (Ffr 120) and cancellation insurance (35).

Book this site
01892 559898

THE ALAN ROGERS'
travel service

6409 Airotel La Chêneraie, Bayonne

Quality site in pleasant situation, 8 km. from sea.

La Chêneraie is only 8 km. from the coast at Anglet with its long sandy beach and large car park., but with the calm and tranquillity of the site, you would think you were much further away from all the hustle and bustle of the coast. The site has a medium sized swimming pool open June - end August (longer if the weather is good). The distant views of the Pyrénées from various points all add to the feeling of peace. The 210 pitches are arranged on neat grass, mostly partially divided by trees and shrubs so quite well shaded. Many have electricity connections, some water and drainage also. One area is very sloping but has been terraced to give level pitches. Wooded walks lead to a small lake which can be used for inflatables or fishing (no swimming). A large, central sanitary block provides British style WCs, washbasins in cabins and controllable showers, with three smaller blocks around the site providing additional facilities. In high season these facilities are under pressure and maintenance can be variable. There are dishwashing and laundry sinks, a washing machine and dryers, baby baths, chemical disposal and facilities for disabled people. Near reception at the entrance to the site are a shop, restaurant with all day snacks and a takeaway (all 1/6-15/9). There are tennis courts (free outside July/Aug), TV room, table tennis and a children's playground on sand. Bicycle hire 5 km, riding 6 km, golf 7 km. Fully equipped tents, bungalows and mobile homes for hire and a tour operator has 20 pitches. English is spoken. This is a useful site to know and it will usually have room if you arrive by early afternoon.

Directions: Site is 4 km. northeast of Bayonne just off main N117 road to Pau, signed at traffic lights. From A63 take exit 6 marked `Bayonne St. Esprit'.

Charges 2001:
-- Per pitch Ffr. 62.00 - 75.00, tent pitch 50.00 - 58.00; pitch with water and electricity 70.00 - 105.00; person 24.00 - 28.00; child (under 10 yrs) 14.00 - 18.00; dog 15.00; local tax (over 18s) 1.10; electricity 23.00.
-- Less 10-20% outside 1/6-1/9.
-- No credit cards.

Open:
Easter - 30 September, full services 1/6-15/9.

Address:
Chemin de Casenave, 64100 Bayonne.

Tel:
(0)5.59.55.01.31.
FAX: (0)5.59.55.11.17.

Reservations:
Made for min. 1 week with deposit (Ffr. 400) and fee (100).

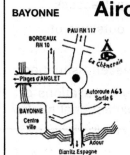

BAYONNE

Airotel La Chêneraie ★★★★

Camping Caravaning

Tel. 0033 559 55 01 31- Fax: 0033 559 55 11 17

★

SWIMMING POOL ON SITE
Beaches only a few minutes drive - Tennis
Archery - Entertainment - Fishing

Fully equipped
BUNGALOWS - CHALETS - MOBILHOMES for hire.

Absolute quiet - View of Pyrénées

6421M Camping Municipal Chibaou-Berria, St Jean-de-Luz

The first impression of this large site beside the beach is one of neatness. From the entrance tarmac roads lead to the spacious pitches which are divided by hedges with plenty of room for awnings. Pitches to the left hand side beyond reception are placed at different levels, whilst those to the right have a sea view. There are 221 pitches in all, all with electrical hook-ups. There are also 10 water points and rubbish points, with night lights distributed around. Sanitary facilities were spotlessly clean when we visited and include showers (some with washbasins), individual wash cabins and hot water. WCs are a mixture of British and Turkish style. Dishwashing sinks are in an open position and there are laundry facilities including washing machines and an ironing room. There is direct access to the beach for surfing and windsurfing. Nearby are discos, tennis courts and often Basque folk festivities or Corridas with Landes cows.

Directions: Follow the RN10 from Bayonne for 2 km. After Guéthary take third road to the right. From the south take motorway exit St Jean-de-Luz north in the direction of Bayonne, then first road to the left.

Charges 2000:
-- Per person Ffr. 30.00; child under 4 yrs 16.50, 4-10 yrs 17.00; pitch 31.00; electricity 16.50; local tax incl.

Open:
1 June - 15 September.

Address:
64500 St Jean-de-Luz.

Tel:
(0)5.59.26.11.94 or (0)5.59.51.61.71.

Reservations:
Contact site.

6401 Europ Camping, St Jean-Pied-de-Port

Neat, tidy site in the foothills of the Pyrénées with superb views.

Europ Camping is a neat, orderly, family run site with wonderful views of the vine-covered closer hills and the distant high Pyrénées. Each of the 93 pitches is clearly marked and separated by shrubs and all have electricity (6A), water and drainage. The swimming pool, which is near the entrance beside reception and the bar/restaurant, is of a decent size and has a smaller children's pool alongside. Surrounded by fine gravel, table and chairs are provided. There is also a sauna. The central toilet block is modern and very well appointed, with pre-set hot water in roomy showers, washbasins in cubicles, British style WCs and good facilities for disabled visitors. Two washing machines, a dryer and dishwashing sinks (with an excellent supply of hot water) are outside, but under cover. The bar/restaurant is open all season with a reasonably priced meal of the day and takeaway. The small shop is limited but St Jean-Pied-de-Port is only 2 km. On site are a children's play area, volleyball and petanque. Tennis near, fishing 200 m, bicycle hire 2 km, riding 10 km. A barbecue area is near the entrance. Motorcaravan service point, free car wash and chemical disposal. The area is good for walking or mountain biking and there is rafting on a local river. The site is only 20 km. from the forest of Iraty with its lakes and ski-runs, and the Spanish border on the route de St Jacques-de-Compostelle, is 8 km. Mobile homes for rent (10).

Directions: Site is 2 km. northwest of St Jean-Pied-de-Port in the hamlet of Ascarat and is signed from the D918 Bayonne road.

Charges 2000:
-- Per adult Ffr 34.00; child (under 7 yrs) 17.00; pitch and car 48.00; dog 13.00; electricity (6A) 24.00; local tax 1.50.
-- Credit cards accepted.

Open:
Easter - 30 September.

Address:
Ascarat, 64220 St Jean-Pied-de-Port.

Tel:
(0)5.59.37.12.78. FAX: (0)5.59.37.29.82.

Reservations:
Made in writing with 30% deposit and Ffr. 140 fee.

Book this site
01892 559898

THE ALAN ROGERS'
travel service

6404 Camping des Gaves, Laruns

Small, all year site set high in Pyrennean walking country on the route to Spain.

Des Gaves is a clean, well managed site with very friendly owners and staff. Of the 48 touring pitches, 38 are fully serviced, all are level, numbered and separated. The sanitary block is rather reminiscent of a school dormitory but, nevertheless, has modern fittings, with roomy controllable showers (one in the ladies' suitable for showering children). Washbasins for ladies are in cubicles with a curtain, there is plenty of hot water and the building is heated in cool weather. The laundry room has a washing machine and indoor lines, dishwashing and laundry sinks are indoors too. Chemical disposal. There is a small bar with a large screen TV, pool and video games (July/Aug). Outside is a boules pitch, volleyball and a small play area. A larger bar houses three table tennis tables. The river runs alongside the site (well fenced) and fishing is possible. No shop but the baker calls and the busy little tourist town of Laruns is only a short walk. Tourist information will suggest many and varied things to do. Bicycle hire 800 m. Laruns is only 25 km. from the Spanish border. Mobile homes, apartments and chalets to hire. Caravan storage.

Directions: Take N134 from Pau towards Olorons and branch left on D934 at Gan. Follow to Laruns and just after town, turn left following signs to site.

Charges 2000:
-- Per pitch Ffr. 60.00; person 23.00; child (under 10 yrs) 15.00; electricity 3A 16.00, 6A 20.00, 10A 25.00; local tax 1.00 (child 0.50).
-- Less in low seasons.
-- No credit cards.

Open:
All year.

Address:
64440 Laruns.

Tel:
(0)5.59.05.32.37. FAX: (0)5.59.05.47.14.

Reservations:
Necessary for most of the year.

6402 Camping-Caravaning Ametza, Hendaye Plage

Large, spacious site, near beach and the Spanish border, very reasonably priced.

Ametza is a neat, well laid out site on mainly sloping ground which is terraced in places. Some areas have views of the sea, others the inland Basque countryside. There are 320 pitches on grass, some with shade and most with electricity. The swimming pool is large with a paddling pool and sunbathing areas (it is a little plain and could be enhanced by some well placed flowers). The two modern toilet blocks have roomy controllable showers, washbasins in cubicles and British style WCs (plus three Turkish). Dishwashing and laundry sinks have hot water. There are washing machines and dryers, facilities for disabled people and one block has a baby room. The small shop caters for most needs, the local shops are not too far. Bar/restaurant and takeaway. Small play area, tennis and table tennis. The site is within walking distance of the beach (900 m) and in high season tournaments and entertainment are organised. Mobile homes for hire.

Directions: Coming from Bayonne, use RN10 and the D913/912 Corniche road to Hendaye Plage, turning left in the direction of Hendaye town before the beach. Site is immediately on left over railway line. If using autoroute, take exit for St Jean-de-Luz (sud).

Charges guide:
-- Per pitch incl. 2 persons and car Ffr. 85.00 - 105.00; extra person 20.00 - 25.00; child (2-10 yrs) 10.00 - 15.00; electricity (10A) 20.00; dog 8.00; local tax 2.00.

Open:
15 June - 15 September.

Address:
64700 Hendaye.

Tel:
(0)5.59.20.07.05. FAX: (0)5.59.20.32.16.

Reservations:
Advised for July/Aug. and made with deposit and Ffr. 24.00 insurance.

DORDOGNE / AVEYRON

We have again rearranged the French départments and regions to give us what we believe the British think of as 'the Dordogne' and have lifted the following départements from these official French regions:

AQUITAINE	MIDI-PYRENEES	POITOU-CHARENTES
Départements:	**Départements:**	Département: 16 Charente
24 Dordogne	12 Aveyron, 46 Lot	
47 Lot et Garonne		

The history of the Dordogne goes back many thousands of years when man lived in the caves of the Périgord and left cave paintings at sites such as Les Eyzies and Lascaux. The ancient dukedom of Aquitaine was ruled by the English for 300 years following the marriage of Eleanor of Aquitaine to Henry Plantagenet, who became King of England in 1154. The fortified villages and castles of the area bear evidence of the resulting conflict between the French and English for control of Aquitaine, and today add charm and character to the countryside. Monpazier is the best surviving example of the bastides (fortified towns). It is a diverse region of mountains, vineyards, and fertile river valleys, rolling grasslands and dense forests. Within its boundaries are the beautiful valleys of the Dordogne and Vézère.

To the south of the cultivated fields and cliff-side villages beside the river Lot lie the higher, stony lands of the Quercy Causse and the rocky gorges of the Rivers Aveyron and Tarn. Centred around Millau, there are tortuous gorges and valleys, spectacular rivers, underground caves and grottes, and thickly forested mountains. This is the home of Roquefort cheese.

To the north west is the old province of Poitou, or Charente, heartland of the domains of Eleanor, Duchess of Aquitaine, where the river Charente was once a busy industrial waterway bringing armaments from Angoulême to the naval shipyards of Rochefort. Today it is Cognac beside the River Charente which springs to mind. Untouched by any recession 80% of the production is exported. The Hennessy warehouse is worth a visit. The first Hennessy, seven generations ago, was an Irishman!

Note: The site reports are laid out by département in numerical order not by region.
See map on page 315.

Cuisine of the region

Cagouilles – snails from Charentes
Foie Gras – specially prepared livers of geese and ducks, seasoned and stuffed with truffles
Cassoulet – a hearty stew of duck, sausages and beans
Confit de Canard (d'oie) – preserved duck meat (goose)
Magret de canard – duck breast fillets
Confits – (preserved goose and duck) are a key ingredient in a number of dishes
Fish and seafood – like carp stuffed with foie gras, mullet in red wine and besugo (sea bream)
Chorizos – spicy sausages
Cèpes – fine, delicate mushrooms; sometimes dried
Chou farci – stuffed cabbage, sometimes aux marrons (with chestnuts)
Huile de noix (walnut oil) – many magnificent walnut trees in the Dordogne area
Mouclade – mussels cooked in wine, egg yolks and cream, served with Pineau des Charentes

Places of interest

Agen – rich agricultural area, famous for its prunes
Angoulême – Hill-top town surrouded by ramparts; cathedral, Renaissance château
Cognac – the most celebrated 'eau de vie' in the world, cellars, Valois Castle
Cordes – medieval walled hilltop village
Monflanquin – well preserved fortified village
Rocamadour – cliffside medieval pilgrimage site
Saint Cirq-La Popie – medieval village perched on a cliff

1201 Castel Camping Val de Cantobre, Nant d'Aveyron, nr Millau

Attractive, terraced site in the valley of the Dourbie.

This site which has been imaginatively and tastefully developed by the Dupond family over a 25 year period, offers a bar, restaurant, pizzeria and takeaway facility. In particular, the magnificent carved features in the bar create a delightful ambience, complemented by a recently built terrace. True, the ground is hard in summer but reception staff supply robust nails if your awning pegs prove a problem. Most of the 200 pitches (all with electricity and water) are peaceful, generous in size and blessed with views of the valley. The three adjoining pools have a new surround, bedecked by flowers and crowned by a large urn which dispenses water into the paddling pool. The shop, although small, offers a wide variety of provisions; including many regional specialities. Comparisons showed that quality and cost of produce was always as good, and quite often, better than could be found in local shops or markets. The new sanitary block is impressive and is beautifully appointed, with British style WCs and a huge indoor dish-washing area. But it is the activity programme that is unique at Val de Cantobre. Adventurous visitors relish sports like river rafting, white water canoeing, rock climbing or jumps from Millau's hill tops on twin seater steerable parachutes. Around 15 such activities, all supervised by qualified instructors, some arranged by the owners and some at a fair distance from the site. Passive recreationists appreciate the scenery, especially Cantobre, a medieval village that clings to a cliff in view of the site. Nature lovers will be delighted to see the vultures wheeling in the Tarn gorge alongside more humble rural residents. Butterflies in profusion, orchids, huge edible snails, glow worms, families of beavers and the natterjack toad all live here. It is easy to see why - the place is magnificent. Fishing. Torches would be useful. Although tour operators occupy around 40% of the pitches, the terrace design provides some peace and privacy, especially on the upper levels. Mobile homes and chalets for hire (18). A warm welcome awaits from the Dupond family.

Directions: Site is 4 km. north of Nant, on D991 road to Millau.

Charges 2001:
-- Per unit incl. 2 persons and 4A electricity 120.00 - 162.00; extra person (4 yrs and over) 20.00 - 37.00; extra car free - 10.00; dog free - 15.00; electricity 10A 20.00.
-- Credit cards accepted.

Open:
12 May - 15 September, with all facilities.

Address:
12230 Nant d'Aveyron.

Tel:
(0)5.65.58.43.00.
FAX: (0)5.65.62.10.36.

Reservations:
Made for any length with 25% deposit, fee (Ffr. 120) and optional cancel-lation insurance (37).

`Camping Cheque'

Book this site
01892 559898

THE ALAN ROGERS'
travel service

see colour advert
between pages 192/193

1202 Camping-Caravaning Les Rivages, Millau

Large site on town outskirts close to Tarn Gorges with good range of sporting facilities.

Les Rivages is well organised and well situated, being close to the high limestone Causses and the dramatic gorges of the Tarn and Dourbie, the latter of which runs past the back of the site. Smaller pitches, suitable for tents and small units, abut a pleasant riverside space suitable for sunbathing, fishing or picnics. Most of the 314 pitches are larger, 100 sq.m. or more, and are well shaded. A newer part of the site (on the right as you go in) has less shade but pitches are larger. All pitches have electricity (6A), and 98 have their own water and drainaway. Four modern toilet blocks have all necessary facilities, and are kept very clean. A special block for children includes baby baths, small showers, children's toilets as well as ironing facilities. Expecting children to do the ironing may be optimistic. A wide range of sporting activities is available, close to 30 in all, and including tennis (indoor and outdoor), squash (can be viewed from the bar), table tennis, floodlit petanque, a variety of river activities, walking, bird watching and fishing. Off-site activities, including rafting and canoeing, are arranged frequently. A children's play area, and much evening entertainment, largely for children, along with child minding and a mini-club, all help to take the pressure off parents. A terrace restaurant and bar overlook the good-sized main pool and children's pool (from 10/5). Bicycle hire 1 km, riding 10 km, golf 40 km. The shop has most essentials (20/5-15/9), and there is a hypermarket in Millau, which is a bustling and pleasant town. Don't miss the night markets, but don't eat before you get there – there are thousands of things to taste, many of them grilled or spit roasted. Gates shut 10 pm.- 8 am, with night-watchman. Mobile homes to rent.

Directions: From Millau, take D991 road south towards Nant. Site is about 400 m. on the right.

Charges 2001:
-- Per pitch incl. 2 persons Ffr. 80.00 - 120.00, with electricity 93.00 - 141.00, with water and drainage also - 106.00 - 152.00; extra person (over 3 yrs) 20.00 - 25.00; pet 15.00 - 17.00; local tax (15/6-15/9) 2.00.
-- Credit cards accepted.

Open:
1 May - 30 September.

Address:
Avenue de l'Aigoual, 12100 Millau.

Tel:
(0)5.65.61.01.07.
FAX: (0)5.65.59.03.56.
E-mail:
campinglesrivages
@wanadoo.fr.

Reservations:
Made with deposit (Ffr. 400) and fee (100).

Book this site
01892 559898

THE ALAN ROGERS'
travel service

see colour advert
between pages 96/97

DORDOGNE / AVEYRON - 12 Aveyron

1200 Camping Peyrelade, nr Millau

Attractive site by a pebble beach in the Gorges du Tarn.

Situated at the foot of the Tarn gorges, on the banks of the river, this site is dominated by the ruins of the Château de Peyrelade. Bathing from the pebble beach is safe and the water is clean. The 124 touring pitches are terraced, level and shady with 6A electricity (long leads may be required for riverside pitches). One of the two toilet blocks has been refurbished. Young children are catered for, also people with disabilities and there are chemical disposal points, washing machines and dryer. There is a paddling pool, an attractively designed swimming pool (no shorts), plus a good playground. Facilities in the adjacent leisure centre can be booked at reduced charges. Amenities include a games room, mini-club and barbecue area. A bar, restaurant, pizzeria and takeaway are near reception (all from 1/6). Fishing on site, bicycle hire 100 m, riding 3 km. The site is ideally placed for visiting the Tarn, Jonte and Dourbie gorges, and centres for rafting and canoeing are a short drive up the river. Nearby are the Caves of Aven Armand, the Chaos de Montpellier, Roquefort and the pleasant town of Millau, with its hypermarket, shops and night markets. The road to/from Millau is often jammed at peak hours. Many roads along and between the Gorges are breathtaking for passengers, scary for drivers who don't like looking down!

Directions: Take autoroute A75 to Sévérac. From N9 Sevérac - Millau road, turn east from Aguessac on D907 (follow Gorges du Tarn signs). Site is 2 km. past Rivière sur Tarn, on the right - the access road is quite steep.

Charges 2001:
-- Per unit incl. 2 persons Ffr. 85.00 - 116.00; extra adult 16.00 - 25.00; child (under 5) 12.00 - 15.00; dog 8.00; electricity (6A) 19.00; local tax 1.00.
-- Credit cards accepted.
Open:
15 May - 15 September.
Address:
12640 Rivière-sur-Tarn.
Tel:
(0)5.65.62.62.54.
FAX: (0)5.65.62.65.61.
Reservations:
Made with deposit (Ffr. 450) and fee (100).

*see colour advert
between pages 96/97*

1208 Camping Club Les Genêts, Lac de Pareloup, Salles Curan

Lakeside site in attractive area, with own swimming and spa pools.

This family run site is on the shores of Lac de Pareloup and offers both family holiday and watersports facilities. The main building houses reception, a restaurant, bar and a well stocked shop. The 162 pitches include 102 mostly individual pitches for touring units. These are in two areas, one each side of the entrance lane, and are divided by hedges, shrubs and trees. Most have electricity (6A) and many also have water and waste water drain. Two main sanitary units provide British style WCs, washbasins (many in cubicles), hot showers with small dividers and shelf, a suite for disabled people, chemical disposal, plus dish-washing and laundry sinks. All hot water is free. Refurbishment of the older unit is planned, whilst the other unit is newer and modern. A building opposite reception contains the laundry, with washing machine and dryer, and a baby room. The terrace has views over the pool and the lake beyond and there is also a spa pool (both 1/6-15/9; unsupervised). A snack bar is adjacent in main season. The site slopes gently down to the beach and lake with facilities for watersports including water skiing. Pedaloes, windsurfers and kayaks can be rented, and fishing licences are available. Minigolf, volleyball, boules, bicycle hire and, for children, Red Indian style tee-pees, pony riding and a playground. An animation and activities programme is available in high season, and there is much to see and do in this very attractive corner of Aveyron. Mobile homes for rent (26). Used by tour operators (40 pitches). Winter caravan storage. A `Sites et Paysages' member.

Directions: From Salles-Curan take D577 for 4 km. approx., turning right into a narrow lane immediately after sharp right hand bend. Site is signed at junction.

Charges 2000:
-- Per unit incl. 2 or 3 persons and electricity Ffr. 90.00 - 180.00 acc. to season and location; extra person 18.00; extra tent, vehicle or animal 15.00; local tax 1.00.
-- Credit cards accepted.
Open:
1 June - 15 September.
Address:
12410 Salles Curan.
Tel:
(0)5.65.46.35.34.
FAX: (0)5.65.78.00.72.
E-mail: contact@
camping-les-genets.fr.
Reservations:
Advised for July/Aug.

**Book this site
01892 559898**

THE ALAN ROGERS'
travel service

1209 Camping La Boissière, Saint Geniez d'Olt

Riverside site in the Upper Lot valley.

With trout in the river and carp in the lakes, La Boissière is a fisherman's paradise. Situated on the banks of the River Lot, surrounded by wooded hills, walking, swimming, canoeing or cycling are alternative pursuits. Mature trees provide plenty of shade on the generous, partly hedged, grassy pitches, all of which have electricity connections (6A) and frequently placed water points. Two modern sanitary blocks offer all the necessary facilities at a high standard. These include British style WCs, hot showers and washbasins in private cubicles, plus the novel luxury of 'litter flaps' for dry waste. A washing machine and dryer provided. There is direct access through the site to the river, which is suitable for swimming and canoeing. Reception is housed in an old, converted farmhouse, where basic provisions are stocked (milk and bread in high season only). There is also a bar with a terrace here and nearby are a bouncy castle and children's playground. A large, heated swimming pool (no Bermuda style shorts) has a paved sitting out area and a paddling pool. Entertainment is organised in July/Aug. The nearby old town of St Geniez d'Olt should satisfy all shopping needs, and day or longer fishing licences can be obtained there (the helpful site staff will advise). Mobile homes and bungalow tents to rent.

Charges 2001:
-- Per unit incl. 2 adults Ffr 58.00 - 98.00; extra person 21.00 - 31.00; child (2-7 yrs) 13.00 - 20.00; extra vehicle 25.00; animal 10.00; electricity 20.00.
-- Credit cards accepted.

Open:
20 April - 30 September.

Address:
Rte de la Cascade, 12130 St Geniez d'Olt.

Tel:
(0)5.65.70.40.43.
FAX: (0)5.65.47.56.39.

Reservations:
Contact site.

Directions: Site is off the D988 east of Saint Geniez d'Olt.

1205 Camping Les Terraces du Lac, Pont de Salars, nr Rodez

Terraced site overlooking lake between Millau and Rodez.

At an altitude of some 2,000 ft. on the plateau of Le Lévézou, this outlying site enjoys attractive views over Lac de Pont de Salars. The site is terraced, providing 180 good sized, level pitches with or without shade, all with electricity. The site seems largely undiscovered by the British, perhaps as it is only open for a short season. There is an attractive, quite large (200 sq.m.) heated pool and children's pool (15/6-15/9), with paved and grass sunbathing terraces and good views over the lake which has direct access from the site at two places - one for pedestrians and swimmers, the other for cars and trailers for launching small boats. A large bar/restaurant with a lively French ambience serves full meals in high season and snacks at other times, with takeaway and there is a shop (all 1/7-31/8). The four sanitary blocks are of varying ages but all have free hot showers, British style WCs and some washbasins (H&C) in private cabins, plus washing up areas under cover and laundry facilities. There are fridges for hire. Amenities on site include a solarium, children's playground, volleyball, pétanque, table tennis, billiards, games and TV rooms, with entertainment and activities organised in high season. Tennis 3 km. This site is well placed for excursions into the Gorges du Tarn, Caves du Roquefort and nearby historic towns and villages.

Charges 2001:
-- Per pitch incl. 2 persons Ffr. 70.00 - 105.00; extra person 21.00 - 25.00; child (2-7 yrs) 15.00; electricity (6A) 20.00; water, drainage and electricity 25.00; local tax 1.00.
-- Credit cards accepted.

Open:
1 June - 30 September.

Address:
Route du Vibal, 12290 Pont de Salars.

Tel:
(0)5.65.46.88.18 (when closed (0)5.65.74.32.85).
FAX: (0)5.65.46.85.38.

Reservations:
Made with deposit (Ffr. 400) and fee (100).

Directions: Using D911 Millau - Rodez road, turn north at Pont de Salars towards the lake on the D523. Follow camp signs. Ignore first site and continue following lake until Les Terraces (approx. 5-6 km).

1210M Camping Municipal du Lauradiol, Campouriez, nr Entraygues

A strikingly neat and pretty little site, tucked into a wooded gorge in the Aveyron hills, Lauradiol is alongside the La Selves river (fishing possible), 500 m. from the Cambeyra barrage. The 34 pitches, 21 with electricity, are arranged on flat grass, neatly separated by trim hedges. Many are quite large, although those actually along the river bank are somewhat smaller. There is quite good shade from a variety of trees. Surprisingly for such a small site, there is even a swimming pool, plus paddling pool, and a well kept tennis court - both free to campers. There is not much else by way of facilities, but there are several villages within 5 or 6 km. for restaurants, shopping, etc. The sanitary facilities include hot showers, some washbasins in private cabins, British style WCs and chemical disposal - recently refurbished and all very clean when inspected.

Charges guide:
Per caravan incl. 1 or 2 persons and electricity Ffr. 80.00, 3 or 4 persons 90.00; tent incl. 1 or 2 persons 60.00.
-- No credit cards.

Open:
20 June - 10 September.

Address:
12460 Campouriez.

Tel:
(0)5.65.44.53.95.
Winter (La Mairie):
(0)5.65.44.85.31.

Reservations:
Advised for July/Aug. Write or phone La Mairie de Campouriez.

Directions: Site is between Entraygues sur Truyère and Campouriez on the D34 at the hamlet of Lauradiol. Site entrance is by the river bridge at junction of D34 and D572.

1204 Castel Camping Les Tours, St Amans-des-Cots

Attractive, friendly and efficiently run site on shores of Lac de la Selves.
This spacious site now has 95 individual pitches on gently sloping grass, separated by low wooden rails and attractive new planting. All have access to electricity (6A), water and waste water connections. They include 21 chalets and tents for rent. The central sanitary building is modern, spacious and clean, with British style WCs, controllable showers, and washbasins all in cubicles. There are facilities for babies and disabled people and chemical disposal. Dishwashing and laundry sinks are at the end of the building in a covered loggia area, and hot water is free throughout. A washing machine and dryer are in a room at the reception building, where you will find plenty of local tourist information. The owner will advise you about the visits to a château evening with candlelight banquet, an angora farm, and a local pottery which he runs weekly in main season, and music or groups feature in the site's bar. The original swimming pool and sun terrace has its own sanitary unit and changing rooms below, and a pool-side snack-bar serves pizzas, grills etc. in high season A further new pool has been added. Other organised activities include a children's club, bicycle hire and archery lessons. Fishing 2 km, riding 9 km. There is a large well equipped children's playground plus plenty of grassy space for ball games. Fresh bread, croissants and regional produce are available from the épicerie at reception (1/7-31/8). An evening stroll around this delightful village is a must, and Sévérac Le Château (21 km), Rodez (28 km), and the many other pretty towns and villages in the region should satisfy all shopping, sightseeing and cultural needs.

Directions: Take the D34 from Entraygues-sur-Truyère to St Amans-des-Cots (14 km.). In St Amans take D97 to Colombez and then the D599 to Lac de la Selves (site is signed). Site is 5 km. from St Amans. Alternatively, if using autoroute A75, take St Flour exit and follow D921 south for 41 km. Go 1.5 km. past Lacalm and turn right on D34 signed St Amans-des-Cots. Follow signs for 23 km.

Charges 2001:
-- Per unit, incl. 2 persons Ffr. 149.00; extra person 30.00; child (under 7 yrs) 21.00; electricity 18.00; water and drainage 10.00.
-- Less 10-20% outside July/Aug.
-- Credit cards accepted.

Open:
20 May - 9 September.

Address:
12460
St Amans-des-Cots.

Tel:
(0)5.65.44.88.10.
FAX: (0)5.65.44.83.07.

Reservations:
Made and are advisable for July/Aug. - write for details.

`Camping Cheque'

Book this site
01892 559898

THE ALAN ROGERS'
travel service

CASTEL CAMPING

LES TOURS
★★★★

Don t hesitate, ask for our free brochure!

1207 Camping La Grange de Monteillac, Sévérac L'Église

Modern well equipped site, in beautiful, well preserved small village.

This spacious site now has 95 individual pitches on gently sloping grass, separated by low wooden rails and attractive new planting. All have access to electricity (6A), water and waste water connections. They include 21 chalets and tents for rent. The central sanitary building is modern, spacious and clean, with British style WCs, controllable showers, and washbasins all in cubicles. There are facilities for babies and disabled people and chemical disposal. Dishwashing and laundry sinks are at the end of the building in a covered loggia area, and hot water is free throughout. A washing machine and dryer are in a room at the reception building, where you will find plenty of local tourist information. The friendly owner and his welcoming staff will advise you about the visits to a château evening with candlelight banquet, an angora farm, and a local pottery, which are run weekly in main season. Music or groups feature in the site's bar. The original swimming pool and sun terrace has its own sanitary unit and changing rooms below, and a pool-side snack-bar serves pizzas, grills etc. in high season A further new pool has been added. Other organised activities include a children's club, bicycle hire and archery lessons. Fishing 2 km, riding 9 km. There is a large well equipped children's playground plus plenty of grassy space for ball games. Fresh bread, croissants and regional produce are available from the épicerie in season (1/7-31/8). An evening stroll around this delightful village is a must, and Sévérac Le Château (21 km), Rodez (28 km), and the many other pretty towns and villages in the region should satisfy all shopping, sightseeing and cultural needs.

Charges 2001:
-- Per unit incl. 2 persons and electricity Ffr. 120.00; extra adult 21.00; child (3-7 yrs) 17.00; `confort' pitch plus 30.00; extra car 17.00; animal 8.00.
-- Less 30% outside July/Aug.
-- Credit cards accepted.
Open:
1 May - 15 September.
Address:
12310 Sévérac L'Église.
Tel:
(0)5.65.70.21.00.
FAX: (0)5.65.70.21.01.
E-mail: info@la-grange-de-monteillac.com.
Reservations:
Contact site.

Directions: Site is on the edge of Sévérac L'Église village, just off N88 Rodez - Sévérac Le Château road. From A75 use exit 42.

1605M Camping Municipal de Cognac, Cognac

If you're a lover of brandy, this area is a must, with abundant vineyards and little roadside chalets offering tastings of Pineau (a Cognac based aperitif) and a vast range of Cognacs. This municipal site by the Charente river is convenient as a night stop or longer stay to visit the area, and for sleeping off the effects of the 'tastings' – you probably won't even notice the slight noise from the nearby road! The 160 large pitches, all with electricity (5/6A), are neatly laid out and separated by shrubs and trees. Two good, modern toilet blocks have mixed British and Turkish style WCs, including children's toilets and chemical disposal. Push-button showers with free hot water, washbasins in private cabins, dishwashing and laundry sinks and a washing machine. There is a small swimming pool on the site or the municipal pool is nearby. Restaurants, bars and shops may be found in the town centre, although the site offers a snack bar and entertainment (15/6-15/9). Other on-site amenities include fishing, volleyball, table tennis, a children's play area on grass and a sand pit. Bicycle hire 2 km, riding 6 km, golf 5 km. The famous Cognac Houses (Pineau, Hennessy, Martell, Remy Martin, etc.) and the Cognac Museum may be visited but there is no public transport to the town centre (2.3 km). Riverside walks.

Charges guide:
-- Ffr: Per pitch incl. 2 persons Ffr. 67.00 - 78.00; extra person 16.00; child (0-7 yrs) 11.00.
-- Credit cards accepted.
Open:
1 May - 15 October.
Address:
Bvd. de Chatenay, Rte. de Ste-Sèvre, 16100 Cognac.
Tel:
(0)5.45.32.13.32.
FAX: (0)5.45.36.55.29.
Reservations:
Advised in high season. Write for more information to:
Office de Tourisme de Cognac, 16 Rue du 14 Juillet, 16100 Cognac. Tel: (0)5.45.82.10.71. FAX: (0)5.45.82.34.47.

Directions: Site is signed from N141 Saintes - Angoulême road following signs for town centre. It is to north of the town beside the river on road to Ste-Sévère.

1601M Camping Municipal de Bourgines, Angoulême

This little site on flat grassy terrain provides a convenient and satisfactory night halt close to the town and to the main routes to the southwest. With the municipal swimming pool complex next door, you might even stay an extra day or so. There are 160 neat, flat pitches, most separated by bushes and trees, 100 with electricity (5/15A) and 11 with drainage. The two toilet blocks can be heated and give a satisfactory total supply with mostly Turkish style WCs, washbasins in cubicles, free hot showers, chain operated in the newer block, with taps in the old block by reception, and chemical disposal. Bread and basic supplies are available from reception and there is a children's playground and table tennis. Good security (gates locked from 8 pm. in low season with parking outside). Motorcaravan service point (drive-over). The river runs close by and is used for fishing, canoeing and boat trips. Bicycle hire 100 m. riding or golf 5 km. Caravans to rent.

Directions: From N10 (town by-pass) west of Angoulême, turn towards centre of town at junction with N141 (Cognac road). At first roundabout turn left (site signed) and continue round inner ring. Turn right again where site is signed.

Charges 2001:
-- Per pitch incl. 2 adults Ffr. 60.00; adult 18.00; child (under 7 yrs) 10.00; dog 6.00; electricity 5A 17.00, 15A 27.00.
-- Credit cards accepted.
Open:
1 April - 30 September.
Address:
Ile de Bourgines, 16000 Angoulême.
Tel:
(0)5.45.92.83.22.
FAX: (0)5.45.95.91.76.
E-mail: campingan-gouleme@wanadoo.fr.
Reservations:
Write to site or L'Office de Tourisme, 7B Rue du Chat, B.P. 222, 16007 Angoulême.

1602 Castel Camping Gorges du Chambon, Eymouthiers, Montbron

Family site in pretty, rolling Perigord Vert countryside.

Under new ownership, this site is arranged around a restored Charente farmhouse and its outbuildings. It provides an attractive, spacious setting with 120 large, marked pitches with electrical connections, on gently sloping grass and enjoying extensive views over the countryside. The pitches are arranged in two circular groups with a sanitary block at the centre of each. Built in a traditional style, the blocks provide unisex facilities with British style WCs, hot showers and washbasins in cabins. Facilities for disabled people, baby bath, chemical disposal, laundry facilities including a washing machine and dryer, and good dishwashing rooms. To one side is a swimming pool (18 x 7 m), a children's pool and minigolf. Converted from an old barn with an interesting gallery arrangement, are a bar and restaurant, plus takeaway that includes pizzas (1/6-31/8). Reception stocks some basic supplies and bread can be ordered. A butcher calls each Wednesday evening. Animation is organised in July/Aug. including a children's club, youth disco and teenagers' corner. Visits to local producers and day trips (low season) are organised. Amenities include a games room, TV and table tennis, tennis, archery, bicycle hire and a children's play area. Fishing and riding within 200 m, golf 4 km. The site also offers canoe hire on the river and a footpath has been created to the river with two beaches where swimming is possible. Mobile homes, gite, tents and chalets to let. No animals are accepted.

Directions: From N141 Angoulême - Limoges road at Rochefoucauld take D6 to Montbron village. Follow D6 in direction of Piegut-Pluviers and site is signed down country road past holiday complex.

Charges 2001:
-- Per pitch Ffr. 35.00 - 42.00; person 27.00 - 33.00; child (1-7 yrs) 12.00 - 15.00; car 12.00; electricity (6A) 20.00.
-- Credit cards accepted.
Open:
28 April - 15 September.
Address:
Eymouthiers, 16220 Montbron.
Tel:
(0)5.45.70.71.70.
FAX: (0)5.45.70.80.02.
E-mail: gorges.chambon @wanadoo.fr.
Reservations:
Necessary for July/Aug; contact site quoting Alan Rogers.

Book this site
01892 559898
THE ALAN ROGERS'
travel service

THE **LOW** COST **LOW** SEASON HOLIDAY SOLUTION

Looking for a Go-As-You-Please holiday?

Looking for low season prices but high season quality?

Looking for rock bottom ferry prices?

Enjoy **HUGE** Ferry Savings

Ferry-inclusive prices
from

£**239**
per party

- 10 Camping Cheques
- Return Dover-Calais crossing for car and up to 5 passengers

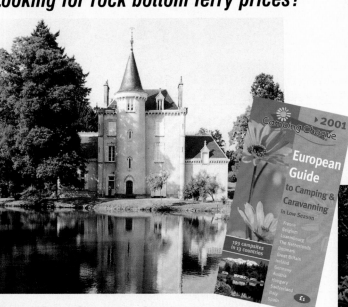

Camping Cheque is the answer.

Camping Cheques offer a choice of nearly 200 of Europe's finest sites – all at an incredible fixed price of just £7.95 per night for pitch + 2 adults. That's a saving of up to 50% off normal site tariffs. What's more they guarantee fully open services (and a cheerful welcome!) throughout the low season.

For a **FREE** colour brochure

01892 55 98 55

We're waiting to hear from you

www.campingcheque.com

ABTA
W1610

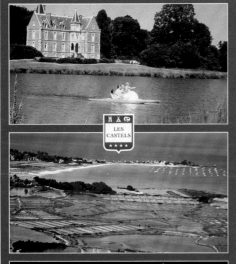

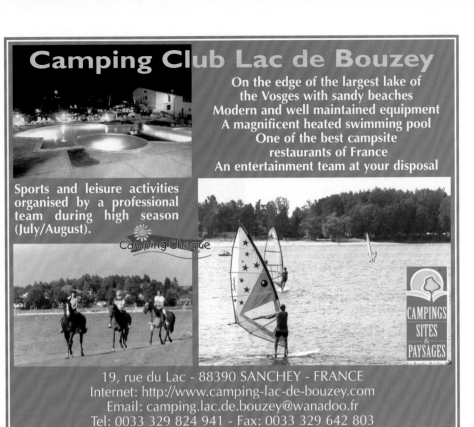

Camping La Yole ★★★★

Camping Cheque

Wake up to the sound of birdsong in a wooded park of 17 acres with four star comfort. Space, security, informal atmosphere: LA YOLE, tucked away between fields and pine trees, only 1 km from the beach.

– Chemin des Bosses - Orouet - F 85160 Saint Jean de Monts –
– Tel: 0033 251 58 67 17 - Fax: 0033 251 59 05 35 –
– camping.layole@wanadoo.fr –

FUTURISTE

Panoramic view over the Futuroscope situated at 2 kms.
Heated swimming pool, pond, snack.
Chalets for hire.
Open all year.

Camping Cheque

86130 St-Georges les Baillargueaux
Tel/Fax: 0033 549 52 47 52

On the route of the castles of the Loire
2 campsites at your disposal

CAMPING DE CHANTEPIE ★★★★
49400 St-Hilaire-St-Florent - SAUMUR
Tél. 02 41 67 95 34 - Fax 02 41 67 95 85
e-mail : camping.chantepie@wanadoo.fr

The same spirit of hospitality

CAMPING DE L'ÉTANG ★★★★
49320 St-Saturnin-sur-Loire - BRISSAC
Tél. 02 41 91 70 61 - Fax 02 41 91 72 65
e-mail : camping.etang@wanadoo.fr

Camping Cheque

ISTA - Atelier protégé "Guiderries" N° 94 DRTE 49

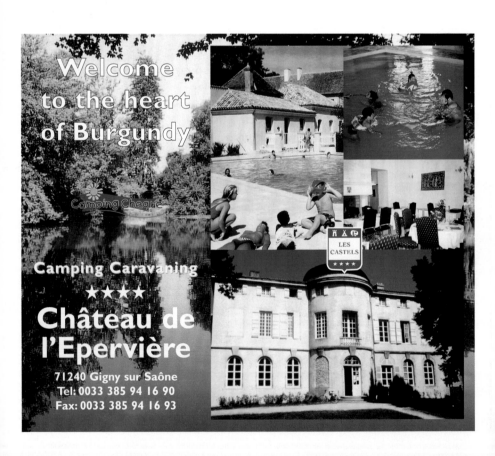

Welcome to the heart of Burgundy

Camping Cheque

Camping Caravaning
★★★★
Château de l'Epervière
71240 Gigny sur Saône
Tel: 0033 385 94 16 90
Fax: 0033 385 94 16 93

LES CASTELS
★★★★

1603M Camping Municipal Le Champion, Mansle

Le Champion is a convenient stop-over from the N10 or a good base to explore the northern Charente area. Beside the Charente river, the site has a cool, relaxing atmosphere created by its attractive location. The site, with 120 average size, separated pitches, is mostly open with little shade. All pitches have electricity (16A) and water points. The main modern sanitary block is well maintained and provides push-button showers, some washbasins in cabins, British style WCs and facilities for disabled people. There are dishwashing and laundry areas and a small free washing machine. An additional smaller, older block is in the tenting area at the rear of the site. Two privately owned restaurants are at the site entrance. One is attractively canopied and has 'al fresco' facilities and snack bar priced food. The town and shops are 200 m. Swimming pool in town, recreational area next to the site. Information on opportunities for cycling, walking, canoeing or fishing is available from the local Syndicate d'Initiative (500 m). Motorcaravan service point at entrance. Some road noise from the N10.

Directions: Site is well signed off the N10 (in town of Mansle), 30 km. north of Angoulême.

Charges guide:
-- Per pitch Ffr. 16.00; adult 12.00; child (under 7 yrs) 6.00; caravan or tent 11.00; vehicle 11.00; electricity 16.00.

Open:
15 May - 15 September.

Address:
16230 Mansle.

Tel:
(0)5.45.20.31.41.
FAX: (0)5.45.20.30.40.

Reservations:
Bookings accepted without deposit on Alan Rogers' booking form, although not usually necessary.

Mansle Town — *Charente River* — *Le Champion Camp Site*

DORDOGNE / AVEYRON - 24 Dordogne

2401 Castel Camping Château Le Verdoyer, Champs Romain

Dutch owned site developed in park of restored Château Le Verdoyer.

We particularly like this site for its beautiful buildings and lovely surroundings. Le Verdoyer is situated in this lesser known area of the Dordogne sometimes referred to as the Périgord Vert, with its green forests and small lakes. The 37 acre estate has two such lakes, one in front of the Château for fishing and one accessed by a footpath, with sandy beach and safe swimming area where canoeing and windsurfing for beginners are also possible. There are now 150 marked, level and terraced pitches (some a little rocky). Mostly of a good size (100-150 sq.m), all have electricity (5/10A), with a choice of wooded area or open field, where hedges have been planted and have grown well; 120 are 'confort' pitches with more planned. There is a swimming pool complex with two pools (25 x 10 m. and 10 x 7 m; the smaller one can be covered in low season) and a paddling pool. In high season activities are organised for children (5-13 yrs). There is definitely no disco! The modern toilet block housed in the old barn buildings is of good quality, containing showers with dividers and hooks, washbasins in cabins and British style WCs. There is another very well appointed block and both have facilities for disabled people, baby baths and hot water also for dishwashing. Serviced launderette, motorcaravan service point and fridges can be rented. Multi-purpose shop with gas. The courtyard area between reception and the bar is home to evening activities, and provides a pleasant place to enjoy drinks and snacks from the bar, with takeaway facilities. A good value bistro serves meals in July/Aug. Activities include an all-weather tennis court, volleyball, basketball and badminton, table tennis, minigolf and bicycle hire (tennis and bicycles are free in low season). Children's play areas. Small library. Barbecues are allowed. The Château itself has rooms to let and its excellent lakeside restaurant is also open to the public. Bungalows and mobile homes to rent. Used by a Dutch tour operator (15 pitches).

Directions: Site is 2 km. from the Limoges (N21) - Chalus (D6bis-D85) - Nontron road, 20 km. south of Chalus and is well signed from the main road. Site is on the D96 about 4 km. north of village of Champs Romain.

Charges 2000:
-- Per unit incl. 2 persons and electricity Ffr. 99.00 - 150.00; extra person 30.00 - 40.00; child (2-7 yrs) 20.00 - 30.00; full services free - 29.00; without electricity less 17.00; animal 20.00.
-- In low season, 7th night free.
-- Credit cards accepted.

Open:
1 May - 30 September.

Address:
24470 Champs Romain.

Tel.
(0)5.53.56.94.64.
FAX: (0)5.53.56.38.70.
E-mail: chateau@verdoyer.fr.

Reservations:
Write to site.

Book this site
01892 559898

THE ALAN ROGERS'
travel service

2418 Camping-Caravaning Saint Avit Loisirs, Le Bugue

Well appointed site with impressive pool complex close to Dordogne attractions.

St Avit lies in the middle of rolling countryside, well away from towns and holiday congestion. The site is divided into two sections surrounding an excellent pool complex, with 200 sq.m. outdoor pool, children's pool, water slide and a heated indoor pool with jacuzzi and adjacent fitness room. Beside the pool are two table tennis tables, floodlit minigolf and a boules area. A good quality tennis court is nearby, plus a volleyball pitch, and an extensive children's play area. The main section of the site contains 199 pitches, all with electricity and minimum 100 sq.m, arranged in cul-de-sacs off a main access road. The site can become very crowded in the main season when facilities at the three toilet blocks in this section are stretched. Tour operator tents and mobile homes (with lots of British visitors) occupy 153 pitches, leaving only 46 for touring units. The other section of the site is devoted to chalets, bungalows and further mobile homes. The toilet blocks are modern, each containing push-button showers with temperature controls, washbasins in cabins, British-style toilets with seats, full laundry facilities and baby changing areas. A new reception building is at the entrance and English is spoken. The bar, restaurant, good-value café and takeaway are in a recently built, but traditional-style stone building. The café (highly recommended), shop and bar open onto a large terrace with pergola and hanging baskets, which overlooks the pool complex. Most of the evening entertainment in high season happens here. A disco is behind the bar, and is well sound-proofed from the rest of the site. Canoe trips on the Dordogne are organised, as are many other sporting activities. Good walks can be taken direct from the site. The site is ideally situated for visits to Les Eyzies and Lascaux as well as many other places of interest of the Dordogne region. Sarlat and Perigeux are also within range for markets and hypermarkets.

Directions: Site is 6 km. north of Le Bugue. From south on D710 turn left on the C201 (about 2.5 km. from town). Site is signed from the main road, and at nearby hamlet of St Avit Vialard. The approach road is narrow and bumpy in places.

Charges 2000:
-- Per pitch Ffr. 35.60 - 62.50, with electricity 57.30 - 84.50, with water and drainage 74.80 - 102.50; adult or child over 4yrs 22.70 - 40.50 (under 4 free); dog 11.30 - 20.00; local tax (over 9 yrs) 2.00.
-- Credit cards accepted.

Open:
1 April - 30 September.

Address:
Le Bugue, 24260 Saint Avit de Vialard.

Tel:
(0)5.53.02.64.00.
FAX: (0)5.53.02.64.39.
E-mail: contact@saint-avit-loisirs.com.

Reservations:
Made with deposit (Ffr 300 per week) and fee (Ffr 100).

Book this site
01892 559898

THE ALAN ROGERS'
travel service

2400 Camping La Tuilière, St Rémy-sur-Lidoire

Traditional French site with small lake, swimming pool and lots of space.

La Tuilière is a spacious site with 100 pitches on a gently sloping hillside. Most of the pitches are fairly level with some shade and there are 75 with electricity (6/10A), although long leads may be needed. The entrance building houses reception, a small bar/restaurant for lunches and evening meals (all 1/7-31/8), overlooking the swimming pool and paddling pool. There is a good play area and tennis court. Activities include bicycle hire, archery, minigolf, table tennis and pool tables. In July/Aug. dances, tournaments and karaoke nights are arranged. The small unfenced lake, where there is more play equipment, can be used for fishing and water games. The two toilet blocks, one quite new and both very clean, have British style WCs, some washbasins in cubicles and pre-set showers. There are laundry facilities, a room for babies and a unit for disabled visitors. This is a typical French site with very friendly owners (who encourage British rallies). St Rémy is in the western Dordogne (less crowded with tourists), not far from Ste Foy la Grande, and well positioned to visit the wine areas of St Emilion, Pomerol and Bergerac. Mobile homes for hire.

Directions: From the north on D708 Montpon-Ménestérol to St Foy-la Grande road, site is 5 km. south of Montpon on the right. From the south site is 1.5 km. north of St Rémy on the D708 (on the left).

Charges 2001:
-- Per pitch Ffr. 28.00; person 20.00; child (under 7 yrs) 12.00; animal 8.00; electricity 3A 12.50, 5A 15.00, 10A 20.00.
-- Low season less 20%.
-- Credit cards accepted.
Open:
1 June - 15 September
Address:
St Rémy-sur-Lidoire, 24700 Montpon-Ménestérol.
Tel/Fax:
(0)5.53.82.47.29.
E-mail: la.tuilliere@wanadoo.fr.
Reservations:
Made with Ffr. 65 deposit.

2421M Camping Municipal Le Repaire, Thiviers

This high quality, peaceful municipal site in the heart of the Périgord Vert has been completely refurbished and is being thoughtfully developed by its owner in partnership with the Commune of Thiviers. The 94 pitches are divided by shrubs and a variety of trees have been planted to provide shade, though it will be a year or two before many pitches benefit. There is plenty of space for all units, some pitches being very large and most have access to electricity (6A). There are a few pitches in the woods. The two toilet blocks are modern and kept very clean, with free hot showers and washbasins in private cabins, plus cubicles for disabled visitors, washing machines and drying facilities. There is a small lake for fishing and a new unheated swimming pool and adjacent shallow pool The reception area houses a small shop, terrace bar and snack/ takeaway service (all July/Aug). A small children's playground, new tennis court, boules, table tennis, exercise track, bicycle hire and volleyball. The municipal swimming pool and tennis courts are adjacent to the site. A few bungalows and chalets are for hire in the woods.

Directions: From N21 Limoges - Perigueux road, turn off at traffic lights in centre of Thiviers. Site is signed to left from a quite complex junction, and is about 2 km from the town on the D707 east towards Lanouaille.

Charges 2000:
-- Per pitch Ffr. 25.00 - 35.00; adult 20.00 - 25.00; child (2-12 yrs) 12.00 - 15.00; animal 10.00; electricity 17.00.
-- No credit cards.
Open:
1 May - 30 September.
Address:
24800 Thiviers.
Tel:
(0)5.53.52.69.75.
FAX: as phone..
Reservations:
Not necessary, but possible with a 25% deposit.

2425 Camping Les Tourterelles, Tourtoirac

Countryside site with own equestrian centre

This is a site that will appeal to lovers of the countryside, in an area that is ideal for walking or horse riding. The adjacent riding stables with 30 horses is run by the owner's daughter Angélique. The horses have been selected to be ideal for the local terrain, and to be safe and dependable. There are 125 pitches in total, but the site has some chalets, bungalows and mobile homes for rent, which leaves around 87 grassy pitches for tourists. These are on several different levels most with good shade from mature trees, and all have electricity (6A). Reception is housed in a corner of the bar/restaurant, which is adjacent to the 20 x 10 m. pool with a paddling pool for the youngsters. There is no shop but bread can be ordered, although Tourtoirac (1 km.) has a shop, and there is a supermarket at Excideuil. Freezer pack service. The restaurant serves good value meals, and has a takeaway service. In addition to the riding, activities include tennis, volleyball, badminton, table tennis, fishing, with an animation programme in the main season. In low season the site can organise tours to local walnut farms, dairies etc.

Directions: From Limoges take D704 to St Yrieux (70 km. south), Lanouaille and Cherveix-Cubas. Just after Cherveix-Cubas turn right in village on D5 to Tourtoirac. Turn right in village and fork left on D73 towards Coulaures; site is on left in 1 km.

Charges 2000:
-- Per adult Ffr. 23.50; child (under 9 yrs) 19.50; pitch 56.00; motor-caravan 60.00; animal 13.00; electricity 22.00.
-- Low season discounts for over 55's.
-- Credit cards accepted.
Open:
Easter - 2 October.
Address:
24390 Tourtoirac.
Tel:
(0)5.53.51.11.17.
FAX: (0)5.53.50.53.44.
E-mail: les-tourterelles@wanadoo.fr
Reservations:
Advised for July/Aug.

DORDOGNE / AVEYRON - 24 Dordogne

2407 Camping Lestaubière, Pont St Mamet, nr Bergerac

Small country site with swimming pool, mid-way between Bergerac and Perigueux.

Having direct access from the main N21 (though screened from it by woodland), one thinks first of this as a useful transit site but, in fact, most people stay for a while. It takes 90 units, mostly on fairly flat, shaded wooded ground at the top of the site, with some on more sloping open meadow with views. Pitches are marked and all have electricity (4A) but long leads may be necessary. A swimming pool (unsupervised) and paddling pool encourage longer stays, as does the small lake with diving platform and beach. The two toilet blocks have British style WCs, showers and washbasins with free hot water (in cabins in the larger block). A large room houses ample dishwashing and laundry sinks; there are baby baths, and a large family shower room. There are no facilities for disabled visitors. There is a general room with bar and room for the young with amusement machines, reached via a pleasant, shaded patio terrace under vines and maples. Small shop. Library. Occasional organised activities. Good children's play equipment. Volleyball, boules and fishing on site, tennis near. Many British and Dutch visitors, but no tour operators. Good English is spoken.

Directions: Site is 1 km. north of Pont St Mamet on the N21. Access is off a busy 3 lane highway and care is needed turning across oncoming traffic.

Charges 2000:
-- Per person Ffr. 26.00; child (under 7) 16.50; pitch 28.50; electricity (4A) 15.00.
-- No credit cards.

Open:
1 May - 1 October.

Address:
Pont St Mamet, 24140 Douville.

Tel:
(0)5.53.82.98.15.
FAX: (0)5.53.28.90.70.

Reservations:
Made for exact dates (min. 1 week) without deposit to guarantee admission.

2416 Camping-Caravaning Le Grand Dague, Atur, Périgueux

Good quality site with pool on the outskirts of Périgueux.

Having negotiated the narrow access road, Le Grand Dague is found to be a very spacious, clean and attractive site. There are 93 good sized, slightly sloping pitches, 66 of which are for tourists, and all have electricity (6A). The excellent sanitary facilities are housed in four centrally located, inter-linking units, one of which is heated for use in colder months. These provide mostly unisex facilities and include British style WCs, washbasins in cubicles, push-button showers with divider and shelf, a baby room, facilities for people with disabilities, dishwashing and laundry sinks. The main building houses reception, a small shop providing essentials (15/5-30/9) and the very attractive restaurant and bar with its shady terrace. A takeaway service and an appetising restaurant menu make the most of this provision (all from June). A swimming pool, water slide and paddling pool enjoy a sunny location (from early May). Sports amenities on site include football, volleyball, badminton, petanque, minigolf and table tennis. Fishing, bicycle hire, riding 5 km, golf 10 km. The site is about 6 km. from Périgueux and also close to hypermarkets and tennis. No tour operators. Rally field available. Mobile homes for rent (18) and some attractive chalets. A 'Sites et Paysages' member.

Directions: Site is signed from N89 south of Périgueux. From centre of Périgueux take Brive road.

Charges 2001:
-- Per pitch Ffr. 30.00 - 45.00; adult 25.00 - 34.00; child (0-7 yrs) 15.00 - 20.00; electricity (6A) 18.00; animal 8.00; local tax 1.50.
-- Credit cards accepted.

Open:
Easter - 30 September.

Address:
Atur, 24750 Périgueux.

Tel:
(0)5.53.04.21.01.
FAX: (0)5.53.04.22.01.

Reservations:
Advised for high season and made with deposit (Ffr. 500) and fee (100).

2411 Camping-Caravaning Aqua Viva, Carsac, nr Sarlat

Clean site with good pool complex in heart of the Périgord Noir.

This site is divided into two sections, separated by the access road. One side is very quiet and spacious with 186 pitches (some very large) and 32 chalets terraced in woodland. The other half contains pitches on flat grass and has an excellent, heated main swimming pool, children's pool, small lake (for fishing), table tennis, a floodlit basketball and boules area, high quality minigolf, children's tennis court and under 7s play park. Canoe lessons and guided trips on the Dordogne are organised by the site, as are many other sporting activities. Each part of the site has very modern, very clean and heated toilet blocks, with facilities for disabled people, laundry, baby areas and chemical disposal. Between the two sections is the reception area, with a small reasonably priced restaurant and a bar and terrace where evening entertainment is arranged in season. Small shop and takeaway. Bicycle hire and fishing on site, riding 1 km, golf 5 km. The site is ideally situated for visits to Rocamadour and Padirac. It is also close to Sarlat for markets and hypermarkets. The site is very popular with families, especially those with pre-teen and younger teenage children. English is spoken. No tour operators.

Directions: Site is 6 km. from Sarlat on the D704 road from Sarlat to Souillac. Coming from Sarlat, the entrance is not easy to see.

Charges 2001:
-- Per pitch Ffr. 24.00 - 55.00; person 18.00 - 37.00; child (under 7 yrs) 10.00 - 24.00; animal 10.00; electricity 3A 14.00, 6A 18.00, 10A 25.00; local tax 1.00.
-- Credit cards accepted.

Open:
Easter - 30 September.

Address:
Carsac, 24200 Sarlat.

Tel:
(0)5.53.31.46.00.
FAX: (0)5.53.29.36.37.
E-mail: aqua_viva@ perigord.com.

Reservations:
Made with deposit (Ffr. 50 per day) and fee (100).

2406 Camping Le Paradis, St Léon-sur-Vézère, Montignac, nr Sarlat

Exceptionally attractive riverside site halfway between Les Eyzies and Montignac.

Well placed for exploring the Dordogne, Le Paradis is very well kept and is laid out with mature shrubs and bushes of different types. It has 200 pitches of good size on flat grass, divided by trees and shrubs (164 for touring units). All have electricity, water and drainage, and there are some pitches for motorhomes. The two main toilet blocks are of outstanding quality, although the shower cubicles are small. However, they can be heated and have baby baths and toilets, chemical disposal, extensive laundry facilities and even outside showers for those who have just had a swim or romp in the sand-pit! A very good swimming pool complex is heated in low season, with one deep pool (25 x 10 m), another shallower one (17 x 7 m), plus a paddling pool. There is a well stocked shop (with gas) and the restaurant has a wide choice of menu and a takeaway service. Canoeing on the Vézère river starts from steps adjacent to a small beach; the site organises trips to the surrounding area. Activities include two tennis courts, a football field, BMX track, fishing, bicycle hire, volleyball, table tennis and pool activities, and a well designed children's playground. Riding 2 km. The site welcomes a good quota of British and Dutch guests, many through a tour operator. However, organised games, competitions and evening events are run by the site, who try to maintain a French flavour. English is spoken. A site of real quality, which we recommend.

Directions: Site is by the D706, 10 km. north of Les Eyzies near village of St Léon-sur-Vézère, or south of Montignac (13 km).

Charges 2000:
-- Per person Ffr. 26.60 - 38.00; child under 4 yrs free; pitch 41.70 - 59.50; electricity (6A) 19.00, each extra amp 1.00; local tax (1/7-31/8) 1.50.
-- Low season less 10% for pensioners.
-- Credit cards accepted.

Open:
27 March - 25 October.

Address:
St Léon-sur-Vézère, 24290 Montignac.

Tel:
(0)5.53.50.72.64.
FAX: (0)5.53.50.75.90.
E-mail: le-paradis @perigord.com.

Reservations:
Any length with deposit (Ffr. 500 or 76.25) and fee (Ffr. 100 or 15.25).

2413 Camping Les Grottes de Roffy, Ste Nathalène, nr Sarlat

Well organised site with good pool, restaurant and shop.

This site is some 5 km. east of Sarlat with 166 clearly marked pitches (some very large). With easy access, they are set on very well kept grass terraces, with good views across an attractive valley. Some have plentiful shade, although others are more open, and all have electricity (6A). Two toilet blocks with modern facilities are more than adequate. A very good swimming pool complex comprising two deep pools (one heated), a fountain, a children's pool and a heated jacuzzi. A concrete play space for roller skating and a children's play area is nearby. Close to the main reception are a bar, restaurant (indoor and with terrace) and shop area, all located within converted farm buildings surrounding a courtyard. We were very impressed with the shop, well stocked with a variety of goods and a tempting charcuterie section (prepared on site) with plenty of ideas for the barbecue. The restaurant menus were imaginative and sensibly priced, and takeaway food is available (all amenities from 6/5). Adding to the musical talent of the site owners, a variety of music groups perform throughout the season. Fishing 2 km, bicycle hire 7 km, riding 10 km, golf 15 km. The site is conveniently located for Sarlat and all other Dordogne attractions and is a pleasant place to stay in its own right. It caters well for families. Used by tour operators (73 pitches).

Directions: Site is 5 km. east of Sarlat on the D47 Sarlat - Souillac road.

Charges 2001:
-- Per pitch Ffr. 40.60 - 50.75, with electricity 55.35 - 69.20, services 62.95 - 78.70; adult 31.40 - 39.25; child (2-7 yrs) 22.30 - 27.90; pet 9.80 - 12.30; local tax 1.50.
-- Credit cards accepted.

Open:
1 May - 23 September.

Address:
Ste Nathalène, 24200 Sarlat.

Tel:
(0)5.53.59.15.61.
FAX: (0)5.53.31.09.11.
E-mail: roffy@ perigord.com.

Reservations:
Made with deposit - contact site.

2414 Camping Bel Ombrage, St Cybranet, nr Cénac

Very quiet, clean site with good pool close to river and Dromme.

Bel Ombrage sits in a pretty location by the little River Céou, with a beach onto a backwater that is safe and clean for bathing. There are 180 well shaded, flat grass pitches of good size, marked by trees and bushes. Two modern toilet blocks are kept very clean, with a laundry and facilities for disabled visitors and for babies. The site boasts a good pool, but lacks a bar or restaurant, although soft drinks are sold by the pool and a bread van calls daily. There is a pizzeria next door, and it is a short walk to the village of St Cybranet, where there are restaurants and a well stocked store (at the local garage). There are more shops at Cénac, and a short drive takes you to the beautifully restored village of Daglan. Tennis close. Canoeing and other excursions can be booked at reception. Fishing on site, riding or bicycle hire 3 km, golf 6 km. Bel Ombrage is close to Domme and Castelnaud, and would make a good base for touring the southern Dordogne .

Directions: Take the D57 from Vézac towards Cénac. After St Cybranet, the site is a short distance on the left.

Charges 2000:
-- Per pitch Ffr. 38.00; adult 27.00; child (under 7 yrs) 14.00; electricity 18.00.

Open:
1 June - 5 September.

Address:
24250 St Cybranet.

Tel:
(0)5.53.28.34.14.
FAX: (0)5.53.59.64.64.

Reservations:
Write to site.

2422 Camping Domaine des Chênes Verts, Calviac

Peaceful, family site in the valley of the Dordogne.

The old Périgordian renovated farm buildings complement this peaceful country-side campsite. The spacious grounds which contain many trees provide two areas (150 pitches in total) on either side of the main buildings. The pitches, most shaded, are separated by hedging, all with electricity (6A) and with water nearby. The majority are level but some are gently sloping. The two toilet blocks include British style WCs, roomy, controllable showers, washbasins in cabins, chemical disposal, dishwashing and laundry areas, all with free hot water. A washing machine is available. The medium sized swimming pool has a large sunbathing area and is close to a new children's play area, bar and restaurant (15/6-15/9). A new covered, heated pool was added recently. Shop (in reception low season). TV and games room, large open grassed area for ball games and a tennis court. Forest walks and cycle tracks lead from the site. Chalets (46) and mobile homes (20) for rent. The owners, who speak some English, are very helpful and friendly.

Directions: From Sarlat take D704, then in 3.5 km. turn left on D704A towards Calviac. Site is 5 km.

Book this site
01892 559898

THE ALAN ROGERS'
travel service

Charges 2000:
-- Per pitch Ffr. 44.00; person 27.00; child (under 7 yrs) 14.00; electricity 21.00; dog 10.00; local tax (over 12 yrs) 1.00.
-- Low season less 20%.
-- Credit cards accepted.

Open:
1 May - 28 September.

Address:
Route de Sarlat, 24370 Calviac en Périgord.

Tel:
(0)5.53.59.21.07.
FAX: (0)5.53.31.05.51.

Reservations:
Advised in July/Aug; contact site.

2409 Camping Soleil Plage, Vitrac, nr Sarlat

Spacious site with enviable location beside the Dordogne.

The site is in one of the most attractive sections of the Dordogne Valley, right on the riverside. It is divided into two sections - one section of 56 pitches has its own toilet block and lies adjacent to the reception, bar, shop and restaurant complex (all 12/5-15/9), which is housed in a renovated Perigourdine farmhouse. It is also close to a small sandy river bank and canoe station, from which canoes and kayaks can be hired for down-river trips or transport up-river for a paddle back to the site. Near the reception area is a swimming pool, paddling pool, tennis court and minigolf. The friendly bar provides an extensive takeaway including inter-esting 'plat du jour'. The restaurant (with its attractively extended terrace) serves excellent Périgourdine menus. The larger section of the site (124 pitches) is about 250 m. from the reception area, and offers river bathing from a sizeable pebble bank. All pitches are bounded by hedges and are of good size, and in this section there are a few giant pitches for large families. Most have good shade. Open air table tennis, volleyball and a playground occupy part of a large central recreation space. Fishing on site, bicycle hire 2 km, golf 1 km, riding 5 km. Sanitary facil-ities are provided by two modern blocks, with washing machines, chemical disposal and motorcaravan services. TV room. Activities are organised including walks and sports tournaments, Once a week there is a 'soirée' usually involving a barbecue or paella, with band and lots of wine - worth catching! The site is becoming increasingly popular, though in late August it begins to empty, but reservations are essential for July - early Aug. Used by tour operators (80 pitches).

Directions: Site is 8 km south of Sarlat. Take D704 and it is signed from Montfort castle. Coming from the west on D703, turn first right 1 or 2 km. after the bridge at Vitrac-Port, and follow the signs.

Charges 2001:
-- Per person Ffr. 24.00 - 37.00; child (2-10 yrs) 15.00 - 22.00; pitch 37.00 - 63.00, with electricity 52.00 - 83.00, with full services 70.00 - 113.00; dog 10.00; local tax 1.00 (over 10s) in high season.
-- Credit cards accepted.

Open:
1 May - 30 September.

Address:
Vitrac, 24200 Sarlat.

Tel:
(0)5.53.28.33.33.
FAX: (0)5.53.28.30.24.
E-mail: soleil.plage @wanadoo.fr.

Reservations:
Made for exact dates: min. 1 week with deposit and fee; send for booking form.

2404 Castel Camping Le Moulin du Roch, Sarlat

Family run site midway between Sarlat and Les Eyzies with activities to suit everyone.

You will receive a warm welcome at this family run site where the 210 pitches are carved out of natural sloping woodland which creates shade on its several levels. Site owned mobile homes and tour operator pitches take up many pitches leaving 75 for touring units. All pitches have electricity (6A) and some have water and drainage. Those on the lower plateau tend to be more level than those higher up. The three well equipped toilet blocks have all the usual amenities with free hot water throughout. Laundry facilities include a washing machine and dryer. A swimming pool (proper swimming trunks, no shorts) and paddling pool are open all season and are encircled by a comfortable patio area. There is a small shop, reasonably priced restaurant and a takeaway with extensive menu (all from 12/5). On site are a children's playground, tennis, fishing lake and table tennis. Maps are provided for walking forest trails and bicycle rides in the surrounding area. Canoeing and caving nearby. Bicycle hire or riding 10 km, golf 15 km. Entertainment and activities are organised in high season, with something for everyone from needlework and painting to canoeing and caving for teenagers. Twice weekly disco. Advance booking is essential in July/Aug. Dogs are not accepted.

Directions: Site is 10 km. from Sarlat on D47 road to Les Eyzies.

Charges 2001:
-- Per unit incl. 2 persons 78.00 - 135.00, with electricity 98.00 - 155.00, with full services 113.00 - 170.00; extra person (over 9 yrs) 15.00 - 35.00; child (4-9 yrs) free - 15.00; local tax 1.00 (4-8 yrs 0.50).
-- Credit cards accepted.

Open:
1 May - 16 September.

Address:
Route des Eyzies D47 , 24200 Sarlat en Périgord.

Tel:
(0)5.53.59.20.27.
FAX: (0)5.53.59.20.95.
E-mail: moulin.du.roch @wanadoo.fr.

Reservations:
Accepted with deposit (and Ffr. 120 fee in July/Aug. only).

`Camping Cheque'

Book this site
01892 559898

THE ALAN ROGERS'
travel service

Le Moulin du Roch
Route des Eyzies - 24200 SARLAT
☎ 00 33 553 59 20 27 - Fax: 00 33 553 59 20 95
E-mail:Moulin.du.roch@wanadoo.fr
www.campings-dordogne.com/moulin-du-roch

LES CASTELS

♦ **Large individual emplacements for tents, caravans, camping cars**
♦ **Pool and paddling pool, tennis, table tennis, boules, volley-ball**
♦ **Bar, take-away, shop, launderette, satellite TV**
♦ **Modern sanitary blocks, baby bath and children's toilets**
♦ **Daily children's club, Pot-holing, aqua-gym, aerobics**
♦ **Guided canoe trips, horse-riding, walk.**

"Le Moulin du Roch"

DORDOGNE

2412 Camping La Palombière, Ste Nathalène, nr Sarlat

Clean site with good recreational facilities east of Sarlat.

This is a spacious site in a peaceful valley with 167 quiet, well shaded woodland pitches delineated by trees and bushes and some fully serviced. Two very clean modern toilet blocks are provided with facilities for laundry, babies and disabled people. A large recreational area with high quality sports facilities contains boules pitches, a small football pitch, tennis and volleyball courts. A new children's play area (under 8 yrs) is in shade at the edge of the field, with minigolf set on a higher level by the entrance. The good sized main pool and children's pool are flanked by a raised terrace from which parents can keep an eye on youngsters. Above this again is a larger terrace serving the reception, bar and restaurant complex, from which a good range of meals is available (1/5-16/9). A well stocked shop includes meat, fresh milk and newspapers (1/5-16/9). Bicycles can be hired and canoe trips reserved at reception. The site organises sports competitions and evening activities in season, including talent shows, a weekly disco, cabaret and even giant scrabble! Fishing 3 km, riding or golf 10 km. This is an ideal site for families where children are at an age where they need a wide range of activities, but it nevertheless preserves a relaxed ambience and general tranquillity. Used by tour operators (80 pitches). Mobile homes for rent (15).

Directions: Take D47 east from Sarlat to Ste Nathalène. Site is signed from village and is reached by taking a left turn just beyond it.

Charges 2001:
-- Per pitch: simple Ffr. 39.80 - 52.80, with electricity 56.90 - 70.30, with water and drainage 67.40 - 80.90; adult 26.50 - 37.10; child (0-7 yrs) free - 25.80; animal 13.00; local tax 1.50.
-- Less 10% for senior citizens outside July/Aug.
-- Credit cards accepted.

Open:
14 May - 30 September.

Address:
Ste Nathalène, 24200 Sarlat.

Tel:
(0)5.53.59.42.34.
FAX: (0)5.53.28.45.40.
E-mail: la.palombiere @wanadoo.fr.

Reservations:
Made with deposit (Ffr. 420 or 64.02) and fee Ffr. 80 or 12.20).

DORDOGNE / AVEYRON - 24 Dordogne

2403 Camping Les Périères, Sarlat

Good quality, small site with large pitches and swimming pool very close to town.

This little site is in a pleasant setting amid attractive trees on the edge of the town of Sarlat. It has 100 individual pitches mainly on terraces on a semi-circle of a fairly steep hillside with shade in many parts. They are of very good size and all are equipped with electricity (6A), water connections and drainaway. It becomes full in July/Aug. so reservation is advisable, but a proportion of the site is not reserved, so space could be found if you are early. The main sanitary blocks are of varying size and should be quite sufficient, providing individual washbasins mostly in cabins and free hot water. Washing machines and dryers. On the more level ground there is a swimming pool (no Bermuda style shorts), paddling pool and two tennis courts. A recent addition is an indoor spa pool and sauna, open all season. The main buildings house a small shop, pleasant bar and just beyond these, a terrace restaurant with takeaway (15/6-15/9). Interestingly, the owners have made space for a library, where visitors can read, study or play board games and Dutch billiards. Other activities include table tennis (indoors or out), football pitch, sauna and a fitness track with exercise halts. Bicycle hire 1 km, fishing 5 km, riding or golf 7 km. Motorcaravan service point. Good quality bungalows for let. The site has a spacious air and is quite free from overcrowding, and is one of the most thoughtfully improved sites visited.

Directions: Site is east of the town on D47 road towards 'Sous-Préfecture' and Croix d'Alon.

Charges 2000:
-- Per unit in high season, incl. up to 3 persons Ffr. 164.00, with electricity 188.00, 2 persons 144.00 or 167.00.
-- Per unit in low season incl. up to 2 persons 111.00, with electricity 133.50; extra person 35.00; child (under 7 yrs) 22.00; local tax 2.50.
-- No credit cards.

Open:
Easter - 30 September.

Address:
Rte. Ste Nathalène, 24203 Sarlat Cedex.

Tel:
(0)5.53.59.05.84.
FAX: (0)5.53.28.57.51.

Reservations:
Advised for high season and made for min. 1 week with deposit (Ffr. 650 p/week) and fee (85).

Camping Les Périères

24200 SARLAT, DORDOGNE - PÉRIGORD

The 4-star site in a natural amphitheatre of woods and meadows.
A peaceful oasis in the heart of Black Périgord, yet only half a mile from
the medieval town and gastronomic centre of Sarlat.

LARGE INDIVIDUAL PITCHES - EXCELLENT TOILET BLOCKS
SWIMMING POOLS, one covered and heated - SAUNA
TENNIS COURTS - VOLLEYBALL - TABLE TENNIS
LOUNGE BAR - SHOP - LIBRARY

2402 Camping Les Granges, Groléjac, nr Sarlat

Well shaded site with good pool complex close to Dordogne.

Les Granges is situated on undulating ground in woodland. The pitches are marked and numbered on level terraces which are mostly blessed with good shade from mature trees and shrubs; most have electricity. Sanitary blocks are of a very high standard, with good hot showers and clean toilets. There are toilet and shower facilities for disabled visitors. The local doctor will call if needed. There is a good sized swimming pool, and shallow pool for children. A bridge over a path connects these to a new fun pool, with water slides. Canoes and bicycles can be hired and there are table tennis, volleyball, minigolf and children's play facilities. An enclosed bar/restaurant is supplemented by a terrace where dancing and other entertainment are organised in high season. Close to this is a snack bar which also provides takeaway food. There are shops and restaurants in the nearby town of Groléjac and the hypermarkets of Sarlat or Gourdon are not far away. The site is popular with tour operators, but there is a sensible balance and 'animation' is organised by the site. Les Granges could provide a good base for touring the Dordogne area and the present French owners have created an ambience that will assist in ensuring a pleasant stay.

Directions: Site is signed in village of Groléjac on D704 (Sarlat-Gourdon). From north leave N20 at Souillac towards Sarlat, but later keep left twice for Gourdon.

Charges guide:
-- Per unit incl. 4 persons Ffr. 161.00; extra person 25.00 (child under 2 free); special pitches 25.00 extra; electricity 18.00.

Open:
1 May - 25 September.

Address:
Groléjac, 24250 Domme.

Tel:
(0)5.53.28.11.15.
FAX: (0)5.53.28.57.13.

Reservations:
Made for exact dates with deposit and fee.

2423 Camping Le Moulin de Paulhiac, Daglan

Pleasant family site close to main Dordogne attractions.

Daglan is a very pretty village undergoing a complete renovation, and is becoming something of a tourist centre for this quieter area of the Dordogne. We were very impressed with the friendly welcome from the Armagnac family, who are justifiably proud of their well-kept and attractive site, built in the grounds surrounding an old mill. The 150 numbered pitches are separated by hedges and shrubs, all have electricity, and there is plenty of shade. Many pitches are next to a stream that runs through the site, and joins the River Ceou along its far edge. There is a tent field which slopes gently down to the river, which is well marked and quite shallow. Two toilet blocks were very clean when inspected, and were large enough to be adequate for the site. Sporting visitors will find volleyball, table tennis, badminton and boules on site, with municipal tennis courts adjoining. There is a modern pool complex (no bermuda style shorts) with a main pool (15 x 7.5 m), children's pool (7.5 x 7.5 m), and a slide with landing pool. Canoe trips are organised on the Dordogne. The site has a good value restaurant and takeaway, and local shops and markets complement the well-stocked site shop – you can even buy the owner's home-grown walnuts (delicious!). The site organises evening activities and there is a children's club. It is very close to Domme and La Roque-Gajeac. This is a site that will appeal especially to families with younger children, and was a place where we feel the parents would be able to relax and have a holiday too!

Directions: Crossing the Cenac (near Domme), take D46 south for 6 km, turn right on D60 to Daglan. Turn right on D57, and the site is about 5 km. on the right.

Charges 2000:
-- Per pitch Ffr. 46.00; person 33.00; child under 10 yrs 24.00, under 2 yrs 12.00; electricity (6A) 18.50.
-- Low season reductions.
-- Credit cards accepted.

Open:
15 May - 15 September.

Address:
24520 Daglan.

Tel:
(0)5.53.28.20.88.
FAX: (0)5.53.29.33.45.

Reservations:
Made for any length with deposit.

**Book this site
01892 559898**

THE ALAN ROGERS'
Travel service

2410 Camping-Caravaning Le Moulinal, Biron

Lakeside site with wide range of activities for all ages.

Not only does Le Moulinal provide a good base for exploring the southern Dordogne, but it has extensive wooded grounds to explore with picnic areas. The 280 grassy pitches (60 for touring units), all with electricity (3/6A), are level but of varying size, some a little cramped where access may be difficult for larger units. The sanitary facilities have been built to harmonise with the surroundings and provide British and Turkish style toilets (most in one block), washbasins (some in cabins), and hot showers. There is a good supply of hot water for dish-washing sinks, a laundry with washing machines and dryers, chemical disposal aand facilities for disabled people and babies. The 5-acre lake has a sandy beach and is suitable for boating (canoes available), swimming and fishing. An excellent restaurant serves regional meals (including a four course 'menu enfant'), there is a bar, also serving snacks and light meals (all season) and a snack bar/takeaway on the other side of the lake. A rustic children's play area on grass overlooks the lake. There is a large, heated swimming pool with jacuzzi and children's pool. Ambitious, well organised animation is run as a series of programmes; the 'baby club' (ages 2-6) offering amongst other things ball games, painting and pottery; there is a 'kid's club' for 6-10 year olds, including swimming lessons and football; the 'junior club' for 11-15s, including mountain biking and ball games, and a 'sport-club' for active young people or adults - pot-holing and rock climbing feature. The 'tourist club' and 'art club' add to the variety of programmes. Sport and leisure facilities include canoeing, potholing, tennis, diving and archery (small charges), volley-ball, table tennis, fishing, dance, football and hockey (all free). Bicycle hire. Excursions are organised on foot, on horseback, by car or bicycle. There is a full programme of evening entertainment in high season. Tents, mobile homes, chalets and bungalows for hire. Motorcaravan service point. The site is also popular with tour operators (80 pitches), although the owner has reduced their presence.

Directions: Biron is 53 km. southest of Bergerac. From Biron take D53/D150 south to Lacapelle Biron (4.5 km). Site is 1.5 km. west of the village beside the D255 to Villeréal.

Charges 2000:
-- Per pitch incl. 2 persons: normal Ffr. 59.00 - 144.00, near lake 69.00 - 154.00. with water and drainage 79.00 - 169.00; extra person (over 7 yrs) 13.00 - 42.00; child (2-7 yrs) free - 36.00; animal free - 14.00; electricity 3A 21.00, 6A 27.00; local tax 1.00 (under 7 yrs 0.50).
-- Credit cards accepted.

Open:
14 April - 15 September with all services.

Address:
24540 Biron.

Tel:
(0)5.53.40.84.60.
FAX: (0)5.53.40.81.49.
E-mail: lemoulinal @perigord.com.

Reservations:
Made with deposit (Ffr 250) and for high season, fee (150).

see colour advert between pages 128/129

DORDOGNE / AVEYRON - 24 Dordogne

2408 Camping-Caravaning Le Moulin de David, Gaugeac, Monpazier

Secluded valley site with pool, on southwest of the Dordogne.

Owned and run by a French family who continually seek to improve it, this pleasant little site is one for those who enjoy peace, away from the hustle and bustle of larger sites closer to the main Dordogne attractions, yet is sufficiently close for them to be accessible. Set in 14 ha. of wooded countryside, it has 160 pitches split into two sections; 35 are below the central reception complex in a shaded situation, and 75 above on partly terraced ground with varying degrees of shade. A new section has been opened along the valley, with a brand new sanitary block, and much planting of trees which will soon provide sufficient shade. All pitches have electricity and some are quite large. Spacing is good and there is no crowding. The site has been attractively planted with a pleasing variety of shrubs and trees. All three sanitary blocks are of a good standard, with controllable showers, washbasins in cabins, and facilities for disabled visitors and babies in each. There are chemical disposal facilities, adequate dishwashing and laundry sinks and there is now a laundry room. The reception block embraces a restaurant (doubling as a games and TV room), bar with shaded patio and takeaway, and a good shop. Two swimming pools, one for small children and the other for adults and older children have a paved sun terrace. Between these and the upper site is a children's play area and a small lake with water toboggan. Some events and games are organised for adults and children. Activities include boules, half-court tennis, table tennis, volleyball, trampolining. A new football area is at the far end of the site. There is a library, and bicycle hire. Money exchange. Canoe trips are organised from the site. Tents, mobile homes and caravans for hire; one tour operator has 15 pitches at present. There is a delightful wooded walk via a long distance footpath (GR 36) to Château Biron, about 2-3 km distance. The Bastide town of Monpazier is also walkable. A 'Sites et Paysages' member.

Directions: Site is just south off D2 Monpazier-Villeréal road, about 2 km. west of Monpazier.

Charges 2001:
-- Per normal pitch Ffr. 29.00 - 53.00, large pitch incl. water and drainage 46.00 - 70.00; person over 2 yrs 21.00 - 37.00 (under 2 yrs free); extra child's tent 8.00 - 15.00; electricity 3A 20.00, 5A 24.00, 10A 33.00; local tax 1.00 (under 12 yrs 0.50).
-- Credit cards accepted.

Open:
19 May - 8 September.

Address:
Gaugeac,
24540 Monpazier.

Tel:
(0)5.53.22.65.25.
FAX: (0)5.53.23.99.76.
E-mail: courrier@moulin-de-david.com.

Reservations:
Advisable for Jul/Aug. with Ffr. 400 deposit plus fee (120).

**Book this site
01892 559898**

THE ALAN ROGERS'
travel service

LE MOULIN DE DAVID ★★★★

Convivial, comfortable, quiet and relaxing in magnificent countryside and an exceptional location

All services, swimming pool complex, entertainment

Mobile homes and tent bungalows to hire

England Eric & Kay SALE, 40 Lindale Mount, Wakefield, West Yorkshire WF2 OBH
Tel: 01924 781503

France Liliane & J.C Ballay, Moulin de David, 24540 GAUGEAC-MONPAZIER
Tel: (0033) 5 53 22 65 25 Fax: (0033) 5 53 23 99 76
E-mail COURRIER@MOULIN-DE-DAVID.COM Web MOULIN-DE-DAVID.COM

2415 Camping Les Deux Vallées, Beynac, Vézac

Developing woodland site in the heart of the Dordogne.

This site is enviably situated almost under the shadow of Beynac Castle. There are 100 flat marked touring pitches, including a newly established, yet shady, section with direct views towards the castle. All are of of good size, some generous, divided by trees and shrubs, all with electricity (6A). There is plenty of shade and the general feel is of unspoilt but well managed woodland. The main modern toilet block gives ample provision, with British style WCs, good access for disabled people and chemical disposal facilities. A second smaller block, which is heated for off-season use, has been added more recently. A good sized pool (1.6 m. deep) and children's pool provide on-site swimming from mid May, and it is a short distance to the Dordogne for bathing or canoeing. A small lake, with island and tree-house, is available for fishing or just sitting beside, and there are facilities for bicycle hire, volleyball, basketball, minigolf, boules, table tennis, table football and an intriguing outdoor pool game. Riding 2 km, golf 8 km. Quiz nights are a regular feature in the main season. Shop and bar/restaurant (both 15/5-30/9) which serves good value snacks and more ambitious meals to take away, eat inside or on the terrace. The site is being steadily upgraded, with more pitches planned, by its Dutch owners, who assure a very friendly welcome. Site owned mobile homes (6) to rent and 10 tour operator pitches (not mobile homes). Winter caravan storage. A single track railway runs along the eastern boundary of the site (trains are relatively infrequent). English spoken.

Directions: Take D703 from Bergerac, go through Beynac and, just past the village, turn left towards Sarlat on D57/D49. Shortly after, turn left and site is signed from here. This route involves a narrow railway bridge - to avoid continue on Sarlat road for a few hundred metres turning left at further site sign, across an unmanned level crossing and on to site.

Charges 2001:
-- Ffr: Per pitch Ffr. 24.00 - 38.00; adult 17.00 - 28.00; child 3-7 yrs 11.00 - 18.00, free under 3; first extra tent free, 2nd 6.00 - 10.00; electricity 6A 16.00, 10A 20.00; dog 4.00 - 6.00; local tax (over 10 yrs) 2.00.
-- No credit cards.

Open:
All year.

Address:
24220 Vézac.

Tel:
(0)5.53.29.53.55. FAX: (0)5.53.31.09.81. E-mail: les2v@ perigord.com.

Reservations:
Advised for July/Aug. and made with deposit (Ffr 550) and fee (50).

2405 Castel Camping Les Hauts de Ratebout, Belvès, nr Sarlat

Country site with excellent pool complex southwest of Sarlat.

There are some stunning views of the surrounding countryside from many of the 200 pitches at this hilltop campsite. The terraced pitches vary in size (80-130 sq.m.) and some are more level than others. Over 180 have electricity (6A) and 160 also have water and drainage. Four toilet blocks offer the usual amenities and are of a high standard. They provide free hot water throughout, showers, private washbasins and British style WCs, and include facilities for people with disabilities. There are washing machines and dryers in each block. The restaurant/bar is housed in the older part of the building and is interestingly furnished. There is a small shop (with gas) and a takeaway service. The pool complex includes a 200 sq.m. unheated pool with slide, a shallow 100 sq.m. pool which is covered and heated as necessary, a fun pool with another slide and a small paddling pool. A stimulating, gravel based adventure playground is nearby. A general room houses a library, pool and football tables, and TV. Sports facilities include volleyball, table tennis, bicycle hire and two tennis courts. Activities are organised in season and include canoe trips, nightly videos and sporting events for families and children up to 16 years. Fishing 6 km, riding 7 km, golf 8 km. Mobile homes to rent (14). Used by tour operators (22 pitches). Caravan storage. The walled town of Belvès is worth a visit.

Directions: From Belvès, take D710 southwards for 2 km. then left on D54 at camp sign and follow through to site.

Charges 2000:
-- Per unit incl. 2 adults Ffr 85.00 - 135.00; extra person 15.00 - 37.00; child 3-7 yrs 7.00 - 26.00, under 3 yrs 7.00 - 17.00; electricity (6A) free - 18.00; electricity, water and drainage free - 35.00.
-- Credit cards accepted.

Open:
1 May - 12 September.

Address:
Ste Foy de Belvès, 24170 Belvès.

Tel:
(0)5.53.29.02.10.
FAX: (0)5.53.29.08.28.
E-mail: camping@ hauts-ratebout.fr.

Reservations:
Made for a few days or more, with deposit Ffr. 420 per week (or 60 per day) and fee (90).

N2419 Centre Naturiste Le Couderc, Naussannes, nr Beaumont

Friendly, welcoming naturist site based on old coaching inn.

Le Couderc (from the 12C Occitan 'gathering place') is set at a crossroads on the route of the 'bastide' (fortified) towns of the Dordogne. Issigeac with its Sunday market is 8 km, Beaumont 7 km. Five castles are within walking distance and there are cave paintings at Lascaux and Padriac. The original inn provides a home for the extended family of Marieke, Nico and Olivier, whilst the stables have been sensitively converted to provide a bar and clubroom complete with a large, open fire for cooler evenings. Rather than fell a large tree when connecting two buildings to provide the restaurant, the trunk grows through the dining room. The bar and snack bar open throughout the season, the restaurant closes each Wednesday. The Dutch chef produces excellent French dishes. There is a covered terrace, a small museum and art display and a small shop with local produce. The 180 large pitches are around the edges of three gently sloping valleys radiating from the old inn. All pitches are level and have electricity. Unisex sanitary blocks in each of the valleys are of good quality with British style WCs and free hot water in washbasins and showers (some controllable), all of which are kept very clean. Washing machine, facilities for disabled people in some blocks and chemical disposal. There is always something going on here - fixed facilities for leisure include a solar heated pool, small lake with sandy beach, petanque (with competitions organised), volleyball, bicycle hire, play areas and a paddling pool with a little terrace for parents. A children's club offers painting, poetry, circus skills, etc. and there are adult painting and sculpture classes, a talent evening at the impressive 'podium' on Wednesdays and enjoyable theme evenings on Fridays. There is a small library, plus a photocopying and fax service. A wooded area not used for camping has paths for walks. Torches are required at this site. Fishing 5 km, riding 4 km, golf 15 km. The famous Dordogne wines such as Bergerac and Monbazillac are waiting at the local wine châteaux! Bungalows for rent. Good English is spoken by the Dutch family and the site is extremely popular with the Dutch. Cars are left outside the site in peak season.

Directions: 10 km. east of Bergerac on D660 Sarlat road, turn into Mouleydier and take D21 to St Aubin-de-Lanquais. In that village turn left on D19 to Faux and in Faux follow signs to Naussannes. Pass Micalie and 300 m. after second crossing to Monsac, turn left at camp sign and follow rough track for 1 km. to site.

Charges 2000:
-- Per adult Ffr. 29.00; child (under 14 yrs) 19.00; pitch 59.00; dog 18.00; electricity 18.00.
-- Less 10-30% for longer stays outside 14 June - 29 Aug.
-- Credit cards accepted (not Amex).

Open:
1 April - 30 September.

Address:
Naussannes, 24440 Beaumont-du-Périgord.

Tel:
(0)5.53.22.40.40.
FAX: (0)5.53.23.90.98.
E-mail: le.couderc@ perigord.com.

Reservations:
Advised for 10 July-15 Aug. with deposit (Ffr 60 per night) and fee (110).

2420M Camping Municipal de la Plage, Saint-Aulaye

This is a gem of a municipal site, well situated with the benefit of very well maintained facilities. Beside the river Dronne, that runs on three sides of it, a sandy river beach is shared with the village community where there is also a bar with snacks and a large playground. Our biggest regret about the site is its short season. There are 65 marked, level touring pitches separated by small hedges and all have electricity. They are well spaced giving a feeling of spaciousness, the ones nearest the river (unfenced) having the most shade. Sanitary facilities are modern with British style WCs and free hot water. Kept very clean, there are washing machines and good facilities for disabled people. On site are bicycle and canoe hire, a water slide, fishing, tennis and minigolf. Riding 5 km; golf 8 km. Reception also doubles as a small shop with bread and basics, but the lovely little town of Saint-Aulaye is only a short walk. It has a weekly market and some interesting tourist type shops. Convenient for the Bergerac and Bordeaux vineyards, this is a little oasis of peace and quiet. Mobile homes (7) and chalets (14) to rent.

Directions: Saint-Aulaye is on the D5 Riberac - La Roche-Chalais road. Site is well signed in the village, located on the river bank on D17 road to Aubeterre.

Charges guide:
-- Per pitch incl. 2 persons Ffr. 45.00; extra person 10.00; child (under 7 yrs) 8.00; dog 6.00; electricity 5A 12.00, 10A 20.00.
-- Less for weekly stays.
Open: 15 June - 15 September.
Address: 24410 Saint-Aulaye.
Tel: La Mairie: (0)5.53.90.62.20. FAX: (0)5.53.90.59.89.
Reservations: Not normally considered necessary.

2428 Camping De Barnabé, Boulazac, nr Périgeux

Memorable site on the River l'Isle, only 2 km. from Périgeux town centre.

A unique site in a unique setting, De Barnabé has a special ambience. A distinctive 1936 Art Deco style building houses the reception, bar, restaurant and games room, complete with an attractive terrace overlooking the river, in the style of the old 'Cafe de Paris'. The bar has its own Wurlitzer juke box, and you will find pool tables and table football in the old ballroom. This site (created by the present owner's father in 1953) has 56 pitches all for tourists, all with access to electricity (4/6A). These are in four areas, with 42 pitches on one side of the river. The other 14 are on the opposite side and use a separate entrance (you will be given a map). Access roads are a little narrow, and larger units will need to take great care. The ground may be rather firm for tent pegs. The six sanitary buildings are not modern, but they have been re-tiled, are well cleaned, and the unisex facilities which include British and Turkish style WCs, are more than adequate. One is heated and is used for the winter months, when the others have been closed down. One is in the smaller section of the campsite on the opposite side of the river. The finishing touch is the old fashioned, passenger operated ferry, resembling a gondola, which allows access between the two sections of the campsite.

Directions: From N2089 on outskirts of Boulazac, turn towards Périgeux at the Memoire roundabout. Go under railway bridge, round a double bend (right hand lane) and turn right. Continue until site signed to right. We suggest continuing to the far end of Rue des Bains using the car park opposite the Barnabé entrance until you have located your pitch.

Charges 2000:
-- Per adult Ffr. 17.00; child (under 7 yrs) 10.00; caravan 16.50; tent 16.50; car 10.00; motorcaravan 25.50; motorcycle 8.00; animal 4.00; electricity 14.50 (4A), 17.50 (6A).
Open: All year.
Address: Rue des Bains, 24750 Périgeux.
Tel: (0)5.53.53.41.45. FAX: (0)5.53.54.16.62.
Reservations: Contact site for details.

2426 Camping Caravaning La Linotte, Le Bugue

Family run, hilltop site with excellent pool complex.

La Linotte is a well designed site where the camping area is well separated from the activities. At the entrance behind reception is the restaurant, a small shop, and the well fenced pool complex (15/5-15/9). This consists of a 200 sq.m. main pool (unheated, except by the sun), a splash pool with two slides and a paddling pool (both heated), and a jacuzzi. There are views of the surrounding countryside from the terrace and the pool area. The bar/restaurant provides takeaway and breakfast, with bread to order from the small shop. There are 60 hedged pitches for tourists, with 32 units for rent (mobile homes, chalet, and tents) hidden amongst them. The pitches are level, and on grass, with 6A electric hook-ups, some having good views. Concealed in the centre of this area is the rather smart sanitary unit, with a bright and cheerful interior, providing a mixture of British and Turkish style WCs, showers and washbasins in cubicles, dishwashing and laundry sinks, plus limited facilities for babies and disabled people. Activities include volleyball, football, table tennis and pétanque tournaments, canoe and walking outings, dancing and pool evenings. A small playground is close to the terrace and pool area.

Directions: From D710 at northern end of Le Bugue turn on D32E where site is signed. After 1 km., turn right (site signed) on minor road for a further 1 km.

Charges 2000:
-- Per adult Ffr. 19.00 - 31.00; child (under 7 yrs) 15.00 - 20.00; pitch 26.00 - 41.00; animal 9.00: electricity 16.00.
-- Credit cards accepted.
Open: 1 April - 15 October.
Address: 24260 Le Bugue.
Tel: (0)5.53.07.17.61. FAX: (0)5.53.54.16.96.
Reservations: Made for July/August with deposit and fee.

DORDOGNE / AVEYRON - 24 Dordogne

2417 Camping Port de Limieul, Limieul

Delightful family site at the confluence of Dordogne and Vézère.

Situated on the banks of the Dordogne, opposite the picturesque village of Limieul, this site exudes a peaceful and relaxed ambience. There are 90 pitches, marked and numbered, some very spacious. All have electricity (5A). The young French owners have been steadily developing first class facilities, including two very well appointed sanitary blocks and a small pool (1/5-15/9). There are plans to build a larger pool for 2001. The reception area is contained in a building which also houses a friendly bar and restaurant with snacks and takeaway (all 25/5-5/9). The buildings are in Périgourdine style and surrounded with flowers and shrubs - it is a very pretty site. Facilities include minigolf, badminton, football, boules and volleyball. The last of these is set up on a large open grassy area between the trees on the river bank and the main camping area, which adds to the feeling of space and provides an additional recreation area. There are places for tents and camper vans along the bank. Mountain bikes and canoes can be hired - the latter are launched from a pebble beach exclusive to the site. Riding 1 km, golf 10 km. This is an ideal location for visiting the west central part of the Dordogne département, and is recommended for long stays. Used fairly unobtrusively by a tour operator.

Directions: Take D51 from Le Buisson towards Le Bugue. The road branches left to Limieul after about 3 km. and site is then signed.

Charges 2001:
-- Per unit incl. 2 persons Ffr. 120.00; extra person 25.00; child (0-10 yrs) 18.00; electricity (5A) 20.00; dog 10.00; local tax 2.00 (5-10 yrs 1.00).
-- Less 20-40% outside July/Aug.
-- Credit cards accepted.

Open:
1 April - 15 October.

Address:
24480 Alles-s-Dordogne.

Tel:
(0)5.53.63.29.76.
FAX: (0)5.53.63.04.19.
E-mail: didierbon-vallet@aol.com.

Reservations:
Advised for mid July - end Aug; contact site.

2427 Camping Le Mas, Sireuil, nr Les Eyzies

Well established family site in an outstanding hilltop location.

La Mas is situated at the top of the hill above the Beune valley, in the popular Périgord Noir region with its plethora of castles, grottoes and tourist towns. There are tantalising glimpses over the surrounding countryside from the site, which has a total of 140 pitches, with some mobile homes and chalets to rent, leaving around 75 tourist pitches. The individual hedged and grassy pitches have good shade from mature trees and all have electricity (6A). There are two well built, modernised sanitary units, both unisex, providing British and Turkish style WCs, washbasins in cubicles, push-button showers, dishwashing and laundry sinks, and facilities for babies. The main swimming pool is 16 x 7m, with a paddling pool and sun terrace, facilities include tennis, volleyball, pétanque and a woodland fitness circuit., plus a programme of activities for children in the main season. Also on-site are a snack bar and takeaway, bar, shop, and the adjacent Auberge du Mas which serves local specialities. All facilities fully open 15/5 - 15/9.

Directions: From D47 between Sarlat and Les Eyzies, turn on to C2 towards Sireuil village. Site is signed on right after 2.5 km. approx. (well signed).

Charges 2000:
-- Per adult Ffr. 27.00; child (3-7 yrs) 22.00; pitch 47.00; dog free; electricity 17.00.
-- Credit cards accepted.

Open:
15 May - 15 September.

Address:
Sireuil, 24620 Les Eyzies.

Tel:
(0)5.53.29.68.06.
FAX: (0)5.53.31.12.73.
E-mail: CAMPING-LE-MAS@wanadoo.fr

Reservations:
Made for min. of 1 week.

2424 Camping Les Bö-Bains, Badefols-sur-Dordogne

Peaceful riverside site.

Les Bö-Bains is very well kept, laid out with mature trees and neat pitches along a 700 m. stretch of the river bank. The 97 hedged pitches are on terraces accessed by tarmac roads. The riverside terrace is particularly pleasant, and perfect for anglers, though families with young children may prefer to be in the next terrace up. River bathing is possible, though further out the current can be quite strong. Pitches are of a good size, and on flat grass. All have electricity, with water taps and drainaway points between each pair. There are one or two extra large pitches for big motorhomes, and two with hardstanding. The two main toilet blocks are of good quality with baby rooms and laundry facilities. The pool complex contains a main pool (18 x 9 m), another shallower one (5 x 5 m), plus a toboggan and landing pool (14 x 7 m). Small shop at reception. The restaurant has a takeaway service. Canoeing on the Dordogne or Vézère can be arranged and there are places to launch one's own small craft. Sports facilities include a tennis court, a small football field, minigolf, boules, trampoline, volleyball, table tennis and pool activities. There is a well designed children's playground and a TV room. The site welcomes a good quota of French and Dutch clients, but not many British as yet. Games, competitions and evening events are organised. No tour operators, but mobile homes and chalets are to rent on higher terraces.

Directions: Site is on D29 between Lalinde and Badefols, 27 km. east of Bergerac, 35 km. west of Sarlat.

Charges 2000:
-- Per pitch incl. 2 persons simple: Ffr. 75.00 - 130.00, with electricity (5A) 95.00 - 150.00; pitch by river incl. electricity 95.00 - 175.00; extra person over 4 yrs 20.00 - 35.00.
-- Credit cards accepted.

Open:
15 April - 30 September. (chalets all year)

Address:
24150 Badefols-sur-Dordogne.

Tel:
(0)5.53.73.52.52.
FAX: (0)5.53.73.52.55.

Reservations:
Made for any length with deposit.

4601 Castel Camping de la Paille Basse, Souillac

High quality site in rural situation with panoramic views.

Lying some 8 km. from Souillac, this family owned and managed site is easily accessible from the N20 and well placed to take advantage of excursions into the Dordogne. It is part of a large domaine of 80 hectares, which is available to campers for walks and recreation. The site is quite high up, and there are excellent views over the surrounding countryside. The 250 pitches are in two main areas - one is level in cleared woodland with good shade, and the other on grass in open ground without shade. Numbered and marked, they are all a minimum 100 sq.m. and often considerably more. About 80 have individual electricity, water and drainaway, and electricity is available to all the others. The site has a good swimming pool complex, with a main pool (25 x 10 m), a second one (10 x 6 m) and also a paddling pool; they are not heated. A solarium and a crêperie are adjacent to the pools. There is a shop for all essentials, a good restaurant, bar with terrace and takeaway food. A sound-proofed disco room (twice weekly in season), TV rooms (with satellite) and cinema room are situated under the swimming pool area. Sporting activities include archery, tennis (charged), football, volleyball, and there are good quality table tennis tables and a children's playground. Golf 4 km. Laundry facilities. Doctor calls. The main sanitary facilities (there is also a small night unit at one end of site) are in three different sections, all centrally located close to reception. All have modern equipment and are kept very clean. There are chemical disposal and laundry facilities. Activities and entertainment are organised in season, and the animation was of a very high standard when we stayed. Mobile homes for hire (15). For good reason, the site can get very busy in high season and is popular with tour operators (20%), but there is more space available from mid August.

Directions: From Souillac take D15 road leading northwest towards Salignac-Eyvignes and after 6 km. turn right at camp sign on 2 km. approach road.

Charges 2001:
-- Per person Ffr. 33.00; child (under 7) 21.00; pitch 53.00 or with 3 services 65.00; electricity 3A 20.00, 6A 33.00; local tax 1.00.
-- Less 20% outside 15/6-1/9.
-- Credit cards accepted.

Open:
15 May - 15 September

Address:
46200 Souillac-sur-Dordogne.

Tel:
(0)5.65.37.85.48.
FAX: (0)5.65.37.09.58.
E-mail: paille-basse@wanadoo.fr.

Reservations:
Advised mid-July - mid-Aug. and made for min. 1 week with deposit and Ffr. 120 booking fee.

`Camping Cheque'

Book this site
01892 559898

THE ALAN ROGERS'
Travel service

see colour advert
between pages 192/193

4604 Camping-Caravaning Moulin de Laborde, Montcabrier

Small site developed round an old water mill, with swimming pool.

The watermill and its outbuildings at Moulin de Laborde have been sympathetically developed to provide a courtyard and terrace with a small bar, restaurant, takeaway and a shop that stocks basics and gas (all open all season). There are 90 pitches of at least 100 sq.m on level grass, well marked out by shrubs and trees. All have electricity and they are bordered by woods, hills and a small river. There is a swimming pool with sunbathing area and a paddling pool (15/5-15/9). The sanitary block is a good one with well designed showers, British toilets and washbasins in cabins. A covered area provides sinks for dishwashing and laundry, a washing machine and dryer, with a unit for disabled people and a chemical disposal point. Mountain bike hire, fishing and rock climbing lessons are available at the site, plus organised activities every day. Other activities include a rustic children's play area on grass, a small lake for recreation, volleyball and badminton court, boules, a recreation room and table tennis. Riding 5 km, golf 8 km, tennis near and canoeing on the Lot. A gate at the back of the site leads walkers onto a 'Grand Randonée'. The Château of Bonaguil and towns of Fumel and Villefranche du Perigord are close. No mobile homes, no tour operators. Dogs are not accepted. The friendly Dutch owners speak good English and French.

Directions: Site is near Montcabrier, which is just south of the D673, 12 km. from Fumel. Follow D673 north for 1 km. towards Gourdon, and site is on the left.

Charges 2000:
-- Per person Ffr. 34.00; child (under 7) 17.00; pitch 42.00; electricity (4A) 14.00; local tax (over 10 yrs) 2.00.
-- Less 20-30% outside 1/7-20/8.
-- No credit cards.

Open:
1 May - 15 September.

Address:
46700 Montcabrier.

Tel:
(0)5.65.24.62.06.
FAX: (0)5.65.36.51.33.
E-mail: campingmoulin-delaborde@wanadoo.fr.

Reservations:
Write with deposit (Ffr. 35 per night booked).

Book this site
01892 559898

THE ALAN ROGERS'
Travel service

4608 Camping Château de Lacomté, Carlucet

Welcoming English-run site near Rocamadour with excellent pool and restaurant.

Château de Lacomté is the closest site in this guide to Rocamadour; just a 15 minute drive along a back road. A little further on is the Gouffre de Padirac with its underground rivers and concretions. It is close to Gramat and Cahors for supermarkets and other shops. The site is run by an English family, Sheila and Stuart Coe and their children, who have worked hard developing the site and continue to run it and manage the facilities. The restaurant, which has a good reputation, and bar make up part of the converted outbuildings of the Château, which also contain a small shop (1/5-30/9) and the reception area. The restaurant is fronted by a large terrace where guests can eat or take drinks, and where there are steps down to a large swimming pool (from 1/6) with children's paddling area. Views from the terrace over mature woodland are memorable, and the pool and terrace are beautifully lit at night. Below the pool is a tennis court and children's playground, with table tennis by the reception area. The site tries to retain as much of the meadowland as possible for wildlife and flowers. The main camping field is quietly located down a slope to one side of the bar area. The first section contains pitches marked out on slightly sloping ground, most with flat areas, and six have hardstanding. The majority of pitches on this upper terrace have good shade, though most pitches on the extensive lower field are still relatively open. All pitches have electricity, water and drainage. The toilet block is good, clean and well equipped, with laundry facilities. Fridge hire. There are a few mobile homes for hire. Many who have discovered the site have booked to come back, and it is advisable to reserve if you want one of the best pitches. It is very popular with British visitors. The site is a little more out of the way than other Dordogne sites and out of season you may have to travel to the nearest town for bread and other supplies. Torches useful. Fishing 6-10 km.

Charges 2001:
-- Per pitch Ffr. 45.00; person 35.00; child (under 12 yrs) 20.00; dog 20.00; electricity 25.00.
-- Less 20-35% in low seasons.
-- Credit cards accepted.

Open:
1 April - 30 October.

Address:
46500 Carlucet.

Tel:
(0)5.65.38.75.46.
FAX: (0)5.65.33.17.68.
E-mail: ccl@easynet.fr.

Reservations:
Made with 25% deposit and Ffr. 50 fee; contact site.

Book this site
01892 559898

THE ALAN ROGERS'
travel service

Directions: From N20, 8 km. south of Peyrac, take D1 towards Gramat. After 12 km. turn left on D677, then after 1.5 km. left on D323 to Carlucet where site is signed. The D32 (Rocamadour - Carlucet) is not recommended for caravans or large motorcaravans.

4609 Domaine de l'Evasion, Martignac

Unusual site with family club atmosphere near River Lot.

Situated about 10 km. north of the river in rolling countryside, this site will suit those who like to mix lazy days with light-hearted activity in the evenings. In high season you will undoubtedly be met by the very charming Etienne, son of the owners, who will be on vacation from his tourism course at University. For many this alone will justify the visit. About half the holidaymakers are housed in cabins and mobile homes. There are roughly 90 camping places, neither marked and numbered, but all units seemed to have plenty of space, some almost acres of it. All have or can have electrical connections, and there are convenient water points. The French owners have been steadily developing good quality facilities, including two very well appointed sanitary blocks and a good sized pool, with water slide and separate children's pool. The reception area is contained in a small building situated about as far away from the entrance road as you can get, but most activity happens in the main concourse building, including the very low priced restaurant, takeaway and bar. Facilities include a sauna, children's playground, tennis, badminton, billiards, table tennis, boules and volleyball. Night swimming after the paella evening sounds like fun, though may not aid digestion. There is a barbecue area, though campers are welcome to have their own. Mountain bikes can be hired. This is an ideal location for visiting the area south of the Dordogne, and exploring this developing but still relatively quiet section of the Lot.

Charges guide:
-- Per person per week Ffr. 175.00 - 280.00; extra day 25.00 - 40.00.
-- Per child (under 10 yrs) per week Ffr. 140.00 - 225.00; extra day 20.00 - 30.00.
-- Electricity 14.00.
-- Credit cards accepted.

Open:
1 May - 15 October.

Address:
46700 Puy-L'Eveque.

Tel:
(0)5.65.30.80.09.
FAX: (0)5.65.30.81.12.

Reservations:
Advised for mid July - end Aug; contact site.

Directions: From the D911 in Puy L'Eveque take D28 northwards for Martignac and watch for site signs.

4603 Camping Les Pins, Payrac-en-Quercy

Site in wooded park suitable for a Dordogne holiday or overnight stop on way south.

Camping Les Pins, named after its magnificent pine trees, has impressive views. There are 125 clearly marked, level pitches (100 sq.m), of which 55 are available for touring units. All have electricity, most with water and drainage, Many pitches are shady although there is a fair number of sunny places. The site has recently developed its pool complex with a heated swimming pool (15 x 17 m.) with sunbathing area, three new water slides and a smaller children's paddling pool (15/5-15/9). The three toilet blocks, two recently modernised, are very well maintained providing British style WCs, showers with stool, washbasins in cabins, good baby bath facilities, dishwashing and laundry sinks with plenty of hot water, washing machines and dryers (with plenty of drying lines) and chemical disposal. There is a motorcaravan service point. Sports facilities include a good quality tennis court, table tennis, pétanque and volleyball. Shop (1/6-31/8) and good value bar/restaurant with views over the surrounding countryside, reasonably imaginative menus, and a good range of takeaway food (1/6-31/8). Equally imaginative are the site's new options of half-board and full-board camping tariffs. There is some entertainment in season, including weekly family discos. TV and library. Fishing 7 km, riding 10 km. The site is used by tour operators. Mobile homes for hire (40).

Directions: Site entrance is on western carriageway of the N20 just south of Payrac-en-Quercy, 16 km. from Souillac.

Charges 2000:
-- Per person Ffr. 32.00; child (under 7 yrs) 20.00; pitch 48.00, with electricity 65.00; local tax (adult) 2.00.
-- Less 30% outside 15/6-1/9.
-- Credit cards accepted (not in restaurant).

Open:
1 April - 15 September.

Address:
46350 Payrac.

Tel:
(0)5.65.37.96.32.
FAX: (0)5.65.37.91.08.
E-mail: info@les-pins.camping.com.
In UK: 01722-322583.

Reservations:
Made for min. 1 week with deposit (25%) plus fee (Ffr. 100).

4605 Camping Le Rêve, Le Vigan

Very peaceful, clean site with pool far from the madding crowd.

Le Rêve is situated in the heart of rolling countryside where the Perigord runs into Quercy. Pitches are divided by shrubs, and a variety of attractive trees have grown well to provide some shade. There is plenty of space for all units and some of the 60 pitches are very large. Most have access to electricity connections (6A) and there are now 9 pitches in the woods. The toilet block is modern, kept very clean and has been extended to include a heated enclosed area. There are free hot showers and washbasins in cabins, plus cubicles for disabled people and a baby room. Washing machine and dryers, chemical disposal. The small (solar heated) swimming pool, also very clean, has a large separate children's paddling pool with 'mushroom' fountain. The reception area has been extended and houses a small shop, a pleasant bar and restaurant and takeaway, serving snacks and more substantial dishes (all open all season). A small shaded children's playground, boules area, bicycle hire, table tennis and volleyball complete the amenities. Fishing 5 km, riding 2 km. There are a few chalets for hire. Le Rêve continues to impress us with its tranquillity and the young Dutch owners are keen to develop the site in such a way that this will not be lost. A site particularly suitable for families with very young children. Winter caravan storage.

Directions: Follow N20 from Souillac towards Cahors. About 3 km. south of Payrac, turn right on D673 (signed Le Vigan and Gourdon). After about 2 km, Le Rêve is signed on right down a small lane and the site is some 3 km. further on.

Charges 2000:
-- Per adult Ffr. 23.00; child (under 7 yrs) 12.00; pitch 30.00; electricity (6A) 15.00.
-- Less 20-35% outside July/Aug.
-- No credit cards.

Open:
25 April - 23 September.

Address:
46300 Le Vigan en Quercy.

Tel:
(0)5.65.41.25.20.
FAX: (0)5.65.41.68.52.
E-mail: campinglereve @yahoo.fr

Reservations:
Advised for high season and made for any length with deposit (Ffr. 400) and fee (30).

DORDOGNE / AVEYRON - 46 Lot / 47 Lot-et-Garonne

4607 Camping de la Plage, Saint-Cirq-Lapopie

Activity site on the bank of the River Lot.

Due to its unusual position adjacent to the River Lot, this site is a good base for those looking for an active holiday, with many sporting activities either on site, or in the immediate area. It attracts organised groups of young people and can be quite lively at times. The site is a rental base for canoeing and kayaking (life-jackets included in hire charge), with riding, climbing, canyoning and caving all available close by. Swimming is possible from the beach at the rear of the site, with a lifeguard in July/Aug. The site has 120 pitches with electricity (6/10A) to all, a few serviced pitches and some hardstandings. Most are on a very slight slope, with good shade from mature trees. The two sanitary units are practical, providing British style WCs, washbasins in cubicles and controllable hot showers, both have dishwashing and laundry sinks. There is a unit for disabled people, although the local terrain is not ideal. There is a motorcaravan service point (usual services and toilet block, charged for) outside at the rear of site on the river bank. Mobile homes (4) and chalets (4) for rent. NB. This site is open all year and may be subject to flooding in the winter months - contact site before travelling.

Directions: From Cahors take D653 east to Vers, then take D662 for 17 km. to Tour de Faure. Cross river on narrow bridge and site entrance is on right by bar/restaurant. Do not approach via Saint-Cirq-Lapopie.

Charges 2000:
-- Per adult Ffr. 30.00;
child (under 7 yrs) 15.00;
pitch 20.00 - 30.00;
electricity (6A) 18.00.
-- Credit cards accepted.
Open:
All year.
Address:
46330
Saint-Cirq Lapopie.
Tel:
(0)5.65.30.29.51.
FAX: (0)5.65.30.23.33.
E-mail: camping.laplage
@wanadoo.fr.
Reservations:
Advised for high season;
contact site.

4610M Camping Municipal Soulhol, Saint-Céré

Saint-Céré is an interesting small town, overlooked by the old château of the same name. It is actually situated in the département of Lot but is still in that area considered by the British to be the 'Dordogne'. The municipal site is now under privatised management, an increasingly popular system in France. It is well located, less than 100 m. from the swimming pool and tennis courts and only about 300 m. from the village centre with its shops, restaurants, etc. The site is neatly and attractively arranged with 180 large, flat pitches of which half have 10A electrical connections. They are marked by rose bushes and have shade from the avenues of mature trees which extend down the sides and middle of the site. Despite its close proximity to the town, the site has its own small shop (with gas), snack bar and takeaway and bread can be ordered. A further separate area is used mainly for rallies, etc. with its own elderly sanitary block. There are two other blocks, one new in '99 and an older, more central unit. These provide hot showers with dividers, washbasins (H&C) in cabins, British type WCs, dishwashing (H&C), a washing machine and chemical disposal facilities. Boules, fishing and bicycle hire are on site. The adjacent pool (July/Aug). and is free for campers.

Directions: Site is off the D48 road towards Lacapelle and is well signed from the centre of Saint-Céré. If entering from Figeac on D940 turn right before crossing bridge (not signed at this point).

Charges 2000:
-- Per person Ffr. 20.00;
child (4-7 yrs) 10.00;
pitch 17.00; electricity
5A 15.00, 10A 20.00;
animal 8.00; local tax
2.00 (child 2-7 yrs 1.00).
-- Discounts for long
stays.
-- Credit cards accepted.
Open:
1 April - 30 September.
Address:
46400 Saint-Céré.
Tel:
(0)5.65.38.12.37.
FAX: (0)5.65.10.61.75..
Reservations:
Made with deposit (Ffr.
250) and fee (90); contact
site.

4710M Camping Municipal, Tonneins

Close to the River Garonne, this small site has a rather formal charm, with neat flower beds, well mown lawns and a generally extremely well cared for appearance. It only has 40 pitches (many occupied by seasonal units), all with electricity (15A) plus a meadow for camping. Pitches are of a reasonable size, mostly separated by hedges and shrubs, with shade from many poplar trees. The sanitary facilities were very clean when seen (in high season) and include hot showers, some British style WCs, washbasins in private cabins, and dishwashing sinks (H&C) under cover. They are purpose built but of a fairly old design and adequate rather than luxurious and there is no proper chemical disposal point. Other than a children's play area, sandpit and table tennis, there is little by way of leisure facilities. However, the site is on the outskirts of the town with a fair choice of shops, restaurants, etc, and only a 15 minute drive from the charming old riverside town of Port Ste Marie. There is some road and rail noise at times. Torches required. Ice and cold drinks available. Gas barbecue provided (supply your own gas!) This is a good stopping off point.

Directions: Use RN113 in direction of Agen from the town of Tonneins. Take either exit 5 from autoroute to Marmande then the N113 south or exit 6 to Aiguillon and the N113 north. Site is off the road leading out of Tonneins.

Charges 2000:
- - Per unit incl. pitch and
2 persons Ffr. 62.00;
extra person 12.00;
electricity included.
Open:
1 June - 30 September.
Address:
47400 Tonneins.
Tel:
(0)5.53.79.02.28.
Reservations:
Contact site.

DORDOGNE / AVEYRON - 47 Lot-et-Garonne

4701 Camping-Caravaning Moulin du Périé, Sauveterre-la-Lémance

Pretty, family run site set in wooded countryside.

Set in a quiet area and surrounded by woodlands this peaceful little site is well away from much of the tourist bustle. Its 125 grass pitches, divided by mixed trees and bushes, are reasonably sized and extremely well kept, as indeed is the entire site. All pitches have electricity (6A) and most enjoy good shade, with younger trees and shrubs rapidly filling out in the new area. The picturesque old mill buildings adorned with flowers and creepers, now form a bar/reception, restaurant (including takeaway) and small, indoor play area. The attractive front courtyard is complemented by an equally pleasant terrace at the rear. Two small, clean pools (no bermuda-style shorts) overlook a shallow, spring water lake, ideal for inflatable boats and paddling. Bordering the lake is a large grass field, popular for football and volleyball, with other amenities including boules, table tennis, outdoor chess, a new playground and a trampoline. The three toilet blocks are clean, modern and well maintained, incorporating facilities for disabled visitors, babies and laundry. There are chemical disposal and motorcaravan service facilities. The site shop stocks essentials (with gas) with a small supermarket in the village and larger stores in Fumel. In season various activities, on and off site, are arranged; including canoeing, bicycle hire, riding, wine tasting visits, sight seeing trips plus weekly barbecues and gastronomic meals. The food is to be recommended as is the owner's extensive knowledge of wine that he is pleased to share with visitors. Fishing 1 km. No tour operators, but tents (14), chalets (4) and mobile homes (20) for hire. Winter caravan storage. A quiet, friendly site with regular visitors - reservation is advised for July/Aug. A Sites et Paysages member.

Charges 2000:
-- Per person Ffr. 34.00; child (under 7 yrs) 18.50; pitch and car 47.50; animal 21.00; electricity (6A) 20.50.
-- Credit cards accepted.

Open:
5 May - 24 September.

Address:
Sauveterre- la-Lémance, 47500 Fumel.

Tel:
(0)5.53.40.67.26.
FAX: (0)5.53.40.62.46.

Reservations:
Advised for July/Aug.

`Camping Cheque'

Book this site
01892 559898
THE ALAN ROGERS'
travel service

Directions: Sauveterre-la-Lémance is by the Fumel - Périgueux D710 road, midway between the Dordogne and Lot rivers. From D710, cross railway line, straight through village and turn left (northeast) at far end on C201 minor road signed Château Sauveterre, Loubejec and site. Site is 3 km. up this road on right.

4705 Moulin de Campech, Villefranche du Queyran

British owned site with superb trout fishing lake and pool.

This site is run by Sue and George Thomas along with Sue's parents, Dot and Bob Dunn. A cheery welcome and a free drink awaits you and a determination to ensure that you enjoy your stay. A fabulous view also awaits as you descend the drive from the entrance. The trout lake with graceful weeping willows feeds under the restored mill house which is home to the owners, the main administration area alongside and the bar and restaurant. Enjoy the fare produced by Sue on the pretty terrace as the trout jump (fresh trout is always a menu option, and several were caught when we were there - a rod costs Ffr. 30 daily or 100 weekly, a discounted rate for campers). The river continues through one side of the site. Children will need supervision around the lake and at the pool which is on an elevated area above the mill house. The single sanitary unit is rather ordinary but can be heated and has modern fittings. It provides both British and Turkish style WCs, some washbasins in cubicles with hot water, or open washbasins (cold only in men's section), and hot showers. Dishwashing and laundry sinks (H&C) are outside under cover at the side of the building, together with two washing machines and a dryer. The 60 pitches are mostly divided by hedges, with electricity available (2/6A, long leads may be necessary in places). There is a good playground for children together with an open grassy area for volleyball and other games, table tennis and baby-foot in a tent outside. Board games, boules and a small library are provided. In the main season barbecue and gourmet nights are organised. There are markets every day in the villages and towns around the region. Watersports, bicycle hire, golf or riding 10 km. Torches are required in some areas.

Charges 2001:
-- Per pitch Ffr. 39.00 - 49.00; adult 20.00 - 28.00; child (under 7 yrs) 15.00 - 19.00; electricity 2A 15.00, 6A 25.00; dog 15.00; extra car 30.00.
-- Credit cards accepted.

Open:
Easter - 31 October.

Address:
47160 Villefranche du Queyran.

Tel:
(0)5.53.88.72.43.
FAX: (0)5.53.88.06.52.
E-mail: campech@ fr.packardbell.org.

Reservations:
Recommended for July/Aug; contact site

Book this site
01892 559898
THE ALAN ROGERS'
travel service

Directions: Take A10 south to Bordeaux. Join A62 for Toulouse and take exit 6 for Damazan. Follow D8 to Mont de Marsan, at Cap du Bosc turn right onto D11 for Casteljaloux. The site is 10 km on the right and signed.

4703 Castel Camping Château de Fonrives, Rives, Villeréal

Neat, orderly site with swimming pool, in southwest of the Dordogne.

This is one of those very pleasant Dordogne sites set in pretty part-farmed, part-wooded countryside close to the delightful old town of Villeréal. The park is a mixture of hazelnut orchards, woodland with lake, château (mostly 16th century) and camping areas. An attractive entrance avenue leads to the barns adjacent to the château which have been tastefully converted (the restaurant particularly so) to house the reception, bar, B&B rooms, shop and games areas. The swimming pool (no bermuda style shorts) is on the south side of this. There are 200 pitches, 140 for touring units. Of 100-150 sq.m, all have electricity (4, 6 or 10A) and 60 have water taps also. Pitches near the woodland receive moderate shade, but elsewhere there is light shade from hedges and young trees. Some 'wild' camping is possible in one or two areas. The two main sanitary units are clean and adequate with free hot water, push-button showers, washbasins in well appointed private cabins and British style WCs. There are also some private bathrooms (for hire by the week), facilities for children and babies, laundry rooms, chemical disposal and motorcaravan services. The lake can be used for fishing or boating. A small field is set aside by the pool for volleyball and football. Other activities include children's play areas, a paddling pool and trampolines, a reading room, minigolf and bicycle hire. There is a shop, and elegant restaurant, plus takeaway meals, a bar and snacks (all 10/6-10/9). Plenty of activities are organised for children and adults in season, including excursions and walks. Riding 8 km. Caravan storage available. Mobile homes, bungalows and chalets in the wood for hire.

Directions: Site is about 2 km. northwest of Villeréal, on the Bergerac road (D14/D207).

Charges 2000: -- Per unit incl. 2 adults Ffr. 86.00 - 135.00; extra person 25.00 - 33.00; child (under 7 yrs) 15.00 - 20.00; electricity 4A 18.00, 6A 20.00, 10A 25.00; dog 10.00; private bathroom 350 per week. -- Credit cards accepted.

Open: 8 May - 18 September.

Address: 47210 Rives.

Tel: (0)5.53.36.63.38. FAX: (0)5.53.36.09.98. E-mail: chateau.de.fonrives@wanadoo.fr.

Reservations: Advisable for July/Aug.

 Book this site 01892 559898

THE ALAN ROGERS' travel service

Book your site with the experts Call for an instant quote **01892 55 98 98**

 Low cost ferries guaranteed!

LIMOUSIN / AUVERGNE

We have combined two of the French official regions for our Tourist region:

LIMOUSIN

Major cities: Limoges, Brive-la-Gaillarde

Départements: 19 Corrèze
23 Creuse, 87 Haute-Vienne

AUVERGNE

Major city: Clermont-Ferrand

Départements: 03 Allier, 15 Cantal
43 Haute-Loire, 63 Puy-de-Dôme

We have also included département **48 Lozere** which is actually part
of the offical French region of **MIDI-PYRENEES**

Limousin is an unspoilt, thinly populated region on the western side
of the Massif Central. With hills and gorges and lush green
meadows grazed on by the Limousin breed of cattle,
numerous ancient village churches dot the
landscape as well as more imposing abbey
churches and fortresses. Its moorland has made
the region popular with horse breeders. The
Anglo-Arab horse originated from the famous
studs at Pompadour. The city of Limoges, synonymous
with porcelain, produced the finest painted enamelware
of Europe in the 16th and 17th centuries and today
remains the porcelain capital of France, and Aubusson is
known for beautiful and intricate tapestries.

The Auvergne, set in the heart of the Massif Central, is a
dramatic region of awe-inspiring non-active volcanoes,
lakes, rivers and forests. It is a wonderful destination for
nature lovers, those who enjoy active outdoor pursuits or for people who want to 'take the
waters' at the spa resorts. The 'Parc Naturel Régional des Volcans d'Auvergne' – the
Auvergne Volcano Park – is the largest natural park in France and is a protected environment
for exceptional flora and fauna. An area once fairly isolated and inward looking, it is now
realising its potential as a holiday area.

Note: site reports are laid out by département in numerical order not by region.
See map on page 316.

Cuisine of the region

Limousin is known for a soup called 'bréjaude', eaten with rye bread, and so thick with
cabbage and other vegetables that a spoon will stand up in it. Also for traditional dishes
which include a varity of stews such as potée, cassoulet, beans and pork and sauced dishes
accompanied by chestnuts or rye pancakes.

The beef (Limousin) of the region is extremely tender and full of flavour

Desserts include thick home-made cakes, almond cake of the Creuse, galette Corrézienne

Local specialties in the Auvergne include ham and andouille sausages, stuffed cabbage, and
bacon with lentil and cèpes (mushrooms) and fresh river fish such as trout and pike are much
used

Aligot – purée of potatoes with Tomme de Cantal cheese, cream, garlic and butter

Friand Sanflorin – pork meat and herbs in pastry

Jambon d'Auvergne – a tasty mountain ham

Perdrix à l'Auvergnate – partridge stewed in white wine

Potée Auvergnate – a stew of vegetables, cabbage, pork and sausage

Le Puy is famed for its lentils and Vereine du Velay – yellow and green liqueurs made from
over 30 mountain plants

Places of interest

Aubusson – long tradition of tapestry making, Hotel de Ville tapestry collections

Clermont-Ferrand – old city centre, 11th and 12th century Notre Dame du Port Basilica,13th
century cathedral; known as 'ville noire' for its houses built in local black volcanic rock

Limoges – porcelain, enamel and faience work, château, church of St Michel-de-Lions,
cathedral of St Etienne

Vichy – spa, natural spring park, seat of the collaborationist government in 1940

LIMOUSIN / AUVERGNE - 03 Allier

0301 Camping de la Filature, Ebreuil

Small peaceful riverside site with a difference.

Situated near the spa town of Vichy and bordering the Massif Central area, this site provides the opportunity to explore this lesser known and unspoilt area of France known as the Auvergne. Originally developed around a spinning mill (even today the hot water is provided by log burning - note the chimney), the rural setting is home to peacocks and some free range poultry and has an individuality not normally evident in French sites which is being perpetuated by its English owners. The site lies beside the River Sioule and there are 80 spacious, grassy pitches, some with shade from mature fruit trees. All the pitches can be supplied with electricity (3/6A). The sanitary facilities, with brightly painted doors, are housed in the original buildings, all with external access opening into an alley . They provide free hot water, mostly British type toilets, showers, a bathroom, wash cabins, plus chemical disposal, a washing machine and ironing facilities. River bathing alongside the site is possible (although it may be a little shallow at the height of the summer) and there are fishing facilities. The area is good for bird-watching and botany, ideal for cycling and walking. Riding, canoeing and tennis nearby. Bread can be ordered. Excellent takeaway food (traditional French cooking or straightforward English) and bar (both 1/5-30/9). There are barbecue facilities on site and a weekly barbecue is organised in high season. Activities include minigolf, table football, table tennis and children's play area. Mobile homes for hire (details from site).

Directions: Site signed at exit 12 of A71 autoroute to Clermont Ferrand in the direction of Ebreuil. Site is west of Ebreuil beside the river, 6 km. from the A71 and beside the D915 towards the Chouvigny gorges. It is well signed.

Charges 2001:
-- Per unit incl. 2 persons Ffr. 85.00; extra adult 25.00; child (under 16 yrs) 12.00; extra car 20.00; electricity 3A 10.00, 6A 18.00.
-- Low season reductions (10-50%) and 'meals included' arrangements.
-- Credit cards accepted.

Open:
31 March - 1 October.

Address:
03450 Ebreuil.

Tel:
(0)4.70.90.72.01.
FAX: (0)4.70.90.79.48.
E-mail: john.shaw @libertysurf.fr.

Reservations:
Made with deposit (Ffr 200 or 30 per week of stay or full amount if stay costs less). Credit card bookings accepted (English staff).

Don't wait to die to go to heaven, come to:

CAMPING DE LA FILATURE DE LA SIOULE

03450 EBREUIL, FRANCE

Tel: 0033 (0)4 70 90 72 01 Fax: 0033 (0)4 70 90 79 48

- Very clean facilities and a bathroom
- Really hot water • Excellent take away with pizza and barbecue evenings in high season • Bar and terrace
- Low season bargains for long stays
- Children up to 16 charged child rate
- Near to exit 12 of A71 for stopover or long stay

See us on website www.campingfilature.com

0306 Camping Deneuvre, Châtel de Neuvre

Quiet, riverside site, ideal for water lovers.

Anyone looking for a quiet, unsophisticated family site need look no further. Situated on the banks of the Allier and alongside a nature reserve makes this the ideal spot for both bird-watchers and water lovers alike. The site hires out canoes and takes parties of canoeists on the river, but the fish are very wily by all accounts and are not easily caught. What a challenge! The 75 pitches are about 80 sq.m. with some a little larger, and all are on grass. The ones overlooking the river are naturally the most popular. There is little shade as yet and 52 pitches have electricity (4A). The unisex toilet blocks are tiled with hot showers, some wash-basins in cabins and British style WCs, a baby room with bath, a good unit for disabled people and chemical disposal. A small pool, table tennis, darts and a play area are provided for the children, but the main attraction in decent weather is messing about on the river. Boules competitions and games for children are organised in July/Aug. and there are bicycles to hire. Riding 8 km, golf 12 km. Reception doubles as the bar and restaurant and a few essential groceries can also be bought there. English is spoken by the Dutch family owners.

Directions: Site is at northern end of Châtel de Neuvre on RN9 Moulins - St Pourcain road, signed from the main road. Site is 500 m.

Charges 2000:
-- Per person Ffr. 18.00 - 22.00; child (2-10 yrs) 11.00 - 15.00; pitch 18.00 - 22.00, first night 25.00 - 27.00; dog 6.00; electricity (4A) 14.00.
-- No credit cards.

Open:
1 April - 1 October.

Address:
Les Graves RN9, 03500 Châtel de Neuvre.

Tel:
(0)4.70.42.04.51.
FAX: as phone:
E-mail: camping-deneuvre@wanadoo.fr.

Reservations:
Made with Ffr. 300 deposit.

0305 Camping-Caravaning La Petite Valette, Sazeret, Montmarault

Attractive, neat and tidy site with good facilities.

Originally a working farm, La Petite Valette has been transformed in three years by its hard working Dutch and German owners into a very attractive and peaceful campsite. The toilet facilities are housed in original outbuildings, each block having good modern fittings, tiling, free hot water, chemical disposal, a large separate room with full facilities for disabled people and a new laundry. There are 55 level grassy pitches each with an electricity point (6A) and separated by new bushes and trees. There are only a few old trees so, as yet, there is little shade. A small fenced play area with a seat and 'brolly' for Mum will keep the toddlers happy, whilst older children have table tennis in one of the barns, mountain bike hire and organised activities in July/Aug. There is a small lake in one of the lower fields stocked with fish for anglers. Ponies and small livestock (rabbits, chickens and ducks) keep the farm feeling alive. There is no shop but bread can be ordered. Meals and snacks are served all day in the farmhouse restaurant, also at outside tables in the cottage garden which overflows with flowers. A small swimming pool has been added with a tiled sunbathing area alongside. Two chalets for hire. Montmarault is only 4 km. for your shopping needs and you will find tennis, riding and sailing in the area.

Charges guide:
-- Per adult Ffr. 22.00; child (0-8 yrs) 15.00; pitch 42.50; motor-caravan plus 19.50; dog 9.00; electricity (6A) 16.00.
-- For one night stay 9/7-27/8, plus 10%.

Open:
1 April - 30 October.

Address:
Sazeret,
03390 Montmarault.

Tel:
(0)4.70.07.64.57.
FAX: (0)4.70.07.25.48.
E-mail: la.petite.valette
@wanadoo.fr.

Reservations:
Essential for July/Aug. and made with 50% deposit.

Directions: From N145 Montmarault - Moulins road, turn right at first roundabout on D46 signed St Pourcain. Left at next roundabout on minor road signed Deux-Chaises and La Valette. After 2.5 km. left at site sign and site is approx. 1 km.

0320M Camping Municipal du Lac, Neris Les Bains

This is a modern site on the edge of a very attractive, small spa town. Offering a total of 150 mainly flat, grassy pitches, all with 10A electrical connections, this site is actually a combination of two smaller sites. Situated within walking distance of the centre of the town, it is on two levels alongside a small lake and is pleasantly laid out with pitches mainly in small bays. The three sanitary blocks, of modern purpose-built construction are of a generally good standard which varies slightly from block to block. They provide mostly British type WCs, hot showers with dividers, hooks, etc., washbasins in cabins, washing machine and dryer. Although close to the town's many and varied facilities, the site has its own attractive bar with snacks and restaurant, beside a stream which runs through the lower part of the site. Chalets to rent.

Charges guide:
-- Per unit incl. electricity and 1 person Ffr. 53.50; double axle unit 100.00; extra person 20.40; child (4-10 yrs) 10.20; dog 6.70; local tax 2.20.

Open:
11 April - 24 October.

Address:
Avenue Marx-Dormoy,
03310 Neris Les Bains.

Tel:
(0)4.70.03.17.69 or
(0)4.70.03.24.70.

Reservations:
Contact site for details.

Directions: Site is 500 m. from the RN144, signed in the town centre.

0304 Camping Champ de la Chapelle, Braize, St Bonnet Troncais

Very quiet, rural site with large pitches in the 10,500 hectare Forest of Troncais.

This small site is the perfect answer for those who want to get away from it all. With only 80 pitches set in 5.6 hectares, they are large (up to 250 sq.m.) with plenty of shade and open space. It is the policy of the owner to keep the site small, quiet and unsophisticated. The reward is the wealth of wild life - you may see red squirrels, deer, bee-eaters or hoopoes. Of the 80 pitches, 62 have electricity (16A) and water. The sanitary block is modern and well appointed with British style toilets, washbasins in cabins, pre-set, push-button type showers, and low toilets for children. Dishwashing facilities are good and there is a washing machine and dryer. There is a small snack kiosk. Bread is sometimes available but there is no shop - nearest supermarket is 5 km. at St Bonnet. Facilities include a small pool (from 15/5), children's play area and courts for volleyball, flip-ball and petanque. There are many lakes in the area - one at 5 km. offers fishing, bathing, pedaloes, canoes, sail-boarding, minigolf, volleyball, tennis and, in high season, organised rambles every day. At 6 km. there is riding and archery and the whole area is a paradise for nature lovers, cyclists and walkers. The museum at nearby St Armand-Montrond traces 100,000 years of local history and at Ainay-le-Viel you can visit 'Little Carcassone'. Mobile home and caravan for rent.

Charges 2001:
-- Per unit incl. 1 person Ffr. 46.00; extra person over 5 yrs 16.00, under 5 yrs 7.00; pet 5.00; electricity 16.00.
-- No credit cards.

Open:
14 April - 16 September.

Address:
Braize, 03360 St Bonnet Troncais.

Tel:
(0)4.70.06.15.45.
FAX: (0)4.70.06.54.44.
E-mail: ccdlp@aol.com.

Reservations:
Any period with deposit (Ffr. 600) and fee (60).

Book this site
01892 559898

THE ALAN ROGERS'
travel service

Directions: From N144 Bourges-Montlucon road take D978A east and at round-about take D28 signed Braize. Site signed in 3 km. on right with sign for church and campsite. Follow site signs for 3 km. (single track with passing places).

LIMOUSIN / AUVERGNE - 03 Allier / 15 Cantal

0302 Castel Camping Château de Chazeuil, Varennes sur Allier

Convenient night-stop in central France, adjacent to main road.

Set amongst parkland, this site is located on level lawns in front of the château. The 60 marked pitches all have electricity (6A), with many mature trees providing shade.The facilities are very adequate, the modern sanitary block providing showers, British style WCs and washbasins in cabins, and it is maintained to a satisfactory level. There is a children's play area, table tennis and a reading room. The secluded unheated swimming pool is a short walk from the main site. Although adjacent to the main N7, traffic noise should be no problem and the site provides a pleasantly relaxing night stop. A one-way road system operates to ensure a safe exit from the site.

Directions: Site is on the eastern side of the main N7, 25 km south of Moulins, almost opposite the D46 turning for St Pourcain.

Charges 2000:
-- Per person Ffr. 28.00; child (under 7 yrs) 18.00; pitch 25.00; car 18.00; m/cycle 11.00; electricity 18.00; animal 7.00.
-- Credit cards accepted.

Open:
15 April - 15 October.

Address:
03150 Varennes-sur-Allier.

Tel/Fax:
(0)4.70.45.00.10.

Reservations:
Made for min. 3 days with Ffr. 300 deposit.

0317M Camping Municipal, Dompierre-sur-Besbre

A popular little site with a cosmopolitan clientele, this very attractive, floral site has large, individually hedged, grassy pitches. It is located adjacent to the municipal sports fields, and within easy walking distance of the town centre and supermarket (700 m). There are 70 pitches with only a few long stay units, leaving about 65 for tourists; 60 have electricity (10A) and most have full service facilities. The warden is very proud of his site, and the sanitary unit is kept very clean. It provides push-button hot showers, washbasins (some in curtained cubicles for ladies), with Turkish and British style WCs, dishwashing and laundry sinks plus a washing machine. Motorcaravan service point. The Vallée de la Besbre has a wealth of activities, with tennis and a swimming pool close by, the Canal Latéral de la Loire for boating, several 'plan d'eau' in local villages for fishing, cycle tracks and footpaths, and several equestrian centres. Do visit the nearby vertical boat lift on the canal, and the rose gardens in the adjacent park.

Directions: Site is southeast of town centre just before the junction of N79 and D55.

Charges guide:
-- Per adult Ffr. 11.00; child (5-14 yrs) 5.50; pitch 4.50; car 4.50; motorcaravan 6.00; electricity 10.00.

Open:
1 May - 30 September.

Address:
03290 Dompierre-sur-Besbre.

Tel:
(0)4.70.34.55.57.

Reservations:
Advised for high season, contact site.

N1502 Domaine Naturiste de la Taillade, Neuvéglise

Delightful naturist site in superb Cantal surroundings.

In the words of the jovial and enthusiastic owner, Noel Brun, 'this is a site where comfort comes second to activities'. This may be partly true, as the activities are very important, but we spent a very comfortable 36 hours here doing very little! Approached along a very minor road through beautiful countryside, this is a superbly situated site, with wonderful views across the Auvergne landscape and part of the Gorges de la Truyère. For such a rural site it is surprisingly large, with 120 reasonably flat pitches, of variable size, on several terraces, many of which enjoy the views. A fair number have electrical connections. Facilities include an attractive swimming pool with sunbathing area, small epicerie for basics and a snack bar - the epicerie and snack bar only open when the owner is ready! Sanitary facilities are in three small blocks, one of which is of the 'portacabin' variety. These are fairly basic, but provide all the essentials, with typically naturist open showers as well as traditional, private (hot) indoor ones, some British style WCs, washbasins, washing up sinks (both H&C), etc. For those looking for a countryside hide-away with a range of activities, from the energetic (eg. canoeing or sailing in the lake, fishing, hill walking, riding, rock climbing) to studying the flora and fauna, this site has a lot to offer. In particular it may appeal to the first time naturist as, although the campsite itself is naturist, the activities take place mainly in the non-naturist surrounding countryside. Chalets to let (10).

Directions: Site is signed to right from D921 (St Flour - Chaudeaigues) on bad bend just before Pont de Lanau at Hotel Bélvèdere. Pass Camping Bélvèdere and take small, unclassified road through hamlet of Gros. Follow site signs very carefully for about 5 km. to site.

Charges 2000:
-- Ffr: per pitch incl. 2 persons Ffr. 100.00; extra person (over 3 yrs) 18.00.
-- Euro: per pitch incl. 2 persons 15,24; extra person (over 3 yrs) 1,52.
-- Less 10% for stays over 10 days.
-- No credit cards.

Open:
1 July - 31 August.

Address:
15260 Neuvéglise.

Tel:
(0)4.71.23.80.13.
FAX: (0)4.71.23.86.94.

Reservations:
Advised from mid-July. and made with Ffr. 500 (76.22) deposit.

1901 Camping Intercommunal de l'Abeille, Merlines, nr Ussel

Pleasant site for a short halt between Clermont-Ferrand and Brive.

L'Abeille is in the grounds of and part of a 'village de vacances' complex. Most of the 75 pitches are over 100 sq.m, the 49 with electric hook-up (6A) being the largest and also having hedges to separate them. Long leads may be needed for some hook-ups. All pitches are numbered, some are gravel and some grass. The two modern small toilet blocks are well appointed and tiled throughout. They have British style WCs, washbasins in cubicles and really large showers. There are washing machines in each block, a dryer in one, and both blocks have dish and clothes washing sinks. There are children's play areas dotted about the complex and in season games and competitions are organised for both adults and children. The new manager was happy to point out that all the facilities of the Village are available to campers. The bar and restaurant have been refurbished and there is a very pleasant swimming pool and sunbathing area. There is a charge for the gymnasium and jacuzzi, and also for the hire of bicycles, pedaloes and boats, but tennis is free. Details about riding and fishing permits are at reception. There is no shop on site but the village for bread is only 500 m. and there is a supermarket at Bourg-Lastic (5 km).

Directions: Site is signed on the eastern edge of the village of Merlines which is 20 km. northeast of Ussel on the N89 road.

Charges guide:
-- Per pitch incl. 4 persons Ffr. 65.00 - 85.00; extra adult 18.00 - 21.00; child (over 7 yrs) 10.00 - 11.00; electricity 16.00; pet 16.00.
Open:
7 June - 13 September.
Tel:
(0)5.55.94.31.39.
FAX: (0)5.55.94.41.98.
Reservations:
Write to Village VAL 'L'Abeille', 19340 Eygurande or phone (0)4.73.43.00.43 (head office in Clermont-Ferrand) or site in season. Probably easiest just to turn up.

1903 Camping La Plage, Treignac sur Vézère

Well maintained, terraced site overlooking lake.

Carved out of the wooded hillside, Camping La Plage sits alongside Lac Variousses and the D940 road. Mature trees provide a filigree of sunlight and shade on the four terraces which overlook the lake. The 130 pitches are numbered and separated, all with electricity connections (8A). The two sanitary blocks can be heated and afford very satisfactory facilities including British style WCs, washbasins in cabins and push-button showers with dividers. Dishwashing and laundry sinks, a washing machine, chemical disposal and motorcaravan services are all provided. A small shop, combined with a reception area, provides essentials although bread is only available in July/Aug. A library of English and French books is an interesting feature and a TV/games room is adjacent. An underpass leads to the attractive sandy beach beside the lake where bathing is safe with permitted areas well marked. A largely new children's play area is situated here. Pedaloes, canoes, etc. may be hired. Fourteen walks have been planned from the site and copies of these are available from reception. A children's club is organised (4-10 yrs). Riding 5 km, bicycle hire 3 km. Sailing near. Mobile homes to rent.

Directions: From A20 take exit for Uzerche and Treignac. Site is 3 km. north of Treignac on D940 beside Lac Vamousses.

Charges 2001:
-- Per pitch Ffr. 24.00 - 27.00; person 22.00 - 25.00; child (4-10 yrs) free - 15.00; dog 8.00; electricity 15.00.
-- Credit cards accepted.
Open:
1 April - 30 September.
Address:
19260 Treignac.
Tel:
(0)5.55.98.08.54.
FAX: (0)5.55.98.16.47.
E-mail: la-plage-treignac @wanadoo.fr.
Reservations:
Made with deposit (Ffr 200); contact site.

1905 Camping La Rivière, Donzenac

Former municipal site on outskirts of attractive small town.

The Corrèze is not nearly as well known as the Dordogne to the immediate south, but it is, in fact, a beautiful area, deserving of more attention. Donzenac itself is an attractive small town with a variety of shops, restaurants, etc. This former municipal site is situated on the outskirts, somewhat less than a mile from the centre (an uphill walk). It is quite small with 77 fairly large pitches on level grass, the majority with electricity and many with shade from tall trees. It is next door to the town tennis courts and swimming pool (July/Aug. only; free to campers). On site are a children's play area, table tennis, boules, minigolf and a small takeaway. Fishing and bicycle hire on site, riding 4 km, golf 10 km. Other facilities are all close by in the town and a baker calls at the site in July/Aug. The sanitary facilities which have been modernised and are very good, include a laundry room and chemical disposal facilities. Chalets to rent.

Directions: Site is signed 'Village de Vacances', off the D920 at the bottom of the hill 2 km. south of Donzenac (7 km. north of Brive).

Charges 2001:
-- Per person Ffr. 22.00 - 25.00; pitch 24.00 - 27.00; electricity (5A) 15.00; dog 8.00.
-- Credit cards accepted.
Open:
1 April - 30 September.
Address:
Route de Brive, 19270 Donzenac.
Tel:
(0)5.55.85.63.95.
FAX: as phone.
Reservations:
Probably unnecessary, but if in doubt telephone.

LIMOUSIN / AUVERGNE - 23 Creuse

2301 Castel Camping Le Château de Poinsouze, Boussac-Bourg

Well designed, high quality site, set in a beautiful château parkland.

Le Château de Poinsouze is a recently developed site with 102 pitches arranged on the open, gently sloping, grassy park to one side of the château's main drive - a beautiful plane tree avenue. The 94 touring pitches, some with lake frontage, all have electricity (6, 10 or 16A), with water, waste water and sewage connections to many. A high quality, double glazed sanitary unit is entered via a large utility area equipped with dishwashing and laundry sinks, foot-pedal operated taps, sinks accessible for wheelchair users, a drinks machine, and two smaller rooms with washing machines, dryer and ironing. Four spacious rooms house British WCs, washbasins (some in cubicles), and roomy showers. There are soap and seat cover dispensers, paper towels or hand dryers, hairdryers, and plenty of hooks, mirrors, lights and sockets. Baby baths, changing mats and child's WC, and two suites for disabled people are provided. Hot water is free throughout. The fenced children's playground has been designed with safety in mind - slides set into grassy banking, and a variety of nets, towers and swings. Behind reception is a good motorcaravan service point and car wash. The château (not open to the public) lies across the lake from the site and the exceptionally well restored outbuildings on the opposite side of the drive house a new restaurant, well stocked shop, takeaway, and a comfortable bar with games and TV and library room above. These surround the attractively designed, well fenced swimming pool with slide, children's pool and terrace, and are within an easy stroll of the camping area. Children wear colour coded bracelets (deposit required) for the pool. Other amenities include table tennis, petanque, pool table and table football games, bicycle hire, free fishing in the lake (if you put the fish back); boats and lifejackets can also be hired. The site has a friendly family atmosphere, there are organised activities in main season including dances, children's games and crafts, family triathlons, and there are marked walks around the park and woods. A large area is set aside for football, volleyball, basketball, badminton and other games. Dogs are not accepted in high season (6/7-21/8). All facilities open all season, though times may vary. Mobile homes and tents for rent. Gîtes to rent all year. This is a top class site with a formula which should ensure a stress-free, enjoyable family holiday. Boussac (2.5 km) has a market every Thursday morning. The massive 12/15th century fortress, Château de Boussac, is open daily all year.

Directions: Site entrance is 2.5 km north of Boussac on D917 (towards La Châtre).

Charges 2001:
-- Per unit incl. 2 persons Ffr. 75.00 - 115.00; pitch with electricity (6A), water, waste water 100.00 - 160.00; pitch with electricity (10A), water, waste water, sewage connection 120.00 - 165.00; extra adult 20.00 - 30.00; child (2-7 yrs) 15.00 - 27.00; extra car or caravan free - 15.00; electricity 10A 15.00, 16A 25.00; dog 15.00 (low and mid-season only).
-- Credit cards accepted.

Open:
18 May - 16 September.

Address:
BP 12,
Route de la Châtre,
23600 Boussac-Bourg.

Tel:
(0)5.55.65.02.21. FAX:
(0)5.55.65.86.49.

E-mail: info.
camping-de.poinsouze
@wanadoo.fr.

Reservations:
Advisable for July/Aug; made with 30% deposit and Ffr 120 fee.

`Camping Cheque'

Book this site
01892 559898

THE ALAN ROGERS'
travel service

see colour advert
between pages 192/193

2305M Camping Municipal du Plan d'Eau de Courtille, Guéret

A small site on gently sloping ground set in a valley beside a lake, about 3 km. from the centre of Guéret itself, this site offers few facilities. However, there is a restaurant within walking distance and it is possible to swim from the small beaches around the lake, also sailing and windsurfing. There are 70 good sized, individual, willow hedged pitches, all slightly sloping and with electricity (3 or 10A). These are arranged in six circular clusters around 2 purpose built sanitary units which provide all Turkish style WCs, washbasins in cubicles, push-button showers, facilities for disabled people, plus dishwashing and laundry sinks. Facilities for swimming, riding, forest walks, cycling and canoeing near.

Directions: Site is well signed from the town centre and is beside the Etang de Courtille, southwest of the town.

Charges guide:
-- Per pitch incl. electricity Ffr. 34.00; person (over 7 yrs) 11.00; child 2-7 yrs 5.00; car 7.00; animal 5.00.

Open:
1 June - 30 September.

Address:
23000 Guéret.

Tel:
(0)5.55.81.92.24 or
(0)5.55.52.99.50 (high season).

Reservations:
Probably unnecessary but are made - details from site.

4303 Camping-Caravaning du Vaubarlet, Sainte-Sigolène

Spacious riverside site in beautiful location, with swimming pool.

This peacefully located, family site has 130 marked, level, grassy and open pitches, with perimeter shade and electricity (6A). With 109 pitches for tourists, the remainder are occupied by site owned rental tents or mobile homes. Those who really like to get away from it all can use a small `wild camping' area on the opposite side of the river with its own very basic sanitary unit and campers' kitchen with cooker. This area is reached either by footbridge or separate road access. The main site is served by two sanitary units with British and Turkish style WCs, showers (pre-mixed), washbasins (some for ladies in cubicles), baby room, laundry with washing machine and dryer and dishwashing sinks. Two family bath-rooms (WC, basin, shower) to the rear of the bar, are also suitable for disabled people. Hot water is free. Small shop, bread can be ordered. Takeaway in main season. Two supermarkets (7 days per week) in Ste Sigolène (6 km). The main site is separated from the river (unfenced) by a large field which has the playground, motocross track, volleyball net and space for ball games. Organised activities in the main season include camp fire and music evenings, canoeing lessons for children, pony riding and mini-motorbike motocross. Other facilities include a fenced swimming pool with children's pool, bicycle hire, table tennis, boules, trout fishing (licenses available), birdwatching and walking. This is an attractive site for those seeking a quieter late break in September. It can be warm and sunny with the swimming pool, rooftop sun-deck, delightful modern bar with covered terrace all open. Golfing devotees can be directed to any one of three challenging courses in the area. Tourist attractions in and around the region include a textile museum in Ste Sigolène, an `escargot' farm in nearby Grazac, the stunning scenery, chateaux and churches of the Haute-Loire, and the annual medieval festival in Le Puy each September. A Sites et Paysages member.

Charges guide:
-- Per unit incl. 2 persons Ffr. 80.00; extra adult 20.00; child (2-7 yrs) 10.00; electricity 15.00.
-- Less 10% outside July/Aug.

Open:
1 May - 30 September.

Address:
43600 Sainte-Sigolène.

Tel:
(0)4.71.66.64.95.
FAX: (0)4.71.75.04.04.

Reservations:
Advised for high season and made with 25% deposit and Ffr. 130 fee.

**Book this site
01892 559898**

THE ALAN ROGERS'
travel service

Directions: Site is 6 km. southwest of Ste Sigolène on the D43.

4301 Camping La Fressange, St Didier en Velay

Pretty site in rolling Haute-Loire countryside, with swimming pool.

This site is worth considering as a base for touring this area or as a night-stop to visit St Didier. It has the advantage of being situated some 2 km from the town centre, opposite the municipal swimming pool complex, which includes one pool of Olympic size (open mid-June for the main season only) and tennis courts. This sheltered site is attractively laid out on a series of grassy terraces - despite this, many pitches are on quite a slope and are difficult for motorcaravans. The 100 or so pitches (some occupied by long stay units) all have electricity (5A). There is some shade from the trees that border the site and some from smaller trees within it. Two modern sanitary blocks include showers with dividers, British type WCs, washbasins in cabins (warm water), dishwashing sinks, washing machine, facilities for disabled visitors, but no proper chemical disposal point. There are no tour operators and the site is extensively used by the French. Apart from a small children's playground, there are few other facilities, but the site is only 5-10 minutes walk from the town. Fishing, tennis 200 m. Barrier card deposit Ffr. 200.

Charges guide:
-- Per adult Ffr. 14.00; child (2-7 yrs) 7.00; pitch 11.00; vehicle 10.00; electricity 15.00; local tax 1.50; dog 4.00.

Open:
1 May - 30 September.

Address:
43140 St Didier en Velay.

Tel:
(0)4.71.66.25.28 or (0)4.73.34.75.53.

Reservations:
Advised in high season - contact site.

Directions: Site is signed from the N88 via La Séauve, southwest of Semène. Alternatively from Firminy, southwest of St Etienne, take the D500 to St Didier.

4311M Camping Municipal Les Prades, La Chaise-Dieu

This very attractive municipal site is 1.5 km. north of the town, situated in pleasant countryside next to woodland and a lake with public footpaths adjacent. The site provides 100 pitches, some with electricity (10A), arranged on well cut grass which is landscaped with numerous pine trees (mature and with character) and tarmac roads. All is well tended and rather park-like. Two modern sanitary blocks have washbasins in cubicles, toilets (Turkish type for men) and plenty of hot water; finding a cold water tap is a different matter. Only one block is open in low season. Children's play area. Fishing and windsurfing facilities near. A spacious and well run site, the guardian Mme. Delorme, lives on site.

Charges guide:
-- Per person Ffr. 18.00; child (under 7) 12.00; pitch 18.00; electricity 18.00; local tax 1.00.

Open:
1 June - 30 September.

Address:
43160 La Chaise-Dieu.

Tel:
(0)4.71.00.07.88 or (0)4.71.00.03.64.

Reservations:
Advised - contact site.

Directions: La Chaise-Dieu is approx. 40 km. north of Le Puy on the D906. Site is signed 1.5 km. north of the town.

187

LIMOUSIN / AUVERGNE - 43 Haute-Loire / 48 Lozère

4302 Camping Bouthezard, Le Puy-en-Velay

Well run site with good facilities, and an aire de service for motorcaravans.

Once a municipal campsite, Bouthezard has been under private management since 1991. It has a good security barrier, a warden who lives on site, tarmac roads and around 70 grassy pitches with 6A electricity. The main sanitary unit, recently refurbished and extended, is well equipped with British style WCs, washbasins (some in cubicles), push-button hot showers, facilities for disabled persons, dishwashing and laundry sinks. An older unit at the rear of the site is only used in peak season. A 'salle' by reception has tourist information and a TV set, and there is table tennis, boule, volleyball and badminton. The motorcaravan service point is adjacent with its own security barrier - apply to campsite reception for a barrier key to use the services, or for an overnight stop (reception open 08.00-21.00). The town of Le Puy with its historic sector is within walking distance and is well worth the effort. The Office de Tourisme is on the southern side in Place du Breuil.

Directions: Site lies NW of town centre, close to where N102 crosses the River Borne, and the Rocher St. Michel d'Aiguilhe (a church on a rocky pinnacle). Site is well signed from around the town.

Charges 2000:
-- Per unit incl. 2 persons Ffr. 46.00, 4 persons 60.00; adult 14.00; child (2-10 yrs) 7.00; tent 14.00; caravan 16.50; car 9.50; motorcaravan 21.50; m/cycle 8.50; electricity 18.00; local tax 2.00.
-- Aire de service Ffr. 33.00 + 2.00 p/person p/night. Services only Ffr. 17.00.
-- No credit cards.

Open:
Mid-April - 15 October.

Address:
Avenue d'Aiguilhe, 43000 Le Puy-en-Velay.

Tel:
(0)4.71.09.55.09.

Reservations:
Contact site for details.

4800 Camping-Caravaning Le Champ d'Ayres, Meyrueis

Quiet, neat site for young families and couples, amongst wonderful scenery.

The road to Meyrueis is not for the fainthearted, although we managed in quite a large motorhome, with only a few stretches being a little on the narrow side, and the return seemed even easier. This is a traditionally French style site with a modern feel to it, set in the heart of the Cevennes. Le Champ d'Ayres is very neat, tidy and well kept, run by a young family with young families in mind (teenagers might be bored). The site is slightly sloping with 70 grass pitches, the majority hedged with well trimmed bushes and most with some shade. All have electricity (6/10A) but may require long leads. The sanitary block is central and kept exceptionally clean. It provides mainly British style WCs, pre-set showers and some washbasins in cabins; there is also a family sized shower room, a room with facilities for disabled visitors, baby room, chemical disposal, laundry and dishwashing sinks, plus a washing machine and dryer. In a sunny location, the swimming and paddling pools have tiled sunbathing surrounds (open 25/5-15/9). Reception is at the entrance and incorporates a small bar (1/6-15/9) which also sells ices and bread. There is a play area on grass for 5-10 yr olds, a small games room, table tennis, basketball, netball and a boules pitch. In July/Aug. various activities are arranged for children, as well as family activities such as walking and caving. The area is surrounded by mountains and gorges but the river Jonte is not a canoeing river so a trip to the Tarn would be needed for that. The Gorges de Jonte has an observatory from which vultures can be observed flying the thermals. Being very central there are many attractions in the area - wild horses have been introduced on the causses a few miles to the north, the observatory at the top of Mt Aigoual is well worth a visit and there are many caves in the region. The pretty small town of Meyrueis has many good restaurants. Cabins and mobile homes to hire.

Directions: From N9 at Aquessac (5 km. north of Millau) take D907 signed Gorge du Tarn. At Rozier turn right on D996 signed Meyrueis and Gorges de la Jonte. In Meyrueis follow signs for Château d'Ayres and campsite signs. Site is 500 m.

Charges 2000:
-- Per unit incl. 2 persons Ffr. 60.00 - 84.00; extra person 14.00 - 21.00; child (under 7 yrs) 10.00 - 14.00; electricity (6A) 15.00; local tax (15/6-15/9) 1.50.

Open:
1 April - 30 September.

Address:
48150 Meyrueis.

Tel:
(0)4.66.45.60.51. FAX: as phone.

Reservations:
Contact site for details.

For a list of sites which are open all year - see page 262

188

6304 Château Camping de Grange Fort, Les Pradeaux, Issoire

Good site with modern facilities but plenty of character.

This site has good modern facilities, yet is oozing with character. The 15th century castle is impressive, more British in style than the usual French château. Reception is small but has tourist information, plus a few groceries (bread to order), and the Dutch owners at this very popular site are welcoming. The main toilet facilities have been created in the old stable buildings and are modern, heated and fully tiled. Both ladies' and men's have baby rooms, the men's also has facilities for disabled visitors and a `hydra shower' (Ffr 10). A laundry has washing machines, dryer and iron, hot water is free throughout and there is a chemical disposal point. The bar (1/6-15/9) has a takeaway and a games room and the old stable stalls and hay racks have been left in place. An indoor pool has sliding glass doors and a sauna and massage table (15/4-15/10). The restaurant in the castle, originally the kitchen and dining hall, also has great atmosphere and B&B is offered. The 120 pitches are of average size on grass, connected by rather narrow roads. Some are in sunny fields around the castle, others in bays with hedges and trees and all with 4A hook-ups. Two outdoor pools (15/6-1/10) have grassy sunbathing areas. Tennis, minigolf, table tennis, volleyball, football field, boules and a children's play area, plus walks in the extensive grounds. In season organised activities include archery, canoeing, riding and cycling (horses and bikes provided). Fishing 250 m. Caravan storage.

Directions: From A75 exit 13 at Issoire, go east on D996 to Parentignat. In village turn right (D999). After 200 m. right again on D34 signed Nonette. Site is 3 km.

Charges 2001:
-- Per adult Ffr. 29.00; child (under 7 yrs) 16.50; pitch 45.00; dog 9.00; electricity 16.50.
-- Less in low season.
-- Credit cards accepted.
Open:
1 March - 1 November.
Address:
Les Pradeaux, 63500 Issoire.
Tel:
(0)4.73.71.02.43 or (0)4.73.71.05.93. FAX: (0)4.73.71.07.69. E-mail: chateau@ grangefort.com.
Reservations:
Contact site for details.
`Camping Cheque'

6310M Camping Municipal du Grand Mas, Issoire

This site is located a few hundred metres from exit 12 (Issoire) on the A75 autoroute - there could be some road noise, but it was not intrusive when we visited in late June. The nicely spacious site is on fairly level grass, with most of the 140 pitches arranged in bays of two or four, about half with 6A electrical connections, and having some shade – very welcome in the heat! A useful grassy area beside a lake is immediately opposite the site for sunbathing or picnicking under the trees. The lake is used for fishing and is probably unsuitable for swimming. A sports complex is nearby. The site has a 'salle de reunion' with TV and cold drinks machine, a children's play area, minigolf and table tennis - not much else, but Issoire is only a short drive away and a supermarket is within a longish walk. Sanitary facilities in three blocks, one heated in cool weather, were quite adequate with large hot showers (no dividers), mostly Turkish style WCs and some washbasins in private cabins (H&C), dishwashing and laundry sinks (cold water only) and two washing machines. Not all blocks are open in low season. A recent addition is a good motorcaravan service point.

Directions: Take exit 12 from the A75 towards Orbeil, just beside the autoroute.

Charges guide:
-- Per person Ffr. 14.30; child (under 7 yrs) 7.30; tent 7.30; caravan 9.50; car 7.30; m/cycle 5.00; motorcaravan 16.70; electricity (6A) 10.00.
Open:
1 April - 31 October.
Address:
63500 Issoire.
Tel:
(0)4.73.89.03.59 (or Mairie (0)4.74.89.03.54).
Reservations:
Seldom required and discouraged.

6303 Hotel de Plein Air L'Europe, Murol

Spacious site with pool high in the Auvergne.

This site is just a few minutes from the centre of the village, and only 15 minutes walk over the hill from the delightful Lac Chambon with a sandy beach and watersports. On the site are a swimming pool, water slide and paddling pool, tennis court, a large football field and also a volleyball court at one end of the site, close to one of the three toilet blocks. These blocks are adequate (the supply of hot water may come under pressure at peak times). There are 219 grassy pitches of differing sizes marked out by trees and bushes, with plenty of shade. A small shop sells basics, some local specialities, and bread in the morning. The takeaway food service also operates from the shop, which abuts a bar/restaurant with pool-side terrace. Fishing, bicycle hire or riding within 1 km, golf 10 km. This busy, bustling site is ideal for visits to the southern Auvergne, being only a short drive from St Nectaire, the Puy de Sancy, Le Mont Dore, or the pretty spa town of La Bourboule – you could of course hike, since this is famous walking country, and a number of excursions are organised. Local markets at Murol (Wednesday), Chambon (Friday) and Saint-Nectaire (Sunday). Mobile homes to rent (48).

Directions: From A75 autoroute take exit 6 and drive through St Nectaire and on to Murol. The left turn towards the site is signed in the village.

Charges guide:
-- Per unit incl. 1 person Ffr. 80.00; extra person 25.00; child (under 5 yrs) 19.00; animal 6.00; electricity 3A 19.00, 5A 27.00, 10A 32.00.
-- No credit cards.
Open:
3 June - 2 September.
Address:
Rte de Jassat, 63790 Murol.
Tel:
(0)4.73.88.60.46. or (0)6.08.26.27.02. FAX: (0)4.73.88.69.57.
Reservations:
Made for min. 1 week with 25% deposit.

189

LIMOUSIN / AUVERGNE - 63 Puy-de-Dôme

6305 Camping La Ribeyre, Murol

Picturesque, family run site just outside Murol.

About a kilometre from the centre of Murol, La Ribeyre has a charm about it. The owners, Mme Pommier and her two sons, originally farmers, have put a lot of effort in constructing the site, even the 200 sq.m. heated swimming pool (1/5-1/9). Many young trees have been planted to add to those already on site. A man-made lake at one end provides facilities for swimming, canoeing and surf boarding (lifeguard in July/Aug), while fishing is possible from a nearby stream. There is a picturesque reception area, with a fountain and floral decorations. Six excellent, very clean toilet blocks provide British and Turkish style WCs, washbasins (some in cubicles), good hot showers and chemical disposal. The site provides 400 level, grassy pitches, 300 with electricity (3/6A), 64 with electricity, water and drainage. Although not normally advertised, there are 10A outlets if you ask. There is a TV and games room and a snack bar in peak season (20/6-1/9), plus tennis and volleyball. Bicycle hire 1 km. The surrounding area is very much worth a visit. From mountains rising to over 6,000 ft, to lakes, cavernes and many local craft centres, this site is a superb centre. It is only 5 or 6 km. from St Nectaire, about 10 km. from Besse and the thermal spa town of La Bourboule is also a short drive. The Mont Dore, a starting point for the Puy de Sancy, the highest peak in the area is only a little further. The atmosphere on site is extremely friendly.

Charges 2000:
-- Per unit incl. 1 adult Ffr. 48.00 - 68.00; extra person 19.00 - 27.00; child (under 5 yrs) 14.00 - 20.00; electricity (6A) 20.00 - 25.00; pitch with full services plus 35.00; local tax 2.00 (child 5-16 yrs 1.00).
-- No credit cards.
Open:
1 May - 15 September.
Address:
Route de Jassat, 63790 Murol.
Tel:
(0)4.73.88.64.29.
FAX: (0)4.73.88.68.41.
Reservations:
Contact site.

Directions: From A75 take exit 6, signed St Nectaire and go on to Murol. Turn left and then, opposite Syndicat d'Initiative, turn right. La Ribeyre is the second site along, just after the entrance to Jassat and is well marked on left.

6306 Camping Le Clos Auroy, Orcet, nr Clermont Ferrand

New and popular site close to A75 close to typical Auvergne village.

Orcet is a typical Auvergne village just south of Clermont Ferrand and, being fairly close to the A75, makes an excellent stopping off point on the journey south (the A75 is free of charge from here, southwards to Montpellier). The campsite is only 300 m. from the shops in the village, but has a small shop in high season and a takeaway (both 1/7-15/9). The 90 pitches are on level grass, separated by high hedges, all with electricity (5A), and many fully serviced. Close to reception is a fenced, heated pool (12 x 6 m; 15/5-30/9) and a playground. The two modern sanitary units provide British style WCs, washbasins in cubicles, controllable hot showers, dishwashing and laundry sinks. A smaller unit at reception is heated and used mainly in winter. Chemical disposal is at the motorcaravan service point, close to the entrance (a long walk from some pitches, as is the fresh water tap). Activities include coffee mornings, tennis and boule (50 m), fishing and canoeing (500 m), there are wine 'caves' in the village, a large playground is nearby and a riverside walk is just outside the gate. In winter only 20 pitches are available.

Charges 2001:
-- Per person Ffr. 21.00; child (1-7 yrs) 13.00; pitch 37.00; animal free - 6.00; electricity 15.00 - 22.00; local tax 1.80.
-- No credit cards.
Open:
All year.
Address:
Rue de la Narse, 63670 Orcet.
Tel/Fax:
(0)4.73.84.26.97.
E-mail: camping.le.clos.auroy@wanadoo.fr.
Reservations:
Advised for July/Aug.

Directions: From A75 take exit 4 or 5 towards Orcet and follow campsite signs.

6307 Camping Le Pré Bas, Lac Chambon, nr Murol

Family site in the heart of the Parc des Volcans d'Auvergne.

Almost on the edge of Lake Chambon this site is very suitable for families with younger children and those seeking the watersports that the lake provides. Large, level, grassy pitches are divided up by mature hedging and trees and, with 36 mobile homes for rent, around 144 pitches are available for tourists, all with electricity (4A). One large central sanitary building with four smaller units around the site, provide British style WCs, washbasins (some cubicles), push-button showers, facilities for disabled guests and dishwashing. A building opposite reception houses a laundry and a baby room. Motorcaravan service point. Games room with table tennis, table football, etc, a large 'salle' with giant TV screen, library and a playground. Organised activities in the main season include guided walks, archery and climbing. The well fenced, open air pool complex (10/6-10/9) has three pools and has a lifeguard in July/Aug. At the lower end of the site is a snack bar with a small terrace (10/6-10/9 and some weekends in low season). Close by is a gate leading on to the lakeside, where there is windsurfing, pedaloes, canoes or fishing, and 50 m. away is a beach with supervised bathing.

Charges 2000:
-- Per pitch incl. 2 adults Ffr. 87.00; extra person 24.00; child (1-5 yrs) 12.00; electricity (4A) 18.50; local tax 2.00.
-- Less 30% in May, 20% in June and Sept.
Open:
1 May - 30 September.
Address:
Lac Chambon, 63790 Murol.
Tel/Fax:
(0)4.73.88.63.04.
E-mail: prebas@lac-chambon.com.
Reservations:
Essential for high season, with Ffr. 250 deposit.

Directions: Site is located on D966, 3 km. west of Murol towards Le Mont Dore.

8701M Camping Municipal de Montréal, Saint Germain-les-Belles

Situated on the edge of the town with good views across the small lake, this pleasant municipal site is ideal for an overnight stop or a for a longer stay in the beautiful Limousin countryside between Limoges and Brive. There are 60 tourist pitches, all over 100 sq.m. and separated by well kept hedges, which afford good privacy and views of the lake. They are arranged on two grassy terraces, most with electricity (10A). The modern toilet block is well designed to be quiet and draught free and it is well appointed. Toilets are British style and the washbasins, some communal, some in cabins, have razor points, mirrors and hot water. The showers are controllable (space for dressing, but not partitioned), good facilities for disabled people, dishwashing under cover and laundry sinks, but no washing machine or dryer. A restaurant with terrace and bar overlooks the lake (open to the public) and there is a takeaway service. No shop but the baker calls mornings in July/Aug. and a supermarket, restaurants and a good range of shops are in the town 10 minutes walk away. Leisure facilities are centred on the 5 hectare lake with its 150 m. long sandy beach. A bathing area is marked out by two diving boards, there are pedaloes for hire, fishing, a large children's play area and two tennis courts. The tourist office on site gives updated information to local events.

Charges 2000:
-- Per person Ffr. 13.00; child (under 7 yrs) 8.00; vehicle 7.00; pitch 8.00; electricity 14.00.
-- No credit cards.

Open:
1 April - 30 September.

Address:
87380 St Germain-les-Belles.

Tel:
(0)5.55.71.86.20 or (0)5.55.71.88.65.

Reservations:
Made by phone or letter (letter preferred) to the Tourist Office (address as site); no booking fee.

Directions: From Limoges take A20 south and shortly after Magnac-Bourg (18 km.) take exit 42 onto D7. Continue about 6 km. to St Germain-les-Belles from where the site is well signed on a side road to La Porcherie.

8702 Castel Camping du Château de Leychoisier, Bonnac-la-Côte

Elevated site in the grounds of a château, 10 km north of Limoges.

This large estate offers the opportunity to explore the château grounds and to walk down to the four hectare lake. It is ideally situated only 2 km. from the A20/N20 and 10 km. north of Limoges. There are 90 large grass pitches, some partly sloping with a mixture of sun and shade, and 76 having electrical connections (10A). The partially refurbished sanitary block is housed behind the bureau in an old building. There is a good supply of hot water and the facilities are very clean, but they are rather cramped and need extending and updating to cope with demand at busy times. They include push-button showers, washbasins (some in private cabins) and British style WCs. There is provision for disabled visitors, a washing machine and chemical disposal. Adjacent to the toilet block is a restaurant (from 20/6) with a very pleasant terrace. The snack bar and bar are housed in an open-ended barn, partly protected by a canopy and attractive gazebo. An inviting sun-bathing area surrounds the swimming pool (proper swimming trunks, no shorts). Activities on site include bicycle hire, table tennis, tennis and boules courts (both in need of repair when we visited), volleyball and bar billiards, and there is also a children's play area. The lake provides free fishing, boating, canoeing and a marked off area for swimming. Basic food provisions are sold from reception; bread and croissants must be ordered the night before. Mini-market 2 km, super-market 5 km. Golf 20 km, riding 7 km. Torches are useful. Winter caravan storage. This is a quiet site where you have plenty of space and where there are no letting units and many people like it for these reasons.

Charges 2001:
-- Per pitch Ffr. 44.00 - 52.00; motorcaravan +10.00 - 15.00; person 28.00 - 35.00; child (under 7) 17.00 - 20.00; electricity 21.00; local tax 2.00.
-- No credit cards.

Open:
15 April - 20 September.

Address:
87270 Bonnac-la-Côte.

Tel/Fax:
(0)5.55.39.93.43.
E-mail: leychoisier @wanadoo.fr.

Reservations:
Made with deposit (Ffr. 100) and fee (80), though short bookings accepted without charge in low season.

Book this site
01892 559898
THE ALAN ROGERS'
travel service

Directions: From A20 take exit 27 (west) signed Bonnac-La-Côte. Site is well signed from the village.

RHONE VALLEY

Major city: Lyon
Départements: 01 Ain, 07 Ardèche
26 Drôme, 42 Loire, 69 Rhône

The Rhône Valley is one of Europe's main arteries – this traditional route carries millions of travellers and millions of tons of freight by rail (TGV), by autoroute and by water to the Mediterranean. However, either side of this busy corridor are areas of great interest and natural beauty. From the sun-baked Drôme, with its ever-changing landscapes, culminating in the isolated mountains of the Vercors; the deep gorges and high plateaux of the Ardèche, studded with prehistoric caves to lush valleys filled with orchards and the vineyards of the Beaujolais and the Rhône Valley. The region's 2,000 year 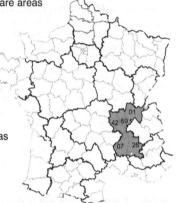 history as a cultural crossroads has blessed the area with a rich blend of customs, architecture and sights of interest. The city of Lyon was developed by the Romans as a trading centre, andwas once the capital. It is now the second largest city of France. Although heavily industrialised, it has a charming old quarter and is renowned for its gastronomy. The Place de la Terreur in the centre of the city is where the guillotine was placed during the French revolution – until it wore out through over-use. There are also reminders of the city's role in World War 2 as a resistance centre. Not far from Lyon lies the Dombes, the 'land of a thousand lakes', the medieval village of Pérouges and the Roman ruins of Vienne with its yearly jazz festival.

Note: the site reports are laid out by département in numerical order not by region.
See map on page 317.

Cuisine of the region

From Lyon to Bresse and Bugey by way of the Dombes, food is an art and a science. The poultry, cheese, freshwater fish, mushrooms and wines are superb

Bresse (Poulet, Poularde, Volaille de) – the best French poultry, fed on corn and when killed bathed in milk; flesh is white and delicate

Gras-double – ox tripe, served with onions

Poulet demi-deuil (half-mourning) – called this because of thin slices of truffle placed under the chicken breast

Poulet au vinaigre – chicken, shallots, tomatoes, white wine, wine vinegar and a cream sauce

Rosette – a large pork sausage

Sabodet – Lyonnais sausage of pig's head, pork and beef, served hot

Wine

Beaujolais, Côte Rotie, St Julien, Condrieu, Tain-Hermitage, Chiroubles and Julienas are some of the wines produced in this region

Places of interest

Beaujolais – vineyards and golden-stone villages

Bourg-en-Bresse – 16th/17th century church of Notre-Dame, craft shops, museum of Ain; also famous for its yellow, corn-fed chickens

Dombes – land of a thousand lakes, ornithological park

Lyon – Gallo-Roman artifacts, Renaissance quarter, historical Fabric Museum, silk museum.

Montélimar – nougat capital of France

Pérouges – lovely medieval village, Galette de Pérouges

St Etienne – museum of Modern Art

Vallon-Pont d'Arc – base from which to visit Gorges de l'Ardèche; canoe and rafting centre

Vienne – Roman remains, Gothic style cathedral, 6th century church St Pierre

Centre de Loisirs
Camping - Caravaning
★★★★

Bois de Reveuge

A camping surrounded by the famous Jura and Vosges mountains, near the Alsace and Swiss, in a 50 acres park, with an inside and an outdoor swimming pool, 4 waterslides, playgrounds for children, a sport place lighted at night, minigolf, archery, fishing, canoeing, pedal boats, horse and pony tour, rock climbing, musical activities.

SNACK BAR - PIZZERIA

Camping du Bois de Reveuge
25680 HUANNE-MONTMARTIN (France)
Tel: 0033 381 84 38 60 from May to September
Tel: 0033 381 84 12 42 from September to May
Fax: 0033 381 84 44 04 - Internet: www.fc-net.fr/huanne

La Pergola
39130 Marigny

Campsite La Pergola is situated on one of the banks of the lake of Chalain and offers very modern facilities completely adapted to current requirements. The heated swimming pools overhanging the lake offer superb moments of relaxation. At the restaurant (underneath our vineyard) you can taste our regional specialities. You will appreciate the beauty of the site, the turquoise water of the lake, the dark green of the beautiful forests and the famous white wine of the Jura Region.

Access: A5 motorway until Dijon.
Then follow signs to Dôle, Poligny, Champagnole.
Tel: 0033 384 25 70 03 - Fax: 0033 384 25 75 96
www.lapergola.com • e-mail: contact@lapergola.com
Open from 13th May.

Airotel Camping Caravaning
de la Côte d'Argent
33990 Hourtin Plage
Tél : 05.56.09.10.25 Fax : 05.56.09.24.96
internet : www.camping-cote-dargent.com

**Swimming pool complex of 3 500 m2
with water slides**

Caravans and mobile homes to rent

Camping de la Côte d'Argent occupies an area of 20 hectares, situated in the heart of a pine forest, but only 300 m from a huge beach, and just 4 km away from one of the biggest natural lakes in the whole of France. A characterful site, protected from the wind by the forest and nearby sand dunes, this site in natural surroundings also enjoys the benefit of an ideal climate. Facilities include a large (3500 sq m) swimming pool complex with water slides. Caravans and mobile homes to rent.

La Rive ★★★★

BISCARROSSE

LE DOMAINE DE LA RIVE, IN THE MIDDLE OF THE LANDES FOREST, ON THE SHORE OF THE HUGE BISCARROSSE LAKE HAS A PRIVATE BEACH AND HARBOUR. YOU CAN RENT PITCHES, MOBIL-HOMES, LOGHOUSES OR BUNGALOW-TENTS. ANIMATIONS.

Camping Cheque

Camping du Domaine de La Rive
Route de Bordeaux - 40600 BISCARROSSE
Tél : (0)5 58 78 12 33 - (0)5 58 82 80 70
Fax : (0)5 58 78 12 92
http://www.camping-de-la-rive.fr

4010

La Colombière
Camping Caravaning ★★★ 74160 Neydens

The campsite is situated in the heart of a small village at the edge of Geneva, on an old roman road. There is still a military post. Near the campsite, there is a 19th century cross, classified as a historical monument due to its unusual architecture and it's remarkable signs of Passion. The grounds of the campsite are checkered with Roman foundations, and it is the first french step on the route of Saint Jacques de Compostelle, from Geneva to Puy en Velay. The excellent quality restaurant proposes local specialities, house wines and a pleasant reception. Also available on the campsite are a basic shop, very comfortable toilets and showers, a laundrette, a heated swimming pool...

Tel: 0033 450 35 13 14 • Fax: 0033 450 35 13 40
www.CAMPING-LA-COLOMBIERE.com • e-mail: la.colombiere@wanadoo.fr

L'Escale★★★

Welcome at the camping site l'Escale in Le Grand-Bornand, a genuine village in the Haute Savoie. In the centre of the village (at ±200m) you can find a lot of sporting and cultural activities for all ages, as well in summer as in winter season. The camping site is situated near the cross country tracks and 500m from the gondolalift.

Camping-Caravaning L'Escale - 74450 Le Grand-Bornand
Tél. 0033 450 02 20 69 - Fax 0033 450 02 36 04

Camping Cheque

Val de Cantobre
Camping Caravaning ★★★★

LES CASTELS
★★★★

Domaine de Vellas
12230 Nant-d'Aveyron
Tel: 0033 565 58 43 00
Fax: 0033 565 62 10 36

A Castels site in unspoilt surroundings.
Pitches with stunning views...
Facilities in medieval farm buildings... in a
region between the Tarn Gorges and
Cevennes... Fauna, flora and history in
abundance... The Dupond family are
waiting to welcome you...

**It's sure to be an unforgetable
holiday with many lasting
memories.**

Mobil-homes and chalets for hire.
Special low season rates.

Le Domaine de la Paille
Basse, half way between
Rocamadour and the
caves of Lascaux, is an
excellent base for
excursions enabling you
to visit the highlights
of two régions.
Situated at the top of a
hill, La Paille Basse is a
restored medieval village
in the heart of 200 acres
of wooded land.
La Paille Basse has
carefully combined
architectural beauty and
modernity, fitting its
facilities within the
original buildings.

Castel Camping La Paille Basse
★★★★

46200 Souillac
Tel: 0033 565 37 85 48
Fax: 0033 565 37 09 58

LES CASTELS
★★★★

Camping Cheque

Camping Cheque

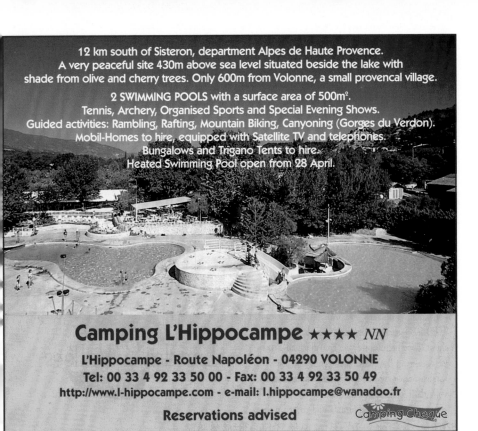

Domaine d'Arnauteille

11250 Montclar

(15 mins from the city of Carcassonne and 9 miles from the airport with direct flights to Paris and London)

In the heart of a 115 ha estate with 7 ha for camping in an exceptional setting with magnificient views of the surrounding hills.
25m swimming pool, walking, rambling & riding.
Comfortable sanitary facilities.
Restaurant & shop.
Caravans, mobil-homes, chalets and André Trigano canvas bungalows, all fully equipped for hire.
Open: 01/04 - 30/09

Tel: 0033 468 26 84 53
Fax: 0033 468 26 91 10
E-mail: arnauteille@mnet.fr
www.arnauteille.com

YOUR HOLIDAYS AT THE SEASIDE

Le Sérignan - Plage is like an open air inn with the Mediterranean Sea at its doorstep.

-heated lagoon swimming-pool, 750 m²
-heated and sheltered swimming-pool
-activities and shows
-every day mini-club
-tennis, water-sports club...

Camping Le Sérignan plage
34410 Sérignan. Languedoc-Roussillon.
tel. + 33 467 32 35 33. fax. +33 467 32 26 36
www.leserignanplage.com

Haute Saison

Le sérignan plage
CAMPING VILLAGE
MÉDITERRANÉE

Camping Les Pêcheurs****

Family campsite with warm atmosphere,
situated at the foot of the Rock of Roquebrune,
Côte d'Azur beaches at short distance.
Large and shady pitches, river,
swimming pools.

83520 Roquebrune sur Argens
Tel: 0033 494 45 71 25 - Fax: 0033 494 81 65 13
E-mail: pecheurs@worldonline.fr

3407

ARINELLA
Bianca

Camping Caravaning
20240 Ghisonaccia

Arinella Bianca is a family site with a lively atmosphere. Situated beside the sea, there is direct access to a magnificent 100 km beach. This shady site provides spacious and clearly marked pitches. The chalets can house 5 to 6 persons, they are close to the sea and the swimming pool. The mobil-homes are a bit more set back and are for 4 persons.
The sanitary blocks are kept impeccably clean, the facilities are open from the start of May until the end of September. We rent out bikes, we speak all languages and are always at your service. There are excursions to all of the beautiful sites on the island. We will give you all the advice you need. We stand for quality, decency and a good atmosphere.
New mobil-homes 6 persons.

For a splendid holiday, come and see us !

Tel: 0033 495 56 04 78 - Fax: 0033 495 56 12 54

0101 Camping La Plaine Tonique, Montrevel en Bresse

Large site by lake with watersport opportunities.

This site belongs to a syndicate of several local villages. Neat and well maintained, it is a large site with 560 marked and numbered pitches, all with 10A electricity. The majority are of a good size, hedged and on flat grass, with reasonable shade in most parts. Although large, the site is spacious and certainly did not feel too pressurised when we visited in late June. It is on the edge of a large, 250-acre lake with its own beach and adjacent public beach, and a variety of watersports, including sailing, windsurfing, swimming, canoeing and, on other parts of the lake, water-skiing and fishing. Campers may bring their own boats, but not motor boats. Minigolf and several tennis courts are on or adjacent to the site, an adventure play area is on the beach. Added in '98, an 'Aquatonic' centre has five pools (reduced charge). There are games and TV rooms, archery, bicycle hire and a new roller skating area. A restaurant and bar (all season) and shop (July/Aug) are adjacent to the site, but Montrevel itself is an attractive, small town, only 300 m. walk. Riding 2 km. Sanitary facilities are in 11 blocks, with 7 now renovated and enlarged. The actual facilities are functional rather than luxurious and include hot showers with dividers, some washbasins in cabins, British type WCs, washing machines and chemical disposal. All have a slightly formal feel but seem to be adequate in terms of number, facilities and cleanliness. Motorcaravan service point. The site is used by Dutch tour operators (100 pitches). The area has strong Rugby connections.

Directions: Site is 20 km. north of Bourg-en-Bresse and 25 km. east of Macon. Montrevel is on the D975; site is signed in town centre towards Etrez on D28.

Charges 2001:
-- Per unit incl. electricity Ffr. 42.00 - 65.00; person 16.00 - 25.00; child (3-7 yrs) 8.00 - 13.00; pet 10.00; extra vehicle 30.00.
-- Credit cards accepted.

Open:
14 April - 28 September.

Address:
Base de Plein Air, 01340 Montrevel en Bresse.

Tel:
(0)4.74.30.80.52.
FAX: (0)4.74.30.80.77.
E-mail: plaine-tonique @wanadoo.fr.

Reservations:
Required mid July - end Aug; write with 25% deposit.

 Book this site 01892 559898

THE ALAN ROGERS' travel service

0709 Castel Camping Domaine des Plantas, Les Ollières-sur-Eyrieux

Good quality campsite in a spectacular setting on the banks of the Eyrieux river.

This site offers an attractive alternative to those in the more popular, and often crowded, southern parts of the Ardèche. The Eyrieux valley is less well known, but arguably just as attractive as those further south and a good deal less crowded, particularly in the main season. Perhaps the only drawback to this site is the narrow twisting 3 km. approach road which, although by no means frightening, may present something of a challenge to those with large outfits - however, the helpful owners have an ingenious system designed to assist campers on departure. There is a sandy beach beside the quite fast-flowing, but fairly shallow, river (used for bathing) and a heated, kidney-shaped swimming pool and a paddling pool were added in 2000 with tiled surrounds for sunbathing. The bar, restaurant and disco are housed in an original building that is quite impressive with its Protestant history and visible from the main road across the river long before you reach it. The restaurant terrace provides a stunning viewpoint. Many activities are possible including mountain biking, canoeing, canyoning, horse riding and 'randonnées pedestres' (sounds better in French!). The 127 pitches are terraced and shaded, so some up and down walking is required. They have electricity connections (10A, long leads may be needed) and water points are very accessible. One large, modern toilet block, centrally situated, is in courtyard style with colourful doors and is well equipped with washbasins in cubicles, push-button showers, British style toilets and good facilities for children with small toilets and baby baths. An additional smaller block serves the higher terraces. Dishwashing and laundry sinks (both with H&C), a washing machine, chemical disposal and motorcaravan service point are provided. A small shop is open from 15/5, otherwise you can order bread and milk. Only gas barbecues are allowed. Activities are arranged according to the campers' motivations, including excursions. An adventure play area is beside the river. In high season animation for children is organised six days a week, and discos for 14-18 year olds held in the cellar twice weekly (strictly no alcohol). Mobile homes for rent (25).

Directions: South of Valence exit N86 at La Voulte and follow D120 west for Les Ollières sur Eyrieux (20 km). After bridge in the village, turn left and follow site signs - the road is single track and could be difficult for large units with bends and twists for 3 km. Units leave the site in timed convoys, otherwise a site car goes in front of you.

Charges 2000:
-- Per unit incl. 2 persons Ffr. 88.00 - 125.00; extra person 16.00 - 25.00; child (under 8 yrs) 10.00 - 15.00; animal 10.00; electricity (5A) 20.00; local tax (over 10 yrs) 2.00.
-- Credit cards accepted.

Open:
20 April - 21 September.

Address:
07360 Les Ollières-sur-Eyrieux.

Tel:
(0)4.75.66.21.53.
FAX: (0)4.75.66.23.65.
E-mail: plantas.ardeche @wanadoo.fr.

Reservations:
Made with deposit (Ffr. 400) and fee (120).

'Camping Cheque'

see colour advert between pages 192/193

RHONE VALLEY - 07 Ardèche

0710 Camping La Garenne, St Laurent-du-Pape

Family run site with a variety of activities for families.

This orderly site in the southern Ardèche is owned and run by Dutchman Tim Martojo. Clients are predominantly Dutch but English is widely spoken. Visitors' pursuits have been carefully considered resulting in a variety of activities. People with diverse interests are therefore attracted throughout the season, for example, bridge evenings are organised during May, June and Sept, a boules instructor visits mid May - end June, there is a daily children's club in July/Aug. and also a sports camp for 7-10 year olds. A playground for young children has a variety of equipment including a sand pit and a small paddling pool with slide (fenced for safety) is adjacent to the large swimming pool (15/5-30/9). There are also facilities for tennis and volleyball. Details for excursions to local places of interest and also for canoeing are available at reception and a small shop stocks basic provisions (15/5-15/9). However, it is only a short stroll to the village where most necessities are catered for. Fishing 1 km, riding 2 km. Two modern sanitary blocks provide British style WCs, pre-set, free hot showers, washbasins (in cubicles) and a larger shower with washbasin for parents with young children. Most cubicles are rather cramped. Laundry with washing machines, a dryer and ironing. The 116 grass pitches are 80-100 sq.m, some separated by hedges and have 3A electricity (some need long leads). No tour operators and no mobile homes to let.

Directions: South of Valence on N7, head west over the Rhône on N304 to Le Pouzin. Turn right onto N86 signed Voulte sur Rhône. At Voulte follow signs for St Laurent on D120; site is in village, well signed on the right.

Charges 2000:
-- Per unit incl. 2 persons Ffr. 65.00 - 122.00, with electricity 83.00 - 140.00; extra person (over 3 yrs) 29.00; extra tent 10.00; extra car (on parking only) 15.00; dog 10.00; local tax 2.00 (4-10 yrs 1.00).
-- Special low season tariff for over 55s staying at least 10 days.
-- No credit cards.

Open:
1 March - 1 November.

Address:
07800 St Laurent-du-Pape.

Tel:
(0)4.75.62.24.62.

Reservations:
Advised and made with deposit (Ffr. 510) and fee (90).

0707 Castel Camping Les Ranchisses, Chassiers, Largentière

Friendly, family site in an attractive peaceful location on the Route de Valgorge.

Combining farming, wine-making, running an Auberge and a friendly family campsite is no simple task, but the Chevalier family seem to manage it quite effortlessly. Well run and with the emphasis on personal attention this is a highly recommended site. In a somewhat lesser known area of the Ardèche at Chassiers, the site has developed from an original 'camping à la ferme' into a very well equipped modern campsite. There are 150 good-sized, level, grassy pitches, most with electricity (6A), with some multi-serviced pitches (electricity, water, waste water). They are in two distinct areas - the original site which is well shaded, and the lower part which is more open with less shade, serviced by tarmac and gravel access roads. There is frontage onto a small lake which is connected to the river, providing opportunities for fishing or canoeing (free life jackets provided) and, judging by appearances, at least one part of this is quite safe for youngsters (supervision recommended). The two sanitary buildings are modern and comprehensively equipped with British style WCs, showers and washbasins (all in individual cubicles), dishwashing and laundry sinks and facilities for babies and disabled persons. Splendid provision indeed and at the time of our visit in July they were immaculate. The laundry is in a separate building and there is a new motorcaravan service point. The excellent swimming pool complex, with a large tiled patio surround, consists of two large pools (one is 20 x 10m, the second 15 x 7.5 m), both heated and open all season and a paddling pool. Overlooking the pool area, the main building contains reception, a small shop, takeaway, bar and terrace. Other on-site facilities include a tennis court, a children's adventure style playground, with organised amusements for the children in high season. Set in a room of the original 1824 building, that once used to house silk worms, the Auberge serves food at lunch-time and evenings (all season), either inside or outside on the attractive, shaded terrace. The food, which is traditional to the region, is to be recommended, being both reasonably priced and extremely good quality. Bicycle hire. Mobile homes and chalets for rent. Canoe and kayaking on the Ardèche is arranged from the site each Wednesday (mid -June to end Aug). The medieval village of Largentière (1 km.) is well worth a visit, with a Tuesday market and a medieval festival in July.

Directions: Largentière is southwest of Aubenas and is best approached using the D5 from its junction with the D104, 16 km. south of Aubenas. From Largentière take Route de Valgorge (D5) and Les Ranchisses is the first site on the left.

Charges 2000:
-- Per unit incl. 2 persons Ffr. 95.00 - 120.00; serviced pitch 125.00 - 155.00; extra person 19.00 - 29.00; child (under 10 yrs) 14.00 - 24.00; animal free - 9.00; electricity 19.50.
-- Credit cards accepted.

Open:
14 April - end September.

Address:
Route de Valgorge, Chassiers, 07110 Largentière.

Tel:
(0)4.75.88.31.97. FAX: (0)4.75.88.32.73. E-mail: reception@ lesranchisses.fr.

Reservations:
Contact site for form; made with Ffr. 600 deposit.

'Camping Cheque.'

Book this site
01892 559898

THE ALAN ROGERS'
travel service

see colour advert
between pages 192/193

0702 Camping-Caravaning L'Ardèchois, St Sauveur-de-Montagut

Well equipped site in spectacular setting.

This site is quite a way off the beaten track and the approach road is winding and narrow in places. It is worth the effort, however, to find such an attractive hillside site offering good amenities and several different types of pitch that vary in size (85-140 sq.m). All 83 touring pitches have electricity (6, 10 or 15A). Some are alongside the small fast-flowing river, while the rest (60%) are on higher, sloping ground nearer the restaurant/bar. The main site access roads are tarmac but are quite steep and larger units may find access difficult to some terraces. Many are separated by trees and plants. The main sanitary block, bar/restaurant, shop and new soundproof 'salle de jeux' have been created by the careful conversion of old buildings and provide modern amenities in an attractive style (all from 1/5). Amenities include a TV room, table tennis, volleyball, bicycle hire, archery and fishing on site. The swimming pool is heated from 1/5 (no bermuda style shorts) and has an adjacent bar, snack bar and terrace, plus a new paddling pool for children. The sanitary facilities, all recently renovated, are good, providing British type toilets, hot showers, washbasins in private cabins etc. and another block of equal quality is near to the riverside pitches. They provide baths and showers for babies, facilities for people with disabilities, chemical disposal, dishwashing and laundry rooms, plus a motorcaravan service point. The owners have developed an extensive and unusual excursion programme for exploring this attractive area on foot or by car. Canyoning, climbing, and canoeing trips are organised. The site is popular with the Dutch. Chalets (9) and mobile homes (14) for hire. A Sites et Paysages member.

Directions: From Valence take N86 south for 12 km, turn right onto D120 to St. Sauveur de Montagut, then take D102 towards Mézilhac for 8 km. to site.

Charges 2001:
-- Per unit incl. 2 persons Ffr. 88.00 - 120.00, with electricity 108.00 - 140.00; extra person (incl. children) 20.00; animal 10.00 - 20.00.
-- Credit cards accepted.

Open:
14 April - 25 September.

Address:
07190 St Sauveur-de-Montagut.

Tel:
(0)4.75.66.61.87.
FAX: (0)4.75.66.63.67.
E-mail: ardechois.
camping@wanadoo.fr.

Reservations:
Write with deposit (Ffr. 600) and fee (150); min. 10 days 7/7-25/8.

`Camping Cheque'

Book this site
01892 559898

THE ALAN ROGERS'
travel service

see colour advert
between pages 192/193

0703 Camping Soleil Vivarais, Sampzon, nr Ruoms

Large, quality site bordering the River Ardèche.

Situated beside the River Ardèche, complete with a sandy beach, Soleil Vivarais offers much to visitors, particularly families with children, be they teenagers or toddlers. The 200 generously sized, level pitches (40 with full services) all have 10A electricity and many are shaded. Four modern, extremely clean sanitary blocks cope well with the demands placed upon them. With a heated babies' and children's room (incorporating several facilities at child height), four units for people with disabilities, ample areas for dishwashing (free hot water), washing machines and dryers, and chemical disposal, there is undoubtedly a full complement of facilities. During the day the proximity of the heated main and toddlers' pools (22.5x10.5 m and 100 sq. m, respectively, no bermuda style shorts) to the terraces of the bar and restaurant make it a pleasantly social area. In the evening the purpose built stage, with professional lighting and sound system, provides an ideal platform for a varied entertainment programme, again incorporating those dining or relaxing nearby. The disco adjacent to the bar (capacity 100-120) is popular with teenagers, although concerns about noise are groundless as it is well sound-proofed. The bar/restaurant complex is bright and modern and, in addition to takeaways and pizzas (cooked in a wood burning oven), the restaurant offers a range catering for all appetites and budgets, from set 'table d'hôte' to full 'à la carte' meals. The large shop also has its own oven for baking bread and croissants. An extensive on-site 'animation' programme in June, July and August offers water polo, aqua-aerobics, pool games and archery. Tennis (charged), fishing, basketball, petanque, table tennis and volleyball. Activities nearby, many with qualified instruction and supervision, include mountain biking (bicycle hire from site), walking, canoeing, rafting, climbing and caving. Riding 2 km, golf 10 km. Used by tour operators (62 pitches). Chalets, mobile homes and tents for hire. A `Sites et Paysages' and 'Yelloh Village' member.

Directions: From Le Teil (on N86) take N102 westwards towards and through Villeneuve-de-Berg, disregarding first sign for Vallon-Pont-d'Arc. Continue on N102 before turning left on D103, toward Vogue and Ruoms, then left on D579 to Sampzon. Access to site is via bridge across the river, controlled by lights.

Charges 2000:
-- Per unit incl. 2 persons and electricity Ffr. 114.00 - 205.00; extra person 25.00 - 42.00; child (under 10 yrs) free - 38.00; animal free - 17.00; local tax 2.00 (over 10s).
-- Credit cards accepted.

Open:
1 April - 20 September.

Address:
Sampzon, 07120 Ruoms.

Tel:
(0)4.75.39.67.56.
FAX: (0)4.75.93.97.10.
E-mail: camping.soleil.
vivarais@wanadoo.fr.

Reservations:
Made by fax and credit card or write to site with deposit (Ffr 600) and fee (195).

see colour advert
between pages 128/129

RHONE VALLEY - 07 Ardèche

0708 Castel Camping Domaine de la Bastide, Sampzon, Ruoms

Good quality, family run site near Vallon-Pont-d'Arc.

The Cargnelutti family are very keen to maintain high standards on their site and this is evident as soon as you drive in with its neat and tidy appearance and with flowers everywhere. When you first drive down to your pitch it seems that there are lots of mobile homes. Actually there are only 31 mobile homes and 25 small chalets, which out of 300 pitches is really not many. Once past these, the site opens up to reveal pleasant pitches, all with some shade, good sized and bordered by flowering trees and bushes. All have electricity connections (3/5A) and 80 are fully serviced. There are two toilet blocks, the newest one with very high quality fittings including pre-set showers, British style WCs, washbasins in cubicles, a baby room and facilities for people with disabilities. There are washing machines, dryers and irons and hot water to laundry and dishwashing sinks. The older block is only open in high season and has mainly Turkish style WCs, plus showers, etc. The heated swimming pool has a pleasant sunbathing area and is surrounded by flowers. There is a children's play area, table tennis, boules, volleyball, football, basketball and tennis courts. In July/Aug. games and competitions are organised and there is a disco in a soundproof cellar at the entrance (with security patrols of the site to ensure quiet nights). Canoe trips can be arranged down the Gorge d'Ardèche and in mid-June every year a large section of the river bank is cleared of boulders and sand put down - just the job for the children. A hairdresser visits weekly in July/Aug. and a doctor daily. The restaurant (with high chairs, weekends from 15/5, daily 20/6-31/8) is very attractive with its white tiled floor and there is also a pizzeria, bar and shop. Free sauna and gymnasium with an instructor. Fishing on site, riding near, golf 6 km. The small town of Ruoms is 4 km, Vallon-Pont-d'Arc 7 km. Barbecues are not permitted. Used by tour operators (16 pitches). Chalets for rent.

Directions: Going south from Ruoms on the D579, bear right on the D111 signed Ales. Cross the Chassezac river bridge and site is 200 m. on the left.

Charges 2000:
-- Per unit incl. 2 persons Ffr. with electricity 120.00 - 168.00, with water and drainage also 140.00 - 190.00; extra person over 3 yrs 22.00 - 33.00; dog free - 25.00; local tax (over 10 yrs) 2.00.
-- No credit cards.

Open:
1 April - 10 September.

Address:
Sampzon, 07120 Ruoms.

Tel:
(0)4.75.39.64.72. FAX: (0)4.75.39.73.28. E-mail: campingbastide @wanadoo.fr.

Reservations:
Made with deposit (Ffr. 500) and fee (200).

0706 Mondial Camping, Rivière Ardèche, Vallon-Pont-d'Arc

Attractive family run site beside the river, close to popular, busy resort.

Mondial is a good quality site catering for active families. It is close to the popular Ardèche resort of Vallon-Pont-d'Arc but is less frenetic than some of the other sites in the area. Shrubs are being planted to separate the 240 pitches, and the majority have some shade from mature trees. Neatly arranged in short rows, all are of a good size and have access to electricity (6/10A), with some pitches also having water and drainage. The site itself is quite long and narrow, with direct access at the far end to the river for bathing, fishing or canoeing (canoes for hire from site) or just watching the river activities. There is a modern restaurant and a bar (1/4-10/9) where evening activities take place until midnight in high season. Some noisy activities may also be heard from nearby sites. An attractive heated pool (no Bermuda style shorts) has sunbathing areas (1/4-25/9) and activities include tennis, volleyball, children's play area and archery beside the river. Shop (1/4-25/9). Three modern sanitary blocks are of a high standard, very clean when we visited and with unusually excellent facilities for disabled people. They can be heated and provide comfortable hot showers, a mixture of British and Turkish style WCs (no paper), washbasins in private cabins, washing machine and dishwashing facilities. Chemical disposal and motorcaravan services. Bicycle hire 300 m, riding 200 m, golf 6 km. The pretty village with shops, restaurants and bars is just a short walk. The famous Pont d'Arc is 2 km. Used by tour operators (30 pitches). Mobile homes to rent.

Directions: From Vallon-Pont-d'Arc take D290 towards Pont St. Esprit - site is on the right of this road. From A7 use Montelimar-Sud or Bolléne exit and take D4 through Bourg St Andéol and St Reméze to Vallon-Pont-d'Arc, then as above.

Charges 2001:
-- Per unit incl. 2 persons Ffr. 105.00 - 156.00; extra person (any age) 32.00 - 38.00; dog 15.00 - 28.00; electricity 23.00; water and drainage 32.00; local tax 3.00 p/person (over 10 yrs).
-- Credit cards accepted.

Open:
15 March - 10 October.

Address:
Route Touristiques des Gorges de l'Ardèche, 07150 Vallon-Pont-d'Arc.

Tel:
(0)4.75.88.00.44. FAX: (0)4.75.37.13.73. E-mail: reser-info@ mondial-camping.com.

Reservations:
Made with deposit (Ffr. 600) and fee (100).

0704 Camping La Rouveyrolle, Casteljau, nr Les Vans

Attractive, family run site in peaceful surroundings beside the Chassezac river gorge.

Family run and aimed at families, this is a very tranquil site by the river in attractive countryside surrounded by vineyards and orchards. Of the 100 good sized pitches here, 53 are available for tourists. These are on flat grass, most with ample shade, the remainder with less for those preferring the sun, and all have electricity (4/5A). The site has a relaxed atmosphere and provides good facilities for families, including tennis courts, bicycle hire and a large children's adventure playground, with the river beach (100 m.) providing swimming and canoeing in July/Aug. Fishing also possible. Positioned to catch the sun all day, the attractively shaped and extremely clean swimming pool will be further enhanced by a new waterfall and rock feature. The site offers a pleasant bar/restaurant (1/5-1/9) serving a 'dish of the day' and including takeaway, plus animation and entertainment (July/Aug). The sanitary facilities are in two modern blocks, with free hot showers in cubicles with separator and some British style WCs, although the majority are the Turkish type. These are supplemented by additional WCs and facilities for the disabled by the pool. Not all the sanitary facilities are open in low season and cleaning may be variable, but at the time of our visit in July all was most acceptable. There are part covered washing-up and laundry areas, including a washing machine. Shop (1/7-31/8, 8.00-12.30 and 4.30-7.30) - the village is 500 m. The Cèvennes and the Gorges of the Ardèche (20 km) are near. Riding 4 km. Pot-holing and rock climbing (with guides) are available nearby and excursions can be arranged. Mobile homes (6 persons) for hire. Used by tour operators.

Charges 2001:
-- Per unit incl. 2 persons Ffr 65.00 - 130.00; extra person 23.00 - 37.00; child under 7 yrs free, 7-16 yrs 18.00 - 28.00; electricity 23.00; local tax 1.00.
Open:
1 April - 30 September.
Address:
Casteljau, 07460 Berrias et Casteljau.
Tel:
(0)4.75.39.00.67. FAX: (0)4.75.39.07.28. E-mail: rouv@club-internet.fr.
Reservations:
Write to site.

Directions: From A7 at Montelimar, take D102 west to Aubenas, then D104, south through Joyeuse and hamlet of Chandolas/Maison-Neuve. Turn right just after bridge over the Chassezac on D252. Turn right after 1.75 km. (site signed) then right at next crossroads. Site is 1 km. Signed to right (do not turn into village La Rouveyrolle).

0705 Camping-Caravaning Le Ranc Davaine, St Alban Auriolles

Busy, family oriented site in southern Ardèche.

Le Ranc Davine is quite a large site, set in two areas separated by a reasonably quiet road. The larger area provides all the entertainment facilities and most of the 356 pitches. They are arranged on fairly flat, rather stony ground under a variety of trees giving much needed shade and all are supplied with electricity (6 or 10A). The lower part is beside the river (unfenced). The attractive large, irregularly shaped swimming pool (no bermuda-style shorts or shirts) is heated in cool weather and supplemented by two small square pools. Sunbathing areas surround the pools, overlooked by the terrace of the bar/restaurant. This serves a good range of meals in very pleasant surroundings, especially with its evening floodlighting. There is also a pizzeria and takeaway. The lively entertainment programme (July/Aug) is aimed at young children and teenagers (with discos!). The five sanitary blocks have British style WCs, hot showers with dividers and many washbasins in cabins. However, outside the main season not all blocks are open, in high season they get very busy. The lower area has a new, unisex sanitary block with hot showers, WCs, washbasins in cubicles and full facilities for disabled visitors, plus dishwashing and laundry sinks. Washing machines, dryers and irons are provided. The large shop will cater for most needs and there is a cash point in the new reception building. There is a play area, tennis, table tennis, minigolf, fishing and an extensive programme of water sports in the pools. Canoes may be hired for excursions down the River Ardèche. Riding 2 km. The site is popular with tour operators (120 pitches) and can get very busy for much of the season. Mobile homes (90) and chalets (21) to rent. A Sites et Paysages member.

Charges 2000:
-- Per unit incl. 2 persons Ffr. 110.00 - 160.00, with electricity 134.00 - 185.00; extra person over 2 yrs 30.00 - 38.00; plus local tax; animal free - 15.00.
-- Credit cards accepted.
Open:
1 April - 17 September.
Address:
St Alban Auriolles, 07120 Ruoms.
Tel:
(0)4.75.39.60.55. FAX: (0)4.75.39.38.50. E-mail: camping.ranc-davaine @wanadoo.fr.
Reservations:
Made with deposit (Ffr. 620, 94,51) and fee (180 27,44).

Directions: Continue south on D111 after Ruoms. Turn right just before Grospierres on D246, across bridge (2.5 m. width restriction) and then left on D208 towards Chandolas and site.

RHONE VALLEY - 26 Drôme

2602 Castel Camping Château de Sénaud, Albon, nr Tournon

Pleasant site convenient for the autoroute or a longer stay.

Château du Sénaud, near the N7 south of Vienne, makes a useful stopover on the way south, but one could enjoy a longer stay to explore the surrounding villages and mountains. It is one of the original sites in the Castel chain and is still run with character and hands-on attention by Mme. Comtesse d'Armagnac. There are a fair number of permanent caravans used at weekends, but it also has some 85 pitches in tourist areas, some with shade, some with views across the Rhône valley, and electricity and water connections are available on all pitches. There is a swimming pool with water toboggan (1/5-15/9, depending on the weather) and a new jacuzzi. Four sanitary blocks have constant hot water in washbasins, showers and sinks, British and one Turkish style toilets, washbasins in private cabins, some en-suite with shower in one block, and facilities for babies. There are washing machines, chemical disposal and motorcaravan service point. Shop (15/5-15/9). Bar, takeaway and good value small restaurant with simple menu (all 15/6-15/9). Activities available on site include a tennis court, fishing, bicycle hire, table tennis, a bowling alley and minigolf. A golf course is adjacent and there are walks. Riding 10 km. Possibly some noise from the autoroute. Mobile homes and chalets to rent. Caravan storage.

Directions: Leave autoroute at Chanas exit, proceed south on N7 for 8 km. then east on D301 from Le Creux de la Thine to site. From south, exit autoroute for Tain-Tournon and proceed north, approaching site on D122 through St Vallier then D132 towards Anneyron to site.

Charges 2000:
-- Per person Ffr. 29.00; child (under 7) 16.00; pitch 40.00; dog 10.00; electricity (6A) 20.00.
-- No credit cards.

Open:
1 March - 31 October.

Address:
26140 Albon.

Tel:
(0)4.75.03.11.31.
FAX: (0)4.75.03.08.06.
E-mail: camping.de.
senaud@libertysurf.fr.

Reservations:
Made with deposit for min. 3 nights.

`Camping Cheque'

see colour advert between pages 192/193

2603 Camping Le Grand Lierne, Chabeuil, nr Valence

Conveniently and attractively situated family site on the route south.

In addition to its obvious attraction as an overnight stop, fairly convenient for the A7 autoroute, this site provides a pleasant base to explore this little known area between the Ardèche and the Vercors mountains and the Côte du Rhône wine area. It has 140 marked pitches, 76 for touring units. Mainly separated by developing hedges or oak trees, with good shade, some on flat grass, all have electricity (6/10A). A more open area exists for those who prefer less shade and a view of the mountains. A varied entertainment programme has a particular emphasis on activities for children, with a range of activities and excursions. There are two swimming pools, one covered and heated in low season (no bermuda shorts allowed in pool), a paddling pool and a 50 m. water slide. A bar/snack bar with terrace provides both `eating in' and takeaway (all season). Two modern sanitary blocks have hot showers, British style WCs and washbasins in private cabins. Facilities for disabled people, a small WC for children, chemical disposal, dishwashing area under cover (H&C) and washing machines and dryer (washing powder provided). Outdoor lines are provided by the blocks. Other amenities include a shop, mini-tennis, children's playgrounds and trampoline, minigolf, table tennis, volleyball, a football field, small climbing wall and bicycle hire. Library. Bureau de change. Fridge rental. Motorcaravan service point. Fishing 3 km, riding 7 km, golf 3 km, archery and hang gliding near. Barbecues are permitted in special areas. The owners wish to keep a balance between nationalities and are also keen to encourage rallies and will arrange visit programmes. Dogs and other pets are not accepted in high season (1/7-21/8). English spoken. Used by tour operators (30%). Bungalows, chalets and tents for hire. Caravan storage. A 'Sites et Paysages' member.

Directions: Site signed in Chabeuil about 11 km. east of Valence (18 km. from autoroute). It is best to approach Chabeuil from the south side of Valence via the Valence ring road, thence onto the D68 to Chabeuil itself. Site is off the D125 to Charpey, 5 km. from Chabeuil, but well signed.

Charges 2001:
-- Per unit incl. 2 adults Ffr. 90.00 - 147.00; extra person 35.00 - 42.00; child (2-7 yrs) 16.00 - 32.00; electricity 6A 22.00, 10A 32.00; animal (excl. 1/7-25/8) 14.00; local tax 1.00.
-- Credit cards accepted.

Open:
15 April - 15 September, with all services.

Address:
BP.8, 26120 Chabeuil.

Tel:
(0)4.75.59.83.14.
FAX: (0)4.75.59.87.95.
E-mail: contact@
grandlierne.com.

Reservations:
Accepted with deposit (Ffr. 600) and fee (180).

`Camping Cheque'

Book this site
01892 559898

THE ALAN ROGERS'
travel service

see colour advert between pages 192/193

2604 Camping-Caravaning Le Couspeau, Poët Célard

Pleasant small site in picturesque area, near village of Bourdeaux (not for large units).
The approach to this site is via a steep road, and with several hairpin bends to negotiate - large motorcaravans or twin-axle caravans should not attempt this hill. However, for other units the views are reward enough, as a magnificent landscape of mountains and valleys unfolds. Developed from a hillside farm, with some buildings being 250 years old, the overall impression of beauty and tranquillity is reflected in the amiable attitude of the owners, who maintain a helpful, yet low profile, relaxed presence. Access to the 67 pitches (all with electricity) is reasonably easy; levelling blocks may be handy as some of the terraced pitches are slightly sloping. Mature trees provide shade. The two sanitary blocks were spotless when seen. There are laundry and dishwashing sinks, along with washing machines and a dryer in one block; this block also houses facilities for disabled campers. A small shop meets basic needs (15/6-30/9) and a little restaurant/bar provides inexpensive meals and takeaway dishes (15/6-31/8), plus entertainment on two evenings per week. In addition to the main pool is another smaller, under cover one (heated in low seasons) plus a toddlers' pool. The proximity of the pools to the splendid children's play area means a watchful eye can be kept at all times. In high season an animation programme is arranged for young children, although teenagers may find the opportunities and location of the site rather restricting. Amenities include tennis and minigolf, supplemented by supervised family walking and cycling trips in the immediate area. Mountain bikes are for hire, with guidance and advice on route. Rafting and canoeing nearby, riding 5 km, fishing 5 km. In low season painting and pottery activities are arranged. Those who seek to unwind and relax should appreciate the delightful scenery and setting of this small site. Chalets and mobile homes for hire. A 'Sites et Paysages' member.

Charges guide:
-- Per unit incl. 2 persons Ffr 72.00 - 120.00; extra person 22.00 - 35.00; child 10.00 - 25.00; animal free - 6.00; local tax 1.00; electricity (6A) 18.00.
-- Credit cards accepted.
Open:
1 May - 26 September.
Address:
26460 Le Poët Célard.
Tel:
(0)4.75.53.30.14.
FAX: (0)4.75.53.37.23.
E-mail: couspeau@wanadoo.fr.
Reservations:
Advised for July/Aug. and made with deposit (Ffr 500) and fee (100).

Directions: From Crest take D538 signed Bourdeaux and turn right onto D328B, signed Le Poët Célard. At T-junction turn right on D328 towards village then left onto D328A. The site is a short distance on the left. (Large motorcaravans or twin-axle caravans should not attempt the hill.)

2610 Camping Les Bois du Châtelas, Bourdeaux

New family site with swimming pool and dramatic views of the mountains.
Les Bois du Châtelas was opened in 1998 and is already becoming very popular. On a hillside 1 km. above the village of Bourdeaux, it is a steep site with terraced levels for the pitches. Most of these will be easy to manoeuvre onto but there may be a little difficulty with some. All have electricity (10A), water and drainage and are of a decent size (many extra large), some with shade and most with the view. The pool, bar/restaurant, shop and one toilet block are at the entrance which is at the highest level - anyone with a disability would be advised to ask for a pitch at the top. The pool complex is on a terrace below the bar restaurant which offers reasonably priced meals to eat in or take away. Both, again, have the wonderful views. The pool has a bridge over the narrow part, a small paddling pool with waterfall, a jaccuzi and a tiled sunbathing area, plus a little grass. The small shop is stocked with basics and bread is available all season with croissants baked daily on the premises. The sanitary facilities are of excellent quality with washbasins in cubicles, British style WCs and well equipped, adjustable showers. There are baby baths, chemical disposal, dishwashing and laundry sinks with plenty of hot water, plus a washing machine. Facilities for disabled visitors are at the top toilet block. A children's play area is on sand and there are boules, volleyball, table tennis and bicycle hire. Entertainment and activities are organised in July/Aug. - boule competitions, guided walks and mountain bike rides and dances. Children have their own entertainment. Other activities include riding, canoeing and climbing. The village is 1 km. with a few shops and restaurants. Crest, 25 km. to the north, has a castle with the highest keep in France giving exceptional views of the Pre-Alps of the Drôme region, the foothills of the Vercors, the Rhône valley and the forest of Saôu. Mobile homes for rent. English is spoken. This is an easy site to get to with no serious hills or hair-pin bends.

Charges 2000:
-- Per unit incl. 2 persons Ffr 76.00 - 93.00; extra person 25.00; child (under 7 yrs) 15.00; animal 15.00; electricity (10A) 23.00; local tax 1.00.
-- Credit cards accepted.
Open:
1 April - 30 September.
Address:
Route de Dieulefit, 26460 Bourdeaux.
Tel:
(0)4.75.00.60.80.
FAX: (0)4.75.00.60.81.
E-mail: bois.du.chatelas@infonie.fr.
Reservations:
Advised for July/Aug. and made with 30% deposit; contact site.

Directions: From A7 exit 16 take D104 Crest road. At Crest take D538 south to Bourdeaux (about 25 km). Go through Bourdeaux continuing on D538 signed Dieulefit and site is signed on left in 1 km.

RHONE VALLEY - 26 Drôme

2609 Camping Les Truffieres, Grignan

Delightful, quiet country site between Grignan and Chamaret.

This is a small country site in a truly rural setting with wonderful views and providing peace and tranquillity. The 80 marked pitches are level and shaded and separated by hedges of rosemary or laurel. Water, waste water and refuse disposal are close at hand and each pitch has electricity (10A). The main sanitary block provides satisfactory facilities with hot pre-set, push-button showers, British style WCs and washbasins. Dishwashing and laundry (H&C) facilities are undercover, a washing machine is available and there is a motorcaravan service point. Extra sanitary provision is opened near the swimming pool in July/Aug. The pool has an attractive terrace, sun-beds and parasols for clients' use, and there is a smaller pool for young children (no bermuda style shorts). The Croze family are most welcoming and achieve a high standard of cleanliness and order while maintaining a friendly and relaxed atmosphere. The restaurant offers a limited menu of dishes at mid-day and evening in a congenial atmosphere (June - Sept). No dogs are accepted.

Charges 2001:
-- Per unit incl. 2 adults Ffr. 75.00 - 90.00; extra person 27.00; child (under 7 yrs) 17.00; electricity (10A) 22.00.
-- Credit cards accepted.

Open:
1 April - 30 September.

Address:
Lieu-dit Nachony, 26230 Grignan.

Tel:
(0)4.75.46.93.62.
FAX: as phone.

Reservations:
Contact site.

Directions: From N7 (exit 18 A7) south of Montélimar, take D133 (changes to D541) signed Grignan, Gap. After 9 km. take D71 to Chamaret and site is on left after 1 km.

2611 Les 4 Saisons Camping de Grâne, Grâne

Small hillside site, just off the Rhône valley.

Opened six years ago, this small terraced site nestles in the hillsides of the lower Drôme valley. With its 55 pitches, it provides mainly overnight accommodation but it is worth a longer stay. The main building is modern, housing on the top floor the reception, a snack bar and games room, and it provides commanding views across the valley towards Crest and the Vercors. A short flight of steps to a lower level leads to the very adequate sanitary facilities which provide roomy showers, British style WCs, washbasins in cabins, dishwashing and laundry facilities and two washing machines. There are facilities for disabled visitors but the site is very sloping and not suitable for wheelchairs. The pitches are level, cut out of the hillside and reached by a one-way system on tarmac roads. All the pitches have electricity (6/16A), water and waste water drain. There is a chemical disposal point. The small, unheated swimming pool has a sunbathing area. Bicycle hire on site; riding 3 km. The village is nearby and provides shops that cater for most needs. This is an excellent base for exploring the Drôme valley. Chalets to rent.

Charges 2000:
--Per unit incl, 2 persons Ffr. 53.00 - 77.00; small tent incl. 2 persons 46.00 - 73.00; extra person 18.00 - 26.00; child (under 10 yrs) 11.00 - 16.00; electricity 6A 22.00, 16A 26.00; electricity and water 29.00; animal 19.00; local tax 1.00.
--Credit cards accepted.

Open:
15 April - 15 October.

Address:
Rte. de Roche-sur-Grâne, 26400 Grâne.

Tel:
(0)4.75.62.64.17.
FAX: (0)4.75.62.69.06.

Reservations:
Advised for July/ Aug; contact site for details.

Directions: From A7 take exit 17, or N7 Loriol, onto D104 Crest road. After 8 km. take D113 south from Grâne. Go through village for 600 m. to site on left.

2606M Camping Municipal St Nazaire-en-Royans, nr Romans

The pretty village of St Nazaire-en-Royans is to be found on the western perimeter of the Parc Régional du Vercors, on the route between Romans and Grenoble, and is distinguished by its impressive bridge which straddles the Isère river. The municipal site here is on the D76 road, 500 m. from the village and is fronted by the municipal tennis courts and boules area. With a well laid out, tidy and organised appearance, the site's 75 grass pitches are of a good size, numbered and separated by hedges. Some, towards the bottom left, overlook the river and lots of trees give shade. Most pitches have access to electricity (3 or 6A). There is night lighting and a security gate (locked 10 pm.-7 am). The sanitary block is basic with white tiles, but in good condition and clean. It provides British style WCs, washbasins with some private, curtained cabins, facilities for disabled visitors, and dishwashing and laundry sinks, plus a washing machine. Chemical disposal. Children's play area with grass base. This is a convenient base for exploring this not so well known, but scenically magnificent area.

Charges guide:
-- Per unit incl. 2 persons Ffr. 45.00; extra person 17.00; child (7 yrs or under) 10.00; dog 8.00; electricity 3A 16.00, 6A 23.00.

Open:
1 May - 30 September.

Address:
26190 St Nazaire-en-Royans.

Tel:
(0)4.75.48.41.18 or Mairie: (0)4.75.48.40.63.

Reservations:
Contact site.

Directions: From Romans-sur-Isère take N532 for 18 km. to St Nazaire-en-Royans. Site clearly signed in village on D76 (500 m). The turn to site from St Nazaire is a left turn on the brow of a hill on a corner - take care.

2608 Camping Le Gallo-Romain, Barbières, nr Valence

Small, quiet, rural site with mountain views close to the Vercors.

Surrounded by wooded hills and mountains, this small simple site makes a good base from which to explore the spectacular Vercors plateau. It is quiet and peaceful, in a lovely location with pitches set on terraces which descend gradually to a small stream. There are 80 grassy pitches all with electricity (6A) and most with some shade at some part of the day. Two sanitary blocks have British style WCs, hot showers and washbasins in cubicles. They are kept very clean but we found the facilities a little stretched when we visited in August. A small bar/ restaurant offers well cooked local dishes at very reasonable prices (booking essential), plus a range of takeaway food. In high season a small shop operates, otherwise there are others in Barbières (1 km). However, fresh bread and croissants are available on site all season. Other facilities include a swimming pool (17 x 8 m) and paddling pool with sunbathing area, games room, pool table, table tennis, volleyball and a small play area. Bicycle hire in the village 1 km, riding or golf 6 km. The area is ideal for walking or mountain biking with many special cycle tracks in the hills, or for wild flower or butterfly enthusiasts. Mobile homes for rent (14). English is spoken.

Directions: Leave A49/E713 autoroute at exit 7 (Romans-sur-Isère) and turn south on D149, following signs to Col de Tourniol. Barbières is approx. 12 km. along this road. Drive carefully through narrow streets in the village; the site is a little way past it on the right.

Charges 2000:
-- Per adult Ffr. 18.00; child (under 7 yrs) 12.00; pitch 60.00; electricity (6A) 15.00.
-- No credit cards.

Open:
1 May - 15 September.

Address:
Rte du Col du Tourniol, 26300 Barbières.

Tel:
(0)4.75.47.44.07.
FAX: as phone

Reservations:
Advised for high season; made for exact dates with deposit and fee.

4201M Camping Municipal de Charlieu, Charlieu

Charlieu is an attractive little town, well worth a visit, and the municipal site here would make a good base for exploring the area. The 100 pitches (30 occupied by seasonal units), all have electricity (4, 6 or 10A). The pitches are reasonably large and well spaced, on level grass. Most are separated by trim hedges with some shade. Immediately opposite the site is an open-air, heated, municipal swimming pool (1/6-31/8) with a grass bank for sunbathing, which was very popular when we visited in late June. Sanitary facilities are reasonably adequate with both British and Turkish style WCs, facilities for disabled visitors, dishwashing and laundry facilities and chemical disposal point. Bicycle hire, volleyball, boules, a children's playground and fishing on site. There are few other facilities as the lovely little town is within about 5 minutes walk. A card from reception gives free entry to the swimming pool and tennis court, plus discounts for the cinema, museums and attractions plus other activities in and around the town.

Directions: Charlieu is 20 km. northeast of Roanne. Site is southeast of the town next to a sports stadium and is signed from the town centre. From Pouilly, on the D482, take D487 to Charlieu (5.5 km).

Charges guide:
-- Per caravan Ffr. 7.00 (twin axle 270.00); tent 6.00; car or m/cycle 5.00; motorcaravan 13.00; electricity 4A 9.00, 6A 10.50, 10A 21.00; adult 11.00 - 12.50; child 5.50 - 7.00; local tax incl.
-- No credit cards.

Open:
1 May - 15 October.

Address:
Rue Riottier, 42190 Charlieu.

Tel:
(0)4.77.69.01.70.

Reservations:
Made without fee.

4202M Camping Municipal Le Surizet, Montbrison

This useful municipal site in the outskirts of the town, has 92 pitches of which about 20 are available for tourists. All are on level grass with some neat hedging and a reasonable amount of shade from mature trees, most with electricity (5/10A). The site has its own open-air swimming pool (fenced but unsupervised) with paved surround, which is reserved for campers. The modern heated sanitary unit includes rather small hot showers with dividers, washbasins in cubicles, British type WCs, dishwashing sinks, and chemical disposal. There are additional WCs at reception and in the picnic area. Plans are in hand for a small unit with facilities for disabled people. Motorcaravan services. A large 'salle de reunion' opposite the site entrance is used for table tennis, discos, etc.

Directions: Site is signed in the direction of Moingt, 2 km. southeast of Montbrison on the D8 (towards St Etienne). Turn right at new roundabout where site is signed.

Charges guide:
-- Per person Ffr. 10.20; child (under 7 yrs) 5.10; car 5.10; tent or caravan 5.10; motorcaravan 10.20; electricity 5A 15.00, 10A 30.00.

Open:
1 April - 31 October.

Address:
42600 Montbrison-Moingt.

Tel:
(0)4.77.58.08.30.

Reservations:
Advised in summer; contact site.

6901M Camping International Porte de Lyon, Lyon

Camping International is a modern overnight site just off the A6 autoroute. Kept busy with overnight trade, reception and the café (in main season) open until quite late. There are 150 separate numbered plots with electricity in most parts. Those for caravans are mostly on hardstandings on a slight slope, with another small grassy part, while those for tents are on a flatter area of grass. The three sanitary blocks are good, with free hot water (solar heated) in all washbasins (in cabins), good showers and sinks. The block under reception has baby changing facilities and washing machines. Amenities on site include a TV room, children's playground, table tennis, medical service and an unheated swimming and paddling pools. Basic provisions kept in the café, but a very large commercial centre has been developed just outside the site, with 8 hotels, restaurants, supermarket, petrol station etc. Some road noise. Mobile homes to rent. Bus for Lyon nearby.

Directions: Going south don't take new A46 motorway around Lyon, but continue on A6 autoroute and take exit marked 'Limonest, Dardilly, Porte de Lyon' about 8 km. north of the Lyon tunnel; at once turn left for Porte de Lyon. Porte de Lyon is well signed from most directions.

Charges 2000:
-- Per person Ffr. 19.00; child (7-15 yrs) 14.50, under 7 free; tent 40.00; motorcaravan 50.00; caravan: 1 axle 50.00, 2 axles 100.00; extra car 70.00; extra tent 20.00; electricity 20.00 - 40.00 (winter); local tax 1.00 (child 0.50).
-- Credit cards accepted.

Open:
All year.

Address:
Porte de Lyon, 69570 Dardilly.

Tel:
(0)4.78.35.64.55.
FAX: (0)4.72.17.04.26.

Reservations:
Made if you write, but there is usually space.

6902M Camping Municipal La Grappe Fleurie, Fleurie-en-Beaujolais

With easy access from both the A6 autoroute and the N6, this site is ideally situated for night stops or indeed for longer stays to explore the vineyards and historic attractions of the Beaujolais region. Virtually surrounded by vineyards, but within walking distance (less than 1 km) of the pretty village of Fleurie, this is an immaculate small site, with 96 separated touring pitches. All are grassed and fairly level with the benefit of individual access to water, drainage and electrical connections (10A). Sanitary facilities are in two blocks with British and Turkish style WCs and very satisfactory shower and washing facilities (showers are not available 22.00-07.00 hrs). Two cold showers are provided for those wishing to cool down in summer. A small children's playground, table tennis, tennis and volleyball areas are on site. Restaurant and shopping facilities are available in the village, although the nearest swimming pool is 8 km.

Directions: From N6 at Le Maison Blanche/Romanech-Thorins, take D32 to village of Fleurie from where site is signed.

Charges 2000:
-- Per adult Ffr. 20.00; child under 5 yrs free, 5-10 yrs 10.00; caravan or motorcaravan 32.00; tent 19.00.
-- Credit cards accepted.

Open:
16 March - 27 October.

Address:
69820 Fleurie.

Tel:
(0)4.74.69.80.07 or the Mairie: (0)4. 74.04.10.44.
FAX: (0)4.74.69.85.71.
E-mail: info@fleuri.org.

Reservations:
Advised in high season.

PROVENCE

Perhaps we should have called this tourist region the Provence Alpes because we have only included the départements from the mountainous hinterland of the official French region of Provence. The capital city of Provence is Marseille, but this now falls into our Mediterranean region.

Départements: 04 Alpes-de-Haute-Provence
05 Hautes-Alpes, 84 Vaucluse

The river valleys provide natural routes through the mountain barrier, as the Romans recognised. Their influence is strong through the region, reminding one that the area was the first Province of Rome, which is why it is now called Provence. Roman monuments can be seen at Orange, and Vaison-la -Romaine, where a 2,000 year old bridge is still in use. Avignon was the site of the papal court and the Palais des Papes at Avignon is a spectacular construction.

The Hautes-Alpes will reward with scenic pleasures, peace and quiet. Briançon is the highest town in Europe and many of the high passes are not for the faint-hearted – Hannibal used one of the routes!

The Vauclause, the area made famous by Peter Mayle's book on the Luberon, where in the late spring the southern slopes of the Montagne du Luberon are a mass of colour from the glades of wild flowers. The extinct volcanic cone of Mont Ventoux, of Tour de France fame provides dramatic views. The scents and colours with an amazing intensity of light, have encouraged artists and writers to settle amidst the sleepy villages, with narrow streets and ancient dwellings topped with sun-baked terracotta tiles, where the air is fragrant with the smell of wild herbs and lavender.

Note: Site reports are laid out by département in numerical order.
See map on page 318.

Cuisine of the region
Influenced by the Savoie area to the north and the Côte d'Azur to the south, the cuisine emphasizes seasonings, such as herbs and garlic, and fish
Aigo Bouido –garlic and sage soup with bread (or eggs and cheese)
Farcement (Farçon Savoyard) –potatoes baked with cream, eggs, bacon, dried pears and prunes; a hearty stomach filler
Plat Gratinée –applies to a wide range of dishes; here this means cooked in breadcrumbs; gratins of all sorts show how well milk, cream and cheee combine together
Pissaladière – Provencal bread dough with onions, anchovies, olives, etc.
Ratatouille – aubergines, courgettes, onions, garlic, red peppers and tomatoes in olive oil
Tartiflette –potato, bacon, onions and Reblochon cheese

Wine
The Côtes de Provence wine region is mainly known for its dry, fruity rosé wines: Bandol, Bellet, Palette, Cassis. Red wines include Côtes du Rhône and Châteauneuf-du-Pape.

Places of interest
Avignon – ramparts, old city, Papal Palace, old palace, Calvet museum
Mont Ventoux – near Carpentras, one of the best known stages of the classic Tour de France annual cycle race
Orange – Roman city, gateway to the Midi, Colline St Europe
Vaison la Romaine – Roman city, the French Pompei

PROVENCE - 04 Alpes-Haute-Provence

0401 Hotel de Plein Air L'Hippocampe, Volonne, nr Sisteron

Friendly site with good pool complex and lots of activities.

Hippocampe is situated in a beautiful area of France which is not well frequented by the British. The perfumes of thyme, lavender and wild herbs are everywhere and the higher hills of Haute Provence are not too far away. This is a family run site with families in mind, with games, aerobics, competitions, entertainment and shows, plus a daily club for younger family members in July/August. A sound-proof underground disco is set well away from the pitches and is very popular with teenage customers. Sports facilities are good with a large selection to choose from, some with free instruction, including archery in high season. Tennis is free outside high season (3/7-21/8). Fishing, canoeing and bicycle hire are available on site with riding 500 m. There are 447 level, numbered pitches (271 for touring units), most with electricity (6A) and many also with water. Most are separated by bushes and cherry trees (June is the time for the cherries and you may help yourself). The toilet blocks vary from old to modern but we have always found them clean. The WCs are British style, all hot water is free and washbasins are in cabins. There are washing machines, chemical disposal and a motorcaravan service point. The bar (1/5-30/9), restaurant, pizzeria and barbecue chicken shop (all 12/5-15/9) are reasonably priced. Small shop (30/6-1/9). The village of Volonne is only 600 m. The swimming pool complex (from 1/5) is very large and attractive, comprising various pools of differing sizes and depths; it is heated in early and late seasons. The site is much quieter in low season with good discounts and these are the months for people who do not want or need entertaining. The Gorge du Verdon is a sight not to be missed and rafting, paragliding or canoe trips can be booked from the site's own tourist information office. Being on the lower slopes of the hills of Haute-Provence, the surrounding area is good for both walking and mountain biking. Charcoal barbecues are not permitted. Mobile homes (90), bungalow tents (43) and chalets (9) to rent. Used by tour operators (20 pitches). English is spoken.

Directions: Approaching from north turn off N85 across river bridge to Volonne, then right to site. From the south right on D4 1 km. before Château Arnoux.

Charges 2000:
-- Per unit with 2 persons simple pitch: Ffr. 78.00 - 124.00, with electricity (10A) 95.00 - 152.00, with water/drainage 100 sq.m. 95.00 - 165.00, 140 sq.m. 95.00 - 190.00; extra person (over 4 yrs) 15.00 - 30.00; extra car or m/cycle free - 15.00; dog free - 15.00; local tax 0.50 - 1.50.
-- Low season offers.
-- Credit cards accepted.

Open:
1 April - 30 September.

Address:
Rte Napoléon,
04290 Volonne.

Tel:
(0)4.92.33.50.00.
FAX: (0)4.92.33.50.49.
E-mail: l.hippocampe
@wanadoo.fr.

Reservations:
Made with deposit and booking fee (Ffr. 150).

`Camping Cheque'

Book this site
01892 559898

THE ALAN ROGERS'
travel service

*see colour advert
between pages 192/193*

0403 Camping Lac du Moulin de Ventre, Niozelles, Forcalquier

Small, peaceful lakeside site, close to the Luberon.

In the heart of Haute-Provence, near Forcalquier, a busy French town, this attractive site is beside a small lake (with pedalo hire) and 28 acres of wooded, hilly land available for walking. Trees and shrubs are labelled and the herbs of Provence can be found growing wild. A nature lover's delight - birds and butter-flies abound. Some 80 of the 100 level, grassy pitches have electricity (6/10A) and there is some shade from the variety of trees. There is a bar/restaurant with waiter service, takeaway meals and themed evenings (high season), plus a pizzeria. Sanitary facilities are good, with hot showers, washbasins in cabins and some en-suite cubicles with showers and washbasins. There are facilities for disabled people, a baby bath, washing machines and fridges for hire. Amenities include a shop for essentials (supermarket 5 km), a library and a children's playground. Activities are organised in high season. There is a swimming pool with a large shallow area (from 1/5), fishing and boules. Only electric or gas barbecues are permitted. The site is well situated to visit Mont Ventoux, the Luberon National Park and the Gorges du Verdon. Apartments, bungalows and caravans to let. Used by tour operators (8%). General site maintenance can be variable. A 'Sites et Paysages' member.

Directions: From A51 take exit for Brillanne (on the N96) then the N100 west for about 3 km. Site is signed on left and is near Forcalquier, 3 km. SE of Niozelles.

Charges 2000:
-- Per unit, incl. 2 persons Ffr. 105.00, with electri-city 138.00; extra person 33.00; child (under 4 yrs) 18.00; dog 20.00.
-- Low season less 20%, 20-60% for longer stays.
-- No credit cards.

Open:
1 April - 20 October.

Address:
Niozelles,
04300 Forcalquier.

Tel:
(0)4.92.78.63.31.
FAX: (0)4.92.79.86.92.

Reservations:
Advised for July/Aug; made with deposit (30%) and fee (Ffr. 150).

`Camping Cheque'

Book this site
01892 559898

THE ALAN ROGERS'
travel service

*see colour advert
between pages 192/193*

0402 Castel Camp du Verdon, Castellane

Good site with swimming pool close to 'Route des Alpes' and Gorges du Verdon.

As you drive into Camp du Verdon, the neat and tidy air of the place is very striking. This is a very popular holiday area, the gorge, canoeing and rafting being the main attractions. Two heated swimming pools and numerous on-site activities help to keep non canoeists here. It is a large level site, part meadow, part wooded. The 500 pitches are numbered and separated by newly planted bushes. They vary in size (but mostly over the average), 420 have 6A electricity, and 120 also have water and waste water points. The site is lit and some lights are left on all night. The sanitary blocks are being refurbished. One is already finished with British style WCs and all the latest, easy to clean equipment and, as the rest are upgraded the Turkish style toilets will be replaced. Showers are pre-set and all facilities have hot water. Each block has a resident cleaner who keeps them spotless. One block has facilities for disabled visitors. Washing machines and irons, chemical disposal and motorcaravan service point. The site restaurant is very popular, a takeaway opens twice daily and there is a pizzeria/crêperie. Beside the restaurant is a terrace and a bar including a room with a log fire for the cooler evenings. The two heated swimming pools are open all season. A new paddling pool with a 'mushroom' style fountain opened in 2000. A small fishing lake for children is restocked regularly and younger children have playgrounds and minigolf. For the rest there is a wide variety of activities - archery, basketball, volleyball, bicycle hire, riding and table tennis to name but a few. Entertainers provide games and competitions for all during July/Aug. Dances and discos suit all age groups (the latest finishing time is 11 pm. and after that someone patrols the site to make sure all is quiet). The river Verdon runs along one edge of the site, so watch children. There is now a walk to Castellane without using the main road. With the facilities open all season, the site is very popular and is used by tour operators (110 pitches). Mobile homes to hire (48).

Directions: From Castellane take D952 westwards towards Gorges du Verdon and Moustiers. Site is 1 km. on left.

Charges 2000:
-- Per unit with up to 3 persons Ffr. 90.00 - 185.00, acc. to season, size and facilities; extra person over 4 yrs 30.00 - 40.00; extra car, tent or caravan 20.00 - 30.00; dog 15.00; local tax 2.00, child (4-12) 1.00.
-- Credit cards accepted.

Open:
15 May - 15 September.

Address:
Domaine de la Salaou, 04120 Castellane.

Tel:
(0)4.92.83.61.29.
FAX: (0)4.92.83.69.37.

Reservations:
Made for any length with deposit (Ffr. 550 - 800, which includes booking fee of Ffr. 130).

Book this site
01892 559898

THE ALAN ROGERS'
travel service

see colour advert between pages 224/225

0406 Camping-Caravaning Le Haut-Verdon, Villars-Colmars

Family site on the river bank only open for a short season.

Situated on the banks of the Verdon, a good trout river which then flows through the spectacular gorge, the Haut-Verdon is a family site surrounded by the majestic peaks of the Alpes-de-Haute-Provence, on the doorstep of the Mercantour National Park. All the buildings are in the style of the high Alps which gives a very authentic feel to the site. The 130 pitches set amongst the pines are mostly on the large size and all have electricity available (6/10A) but some will require long leads. The main toilet block, recently refurbished, is heated and very well appointed. There are bidets, pre-set showers and washbasins in cabins, and most of the WCs are British style, with just a few Turkish. This block also contains washing machines and irons, plus dishwashing and laundry sinks, all with hot water. At the back is a freezer for ice packs and a room for tenters to eat in when inclement weather strikes. Chemical disposal and motorcaravan service point. A small play area keeps children amused and there are entertainers to organise games and competitions. Amenities which include volleyball, basketball, giant chess, a bowling alley, table tennis, tennis and TV, plus swimming and paddling pools, will surely ensure something for everyone. There are barbecue areas around the site (portable ones are banned). The small shop has fresh food and is open all day, as is the attractive bar/restaurant and takeaway. Fishing on site, bicycle hire 3 km, riding 10 km. Chalets for hire. Caravan storage available. There is a small village near but the town of St André is 23 km. English is spoken. A `Sites et Paysages' member.

Directions: Follow D955 north from St André les Alpes towards Colmar. After about 11 km. the road number changes to D908. Site is on right at the southern edge of Villars-Colmars. Caravans are not advised to use the D908 from Annot.

Charges 2001:
-- Per person over 4 yrs Ffr. 20.00 - 26.00; child (2-6 yrs) 10.00 - 15.00; pitch (80-100 sq.m.) 40.00 - 56.00; dog 10.00; electricity 6A 15.00; 10A 20.00; local tax 1.00.
-- Credit cards accepted.

Open:
26 June - 28 August.

Address:
04370 Villars-Colmars.

Tel:
(0)4.92.83.40.09 (or when closed
(0)1.48.72.79.43).
FAX: (0)4.92.83.56.61
(or (0)1.48.72.50.19).

Reservations:
Made with deposit (30%) and fee (Ffr. 100).

0407 Camping du Plan, Barcelonnette

Small, clean site, a cut above other sites in the area.

The area around Barcelonnette is not high in the holiday popularity table, but it is appealing to those who like dramatic mountain scenery and the more rugged pursuits of mountaineering, mountain cycling and white water canoeing. Few caravanners and motor caravanners find their way in to this mountainous region, but it is popular amongst campers with cycles or motorcycles. In an area where most of the sites are rather crowded and basic, Camping du Plan has fairly generously sized pitches and these are defined by mature trees which provide welcome shade in high summer. The toilet block is old fashioned with mostly Turkish style toilets, but it is kept spotlessly clean and there is an unlimited supply of hot water for showers, apart from a two hour maintenance period in the middle of the day. For two wheel campers the bar, which doubles as reception, serves breakfasts and a fairly basic but filling evening menu. Pitches near the road can be fairly noisy during the day, mostly because of motorcycles passing on their way to tackle Col d'Allos. Eight kilometres from Barcelonnette is the other infamous mountain pass, the Col de la Bonette which is the highest paved road in Europe. This pass is really only suitable for two wheeled vehicles. For motor caravanners there is a community service point at Barcelonnette aeroport, and from there the brave can take a brief powered or gliding tour of the surrounding mountains. This site is not suitable for large motorcaravans and twin axle caravans.

Charges guide:
-- Per unit incl. 2 persons Ffr. 65.00; extra person 21.00; child under 5 yrs 12.20; electricity 3A 16.80, 6A 22.20.
Open:
May - end September.
Address:
04400 Barcelonnette.
Tel:
(0)4.92.81.08.11.
Reservations:
Contact site.

Directions: From new Barcelonnette bypass turn right (if coming from Gap) over the bridge and right again at T-junction on D902 signed Allos. Camping du Plan is the first site on the right after 300 yards.

0500 Camping des Princes d'Orange, Orpierre

Attractive, terraced site within walking distance of charming medieval village.

This site, situated on a hillside above the village, has been gradually and thoughtfully developed over 20 years by its owners. Their genuine, friendly welcome means many families return year upon year, bringing in turn new generations. Divided into five terraces, all of its 120 generously sized pitches enjoy good shade from trees and wicker canopies and have electricity connections (4A). Six sanitary blocks with mostly British style WCs, showers and washbasins in cubicles, baby bath, dishwashing and laundry sinks, are extremely clean and accessible from all levels; laundry facilities are near reception. Other amenities include a swimming pool (20 x 10 m.) and paddling pool (15/6-15/9), children's play area including small trampoline with safety net, table tennis and games room. Bicycle hire 500 m. A reasonably priced takeaway service is available from the bar in high season. There is no on-site shop, although bread is available from the bar each morning, and other basics from village (the nearest shopping centre is in Laragne, 12 km). Only gas barbecues are permitted. Renowned as a serious rock climbing venue, Orpierre also has an enchanting maze of medieval streets and houses, a walk through which is to be recommended - almost like a trip back through the centuries. Whether you choose to drive, walk or cycle there is plenty of wonderful scenery to discover in the immediate vicinity, whilst not far away, some exhilarating hang gliding and parascending can be enjoyed. Whilst the steepness of the terrain and its somewhat remote location may not suit all, there can be no doubt that you will be made most welcome and will enjoy the quiet splendours the region has to offer. Chalets (4) and mobile homes (10) for hire.

Charges 2000:
-- Per unit incl. 3 persons Ffr. 115.00, 2 persons 105.00; extra person 23.00; child (under 7 yrs) 15.00; electricity 15.00; local tax (over 16 yrs) 1.00.
-- Less 25% in low season.
-- No credit cards.
Open:
1 April - 1 November.
Address:
05700 Orpierre.
Tel:
(0)4.92.66.22.53.
FAX: (0)4.92.66.31.08.
Reservations:
Made with deposit (Ffr. 550) and fee (60).

Directions: Turn off N75 road at Eyguians onto D30 - site is signed at turning in centre of village of Orpierre.

For lists of sites that offer facilities on site for FISHING, GOLF, HORSE RIDING or BICYCLE HIRE see pages 263 - 265

0501 Camping-Caravaning Les Grillons, Embrun

Well located site for exploring beautiful region.

The town of Embrun, 'le petit Nice' of the Alps, lying in the Durance valley between Les Ecrins (largest National Park in France) and the Queyras valley, is a pivotal point for exploring this area of outstanding natural beauty. Situated between Gap and Briançon, the roads are well marked and easily negotiated. The resorts in the area are well known for winter recreation. The summer season is particularly short - the possibility of quite cool nights contrasting sharply with hot days. Les Grillons, family owned, although lacking somewhat in sophistication, has a friendly ambience (no English). Across the valley from Embrun, it has 93 grass pitches set in alcoves with trees giving demarcation and some shade. The basic sanitary provision offers the usual facilities with warm water, British and Turkish style toilets, chemical disposal, laundry and dishwashing and a washing machine and dryer. There are two medium sized unheated swimming pools, two tennis courts, a children's play area and a large adjoining field for extra activities. Les Grillons is 2,600 ft high and a short ride gives access to alpine meadows of stunning beauty - a paradise for keen walkers and cyclists. There are many leisure activities in the area, including biking, riding, canoeing and paragliding. No shop on site (bread may be ordered), but Embrun caters for all shopping needs.

Directions: From Gap take N94 towards Briançon. Approaching Embrun, at first roundabout, turn right on D40. After 1 km. turn left on N340 and site is on left after 400 m. down long drive. Site is well signed.

Charges 2000:
-- Per unit incl. 1 or 2 persons Ffr. 84.00; small tent incl. 1 or 2 persons 55.00; extra person 23.00; child (3-10 yrs) 12.00; extra car 10.00; dog 10.00; electricity 3A 16.00, 6A 20.00, 10A 26.00; local tax 1.00 (4-10 yrs) 0.50.
Open:
15 May - 15 September.
Address:
Rte de Madeleine, 05200 Embrun.
Tel:
(0)4.92.43.32.75.
Reservations:
Made with deposit (Ffr. 600) and fee (60); contact site.

8403M Camping Le Brégoux en Provence, Aubignan, nr Carpentras

Generally speaking, reasonably priced sites of a good standard in this area are few and far between. This attractive municipal site is an exception and well worth considering as a base for exploring this region, being conveniently situated for visiting Mont Ventoux and the Dentelles de Montmirail, Orange, Carpentras, Vaison la Romaine, Avignon and even Aix-en-Provence. The site itself is about 10 minutes walk from the town, is on level grass and fairly well shaded. The 177 or so pitches, most with electrical connections (6A), are of a reasonable size and are partially separated. Sanitary facilities, in three blocks, include pre-set hot showers, with dressing area, some washbasins in private cabins, British style WCs, covered washing up areas, and two washing machines, all very clean when inspected in July. A machine provides drinks and ice creams all season.

Directions: Site is on the southern outskirts of the small town of Aubignan, 6 km. north of Carpentras via the D7. Signed in Aubignan and is off the D55 to the right.

Charges 2000:
-- Per person Ffr. 16.00; child (under 10 yrs) 9.00; pitch 16.00; dog 8.00; electricity 15.00.
-- Credit cards accepted.
Open:
1 March - 31 October.
Address:
Chemin du Vas, 84810 Aubignan.
Tel:
(0)4.90.62.62.50.
FAX: (0)4.90.62.65.21.
Reservations:
Contact site.

8408 Camping-Caravaning La Simioune, Bollène

Unsophisticated, rural site, a paradise for horse lovers, open all year.

Please don't go to La Simioune if you prefer a regimented site with neat lawns and flower beds or lots of entertainment. In fact, first impressions here are of it being untidy. It will appeal to lovers of nature and the country, with half tame rabbits running around and well cared for horses in the nearby yards. This is actually a riding school with local children coming for lessons. Campers can also hire horses by the hour, although the favourite seems to be the day-long trek with a river crossing and picnic lunch (all at reasonable prices). The site is set amongst tall pines on sandy, undulating ground, bordered on one side by a vineyard. The 80 pitches are of varying size and unmarked, most with electricity (6A). The sanitary block is basic, but clean and adequate, with British style WCs, washbasins and adjustable showers in tiled cubicles, all free. A small room for babies, a child's WC and a room for disabled people. The site itself may be difficult for wheelchairs due to the sandy terrain. There are laundry and dishwashing sinks with two hot taps to draw from and an old washing machine. A motorcaravan service point is planned. The small bar serves simple meals in July and Aug. and there is a small swimming and a paddling pool. The English speaking owner is very helpful. The area has many lovely medieval villages and some (not all!) will visit the nearby crocodile farm down on the Rhone. Barbecues are not permitted.

Directions: From A7 exit 19, at first roundabout, follow signs for Carpentras (site signed). Take third left signed Lambisque and follow site signs for 5 km.

Charges 2000:
--Per pitch Ffr. 20.00; adult 22.00; child (under 7 yrs) 10.00; animal 10.00; electricity (6A) 15.00; local tax incl. In season: pitch incl. 2 persons and electricity 75.00.
-- No credit cards.
Open:
All year.
Address:
84500 Bollène.
Tel:
(0)4.90.33.44.62.
Reservations:
Contact site for details.

PROVENCE - 84 Vaucluse

N8402 Domaine Naturiste de Bélézy, Bédoin, nr Carpentras

Excellent naturist site with many amenities and activities, at the foot of Mt Ventoux.

We continue to be impressed by this site with its policy of annual refurbishment, its management, the French approach to naturism, and the extent to which the natural environment has been managed in harmony with the Provencal countryside. The ambience is essentially relaxed and comfortable. English is spoken widely amongst staff and customers although some activities may be conducted solely in French. The site has two areas joined by a short pedestrian tunnel and the 230 marked and numbered pitches are set amongst many varieties of trees and shrubs – oaks, olives, pines, acacias, broom, lavender, etc. There are a few pitches set aside for wheelchair users. Electricity points (16A) are plentiful but you may need a long cable in places. The emphasis is on informality and concern for the environment, and during high season cars are banned from the camping area to the supervised parking areas nearby. This not only provides an air of tranquillity, but safety for children. Dogs and pets are banned from the camping area all season. Barbecues are only permitted in a communal area. So far as naturism is concerned the emphasis is on personal choice (and weather conditions!), the only stipulation being the requirement for complete nudity in the pools and pool area. The facilities in general are what you would expect from a four star site, although some of the sanitary blocks are a little different. The newer ones are of a standard type and excellent quality, with free hot showers in cubicles with separators, washbasins (H&C) in private cabins and British WCs. One block has an attractive children's section with baby baths, sinks and showers at different heights, children's toilets and is decorated with tiles painted with animals. In the same area the adult block has hot showers in the open air, separated by natural stone dividers and washing up areas (H&C), again mostly in the open air.

The leisure park side of the site is also used for camping and is an area of natural parkland with an orchard, fishpond and woodland (complete with red squirrels) and blends well with the surrounding countryside. A good range of sports facilities includes two tennis courts and three swimming pools. The largest pool is for swimming and relaxation and is accessed by steps, as is the smaller pool (heated 11/3-8/10) which is also used for watersports and aquarobics. The smallest is for children supervised by parents. The area around the pools has been attractively landscaped so that parents can watch their children in the adjacent adventure play area. Near the pools is the smart restaurant, with terrace, and the old Mas (Provencal farmhouse) which houses many activities, as well as the library, near soundproof disco, information centre and children's club. The restaurant provides excellent food, waiter service, and takeaway meals at affordable prices. The shop is also reasonably priced (all 1/4-30/9). It is possible to walk into Bedoin - the market is the best we have shopped at. You will find yourself spoilt for choice here with the extensive range of activities. To mention but a few, they include painting and pottery courses, language lessons, archery, music (bring your own instrument) and guided walks. There are, of course, the usual boules and table tennis. We took advantage of the hydrotherapy centre (1/4-30/9) to tone up and revitalise with qualified diagnosis. Treatments include steam and spa baths, massage and seaweed packs, osteopathy and Chinese medicine , and acupuncture for a reasonable fee. New sauna. Child minding. Mobile homes, bungalows, etc. to let. There is a 'gardien' on call in the Mas during the night for emergencies. The Maison d'Animation offers a restaurant booking service with certain restaurants in the scheme offering a complimentary aperitif. Bélézy operates in four seasons (low, inter, mid and high), booking is recommended. A comprehensive booklet clearly details exactly what is available and when.

Directions: From A7 autoroute or the RN7 at Orange, take the D950 southeast to Carpentras, then northeast via D974 to Bédoin. Site is signed in Bédoin, being about 2 km. northeast of the village.

Charges 2001:
-- Per 1 adult Ffr 50.00 - 125.00, 2 adults 70.00 - 170.00, 3 adults 120.00 - 210.00; extra adult 31.00 - 49.00; child (3-8 yrs) 18.00 - 36.00; electricity (12A) 22.00; large pitch + 25.00; pitch with water, drainage and sink + 30.00; local tax 2.00 adult, 1.00 child.
-- Recreation fee 5.00 - 7.00 per night, per person (child 3.50 - 5.00).
-- Various offers and reductions outside high season.
-- Credit cards accepted.

Open:
11 March - 8 October.

Address:
84410 Bédoin.

Tel:
(0)4.90.65.60.18.
FAX: (0)4.90.65.94.45.
E-mail: belezy@ pacwan.net.

Reservations:
Write with deposit (Ffr 400 per week booked) and fee (180).

Book this site
01892 559898

THE ALAN ROGERS'
travel service

8405 Camping-Caravaning La Sorguette, L'Isle sur la Sorgue

Former municipal site with reasonably long season, 1.5 km. from attractive town.

The entrance and access roads at La Sorguette, a former municipal site, are wide giving the whole site a spacious feel. The 164 level pitches are all of a good size, arranged in fours and hedged with various types of shrubs and trees, mostly having a little shade at some part of the day. All have electricity connections (4/10A). Three strategically placed toilet blocks provide roomy, pre-set hot showers, washbasins with hot and cold water (in cubicles for ladies) and mainly British style WCs. Dishwashing and laundry sinks have hot water and two blocks have washing machines, dryer, ironing boards and clothes lines. There is a unit for disabled people and chemical disposal at all three and a motorcaravan service point. Fridges to hire. All these facilities are kept very clean and well maintained. A children's play area, volleyball, half-court tennis and basketball are in the centre of the site, together with a barbecue area (no pitches overlook this area). A shop and a bar with snacks (1/7-25/8) are set well away from the pitches, outside the entrance which ensures that the occasional entertainment in July/Aug. does not disturb campers. In high season a few competitions are organised (boule or volleyball), plus some children's entertainment, but this is quite low key and the general feel of the site even in high season is of calm and peace. The river Sorgue runs alongside a part of the site (fenced with a gate). This is only 6 km. from its source in the mountains at Fontaine de Vaucluse (a big tourist attraction) and consequently it is still very clear and can be used for canoeing, swimming or fishing. Isle sur la Sorgue is a very attractive small town, dominated by the river which forms small canals and waterways, interspersed with a number of water wheels. There are many bars and restaurants, some with seating overlooking the water which has a cooling effect in the height of summer. Its two well-attended market days provide even more colour and virtually fill the old streets of the town, and brightly coloured pottery, table covers, fruit and vegetable make it a photographer's paradise. This area of Provence has many pretty villages to explore within a 20 mile radius and the many quiet D-class roads are ideal for cycling. The site staff are very friendly and English is spoken. Canoe and bicycle hire. Mobile homes to rent.

Directions: Site is on the N100 to Apt, 1.5 km. east of L'Isle sur la Sorgue and is well signed.

Charges 2001:
-- Per unit incl. 2 persons Ffr. 81.20; extra person over 7 yrs 28.10; child 1-7 yrs 14.00; animal 10.00; electricity 4A 19.00; local tax 1.40.
Open:
15 March - 15 October.
Address:
Route d'Apt (RN100), 84800 L'Isle sur la Sorgue.
Tel:
(0)4.90.38.05.71. FAX: (0)4.90.20.84.61. E-mail: sorguette@wanadoo.fr.
Reservations:
Made with deposit (Ffr. 400 or 60,98) and fee (Ffr. 80 or 12,20).

8407 Camping Club International Carpe Diem, Vaison-la-Romaine

Developing site with marvellous views.

Perhaps Carpe Diem is a shade pretentious with its Greek statues and amphitheatre surround to its main pool. The site is only a few years old and will no doubt mellow as the trees and shrubs grow and old and new blend together. The situation is quite impressive with magnificent views and yet only 800 m. from the village of Vaison Romaine. There are 180 grass touring pitches with electricity (6/10A), that are rather on the small side, divided by small shrubs and young trees. A separate terraced area has some mobile homes and chalets to rent. The central toilet block - with fountain - provides mainly British and a few Turkish style toilets, washbasins in cabins (H&C), pre-set showers with an unusual cupboard for your clothes. Also included are washing up and laundry sinks (H&C) with small editions of everything provided for children, even covering washing and laundry sinks! Washing machine and chemical toilet disposal. Extra facilities are located behind the main pool. Reception provides tourist information with small shop next door. A bar near the main pool is open in the main season and there is a pizzeria and TV room. This main pool is impressive with its tiered seating, plants, etc, and there is a simpler square pool with grass surrounds near the play area. Other on site activities include minigolf, archery (cross-bow type), volleyball, football and basketball. Mountain bikes are for hire. A mini-club and entertainment are organised in high season and can be noisy. There is a charge for participation in sports and entertainment. Mobile homes and chalets to rent. Used by tour operators (5 pitches).

Directions: Follow Campings signs on approaching village. Site is on south side.

Charges 2000:
-- Per pitch Ffr. 32.00 - 49.00; small tent pitch 27.00 - 43.00; adult 22.00 - 25.00; child (2-10 yrs) 14.00 - 17.00; electricity 6A 18.00, 10A 25.00; dog 13.00; local tax 1.10.
-- Obligatory charge for sports and entertainment Ffr. 6.00 per day per person (over 5 yrs).
-- Credit cards accepted.
Open:
1 March - 31 October.
Address:
Route de St Marcellin, BP 68, 84110 Vaison-la-Romaine.
Tel:
(0)4.90.36.02.02. FAX: (0)4.90.36.36.90. E-mail: camping.carpe. diem@wanadoo.fr.
Reservations:
Made with deposit and fee (Ffr. 500).

`Camping Cheque'

MIDI-PYRENNEES

Major city: Toulouse

Départements: 09 Ariège, 31 Haute-Garonne, 32 Gers,

65 Hautes-Pyrénées, 81 Tarn, 82 Tarn-et Garonne

We have left the official region of the Midi-Pyrénées almost intact except for départements of Aveyron (12) and Lot (46) which we believe sit better in our Tourist region of the Dordogne / Aveyron.

Home of Armagnac, Rugby and the Three Musketeers, the Midi-Pyrénées is the largest region of France, extending from the Dordogne in the north to the Spanish border. It is blessed by bright sunlight and a fascinating range of scenery. High chalk plateaux, majestic peaks, tiny hidden valleys and small fortified sleepy villages, which seem to have changed little since the Middle Ages, contrast with the high-tech, industrial and vibrant university city of Toulouse; also rich in art and architecture. Lourdes is one of the most visited pilgrimage sites in the world. Toulouse-Lautrec, the artist, was born at Albi the capital of the département of Tarn. Much of the town is built of pink brick which seems to glow when seen from the distance. In the east, the little town of Foix, with its maze of steep, winding streets, is a convenient centre from which to explore the prehistoric caves at Niaux and the Aladdin's Cave of duty-free gift shops in the independent state of Andorra. The Canal du Midi that links Bordeaux to the Mediterranean was commissioned by Louis XIV in 1666 and is still in working order to day.

Note: Site reports are laid out by département in numerical order.

See map on page 319.

Cuisine of the region

The cuisine of the Midi-Pyrénées is rich and strongly seasoned, making generous use of garlic and goose fat

Foie Gras – specially preserved livers of goose and duck

Cassoulet – a hearty stew of duck, sausages and beans

Confit de Canard (d'oie) – preserved duck meat (goose)

Magret de canard – duck breast fillets

Poule au pot – chicken simmered with vegetables

Seafood such as oysters, salt-water fish, or piballes from the Adour river

Ouillat (Ouliat) – Pyrénées soup: onions, tomatoes, goose fat, garlic

Tourtière Landaise – a sweet of Agen prunes, apples and Armagnac

Grattons (Graisserons) – a mélange of small pieces of rendered down duck, goose,and pork fat; served as an appetiser – very filling

Wine

There are some excellent regional wines, such as full-bodied red Cahors and, of course, Armagnac to follow the meal. Try 'Floc', a mixture of Armagnac and grape juice

Places of Interest

Albi – birthplace and Museum of Toulouse-Lautrec, imposing Ste Cécile cathedral with 15C fresco of 'The Last Judgement'

Collonges-la-Rouge – picturesque village of Medieval and Renaissance style mansions and manors in red sandstone

Conques – 11th century Ste Foy Romanesque church

Cordes – medieval walled hilltop village

Foix – 11th/12th century towers on rocky peak above town; 14th century cathedral.

Lourdes – famous pilgrimage site where Ste Bernadette is said to have spoken to the Virgin Mary in a grotto and known for the miracles said to have been performed there

Auch – capital of ancient Gascony, boasts a fine statue of d'Artágnan

0903 Camping Le Montagnou, Le Trein d'Ustou

New small site in spectacular mountain setting.

The road going south out of St Girons appears to lead to nowhere other than Guzet, but it is well worth the short detour over easy roads to the little village of Le Trein d'Ustou, which is no more than 15 minutes short of the up and coming winter sports resort of Guzet. Just before Le Trein d'Ustou you find a delightful small campsite, Le Montagnou, nestling among the lush lower slopes of the mountains. Robert and Daniel are a jolly couple who have created this charming site from the forest during the last few years. It is an attractive proposition either as a base for winter sports activities or for touring this lovely area, with 60 level pitches on grass, all with electricity (6, 10 or 16A). Developed on modern lines, it has good quality installations, including two identical heated sanitary blocks (one open in low season). Spotless, they have controllable showers, washbasins in private cabins, British style WCs, covered dishwashing area (H&C), two washing machines, two dryers, and excellent facilities for disabled visitors. Other facilities include a snack bar with takeaway; there is a restaurant 50 m. away in the village. At a lower level there is an area of the river running alongside the site which the locals use for swimming, but really the attraction here is the surrounding area with excellent winter sports facilities that include a ski-lift (10 minutes drive) and no less than 24 pistes! Fishing on site, riding 15 km. There are also many places of interest which Robert will be pleased to tell you about, tourist brochures are available. The walks in this area are renowned - watch out for bears! Robert will brief you about these and about other local wildlife such as the marmot.

Directions: From St Girons follow signs for Guzet; take first right at roundabout (Guzet), second right at next roundabout (Guzet, Seix) and second right at third roundabout to Seix. Go through Seix (the river is on your right) and at Pont de la Taule turn left towards Trein d'Ustou. Site is on left before village.

Charges 2000:
-- Per caravan and car incl. 2 persons and 6A electricity Ffr. 80.00 (summer) - 90.00 (winter); motorcaravan 100.00 - 110.00.
-- Pitch no electricity (all year): caravan 21.50; tent 16.00; person 23.50; child (2-7 yrs) 15.00; car 6.50; dog 6.50.
-- No credit cards.

Open:
All year.

Address:
Route de Guzet, 09140 Le Trein d'Ustou.

Tel:
(0)5.61.66.94.97.
FAX: (0)5.61.66.91.20.
E-mail: campinglemontagnou@wanadoo.fr.

Reservations:
Contact site by letter. Resrvation will be made with fee (Ffr 35) payable on arrival.

0906 Camping Le Pré Lombard, Tarascon-sur-Ariège

Well managed site in popular area and 800m. walk from town.

Didier Mioni, the manager here follows the town motto 'S'y passos, y clemoris - if you wish to come here, you will stay here' in his aim to ensure your satisfaction on his site. This busy site is beside the river Ariége on the outskirts of the town, with a supermarket just a level stroll. There are 180 level, grassy, numbered pitches with shade provided by a variety of trees. Some hedged pitches are at the rear of the site and there are 39 site-owned tents and mobile homes. Electricity (4, 6, or 10A) is available to all. The site is well served by six sanitary units of varying age, design and size, although not all may be open off season. These provide mostly British WCs, both open and cubicled washbasins, showers (pre-mixed hot water), dishwashing and laundry sinks, chemical disposal, good motor-caravan service point and facilities for disabled people. Hot water is free. Separate laundry with washing machines, dryer and ironing. There is a good restaurant with entertainment, dancing and an enjoyable French ambience (1/5-30/9). Bar and takeaway (open according to demand). Bread, gas, papers and daily requirements are sold in the bar. Fenced, unsupervised, open-air swimming pool (1/5-30/9 when weather permits, a covered pool is planned), separate playgrounds for toddlers and older children, video games machines, table tennis, table football, boules and volleyball courts. A full programme of entertainment for families is provided in main season. A gate in the fence gives access to the river for fishing (licences required), the ducks here are adept at being uninvited guests at your table if you are parked close to the river, and they provide an amusing diversion. As this is a town site there is some traffic noise during the day and evening. This good value site is open all year and is an excellent choice for early or late breaks, or as a stop-over en-route to the winter sun destinations in Spain. This region of Ariège is in the foothills of the Pyrénées and 45 km. from Andorra. At Tarascon itself you can go underground at the Parc Pyrénéen de l'Art Préhistorique to view rock paintings, or the really adventurous can take to the air for paragliding, hangliding, or micro-lighting. The Vallées Ax famous for cross country ski-ing are within reasonably easy reach for winter sports enthusiasts.

Directions: Site is 800 m. south of the town centre adjacent to the river. Turn off main N20 into the town centre and there are prominent camp signs.

Charges 2001:
-- Per unit incl. 2 adults and 6A electricity Ffr. 80.00 - 130.00, 10A electricity 90.00 - 140.00; extra person over 4 yrs 20.00 - 35.00; animal 5.00 - 10.00; extra vehicle 15.00 - 25.00; electricity 4A 15.00, 6A 20.00, 10A 25.00; local tax per adult 2.00; child (4-10 yrs) 1.00 (July/Aug only).
-- Family rate for 4 persons and 6A electricity Ffr. 100.00.
-- Credit cards accepted.

Open:
All year.

Address:
09400 Tarascon-sur-Ariège.

Tel:
(0)5.61.05.61.94.
FAX: (0)5.61.05.78.93.
E-mail: camping@camping.le.prelombard.com.

Reservations:
Advised for high season and made with 25% deposit and Ffr. 100 booking fee.

`Camping Cheque'

MIDI-PYRENNEES - 09 Ariège

0908 Camping du Lac, Foix

New lakeside site with pool close to Foix.

This is a large sprawling site with many facilities and is just 3 km. north of the very pretty town of Foix. There is some road noise as the site is alongside the busy N20 but there is lots of room to manoeuvre at the entrance and a smart air conditioned reception building. The pool is opposite the entrance and is in a fenced area with sunbathing space on the pool-side with loungers or on a grassed area. There is a separate paddling pool. Reception sells basic goods but no fresh food and there is a pizza hut and bar/drinks stall close to the pool (a restaurant is planned for 2001). The four unisex sanitary blocks are of different designs, all new, some of brick and some resembling pretty 'wendy houses' made of wood. The facilities are modern and clean with free hot water, good showers and British style WCs. One of the little blocks contains excellent facilities for disabled campers and a well equipped baby room. Another hut is the TV room. The site is informally divided into four areas, one given over to parking. The others are generally flat and some shade can be found under mature trees. There are 135 pitches, most with electricity (4, 8 or 13A) but the site is so big there appear to be more, there is lots of room. Electricity distribution boxes and water points are strategically placed. Access to the lake is through a gate that is locked at night. Children's play areas are round the site and another is by the lake. Children will need supervision in the lake area. The lake is owned by a separate company but campers have free use of the attractive area. Here you will find canoeing and pedaloes, along with fishing or just picnics and barbecues. A small bar operates. The lake is not for swimming as there is a fair amount of forbidding green surface weed but there is a clear area for canoe instruction (charges apply). The site has some animation in high season and is ideal for visiting Foix and exploring the local area, especially the prehistoric relics that abound here. Reception will assist in booking the many local attractions such as cycling and walking tours, riding, golf or even white water rafting. A tennis court and boules pitch are on site. Torches are necessary.

Directions: From Foix stay on N20 north for 3 km. Site is well signed on left.

Charges 2000:
-- Per unit incl. 1 person and electricity Ffr. 44.00 - 55.00; extra person 16.00 - 21.00; child (under 7) 11.00 - 14.00; electricity 15.00 - 35.00.
-- Credit cards accepted (you may be asked to pay in advance).
Open:
1 April - 13 October.
Address:
RN 20, 09000 Foix.
Tel:
(0)5.61.65.11.58.
FAX: (0)5.61.05.32.62.
E-mail: camping-du-lac @wanadoo.fr
Reservations:
Advised July & Aug; contact site.

0909N Camping Millfleurs, Varilhes

Peaceful naturist site in superb location for mature naturists.

Millfleurs is owned by a Dutch couple, Gert and Annie Kos who speak excellent English. This is camping at a relaxed and sublime level. It is so peaceful here and there are some 70 acres of woods and meadows to explore with guided naturist walks in total privacy. The long drive leads to a traditional farmhouse housing the campsite administration facilities. Bread is available to order in high season but after that shopping is done locally. Guests dine together in the 'salle de reunion' within the farmhouse two nights a week (Sat/Wed) or you can just relax and meet friends there for a drink. There is a refrigerator with drinks operated on an honesty system. The new central unisex sanitary block is superb and well thought out, including great facilities for disabled campers, the attractive and abundant flowers and potted plants within are really cheery. There is free hot water throughout, British style WCs and superb inside and outside showers. The site has 45 large flat pitches (26 with 4/6A electricity) on well spaced terraces, but there are also very secluded pitches in wooded areas with shade, or you can pitch a tent in the meadows if you prefer. Long leads are required if you pitch off the terraces. There are few of the normal camping leisure facilities here and the site is definitely aimed at the more mature naturist camper. There is a petanque court and a guide book for walks and cycle rides in the local area. Transport is required here as there is no bus service. Explore the nearby mediaeval town of Foix with its stunning castle towering over the busy centre, and investigate the history of the Cathares and the region with its underground rivers and caves. With its temperate climate, the Foix valley is a prime area for growing the grapes for the white wine used in the production of the famous Cava, and the vineyards are worth a visit. The coast is approximately 1½ hours away. Torches are essential at night. Pick ups from airports and stations can be organised by the site.

Directions: Approaching Foix on N20, from north take D1 towards Lavalanet. After 6 km. turn left on D13 for Gudas (watch carefully for sign). The site is now signed at junctions and is 2 km. before Gudas. The entrance is on the left.

Charges 2000:
-- Per pitch Ffr. 25.00 - 35.00; per person all ages 22.50 - 27.50; electricity 15.00.
-- No credit cards.
Open:
1 April - 15 October.
Address:
Le Tuilier Gudas, 09120 Varilhes.
Tel:
(0)5.61.60.77.56.
FAX: as phone.
E-mail: ag.kos@ wanadoo.fr.
Reservations:
Not necessary.

0902 Camping L'Arize, La Bastide-de-Sérou

Small, quality site in strategic location for touring this part of the Pyrénées.

You are assured of a warm welcome from Dominique and Brigitte at this friendly little family site; Brigitte speaks excellent English. The site nestles in a delightful, tranquil valley among the foothills of the Pyrénées and is just east of the interesting village of La Bastide de Sérou beside the River Arize (good trout fishing). The river is fenced for the safety of children on the site, but may be accessed just outside the gate. Deer and wild boar are common in this area and may be sighted in quieter periods. The owners have built this site from ground level over the last five years and have put much love and care into its development. The 70 large pitches are neatly laid out within the spacious site, which is on level grass. All have 3/6A electricity (French type sockets) and are separated into bays by hedges and young trees. There is a small swimming pool with paved sunbathing area, a juice bar and a children's play area. The central sanitary block (unheated) offers spacious showers with free hot water throughout, separators, shelves, washbasins in cabins, a laundry room, dishwashing under cover and good facilities for babies and disabled people. The only omission is a chemical disposal point – the organic sewage system is incompatible with chemicals. Fishing, riding and bicycle hire are available on site. There is entertainment in high season, weekly barbeques and charming welcome drinks on Sundays. Several restaurants and shops are within a few minute's drive and the nearest restaurant, which is located at the national stud for the famous Merens horses just 200 m. away, will deliver takeaway meals to your pitch. There are interesting local activities including golf (5 km). The owners have negotiated discounts at several local attractions, details are provided in the comprehensive pack provided on arrival - in your own language. Equipped bungalow tents and modern mobile homes for rent. This is a comfortable and relaxing base for touring this beautiful part of the Pyrénées with easy access to the medieval town of Foix and even Andorra for duty-free shopping. Caravan storage.

Charges 2001:
-- Per pitch incl. 2 persons and electricity 78.00 - 102.00; extra adult 20.00 - 29.00; child (0-7 yrs) 13.00 - 19.00; dog 5.00
-- Discounts for longer stays in mid and low season.
-- Credit cards accepted.

Open:
1 March - 31 October.

Address:
Lieu-dit Bourtol, 09240 La Bastide-de-Sérou.

Tel:
(0)5.61.65.81.51.
FAX: (0)5.61.65.83.34.
E-mail: campingarize @aol.com

Reservations:
Made with 25% deposit and fee (Ffr 60).

Book this site
01892 559898

THE ALAN ROGERS'
travel service

Directions: Site is southeast of the village La Bastide-de-Sérou. Take the D15 towards Nescus and site is on right after approx. 1 km.

0905M Camping Municipal, Sorgeat, nr Ax-les-Thermes

Superbly situated high up on the mountainside overlooking the valley this site has magnificent views, with the river 300 m distant and a lake at 2 km, this small site provides just 38 pitches on terraces with electricity (5/10A). Well supervised, with the warden present all evening, it is kept very clean. It has a rather small sanitary block with only two showers and two WCs (one British, one Turkish) in each half. Hot water is provided for dishwashing. Facilities for disabled people are also very good with special washbasin and a very large shower suite. A small stream tinkles through the centre of the site and the attractive hills towering above the site reverberate with the sounds of goat bells. There is a separate area with brick barbecues for campers and picnic tables are provided. Small children's play area.

Charges guide:
-- Per pitch 9.00; adult 17.00; child 10.00; electricity 5A 13.00, 10A 23.00; local tax 1.00.

Open:
All year.

Address:
09110 Sorgeat.

Tel:
(0)5.61.64.36.34 or (0)5.61.64.21.93.

Reservations:
Advised for high season - contact site.

Directions: From N20 (Foix - Andorra) through Ax-les-Thermes, in the centre of the village take D613 to left, signed Quillen (hairpin bends) for 5 km. Site is signed on right. The last km. is a narrow two way winding road.

0907M Camping Municipal, Lavelanet

This quiet, neat site is adjacent to the municipal pool and sports complex. It has a very nice modern sanitary unit with an open central atrium. The unit provides mostly British style WCs, washbasins (a few in cubicles), push-button showers (no divider), free hot water, dishwashing and laundry sinks, a WC/washbasin cubicle for disabled people, a washing machine plus iron, and chemical disposal. There are 100 neatly numbered level pitches, about half separated by hedges, some very private, and most with electricity (15A). The site has minigolf (free), table tennis, barbecue areas, archery and volleyball. Activities are arranged (with a guide) including walking, canoeing, canyoning and caving. Shops and other services are close in the town. The notice board at reception gives details of entertainment and local activities. The pool is open July/Aug. Torches are necessary here and unusually dogs are allowed to run free.

Charges 2000:
-- Per pitch Ffr. 18.00 - 23.00; adult 18.00 - 23.00; child (0-7 yrs) 15.00; electricity 15.00.
-- No credit cards.

Open:
15 June - 31 August.

Address:
09300 Lavelanet.

Tel:
(0)5.61.01.22.20.
FAX: (0)5.61.03.06.39.

Reservations:
Write to Service Tourisme,BP 89, 09300 Lavelanet.

Directions: Lavelanet is 27 km. east of Foix. The site is just off the D117 at the western end of the town. Signed at the entrance to town.

3105M Camping Municipal Bélvèdere des Pyrénées, Saint Gaudens

Suitable for an overnight stop, this is a well organised, neat site with marvellous views to the Pyrénées, within walking distance of town. There are 96 pitches of average size on level grass, most with electricity (4/6A) and partially separated by shrubs and trees which give a fair amount of shade. There are also some small pitches for tents. A modern tiled sanitary block has large showers (without shelves or dividers; hot water available 7-11 am and 5-9 pm), washbasins in private cabins, British style WCs, a unit for disabled visitors, plus good dishwashing and laundry facilities.

Charges guide:
-- Per person Ffr. 17.50; pitch 22.00; electricity 4A 16.00, 6A 27.50.

Open:
All year.

Address:
31800 St Gaudens.

Tel:
(0)5.61.89.15.76.

Reservations:
Contact site.

Directions: Site is west of the town off the RN117, signed from a small round-about. Exit either north or south of new autoroute following N117 towards Tarbes.

3206 Camping-Caravaning Lac des Trois Vallées, Lectoure

Large 40 hectare lively, multi-activity holiday village with many facilities.
This site is set in the Gers countryside in the heart of Gascony, a land of fortified villages wine and 'foie gras', near the town of Lectoure which was once the main seat of the Counts of Armagnac and is now a spa town. Lac des Trois Vallées, with its attractive ivy covered reception, is popular with those who like activities and entertainment. It is, in fact, a large holiday complex and good for families with teenage children. The emphasis is on water sports and you can choose between the multiple activities on the lakes and the excellent pool complex. Lake activities range from water sports, to fishing and swimming in the multiple pools with diving platforms or the four water chutes. There is a large safe paddling area (open to the public, from 15/5) The impressive pool complex (from 20/5) has separate paddling pools, hydro-massage facilities, plus pleasant grass and paved areas with small trees for sunbathing. Lifeguards supervise both swimming areas in season. Activities include tennis, archery and mountain biking (bikes to hire), with cabaret, shows at the lakeside amphitheatre and craft activities for all ages. A disco and cinema are on site and a children's 'Tepee Club'. There are three restaurants, one under bright white canvas beside the pool, one opposite reception for fast food, one by the lake and finally a chip bar by the lake plus a drinks kiosk. These are supported by three bars including the 'Pub' (hours according to season). Mini-market (from 1/5) and launderette. The eight sanitary blocks, one of ultra-modern design, have pre-set hot water, mixed style British and Turkish toilets, open air baby baths and chemical disposal. They receive heavy use but when we visited all was in order (some are a little dark inside). Motorcaravan services. There are some steep inclines from the lake to the pitches. There are 500 pitches with over 300 for touring units on shaded or open ground, all with electricity (10A). Used by tour operators (143 pitches). Mobile homes and tents for rent. Riding 4 km, golf 10 km. Caravan storage. A 'Yelloh Village' member.

Charges 2001:
-- Per unit incl. up to 3 persons and electricity Ffr. 125.00 - 215.00; extra person 35.00 - 55.00; dog 7.00 -12.00.
-- Many special rates available for couples, families, etc. and low season discounts
-- Credit cards accepted.

Open:
Easter - 16 September.

Address:
32700 Lectoure.

Tel:
(0)5.62.68.82.33.
FAX: (0)5.62.68.88.82.
E- mail: lac.des.trois.
vallees@wanadoo.fr.

Reservations:
Made with deposit (Ffr. 550) and non-refundable fee (150).

`Camping Cheque'

see colour advert between pages 192/193

Directions: Site well signed 2 km. outside Lectoure to the south, off the N21.

3208 Camping Le Talouch, Roquelaure

Family run site in the Gers valley countryside.
Although enjoying an away from it all location, Auch the region's capital is within a 10 km. drive from this site, which takes its name from the small Talouch river. The entrance, off the D148, is fronted by a parking area with reception to the right and the bar/restaurant facing. Beyond this point lies the top half of the touring area which has generous pitches (at least 120 sq.m.) located between mature trees and divided by hedges. There are 105 pitches with electricity (4A) and 10 of these also have water and drainage. The lower half of the site offers contrast, with unshaded pitches in a more open aspect. There are two very well kept sanitary blocks. The larger refurbished building offers modern units with emphasis on bright colours. The smaller is of a more modern and unusual style and is to the rear of the site. Showers are well fitted and facilities include a baby bathroom/shower which can be used by people with disabilities. On site are two swimming pools, a sunbathing area, two play areas, volleyball, tennis, basketball, bicycle hire, a 9 hole swing golf course and organised entertainment in the high season. A small shop sells basic foodstuffs and snacks are available (1/5-30/9). Chalets for rent.

Charges 2001:
-- Per unit incl. 2 adults Ffr. 107.50, with electricity 126.00; extra adult 33.00; child (3-7 yrs) 27.00; animal 8.00.
-- Less in low season.
-- Credit cards accepted.

Open:
1 April - 30 September.

Address:
32810 Roquelaure.

Tel:
(0)5.62.65.52.43.
FAX: (0)5.62.65.53.68.
E-mail: info@
camping-talouch.com.

Reservations:
Advisable for July/Aug; contact site.

Directions: From Auch take N21 for 8.5 km. north and turn east on D272 to Roquelaure village. Then follow signs to site 2 km. south of village on D148.

3201 Le Camp de Florence, La Romieu

Attractive site on edge of historic village in pleasantly undulating Gers countryside.

Camp de Florence is run by the Mynsbergen family who are Dutch (although Susan is English) and they have sympathetically converted the old farmhouse buildings to provide facilities for the site. There are 173 pitches, with 100 for tourers, all of 100 sq.m. plus, all with electricity, three with hardstanding (these are rather small) and terraced where necessary, arranged around a large field (full of sunflowers when we visited) with rural views, giving a feeling of spaciousness. The older pitches near the main buildings have good shade but it gets progressively less the newer the pitch. However, 25 of these are fully serviced and shade will develop. Two unisex toilet blocks have British style toilets, free hot water, showers and washbasins, some in cabins. These facilities may be under pressure at peak times and are a long walk from some corners of the site. Washing machine and dryer, chemical disposal and motorcaravan services. Water points are limited. An excellent upstairs, air-conditioned restaurant, also open to the public, serves a range of food, including local specialities and an à la carte menu (15/5-30/9, closed Weds, with a barbecue instead). The site's pool area is an attractive feature, with a jacuzzi, central island, a protected children's pool and a large terrace with drinks kiosk. The pool is open to the public in the afternoons. There is a children's adventure play area, games area and a pets area typical of Dutch owned sites. Takeaway food is available from the snack bar. Activities include a games room, tennis, table tennis, volleyball, petanque and bicycle hire. Video shows, discos, picnics, animation and musical evenings and excursions are organised. Exchange facility. Shop in nearby village (bread shop on site in season). The 13th century village of La Romieu is on the Santiago de Compostela pilgrim route and the collegiate church, visible from the site, is well worth a visit (the views are magnificent from the tower). The Pyrénées are a two hour drive, the Atlantic coast a similar distance. Fishing 5 km, riding 10 km. The site arranges walking tours, excursions and wine tasting. A few tour operator pitches (18). Mobile homes, tents and chalets for hire (1 night stay possible outside July/Aug. with breakfast).

Directions: Site is signed from D931 Agen - Condom road. Small units can turn left at Ligardes (signed) and follow D36 for 1 km. and take right turn for La Romieu (signed). Otherwise continue until outskirts of Condom and take D41 left to La Romieu and pass through village to site.

Charges 2001:
-- Per unit incl. 2 persons Ffr. 65.00 - 126.00; extra person 22.00 - 37.00; child (4-9 yrs) 16.00 - 27.00; electricity (6A) 20.00; water and drainage plus 13.00; dog 10.00; local tax 1.00 (child 4-9 yrs 0.50).
-- Special prices for groups, rallies, etc.
-- Credit cards accepted.

Open:
1 April - 31 October.

Address:
32480 La Romieu.

Tel:
(0)5.62.28.15.58.
FAX: (0)5.62.28.20.04.
E-mail: info@
campdeflorence.com.

Reservations:
Write or phone for information (English spoken).

`Camping Cheque'

**Book this site
01892 559898**

THE ALAN ROGERS'
travel service

*see colour advert
between pages 192/193*

N3204 Centre Naturiste Deveze, Gaudonville, nr Saint-Clar

Relaxed, well equipped naturist site in beautiful Gers countryside.

This is a well established and very pleasant site in 50 acres of lovely countryside. The 180 pitches, the majority with electricity and many terraced, are in several different areas. All are separated by mature hedges and trees, the amount of shade available varies from area to area and some pitches are flatter than others. In many respects this site would be an excellent introduction to naturist camping, being quite 'laid-back' in terms of rules and regulations, but offering a range of activities for those that want them without any pressure to join in if you don't want to! Deveze has an attractive swimming pool and children's pool (1/6-15/9) and its own 4 acre lake for fishing (free) and woodland area. Other activities include tennis, volleyball, boules, a children's play area, boating, badminton, bicycle hire, archery, film shows and a small gym for working out. There is a simple outdoor restaurant and takeaway, but with quite a varied menu, and a well stocked shop (all 1/7-31/8). Two TV rooms, one satellite and one French. Sanitary facilities are in three blocks and include hot showers (communal), washbasins (cold water only, but hot tap nearby), British type WCs, hairdryers and chemical disposal, all fitted out to a high standard and very well maintained. The ambience at Deveze is warm and friendly with the centre-piece bar and terrace in the original farm buildings somewhat reminiscent of an English country pub (1/6-15/9). A restaurant has been added recently. Campers are encouraged to provide their own entertainment and their efforts provide much fun and enjoyment. Exchange facilities. Caravan storage. Gas available. Mobile homes, bungalows and caravans for hire.

Directions: From Agen or Auch use N21 to Lectoure and D7 to St Clar. From St Clar take D13 (site signed) to Gaudonville. From Montauban D928 southwest then D27 at Beaumont de Lomagne for Gaudonville.

Charges 2000:
-- Per unit incl. 1 person Ffr. 50.00, 2 persons 95.00; extra adult 35.00; child 3-10 yrs 20.00, over 10 yrs 24.00; electricity (5A) 22.80; dog 9.00.
-- Less 50% outside 1/7-31/8, excl. electricity.
-- Credit cards accepted.

Open:
All year (limited facilities Oct-May).

Address:
Gaudonville,
32380 Saint-Clar.

Tel:
(0)5.62.66.43.86.
FAX: (0)5.62.66.42.02.
E-mail: bernard.lautier
@wanadoo.fr.

Reservations:
Made with deposit (Ffr 300) and fee (70).

MIDI-PYRENNEES - 65 Haute-Pyrénées

6505M Camping Municipal, St Lary-Soulan

This upmarket 4 star municipal site is centrally situated in the tourist village, surrounded by wooded mountains with a ski centre and spa village catering for winter and summer trade. There are 76 pitches with electricity available, over half of which are well shaded for summer, the others more open for winter time. A futuristic and impressive heated toilet block is kept clean and provides all facilities with free showers, British style WCs and good dishwashing and laundry facilities. Children's play area. All other needs are close by and a reader reports that the wardens were very helpful.

Directions: From Arreau take D929 road south, via Vielle-Aure, to St Lary-Soulan (13 km.) and 4 star municipal site is well signed off the main road.

Charges guide:
-- Per pitch Ffr. 24.00 - 27.00; adult 24.00 - 27.00; child 11.00 - 12.00; electricity (2-10A) 15.00 - 33.00; local tax 1.10.

Open:
All year excl. 21/10-3/12.

Address:
65170 St Lary-Soulan.

Tel:
(0)5.62.39.41.58.
FAX: (0)5.62.40.01.40.

Reservations:
Are advised, contact site.

6506 Castel Camping-Caravaning Pyrénées Natura, Estaing

Small friendly site, with the emphasis on enjoying the countryside.

Opened in 1997, Pyrénées Natura is the perfect site for lovers of nature, at an altitude of 1,000 m. on the edge of the National Park. Eagles and vultures soar above the site and a small open air observatory with seats and high power binoculars is provided to observe the wildlife and sometimes a rare breed of bird. The Ruysschaert family's aim is that you go home from a holiday here feeling at peace with the world, having hopefully learned something about the flora and fauna of the High Pyrénées. Tristan, their son, is qualified to take groups walking in the mountains to see chamois, marmots and the varied flora and fauna (there are even a few bears but they are seen very rarely). The 60 pitches, all with electricity, are in a large, level, open and sunny field. Around 75 varieties of trees and shrubs have been planted - not too many to spoil the view though, which can only be described as fantastic. In the past reception was in a large barn, now replaced by a large airy room with beautiful timber floors and an open staircase. Downstairs is a small bar (15/5-15/9) and lounge area, upstairs is another lounge, library and TV (mainly used for videos of the National Park). There is a small shop which is quite unique. Housed in the old water mill (the millstone is part of the shelving) it stocks a variety of produce, including wine. This is all left unmanned and open all day and, after you have chosen your goods, you go to reception to pay – very trusting, but they have not been let down yet. The sanitary facilities are first class with high quality fittings including a cubicle for children with shower, WC and washbasin, full facilities for disabled visitors and, in the same large room, baby bath, shower and changing mat. The showers are large and roomy, WCs have individual paper seat covers. Washing up and laundry sinks are inside and each block has a washing machine with airers provided to avoid unsightly washing lines. A motorcaravan service point, chemical disposal and even a dog shower complete the facilities. There are a few things to keep teenagers occupied (table tennis, boule and giant chess) and a small play area for the very young, but this is a site for nature lovers not really the place for discos and entertainment. In May, June and September the site puts on the occasional evening meal, or the village has two restaurants. The last weekend in May is a special time when the local shepherds take their flocks up to the lake and on to the high pastures. All the campers help by walking up with them and then helping to separate the different flocks. Returning to the site by bus, with a good old sing-song with the shepherds, the site provides food for everyone. That sounds like a trip worth making.

Directions: From Lourdes take N21 to Argelès-Gazost. At the roundabout at Argelès, take D918 signed Aucun, turning left after 5.5 km. onto D13 to Bun. After Bun cross the river and right onto D103 to site (5.5 km). Some parts are narrow but with passing places.

Charges 2000:
-- Per unit incl. 2 persons and electricity (6A) Ffr. 110.00; extra person 25.00; child (under 8 yrs) 10.00.
-- Less in low season.
-- Credit cards accepted.

Open:
1 May - 30 September.

Address:
Route du Lac,
65400 Estaing.

Tel:
(0)5.62.97.45.44.
FAX: (0)5.62.97.45.81.

Reservations:
Made with deposit (Ffr 360); contact site.

`Camping Cheque'

**Book this site
01892 559898**

THE ALAN ROGERS'
travel service

N6501 Domaine Naturiste L'Eglantiere, Ariès-Espénan

Pretty, riverside site in the Vallée du Gers.

This site is situated in the valley between the Pyrénées and the plain, within easy reach of Lourdes and the mountains, alongside a small, fast flowing river, in wooded surroundings. It comprises 12 ha. for camping and caravanning, with a further 32 for walking and relaxing in woods and fields. The river is said to be suitable for swimming and canoeing, with fishing nearby. The 120 pitches are of mixed size on fairly level grass, the older ones secluded and separated by a variety of tall trees and bushes, the newer ones more open, with a natural tenting area across the river. About 100 pitches have 8A electrical connections. An attractive, central, medium sized swimming pool (open mid May - Sept) has sunbathing areas both on paving and grass, and a children's pool, overlooked by the attractive, traditional style clubhouse and terrace. The clubhouse provides a bar and simple restaurant (June - mid Sept), an indoor activities/disco area, play room for young children and table tennis for the older ones. There are restaurants in the nearby village. The two existing sanitary blocks for either end of the site are in typically naturist style, providing under cover, open plan, controllable hot showers, washbasins (H&C) in vanity units, British style WCs and sinks for dishwashing (cold water). Shop (June - Sept). A children's play area is beside the pool with children's animation in season. Activities include volleyball, table tennis, badminton, pétanque, archery, activities on the river. Canoe and mountain bike hire, with trekking and cross-country cycling. Telephones. Studios, mobile homes, chalets and tents to rent. A torch would be useful.

Directions: From Auch take D929 south in direction of Lannemezan. Just after Castelnau-Magnoac watch for signs to hamlet of Ariès-Espénan on left and follow site signs.

Charges guide:
-- Per pitch incl. 2 persons - 'traditional' Ffr 78.00 - 120.00, `wild' 67.00 - 94.00; young person (over 8 yrs) 20.00 - 28.00; child (3-8 yrs) 10.00 - 17.00, under 3 yrs free; animal 9.00 - 12.00; electricity 20.00; leisure card (obligatory) 2.50 - 4.50.

Open:
1 April - 3 October.

Address:
Ariès-Espénan, 65230 Castlenau-Magnoac.

Tel:
(0)5.62.99.83.64 or (0)5.62.39.88.00. FAX: (0)5.62.39.81.44. E-mail: infos@ leglantiere.com.

Reservations:
Made with Ffr. 600 deposit.

Book this site
01892 559898

THE ALAN ROGERS' travel service

6502 Camping Les Trois Vallées, Argelès-Gazost

Developing site with good swimming pool between Lourdes and the mountains.

We felt this was the most promising site along the valley road from Lourdes into the Pyrénées, and one of few with room and plans for development. It has a rather unprepossessing entrance and pitches near the road suffer from noise, but at the back, open fields have views of surrounding mountains on all sides. The swimming pool complex (from 1/6) includes two pools, a paddling pool and two water slides. Recent additions are a bar/disco and two jacuzzis, and future plans include an indoor pool, a new reception building, TV room and laundry room. Bread is available on site, with a supermarket across the road. Recently extended, the site now has 400 flat, grassy, marked out pitches of reasonable size, all with electricity. Water points were scarce, but the owner hoped to remedy this, given the go-ahead by local officialdom. The two toilet blocks were clean and modern (unisex) and also have facilities for disabled people and chemical disposal. Activities include volleyball, football, boules and archery, with a good children's playground. Fishing 500 m, bicycle hire 50 m, riding 3 km. The proximity to the road is at least advantageous for touring the area, being by a roundabout with Lourdes one way, Luz-St-Sauveur and mountains another way, and the dramatic Pyrénées Corniche Col d'Aubisque going off to the west. Argelès-Gazost is an attractive town with excellent restaurants and cultural interests. Mobile homes to rent all year (30). Used by a tour operator (15 pitches).

Directions: Take N21 from Lourdes to Argelès-Gazost. As you approach Argelès, pass a Champion supermarket on your right, and then a roundabout – take the furthest left exit and the site entrance is 100 m. or so on the left.

Charges 2001:
-- Per pitch Ffr. 21.00 - 31.00; person 21.00 - 37.00; child (under 7 yrs) 12.00 - 21.00; electricity 3A 15.00, 6A 30.00.
-- Credit cards accepted.

Open:
Easter - 30 September.

Address:
65400 Argelès-Gazost.

Tel:
(0)5.62.90.35.47. FAX: (0)5.62.90.35.48.

Reservations:
Advised for July/Aug. and made with deposit (Ffr 500) and fee (100).

THE ALAN ROGERS' travel service

Book your site with the experts
Call for an instant quote 01892 55 98 98

Low cost ferries guaranteed!

MIDI-PYRENNEES - 65 Haute-Pyrénées / 81 Tarn

6503 Airotel Pyrénées, Esquièze-Sere, Luz-St-Sauveur

Small good quality, all year site with pools in the heart of the Pyrénées.

Airotel Pyrénées is located on the main road into the mountains, south from Argelès-Gazost and surrounded by the high peaks (some pitches will have daytime road noise). There are 165 level pitches, all with electricity and 35 fully serviced. They are on terraced ground and separated by bushes. Toilet facilities are in two blocks, both modern and well appointed. The block adjoining the indoor swimming pool and sauna has full facilities for disabled people, which also double as baby room with baby bath and shower. Washbasins are in cubicles, pre-set showers are roomy and there are indoor washing up and laundry sinks. The other block below the takeaway has similar high quality fittings and both blocks are heated in winter. Other activities include a practice climbing wall, half court tennis, boule, table tennis, volleyball and indoor archery and there is a sauna and fitness room at the indoor pool (closed 16/10-30/11). The outdoor pool (15/6-15/9) is near the entrance and rather near the road. A third pool has been added with water slides. In high season a programme of activities and tournaments is arranged, from walking and mountain bike trips to rafting. Skiing 10 km. The shop (1/7-31/8) is quite small and limited, but bread is available 15/5-15/9. There are tour operator pitches and mobile homes to hire.

Directions: Take N21 from Lourdes through Argelès-Gazost towards Luz-St-Sauveur. The site is on left at Esquièze-Sere, just outside Luz-St-Sauveur. Site is on left immediately after Camping International.

Charges 2001:
-- Per unit incl. 2 persons Ffr. 90.00 - 100.00, 1 person 65.00 - 75.00; extra person 25.00; child (up to 2 yrs) 10.00; electricity 3A 18.00, 4A 22.00, 6A 32.00; dog 8.00; local tax 2.20 (child 5-11 yrs 1.10).
-- Credit cards accepted.

Open:
All year.

Address:
65120 Esquièze-Sere.

Tel:
(0)5.62.92.89.18.
FAX: (0)5.62.92.96.50.
E-mail: airotel.pyrenees
@wanadoo.fr.

Reservations:
Advised for most periods and made with deposit (Ffr. 300) and fee (125).

Book this site
01892 559898
THE ALAN ROGERS'
travel service

8101 Camping Relais de l'Entre Deux Lacs, Teillet, nr Albi

Small, quiet, family run site between the Rassisse and Bancalié lakes.

This little site, run by the Belgian family of Lily and Dion Heijde-Wouters, is situated in part meadow, part semi-cleared woodland, with a small farm alongside. It offers a range of modern amenities including a good sized swimming pool and a bar/restaurant specialising in Belgian cuisine and serving a range of Belgian beers (all 1/5-30/9). A small library in reception includes some English books and board games. The 65 pitches, all with electricity (3, 6 or 10A, long leads may be required), are on level terraces and of varying size (up to 100 sq.m), mostly with ample shade from mature trees. Those near the bar/restaurant could experience some noise. Late arrivals or those wishing to leave before 8 am. are sited in an adjacent small meadow (although there may be some village traffic noise). There are two sanitary blocks, with extra toilets at the lower part of the site. The main one is of modern style and provides free, pre-set hot showers, washbasins in private cabins, British type WCs and dishwashing sinks under cover (H&C). This block is only open in the main season and is closed at 22.00 hrs each night. The older, smaller block, in the converted pigeon house with similar, though older style fittings, should be heated in winter. This also has facilities for disabled people and washing machines. Bread to order, shop in the village. Volleyball, table tennis, boules, bicycle hire, a playground and a children's farm (they can help feed the animals). Fishing 2 km. Canoes and kayaks for hire on the Rassisse lake. Charcoal barbecues are not permitted. Caravans and chalets to rent. Caravan storage available. This site is well situated for a variety of interesting excursions in an area not that well known to British visitors.

Directions: From Albi ring-road, take D81 going southeast to Teillet (approx. 20 km). Continue through village on D81 and site is on the right.

Charges 2001:
-- Per unit incl. 2 adults Ffr. 80.00, with electricity 105.00; extra person 25.00; child (under 7 yrs) 12.00; extra tent 11.00; dog 11.00.
-- Less 20% outside July/Aug. for stays of min. 5 days.
-- Credit cards accepted.

Open:
All year.

Address:
BP 120, 81120 Teillet.

Tel:
(0)5.63.55.74.45.
FAX: (0)5.63.55.75.65.
E-mail: entre-deux-
lacs@wanadoo.fr.

Reservations:
Made with deposit (Ffr. 300 or 45,73) and fee (Ffr. 80 or 12,20).

Book this site
01892 559898
THE ALAN ROGERS'
travel service

MEDITERRANEAN Part 1

Our 'Mediterranean' Tourist region includes all the areas which border the Mediterranean. It has been put together from the following official French regions and divided into Parts 1 and 2. Part 1 covers the south west coastal region.

LANGUEDOC-ROUSSILLON

Major cities: Montpellier, Perpignan, Nîmes, Carcassonne
Départements: 11 Aude, 30 Gard, 34 Hérault, 66 Pyrénées-Orientales

Once an independent duchy, the ancient land of Languedoc combines two distinct regions: the vineyards of the Corbières and Minervois and the coastal plain stretching from the Rhône to the Spanish border. Much of the region is rugged and unspoilt and there is ample evidence of the dramatic past. Ruins of the former Cathar castles can be seen throughout the region. The walled city of Carcassonne with its towers, dungeons, moats and drawbridges is one of the most impressive examples of medieval France. Today, Languedoc and Roussillon (the area between Narbonne and the Pyrénées) are wine and agricultural regions. Languedoc, with considerable success, is a producer of much of the nation's cheap table wine.

On the coast the vast sandy beaches/resorts, for example La Grande Motte, Cap d'Agde and Canet, are being promoted as an alternative to the more famous Mediterranean stretches of the Côte d'Azur. It is interesting to note that this far south there is a strong Spanish influence – in the look of the people, their culture, accent and in their language too. The local tongue, the ancient 'Occitan' is still spoken in rural areas, while down the coast in the Roussillon area, Catalan is spoken almost as much as French.

Note: site reports are laid out by département in numerical order. **_See map on page 320._**

Cuisine of the region

Cooking is Provençal, characterised by garlic and olive oil with sausages and smoked hams
Fish is popular along the coast – fish soup bourride in Sète
Aïgo Bouido – garlic soup; the garlic is boiled so its impact is lessened; served with bread
Boles de picoulat – small balls of chopped-up beef and pork, garlic and eggs, served with tomatoes and parsley
Bouillinade – a type of 'bouillabaisse' with potatoes, oil, garlic and onions
Boutifare – a sausage-shaped pudding of bacon and herbs
Cargolade – snails, stewed in wine
Ouillade – heavy soup of bacon, 'boutifare' (see above), leeks, carrots, and potatoes
Touron – a pastry of almonds, pistachio nuts and fruit

Wine

Wines include the reds of Corbières, Minervois, and the sweet Banyuls and Muscat

Places of interest

Aigues-Mortes – medieval city
Béziers – wine capital of the region, St Nazaire cathedral, Canal du Midi
Carcassonne – largest medieval walled city in Europe
Limoux – medieval town, Notre Dame de Marseilla Basilica, St Martin church
Montpellier – famous for universities, Roman sites; Gothic cathedral
Narbonne – unfinished Gothic cathedral dominates the town. Excellent archeological museum near the cathedral which shows how Rome and North Africa have influenced the area.
Nîmes – Roman remains and amphitheatre, Pont du Gard
Perpignan – Kings Palace; Catalan characteristics; the old fortress dominates the centre of the city and many of the side streets are more Spanish than French
Pézenas – Molière's home
Villeneuve-lès-Avignon – Royal City and residence of popes in 14th century

MEDITERRANEAN - 11 Aude

1101 Camping Eden II, Villefort, nr Chalabre

Most attractive site in spectacular scenery, near the Pyrénées.

Set in beautiful surroundings, this well equipped modern site is in the foothills of the Pyrénées and provides an ideal location to explore this area; there is a ski station 30 km. away. Growing trees provide some shade on a number of terraced pitches, with the other large, marked pitches on the lower, level part mostly provided with good natural shade (75 pitches in total). All have electricity (6/10A) and the majority have drainage, of which 8 are very large 'super-pitches' with their own sanitary facilities including hot showers. These and the main, large sanitary block have been built to very high standards; the amenities include British style WCs, a small unit for disabled people, a free washing machine, ironing facilities and chemical disposal. Motorcaravan service point. An attractive, partly shaded swimming pool (25/5-15/9, depending on the weather) and sunbathing terrace are just above reception, which is on a fairly steep slope and the tennis courts are further up the slope at the top of the site. Adjacent to reception are the small bar, mini-shop, restaurant, snacks and takeaway (all 15/5-15/9). Refrigerator for ice packs. Activities include archery, table tennis, volleyball, tennis, golf practice, a children's playground, fishing and bicycle hire. Watersports are near. Comprehensive literature and ideas about activities in the area are provided. Mobile homes (2) and chalets (9) for rent.

Directions: Site is between Quillan and Lavelanet, off the D117. Take the D16 north at Puivert towards Chalabre; site is on left before village of Villefort.

Charges 2000:
-- Per pitch incl. 2 adults: basic (tent) Ffr. 58.00 - 76.00; pitch + electricity (6-10A) 79.00 - 111.00; 3 services 103.00 - 141.00; plus individual sanitary facility 124.00 - 174.00; extra person 19.00 - 20.00; child under 4 yrs free; animal 11.00 - 14.00; local tax 1.00.
-- Credit cards accepted.

Open:
1 April - 30 September.

Address:
Domaine de Carbonas, Villefort, 11230 Chalabre.

Tel:
(0)4.68.69.26.33. FAX: (0)4.68.69.29.95.

Reservations:
Advised for July/Aug. with min. Ffr. 200 deposit and fee (150).

1111 Camping Val d'Aleth, Alet les Bains

Small family run site alongside medieval wall of the town of Alet les Bains.

This small site, located in the gateway to the upper valley of the Aude, is operated by Christopher and Christine Cranmer and here you will receive a warm welcome and a personal service from this charming English couple. Open all year, the site has a pleasant atmosphere and in season is bedecked with flowers (which have gained Christine a local prize). Unusually the northeast boundary of the site is the towering medieval wall of the town of Alet les Bains, which used to be classed as a city and has the remains of an abbey and cathedral. Thus there are attractive views of the associated illuminated spires and towers just beyond the wall at night. The ancient church bells are a quaint reminder of the passage of time (but are not disturbing at night). The opposite side is bounded by the river Aude which is fenced for safety but may be used for fishing. Beyond this is the D118 and there is some resultant road noise. Alet is a pretty spa town where roofs reach within one metre of each other across fascinating narrow streets within the old city walls and there is also the thermal pool where the French take 'the cure'. The sanitary block is close to the entrance and although unsophisticated, is adequate. The showers offer high pressure and very hot water at all times. Clean WCs are mostly British type, with some Turkish, laundry and dishwashing sinks are under cover with hot water. Reception stocks essentials with shops two minutes from the gates for all requirements. These include a selection of professionally ready cooked meals (including vegetarian) from the local butcher/charcuterie/traiteur – the patron is a trained butcher and chef. Three restaurants serve the town, or if you are inclined there is a Casino close by (an unexpected remnant of past heady days of aristocratic enthusiasm for spa towns) with piano bar and ATM machine – gambling is optional! (open 11.00 – 03.00). The 37 numbered pitches of varying sizes are separated by hedges and the extremely tall mature trees give shade to the whole site. Electricity (4-12A) is available on all pitches. There is a small children's play area and tourist information in a separate room by reception. The owners are keen to assist, books, guides and walking maps are available on loan along with brochures (in English) of attractions in the area. White water sports are available nearby and this is a Mecca for walkers or mountain-bikers. Mountain bike hire on site. There are bus and train services to Carcassonne and Quillan. The owners operate a B&B from their listed house.

Directions: From direction of Narbonne, use D118 towards Alet and Quillan. On approaching Alet ignore first sign to Alet (to avoid narrow stone bridge) and instead cross the river on the D118. Turn immediately left (by Casino), the site is signed and is 800 m. on the left.

Charges 2000:
-- Per unit incl. 2 persons Ffr. 55.00; extra person 13.00; child (under 8 yrs) 9.00; electricity 4A 14.00, 6A 19.00; dog 6.00; extra car 7.00.
-- Travellers cheques accepted, but not credit cards.

Open:
All year.

Address:
11580 Alet les Bains.

Tel:
(0)4.68.69.90.40. FAX: (0)4.68.69.94.60. E-mail: camping-valdaleth@wanadoo.fr.

Reservations:
Contact site.

1106 Camping Le Domaine d'Arnauteille, Montclar, nr Carcassonne

Peaceful, spacious site with superb views to the Corbières and beyond.

Enjoying some of the best and most varied views of any site we have visited, this rather unusual site is ideally situated for exploring, by foot or car, the little known Aude Département, the area of the Cathars and for visiting the walled city of Carcassonne (10 minutes drive). However, access could be difficult for large, twin axle vans. The site itself is set in 115 hectares of farmland and is on hilly ground with the original pitches on gently sloping, lightly wooded land and newer ones with water, drainage and electricity (5/10A), semi-terraced and partly hedged. A swimming pool (25 x 10 m.) with children's pool and paved sunbathing area is in a hollow basin surrounded by green fields and some newly developed pitches. The main, heated sanitary block is now a distinctive feature, rebuilt to a very high specification with a Roman theme. Three other smaller blocks are located at various points. They include British WCs, hot showers, washbasins in cabins, dishwashing under cover (hot water), laundry and chemical disposal. Facilities for disabled people and a baby bath are other features in what is a good overall provision. Motorcaravan services and gas supplies. A restaurant in a converted stable block offers 'plat du jour', grills, takeaway (15/5-30/9) and a terrace. There is also a small shop (15/5-30/9 – the site is a little out of the way) and a new children's play area. The reception building is vast; originally a farm building, with a newer top floor being converted to apartments. Although architecturally rather strange, from some angles it is quite attractive and mature trees soften the outlines. Table tennis and volleyball. Bicycle hire 8 km, fishing 3 km, golf 10 km, rafting and canoeing near, plus many walks with marked paths. Chalets, mobile homes and bungalow tents to let. A developing site with enthusiastic owners for whom riding is the principle theme with stables on site (open 15/6-15/9, remember that the French are more relaxed about hard hats, etc).

Charges 2000:
Per pitch incl. 2 persons Ffr. 81.00 - 107.00, with electricity 99.00 - 125.00, with water and drainage 115.00 - 145.00; extra person 18.00 - 27.00; child (under 7 yrs) 12.00 - 17.00; dog 7.00 - 10.00. -- Credit cards accepted.
Open: 1 April - 30 September.
Address: 11250 Montclar.
Tel: (0)4.68.26.84.53. FAX: (0)4.68.26.91.10. E-mail: arnauteille @mnet.fr.
Reservations: Made with deposit (25%) and fee (Ffr. 150 or 23).
`Camping Cheque'

see colour advert between pages 192/193

Directions: Using D118 from Carcassonne, after bypassing the small village of Rouffiac d'Aude, there is a small section of dual carriageway. Before the end of this, turn right to Montclar up a rather narrow road for 2.5 km. Site is signed sharp left and up hill before the village.

1104 Camping Le Martinet Rouge, Brousses-et-Villaret

Very pretty, rather quaint retreat in Aude countryside north of Carcassonne.

This is a very pretty little site and the owners have been working hard to improve the facilities. The three sanitary blocks have British WCs, large hot showers, washbasins (hot water) in private cabins, facilities for the disabled, baby bathroom and dishwashing and laundry facilities, including a washing machine. The most striking features of the site are the massive granite boulders (outcrops of smooth rock) throughout the area used for sunbathing and for children's games. The site offers only 35 pitches, all with electricity, in two contrasting areas - one is well secluded with irregularly shaped, fairly level, large pitches amongst a variety of trees and shrubs, while the other is on open meadow with mature oaks more typical of English rather than French sites. This area has a lovely swimming pool (15/6-15/9, no bermuda style shorts), attractively landscaped with flowers and original boulders, with a terrace area and sun loungers. Other activities include croquet, volleyball, new half court tennis, table tennis and a small play area. Small 'pub' bar with terrace serving snacks and a small shop (no others locally) both open 15/6-15/9. Barbecue area. Restaurants 50 m. Tennis, riding and fishing quite close. Caravans (4) and bungalows (2) to let. This is a useful situation from which to visit Carcassonne and to follow the Cathar trail.

Charges 2001:
-- Per standard pitch incl. 2 persons and car Ffr. 70.00, with electricity 85.00; extra person 21.00; child (under 7 yrs) 14.00; animal 5.00. -- No credit cards.
Open: 1 April - 31 October.
Address: Brousses-et-Villaret, 11390 Cuxac-Cabardes.
Tel: (0)4.68.26.51.98. FAX: as phone.
Reservations: Made with deposit of 20%.

Directions: Using N113 going west from Carcassonne, turn right onto D35 just after the village of Pezens (6 km), then almost immediately take left fork on D48. Follow D48 for approx. 10 km. (surface not so good) and site is signed just before the village of Brousses-et-Villaret.

1110 Camping de la Cité, Carcassonne

Remarkably quiet city site with extra large pitches.

Carcassonne has had a turbulent history and the old city was saved from demolition in 1850 by three far-sighted Carcassonne residents. It can now be admired as one of Europe's most complete examples of a fortified medieval city. Camping de la Cité is extremely well placed for such visits, being within l km. of the town along a shaded footpath beside a stream. Being a city site there is much movement and places can usually be found in mid afternoon - in mid July we had a choice of pitches. The majority are very large, separated by bushes and with a little shade. There are also undefined places in deep shade under trees for small tents. Electricity (10A) is available on 100 pitches and there are a few bungalow tents to hire. The toilet blocks are basic and functional, but are kept very clean and well maintained. They provide mainly British style toilets, washbasins in cabins and rather small and basic, pre-set showers, tiled and clean but with no seat or shelf. Chemical disposal points. The site has a swimming pool (May - end Sept) which is quite plain with a small sunbathing area, but is a welcome haven after a hot day's sightseeing. The shop is very limited with bread, wine and a few basic camping supplies. The bar is open all day for bread and snacks, but no alcohol unless food is bought and eaten there. Well equipped laundry room with washing machines, dryers and irons, also large fridges for hire (Ffr. 15 per day). Small children's play area, table tennis, petanque, volleyball and a field for football. Within 100 m. there is a fitness track and fishing. This site is worth considering for a day or two to sample the sights of Carcassonne.

Charges guide:
-- Per unit incl. 2 persons Ffr. 72.00 - 93.00; extra person 22.00 - 27.00; child (2-7 yrs) 11.00 - 16.00; extra car 20.00; electricity 18.00.
-- Credit cards accepted.

Open:
1 March - 8 October.

Address:
11000 Carcassonne.

Tel:
(0)4.68.25.11.77.
FAX: (0)4.68.47.33.13.

Reservations:
Not normally necessary.

Directions: From A61 autoroute take exit 24 onto N113 following signs for city centre. Site is well signed (look carefully) from all roads into the city.

1103M Camping Municipal La Pinède, Lézignan-Corbières

Within walking distance of the little town and only 35 km. from Narbonne Plage, La Pinède is laid out in terraces on a hillside, with good internal access on made-up roads. The 90 individual, level pitches, with electricity (6A) available, vary in size and are divided up mainly by shrubs and bushes. There are three sanitary blocks of good quality (recently refurbished) providing free hot water for showers and sinks. Not all the blocks are opened outside high season. The site has a small shop with gas, and a pleasant bar which also provides decently priced hot food that can be eaten on the terrace (all July/Aug). A barbecue functions here in season (private barbecues are not permitted). Washing machine. Outside the gates are a municipal swimming pool (July/Aug), a disco and restaurant and tennis courts. Local wine can be tasted and there is a vegetable patch in one corner of the site where you can sample really fresh vegetables (charged). This is generally better than many municipal sites in season - it is uncomplicated and peaceful. Fishing 4 km, bicycle hire or riding 2 km. Mobile homes, chalets and caravans for rent. Torches are necessary. Caravan storage.

Charges 2001:
-- Per adult Ffr. 18.00 - 22.00; child 12.00 - 14.00; pitch 36.00 - 40.00; animal 7.00.
-- No credit cards.

Open:
15 March - 15 October.

Address:
11200 Lézignan.

Tel:
(0)4.68.27.05.08.
FAX: as phone.

Reservations:
Advisable in season.

Directions: Access is directly off the main N113 on west side of Lézignan-Corbières.

THE ALAN ROGERS'
travel service

Book your site with the experts
Call for an instant quote
01892 55 98 98

Low cost ferries
guaranteed!

1107 Camping Club Les Mimosas, Narbonne

Lively site on Mediterranean Littoral, close to beaches at Narbonne Plage and Gruissan.

Being some 6 km. inland from the beaches of Narbonne and Gruissan, this site benefits from a somewhat less hectic situation than others in the popular seaside environs of Narbonne. The site itself is, however, quite lively with plenty to amuse and entertain the younger generation while, at the same time, offering facilities for the whole family.the 250 pitches are mainly of good size, most with electricity (6A), including a few 'grand confort', and they benefit from a reasonable amount of shade. Facilities at the site include a large swimming pool (1/5-30/9) and a smaller one (open earlier) with sunbathing areas, overlooked by a mezzanine level which includes a small lounge, amusements, etc. Plans for 2001 include a new pool complex. There are three tennis courts, a sauna, gym, bicycle hire and minigolf, with riding nearby. A lagoon for boating and fishing can be reached via a footpath (about 200 m). The site also includes the rather attractive Auberge Mandirac which offers a comfortable environment and interesting menu for meals (1/4-15/10). There are four sanitary buildings, all refurbished to a high standard with baby baths, etc. The facilities include showers with dividers, some British WCs, washbasins in cabins, hot and cold water, laundry and dishwashing sinks, washing machines and chemical disposal. Shop (1/4-15/10). This could be a useful site offering a variety of possibilities, entertainment (including an evening on Cathar history), and easy access to popular beaches, interesting towns such as Narbonne itself, Béziers or the 'Cité de Carcassonne', the Canal du Midi and Cathar castles. Chalets and mobile homes to rent. Caravan storage.

Charges 2001:
-- Per basic pitch incl. 1 or 2 persons Ffr. 74.00 - 108.00, pitch with electricity 90.00 - 128.00; extra person 17.00 - 23.00; child (2-7 yrs) 10.00 - 15.00; animal 7.00 - 11.00.
-- Credit cards accepted.

Open:
29 March - 31 October.

Address:
Chaussée de Mandirac, 11100 Narbonne.

Tel:
(0)4.68.49.03.72.
FAX: (0)4.68.49.39.45.
E-mail: info@ lesmimosas.com.

Reservations:
Made with Ffr. 500 deposit (and 120 fee in July/Aug only).

Directions: From A9 take exit 38 (Narbone Sud) and go round roundabout to last exit taking you back over the autoroute (site signed from here). Follow signs to La Nautique and then Mandirac and site (total 6 km. from autoroute).

see colour advert between pages 224/225

1108 Camping-Caravaning Le Relais de la Nautique, Narbonne

Family site with lots of space and excellent windsurfing facilities.

Owned and run by a Dutch family, this extremely spacious site is situated on the Étang de Bages, one of the best windsurfing areas in France. The site is fenced off from the water for the protection of children and windsurfers can have a key for the gate (with deposit) that leads to launching points on the lake. La Nautique has 390 huge (a small one is 130 sq.m), level pitches (with 49 site-owned mobile homes for hire and 60 tour operator pitches). Each pitch is separated by hedges making some quite private and trees and bushes give shade. All have electricity (10A) and water. The difference between this and other sites is that each pitch has an individual toilet cabin. Each cabin has a toilet, shower and washbasin (key deposit) and, as each pitch empties, the facilities are cleaned in readiness for the next. There are also pitches for disabled people with facilities fitted out to cater for their needs. Two laundries have washing machines, dryers and ironing facilities and additional dishwashing sinks are around the site. The solar heated pool has a large terrace with sun loungers, a bar and takeaway,. There is a water slide and a paddling pool with fountain and slide, and a third pool is planned. Other amenities include a bar/restaurant (evenings only May and Sept). Entertainment is organised in July/Aug, plus a sports club for supervised surfing, sailing, rafting, walking and canoeing (some activities are charged for). Two children's play areas are on fine sand and there is an active children's club. Free activities such as tennis, table tennis, basketball, volleyball, football, minigolf and boules will meet the needs of most families. A teenagers' disco is organised in high season and there is a recreational area with TV for youngsters. The shop at the entrance (1/6-15/9) has a reasonable stock. Reception provides safety deposit boxes and tourist information. Torches are needed in some areas. Only electric barbecues are permitted. The Étang is ideal for windsurfing with flat water combined with strong winds, but for swimming go to the large sandy beaches at Gruissan (10 km) and Narbonne Plage (15 km). The unspoilt surrounding countryside is excellent for walking or cycling and locally there is riding and fishing. Narbonne is only 4 km. English is spoken in reception by the very welcoming Schutjes family.

Charges 2001:
-- Per unit incl. 1 or 2 persons, electricity, water and ind. sanitary unit Ffr. 90.00 - 148.00; extra person 23.00 - 30.00; child (1-7 yrs) 10.00 - 18.00; extra car on pitch 10.00 - 12.00; dog or cat 8.00 - 12.00; local tax (over 18 yrs) 2.00.
-- Credit cards accepted.

Open:
1 March - 15 November.

Address:
La Nautique, 11100 Narbonne.

Tel:
(0)4.68.90.48.19.
FAX: (0)4.68.90.73.39.
E-mail: relais.de.la. nautique@wanadoo.fr.

Reservations:
Made with deposit (Ffr. 450) and fee (100).

Book this site
01892 559898

THE ALAN ROGERS'
travel service

see colour advert between pages 224/225

Directions: From A9 take exit 38 (Narbonne Sud). Go round roundabout to last exit and follow signs for La Nautique and site, then further site signs to site on right in 4 km.

N1109 Centre Naturiste Le Clapotis, La Palme

Unusual naturist site in protected surroundings with lagoon beaches and pool.

This site is very different from our other Mediterranean naturist site, Sérignan Nature (N3408). It is small and tranquil, situated between Narbonne and Perpignan in a secluded pine wood. It has direct access to a large sea lagoon which is popular with those in pursuit of the ideal conditions for windsurfing (with appropriate clothing!). The lagoon has large, secluded sandy 'beaches' and, if you tire of that, the excellent pool (full nudity required) is directly alongside the beach. Comprising 230 pitches, most with electricity (4A), some are in the pine wood, others on more open ground with trees and shrubs separating them; the pitches in the open are very large. There is a small and pretty bar and restaurant offering a menu of the day and a takeaway facility. It boasts two terraces, one of which gives wonderful views over the lagoon, especially at sunset. A cosy, well stocked shop selling food, hardware and general goods ensures that there is no real requirement to leave the site during your stay. The sanitary facilities (including washing machines) are in rustic style buildings with British and Turkish style WCs, and facilities for children and disabled campers. All other facilities are very natural and simple and this preserves the feeling of harmony and freedom which is exceptional here. There is tennis, volleyball, basketball, petanque and table tennis. Caravans and mobile homes to rent. Torches are required. The Pyrénées are less than an hour away and for wine enthusiasts the Corbières valley has many interesting cellars. If your wish is for peace and serenity then Clapotis is recommended as synonymous with sun and nature.

Charges 2000:
-- Per pitch incl. 2 adults Ffr. 94.00 - 136.00; extra person 18.00 - 20.00; child under 4 yrs free; electricity 28.00.

Open:
Easter, then 5 May - 15 October.

Address:
11480 La Palme.

Tel:
(0.)4.68.48.15.40.
FAX: 0)4.68.48.54.54.

Reservations:
Advisable in high season; contact site.

Directions: Head north from Perpignan towards Narbonne on the N9 and take the D709 to Port La Nouvelle. Site is well signed to the south of the town.

N3010 Domaine de la Sablière, Saint-Privat-de-Champclos, nr Barjac

Spectacularly situated naturist site in the Cèze Gorges.

This site, occupying a much larger area than its 250 pitches might suggest, enjoys a spectacular situation and offers a wide variety of facilities, all within a really peaceful, wooded and dramatic setting. Pitches are grouped in areas - `Mesange', at the bottom of the gorge (mainly for tents) alongside the river (good for swimming and canoeing), at some points close to the main access road, which is well surfaced but steep and winding. A newer area, `Pinson', is near the top of the hill, the whole side of which forms part of the site. A further area, `Fauvette', isalong the river. The pitches themselves are mainly flat on terraces, many of good size, with electricity (6/10A). During high season cars are banned in this area but parking is provided 200 m. away. All pitches are attractively situated among a variety of trees and shrubs. Six unisex sanitary blocks with excellent free hot showers in typical open plan, naturist site style, British style WCs and washbasins (cold water). Washing up and laundry sinks are also open plan. There is chemical disposal and a laundry. Reception at the entrance has tourist information. An open air, covered restaurant (all season) provides good value waiter service meals and a takeaway in an attractive setting. A useful small café/crêperie is in the Fauvette area. A supermarket, charcuterie, bureau de change and pool complex (dynamited out of the hill and built in local style and materials) complete the facilities. The complex provides two large pools (one can be covered by a neat sliding glass dome) and a children's pool, sunbathing terraces, bar, sauna, TV room and a disco. Essentially a family run and family oriented site, the owner, Gaby Cespedes, and her team, provide a personal touch that is unusual in a large site and this no doubt contributes to the relaxed and informal atmosphere. First time naturists would probably find this a gentle introduction into naturism. Activities are varied and numerous, including walking, climbing, canoeing, a fitness track, fishing, archery, tennis, minigolf, volleyball, badminton, boules (including floodlit area), table tennis, pottery lessons, silk painting, bindery, yoga, etc. Activity and entertainment programme for adults and children (28/6-31/8). Mobile homes, caravans, chalets and tents to hire. You must expect some fairly steep walking between pitches, pool complex, restaurant and supermarket (both open Easter-24/9) and a torch would also be handy.

Charges 2000:
-- Per standard pitch incl. 2 persons Ffr. 70.00 - 127.00; extra person (over 8 yrs) 15.00 - 27.00; child (under 8 yrs) free - 18.00; pet 5.00 - 18.00; leisure card (for activities) 4.40 - 7.00; electricity (6A) 22.00; local tax in high season (over 16 yrs) 1.00.
-- Less 20% for stays over 10 nights outside July/Aug.
-- Credit cards accepted.

Open:
1 April - 30 September.

Address:
St-Privat-de-Champclos, 30430 Barjac.

Tel:
(0.)4.66.24.51.16.
FAX: (0.)4.66.24.58.69.
E-mail: sabliere@ club-internet.fr.

Reservations:
Made with deposit (Ffr. 400 per week) and fee (180) - contact site for details.

Book this site
01892 559898

THE ALAN ROGERS'
travel service

Directions: From Barjac take D901 for 3 km. Site is signed just before St Privat-de-Champclos and is approx. 3 km. on narrow roads following camp signs.

mark hammerton
travel

family camping in france
we see things differently

We offer ready-erected, stylish luxury tents and 3 bedroom mobile homes. They're brand new, state-of-the-art and come fully-equipped (down to the corkscrew). Just turn up and move in!

Our sites are small, friendly and convenient for the beaches of Brittany, the Vendee or Charentes, (not forgetting one in the heart of the Dordogne at Sarlat). Most are simply not big enough for the mass-market camping operators (though all are good enough to be included in this guide).

All our sites have excellent swimming pools, many with water slides, and we keep numbers low to preserve the sites' own character. But you will find mature courier couples, seasoned campers themselves, on hand to help you enjoy your holiday.

With incredibly low cross-Channel rates, total flexibility (depart any day of the week, visit as many sites as you like), a comprehensive Travel Pack and an experienced team it makes sense to see things differently in 2001.

make it easy on yourself

FROM **£199**

12 nights tent holiday for 2 adults and up to 4 children starting 10th May, including return Channel crossing

See for yourself!
For full details and a virtual tour of our accommodation visit
wwww.markhammerton.com

Observer
**Travel Awards
2000**

Runner-up
Best Brochure
Runner-up
Best Web Site

For your free brochure

01892 52 54 56
Quote AR01

e-mail: enquiries@markhammerton.com

Caravaning
★★★★
l'Étoile d'Argens

TENNIS AND GOLF FREE LOW-SEASON

TEL: 04.94.81.01.4
83370 ST.AYGULF

l'atelier graphique 94.95.95.36

The MOTOR *Caravanners'* CLUB

™

From the moment you join the club
YOU ENJOY ALL THESE PRIVILEGES AND SERVICES

- Monthly Magazine
- UK. & European Touring Service
- UK. Sites Guide
- Discounted Insurance Rates available
- Breakdown Recovery Service
- Camping Card (CCI) International
- "Snail" Know-How Booklets
- Discounted rates for Cross Channel Ferries and Overseas Travel Insurance
- Year round Social Events, Weekend Meets and Holiday Rallies

It's a great club for enjoyment, interest, making friends, help and advice, weekend meets for you and all the family.

For membership details write:
THE MOTOR CARAVANNERS' CLUB LTD. FREEPOST (1292)
TWICKENHAM, TW2 5BR TEL: 0181 893 3883 (OFFICE HOURS)
E-mail: motorcaravanners@msn.com

MOTOR CARAVANNERS Club
THE ROAD TO ENJOYMENT

F.I.C.

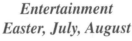

HOTEL DE PLEIN AIR cat. 4 étoiles

CAMP DU VERDON

★ ★ ★ ★

Camping Caravanning

DOMAINE DE LA SALAOU

Excellent site for family-holidays, right on the "Verdon"-River and the entry to the famous "GORGES DU VERDON", the European Great Canyon.

LES CASTELS
★ ★ ★ ★

C4120 CASTELLANE FRANCE
☎ 04.92.83.61.29   Fax: 04.92.83.69.37

Paris

Castellane

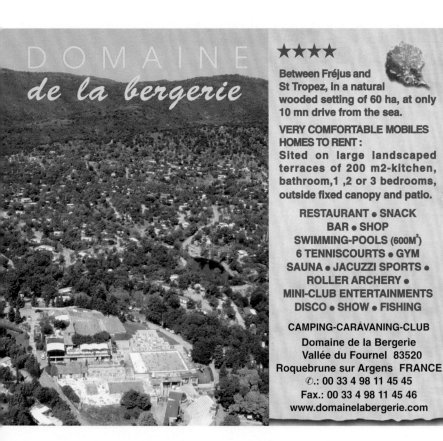

3000 Camping Domaine de Gaujac, Anduze

Woodland holiday site, with lively atmosphere and swimming pool.

This large site is enthusiastically run by the energetic and friendly Holley family. The 293 level, woodland pitches are well shaded and access to some areas, particularly those with hedged pitches, can be difficult for larger units due to narrow access roads, trees and hedges. Larger units should ask for lower numbered pitches (1-148) where access is a little easier. In high season this region is dry and hot, thus grass quickly wears off many pitches leaving just a sandy base. Tour operator or site owned rental tents, chalets and mobile homes occupy 65 pitches, the remainder are for tourists, most with electricity (4/6A). There are four sanitary units of varying ages and design which are opened one by one as the season progresses. They provide mostly British style WCs, both open and cubicled washbasins, showers with pre-mixed hot water, a children's unit with low level showers, toilets and baby baths, dishwashing and laundry sinks, washing machines, dryer and ironing facilities plus units for disabled visitors. Clean and practical rather than luxurious, hot water is free throughout. A small block can be heated in cool weather. Chemical disposal, motorcaravan service point and car wash. A well stocked shop, newsagent, takeaway/crêperie, bar and restaurant are open in main season (on demand other times, 15/5-15/9). The fenced swimming pool and children's pool complex has a lifeguard 5/7-15/8 but is unsupervised at other times, and is open during low season, weather permitting. Organised activities in main season include a children's club, plus cabaret, karaoke, disco, buffet parties and even cinema shows. There is a covered animation area and courtyard terrace. Two tennis courts (free off season), minigolf, children's playground plus sports field for football, volleyball etc. Just across the lane is the river with a small beach where one can swim, boat or fish. Riding 500 m, bicycle hire 5 km, golf 10 km. Tourist attractions in the region include the mining museum at Alès, steam trains run between Anduze and St Jean-du-Gard, a music museum at Anduze, and a number of spectacular caverns and grottoes. Caravan storage available.

Directions: From Alès take N110 towards Montpellier. At St Christol-lès-Alès fork right on D910 towards Anduze, and in Bagard turn left on D246 to Boisset et Gaujac. Site is signed from village.

Charges 2000:
-- Per unit incl. 2 adults Ffr. 91.00; extra adult 17.00 - 21.00; child (under 7 yrs) 12.00 - 15.00; dog free - 15.00; electricity 4A free - 15.00, 6A 5.00 - 20.00.
-- Credit cards accepted.

Open:
1 April - 30 September.

Address:
Boisset et Gaujac, 30140 Anduze.

Tel:
(0)4.66.61.80.65. FAX: (0)4.66.60.53.90.

Reservations:
Necessary in high season and made with deposit (Ffr. 700) and fee (80).

`Camping Cheque'

3006 Domaine des Fumades, Les Fumades, Allègre, nr Alès

Attractive, busy site near thermal springs, with friendly atmosphere.

Reception at des Fumades is a joy to behold. Set in an attractive courtyard, within the farmhouse, it has a central fountain and masses of tubs and baskets of colourful flowers. The entrance as a whole has a very tropical feel with its banana plants and palm trees. The 230 pitches are large and level, all with 4A electricity. A variety of trees add privacy and welcome shade. The three swimming pools with ample sunbathing space and bridges are very pleasantly landscaped. With tennis, volleyball, table tennis and boules, there is certainly plenty to do, and the large, well equipped and fenced playground will keep younger ones busy. July and August can get rather hectic with the well planned animation and entertainment programme, designed to appeal to families. The two well appointed sanitary blocks seem to cope well in high season, providing free hot showers, washbasins in cabins, mainly British style WCs, plus baby baths, facilities for disabled people, laundry and dishwashing. These facilities are clean and well maintained. There are two designated barbecue areas. Catering facilities are set around the entrance and pool area, with a well stocked shop, bar, restaurant and takeaway (all with reasonable prices). A large covered terrace houses a games room, snack bar and a focus for evening entertainment. Riding 2 km. This is a good area for walking, cycling, riding, climbing and fishing. Chalets (20), mobile homes (20) and apartments for rent. Used by tour operators (80 pitches). A Sites et Paysages member.

Directions: From Alès take D16 through Salindres, continue towards Allègre, until signs for Fumades (and thermal springs) on the right.

Charges 2000:
-- Per standard pitch incl. 2 persons Ffr. 79.00 - 141.00, `confort' pitch incl. electricity 99.00 - 161.00; extra person 17.00 - 32.00; child (0-7 years) 10.00 - 14.00; animal 10.00; local tax 1.00.
-- Credit cards accepted (Visa).

Open:
12 May - 9 September.

Address:
Les Fumades, 30500 Allègre.

Tel:
(0)4.66.24.80.78. FAX: (0)4.66.24.82.42. E-mail: domaine.des. fumades@wanadoo.fr.

Reservations:
Made with deposit (Ffr 800) and fee (150).

225

3011 Camping du Mas de Rey, Arpaillargues, nr Uzès

Small, unsophisticated friendly, family run site.

A warm welcome from the English speaking Maire family is guaranteed. Reception has a wealth of tourist information and they are always willing to give advice on the numerous things to see and do in the area. This is a small, 70 pitch site with a friendly feel, most of the large (150 sq.m) pitches separated by bushes and many with shade. All have 10A electricity. Due to the wonderful climate, grass can at times be hard to find. There are two unisex toilet blocks, both tiled and well maintained, one quite new with facilities for disabled visitors, a baby room and family cubicles containing WC, washbasin and shower. Dishwashing and laundry sinks have hot water. A washing machine and an iron are provided, and chemical disposal. Reception, bar, restaurant and shop are in the same large airy building. The shop is only open in high season but bread may be ordered all season. The bar serves a simple 'menu of the day' most evenings and has a terrace overlooking the small circular swimming and paddling pools with sunbathing areas (1/5-15/10). Riding 5 km, golf or fishing 3 km. and canoeing 10 km. Nîmes, Avignon and the Pont du Gard are all near and the owners say the wine festivals in early Aug. at Châteauneuf du Pape and Uzès in mid Aug. are not to be missed.

Directions: From D981 in Uzès take the D982 westwards signed Arpaillargues, Anduze, Sommieres, Moussac. Site is 3 km. on the left, well signed.

Charges 2000:
-- Per unit incl. 2 persons Ffr. 95.00; extra person 22.00; child (under 7 yrs) 15.00; electricity 18.00; animal 10.00.
-- Less 10-20% outside July/Aug.
-- Special senior tariff in low season.
-- Credit cards accepted in July/Aug. only.
Open:
10 April - 15 October.
Address:
Arpaillargues, 30700 Uzès.
Tel/Fax:
(0)4.66.22.18.27.
Reservations:
Made with deposit (Ffr. 300) and fee (50).

3014 Camping Caravaning Soubeyranne, Remoulins

Medium size campsite near Pont du Gard.

This site is well positioned for visiting the Pont du Gard, Nîmes and Uzès, famed for their Roman connections. It is approached by a short tree-lined avenue leading to reception. The 200 pitches offer very generous amounts of shade and keeping the 4.5 hectares watered involves over 5 km. of hose pipe. Pitches are large, level, numbered and separated, with 170 having 6A electricity. The two well appointed, unisex sanitary blocks are basic but clean, providing British style WCs, pre-set showers and washbasins in cubicles. Provision for washing up and laundry, plus a motorcaravan service point and fridges for hire. A small shop sells basic provisions, although Remoulins is only 1.5 km. The pool complex provides a 20 x 10 m. pool and a smaller, toddlers' pool (unsupervised), with paved surround and grass enclosure for sunbathing. Even the pool is partly shaded - greatly appreciated in the heat of the day. Overlooking the pool from an attractive terrace are the restaurant, bar and takeaway (all from 1/5). The menu, although not extensive, is adequate and moderately priced. Play area, table tennis, boules, tennis, volleyball and bicycle hire. An animation programme (July/Aug) is mainly for young children (teenagers may find it rather quiet). Fishing 1 km. Chalets (5) and mobile homes (5) for hire. Whilst the site is quiet in some respects, train noise both by day and night can be an irritant.

Directions: From Uzès take D981 to Remoulins, turn right at lights over river bridge, left at roundabout, then left (D986 Beaucaire). Site is 1.5 km. on left.

Charges 2001:
-- Per unit incl. 2 persons Ffr. 73.00 - 97.00, with electricity 89.00 - 133.00, water 107.00 - 134.00; extra person 16.00; pet 7.00; local tax 1.00.
-- Credit cards accepted.
Open:
7 April - 17 September.
Address:
Route de Beaucaire, 30210 Remoulins.
Tel:
(0)4.66.37.03.21.
FAX: (0)4.66.37.14.65.
E-mail: soubeyranne @wanadoo.fr.
Reservations:
Contact site for details.

Book this site
01892 559898
THE ALAN ROGERS'
travel service

3015M Camping Municipal de la Laune, Villeneuve lès Avignon

Anyone wishing to visit the historic city of Avignon have the ideal site here. It is in a quiet location away from the traffic with just the occasional day-time train to be heard. The 130 pitches are generous in size, on well shaded, level grass and separated by hedges and trees, over half having 6A electricity. The two sanitary blocks are clean and well maintained having British and Turkish style WCs, very roomy hot pre-set showers and washbasins in cabins. There are dishwashing and laundry sinks, plus two washing machines. Fees for the nearby municipal pool are included in the site charges, and tennis, riding, shops and restaurants are close. A 20 minute walk takes you to the boats that sail to Avignon, taking a detour on the return to see the famous bridge. Go in the morning to see the Pope's Palace and return later in the day. There is usually room to park at the landing stage.

Directions: Take Nîmes road, N100, out of Avignon towards Bagnoles-sur-Cèze and turn right after bridge over the Rhône. Take left road beside the river (D980) towards Roquemaure, then signs for Municipal Camping. From west on N100 (Pont du Gard) at roundabout take D900 to Villeneuve and follow straight down to river (Avignon). Site signed right, then immediately left. Then D980 as above.

Charges 2000:
-- Per person Ffr. 21.00; child (3-7 yrs) 9.00; car 11.00; caravan 18.00; tent 17.00; motorvan 28.00; electricity 15.00; animal 5.00; local tax 2.00.
Open:
1 April - 15 October.
Address:
Chemin Saint-Honoré, 30400 Villeneuve lès Avignon.
Tel:
(0)4.90.25.76.06.
FAX: (0)4.90.25.91.55.
Reservations:
Advised for July/Aug. with Ffr. 120 deposit.

3003 Camping Abri de Camargue, Le Grau-du-Roi, nr Montpellier

Pleasant site with both indoor and outdoor swimming pools.

This site has an attractive pool area overlooked by the bar and its outdoor tables on a pleasant sheltered terrace. The larger outdoor pool has sunbathing surrounds and the smaller indoor one is heated. The site's 300 level pitches are mainly 100 sq.m. but there are also smaller ones, with electricity and water available on most. The pitches are well shaded and trees and flowering shrubs are quite luxuriant in parts. Six well appointed toilet blocks, very clean when we visited, provide British style WCs, washbasins in private cubicles, adjustable showers, dishwashing and laundry sinks and all hot water is free. There are chemical disposal facilities and a very convenient motorcaravan service point. Amenities include a bar with TV, restaurant and takeaway with reasonably priced food and a shop. All facilities are available when the site is open. A new children's play area is of the highest quality (one of few with a rubberised EU standard safety base). Petanque pitches and tennis 800 m. Fishing, riding, golf and bicycle hire within 2 km. The site is 900 m. from the nearest beach at Port Camargue and 4 km from the one at L'Espiguette (in July/Aug. a free bus passes the gate to L'Espiguette). A summer fair is within walking distance which can be noisy until quite late. Mobile homes for long or short let. English spoken.

Directions: A road now bypasses Le Grau-du-Roi from the west as well as the approach from Aigues-Mortes. Turn left at sign to Port Camargue and Campings just northeast of Grau-du-Roi. At next crossroads go left again towards l'Espiguette and site is on right after 200 m. If approaching via D979 from north, turn on D62 and D62A towards La Grande Motte at junction north of Aigues-Mortes.

Charges 2000:
-- Per unit incl. 1 or 2 persons and electricity Ffr 115.00 - 250.00, 3-5 persons 130.00 - 250.00; extra person or extra car 30.00 - 60.00; pet, boat or trailer 30.00.
-- Credit cards accepted

Open:
April - October.

Address:
320 Rte. du Phare de l'Espiguette,
Port Camargue,
30240 Le Grau-du-Roi.

Tel:
(0)4.66.51.54.83.
FAX: (0)4.66.51.76.42.

Reservations:
Only required for very high season (10/7-20/8) and made for min. 1 week.

LANGUEDOC MEDITERRANEE
Abri de Camargue
CAMPING CLUB
☆ ☆ ☆ ☆

320, route du Phare de l'Espiguette
Port Camargue
F-30240 Le Grau du Roi
Tel.: 33/(0)4 66 51 54 83
Fax: 33/(0)4 66 51 76 42

from Spring till Autumn

SPECIALISED IN THE RENTAL OF MOBILE-HOMES sleeping 6-persons with all the comforts of home 2 bedrooms + WC + shower + living room SALE OF MOBILE-HOMES New or second-hand YEAR-ROUND PLOT RENTAL Open from April to October with reduced rates for off-season stays

2 swimming pools, one of which indoor and heated. Well-kept, shaded and bordered plots. Restaurant, supermarket, bar. Entertainment during high-season : sporting, evening, children's club. Services for camping cars. Close by : Fine sandy beach and gently sloping dunes, no danger for children (sea 900 meters away).

3012 Camping Campeole Ile des Papes, Villeneuve-lez-Avignon

Very well equipped site, 8 km. from Avignon.

New in '94, Ile des Papes is a large, open site. The railway is quite near but noise is limited to day-time The toilet blocks are of very good quality with free hot water, rooms dedicated to washing and drying hair (this in addition to hairdryers in the shower rooms), baby rooms, washing machines, dishwashing and laundry sinks, chemical disposal and a motorcaravan service point. All 342 pitches are of a good size on level grass and all have electricity (6A). The swimming pool area is extensive with two large pools for adults and one for children, with plenty of sunbathing areas around them. All is overlooked by the terrace of the bar and restaurant. In high season there are entertainers providing games and competitions for all ages. A play area will keep children happy and the lake is used for fishing. There is archery, tennis, table tennis, volleyball, minigolf, basket-ball (all free) and bicycle hire (charged). The shop is well stocked with a very large selection of both food and gifts (limited hours in low seasons). Avignon and its Palace and museums is 8 km. away. Riding 3 km. Mobile home and chalets (130) to rent.

Directions: Take N100 Nîmes road out of Avignon towards Bagnoles-sur-Cèze and turn right after crossing the Rhône. Turn left along the river bank and follow signs for Roquemaure (D980). In about 6 km. turn right onto D228 signed Barrage de Villeneuve and site is 1 km.

Charges 2000:
-- Per unit incl. 2 persons Ffr. 85.00 - 135.00; extra person 25.00 - 30.00; child (2-7 yrs) 15.00; dog 10.00; electricity (6A) 20.00; local tax 2.00 (child 4-7 yrs 1.00).
-- Credit cards accepted.
Open:
1 April - 31 October.
Address:
Zone de L'Islon, 30400 Villeneuve-lez-Avignon.
Tel:
(0)4.90.15.15.90.
FAX: (0)4.90.15.15.91.
E-mail: ile.papes@wanadoo.fr.
Reservations:
Made with deposit (25%) and fee (Ffr. 100).

3005 Camping L'Eden, Le Grau-du-Roi, nr Montpellier

Good modern site close to beaches and Camargue, with swimming pool.

L'Eden is a modern, well run, purpose built 4-star site. It is on flat ground about 500 m. from a sandy beach, with 377 hedged pitches, flowering shrubs and trees making it cool and very pretty. There is shade on many pitches, electricity on most and some are fully serviced. Four modern sanitary blocks are of unusual design, tiled blue or pink, and have free hot water. Toilets, some British style (in shorter supply than washbasins), free pre-set hot showers, some en-suite with washbasins. There is a unit with a baby bath, full facilities for disabled people and chemical disposal inside the blocks. An attractive pool complex includes a bridge, water toboggan and children's pool (from mid April) and a fitness centre next door. Supermarket, boutique, bar and restaurant with takeaway (all open all season). TV and meeting room. Activities include half court tennis, minigolf, archery, bicycle hire, table tennis and a sports area with volleyball and basketball - all free. In high season there are organised sports, excursions and entertainment, a mini club (1/7-31/8) and a play area for 1-8 year olds. Marina with sailing lessons, fishing, riding and tennis near. Free bus service to beach in main season. Some tour operators.

Directions: A road bypasses Le Grau-du-Roi from the west (easier if towing), as well as the approach from Aigues-Mortes. Turn left at sign to `Port Camargue' and `Campings' just northeast of Grau-du-Roi and follow signs for l'Espiguette. In 200 m. right at second sign for l'Eden. Not the site with entrance at turn; for l'Eden go hard right onto access road and a further 200 m. to site on left (it is a busy access).

Charges 2000:
-- Per pitch incl. 2 adults: simple (small tent) Ffr. 138.00 - 178.00, with electricity/water 95.00 - 192.00, with drainage 95.00 - 204.00; extra person 12.00 - 30.00; dog 15.00; local tax 1.00.
-- Less 20% for 2 weeks outside 1/7-26/8 or 5% for 3 weeks high season.
-- Credit cards accepted.
Open:
8 April - 1 October.
Address:
Port Camargue, 30240 Le Grau-du-Roi.
Tel:
(0)4.66.51.49.81.
FAX: (0)4.66.53.13.20.
Reservations:
Made 1/1-15/5 with deposit and fee (Sat.-Sat. in high season).

3002 Camping-Caravaning La Petite Camargue, Aigues-Mortes

Impressive site with large swimming pool on the edge of the Camargue.

This is a large site (605 pitches) with a huge swimming pool complex and other amenities to match, conveniently situated beside one of the main routes across the famous Camargue. Its position alongside this busy road is an advantage for access but could perhaps be a drawback in terms of traffic, although when we stayed overnight in season it was virtually silent. It offers a variety of good sized pitches, regularly laid out, with varying amounts of shade. However, there are more than 200 mobile homes interspersed between the 215 touring pitches, but most are set well back from the road. An attractive L-shaped pool complex and adjacent bar/restaurant with pizzeria and takeaway, range of shops, etc. are situated between the pitches and the road and are attractively designed, providing a wide range of facilities and activities. Four sanitary blocks provide very good, well maintained, modern facilities including many combined showers and washbasins with controllable hot water, British style WCs and chemical disposal. Motor-caravan service point. The site is conveniently situated for visiting the Camargue and not far from the sea, beaches and other sport facilities and activities, and it also provides a range of entertainment with a good activity programme, disco and children's club (July/Aug. 4-12 yrs). Activities include riding at the adjoining large stables, children's play area, football, volleyball, basketball, tennis (charged July/Aug), table tennis and bicycle hire. Laundry facilities. Hairdresser and beauty centre. The nearest beach is 3.5 km, with a free bus service in July/Aug. Fishing 3 km, golf 8 km. Winter caravan storage. Mobile homes to let (222). Used by tour operators (80 pitches). English is spoken at this well run, busy site. A 'Yelloh Village' member.

Directions: From autoroute A9 take exit 26 (Gallargues) towards Le Grau-du-Roi. Continue past Aigues-Mortes on the D62 and site is 2 km. on the right, just before large roundabout for La Grand-Motte and Le Grau-du-Roi junction. Site is approx. 18 km. from exit 26.

Charges 2001:
-- Per unit with 1 or 2 persons: standard pitch Ffr. 73.00 - 166.00, with electricity 90.00 - 198.00, with water and drainage 100.00 - 220.00; extra person (over 4 yrs) 26.00 - 36.00; dog 13.00; local tax 1.00.
-- Credit cards accepted.

Open:
13 April - 23 September.

Address:
BP 21,
30220 Aigues-Mortes.

Tel:
(0)4.66.53.98.98.
FAX: (0)4.66.53.98.80.
E-mail: petite.camargue
@wanadoo.fr.

Reservations:
Made with Ffr 480 deposit and 120 fee.

Book this site
01892 559898
THE ALAN ROGERS'
travel service

3013 Camping Village Les Petits Camarguais, Le Grau-du-Roi

Smaller site with young families in mind.

A smaller sister site of La Petite Camargue (no. 3002) and previously known as Le Salonique, this site is being planned around families with young children. The flumes and slides in the attractive new swimming and paddling pools are only for the under-twelves. There is a large play area with rubber safety base close by. The site has 170 mobile homes and 84 touring pitches, so the tourers could feel a little overpowered. Most of the touring pitches have electrical connections (6/10A) and a few also provide water. The sanitary blocks are of an older design, giving a functional but not luxurious provision. The WCs are mostly Turkish style, the showers are pre-set and the external dishwashing and laundry sinks share one hot water tap. A new laundry provides washing machines, dryers and irons and there is a new baby room with baths and children's toilets. The bar/pizzeria has been refurbished and has a pleasant open air terrace overlooking the pool and its large sunbathing areas. At the entrance is a well stocked shop and reception provides cash machines and safety deposit boxes. Activities include table tennis and a new all-weather court for basketball, football or volleyball. There is a children's club, plus organised entertainment including dances, discos, magic shows and karaoke. Fishing 6 km, riding on Camargue horses 300 m, golf 12 km. The local beach is 1.8 km. with a free bus service in high season. Mobile homes to rent (170). English is spoken. A 'Yelloh Village' member.

Directions: Follow signs from exit 26 towards Le Grau-du-Roi past Aigues-Mortes on D62. Turn off to Port Camargue and campings, then signs for L'Espiguette. Site is on left past several sites and stables.

Charges 2001:
-- Per unit incl. 1 or 2 adults standard pitch Ffr. 73.00 - 166.00, with electricity 90.00 - 198.00, with water and drainage 100.00 - 220.00; extra person (over 3 yrs) 26.00 - 36.00; animal 13.00; local tax 1.20.
-- Credit cards accepted.

Open:
21 April - 23 September.

Address:
Rte de L'Espiguette,
30240 Le Grau-du-Roi.

Tel:
(0)4.66.51.16.16.
FAX: (0)4.66.51.16.17.
E-mail: petite.camargue
@wanadoo.fr.

Reservations:
Made with deposit (Ffr. 550) and fee (50).

Book this site
01892 559898
THE ALAN ROGERS'
travel service

MEDITERRANEAN - 34 Hèrault

3407 Camping Village Le Sérignan Plage, Sérignan

Unusual, well equipped, family run site with superb indoor pool and direct access to beautiful sandy beach.

This is the sister site to Sérignan Plage Naturist (no. 3408N), owned by Jean Paul Amat and his family who you will see around the site. Have a chat - his English is excellent and he likes to practise. This is a large, but very comfortable site, built in a genuinely unique style. Here you will normally find room even in the high season, with 470 touring pitches in several different areas and three different styles to choose from, with the benefit of some of the most comprehensive amenities we have encountered. The touring pitches by the beach have little shade, are sandy and a little smaller. The others are mostly of a very good size on level grass with plenty of shade. All pitches have electricity connections (5A) and are fairly separate from a similar number of seasonal pitches and rented accommodation in the centre section of the site.

Perhaps the most remarkable aspect of this site is the cluster of attractive buildings which form the central amenity area, amongst which is a small indoor heated swimming pool of unusual design. This is not intended for use in the high season, when the beach and sea offer a better alternative, although the imaginative owners have designed and built an amazing new pool complex. With interlinked pool areas, deep parts for swimmers, exciting children's areas with slides, bridges and islands, it is attractively landscaped and surrounded by a very large grass sunbathing area complete with sun loungers. With lifeguards (main season) and an ID card system to prevent abuse, it is a very nice addition. The traditional style buildings are virtually a small village, with pretty bars and a beautiful restaurant serving impressive good value meals, including local specialities plus takeaway choices (all 7/4-10/9). The complex provides market stalls (meat and vegetables), a well stocked supermarket, newsagent/tabac, bureau de change, ATM, an outdoor market, disco, small amphitheatre and even a separate, secluded roof-top bar - ask for a 'Cucaracha'! The whole area has a lively, international atmosphere (well used and perhaps showing some wear and tear). Entertainment is provided every evening in high season, including shows at the amphitheatre, discos most nights and daily sporting activities. Wine and food tastings with tourist information presentations each Monday at 5 pm. Giant screen for news and current affairs. There is something for everyone here and you will not need to leave the site if you do not wish to.

There are no less than nine sanitary blocks (unisex). Three older ones are of circular design which provides roomy pre-set hot showers, open-plan washbasins and a mixture of British and Turkish style WCs. These are nearest the sea and central 'village' area, seasonal units and mobile homes, etc. and thus take the brunt of the wear and tear. The blocks are being systematically updated to a pleasant new design with central shrub and flower units. The touring area furthest from the sea, but near the new pool complex, is peaceful with grass pitches well shaded by tall trees and has three modern toilet blocks of individual design. These are well thought out, have excellent facilities and include a number of large controllable hot showers with washbasin (non-slip floor) and WC en-suite, well equipped baby rooms, facilities for disabled people and chemical disposal. Dishwashing and laundry facilities are in all the blocks and there are four washing machines. Remember, this is a seaside site in a natural coastal environment, so do not expect it to be neat and manicured; in parts nature still predominates. The site has direct access to a superb, large sandy beach and to the adjoining naturist beach, both of which slope very gently and offer safe bathing at most times (lifeguard in high season). A sailing and windsurfing school is on the beach. Bicycle hire on site, riding 2 km, golf 10 km. Used by tour operators (99 pitches). Chalets and mobile homes for rent (60).

Directions: From A9 exit 35 (Béziers Est) follow signs for Sérignan on D64 (9 km). Don't go into Sérignan, but take sign for Sérignan Plage for 4 km. At first camping sign turn right (one way) for approx. 500 m. Bear left past two naturist sites (one the sister to site to this).

Charges 2001:
-- Per unit incl. 1 or 2 persons Ffr. 90.00 - 170.00; extra person 22.00 - 30.00; electricity (5A) 19.00; dog 15.00; plus local tax.
-- Low season offers.
-- Discounts in low season for children under 7.
-- No credit cards.

Open:
7 April - 16 September.

Address:
34410 Sérignan.

Tel:
(0)4.67.32.35.33. FAX: (0)4.67.32.26.36. E-mail: info@ serignanplage.com.

Reservations:
Made from 1 Feb. with deposit (Ffr. 100 - 500, acc. to season) and fee (100).

`Camping Cheque'

Book this site
01892 559898

THE ALAN ROGERS'
travel service

see colour advert between pages 192/193

N3408 Camping Le Sérignan Plage Nature, Sérignan Plage

Very comfortable and distinctly characterful naturist site beside large sandy beaches.

We have long sought good quality naturist campsites with direct access to the Mediterranean beaches and with N1109 Clapotis, we now have two! Sérignan Plage Nature was for many years run as a private club but now the charming, English speaking owner, Jean Guy Amat, has decided to dramatically improve facilities here to make the site a prestige naturist campsite - he is well on the way. The site has 260 touring pitches (out of 500 that includes seasonal pitches and mobile homes) on level grass and all with 5A electricity. This is a very comfortable place to spend a holiday. The pitches do vary in size (80-120 sq.m), the smaller ones nearest to the beach with less shade and sandy, whilst many of the larger grassy ones further back are of a comfortable size with a proportion of shade from the varieties of trees that have been encouraged to grow to a good size (utilising waste water for irrigation). A new area has been added away from the beach and this has young saplings only. The Romanesque architectural style of several of the buildings (one is called the Forum) has been preserved, but the recent improvements have restored them to a pristine condition. The bar/restaurant complex has also been renewed and a cover added to the terrace. The menu is excellent and reasonably priced. A delightful new, themed bar has been added, along with a disco room. The warm and friendly ambience of the bar and restaurant has been retained, and there is a range of entertainment, with several competing attractions held on the same evening in season. This atmosphere is helped in no small measure by the enthusiasm of the restaurant and shop managers. In addition to a surprisingly large supermarket, the site boasts its own market for fresh fruit and vegetables, along with a newsagent/souvenir shop and an ice cream kiosk. The sanitary blocks have all been refurbished, sporting a central display of shrubs and flowers. Of different design, all offer modern facilities with roomy hot showers, some washbasins in private cabins and a choice of British and Turkish style WCs, all of which were clean and well maintained when inspected in July. This is now a very smart, comfortable, well equipped family oriented campsite, with many facilities and good quality entertainment in season. It has the additional benefit of direct access to a superb, safe and virtually private naturist beach of fine sand (with lifeguard in high season).

Directions: From A9 exit 35 (Béziers Est) follow towards Sérignan (9 km). Take road to Sérignan Plage (4 km) watching for first camping signs and turn right (one way) for 500 m. bearing left (note: not the first naturist site, it is the second).

Charges 2001:
-- Per unit incl. 1 or 2 persons Ffr. 80.00 - 165.00; extra person 22.00 - 23.00; electricity (5A) 17.00; dog 15.00; plus local tax.
-- Special discounts in low season.
-- Credit cards accepted.

Open:
1 May - 30 September.

Address:
34410 Sérignan.

Tel:
(0)4.67.32.09.61.
FAX: (0)4.67.32.68.41.
E-mail: info@ serignannaturisme.com.

Reservations:
Made from 1 Feb. with deposit (Ffr. 400), fee (100) and cancellation insurance (70).

Book this site
01892 559898

THE ALAN ROGERS'
travel service

3403 Camping Club International Le Napoléon, Vias Plage

Smaller family site in village bordering the Mediterranean at Vias Plage.

The town of Vias is in the wine-growing area of the Midi, an area which includes the Camargue, Béziers and popular modern resorts such as Cap d'Agde. The single street that leads to Vias Plage is hectic to say the least in season, but once through the new security barrier and entrance to Le Napoléon, the contrast is marked - tranquillity, yet still only a few yards from the beach and other attractions. Not that the site itself lacks vibrancy, with its own new Californian-style, heated pool with lively piped music, bar, restaurant/pizzeria and extensive entertainment programme, but thoughtful planning and design ensure that the camping area is quiet, with good shade from the many tall trees. The 250 partially hedged pitches (80 with hire units), most with electricity, vary in size from 80-100 sq.m. The three sanitary blocks are of a reasonable standard including British WCs, washbasins in private cabins, baby bath, laundry and facilities for disabled people, all well maintained when seen in peak season. Chemical disposal and motorcaravan services. The site has its own well stocked supermarket and there are plenty of other shops, restaurants, etc. all immediately adjacent, including a laundry. Activities include tennis, archery, volleyball, bicycle hire, boules and TV, plus a wide range of entertainment (free). Fridges for hire. Fishing nearby. Chalets, mobile homes and apartments to let. Most facilities available from May.

Directions: From Vias town, take D137 towards Vias Plage. Site is on the right near the beach; watch carefully for turning between restaurant and shops.

Charges 2000:
-- Per unit incl. 1 or 2 persons and electricity Ffr. 115.00 - 170.00; extra person 18.00 - 30.00; extra tent free - 18.00; dog 15.00 - 20.00; local tax 2.00 (4-10 yrs) 1.00.

Open:
30 March - 30 September.

Address:
Ave de la Méditérrane, 34450 Vias Plage.

Tel:
(0)4.67.01.07.80.
FAX: (0)4.67.01.07.85.
E-mail: reception@ camping-napoleon.fr.

Reservations:
Taken from 1 Jan. with 30% deposit and fee incl. insurance (170).

see colour advert
between pages 224/225

N3405 Camping Naturiste Le Mas de Lignières, Cesseras

Peaceful, small, rural site with pool and very large pitches, in the hills of the Minervois.

A delightful find, only 3 km. from the medieval town of Minerve with its Cathar connections, parts of this site enjoy some marvellous views to the Pyrénées, the Corbières and the coast at Narbonne. We recommend that you watch at least one wonderful sunrise over the Pyrénées from the site! The owners Jeanne and Gilles, offer a warm welcome and promote a most enjoyable family atmosphere. It provides 50 large (200 sq.m.) pitches, all with electricity (6A), with 25 designated 'grand-confort' each with water and waste water. Mainly on level grass, they are separated by mature hedges giving considerable privacy. Some smaller pitches (100 sq.m.) are for tents, with cars parked elsewhere. There is natural shade and a variety of fauna and flora including four types of orchid. Within the 50 hectare site there are some good walks with superb views and, although the camping area is actually quite small, the very large pitches and growing trees and hedges give an impression of spaciousness and freedom, creating a very relaxing ambience and a nice introduction to naturist camping. The swimming pool is a bonus (it can get very hot) with a paved area for sunbathing and a new children's paddling pool (1/6-30/9). Tennis, volleyball and boules (all free). A small shop sells the usual essentials, including fresh bread and croissants to order, plus local specialities (15/6-15/9). There is a bar/snackbar (15/7-15/8), a comfortable room for general use with TV, library and tourist information and separate provision for young people. The sanitary block is very pleasant and clean, with hot showers in cabins, British style WCs, washbasins, washing up and laundry sinks (H&C) and washing machine, also en-suite facilities for disabled people. The décor is very tasteful with attractive potted plants and pictures on the walls. Children's playground. Torches are advisable at night. Sailing, riding and canoeing nearby. No dogs are accepted. If you ask nicely, Gilles may take you out in his Landrover (he's a bit of an expert on all things natural) to places you would never find otherwise. The owners are proud that the site has recently been awarded the coveted 'Clef Vert' award for environmental awareness. Mobile homes (4) for hire.

Charges 2000:
-- Per large pitch, incl. 2 persons and electricity, water and drainage Ffr. 135.00; smaller pitch 100.00 (electricity 20.00); extra person 21.00; child (2-7 yrs) 15.00; extra car or tent 15.00.
-- Less for longer booked stays.
-- Credit cards accepted.

Open:
1 April - 31 October.

Address:
Cesseras-en-Minervois, 34210 Olonzac.

Tel:
(0)4.68.91.24.86.
FAX: as phone.
E-mail: lignieres.mas
@libertysurf.fr.

Reservations:
Made until 25/6 with deposit (25%) and fee (Ffr. 70).

Directions: From A61 autoroute take Lézignan-Corbières exit, through the town via the D611 to Homps, then via the D910 to Olonzac. Go through the village following the signs to Minerve (D10). Follow road for approx. 4 km. taking left hand turn to Cesseras (D168). At Cesseras follow signs to Fauzan for approx another 4 km. Site is signed to the right where there is a climb up a winding road, which can be a little narrow in places.

3406 Hotel de Plein Air L'Oliveraie, Laurens

Site with many attractive features at the foot of the Cevennes, open all year.

This lively site has a lot to offer in terms of activities, particularly those for young-sters, including plenty of evening entertainment in the high season, but can be comfortable and quiet at other times. Most of the 116 pitches are large (up to 150 sq.m. in some parts). Arranged in rows on two levels, those on the higher level being older and with more shade from mature trees (mainly olives), all have electrical connections (6/10A). The ground is stony. The large leisure area is slightly apart from the pitches on the lower area, and includes a good sized pool and children's pool (1/6-30/9), with an attractive paved sunbathing area, a tennis court and tennis practice wall, volleyball, basketball, minigolf, bicycle hire, children's play area and adjoining riding stables. There are also good facilities for archery which is quite a feature at the site. Overlooking these facilities is a large terrace with a bar/restaurant serving simple grills in the high season. At other times there is an indoor bar, also used as a lounge for films and activities for younger children. There is a small, well stocked shop (1/7-31/8, local shops at Laurens, 1 km). The main sanitary block on the higher terrace has been renovated to provide hot showers with dividers, washbasins in cabins, British WCs, a new baby bathroom, covered dishwashing areas and a washing machine. A second block on the lower level is opened for high season. All were perfectly adequate and clean when seen in high season. Reception provides a bureau de change and tourist information. Caravan storage available. A 'Sites et Paysages' member.

Charges 2001:
-- Per unit incl. 1 or 2 persons Ffr. 44.00 - 110.00, 3 or 4 persons 58.00 - 150.00, 5 or 6 persons 72.00 - 190.00; dog 10.00; electricity 20.00.
-- Special rates for longer stays.
-- Credit cards accepted.

Open:
All year.

Address:
34480 Laurens.

Tel:
(0)4.67.90.24.36.
FAX: (0)4.67.90.11.20.
E-mail: oliveraie@free.fr.

Reservations:
Contact site.

Directions: Site signed 2 km. north of Laurens off the D909 (Béziers-Bédarieux).

3404 Camping Lou Village, Valras-Plage, nr Béziers

Family owned, busy site with direct access to beach.

Valras is perhaps smarter and is certainly larger than nearby Vias and it has a good number of campsites. Lou Village has direct access to a sandy beach and is a busy site with lots of facilities. Prices are quite competitive and should provide better value than at other sites in the area. However, it will become crowded in the high season as this is a popular area. The pools, restaurant, bar and shops all form part of the 'village centre' where most of the site's activity takes place. There is a raised stage for entertainment, children's club, supermarket, bakery, takeaway, bazaar with daily papers and, in high season, a hairdressing salon. The bar has a large screen for TV and a terrace overlooking the pools. It is a busy area with a pleasant ambience with the swimming pool area attractively redesigned and with heated pools, water slides and a paddling pool. There are 600 pitches (including 200 with mobile homes), all with electricity (10A) and 100 also having water and waste water facilities. Pitches further inland are of grass, partly separated by tall trees which provide good shade; nearer the beach the pitches are smaller, sandy and separated by bushes and bamboo hedges. The four toilet blocks, all recently refurbished, are well situated with reasonable facilities. They provide a mixture of Turkish and British style WCs, free pre-set hot showers with no separator and washbasins, about half in private cabins (H&C). There are baby facilities and provision for disabled visitors. Washing up and laundry sinks are at each block, as are chemical disposal facilities. Considering their heavy use as this is a beach-side site, maintenance (in July) seemed quite satisfactory. Other facilities include a children's playground, football field, bicycle hire, minigolf, volleyball and tennis. There is lots to do off the site – sailing, windsurfing, riding (500 m), canoe kayaking, river fishing (1 km), golf (12 km), bike rides and the history of the Languedoc to discover. Mobile homes (100) and new chalets (20) for rent. English is spoken.

Directions: Site is south of Béziers. From autoroute, take Béziers-Ouest exit for Valras Plage and continue for 13-14 km. Follow 'Casino' signs and site is 1 km south of centre of Valras Plage in the direction of Vendres. Site is signed to the left at the end of Valras Plage and the start of Vendres Plage.

Charges 2000:
-- Per unit incl. 2 persons Ffr. 80.00 - 130.00; extra person (over 7 yrs) 12.00 - 22.00; child under 7 free - 15.00; extra car 15.00; electricity (10A)18.00; dog 15.00; local tax 1.90 (over 4 yrs).
-- Credit cards accepted.
Open:
21 April - 15 September.
Address:
BP 30,
34350 Valras-Plage.
Tel:
(0)4.67.37.33.79.
FAX: (0)4.67.37.53.56.
E-mail:
info@louvillage.com.
Reservations:
Made with deposit (Ffr. 700) and fee (150).

MEDITERRANEAN - 34 Hèrault

3409 Camping-Caravaning Domaine de la Yole, Valras-Plage

Large site with a very relaxed atmosphere.

We were pleasantly surprised when we visited de la Yole – the thought of 1,007 pitches was a little daunting and we expected things to be very hectic when we arrived on a busy day in mid-August. However, everything was calm in the multi-lingual reception and people were enjoying themselves. There are 590 pitches for touring units, the remainder taken by mobile homes and a few tour operator pitches. Most are of a good size, all are level and have electricity, water and waste water points and, very importantly for this area, they all have shade. The site was full but the sanitary blocks were in excellent condition and remarkably clean. Showers are controllable with plenty of changing space, some with washbasins also, most of the WCs are British style and many washbasins are in cubicles. Extra large cubicles with everything including a baby bath can be used by both families or disabled visitors. Seven of the blocks have been recently refurbished and the eighth one is new. All blocks have dishwashing and laundry sinks and all hot water is free. A central laundry provides washing machines and dryers. There is a car wash and motorcaravan service point at the centre of the site and refrigerators can be hired. The extensive pool area is attractive with lots of sunbathing areas, two large pools and a paddling pool, all supervised by a lifeguard in July/Aug. The impressive activities are located in a central area and include two half size tennis courts (free) and two full size (charged July/Aug), large play areas with amusements such as a moto-track and a daily children's club, minigolf, table tennis, boules, volleyball and basketball. A shopping area provides a supermarket, outdoor vegetable stall, fish stall, butchers, wine shop (take your own bottles for really good wines on draught), boutique and a takeaway, all set under low trees very much like a village market. Two good restaurants with huge terraces and an amphitheatre for the daily entertainment (in season). The beach, a long stretch of beautiful sand, is 500 m. and here are trampolining, paragliding and jet-skis. This is a busy site with something for all the family. English is spoken and a doctor calls daily in high season.

Directions: From A9 autoroute take Beziers Ouest exit for Valras-Plage (13-14 km) and follow Casino signs. Site is on left, just after sign for Vendres-Plage.

Charges 2001:
-- Per unit incl. 2 adults Ffr. 102.00 - 184.00; child 0-7 yrs free - 10.00; 7-16 yrs free - 19.00; extra adult 31.00; dog free - 18.00; local tax 2.00 (under 7 yrs 1.00).
-- Credit cards accepted.

Open:
28 April - 22 September.

Address:
B.P. 23,
34350 Valras-Plage.

Tel:
(0)4.67.37.33.87.
FAX: (0)4.67.37.44.89.
E-mail: layole34
@aol.com.

Reservations:
Contact site.

Book this site
01892 559898
THE ALAN ROGERS'
travel service

3410 Camping-Caravaning Mas du Padre, Balaruc Les Bains

Small and quiet family run site with swimming pools.

The Durant family took over this campsite a few years ago and have made many alterations and improvements. It is a small site, just 2.5 km. from Balaruc-Les-Bains, near the Lake of Thau and unusually is part of an estate that has obviously been built around it over the years. Its 116 secluded numbered pitches of varying sizes are enclosed by hedges and mature trees, some are on a very gentle slope and 98 have electrical connections (5A). Two neat sanitary blocks have British style WCs, hot and cold water throughout including for dishwashing and laundry, hairdryers, washing machines, baby changing area and subdued piped music. There are facilities for disabled campers. Car wash. Although set back from the sea, the site offers two small circular pools including one for children around which is a small terraced area with sun-beds (20/5-16/9). Other sporting facilities offered are a tennis half-court, table tennis, four flood-lit boules courts, mini-adventure playground and a sports programme including tournaments, and aquarobics in high season. There is other animation for children in this period, along with a weekly dance when a temporary bar is organised. The site is peaceful and popular with the French who love its simplicity. Torches are necessary in some areas. Reception sells basic provisions (wine of course!), gas and bread (to order in low season), although a large commercial centre is just 500 m. Beaches and many local attractions are close, but if you decide to stay here it would be advisable to have transport. However, there is a bus service to the historic city of Balaruc-Les-Bains from just outside the site. Fishing or riding 2 km, golf 20 km. An industrial area is nearby.

Directions: From A9 take exit for Sete and follow N800 to Balaruc le Vieux, then D2e to Sete. Don't take turn for Balaruc Les Bains but continue following road to Sete where site is signed just after the turn.

Charges 2000:
-- Per unit incl. 1 person and 60 sq.m. pitch Ffr. 44.00 - 93.00, 2 persons, electricity, 80 sq.m. 78.00 - 121.00, 100 sq.m. 98.00 - 177.00, 4 persons 119.00 - 175.00.
-- Credit cards accepted.

Open:
1 April - 21 October.

Address:
4 chemin du
Mas du Padre,
34540 Balaruc-Les-Bains.

Tel:
(0)4.67.48.53.41
FAX: (0)4.67.48.08.94
E-mail: mas-du-padre@wanadoo.fr.

Reservations:
Advised for high season only.

3402 Camping Le Garden, La Grande Motte, nr Montpellier

Useful site close to the sea in modern resort of La Grand Motte.

Le Garden is a mature site, situated 300 m. back from a fine sandy beach and with all the choice of sports, entertainment and other facilities of this popular holiday resort. With space for 117 caravans, 60 tents and 49 mobile homes, the 100 sq.m. pitches are hedged with good shade. All have facilities for electricity (6A), water and waste water. Three well situated toilet blocks provide British and Turkish style WCs, controllable hot showers, washbasins in cabins, plus baby bath and free hairdryers. Dishwashing and laundry sinks have hot water and there are washing machines. Unit for disabled people. A shopping complex is to one side of the site with groceries, cigarettes, newspapers, a boutique, etc. alongside a restaurant, bar and takeaway service. A swimming pool is on site with a children's paddling pool. Reception can exchange money and offers tourist information. Nearby are tennis courts, a riding club, casino and night club.

Directions: Entering La Grand Motte from D62 dual-carriageway, keep right following signs for `campings'. Turn right at Centre Commercial on Ave de la Petite Motte and the site is the first on the right.

Charges guide:
-- Per unit with 1-3 persons Ffr. 150.00, with services 186.00; extra person 30.00 - 32.00; local tax 3.30.
-- Less 20-30% in low seasons.
Open:
1 March - 31 October.
Address:
34280 La Grande Motte.
Tel:
(0)4.67.56.50.09.
FAX: (0)4. 67.56.25.69.
Reservations:
Not made.

6601 Camping-Caravaning California, Le Barcarès, Perpignan

Family site with swimming pool, not far from beach.

Directly off the main road in a popular area near Le Barcarès, California has 256 hedged pitches on level grass and is cool and shaded. Originally an orchard, the site now has a mature look with an attractive terraced pool bar area and an efficient reception area built in local materials. The 150 touring pitches, all with electricity and shade, vary a little in size and shape but average about 100 sq.m. The two toilet blocks are of standard modern construction with British style WCs, with free pre-mixed warm water in the washbasins (shelf and mirror), showers and sinks. There is a baby bath and small toilets, washing machine and ironing room, plus chemical disposal and motorcaravan services. Water points are limited (with push-button). The site is about 900 m. from a sandy beach. It has a swimming pool (200 sq.m.) with palms and sunbathing area, a children's pool and a free water slide in a small separate pool (over 11s only). The restaurant and bar with a large teraced area, takeaway and shop (all 20/6-31/8), a wine store (with degustations) and a pizzeria are at the site entrance. Tennis, volleyball, basketball, table tennis, boules, TV room, small multi-gym, mountain bike hire and archery. Children's animation is organised in season, plus some evening entertainment. Riding or river fishing 500 m, golf 10 km. Car wash. Only gas or electric barbecues are allowed. Torches are useful. Note: some neighbouring sites hold noisy discos. Chalets and mobile homes (85) to let.

Directions: Site is on D90 coast road 2 km. southwest of Le Barcarès centre.

Charges 2000:
-- Per unit with 2 persons Ffr. 110.00, with 10A electricity 128.00; extra person 29.00; child (under 7) 19.00; animal 10.00; local tax 1.00.
-- Less outside July/Aug.
-- Credit cards accepted.
Open:
29 April - 23 September.
Address:
Route de St Laurent, 66420 Le Barcarès.
Tel:
(0)4.68.86.16.08.
FAX: (0)4.68.86.18.20.
E-mail: camping-california@wanadoo.fr.
Reservations:
Made with deposit (Ffr. 500) and fee (90).

**Book this site
01892 559898**

THE ALAN ROGERS'
travel service

6616 Camping Club L'Europe, Le Bacarès

All year site with pools and individual sanitary blocks.

Camping Club Europe is 200 metres from Camping California (no. 6601) but is included because it is open all year. There are 360 level pitches, all with electricity (10A) and all have their own sanitary block. These comprise a British style WC, shower, sink with hot water and a washing up sink outside, and the management state that these are heated in low season. There are mature trees for shade and there should be no problems with access. Three pitches have special facilities for disabled campers. A central building houses a rather sterile set of support facilities. A shop sells bread daily, along with a bar and restaurant with a standard menu with one or two local delicacies and a pizzeria in season. These facilities are provided in July/August (or later depending on custom). Other activities in season include tennis, a large children's play area, weight lifting, trampolines, basketball, and a decent pool with sunbathing area, a few palms and a large paddling pool. A small room has games including pool and games machines. An animation programme is provided in high season only. Chalets and mobile homes to hire.

Directions: From N9 Perpignan road take D81 to Le Bacarès and then junction 9 for Canet. Then take exit for S'Laurent and it the first site on the right.

Charges 2000:
-- Per unit incl. 2 persons Ffr. 50.00 - 175.00; extra person 20.00 - 40.00; child (up to 5 yrs) free - 30.00; sanitary block and electricity (16A) 25.00; dog free - 25.00.
Open:
All year.
Address:
Rte de St Laurent, 66420 Port Bacarès.
Tel:
(0)4.68.86.15.36.
FAX: (0)4.68.86.47.88.
Reservations:
Advised high season; contact site.

MEDITERRANEAN - 66 Pyrénées-Orientales

6606 Camping Les Dunes de Torreilles-Plage, Torreilles

Seaside site near Perpignan with swimming pool and pitches with own sanitation.

This is an unusual site in several respects. It is quite large, with some 600 pitches, all of 100 sq.m. minimum but of varying size and shape, all having electricity and drainage. The pitches are all marked and most are separated by foliage except near the beach and dunes where vegetation is sparse. The site has the advantage of direct access to sandy beaches with good bathing and boating, including a naturist beach 500 m. south of the site. Facilities on site are numerous including a swimming pool (20 x 10 m. 1/5-30/9) and children's pool, with adjacent bar and terrace, bistro and pizzeria with takeaway facilities (1/6-30/9). Small shops for bread, wine, fruit and vegetables (most from 1/5) and a 'centre commercial' with supermarket, shops and restaurant adjacent. Activities include tennis, windsurfing lessons (boards for hire, also pedaloes) and minigolf. Kiosk/bar by beach. Disco. Washing machines and dryers. Treatment room; doctor calls June-Sept. Entertainment programme and organised excursions. Fishing from the beach or rivers (1 km). Another feature of the site is that each pitch has its own small circular sanitary unit with shower (heated and adjustable, but beware instant very hot water), washbasin, British style WC, mirror and hooks. Clients keep these units clean during their stay but the site takes a deposit to ensure that they are left clean, however they are cleaned for incoming clients. Some static units on the site are devoted to tour operators or owner occupiers but, with over 200 pitches for tourists and apart from the mid-July to mid-August peak season, there is usually ample space and the opportunity to choose your own pitch. In many respects this is an ideal site for families, in a still developing tourist area, with plenty of activities on the site and nearby but without being too intrusive for those who prefer just to relax. There may be some evening noise on pitches on the northern side of the site from several nearby discos in high season. This is not a site you are likely to forget but it may not be to everyone's taste - it can be windy and dry.

Directions: From A9 take exit for Perpignan Nord, the D83 towards Le Barcarès for 9 km. then south on D81 towards Canet for 3 km. before turning left to site.

Charges 2000:
-- Per unit incl. 2 persons, sanitary unit and electricity Ffr. 71.00 - 161.00, 3-6 persons 84.00 - 215.00; deposit refunded on departure 600.00; local tax 1.00; dog 12.00.
-- Min. stay 7 days 9/7-22/7 and 30/7-19/8.

Open:
15 March - 15 October.

Address:
66440 Torreilles-Plage.

Tel:
(0)4.68.28.38.29.
FAX: (0)4.68.28.32.57.

Reservations:
Made with deposit (Ffr. 500) and fee (110), min. 1 week in July/Aug.

6607 Camping-Caravaning Le Brasilia, Canet Plage en Roussillon

Excellent, well run site beside beach with wide range of facilities.

We were very impressed with our visit to La Brasilia – it is pretty, neat, tidy and well kept with an amazingly wide range of facilities and activities. It is a large site, but does not seem so, with 807 neatly hedged pitches all with 5A electricity. With a range of shade from mature pines and flowering shrubs, less on pitches near the beach, there are neat access roads (sometimes narrow for large units) and many flowers. The nine modern sanitary blocks are well equipped and maintained, with British style WCs (some Turkish) and washbasins in cabins. One is new, very modern and impressive with good facilities for children (as has one other block). All have washing up and laundry sinks with hot and cold water everywhere, chemical disposal, laundry room with washing machines and dryers, and facilities for disabled people. The sandy beach here is busy, with a beach club (you can hire windsurfing boards) and a naturist section is on the beach to the west of the site. There is a large California type pool (weekly charge in high season), with sunbathing areas bounded by an attractive mosaic wall and bar. A new sports field for football and a smaller games pitch (with 'Astroturf') is beside the tennis courts. There is provision for activities such as aqua gym, aerobics, football, etc. plus a games and video room (club card is required in high season). Bicycle hire and fishing on site, riding 5 km, golf 12 km. The village area with bars and restaurant is busy, providing meals, entertainment (including a night club) and a range of shops. In fact you do not need to stir from the site which is almost a resort in itself providing a cash dispenser, exchange facilities, telephone, post office, gas supplies and even weather forecasts. It does have a nice, lively atmosphere but is orderly and well run - very good for a site with beach access. Torches useful as the lighting is at knee level and sometimes lacking. English is spoken. Bungalows, chalets and mobile homes to rent. A 'Yelloh Village' member.

Directions: Site is north of Canet Port. From Canet Plage follow signs for Port, then 'Campings', and then follow site signs (near the American Park).

Charges 2001:
-- Per unit incl. 2 persons Ffr. 100.00 - 185.00; extra person (over 3 yrs) 25.00 - 40.00; child (under 3 yrs) free - 13.00; dog free - 15.00; electricity (5A) 16.00; local tax (over 3 yrs) 2.00.
-- Credit cards accepted.

Open:
7 April - 6 October.

Address:
BP 204, 66141 Canet Plage en Roussillon.

Tel:
(0)4.68.80.23.82.
FAX: (0)4.68.73.32.97.
E-mail: brasilia@mnet.fr.

Reservations:
Advised for July/Aug - contact site for details.

Book this site
01892 559898

THE ALAN ROGERS'
travel service

*see colour advert
between pages 224/225*

6602 Camping Club Ma Prairie, Canet, nr Perpignan

Excellent site 3 km. back from sea among the vineyards, with various amenities.

The Gill family provide a warm welcome immediately you enter the very pretty ivy covered reception area which boasts an impressive international collection of hats/helmets and uniform caps. Ma Prairie lies some 3 km. back from the sandy Canet beaches, with two excellent swimming pools – a small children's one (120 sq.m.) and a large one for adults (10 x 22 m), across a small road from the camping area. There are 260 pitches of nearly 100 sq.m. average, on flat grassy ground with various trees and bushes separating them and providing shade (possible road noise). Most have electricity, with water and drainage on 35. The three sanitary blocks, two excellent new ones and one more mature, have British type WCs, washbasins in cabins with dividers, shelves and mirrors, and controllable hot showers. Baby bath, washing machines, dryers and chemical disposal. Ample free hot water (and cold) in washbasins, showers, washing-up sinks and clothes sinks. There is extra provision near reception. A large air-conditioned bar overlooks the terraced pool area, which now includes a splendid children's pool. There is satellite TV, table tennis, billiards and amusement machines; dancing evenings, etc. about three times weekly and a busy daily animation programme in season. There is a shop for basics only and a covered snack bar and takeaway next to reception. Tennis, bicycle hire, children's play area, volleyball. The area of the old restaurant is now used for children's entertainment. The Gills have produced another superb touch in their new quality restaurant. A family affair down to mother's cushion designs, grandfather's paintings on the wall, and much more, the chef has been there for many years producing quality food. Tours of the family vineyard with supper are organised weekly (but book early) and the site owners offer wine with their own distinctive label (ask about the clever use of the family name). The attractive Canet Village is within walking distance and has all amenities. Bus/tram services run to the modern resort of Canet, where there are first class restaurants, etc. Riding 600 m, golf 6 km. Caravan storage available. Mobile homes for hire. Used by tour operators (40 pitches). There is a lively family atmosphere. A 'Sites et Paysages' member.

Directions: Leave autoroute A9 at Perpignan North towards Barcares. Site access is from D11 Perpignan road close to the junction with D617 in Canet-Village.

Charges 2000:
-- Per unit with 2 persons Ffr. 82.00 - 142.00; extra person 18.00 - 30.00; child 4-10 yrs 14.00 - 25.00, under 4 yrs 14.00 - 16.00; local tax 2.00; electricity 3A 17.00, 6A 23.00; fully serviced pitch 28.00; dog 16.00; extra car 16.00.
-- Credit cards accepted.

Open:
8 May - 20 September.

Address:
66140 Canet en Roussillon.

Tel:
(0)4.68.73.26.17.
FAX: (0)4.68.73.28.82.
E-mail: ma.prairie @wanadoo.fr.

Reservations:
Made for any length with deposit (Ffr. 400) and fee (80).

`Camping Cheque'

Book this site
01892 559898

THE ALAN ROGERS'
travel service

6603 Camping Cala Gogo, St Cyprien-Plage, nr Perpignan

Site by beach, with own swimming pool and varied amenities.

This is an impressive large and well organised site (sister site to 6604, Le Soleil) and is agreeably situated by a superb sandy beach where there is a beach bar and boats can be launched. The 386 pitches for touring units on flat ground are individual ones of around 100 sq.m. They are fully marked out with easy access, electrical connections everywhere and some shade. The site has now built a most impressive pool complex carefully laid out with palm trees in ample sunbathing areas, three adult pools plus one for children, water-jets, jacuzzi and waterfall. Three of the five toilet blocks are basically good and provide British and Turkish style toilets, washbasins in private cabins with shelves and mirrors, and free hot, controllable showers. The third and fourth blocks nearest the beach have been refurbished to a high standard. There is a large bar complex with disco and TV, which becomes very busy in season (you need a passport photgraph for the night club identity card), and an attractive small shopping mall, wine boutique and a high standard supermarket. Of particular note is a very sophisticated restaurant with excellent cuisine and service, plus a self-service restaurant with simple menu and takeaway food. A small bar by the beach opens in high season. A programme of events is organised in season: sports, etc. during the day, dancing or entertainment on a large stage recently built alongside the bar on some evenings. A large Aquapark, reputed to be amongst the best in southern France, is near. Tennis, table tennis and a children's playground. Fishing, riding, bicycle hire and golf within 5 km. Boat excursions and courses in skindiving, windsurfing or sailing nearby. Treatment room; doctor calls daily in July/Aug. Torches useful. Used by tour operators (135 pitches). Mobile homes to rent.

Directions: Site is south of St Cyprien and is well signed from roads around.

Charges 2001:
-- Per person (over 5 yrs) Ffr. 39.00; pitch (any unit) 58.00; dog 20.00; local tax 2.00 (child 1.00).
-- Less 20% outside July/Aug.
-- Credit cards accepted.

Open:
12 May - 29 September, with all services.

Address:
La Vigie,
66750 St Cyprien-Plage.

Tel:
(0)4.68.21.07.12 (when closed (0)4.68.95.90.11).
FAX: (0)4.68.21.02.19 (or (0)4.68.95.92.82).
E-mail: calagogo@ campmed.com.

Reservations:
Made for Sat. to Sat. and necessary for Jul/Aug, with deposit (Ffr 480) and fee (120).

6604 Camping Le Soleil, Argelès-sur-Mer, nr Perpignan

Busy, family owned site with good size pitches and direct access to beach.

Le Soleil, a sister site to Cala Go-Go (6603), with direct access to the beach, is popular and has grown in the last few years. A large site, more like a small village, it has over 800 individual numbered pitches of ample size, on sandy/grassy ground and with shade (except, perhaps, in the newer extensions) and electrical connections in all areas. Access for caravans sometimes needs care on the narrow tree lined roads. It has a wide range of amenities with Spain and the Pyrénées near enough for excursions. The seven sanitary blocks are of the type with external access to individual units and should give good coverage. They have plentiful pre-set hot showers in four blocks. The other two blocks have undergone a major refurbishment and now offer controllable showers and unusually two additional pressure water outlets at waist level in each. Washbasins in private cabins and hot water is available throughout. A large, impressive swimming pool complex is to one side of the site with a press, tabac and bar nearby. A supermarket, general shop and restaurant for sit down or takeaway food is more centrally situated. Bar with disco (July/Aug - you will need a passport photo for the nightclub identity card) and beach bar. Children's adventure playground, TV room, tennis and bicycle hire on site. Riding on site in high seaosn and nearby and facilities for fishing and mooring boats on the adjacent river. Golf 5 km. Washing machines. Bureau de change and ATM machine. Doctor on site in high season. English is spoken and there is a comprehensive reservation system (advised for most of July/Aug). No dogs are accepted. Used by tour operators (150 pitches). Mobile homes for rent (60).

Directions: Site is at north end of the beach about 1 km. from Argelès-Plage village.

Charges 2000:
-- Per person (any age except babies) Ffr. 41.00; local tax (adults) 2.60; pitch 58.00; electricity (6A) 17.00.
-- Less 20% outside July/Aug.
-- Swimming pool deposit Ffr. 100 per pitch.
-- Credit cards accepted.

Open:
15 May - 30 September.

Address:
Rte du Littoral, 66700 Argelès-sur-Mer.

Tel:
Season: (0)4.68.81.14.48.
FAX: (0)4.68.81.44.34.
Winter: (0)4.68.95.94.62.
FAX: (0)4.68.95.92.81.
E-mail: camping.lesoleil @infonie.fr.

Reservations:
Made from Sat or Wed (min. 1 week) with deposit (Ffr. 480) and booking fee (120).

6613 Hotel de Plein Air L'Eau Vive, Vernet-les-Bains

Well kept small site at the spa town of Vernet in the Pyrénées.

Enjoying dramatic views of the towering Pic du Canigou (3,000 m.), this site is 1½ km. from the centre of Vernet-les-Bains. It is approached via a twisting road through a residential area. Under new ownership, the site is well kept with first class sanitary facilities in two modern blocks with British WCs, hot showers with dressing area, washbasins (hot water) in private cabins, dishwashing (hot water) under cover, chemical disposal, facilities for disabled people. A washing machine is in each block. The 77 tourist pitches, all with electricity (4/10A) and water, are on a slight slope, part hedged and some terraced. Most have some shade. Although there is no swimming pool as such, the site has a more or less natural pool (created by pumping and circulating running water from the nearby stream – very attractive) and even providing a small beach with water slide. There is a central floating safety line across the pool but parents should keep an eye on children around the pool as there is no supervision or safety fence. Bar/reception with pool table, amusement machine, library, etc. There is an attractive open air (but under cover) snack bar with simple food and takeaway (1/6-30/9). Bicycle hire on site, fishing 200 m. Well situated for touring this area of the Pyrénées and with very comfortable amenities, this small site quickly becomes fully booked in season and reservation is essential. The medieval, walled town (Ville Franche de Conflent), the Grottes des Canalettes and Fort Libena with its many steps are well worth visiting. English is spoken by the Dutch owners. Chalets to let.

Directions: On N116 to Andorra, 6 km. after Prades, take turning at Villefranche-de-Conflent for Vernet-les-Bains. Continue up hill for 5 km. and keep right avoiding town centre. Turn right over bridge in direction of Sahorre. Immediately, at one end of small block of shops, turn right into Avenue de Saturnin and follow for about 1 km. past houses to more open area and site is signed.

Charges 2000:
-- Per unit incl. up to 3 persons and electricity (4A) Ffr. 90.00 - 140.00; extra person (over 4 yrs) 15.00 - 20.00; animal 10.00 - 20.00; electricity (10A) 15.00.
-- Discounts for weekly stays.
-- Credit cards accepted 15/6-15/9 only.

Open:
All year except 12 Nov - 15 Dec.

Address:
Chemin de Saturnin, 66820 Vernet Les Bains.

Tel:
(0)4.68.05.54.14.
FAX: (0)4.68.05.78.14.
E-mail: leau@club-internet.fr.

Reservations:
Made with deposit (20% of charges), Ffr. 100 fee (high season only) and cancellation insurance (details from site).

6611 Camping Le Dauphin, Argelès-sur-Mer

Quieter site with views of the Pyrénées and good swimming pools.

Near Taxo in the quieter, northern part of Argelès (a somewhat frenzied resort in season), this site on flat, grassy parkland enjoys good views of the Pyrénées, particularly from the terrace area surrounding its excellent complex of swimming pools. About a third of the 310 level, grassy and well shaded pitches (all with 10A electricity) have the benefit of what amounts to their own individual sanitary block with hot shower, washbasin and WC and with an adjacent washing up sink. The other pitches are served by a central sanitary block which, although mature, provides modern facilities including a number of showers and washbasins en-suite, British style WCs, etc. The site has a good range of facilities in addition to the pools (small charge), including a bar/restaurant, pizzeria with takeaway, shops (all 1/6-15/9), tennis courts, a small children's play area, minigolf, table tennis, a sports ground and games room. An entertainment programme is staged in high season. Although located some 1½ km. from the town and beach, there is a regular connecting 'road train' service to and fro throughout the day and evening up to midnight. Fishing 2 km, riding 1 km. Mobile homes to rent (60). Used by tour operators (70 pitches). Torches are useful in some areas of the site.

Directions: Site is on north side of Argelès. From autoroute take exit Perpignan-Nord for Argelès and follow directions for Plage-Nord and Taxo d'Avall (similarly from the N114).

Charges 2000:
-- Per unit incl. 2 adults Ffr. 145.00; extra person 33.00; child (under 5 yrs) 19.00; electricity 20.00; water and drainage 20.00; individual sanitation 50.00; extra car 12.00; animal 12.00; local tax (over 10 yrs) 2.40.
-- No credit cards.

Open:
25 May - 30 September

Address:
Rte. Taxo d'Avall, 66701 Argelès-sur-Mer.

Tel:
(0)4.68.81.17.54.
FAX: (0)4.68.95.82.60.

Reservations:
Made with deposit (Ffr 500) and booking fee (100).

6600 Camping Pujol, Argelès-sur-Mer

Well managed site with ornamental swimming pool complex.

Argelès is a busy tourist area and in high season it doesn't matter which of the 60 or so sites you are on, there are various loud open air discos and activities which may impinge on the wrong side of midnight for a while. However, it is possible to avoid the standard hectic seaside site in otherwise attractive Argelès, and Pujol may represent the best chance of doing so. There are 310 numbered pitches, all larger than 100 sq.m. on flat grass, nearly all with electricity. They include 100 privately owned British mobile homes, the company 'Allez France' employing a British manager to sell mobile homes on this site. The number of pitches has been increased this year (50) but these will be taken by mobile homes over the next few years, but in the meantime they are useful large pitches with electricity for tourers. The main sanitary blocks, including a new one, contain good modern facilities, including British style WCs, and are kept very clean. A second block (affection-ately known as the Taj Mahal) has been built in an extended section of the site, and is very well appointed in all respects except for its lack of water taps, though there is is another block close by. There are washing machines in each block with free ironing, plus chemical disposal. The site boasts a good terraced restaurant and friendly bar (1/6-15/9). Care is taken to ensure this is a family bar rather than one overrun by youngsters, who are catered for in an attractively covered meeting area that also houses animation and dances. There is some road noise near the entrance to the site. A small supermarket sells cheap wine by the flagon, all basic needs, and excellent hot bread twice a day, baked on the premises (1/6-15/9). The site's pride and joy is a delightful pool complex (1/6-15/9) with a fairly large L-shaped pool, children's pool, and for adults, a spa pool on an overlooking terrace. Semi-tropical shrubs and fountains make the area very attractive. There are table tennis tables, small multi-gym, games room, volleyball, children's playground, boules pitches and minigolf. Fishing, bicycle hire 1 km, riding 500 m. The site is very close to an interesting fortress and only 2 km. from the fast N114, via which the pretty ports of Collioure and Port-Vendres are but a short distance to the south, and Perpignan not far in the other direction (watch for traffic jams in the mornings going north). Argelès Plage and the quiet resort of Racou are a short distance if you want to exchange the pool for a Mediterranean beach.

Directions: From autoroute take Perpignan-Nord exit. Follow N114 from Perpignan and use exit 10 for Argelès. Cross first roundabout onto Chemin de Neguebous (avoiding town). Turn left at second roundabout and site is 200 m. on right opposite Tour de Pujol.

Charges 2001:
-- Per pitch incl. 2 adults Ffr. 130.00, with electricity 160.00; extra person 30.00; child (under 3) 15.00; extra car 10.00; local tax (over 10 yrs) 1.75.
-- Less 20% in June and Sept.
-- No credit cards.

Open:
1 June - 30 September.

Address:
Rte. du Tamariguer, 66700 Argelès-sur-Mer.

Tel:
(0)4.68.81.00.25.
FAX: (0)4.68.81.21.21.

Reservations:
Advised in high season and made with Ffr. 500 deposit. Write or 'phone for information.

N6612 Camping Naturiste La Clapère, Maureillas

Very attractive naturist site in the lower ranges of the Pyrénées.

Situated in a valley in the Albères, this site occupies a large area (50 hectares), includes a fast flowing small river and offers a choice of 200 good sized pitches on no less than eight separate terraces, all very natural. They are all slightly different in character; two for example are alongside the river, one is among fruit trees, another vines. Electricity is available on five of the terraces, the others being more suitable for tents. There is a large swimming pool, a smaller children's pool, and ample paved sunbathing areas. Alongside is the attractive bar and restaurant and a terrace with excellent views of the Pyrénées. The restaurant offers a simple, basic menu, a choice of more sophisticated set menus, and a takeaway service. The shop, although small, is very well stocked (all 1/6-15/9). Activities include table tennis, boules, volleyball and fishing with organised rambles and a good children's playground. There are three modern sanitary blocks of unusual design providing good facilities. The first block is heated by solar panels, so if the weather is not so good, water is cooler. Toilets are both British and Turkish style, washbasins have hot and cold water, as do the washing up and laundry sinks; there are also washing machines in the first block, and chemical disposal. A busy river runs through the site, there is an attractive waterfall and a deep pool for non serious fishing (but you are not allowed to remove the crayfish). The nearby town of Céret has a Saturday morning market. This is one of a small number of very attractive, unspoilt naturist sites located in beautiful, wild countryside. It is little wonder that more and more campers and caravanners are turning to naturist sites for their holidays in these more environmentally conscious times. Mobile homes for hire (8).

Directions: Take last autoroute (A9) exit before Spain (Boulou exit). Leave Boulou on N9 in the direction of Le Perthus for 3 km. Turn right onto N618 to Maureillas-las-Illas, then D13 to site (2 km).

Charges 2000:
- Per unit incl. 2 adults Ffr. 114.00; adult 25.00 - 36.00; child (0-14 yrs) 15.00 - 26.00; animal 7.00 - 10.00; electricity (3A) 19.00; local tax 1.50, child (4-10) 0.75. -- No credit cards.

Open:
1 April - 31 October.

Address:
Route de Las Illas, 66480 Maureillas.

Tel:
(0)4.68.83.36.04.
FAX: (0)4.68.83.34.44.

Reservations;
Made with deposit (30% of charges).

MEDITERRANEAN Part 2

Part 2 covers the eastern coastal region of the Mediterranean. We have used two départements from the official French region of Provence, i.e. those that border the coast, and the official region of Cote d'Azur.

Coastal Provence

Major city: Marseille

Départements:
13 Bouches-du-Rhône, 83 Var

Côte d'Azur

Major cities: Nice, Cannes, Monte Carlo (Monaco)

Départements: 06 Alpes-Maritime

The mention of Provence immediately draws to mind lavender fields and olive groves; it is a sunny bright region backed by mountains, with a glittering coastline. The Romans settled in the region and their legacy remains in the great amphitheatres and monuments of Arles and Nîmes. The Rhône valley divides above Arles into two arms which encircle the marshlands of the Camargue before reaching the sea. The wild white horses which gallop, manes flying, through the shallow waters of the delta are legendary, as are the ragged black bulls and the rose and white flamingos.

The Côte d'Azur, perhaps better known as the French Riviera, is a beautiful stretch of coast studded with sophisticated towns such as Monte Carlo, Nice, and Cannes, not forgetting the other famous resort of St Tropez. The quaint harbours and fishing villages have become chic destinations, now full of pleasure yachts and crowded summertime beaches. Up in the hills are quieter tiny medieval villages of winding streets and white-walled houses with terracotta roofs, which have attracted artists and visitors for many years. In St Paul-de-Vence visitors can browse through shops and galleries set on narrow winding cobblestone streets. Grasse is the perfume capital of the world.

Note: site reports are laid out by département in numerical order not by region.
See map on page 320.

Cuisine of the region

Cuisine emphasizes seasonings, such as herbs and garlic, and fish
Aigo Bouido –garlic and sage soup with bread (or eggs and cheese)
Aïoli (ailloli) – a mayonnaise sauce with garlic and olive oil
Bouillabaisse – fish soup served safran (saffron) and aïoli (see above)
Rouille –an orange coloured sauce with peppers, garlic and saffron
Bourride – a creamy fish soup (usually made with big white fish), thickened with aïoli and flavoured with crawfish
Brandade (de morue) à l'huile d'olive – a mousse of salt cod with cream, olive oil and garlic
Pain Bagna – bread roll with olive oil, anchovies, olives, onions, etc.
Pissaladière – Provencal bread dough with onions, anchovies, olives, etc.
Pistou (Soupe au) – vegetable soup bound with 'pommade'
Pommade – a thick paste of garlic, basil, cheese and olive oil
Ratatouille– aubergines, courgettes, onions, garlic, red peppers and tomatoes in olive oil
Salade Niçoise – tomatoes, beans, potatoes, black olives, anchovy, lettuce and olive oil and sometimes tuna fish

Places of interest

Aix-en-Provence – old town with 17th/18th century character; Paul Cézanne and Tapestry museums
Cannes – popular for conventions and festivals, Cannes Film Festival, la Croisette, old city
Monte Carlo – main city of Monaco, casinos, gardens, Napoleon Museum. motorsport circuit

0605 Camping La Vieille Ferme, Villeneuve Loubet Plage, Antibes

Family owned site with good facilities, open all year, in popular resort area.

La Vieille Ferme is a family owned site with 134 level gravel-based pitches, 116 with electricity (6-10A), water and waste water connections and the majority separated by hedges. Some are only small, simple pitches for little tents. There is also a fully serviced pitch on tarmac for motorhomes. The three toilet blocks (two heated for winter use) provide mainly British style WCs, washbasins (all in cabins) and pre-set, well equipped showers. There are children's toilets, a baby room, two units for disabled people, chemical disposal and motorcaravan services. The blocks are all now of modern style and kept very clean. Dishwashing and laundry sinks have ample hot water and there are three washing machines and a dryer. A shop is open in high season with a drinks, sweets and ices machine in the TV room for all year use. The swimming pool (20 x 10 m.) and a new children's pool are also heated and covered for winter use (closed mid Nov-mid Dec) and beside it is a sunbathing area and jacuzzi. Table tennis, basketball and a boule pitch are available and games and competitions are organised in July/Aug. Fishing 1 km, golf 2 km. Refrigerator hire and safety deposit boxes. The site aims to cater for all year caravanning and, even though the shop is closed in winter, gaz, bread and milk are available to order. There are special winter rates for long stays with quite a few long stay units on site. The entrance to the site is very colourful with well tended flower beds. English is spoken at reception and the whole place has a very friendly feel to it. Chalets to let, available in winter as well. A 1 km. walk beside the road towards Antibes brings you to the railway station, giving access to all the towns along the coast and to the beach.

Directions: From west take Antibes exit from Esterel autoroute and turn left towards Nice when joining the N7 outside Antibes. After 3.5 km. on N7 turn left for site. From east take N7 towards Antibes and turn right after Villeneuve Loubet Plage. The turning off the N7, though signed, is not easy to see particularly at busy times but, coming from Antibes, it is on the left, more or less between the Bonne Auberge and the Parc de Vaugrenier. Site is 150 m. on right. Avoid N98 Route du Bord de Mer. Site has prepared its own small, yellow site signs.

Charges 2001:
-- Per pitch incl. 2 persons: tent and car Ffr. 90.00 - 140.00, caravan (if reserved) 100.00 - 155.00; extra person 23.00 - 29.00; child (under 5 yrs) 15.00 - 19.00; dog 10.00; electricity 2A 15.00, 6A 21.00, 10A 29.00; local tax 2.50.
-- Less 20-30% for longer stays in low season.
-- Credit cards accepted.

Open:
All year

Address:
296 Bvd. des Groules, 06270 Villeneuve Loubet Plage.

Tel:
(0)4.93.33.41.44. FAX: (0)4.93.33.37.28. E-mail: vieilleferme @bigfoot.com.

Reservations:
Advised over a long season and made with 25% deposit and Ffr. 120 (15.24) fee (high season only); Sat.-Sat. only in July/Aug. and at Easter.

**Book this site
01892 559898**

0601 Domaine Sainte Madeleine, Sospel

Attractive, peaceful site, with swimming pool, in spectacular mountain scenery.

Situated about 18 miles inland from Menton, and very near the Italian border, the approach to this site is not for the faint-hearted although having said that, when we visited in late July, the site was very busy with touring caravans so it cannot be too bad. The site itself makes the effort worthwhile - situated on a terraced hillside with mountain views towards Italy. On a fairly steep hillside, manoeuvring within the site presents no problem and the pitches themselves are on level, well drained grass. The lower ones have shade but those higher up on the hill have none. Electricity connections are available to 70 of the 90 pitches. The single sanitary block is of good quality, with British style WCs (seatless), washbasins in cabins, and large hot showers which, unusually for France, are on payment (Ffr. 3). Hot water (often only warm) for dishwashing and laundry sinks is drawn from a single tap. There are washing machines, chemical disposal, motorcaravan services and gas supplies. The popular swimming pool (140 sq.m. and heated in spring and autumn) is in a sunny location with areas for sunbathing. There is no shop or catering facilities on site but bread can be ordered. The attractive small town of Sospel is only 4 km. and here are many restaurants, bars, cafés and shops. Also at Sospel are tennis and horse riding and it is a centre for mountain biking. Fishing 1 km. There are way-marked walks for serious walkers in the surrounding hills. Chalets for rent (April-Oct, depending on the weather) and rooms in the house. Winter caravan storage. English is spoken.

Directions: Site is on D2566, 4 km. north of Sospel. The D2566 can be reached from either the A8 autoroute via Menton exit, or from the N7 at Menton.

Charges 2001:
-- Per unit incl. 2 adults Ffr. 95.00; extra adult 20.00; child (under 6 yrs) 13.00; animal 6.00; electricity (10A) 18.00; local tax (over 12 yrs) 1.00.
-- Less 15% outside July/Aug.
-- No credit cards.

Open:
1 April - 30 September.

Address:
Rte. de Moulinet, 06380 Sospel.

Tel:
(0)4.93.04.10.48.
FAX: (0)4.93.04.18.37.
E-mail: camp@camping-sainte-madeleine.com/

Reservations:
Necessary for July/Aug. and made with Ffr. 300 deposit.

**Book this site
01892 559898**

THE ALAN ROGERS'
travel service

0608 Camping-Caravaning Les Cigales, Mandelieu la Napoule

Quiet haven in centre of Mandalieu, open all year.

It is hard to imagine that such a quiet, peaceful site could be in the middle of such a busy town and so near to Cannes - we were delighted with it. The entrance (easily missed) with reception and parking has large electronic gates which ensures that the site is very secure. All the pitches are level and have much needed shade in summer and the sun will get through in winter when it is needed. There are three pitch sizes, from small ones for tents to pitches for larger units. All have electricity (6A) and some have water and waste water also. There are only 115 pitches, 20 used for mobile homes to hire, so this is really quite a small, personal, friendly site. The swimming pool is quite new and has a large sunbathing area with sun-beds provided. It is open March - Oct, but not heated so it would have to be a good day to entice anyone in early or late season, but the sun can be quite warm then in this part of France. The two unisex toilet blocks are new, very well appointed and kept spotlessly clean. One is heated for the winter months and they provide British style WCs, washbasins in cabins and good size, pre-set showers. All hot water is free and there are facilities for babies and disabled visitors, dishwashing and laundry sinks, a washing machine, chemical disposal and a motorcaravan service point. The restaurant by the entrance also serves takeaways (April - 30 Sept). The only concession to children is a small play area, table tennis and two games machines. There is no entertainment on site so it may not appeal to families with teenagers. The site is alongside the Canal de Siagne and for a fee small boats can be launched at La Napoule, then moored outside the campsite's side gate. Fishing is also possible in the canal, but we were told that there are not many fish! The town is an easy walk. the beach is 800 m. Held in the area are the Monte Carlo Rally, the Cannes Film Festival and the Mimosa Festival, all at quieter times of the year. Railway station 1 km. for trains to Cannes, Nice, Antibes and Monte Carlo. English is spoken.

Directions: From A8 take exit 40 and follow signs for Fréjus along the N7. You will track back to the autoroute and pass under it. Immediately after, at round-about, turn left into Ave de la Mer. Site is on left in 500 m.

Charges 2000:
-- Per adult Ffr. 22.50; child (under 5 yrs) 15.00; caravan or tent 45.00 - 120.00, acc. to season and size of unit; motor-caravan 70.00 - 34.00; two person tent 30.00 - 60.00; car 25.00; m/cycle 12.50; dog free; electricity 3A 15.00, 6A 25.00.
-- Low season for longer stays.
-- Credit cards accepted.

Open:
All year.

Address:
505 ave. de la Mer, 06210 Mandelieu la Napoule.

Tel:
(0)4.93.49.23.53.
FAX: (0)4.93.49.30.45.
E-mail: campingcigales @wanadoo.fr.

Reservations:
Made with deposit (Ffr. 500); contact site.

**Book this site
01892 559898**

THE ALAN ROGERS'
travel service

MEDITERRANEAN - 06 Alpes-Maritimes

0609 Camping-Caravaning Les Gorges du Loup, Le Bar-sur-Loup

Quiet, unsophisticated site in the hills above Grasse.

Les Gorges du Loup is situated on a steep hillside and many of the pitches are only suitable for tents and certainly not for large caravans, mainly due to the steepness of the site roads, but also because of the narrow 1 km. track which leads to the site. All the pitches are on level terraced areas and all have electricity (4/6A). The two tiled toilet blocks are kept very clean and provide pre-set hot showers with dividers and seats, washbasins mostly in cubicles and a majority of British style WCs (no chemical disposal facilities). Dishwashing and laundry sinks have a single hot tap to draw from and there is a washing machine and iron. A TV room with tables and chairs for board games, plus a library may be useful in early and late season. Outside are boules pitches, table tennis, volleyball and skittles. The swimming pool is open all season (no Bermuda shorts) and has a small slide and diving board, although there is no pool for small children. Overlooking the pool is a small bar/restaurant and takeaway (July/Aug). A quiet family site, there is no organised entertainment. Reception also houses a small shop with bread daily. Bar-de-Loup is only a 500 m. walk, with its few shops and restaurants. Grasse (9 km.) is surrounded by fields of lavender, mimosa and jasmine and has been famous for the manufacture of perfume since the 16th century. The Musée International de la Perfume has a garden of fragrant plants and the cathedral in the old town has three paintings by Reubens. Mobile homes to hire. If you find the steepness of the site a little daunting the very friendly owners will site your caravan with their 4 track free of charge. They also speak a little English.

Charges guide:
Per tent incl. 2 persons Ffr. 80.00 - 115.00; large tent, caravan or motor- caravan 90.00 - 145.00; extra person 15.00 - 20.00; child (under 5 yrs) 10.00 - 15.00; dog 10.00; electricity 4A 15.00, 6A 18.00, 10A 24.00.

Open:
1 April - 1 October.

Address:
06620 Le Bar-sur-Loup.

Tel:
(0)4.93.42.45.06. FAX: as phone.

Reservations:
Recommended in high season; contact site.

Directions: From Grasse take D2085 Nice road. At Châteauneuf Pré du Lac take D2210 to Pont-de-Loup and Vence. Site is signed on right about 500 m. after village of Bar-sur-Loup. After a very tight right turn, take 1 km. long, very narrow access road (a few passing places).

0604 Le Grand Saule, Cannes La Bocca

Agreeable, small site with swimming pool, within Cannes limits.

This little site is in a pleasant setting and, although only 200 m. from a busy through road, the intervening wooded area seems to give it sufficient screening to make the camp itself quite peaceful. It is only 1.5 km. from the beach at La Bocca and 4 km. from Cannes town centre, so its position is unusually handy for one of the show-places of the Riviera. A bus stop is close to the entrance gate. There is a small swimming pool of irregular shape beside an attractive terrace bar serving snacks (all from 1/5). With its situation the site obviously deals with much transit trade and many backpackers. It therefore has `young people' areas, formally designed for tents, and a `family area' with individual pitches separated by hedges and with electricity, water points and drainage, all with good shade, with a total of 55 units taken. The small toilet block, though kept busy, is usually well kept and clean, with British WCs, free fully controllable hot showers, washbasins with cold water (some in private cabins) and with hot water in dishwashing and laundry sinks and a washing machine. Chemical disposal and motorcaravan services. No shop but many are very close. Table tennis, children's frames and a sauna on site. Tennis club adjoining, open to clients, fishing, bicycle hire, riding 1.5 km, golf 2.5 km. Only gas barbecues are permitted. Being very close to Cannes, the site is naturally not cheap, but it is easily accessible. Small chalets to let (25).

Charges 2001:
-- Per unit incl. 2 persons Ffr. 114.00 - 154.00; extra person 41.00; child (2-5 yrs) 20.00; electricity 20.00.
-- Credit cards accepted.

Open:
1 May - 30 September.

Address:
24-26 Bd. Jean Moulin, 06110 Le Cannet Cannes.

Tel:
(0)4.93.90.55.10. FAX: (0)4.93.47.24.55. E-mail: le.grand.saule @wanadoo.fr.

Reservations:
Advised and made from any day with deposit equivalent to 1 weeks stay.

Directions: From A8 autoroute take Cannes-Ouest exit, turn towards Cannes, passing airport, left into Ave. de Coubertin, then into Ave. Jourdan; cross under autoroute, then 300 m. to camp on right. Le Grand Saule is signed from most main junctions in La Bocca.

Book this site
01892 559898

THE ALAN ROGERS'
travel service

0603 Camping-Caravaning Domaine de la Bergerie, Vence, nr Nice

Quiet family site with pool and tennis courts in the hills near St Paul de Vence.

La Bergerie, a family owned site, is situated in the hills about 3 km. from Vence and 10 km. from the sea at Cagnes-sur-Mer. This extensive, lightly wooded site has been left very natural and is in a quiet, secluded position about 300 m. above sea level. Because of the trees most of the pitches are shaded and all are of a good size. It is a large site but, because it is so extensive does not give that impression. There are 450 pitches, 250 with 2/5A electricity) and 65 with water and drainage also. Both toilet blocks have been refurbished and provide hot water throughout, washbasins in cabins, British style WCs and excellent provision for disabled people (pitches near the toilet block are reserved for disabled people). A recent addition is a large swimming pool, paddling pool and spacious sunbathing area (5/6-30/9). The site has a small bar/restaurant with takeaway and a shop (all 1/5-30/9). There are no organised activities but there is a children's playground, bicycle hire, table tennis, tennis courts and 10 shaded boules pitches (lit at night) with competitions in season. Riding 6 km, fishing 10 km, golf 12 km. Two chalets to hire but no tour operators and definitely no groups allowed. Caravan storage available. Hourly bus service (except Sundays) from site to Vence.

Directions: From autoroute A8 exit 47 take Cagnes-sur-Mer road in the direction of Vence. Site is west of Vence and it is necessary to follow `toutes directions' signs around the town to join the D2210 Grasse road. Follow this to roundabout (2 km.), turn left and follow site signs for 1 km. Site is on right in light woodland.

Charges 2000:
-- Per unit incl. 2 persons in high season Ffr. 76.00; with electricity (2A) 96.00 - 123.00; with 3 services 115.00 - 143.00; extra person 25.00; child (under 5) 15.00; electricity (5A) 10.00; local tax (over 18) 1.00.
-- Less 5-10% for longer stays in low season.
-- Credit cards accepted.

Open:
25 March - 15 October.

Address:
Rte de la Sine,
06140 Vence.

Tel:
(0)4.93.58.09.36.

Reservations:
Needed only in July/Aug. for the special pitches and made with 25% deposit and Ffr. 85 fee.

Provence Alpes Côte d'Azur

DOMAINE LA BERGERIE
★ ★ ★

Route de la Sine, 06140 Vence
Tel: 04.93.58.09.36

Two pools ~ Tennis ~ Chalets in 13h

N0607 Domaine Naturiste Club Origan, Puget-Theniers, nr Nice

Spectacularly situated naturist site in the mountains behind Nice.

Despite its rather spectacular location, Origan is easily accessible from the coast and you only discover that you are at a height of 500 m. when you arrive! The terrain within the extensive confines of the site is fairly wild and the roads distinctly stony. The scenery is impressive and footpaths in and around the site offer good, if fairly strenuous walks up to a height of 1,000 m. The nearby small town of Puget-Theniers is very pleasant and offers a choice of bars, cafés, shops, etc. although Origan itself provides a bar/restaurant (all season), takeaway and site shop (1/7-30/8). There are two swimming pools, one for children, a jacuzzi, a new sauna and even a disco in the cellars. Fishing and bicycle hire on site. The 50 pitches, some with the possibility of electric hook-up (by long cables) are in three different areas with many wild flowers. They are of irregular size and shape and all have good views. Sanitary facilities, exceptionally clean when we visited, are of a standard and type associated with most good naturist sites - mainly British type WCs, mostly open plan hot showers and ample washbasins with hot and cold water. Chemical disposal. Reservation is necessary in high season.

Directions: Heading east on the N202, just past the town of Puget-Theniers, turn right at camp sign at level crossing; site is 1.5 km.

Charges 2000:
-- Per unit incl. 2 persons Ffr. 75.00 - 139.00, 3 persons 93.00 - 159.00; extra person 16.00 - 22.00; child (5-14 yrs) free - 17.00; electricity (5A) 22.00; entertainment 2.00 - 5.00 per night.
-- Credit cards accepted.

Open:
1 April - 30 September.

Address:
06260 Puget-Theniers.

Tel:
(0)4.93.05.06.00.
FAX: (0)4.93.05.09.34.

Reservations:
Made with deposit (Ffr. 600 p/week) and fee (180). Write to Nat' Azur, 23 avenue J. Médecin, 06000 Nice. (Tel: (0)4.93.88.28.61. Fax: (0)4.93.87.47.49).

Book this site
01892 559898

THE ALAN ROGERS'
travel service

MEDITERRANEAN - 13 Bouches-du-Rhône

1300M Camping Municipal Les Pins, Fontvieille

Peace and quiet amongst the pines is the order of the day at Camping Les Pins. The pitches are all slightly sloping and are separated by hedges. Of the 163 pitches, 57 have electricity (6A), water and waste water points. The toilet blocks are modern but, because the tiles are dark brown, the first impression is not favourable. They are, in fact, clean and well maintained. There are British style toilets and showers are controllable and free. Plenty of laundry and dishwashing sinks with hot water are inside. Chemical disposal. A separate room houses washing machines, dryers and an ironing board. A children's play area is on site. Reception is bright and cheerful with ample tourist information. Try not to arrive during the lunch break as it is forbidden to go on site when reception is closed. There is no shop but the very pretty, floral village of Fontvieille is 15 minutes away on a forest track. The supermarket is small but fills a need, the village tennis courts are open to all, as is the local swimming pool. Arles, Les Baux and St Remy are all only a short drive away if the peace and quiet get too much for you.

Directions: Site signed on eastern edge of Fontvieille, on D17 Arles - Les Baux road (just at end of one way system).

Charges 2000:
-- Per pitch incl. 2 adults Ffr. 60.00; extra person 15.00; child (under 7 yrs) 9.00; dog 8.00; electricity 15.00; local tax 2.00.
-- Credit cards accepted.
Open:
1 April - 15 October.
Address:
Rue Michelet, 13990 Fontvieille.
Tel:
(0)4.90.54.78.69.
FAX: (0)4.90.54.81.25.
Reservations:
Made for min. 8 nights with Ffr. 100 fee.

1301M Camping Municipal Les Romarins, Maussane-les-Alpilles

A well kept, neat municipal site, Les Romarins has been in the guide for several years and remains popular with readers. It has tarmac access roads to the 145 good sized grassy pitches that hedged are by bushes, all with electrical connections (4A). The three toilet blocks are good, especially the newly refurbished one which provides British style toilets, adjustable, roomy showers, washbasins in cubicles and free hairdryers. A baby room, washing machine, laundry and dishwashing sinks and facilities for disabled visitors are included. The two older blocks have some Turkish style WCs and are of an older design, but still kept very clean and well maintained. On-site amenities are very limited - a pleasant reading room for cooler days, telephone (when reception is open), free tennis courts and a children's play area. The municipal swimming pool (with discounts) is near and shops and restaurants are in the pleasant little town. Bicycle hire or golf 1 km, fishing or riding 3 km. Les Baux and St Remy-de-Provence are tourist attractions not to be missed, especially St Remy's Roman ruins. Les Romarins is popular and becomes very busy from 1 July - late August. Caravan storage.

Directions: Site is within the little town of Maussane on the eastern edge.

Charges 2000:
-- Per pitch, incl. 2 adults + 1 child Ffr. 81.50; extra person 18.50; child (0-12 yrs) 10.50; dog 12.50; electricity 15.50 - 19.00; local tax 2.00.
-- Less 10-20% for longer stays.
-- Credit cards accepted.
Open:
15 March - 15 October.
Address:
13520 Maussane.
Tel:
(0)4.90.54.33.60.
FAX: (0)4.90.54.41.22.
Reservations:
Made for any length with fee (Ffr. 52 in low season, Ffr. 115 at Easter and for high season).

1305M Camping Municipal Mas de Nicolas, St Rémy-de-Provence

St Rémy de Provence is a very popular town and this reflects on Mas de Nicolas, as this too is very popular and always reasonably busy. The site has a very spacious feel to it, due mainly to the central area of gently sloping grass, dotted with shrubs, that is kept clear of pitches and used for leisure and sunbathing. The 140 pitches are separated by hedges, 120 with 6A electricity, water and drainage, and access roads are wide. Some pitches are an irregular shape and some are sloping, but many have views and they are mostly organised into groups of two and four. One of the old toilet blocks was refurbished for 2000 to give excellent facilities including British style WCs, washbasins in cabins, pre-set showers, a good chemical disposal point and even a dog shower. The other blocks are of an older design with mainly Turkish style WCs. However, all hot water is free and another block is to be refurbished for 2001. There are dishwashing and laundry sinks (with hot water), washing machines and drying lines. The swimming pool on site has a tile and grass sunbathing area (15/5-15/9) and next door are the municipal gymnasium, tennis and volleyball courts. Fishing 2 km, bicycle hire or riding 1 km, golf 15 km. St Rémy has a wide selection of restaurants and a Wednesday market.

Directions: St Rémy de Provence is located where the D571 from Avignon joins with the D99 Tarascon - Cavaillon road. Site is signed from the village centre on the north side. Leave autoroute A7 at Cavaillon or Avignon-Sud.

Charges 2000:
-- Per unit incl. 2 persons Ffr. 84.00 - 88.00; extra adult 27.00; child (under 10 yrs) 13.00; animal 10.00; extra child's tent 5.00; electricity (6A) 19.00; local tax 3.00
-- Credit cards accepted.
Open:
15 March - 15 October.
Address:
Av. Plaisance du Touch, 13210 St Rémy-de-Provence.
Tel:
(0)4.90.92.27.05.
FAX: (0)4.90.92.36.83.
Reservations:
Necessary for main season and made with Ffr. 110 fee (non returnable).

8302 Esterel Caravaning, Agay, nr Fréjus

Attractive, good site for caravans only, in hills east of St Raphaël, 3.5 km. from sea.

Set among the hills at the back of Agay, in an attractive quiet situation with good views around, this site is 3.5 km. from the sandy beach at Agay, where parking is perhaps a little easier than at most places on this coast. In addition to a section for permanent caravans, it has some 250 pitches for tourists, on which caravans of any type are taken but not tents. Pitches are on shallow terraces, attractively landscaped with good shade and a variety of flowering plants, giving a feeling of spaciousness and all with electricity connection and tap. There are 18 special ones which have their own individual washroom with WC, basin and shower (both with hot water) adjoining. Amenities include five heated, circular swimming pools, one large for adults, one smaller for children and three arranged as a waterfall. They are much used, attractively landscaped (floodlit at night) and open all season. A pleasant courtyard area contains the shop, takeaway and the bar/restaurant and terrace which also overlooks the pools (all 1/4-30/9). Activities include a new disco, archery, volleyball, minigolf, two tennis courts, a children's playground, bicycle hire, pony rides, petanque and, most unusual for France, a squash court. Two toilet blocks, plus one smaller one adjacent to the tourist section, were recently refurbished and are very satisfactory. They can be heated and provide British type WCs, washbasins mostly in private cabins, and free hot water in all facilities, though the temperature varies a little at busy times. Cleaning of these blocks and dustbin emptying are very good. There are facilities for disabled people and a laundry room, plus a motorcaravan service point and car wash. Events and entertainment are organised in season. Good golf courses are very close, and trekking by foot, bicycle or by pony in the surrounding natural environment of L'Esterel forest park. Wild boar come each evening to the perimeter fence to be fed by visitors. For obvious reasons barbecues (or any type of fire) are forbidden. Mobile homes (245) to let. A good site, well run and organised in a deservedly popular area. A member of 'Les Castels' group.

Directions: You can approach from St Raphaël via Valescure but easiest way to find is to turn off coast road at Agay where there are good signs. From Fréjus exit from autoroute A8, follow signs for Valescure throughout, then for Agay, and site is on left. (Reader's comment: If in doubt, follow golf complex signs - or Le Clerc). The road from Agay is the easiest to follow.

Charges 2001:
-- Per pitch incl. 2 persons: standard pitch Ffr. 145.00 - 170.00, deluxe pitch 185.00 - 215.00; extra person 45.00; child (1-7 yrs) 30.00; animal 10.00; local tax 2.00.
-- Credit cards accepted (from 2001).

Open:
1 April - 30 September.

Address:
Rte. de Valescure, 83700 St Raphaël-Agay.

Tel:
(0)4.94.82.03.28.
FAX: (0)4.94.82.87.37.
E-mail:
esterel@FranceNet.fr.

Reservations:
Necessary for high season and made for min. 1 week with deposit (Ffr. 500) and fee (100). CD brochure available from site.

Book this site
01892 559898

THE ALAN ROGERS'
travel service

see colour advert between pages 224/225

8318 Camping-Caravaning Les Rives de l'Agay, Agay

Quiet, family run site without entertainment, with number of caravan holiday homes.

The wide sweep of the beach at Agay is only a 400 m. walk from Les Rives de l'Agay, a quiet family site run by the third generation of the Nore family. The river runs alongside the site on its way to the sea. It is well fenced and there is the option of mooring your boat there, which is very popular with fishermen, both for river or sea fishing. The 96 pitches are shaded and a little smaller than most, but all have 6A electricity. There is a well stocked shop and a bar which also sells snacks and takeaway (both 1/4-30/9). The swimming pool has ample sunbathing areas for when you tire of the beach. The toilet blocks have been reburfished and can be heated, with cabins for washbasins, British style WCs, hot showers and baby baths. There are two washing machines, plenty of hot water in laundry and dishwashing sinks, a unit for disabled visitors and chemical disposal. There is a small games room and table tennis. Agay has many bars and restaurants and the market on Wednesdays is quite a large one in two areas, one along the sea front, the other just below the site. Trains and buses can be caught in Agay giving a wide variety of destinations to visit, from Monte Carlo to St Raphael and all places between. A car ride up the D100 will take you to a number of golf courses (nearest 6 km). Bicycle hire or riding 1 km. This is a quiet family site with no entertainment and quiet nights, although trains can be heard during the day. Mobile homes to rent (39).

Directions: From the N98 in Agay take the D100 northwest. Site is in 1 km. (on a bad bend).

Charges 2000:
-- Per pitch low season incl. 2 persons Ffr. 86.00, high season incl. 4 persons 156.00; extra person (over 3 yrs) 30.00 - 32.00, child under 3 yrs 13.00; dog 10.00; electricity (6A) 16.00; local tax 2.00.
-- Credit cards accepted.

Open:
1 March - early Nov.

Address:
83530 Agay.

Tel:
(0)4.94.82.02.74.
FAX: (0)4.94.82.74.14.

Reservations:
Contact site.

8301 Camping-Caravaning Les Pins Parasols, Fréjus

Family owned site with pool, 5 km. from beach; with some individual sanitary units.

Not everyone likes very big sites, and Les Pins Parasols with its 189 pitches is of a size which is quite easy to walk around. Although on very slightly undulating ground, virtually all the plots are levelled or terraced and separated by hedges or bushes with pine trees for shade. They are of around 100 sq.m. and all with electricity. What is particularly interesting, as it is the most unusual feature of the campsite, is that 48 of the pitches are equipped with their own fully enclosed, tiled sanitary unit, consisting of British WC, washbasin, hot shower and washing up sink, all quite close together. These naturally cost more but may well be of interest to those seeking extra comfort. The normal size toilet blocks, in three different places, are of good average quality and give a plentiful supply with washbasins in cabins, free, pre-set hot showers with push-button, chemical disposal and facilities for disabled people. One block can be heated when necessary. On site is a 200 sq.m. pool with attractive rock backdrop and sunbathing terrace, a separate long slide with landing pool and a small children's pool. Small shop with reasonable stocks and restaurant with takeaway (both 1/5-20/9). General room with TV. Half-court tennis. Tax free exchange facility. Bicycle hire or riding 2 km, fishing 6 km, golf 10 km. There is a bus from the gate into Fréjus. The nearest beach is the once very long Fréjus-Plage, now reduced a little by the new marina, which is some 5½ km. away and adjoins St. Raphaël. (See note on La Baume entry concerning traffic delays at the D4/N7 road junction.) Used by tour operators (10%).

Directions: From A8 exit 38 Fréjus Est, turn right immediately on leaving pay booths on a small road leading across to D4. Right again and under 1 km. to site.

Charges 2000:
-- Per normal pitch with electricity incl. 2 persons Ffr. 114.00 - 135.00, with sanitary unit 141.00 - 169.00; extra person 29.00 - 35.00; child (under 7 yrs) 19.00 - 22.00; dog 11.00 - 13.00.
-- No credit cards.

Open:
Easter - 30 September.

Address:
Route de Bagnols, 83600 Fréjus.

Tel:
(0)4.94.40.88.43.
FAX: (0)4.94.40.81.99.
E-mail: lespinsparasols @wanadoo.fr.

Reservations:
Made for min. 10 days for exact dates with deposit (Ffr 600), no fee.

Book this site
01892 559898

THE ALAN ROGERS'
travel service

CAMPING CARAVANNING ★★★★NN
ROUTE DE BAGNOLS - F-83600 FRÉJUS
Telephone 04.94.40.88.43 Swimming Pool

Supermarket - Snackbar - Individual washing cabins and hot water in all sanitary facilities - Separated pitches (80-100m2) all with electricity. Pitches with individual sanitary facilities (shower, washbasin, sink with hot water, WC) - Children's playground and solarium - Caravan pitches - Water points - Mini-tennis

LES PINS PARASOLS

SUN AND SHADE just 5 kms distance from the beaches of the COTE D'AZUR

8308 Au Paradis des Campeurs, La Gaillarde Plage, nr Fréjus

Agreeable small site with direct access to sandy beach.

Having direct access to a sandy beach via an underpass and being so well maintained are just two of the reasons that Au Paradis is so popular. Family owned and run, it now has 180 pitches, all with 6A electricity and 75 with water tap and drainaway. The original pitches vary in size and shape but all are satisfactory and most have some shade. The new pitches are all large but at present have no shade although trees and bushes are being planted. The two toilet blocks have been refurbished to an excellent standard with high quality fittings. They are well maintained with British style WCs, the majority of the washbasins in cabins, controllable showers and chemical disposal. Children have a shower at a suitable height and there are facilities for babies. All facilities, including dishwashing and laundry sinks, have free hot water and there are two washing machines and a dryer. The shop and restaurant (with takeaway) front onto the main road and are open all season. TV room. Two excellent children's play areas, catering for the under and over 5s, both have top quality safety bases. There is no entertainment which gives peaceful nights. Bicycle hire 2.5 km, riding 3 km, golf 6 km. Motorcaravan service point. The gates are surveyed by TV (especially the beach gate) and a security man patrols all day. The site has become popular and it is essential to book for June, July and August. Mobile homes to rent (8).

Directions: Site signed from N98 at La Gaillarde, 2 km. south of St Aygulf.

Charges 2000:
-- Per unit incl. up to 3 persons Ffr. 80.00 - 124.00, with water and drainage 96.00 - 150.00; extra person 30.00; child (under 4 yrs) 18.00; dog 15.00; extra tent 15.00; electricity (6A) 22.00; local tax (over 10 yrs) 15/6-15/9 2.00.
-- Credit cards accepted.

Open:
20 March - 10 October.

Address:
La Gaillarde Plage, 83380 Les Issambres.

Tel:
(0)4.94.96.93.55.
FAX: (0)4.94.49.62.99.

Reservations:
Advised for main season.

8306 Camping-Caravaning de la Baume + La Palmeraie, Fréjus

Busy, large site back from sea with excellent pool complex and other amenities.

This large site has been well developed, and much money has been spent on it. It lies about 5½ km. from the long sandy beach of Fréjus-Plage, but it has such a fine and varied selection of five swimming pools on site that many people do not bother to make the trip. The pools, with their palm trees, are a feature of this site and were remarkable for their size and variety (water slides, etc.) even before the addition of the latest, very large feature pool that is one of the highlights of the site. This large pool, surrounded by sunbathing areas, is overlooked by the very pretty terracing for the bar, restaurant, etc. The site has nearly 500 pitches of varying but quite adequate size with electricity, water and drainaway, with another 200 larger ones with mains sewerage to take mobile homes; separators to divide plots are being installed. Shade is available over most of the terrain. Although tents are accepted, the site concentrates mainly on caravanning. The seven toilet blocks should be a satisfactory supply, two have recently been enlarged and the others refurbished. They have British style toilets with a few Turkish; washbasins in cabins and free hot showers and sinks for clothes and dishes with hot water at pre-set temperature. Supermarket and several other shops. Bar with terrace and TV. Restaurant and takeaway. Tennis, archery and organised events - sports, competitions, etc. in daytime and some evening entertainment partly in English. Amphitheatre for shows. Discos daily in high season. First aid post. A bus to Fréjus passes the gate. The site becomes full in season, but one section with unmarked pitches is not reserved and there is plenty of space off-peak. La Baume's convenient location has its down-side as there is some traffic noise from the nearby autoroute: somewhat obtrusive at first but we soon failed to notice it. A popular site with tour operators. Adjoining La Baume is its sister site La Palmeraie, which contains self-catering accommodation. It has some 80 small chalet-type units for 4-6 persons (details from site). It also has its own landscaped pool and provides some entertainment to supplement that at La Baume.

Directions: Site is 3 km. up the D4 road, which leads north from N7 just west of Fréjus. From west on autoroute A8 take exit for Fréjus/St Raphaël (junction 37), turn towards them and after 4 km., turn left on D4. From east take exit for Fréjus/St Raphaël (junction 38); after exit turn right immediately on small road marked `Musée' etc. which leads you to D4 where right again.

Charges guide:
-- Per unit incl. 2 persons, 6A electricity, water and drainage Ffr. 98.00 - 180.00; extra person 20.00 - 36.00; child (under 7) free - 25.00; car or m/cycle 20.00 - 22.00; plus local tax.
-- Min. stay 3 nights.
-- Credit cards accepted.
-- For La Palmeraie charges apply to site.

Open:
22 March - 30 Sept, with full services.

Address:
Route de Bagnols, 83618 Fréjus Cedex.

Tel:
(0)4.94.40.87.87.
FAX: (0)4.94.40.73.50.
E-mail: la.baume.
la.palmerie@wanadoo.fr.

Reservations:
Essential for high season, and made for exact dates with substantial deposit and fee (Ffr 195), from 1 Jan.

Book this site
01892 559898
THE ALAN ROGERS'
travel service

Note: In peak season considerable traffic delays may be experienced at the D4/N7 junction if you wish to travel to Fréjus-Plage or to the nearest towns of Fréjus or St Raphaël. To avoid these it is possible to turn off the D4 on a minor road (signed 'Zoo' and 'Daniel Templon') leading past the easterly Fréjus/St Raphaël motorway entrance, which can get you reasonably quickly to the motorway or the eastern part of St Raphaël and areas east of that, but there can still be unwelcome delays in reaching Fréjus-Plage.

8310 Camping de la Plage, Grimaud, nr St Tropez

Popular site by a sandy beach opposite St Tropez.

A site actually on the beach is always in great demand, and Camping de la Plage is no exception and consequently, as such a popular site, it becomes very crowded. The site is divided into two parts by the N98 although a dangerous crossing is avoided by an underpass. All pitches are numbered - pitches away from the beach will be more peaceful. They are mostly of a decent size, with the ones over the road having more grass and more shade. All pitches have electricity (2, 4, 6 or 10A) but long leads may be required. There are three sanitary blocks on the beach side of varying quality, but were all clean when we visited and, according to regulars, cleaned regularly. All hot water is free and there is a satisfactory supply to showers and washbasins (a few in cabins). Baby bath. The majority of the WCs are of the British type. A large, well stocked supermarket is open all season, the bar, restaurant and takeaway open in May. Beach volleyball is popular, as is tennis and a small play area. There is boat hire close to the site. Bicycle hire 2 km, golf and riding 3 km. A first aid room is close to reception and in July/Aug. an English speaking doctor calls daily. Apartments to rent. Ste Maxime is 6 km. and it is not very far to all the familiar names - St Tropez, Port Grimaud, Fréjus and St Aygulf.

Directions: Site is on N98 main coast road about 6 km. southwest of Ste Maxime. Take care - this road is very busy in main season.

Charges guide:
-- Per unit with 2 persons Ffr. 105.00; extra person 28.00; child (under 7) 14.00; extra car or boat 14.00; extra small tent 25.00; animal 8.00; electricity 2A 17.50, 4A 21.00, 6A 26.00 or 10A 37.00; plus local tax.
-- Credit cards accepted.

Open:
8 March - 30 September.

Address:
83310 Cogolin-Grimaud.

Tel:
(0)4.94.56.31.15.
FAX: (0)4.94.56.49.61.

Reservations:
Bookings taken for exact dates with booking fee from Oct.- March only.

MEDITERRANEAN - 83 Var

8307 Camping-Caravaning L'Etoile d'Argens, St Aygulf, nr Fréjus

Large, well equipped site near beach, with good pool complex, suitable for families.

First impressions of L'Etoile d'Argens are of space, cleanliness and calm. Reception staff are friendly and English is spoken. This is a site run with families in mind and many activities are free. There are 493 level grass pitches laid out in typical French style, separated by hedges. There are five sizes ranging from 50 sq.m. (for small tents) to 100, 180 or 250 sq.m. These are exceptionally large and two families could easily fit two caravans and cars or one family could have a very spacious plot. Most pitches are fully serviced with fresh and waste water and 10A electricity. Most have some shade but the site is not over-powered by trees. A new central toilet block was added in 2000, whilst some of the original blocks (one unisex block at the end of each row of 25/30 pitches) have been retiled. Clean and well maintained, they provide British WCs, washbasins (some in cubicles), controllable showers and dishwashing sinks. A central laundry has washing machines, dryers, irons and outside clothes lines. The pool area is quite large with two pools, a paddling pool and a solarium, all surrounded by a sunbathing area. Around the entrance are the bar, restaurant, pizzeria, takeaway and shop. The bar area overlooks the tennis courts and has old olive and palm trees on beautifully manicured and watered grass. Activities include tennis (two courts are floodlit) with coaching, minigolf (both free in low season), aerobics, archery (July/Aug), football and swimming lessons. Volleyball, basketball, table tennis and boule. The play area has a safety base and there is a children's entertainer in July/Aug. An activity programme includes escorted walking trips to the surrounding hills. The river runs along one side of the site and a free boat service (15/6-15/9) runs every 40 mins to the beach. It is also possible to moor a boat or fish. Golf, riding or bicycle hire within 3 km. A good family site for the summer but also good in low season for a quiet stay in a superb location. Tour operators (85 pitches) and mobile homes (30 to rent). Winter caravan storage.

Charges 2000:
-- Per tent pitch (100 sq.m.) with electricity and 3 persons Ffr. 195.00; 'confort' pitch (100 sq.m.) with water and drainage 225.00; 'luxury' pitch 180 sq.m. 305.00 or 250 sq.m. 325.00; extra person 42.00; child (under 7) 31.00; dog 20.00.
-- Less in low season.
-- Credit cards accepted.

Open:
Easter - 30 September, with all services.

Address:
83370 St Aygulf.

Tel:
(0)4.94.81.01.41.
FAX: (0)4.94.81.21.45.

Reservations:
Any period with substantial deposit and fee.

Book this site
01892 559898
THE ALAN ROGERS'
travel service

*see colour advert
between pages 224/225*

Directions: Leave A8 at exit 36 and take N7 to Le Muy and Fréjus. After about 8 km. at roundabout take D7 signed Roquebrune and St Aygulf. In 9.5 km. turn left signed Fréjus. Ignore width and height limit signs as site is 500 m. to right.

8320 Camping-Caravaning Les Pecheurs, Roquebrune sur Argens

Friendly, family run site beside river at the foot of the Roquebrune Rock.

Developed over three generations by the Simoncini family, this peaceful site, in more than 4 hectares of mature, well shaded countryside, will appeal particularly to families who appreciate natural surroundings with many activities. The 110 touring pitches are of a good size with electricity (6/10A) and separated by trees or flowering bushes. Among the many features is an attractively paved, sheltered pool (25 x 10 m) with a paddling pool (with gate and a lifeguard in season). The Provencal style buildings are delightful, especially the bar, restaurant and games room, with its terrace down to the river and the site's canoe station (locked gate). Adjacent to the site, by the lake (path under road bridge) is another restaurant, open to the public. This is near the sandy beach, minigolf and half-court tennis. Other than the beach (no lifeguard), the lake is used exclusively for water skiing. Sanitary facilities are variable, one block being equipped with a baby bath and facilities for disabled visitors. The other two renovated blocks are well maintained with washbasins in cabins, dishwashing and laundry sinks (some with hot water) and a washing machine. Chemical disposal in each block. Overall it is a good provision, opened as required. Activities besides fishing, canoeing and water skiing include climbing the Rock with a guide. We were intrigued with stories about the Roquebrune rock, as unfolded by Sabine Simoncini. The Holy Hole, Three Crosses and the Hermit all call for further exploration which Sabine is happy to arrange, likewise trips to Monte Carlo, Ventiniglia (Italy) and the Gorges du Verdon. The medieval village of Roquebrune is within walking distance. Animation is arranged in the main season with visits to wine caves and sessions at rafting and diving schools. Riding 4 km, golf 5 km, bicycle hire 1 km. Barbecues not permitted. Used by tour operators (40%). Mobile homes for hire (22).

Charges 2001:
-- Per unit incl. 2 persons Ffr. 95.00 - 160.00, 3 persons 110.00 - 170.00; extra person 20.00 - 33.00; child (under 7 yrs) 15.00 - 25.00; dog 10.00; electricity 6A 20.00, 10A 25.00; local tax (over 10 yrs, 15/6-15/9) 2.00.
-- No credit cards.

Open:
8 April - 29 September.

Address:
83520 Roquebrune sur Argens.

Tel:
(0)4.94.45.71.25.
FAX: (0)4.94.81.65.13.
E-mail: pecheurs@worldonline.fr.

Reservations:
Made for touring pitches without fee; contact site.

`Camping Cheque'

Book this site
01892 559898
THE ALAN ROGERS'
travel service

*see colour advert
between pages 192/193*

Directions: From A8 Le Muy exit follow N7 towards Frèjus for 13 km. bypassing Le Muy. Cross over A8 and turn right at roundabout towards Roquebrune sur Argens. Site is on left after 2 km. just before bridge over river.

8316 Parc Camping-Caravaning Les Cigales, Le Muy

Family run site convenient for the attractions of this popular area.

In a natural, shady setting of 10 ha. this site is well tucked in 1 km. from the busy N7, although unfortunately close to the very busy A8 which is noisy if the wind is in the wrong direction. The site itself offers the opportunity for a relaxing stay and it also makes an excellent base for exploring the coast or the hinterland and the Gorges du Verdon. On entering (card-operated gate), reception is on the left. Gravel roads lead off a tarmac circuit to the numbered pitches that vary in size, with some terracing. The terrain is typical of the area with rough, sloped and stony, dry ground, but pitches are mostly level. They benefit from the shade given by the many trees including cork, oak and umbrella pines, plus the sweet smelling mimosa and shrubs that fill the air reminding us that this is Provence. There are six modern sanitary blocks that more than serve the 186 pitches. Facilities include showers, washbasins in cabins and facilities for disabled people. Dishwashing sinks are outside but covered, laundry area with washing machines and ironing, and chemical disposal. A pleasant feature here is the pool and sunbathing area, and also the patio at the restaurant/bar. Entertainment is organised each evening in season, with a disco twice weekly and daytime activities for children and senior citizens. Restaurant (10/6-1/9) and shop (1/5-30/8), but if wanting to get out and about, it is only 2 km. to Le Muy where a Sunday market is held. The N7 is on a bus route or take a train at Les Arcs (8 km). Canoeing, riding and hang-gliding are organised. Charcoal barbecues are not permitted. Fishing 2 km, riding 7 km, golf 10 km. Caravan storage. Chalets to rent (14). A 'Sites et Paysages' member.

Charges 2001:
-- Per unit incl. 2 persons Ffr. 70.00 - 130.00; extra person 18.00 - 30.00; child (under 7 yrs) free - 19.00; electricity 6A 20.00 - 21.00, 10A 25.00 - 31.00; local tax included.
-- Less 5% for stays over 3 weeks.
-- Credit cards accepted.

Open:
1 April - 30 September.

Address:
83490 Le Muy.

Tel:
(0)4.94.45.12.08.
FAX: (0)4.94.45.92.80.
E-mail: contact@ les-cigales.com.

Reservations:
Advised for July/Aug; contact site.

Directions: Site is signed off approach to A8 péage at Le Muy exit and is 2 km. west of Le Muy on N7. Approach toll booth from Le Muy, cross dual-carriageway and site is then 1 km. down small road running parallel to the autoroute.

A pleasant family campsite of 25 acres with 180 shaded places. A terraced park, with parasol pines, oaks, palms and olives trees.
An excellent site for visiting the Côte d'Azur, the Verdon Gorges .
Swimming pool, tennis court, bouladrome, programme of entertainments, bar, restaurant, shop and laundry room
Chalets for Hire

les **Cigales**
Le Jardin de vos Vacances*
*Your holiday's garden

721, chemin du Jas de la Paro - F 83490 LE MUY - Tél. 04 94 45 12 08 - Fax 04 94 45 92 80 e.mail : contact@les-cigales.com - Internet : www.les-cigales.com

8303 Camping-Caravaning Leï Suves, Roquebrune sur Argens

Quiet, pretty site a few kilometres inland from the coast.

This site is 2 km. north of the N7 and is very convenient as a night halt. However, you may decide to stay longer as it has all the conveniences of the coastal sites but without as many people. Close to the unusual Roquebrune rock, it is within easy reach of resorts such as St Tropez, Ste Maxime, St Raphaël and Cannes. The site entrance is appealing - wide and spacious with a large bank of well tended flowers. Mainly on a gently sloping hillside, the pitches are terraced with shade provided by the many cork trees which give the site its name. The 310 pitches are of a decent size, all with electricity and access to water. The two modern sanitary blocks provide hot showers, British type WCs and washbasins in cabins, along with external dishwashing sinks, chemical disposal, a laundry room with washing machines and ironing boards and facilities for disabled visitors. Hot water is free and all is kept very clean. A good sized pool (1/5-30/9) surrounded by sunbathing areas, is overlooked by the bar and its terrace, snack bar and takeaway. Shop (all 15/5-30/9). An outdoor stage is near the bar for evening entertainment in high season. Table tennis, tennis, children's play area and a new sports area. Fishing 3 km, bicycle hire 5 km, riding 1 km, golf 7 km. The beach at St Aygulf is 15 km. Only gas barbecues permitted. Caravan storage. Mobile homes to rent.

Charges 2000:
-- Per unit incl. 2 persons Ffr. 99.50 - 159.00, 3 persons 108.00 - 165.00; extra adult 23.00 - 35.00; child (under 7 yrs) 13.00 - 20.00; electricity 17.00; animal 10.00; local tax 2.00.
-- Credit cards accepted.

Open:
15 March - 15 October.

Address:
Quartier du Blavet, 83520 Roquebrune sur Argens.

Tel:
(0)4.94.45.43.95.
FAX: (0)4.94.81.63.13.

Reservations:
Made with deposit (Ffr. 350) and fee (50).

Directions: Leave autoroute at Le Muy and take N7 towards St Raphaël. Turn left at roundabout on D7 going north signed La Boverie. Site on right in 2 km.

8317 Camping Domaine La Bergerie, Roquebrune-sur-Argens

Well organised site with a holiday environment to suit all ages and tastes.

This is yet another site near the Côte d'Azur which takes you away from all the bustle of the Mediterranean to total relaxation amongst the natural perfumes of Provence. Here, where cork oak, pine and mimosa flourish, is a 60 ha. campsite which varies from landscaped areas for mobile homes to flat, grassy terrain with avenues of 200 separated pitches for touring caravans and tents. All pitches average over 100 sq.m. and have electricity, with those in one area also having water and drainage connections. The four sanitary blocks are kept very clean and include hot showers, washbasins in cubicles, British WCs, facilities for disabled people and for babies, chemical disposal points, plus dishwashing and laundry areas with washing machines. A well stocked supermarket (daily fresh bread, fruit and vegetables) is uphill behind the touring pitches. To the right of this, adjacent to the restaurant, are parking areas as, being a spread out site, walking can be tough going. The restaurant/bar, a converted farm building, is surrounded by shady patios, whilst inside it oozes character with high beams and archways leading to intimate corners. It has a takeaway service. Alongside is an extravagantly designed complex with three swimming pools (15/5-30/9) and a keep fit centre (body building, sauna, gym, etc). There are five tennis courts and two half courts, volleyball, bicycle hire, mini football and more. Tournaments and programmes are organised daily and, in the evening, shows, cabarets, discos, cinema, karaoke and dancing at the amphitheatre prove popular (possibly until midnight). Fishing on site, water skiing and rock climbing nearby - in fact, few activities have been forgotten. Riding or golf 4 km, bicycle hire 7 km. When all that the site has to offer has been exhausted, either St Aygulf or Ste Maxime are 7 km, or drive inland and discover the delights of the hinterland. A good site for families with children and teenagers. Winter caravan storage. Mobile homes for rent (250) available 15 Feb - 15 Nov. Readers report that, in the early season, the touring area is not as well prepared or maintained as the rest of the site.

Directions: Leave A8 at Le Muy exit on N7 towards Fréjus. Proceed for 9 km., then right onto D7 signed St Aygulf. Continue for 8 km. and then right at roundabout onto D8; site is on the right.

Charges 2000:
-- Per unit incl. 2 adults and electricity (5A) Ffr. 95.00 - 135.00; 3 persons and electricity 120.00 - 185.00; 3 persons and electricity, water and drainage 140.00 - 210.00; extra adult 23.00 - 36.00; child (under 7 yrs) 17.00 - 25.00; electricity (10A) 12.00 - 13.00; local tax 2.00.
-- No credit cards.

Open:
1 April - 30 September.

Address:
Vallée du Fournel, 83520 Roquebrune-sur-Argens.

Tel:
(0)4.94.82.90.11. FAX: (0)4.94.82.93.42. E-mail: info@domaine labergerie.com.

Reservations:
Made with deposit (Ffr. 1,000).

see colour advert between pages 224/225

8322 Camping-Caravaning Cros de Mouton, Cavalaire

Quiet, reasonably priced site on a steep hillside in a popular area.

Situated high in the hills 1.5 km. from Cavalaire and its popular beaches, Cros de Mouton is a calm oasis away from the hectic coast. Unfortunately, due to the nature of the terrain, some of the site roads are very steep - the higher pitches with the best views are especially steep. However, Olivier and Andre are very happy to take your caravan up with their 4x4 Jeep if you are worried. There are 199 terraced pitches under cork trees which include 39 for mobile homes, 80 suitable only for tents only with parking close by, and 80 for touring caravans. These have electricity (10A), some also have water. The two toilet blocks are clean and well maintained with all the usual facilities including British style WCs, showers and washbasins in cubicles. There is a washing machine and chemical disposal at each and a fully fitted facility for disabled customers (although we would have thought the site perhaps a little steep in places for wheelchairs). There is a large parking area at reception. Above is the bar/restaurant which serves reasonably priced lunches and evening meals, plus takeaways. Eating on the terrace with its wonderful view of Cavalaire and the bay looked very inviting. Higher again are the swimming and paddling pools with lots of sun-beds on the terrace and a small bar serving snacks and cold drinks, once again with the wonderful views. There is a small play area and games room but nothing much in the way of organised activities. English is spoken. Mobile homes to rent.

Directions: Site is very well signed from the centre of Cavalaire.

Charges 2000:
-- Per adult Ffr. 32.00 - 39.00; child (under 7 yrs) 20.00; pitch 32.00 - 39.00; electricity (10A) 22.00; local tax 2.00 (under 10 yrs 1.00).

Open:
15 March - 31 October.

Address:
B.P. 116, 83240 Cavalaire sur Mer.

Tel:
(0)4.94.64.10.87. FAX: (0)4.94.05.46.38. E-mail: campingcrosde-mouton@wanadoo.fr.

Reservations:
Made with deposit (Ffr. 500) and fee (100).

Camping Cheques

8321 Camping Les Tournels, Ramatuelle

Large site on steep hillside, within 1.5 km. of fine beach.

Les Tournels is set on a hillside and some of the pitches have wonderful panoramic views of the Gulf of St Tropez and Pampelonne beach. The whole hill is covered in parasol pines and old olive trees, so all pitches have some shade. All are reasonably level, although they vary in size and there is electricity on the majority, with water on many (long electricity leads may be required). The rest are reserved for tents. There are very clean and well equipped sanitary blocks within reasonable distance of the pitches, but the swimming pool, play area, shop and bar could turn out to be quite some distance away. Two of the blocks are of an older design but the other six are very good. Showers are very spacious, adjustable and with hook and seat, washbasins are in cubicles, WCs are mainly British style, there are baby baths, children's WCs and facilities for disabled visitors. Three blocks are heated in low season. Chemical disposal and washing and drying machines are provided at five blocks, with refrigerators to rent outside all of them. plus all the usual dishwashing and laundry sinks. The swimming pool is large (600 sq.m, open 25/3-20/10. and heated in low season) and of an unusual shape, the large circular paddling pool has a mushroom shaped fountain and both are surrounded by sunbathing areas with sun-beds. The bar/restaurant (25/3-15/10) serves meals until quite late and provides a takeaway service. Another bar with disco is at the furthest end of the site, well away from the majority of the pitches. There is a large fenced play area with good quality equipment, table tennis, volleyball, basketball and boules pitches, plus a mini-club taking children over 5 years for sporting activities. Competitions and shows are produced for adults and children in July/Aug. A shopping centre 500 m. from the site entrance (owned by the family) contains a supermarket, tobacconist, launderette, rotisserie and a snack bar. Five hundred metres sounds a long way in the heat of summer but there is a shuttle bus which also runs to Pampelonne beach. Reception opens for long hours and has safety deposit boxes to hire, exchange bureau and English is spoken. Only gas barbecues are permitted. The beaches are a big draw, but also who can resist a visit to St Tropez where perhaps you will see someone famous as they parade along the famous waterfront, and the floating 'gin palaces' are a sight to behold. Mobile homes to hire. Doctor visits daily July/Aug.

Directions: From A8 exit 36 take D25 to Ste Maxime, then D98 towards St Tropez. On outskirts of St Tropez, take D93 to Ramatuelle. Site is signed on left in 9 km.

Charges 2001:
-- Per adult Ffr. 31.00 - 42.00; child (2-7 yrs) 17.00 - 21.00; pitch incl. electricity 47.00 - 68.00, with water and drainage 65.00 - 90.00; animal 16.00 - 20.00; electricity 10A plus 22.00; local tax 2.00 (under 7 yrs 1.00).
-- Credit cards accepted.

Open:
All year excl. 1 Jan - 14 Feb.

Address:
Route de Camarat, 83350 Ramatuelle.

Tel:
(0)4.94.55.90.90. FAX: (0)4.94.55.90.99.

Reservations:
Contact site for details.

8311 Camping de la Baie, Cavalaire

Busy site, with pool, within the resort of Cavalaire and only a short way from the beach.

This site is only a short walk from the beach and from the main street of a pleasant, popular holiday resort where there is a harbour, restaurants and shops. A long, sandy beach runs right round the bay and there are plenty of watersports activities nearby. The site has an attractive, free, kidney-shaped swimming pool with sunbathing terrace (open Easter - end Nov.) and a small children's pool. Pitches are individual ones on slightly sloping, sandy ground with terracing and access roads, nearly all with electricity. Trees have grown well to give plenty of shade. There are four modern main toilet blocks with free hot showers, washbasins in tiled private cabins, and four smaller units with toilets and open washbasins behind. Toilets are British style, with some Turkish. A small shop with baker is on site, the town shops are close. Attractive, refurbished restaurant (all season) and bar, with takeaway. 'Animation' with dance evenings. Other facilities include a launderette, children's playground. table tennis, TV room and exchange facilities. Doctor 150 m. Mobile homes and chalets for hire. English is spoken.

Directions: Site is signed from main street of Cavalaire, in the direction of the harbour.

Charges guide:
-- Per unit with 1-3 persons Ffr 118.00 - 163.00; extra person 29.00 - 39.50; child (under 7) 14.50 - 20.00; electricity 26.00; small tent 71.00 - 97.00; local tax 2.00 (4-10 yrs 1.00).
-- Credit cards accepted.

Open:
15 March - 15 November.

Address:
Bd. Pasteur, BP.12, 83240 Cavalaire sur Mer.

Tel:
(0)4.94.64.08.15 or (0)4.94.64.08.10. FAX: (0)4.94.64.66.10. E-mail: campbaie @club-internet.com.

Reservations:
Advised for 15/6-15/9 and made from 1 Jan. (July/Aug. min. 1 week, Sat. to Sat) with deposit (Ffr. 1,000 incl. fee 200).

8312 Camp du Domaine, La Favière, Le Lavandou

Site by a sandy beach with plenty of shade, 3 km. south of town.

Camp du Domaine is a large beach-side site with 1,200 pitches, although surprisingly it does not give the impression of being so big. Most pitches are reasonably level and 800 have 6A electricity. The most popular pitches are at the beach, but the ones furthest away are, on the whole, larger and have more shade, although many of them are more suitable for tents. The beach is the attraction, however, and everyone tries to get as near to it as they can. The sanitary blocks are quite modern and are kept clean but, due to high usage because of the popularity of the site, parts soon begin to show wear and tear. WCs are predominately of the Turkish type (management policy). All facilities have pre-mixed hot water and many of the washbasins are in cabins. There are facilities for disabled visitors (but steep steps) and a block for children. Washing machines are distributed around the ten sanitary blocks. The supermarket is well stocked and there are bars and a pizzeria. The children's play area is excellent with a good safety base, boats and pedaloes may be hired and games and competitions are arranged in July/Aug. Also available are tennis courts, table tennis and minigolf. Bicycle hire 500 m, riding or golf 15 km. American motorhomes are not accepted. Barbecues are strictly forbidden. Fridges to hire. Despite its size, it does not give the impression of being busy except perhaps around the supermarket. This is mainly because many of the pitches are hidden in the trees, the access roads are quite wide and it all covers quite a large area (some of the beach pitches are 600 m. from the entrance). Its popularity makes early reservation necessary over a long season, from about mid June to mid Sept. as regular clients book from season to season. English is spoken. Mobile homes (18) and chalets (10) to rent.

Directions: Just outside and to west of Le Lavandou, at roundabout, turn off D559 towards the sea on road signed Favière. After some 2 km. turn left at camp signs.

Charges 2001:
-- Per unit incl. 2 persons Ffr. 93.00 - 121.00, with electricity and water 140.00 - 165.00; extra person 28.00 - 33.00; child (under 7) 16.00 - 18.00; local tax (over 7 yrs) 2.00.
-- Credit cards accepted.

Open:
6 April - 31 October.

Address:
La Favière
B.P. 207, 83238
Bormes les Mimosas.

Tel:
(0)4.94.71.03.12.
FAX: (0)4.94.15.18.67.

Reservations:
Made with 30% deposit and fee (Ffr. 150).

8315 Camping International de la Sainte-Baume, Nans-les-Pins

Holiday style site with excellent swimming pools.

This is a family oriented 'holiday' site in Provencal countryside, some 30 minutes by car from the coast at Cassis. Somewhat smaller than other sites of this type, there are 160 good sized pitches (50 for touring units). On mainly level, rather stony ground, with variable shade, all have 6/10A electricity. There is an attractive large complex with three swimming pools (one for children), a solarium and jacuzzi, surrounded by an ample paved sunbathing area with some shade from the trees. A restaurant overlooks the pools offering a varied and full menu (20/6-31/8), also snacks and takeaway. A separate, renovated building houses a bar, disco, shop (20/6-31/8) and TV room and is fronted by an entertainment area for shows, cabarets, etc. Sporting facilities include riding, tennis, table tennis, volleyball, archery and boules. The two main sanitary blocks, including a new super deluxe one, are of a good standard with free hot showers, washbasins in private cabins and British WCs, plus dishwashing, laundry and chemical disposal. Although having all the facilities, activities and entertainment expected of a holiday site, the atmosphere is very relaxed and much less frenzied than some other similar sites. Mini-club for children and evening entertainment in season. Mobile homes and bungalows to hire (80). Caravan storage available. Golf 3 km. A 'Sites et Paysages' member.

Directions: Take St Maximin exit from A8 and head for Auriol on the N560, turning after 9 km. for Nans-les-Pins (D80); site is on left just before this village.

Charges 2000:
-- Per unit incl. 2 persons Ffr. 89.00 - 139.00; extra person 19.00 - 35.00; child (2-7 yrs) 17.00 - 29.00; electricity (6A) 23.00, 10A 29.00; drainage/water or extra vehicle 15.00; dog 15.00; local tax (15/6-15/9) 2.50.
-- No credit cards.

Open:
1 May - 5 September.

Address:
83860 Nans-les-Pins.

Tel:
(0)4.94.78.92.68.
FAX: (0)4.94.78.67.37.
E-mail: ste.baume
@wanadoo.fr.

Reservations:
Made with deposit (Ffr. 970).

8313 Castel Camping Le Beau Vezé, Carqueiranne, nr Hyères

Quiet site, with pool, some way inland from the busy resort of Hyères.

The owners of Beau Vezé try to keep this as a family site. On a steep hillside, it has terraced pitches and a plateau with more pitches on the top. It is a quiet location, being inland from the coast, but the superb beaches and hectic coastal areas are within easy reach. The 150 pitches are well shaded but, unfortunately, most will be rather difficult to manoeuvre onto due to over-hanging trees. The medium sized pool, paddling pool and sunbathing area are beside the bar/restaurant and takeaway. The three sanitary blocks are of a reasonable standard, two of them quite modern with heating. All have hot showers and some cubicles also have a washbasin, making them more roomy. There are both British and Turkish style WCs and hot water is provided for everything, including clothes and dishwashing sinks. Two washing machines. The children's play area is very limited, but there is minigolf, bicycle hire, table tennis, volleyball, boule and a tennis court. Riding and golf 2 km. Besides being convenient for the coast the lovely old town of Hyères is only 8 km. away. Caravan storage.

Directions: From D559 between Carqueiranne and Le Pradet, take D76 northwards signed La Moutonne and site is signed on right of D76.

Charges guide:
-- Per unit, incl. 2 persons Ffr. 135.00; extra person 39.00; child (under 7 yrs) 27.00; electricity (6A) 22.00; animal 10.00.

Open:
1 May - 15 September.

Address:
Rte. de la Moutonne, 83320 Carqueiranne.

Tel:
(0)4.94.57.65.30.
FAX: as phone.

Reservations:
Made with deposit (Ffr. 300) and fee (100).

'Camping Cheque'

Book this site
01892 559898

THE ALAN ROGERS'
travel service

8314 Camping-Caravaning Les Lacs du Verdon, Regusse

Conveniently situated site for touring Provence.

In beautiful countryside and within easy reach of the Grand Canyon du Verdon and its nearby lakes, this site is only 90 minutes from Cannes. The 30 acre wooded park is divided in two by a minor road. The part across the road is strictly only suitable for caravans due to the very stony ground. In fact this part of the site takes some getting used to. Besides the ground being so hard and stony, instead of bushes, pitches are separated by large boulders. This gives quite an alien feel to the site and there is not much shade either. The main site is under pine trees and is much more pleasant. The 480 level pitches are marked, some separated, all are of a good size and 250 have electricity (6/10A). Tour operators and mobile homes for hire take up over half of the site. The sanitary blocks are acceptable with mainly British style WCs and some washbasins in cubicles. The block we tried had piping hot water but other campers complained they were not so lucky. All blocks have sinks for clothes and dishes, there are washing machines and dryers, and chemical disposal. Open all season are a well stocked shop, a bar, restaurant and pizzeria, plus swimming and paddling pools. TV and teenage games are off the bar and discos, dances and theme nights are held twice weekly. Tennis, volleyball, table tennis and boule. Sailing and windsurfing available at the site's club at Saint Croix. The village of Regusse is about 2.5 km. and the small town of Aups is 7 km.

Directions: From St. Maximin go via the D560 northeast to Barjols. Turn off at Barjols onto the D71 to Montmeyan, turn right onto the D30 to Regusse and follow site signs.

Charges 2000:
-- Per pitch with 6A electricity, water and drainage, incl. 2 persons Ffr. 94.00 - 110.00; extra person 34.00 - 40.00; child (2-7 yrs) 30.00; electricity 10A 22.00; local tax 2.00.
-- Credit cards accepted.

Open:
1 May - 30 September.

Address:
Domaine de Roquelande, 83630 Regusse.

Tel:
(0)4.94.70.17.95.
FAX: (0)4.94.70.51.79.
E-mail: info@
lacs-verdon.com.

Reservations:
Made with 25% deposit and fee (Ffr. 120)

THE ALAN ROGERS'
travel service

Book your site with the experts
Call for an instant quote
01892 55 98 98

Low cost ferries
guaranteed!

HAVEN EUROPE HOLIDAYS

see colour advert opposite

La Pignade, Ronce-les-Bains

(Vendée/ Charente - 17 Charente-Maritime)

Haven Europe owned park with pool and entertainment facilities, ideal for families.

La Pignade is set in a pine forest, where the river Suedre meets the Atlantic, on the edge of the seaside resort of Ronce-les-Bains with its sandy beaches. The park entrance opens up to a large courtyard piazza around which all the main amenities are grouped. This central area is impressive with its water fountain, neat paved area, well tended, colourful shrubs. In the evening it is particularly alive with the buzz of activity and chatter. The large, brightly decorated bar has seating inside and out. You can also eat inside or out at the restaurant which serves local specialities, together with reasonably priced set menus. A large heated pool has a shallow end for children, and a water chute has its own splash pool. Around the pools are paved areas for sunbathing, backed by tall pines. Entertainment is especially good for children, whatever their age, with the organised games and activities of the PAWs, Tiger and TGO clubs. A large play area, volleyball, table tennis and mini-golf provide amusement. You can practice at the golf driving net before trying one of the local golf courses, or have a go at archery. Tall pine trees give shade to the spacious pitches, most with a paved area for sitting out. The large touring area is within easy reach of the amenities and has its own sanitary block. The shop opens daily with a wide range of provisions and essential holiday items.

Directions: Site is signed 250 m. south of the town of Ronce-les-Bains off the D25 La Tremblade road.   *To be inspected 2001*

Charges 2001:
-- Per pitch incl. up to 2 persons with electricity Ffr. 85.00 - 189.00; extra person 20.00 - 35.00.

Open:
28 April - 14 September.

Address:
Avenue des Monards, 17390 Ronce-les-Bains.

Tel:
(0)5.46.36.25.25.
FAX: (0)5.46.36.34.14.

Reservations:
Accepted at any time for min. 4 days; no booking fee. Contact site or Haven Europe in the UK on 0870 242 7777 for information or reservation quoting FAR01.

La Reserve, Gastes, nr Biscarrosse

(Atlantic Coast - 40 Landes)

Haven Europe park by large lake with pools and watersports, south of Biscarrose.

La Reserve used to be featured in this guide until it was sold a few years ago, and it has now been taken over by Haven Europe. It is a big site set in a pine wood, with access to a large lake with a beach and small harbour (Atlantic beaches are nearby). The lake shelves gradually so provides good bathing for children and good facilities for windsurfing and sailing; powered boats for water ski-ing are also permitted. The site has a covered, heated pool, another unheated outdoor pool (350 sq.m) and a paddling pool. The 700 numbered pitches are of above average size (mostly 120 sq.m.), set on mainly flat ground and marked by stones in the ground. Most have electricity. The five sanitary blocks, some modern and with en-suite facilities in one, provide British style WCs (as often in France, the least plentiful), washbasins in cabins and many fairly basic, pre-set free hot showers. There is a well stocked supermarket, restaurant and large bar where entertainment is organised all season. Activities include a children's club for all ages, two tennis courts (floodlit), minigolf, table tennis and volleyball. There are boats for hire (including powered ones), windsurfing courses and water ski-ing.

Directions: Turn west off D652 Gastes – Mimizan road 3 km. south of Gastes by camp sign.   *To be inspected 2001*

Charges 2001:
-- Per pitch incl. up to 2 persons Ffr. 75.00 - 179.00, with electricity 90.00 - 209.00; extra person 20.00 - 35.00.

Open:
28 April - 14 September.

Address:
40160 Parentis-en-Born.

Tel:
(0)5.58.09.75.96.
FAX: (0)5.58.09.76.13.

Reservations:
Accepted at any time for min. 4 days; no fee. Contact site or Haven Europe in the UK on 0870 242 7777 for information or reservation quoting FAR01.

La Carabasse, Vias-sur-Mer

(Mediterranean - 34 Hèrault)

Haven Europe owned holiday park with two pools and very own beach club.

La Carabasse, situated just outside the Mediterranean resort of Vias Plage, has everything you could want from a holiday in the sun with two pool complexes, bars and a restaurant, together with plenty of activities and clubs for young families and teens, plus golf lessons, aqua-aerobics and tennis tournaments. In the evening you can enjoy live music at the Atoll bar restaurant, or sit at the Arhipel bar and enjoy the animation provided by the Haven Europe team. Tall, airy birch and poplar trees line the avenues around the site and provide partial shade for the spacious pitches. Some have their own private sanitary cabin providing a WC and shower. The Mediterranean beaches are about 2 km. away and the beautiful Canal du Midi a mere three minutes walk. La Carabasse is perfect for all sorts of water-based activities. Those who want to try windsurfing or enjoy a leisurely pedalo journey on the sea can take advantage of La Carabasse's own Beach Club at Vias-Plage. The site is well placed to explore this fascinating region, with medieval towns such as Pezenas (often used as a film set), beautiful ports and lively resorts and inland towns such as Carcassonne and Peyrepertuse.

Directions: Site is south of Vias. From N112 (Agde - Beziers) road turn right at signs for Vias-Plage (D137) and site (on the left).   *To be inspected 2001*

Charges 2001:
-- Per pitch incl. up to 2 persons and electricity Ffr. 90.00 - 209.00, with private sanitary cabin 120.00 - 250.00; extra person 20.00 - 35.00.

Open:
15 April - 14 September.

Address:
Rte de Farinette, 34450 Vias-sur-Mer.

Tel:
(0)4.67.21.64.01.
FAX: (0)4.67.21.76.87.

Reservations:
Accepted at any time. Contact site or Haven Europe in the UK on 0870 242 7777 for information or reservation quoting ARF01.

Carefree
Touring with...

Haven
Europe

Your choice of 6 superb touring parks in some of the most beautiful regions of France. Since we own all our touring parks, we can offer the unique guarantee that our facilities and services are open all season.

- Stay on one park or tour around France and experience all six
- Just one phone call will book your whole holiday
- Superb low season prices
- Resident bilingual staff on park
- Free use of a huge range of sports and leisure activities
- Free use of pool complexes and waterslides
- 3 children's clubs for all ages

For information or reservations call Haven Europe in the UK on

0870 242 7777
quoting code FAR01

Charente-Maritime, Les Charmettes
See page 80 of this guide

Charente-Maritime, La Pignade
See opposite page 256

Finistère, Domaine de Kerlann
See page 23 of this guide

Mediterranean Coast, La Carabasse
See opposite page 256

Landes, La Réserve
See opposite page 256

Vendée, Le Bois Dormant
See page 97 of this guide

Grand Prix Racing

Just Tickets

As the largest suppliers of **Formula One** and **Le Mans 24 Hour** spectator tickets we provide the **best range of seats in this country**.

Our **TICKET ONLY** service covers general admission, grandstand seats and parking at F.1 circuits and Le Mans. At **MONACO** we offer some of the **best viewing of all from private apartment terraces** located at the most advantageous point, and seats and hospitality at a trackside restaurant.

For **SILVERSTONE** we can book seats, hospitality marquees and helicopters.

JUST MOTORING offers inclusive self-drive arrangements with hotels at **European Formula One** events, plus for **Le Mans,** ferry bookings, parking, camping and hospitality marquees.

Just Tickets
1 Charter House
Camden Crescent
Dover, Kent
CT16 1LE
Tel: 01304 228866
Fax: 01304 242550
www.justtickets.co.uk

Mr/Mrs/Ms

Address

Postcode

Event

Ref GCG/00

CHANTILLY

Le Château Musée Condé

Raised up in the middle of the water, in the Renaissance section of the castle, the chambers of the Princes of Condé appear (17th to 18th centuries) and in the section rebuilt by the Duke d'Aumale, the son of the King Louis-Philippe, one finds his collection of paintings. Chantilly is the first French museum of old paintings after the Louvre (Raphaël, Poussin, Watteau, Ingres, Delacroix). Its library reunites unique resource of respected manuscripts of the Middle Ages.

Open every day except Tuesday (grounds open every day)
1st March - 31st October: 10.00 - 18.00
1st November - 28th February: 10-30 - 12.45 and 14.00 - 17.00

Musée Condé – Château de Chantilly – BP 70243 - 60631 – CHANTILLY cedex

Le Musée Vivant du Cheval

The Living Horse Museum, housed in the Princes de Condé great Stables, created withou any subsidy in 1982 by Yves Bienaimé, has become a real institution of international renown. A Living and Pedagogical Museum, thanks to its 30 horses of different breeds, i 31 cultural and educational rooms and its daily educational equestrian demonstrations. Also a Magical Museum with its equestrian shows.

Open every day except Tuesday
1st April - 31st October: 10.30 - 17.30 on weekdays, and 10.30 - 18.00 on weekends and bank holidays (open Tuesdays all in May and June and afternoons only in July and August)
1st November - 31st March: 14.00 - 17.00 weekdays and 10.30 - 17.30 on weekends and bank holidays.

Musée Vivant du Cheval – Grandes Écuries – BP 60242 - 60631 – CHANTILLY cedex

L'Aérphile et L'Hydrophile

Discover, vertically or horizontally, the magnificent Domaine de Chantilly. Fly aboard the world's largest balloon (32 metres high) to 150 metres in altitude without noise or brisk movements (in total security) and taste a new sensation. Navigate, silently, along the gran Canal among the aquatic fauna that has remained wild to take in the monuments and different perspectives of the park.

Open every day from beginning of March to mid-November, and from mid-November to March at weekends only from 10.00 to 19.00

Aérophile – Château de Chantilly – BP 80122 - 60501 – CHANTILLY cedex

---

Directions

By motorway:
A1 – exit 7 Survilliers coming from Paris
A1 – exit 8 Senlis coming from Lille
A16 – exit Champagne sur Oise

By road:
N 16
N 17

insure④europe.com

European Camping Holiday Insurance

Taking your tent, caravan or motorhome abroad?
Looking for the best cover at the best rates?

Whatever your outfit our policies provide exactly the right cover for this type of holiday at exceptionally low rates. What's more, they are normally only available as part of a holiday 'package'. And, if you're planning to take another holiday abroad during the next 12 months, our Annual multi-trip policies offer even better value.

> We've searched for some time for outstanding insurance cover, suitable for our readers.
>
> We believe we've found it – and at the lowest prices around.

THE ALAN ROGERS'
Good camps guide

Total Peace of Mind

To give you total peace of mind during your holiday our insurance has been specifically tailored to cover most potential eventualities on a self-drive camping holiday. Each is organised through Voyager Insurance Services Ltd who specialise in travel insurance for Europe and for camping in particular. All policies are underwritten by UK Insurance, part of the Green Flag group.

The Right Price

Although you can buy low-cost travel insurance policies elsewhere, they do not always provide the right protection for a European camping holiday. Not only are our policies designed specifically for a European camping holiday (specific cover for valuables stored overnight in your vehicle whilst on the campsite* for example) but they are also the best value.

see policy wording

Save with Combined Policies

For even greater value why not buy 'Combined policies', covering personal and vehicle assistance for either a couple or a family.

No Excesses with Premier Plus

For just a little extra, we strongly recommend our Premier Plus policies which offer even higher levels of cover and *no excess charges*. Premier Plus Vehicle Assistance provides higher limits for car hire - particularly important if you have a large car or if you are towing.

One call and you're covered – ask for a no obligation quote
01892 55 98 44

Policies despatched within 24 hours.

European Camping – Single Trip Policies

Our personal insurance provides access to the services of International Medical Rescue (IMR), one of the UK's largest assistance companies. Experienced multi-lingual personnel provide a caring, sympathetic and efficient service 24 hours a day. They are backed by a medical team who include in-house doctors and nurses headed by specialist medical consultants.

★ 24 hour travel advice line and medical assistance

★ Authorisation of medical costs and payment guarantees

★ Air ambulance repatriation/evacuation

★ Repatriation due to serious illness of relatives at home

★ Medical escorts and regular liaison with overseas doctors providing treatment

European vehicle assistance cover is provided by Green Flag who, with over 25 years' experience, provide assistance to over 3 million people each year. With a Europe-wide network of over 7,500 garages and agents you know you're in very safe hands.

Both IMR and Green Flag are very used to looking after the needs of campsite-based holidaymakers and are very familiar with the location of most European campsites, with contacts at garages, doctors and hospitals nearby.

Low Cost Combined Personal and Vehicle Assistance Insurance

Premier Family Package
17 days cover for vehicle, 2 adults
plus dependent children under 16 **£75***

Premier Couples Package
17 days cover for vehicle and 2 adults **£59***

*Motorhomes, cars towing trailers and caravans, all vehicles over 4 years old and holidays longer than 10 days attract supplements as detailed below.

Basic Premiums	Premier Cover - European Camping			
	up to 5 days	up to 10 days	up to 17 days	Over 17 days per wk/part wk
Personal Holiday Insurance				
Adult	£13.95	£16.95	£19.95	£2.95
Child (4-15)	£7.95	£9.95	£11.95	£1.95
Infant (0-3)	FREE	FREE	FREE	FREE
Couple†	£24.00	£29.00	£34.00	£5.00
Family‡	£33.00	£41.00	£49.00	£8.00
Vehicle Assistance Insurance				
Vehicle (0-4 years old)*	£25.95	£29.95	£33.95	£4.00
Combined Personal & Vehicle Insurance				
Couples special package†*	£45.00	£52.00	£59.00	£7.00
Family special package‡*	£53.00	£64.00	£75.00	£11.00

Basic Premiums	Premier Plus Cover - European Camping			
	up to 5 days	up to 10 days	up to 17 days	Over 17 days per wk/part wk
Personal Holiday Insurance				
Adult	£15.95	£19.95	£23.95	£3.95
Child (4-15)	£8.95	£11.95	£14.95	£2.95
Infant (0-3)	FREE	FREE	FREE	FREE
Couple†	£27.00	£33.00	£39.00	£6.00
Family‡	£39.00	£49.00	£59.00	£10.00
Vehicle Assistance Insurance				
Vehicle (0-4 years old)*	£31.95	£35.95	£39.95	£4.00
Combined Personal & Vehicle Insurance				
Couples special package†*	£55.00	£62.00	£69.00	£7.00
Family special package‡*	£63.00	£76.00	£89.00	£13.00

Additional Premiums*	Vehicle Assistance - European Camping			
	up to 5 days	up to 10 days	up to 17 days	Over 17 days per wk/part wk
Vehicle (5-9 years old)	£5.95	£6.95	£7.95	£1.00
Vehicle (10-15 years old)	£12.95	£14.95	£16.95	£2.00
Vehicle (over 15 yearsold)	£21.95	£44.95	£46.95	£10.00
Motorhome	£4.95	£5.95	£6.95	£1.25
Car towing trailer	£7.95	£9.95	£11.95	£2.25
Car towing caravan	£13.95	£16.95	£19.95	£3.25

† Two adults living at the same address
‡ Parents/guardians plus dependent children under 16
* Additional premiums apply for older vehicles, motorhomes, trailers and caravans as above.

Call us to arrange your low-cost travel insurance today or ask us for a no-obligation quote.

Policies despatched within 24 hours

01892 55 98 44
www.insure④europe.com

Save with Annual Policies

If you are likely to make more than one trip to Europe over the next 12 months then our Annual multi-trip policies could save you a fortune. Personal cover for a couple starts at just £79 and the whole family can be covered for just £99.

★ Annual policy cover as for European Camping cover*
★ FREE – 17 days wintersports cover
★ Low cost extensions available to extend cover for European flight-based holidays and Worldwide cover.
★ Includes travel wholly within the UK subject to 2 nights in paid accommodation
★ Covers trips of up to 31 days
★ Adults are insured to travel independently
★ Maximum age 65 at date of purchase
★ No limit to the number of trips abroad in a year

* Cancellation cover is limited to £3,000.

Low Cost Annual Multi-Trip Insurance

Premier Annual Europe self-drive
Per couple including 17 days wintersports **£79** per couple*
Two adults with the same address. Maximum age 65 at date of purchase.

Premier Annual Europe self-drive
Per family including 17 days wintersports **£99** per family*
Parents/guardians plus dependent children under 16

Basic Premiums	Premier Cover - Annual multi-trip		
	Europe	Europe	Worldwide
Personal Holiday Insurance	self-drive	incl. Flights	cover
Adult	£59.00	£75.00	£99.00
Couple†	£79.00	£95.00	£119.00
Family‡	£99.00	£115.00	£139.00
Vehicle Assistance Insurance			
Vehicle (0-4 years old)*	£59.00	£59.00	£59.00
Combined Personal & Vehicle Insurance			
Couples special package†*	£129.00	£145.00	£169.00
Family special package‡*	£149.00	£165.00	£189.00
Basic Premiums	**Premier Plus Cover - Annual multi-trip**		
	Europe	Europe	Worldwide
Personal Holiday Insurance	self-drive	incl. Flights	cover
Adult	£75.00	£89.00	£119.00
Couple†	£99.00	£119.00	£149.00
Family‡	£129.00	£149.00	£179.00
Vehicle Assistance Insurance			
Vehicle (0-4 years old)*	£79.00	-	-
Combined Personal & Vehicle Insurance			
Couples special package†*	£169.00	£189.00	£219.00
Family special package‡*	£199.00	£219.00	£249.00
Additional Premiums*	**Vehicle Assistance - Annual multi-trip**		
	Europe	Europe	Worldwide
	self-drive	incl. Flights	cover
Vehicle (5-9 years old)	£10.00	£10.00	£10.00
Vehicle (10-15 years old)	£40.00	£40.00	£40.00
Motorhome	£20.00	£20.00	£20.00
Car towing trailer	£20.00	£20.00	£20.00
Car towing caravan	£40.00	£40.00	£40.00

† Two adults living at the same address
‡ Parents/guardians plus dependent children under 16
* Additional premiums apply for older vehicles, motorhomes, trailers and caravans as above.

Important Notice:

In accordance with the Association of British Insurance General Business Code of Practice, we would like to draw your attention to some important features of your insurance including:

1. **Insurance document.** You should read this carefully. It gives full details of what is and is not covered and the conditions of the cover. It will be sent with your holiday invoice.
2. **Conditions and exclusions.** Specific conditions and exclusions apply to individual sections of your insurance, whilst general exclusions and conditions will apply to the whole of your insurance.
3. **Health.** This insurance contains certain restrictions regarding pre-existing medical problems concerning health of the people travelling and of other people upon whose health the trip depends. You are advised to read the document carefully.
4. **Property Claims.** These claims are paid based on the value of the goods at the time you lose them and not on a 'new for old' or replacement cost basis.
5. **Limits.** This insurance has limits on the amount the insurer will pay under each section. Some sections also include other specific limits, for example, for any one item or for valuables in total.
6. **Excesses.** Under some sections of this insurance, claims will be subject to an excess. This means you will be responsible for paying the first part of the claim. There are no excesses under our Plus policies.
7. **Reasonable Care.** You need to take all reasonable care to protect yourself and your property, as you would if you were not insured.
8. **Dangerous Sports and Pastimes.** If you are going to take part in dangerous sports or pastimes where there is a risk of injury, check that this insurance covers you.
9. **Customer Service.** We always try to provide a high level of service. However, if you think we have not lived up to your expectations, please refer to the wording which outlines our complaints procedures.
10. **Cooling-off.** This insurance contains a 'cooling-off' period of 14 days during which you can return it and get a refund if you have a justifiable reason for being dissatisfied with the cover provided.

European Vehicle Assistance

	Premier Cover	Premier Plus Cover
Cover before commencement	£1,000	£1,500*
Roadside Assistance	No limit	No limit
Emergency Labour	£250	£250
Loss of use of vehicle		
a) Transport to destination / repatriation to UK	a) Up to costs incurred	a) Up to costs incurred
b) Car Hire	b) £1,000	b) £1,500*
c) Collection of vehicle	c) £600	c) £600
d) Additional overnight costs (per person)	d) £35 per night	d) £45 per night
Provision of Chauffeur	No limit	No limit
Location & despatch of parts	No limit	No limit
Vehicle repatriation	No limit	No limit
Collection of vehicle	£600	£600
Storage charges	£100	£100
Car hire in UK after return	Not Covered	£150
Legal Expenses	£10,000	£10,000
Advance of funds	£1,000	£1,000
Theft break-in indemnity	£175	£175
Additional accommodation following loss of use of own tent	£100 per person	£100 per person
Credit facilities	£400	£400
General Average indemnity	£2,000	£2,000

£2,000 if towing a caravan/trailer tent

Personal Insurance

	Premier Cover	Premier Plus Cover
Medical Expenses	£1,000,000	£2,000,000
Hospital Benefit (per day)	£300 (£10)	£600 (£25)
Personal Accident	£10,000	£20,000
Maximum in the event of death	£5,000	£5,000
Baggage & Money		
Overall limit	£1,250	£2,500
Money (Cash limit)	£300 (£100)	£300 (£200)
Limit per item, pair or set	£200	£250
Total limit for all Valuables	£200	£250
Cancellation/Curtailment	Holiday Cost/£3,000*	Holiday Cost/£3,000*
Abandonment (after 12 hrs)	Holiday Cost/£3,000*	Holiday Cost/£3,000*
Passport Indemnity	£250	£500
Missed Departure	£300	£600
Travel Delay expenses	£100	£200
Personal Liability	£1,000,000	£2,000,000
Legal Expenses	£10,000	£20,000

Cancellation/curtailment/abandonment limited to £3,000 under Annual policies

Personal Holiday Insurance

The above is a summary of cover only. You will receive the full policy wording at the time of purchase, which defines the cover, conditions and exclusions. You have a 14-day cooling-off period during which you can return it and get a refund if you have a justifiable reason for being dissatisfied with the cover provided. The insurance is underwritten by UK Insurance.

Like most Medical and Travel insurances, we will not pay for a claim related to an existing medical condition. However, it is often possible to extend cover to include the conditions if you contact our freephone Medical Pre-Screening Helpline. There is no need to worry about minor short-term illnesses or injuries. To help decide whether you need to contact the helpline, please consider the following questions, at the time the insurance is arranged and each time you make arrangements for a trip. If you are travelling to anywhere other than France and the answer is 'Yes' for any of the questions 1-4 then please contact the Medical Pre-Screening Line on 0800 0133445 (quoting the reference VOY/MH/00) who will advise if cover can be provided.

1. Are you aware of any circumstances which are likely to give rise to a claim? Yes ☐ No ☐
2. Has your medical condition worsened or required you to consult a doctor for anything other than a routine check-up in the past six months? Yes ☐ No ☐
3. If you are taking continuing medication, have the drugs or dosage levels changed in the past six months? Yes ☐ No ☐
4. Are you on a hospital waiting list for in-patient treatment or investigation? Yes ☐ No ☐

You are also not covered for any related claims if you answer 'Yes' to the following:
* Are you planning to travel against the advice of your doctor or with a view to obtaining medical treatment? Yes ☐ No ☐
* Have you been given a terminal prognosis? Yes ☐ No ☐
* Are you pregnant with an anticipated delivery date of less 10 weeks after you plan to return home? Yes ☐ No ☐

If you are only travelling to France and have a pre-existing medical condition you simply need to obtain a medical certificate from your usual treating Doctor confirming that in his opinion you are fit to undertake the planned trip and there is no reason to expect that cancellation or emergency treatment will be required. Please note that the costs of any regular continuing treatment are not covered under this insurance. This certificate should not be sent in advance but will be required in the event of a claim.

CORSICA

Major Cities: Ajaccio, Bastia
Départements: 20 Corse-Sud; Haute-Corse

The island of Corsica is made up of two French départements: Haute Corse (upper Corsica) and Corse du Sud (south Corsica). Over the years there has been much dispute over the ownership of the island. The Phoenician Greeks, the Romans, followed by the Byzantines, Moors and Lombards have all fought over the island, creating a bloody history unparalleled for such a small area. In 1768, Genoa sold Corsica to France. The result is a fiery, lucidly intellectual and music-loving race of people, both superstitious and pious at the same time. It is also the birthplace of Napoleon Bonaparte.

Today about half of its 250,000 inhabitants live in the towns of Ajaccio and Bastia, leaving much of the 8,720 sq.km. island (the fourth largest in the Mediterranean) very thinly populated. Like a mountain in the sea, much of the island is covered with vegetation, pine trees, oaks, chestnut and the famous 'maquis', the variety of scenery is spectacular with mountains rising to 2,706 m and a coastline of 992 km. both dramatic and serenely beautiful. The highest mountains lie to the west, the gentler ranges, weathered in strange and often bizarre shapes, lie to the south and a continuous barrier forms the island's backbone. Beaches curve around scenic bays of white sand and the clear blue waters of the Mediterranean contrast with the stone pines that line the beaches and the multi coloured flowers that flourish on the sandy terrain. The entire island is ablaze with exotic flowers, aided by Corsica's excellent sunshine record.

See map on page 318.

Travel to and from Corsica by ferry is not difficult and SNCM operate a choice of routes from mainland France. On our recent visit we travelled from Nice to Bastia on a comfortable overnight sailing. The fare structure is quite complicated but a study of the ferry guide is worthwhile and can mean picking up a special offer if prepared to travel on given dates and specified sailings. There are also several services to Corsica from mainland Italy and Sardinia. Part of any stay on Corsica should include the 11 km. ferry trip from Bonifacio to Santa Teresa in Sardinia. Many make this short crossing to appreciate the incredible sight of Bonifacio from the sea. For ferry information between France and Corsica contact:
SNCM Southern Ferries, 179 Piccadilly, London WIV 9DB.
Tel. 0207 491 4968 or www.seafrance.com/pages/secretfrance/SNCM

Cuisine of the Island

Corsican cuisine is essentially simple, with the sea providing the most dependable source of food. Freshwater fish abound in the interior and the 'maquis' is game country. Aromatic herbs and berries add a particularly piquant flavour to the meat. The extremes of the climate limit the variety of vegetables available. The Corsicans like hot and strong flavours

Capone – local eels, cut up and grilled on a spit over a charcoal fire

Dziminu – fish soup, like bouillabaise but much hotter. Made with peppers and pimentos

Figatelli – a sausage made of dried and spiced pork with liver. Favourite between-meal snack

Pibronata – a highly spiced local sauce

Prizzutu – a peppered smoked ham; resembles the Italian prosciutto, but with chestnut flavour added

Wine

Red wine is available in abundance, but white and rose are also produced.

Places of Interest

Ajaccio – a dazzling white city full of Napoleonic memorabilia

Bastia – historic citadel towering over the headland. The old town has preserved its streets in the form of steps connected by vaulted passages, converging on the Vieux port (the old port). The new port is the real commercial port of the island

CORSICA

2000 Camping Caravaning U Farniente, Pertamina Village

Well designed, attractive site only 4 km. from Bonifacio.

Irrespective of whether or not you are using the ferry to Sardinia, Bonifacio deserves a visit and it would be difficult to find a more attractive or convenient site than this one at which to pitch for a night stop or longer stay. The 120 pitches, many with electricity (3A), are partially terraced and are hedged with trees and bushes, providing reasonable shade. They are reasonably flat and vary in size, many being well over 100 sq.m. A central feature of the site is the large attractive swimming pool, surrounded by terraces and a bar. A good restaurant serves set meals and an à la carte selection at reasonable prices (with a reduced service, ie. shorter opening hours in May, June and Oct). There is a pizzeria and takeaway and a self-service shop. Sanitary facilities are in two blocks with free hot showers (cabins without dividers), washbasins in semi-private cubicles, both British and Turkish style WCs, dishwashing and washing machines plus drying and ironing facilities. Amenities include tennis, table tennis, a children's play area and TV room. Mobile homes and chalets for weekly hire.

Directions: Site is on RN198, 4 km. north of Bonifacio on the right. Watch for the sign - you come on it quite suddenly.

Charges guide:
-- Per unit incl. 2 adults Ffr. 88.00 - 125.00; extra person 27.00 - 39.00; child (2-8 yrs) 17.00 - 20.00; electricity 18.00 - 23.00; local tax 1.00.
Open:
4 April - 12 October.
Address:
Pertamina Village, 20169 Bonifacio (Corse).
Tel:
(0)4.95.73.05.47.
FAX: (0)4.95.73.11.42.
Reservations:
Contact site.

2006 Camping-Caravaning La Vetta, Trinité de Porto-Vecchio

Family run site in country park setting, yet only minutes from the sea.

In a pleasing position to the north of La Trinité village, La Vetta is only 3 km. from Porto-Vecchio and its magnificent sandy beaches. This 8.5 ha. campsite enjoys a tranquil setting and is a part sloping, part terraced site, that seems to stretch endlessly. It is well maintained and has an abundance of tree varieties including cork oaks. Giving the impression of being off the beaten track, many of the delights of Corsica are only a short drive away. If you want to do no more than relax there is much on offer: a swimming pool for hot days (all season), plenty of trees for shade and a patio area for cool drinks (July/Aug). For the young there is table tennis, table football, snooker table, a play area, TV and entertainment in high season. The site has 100 pitches, most with 16A electrical connections. The clean, modern sanitary facilities are more than adequate and include hot showers, open plan washbasins plus cabins with mirrors and shaver points, British type WCs, chemical disposal, dishwashing and laundry sinks and also a washing machine. Shop (July/Aug) and gas supplies. Barbecues are not permitted in certain weather conditions. The entrance to the site is directly off the main road with security gates closed midnight - 7 am. Riding 4 km, fishing 3 km, bicycle hire 5 km, golf 7 km. New mobile homes to rent.

Directions: Site in La Trinité village, off RN198 (east), north of Porto-Vecchio.

Charges 2000:
-- Per adult Ffr. 34.00 - 37.00; child (under 7) 16.00 - 18.00; tent or caravan 12.00 - 14.00; car 12.00; motorcaravan 24.00 - 26.00; electricity 15.00; local tax 1.00.
-- No credit cards.
Open:
1 June - 25 September.
Address:
Trinité, 20137 Porto-Vecchio.
Tel:
(0)4.95.70.09.86.
FAX: (0)4.95.70.43.21.
E-mail: info@ campinglavetta.com.
Reservations:
Made with 30% deposit.

2007 Camping Santa Lucia, Sainte-Lucie-de-Porto-Vecchio

Friendly, family run site in a delightful southern Corsican setting.

This well appointed campsite is set in a cork oak forest just off the main road, the entrance enhanced by a huge palm tree which characterises the approach to reception. At this point you also find the restaurant and bar which overlook the swimming pool - particularly pleasant in the evening when ornamental lamps light up the patio area. There are 160 pitches, 40 with 6A electrical connections. Pitches are numbered and some are in little enclosed bays which offer privacy. Two sanitary blocks, one to the right of the site, the other on the far left towards the rear, house British style WCs, washbasins (some cubicles), dishwashing and laundry sinks, washing machine, and chemical disposal. Apart from the bar (15/6-15/9), restaurant and takeaway (1/7-31/8), there is a small shop selling bread, milk, etc. A supermarket is opposite the site entrance and services such as a doctor, chemist, grocers and newsagent are available in the village. Other on site activities include table tennis, volleyball, minigolf and a children's play area. Chalets and tents for rent blend unobtrusively with the setting. Barbecues are only permitted in a specific area. Fishing 5 km. Based at this site you are only minutes by car from Porto Vecchio which is surrounded by lovely beaches.

Directions: Site is at south end of Sainte-Lucie-de-Porto-Vecchio village, off N198 and well signed.

Charges 2000:
-- Per adult Ffr. 25.00 - 36.00; child (2-10 yrs) free - 16.00; pitch 13.00 - 20.00, with electricity 28.00 - 38.00; car 9.00 - 14.00; m/cycle 5.00 - 8.00.
-- Credit cards accepted.
Open:
15 May - 10 October.
Address:
Lieudit Mulindinu, 20144 Ste-Lucie-de-Porto-Vecchio.
Tel/Fax:
(0)4.95.71.45.28.
E-mail: santalucia@ wanadoo.fr.
Reservations:
Contact site.

2001 Camping Arinella Bianca, Ghisonaccia

Very well designed, family run, beach side site on Corsica's east coast.

This site is a tribute to its owner's design and development skills as it appears to be in entirely natural glades where, in fact, these have been created from former marshland with a fresh water lake. The 300 marked pitches, 164 for touring units and all with 6A electricity, are on flat grass among a variety of trees and shrubs, providing ample shade. They are irregularly arranged, but are all of a good size. The site is right beside a beach of soft sand which extends a long way either side of the attractive central complex which, together with the swimming pool (from 1/5), forms the hub of this site. The complex comprises a new terraced restaurant, a shop, bar, amphitheatre and snack bar, etc. (all 10/5-15/9) There are four open plan sanitary blocks with free pre-set hot showers in larger than average cubicles (some with dressing area), washbasins in private cabins and mainly British, some Turkish style WCs. There are open air dishwashing areas, a laundry with washing machines and ironing boards and a motorcaravan service point. The large range of sports and leisure facilities at, or adjacent to, the site, includes windsurfing, canoeing, fishing, volleyball, bicycle hire, tennis, riding, children's mini-club and play area and a disco, plus an entertainment programme in the main season. Used by tour operators (76 pitches). Chalets and mobile homes for rent (116). A 'Sites et Paysages' member.

Directions: Site is 4 km. east of Ghisonaccia. From N198 after entering Ghisonaccia look for sign La Plage / Li Mare. Turn east on to D144 and continue for 3.5 km. to roundabout. Turn right and site is on left in approx. 500 m.

Charges 2001:
-- Per unit incl. 2 adults Ffr. 109.00 - 179.00; extra person 32.00 - 42.00; child (up to 7 yrs) free - 22.00; extra car 10.00; animal 15.00; electricity (6A) 20.00; local tax 3.00 (child 1.00).
-- Credit cards accepted.

Open:
Easter - 30 September.

Address:
20240 Ghisonaccia.

Tel:
(0)4.95.56.04.78.
FAX: (0)4.95.56.12.54.
E-mail: arinellab@mic.fr.

Reservations:
Contact site.

'Camping Cheque'

Book this site
01892 559898

THE ALAN ROGERS'
travel service

*see colour advert
between pages 192/193*

N2004 Camping Naturiste de Riva Bella, Aleria

Relaxed, informal naturist site beside glorious beach.

Arguably this is camping and caravanning at its very best. Although offering a large number and variety of pitches, they are situated in such a huge area of varied and beautiful countryside and seaside that it is difficult to believe it could ever become overcrowded. The site is divided into several distinct areas - pitches and bungalows, alongside the sandy beach, in a wooded glade with ample shade, behind the beach, or beside the lake/lagoon which is a feature of this site. The ground is undulating, so getting an absolutely level pitch could be a problem in the main season. Although electric hook-ups are available in most parts, a long cable is probably a necessity. The sanitary facilities have been completely refurbished and are in several blocks. Whilst fairly typical in design for naturist sites, they are fitted and decorated to the highest standards with hot water throughout and facilities for disabled people and babies. Besides the beautiful beach (with sailing school, fishing, sub-aqua and other watersports), there is a wide variety of activities available including volleyball, aerobics, sauna, table tennis, giant draughts, archery, fishing, mountain bike hire, half-court tennis, etc. You can even spend your time observing the llamas. Riding 5 km. An excellent restaurant (all season) with reasonable prices overlooks the lagoon, as well as a snack bar beside the beach during the main season (1/6-30/9). Large well stocked shop (15/5-30/9). Fridges for hire. There is an interesting evening entertainment programme. A recent addition is a therapy centre with treatments and massages based on marine products. Noël Pasqual is fully proud of his site and the fairly unobtrusive rules are designed to ensure that everyone is able to relax, whilst preserving the natural beauty of the environment. There is, for example, a restriction on the movement of cars in certain areas, although there is ample free parking. The police/fire service ban barbecues during the summer as a safety precaution, but generally the ambience is relaxed and informal with nudity only obligatory on the beach itself.

Directions: Site is approx. 8 km. north of Aleria on N198 (Bastia) road. Watch for signs and unmade road to it and follow for 4 km.

Charges 2001:
-- Per unit incl. 2 persons Ffr. 72.00 - 132.00, 1 person 44.00 - 88.00; extra person 28.00 - 44.00; child (0-8 yrs) 16.00 - 25.00; electricity 22.00; local tax 1.00.
-- Special offers and half-board arrangements available.
-- Credit cards accepted.

Open:
6 May - 14 October.

Address:
20270 Aleria.

Tel:
(0)4.95.38.81.10 or (0)4.95.38.85.97.
FAX: (0)4.95.38.91.29.
E-mail: riva-bella@wanadoo.fr.

Reservations:
Made with deposit (Ffr. 500) and fee/cancellation insurance (180).

Book this site
01892 559898

THE ALAN ROGERS'
travel service

CORSICA

N2005 Camping Naturiste Club La Chiappa, Porto-Vecchio

Extensive site set in a naturist reserve with 3 km. of private beach.

This holiday paradise stands in a magnificent setting on the Chiappa Peninsula, which juts out into the bluest of seas. There are 220 pitches for caravans and tents, plus 430 bungalows to hire. Even when full, there should be lots of space and something to suit all tastes - in fact, here you can be as private and relaxed or as convivial as you wish. There are three beaches of golden sand where you are sure to find a quiet spot and where it is safe to swim, or alternatively enjoy the swimming pool. There are extensive grounds and gardens and, for the sports enthusiasts, riding, tennis, fishing, diving, keep fit and much more (some at extra cost). For children: a mini-club and play area. The pitches are large, part shaded and level, and some have 6A electrical connections. There are more than enough sanitary blocks and open plan facilities, which include showers, British style WCs, washbasins, etc. which are clean and modern. Plenty of dishwashing sinks, washing machines, chemical disposal and motorcaravan service point. If you don't want to cook, there are restaurant meals, snacks and three bars and a baby sitting service is available. Well stocked shop.

Charges guide:
-- Per pitch incl. electricity Ffr. 40.00 - 50.00; adult 50.00 - 60.00; child 5-13 yrs 20.00 - 25.00.
-- Less for longer stays in low season.
-- Credit cards accepted.
Open:
15 May - 9 October.
Address:
20137 Porto-Vecchio.
Tel:
(0)4.95.70.00.31.
FAX: (0)4.95.70.07.70.
E-mail: chiappa.club@wanadoo.fr.
Reservations:
Contact site.

Directions: From Bastia on N198 going south, continue through Porto-Vecchio for 2 km. Turn left on minor road to Pnte de la Chiappa and follow camp signs.

2003 Camping Merendella, Moriani, nr San Nicolao

Attractive smaller site with direct access to beach.

This is a smaller, family run site with the advantage of direct access to a pleasant beach. It is peacefully situated on level grass with many trees and shrubs providing shade and colour. There are 133 pitches of a min. 100 sq.m. with electricity available on practically all (although long cables may be needed). The sanitary facilities are in one main block, apart from a couple of individual cabin units near the beach with two showers, two washbasins and a toilet. Facilities are modern and include free hot showers, washbasins in private cubicles and some British style WCs plus further Turkish style ones. There are also washing up and laundry areas including two washing machines. The site is about 800 m. from the village but also has its own well stocked shop. Snack bar. TV and games room. Chalets to hire. Amenities nearby include tennis, riding and various watersports including a diving centre. No dogs or cats are accepted.

Charges guide:
-- Per person Ffr. 30.00 - 35.00; child (2-12 yrs) 18.00 - 21.00; pitch 12.00 - 14.00; motorcaravan 12.00; motorcaravan 27.00 - 31.50; caravan 15.00 - 18.00; tent 12.50 - 14.50; electricity 19.00; local tax (1/7-15/9) 1.00.
Open:
15 May - 15 October.
Address:
20230 Moriani-Plage.
Tel:
(0)4.95.38.53.47.
FAX: (0)4.95.38.44.01.
E-mail: merendel @club-internet.fr.
Reservations:
Advisable; write to site.

Directions: Site is to seaward side of the RN198, 800 m. south of Moriani Plage.

2009 Ferme de Peridundellu - Aire Naturelle de Camping, Venaco

Idyllic small campsite in the mountains.

Just as spectacular as the coastline is Corsica's mountainous interior and by getting off the N200 this exceptional little campsite can be discovered. In a clearing among the trees are 25 pitches, many with electrical connection (20A). Whilst the view, peace and tranquillity are cause enough to be here, the enthusiastic young couple, Mathieu and Angele who run the site have already made it noteworthy. They offer visitors a restaurant service with cuisine of Corsica, prepared from their own farm produce - Mathieu works on the farm, as well as being the chef. The small restaurant is a delight with neatly laid tables, an old stone fireplace, wall hangings and bric a brac all creating a special atmosphere. The local cheeses and wines are superb, but don't expect chips. Farm produce and bread available each day in the shop. The single sanitary block is clean and provides washbasins with mirrors, hot showers and British style WCs. Around the site are picnic tables, water points, night lighting and a central rubbish point. You are not totally isolated at this site - Venaco (with doctor, chemist, boulangerie, etc) is only 4 km. away.

Charges guide:
-- Per adult Ffr. 30.00; child (3-7 yrs) 15.00; tent 17.00; car 15.00; m/cycle 5.00; caravan 24.00; motorcaravan 35.00; electricity 22.00.
Open:
April - 30 October.
Address:
La Ferme de Peridundellu, 20231 Venaco.
Tel:
(0)4.95.47.09.89.
FAX: as phone.
Reservations:
Write to site but probably not necessary.

Directions: From Corte centre take N200 towards Aléria. After 15 km. turn east on the D143 and site is on left after 4 km.

2010 Camping-Caravaning Santa Barbara, Corte

Developing campsite in Corsica's mountainous interior.

Corte, the historical capital of the island, stands at 396 m. altitude in the central mountains where you get a feel of the real Corsica. Camping Santa Barbara is 3 km. east of the town. Already established as a restaurant/bar, the campsite is an ongoing project with, at present, 40 level touring pitches and 12 caravan holiday homes. The pitches are separated by young shrubs and there are 32 electricity connections (12A). The sanitary facilities are being further extended, adding to the already modern and spotlessly clean units with showers, British WCs, facilities for the disabled, dishwashing and laundry sinks, and a washing machine. An excellent swimming pool is an established focal point and very welcome in this hot, mountainous region. The patio area, which overlooks the pool, is popular. The restaurant offers a varied menu and a pizza style hut is outside near the pool. Reception and a mini-market are being located alongside the attractive, well kept restaurant building. Children's play area, table tennis and pool table. The owners of the site are friendly and helpful. There could be some road noise.

Directions: Site is 3 km. southeast of Corte by the N200 Aléria road.

Charges guide:
-- Per adult Ffr. 30.00; child (under 7 yrs) 17.00; tent 16.00; caravan 24.00; car 16.00; motorcaravan 35.00; electricity 24.00; local tax 1.00.
Open:
April - 31 October.
Address:
RN200 Rte. d'Aléria, Aérodrome de Corte, 20250 Corte.
Tel:
(0)4.95.46.20.22. FAX: (0)4.95.61.09.44.
Reservations:
Write to site.

2012 Camping-Caravaning Le Panoramic, Lumio

Simple, family run site in a quiet, elevated position.

On the scenic route that winds inland and upwards from the coast between Calvi and L'Ile Rousse, Le Panoramic, as its name suggests, enjoys magnificent views across the Golfe d'Ambroggio. The 120 pitches are laid out in named avenues (Rue Josephine, etc) and the marked places are shaded by many trees and vegetation, with quite a number having 15A electricity connections. Whilst the ground is level, the site is terraced and hard going if climbing from the bottom towards reception. It is probably best suited for small motorcaravans or tents. There are four sanitary blocks housed in typical rough-cast buildings with basic decor, but they appeared well maintained and kept clean. They include British style WCs, hot showers, washbasins, plus sinks for dishwashing and two washing machines. Chemical disposal can be arranged through reception. There is a good sized shop, takeaway and a bar. Amenities include a swimming pool, table football, pool table and a children's play area. Caravans to hire. Caravan storage available. Bicycle hire 4 km, riding 3 km, golf 5 km. A recommended scenic drive is the 5 km. climb to St Antonino, a mountain village piled upon a rock face.

Directions: From Calvi take N197 towards L'Ile Rousse. Proceed for 10 km. to village of Lumio, then east on D71 and site is 2 km. on the left.

Charges guide:
-- Per adult Ffr. 32.00; child (2-7 yrs) 16.00; caravan 22.00; tent 13.00; car 9.00; m/cycle 7.00; motorcaravan 28.00; electricity 19.00; local tax 1.10.
-- No credit cards.
Open:
1 June - 15 September.
Address:
Rte de Lavatoggio, Lumio, 20260 Calvi.
Tel:
(0)4.95.60.73.13 (or when closed: (0)4.66.68.17.12 or (0)1.46.45.71.52).
FAX: (0)1.40.95.16.01.
Reservations:
Phone or write.

2013 Camping San Damiano, Biguglia

Family run site convenient for the port of Bastia.

What we found pleasing about this site was the friendly reception we received and also its convenient situation only 9 km. from the port of Bastia. It makes an excellent night halt, or alternatively a suitable base for visiting Bastia, the northeast of the island or its mountainous interior. Despite being on the outskirts of a city, it enjoys an ideal location off the busy N193, situated between the Etang de Biguglia and the golden sands of Corsica's east coast. It is divided in two by a public access road to the beach and is a sprawling site with 280 pitches which are shaded by trees, with many separated by shrubs. There are 180 electricity connections (10A). The facilities are basic (but clean when we visited) and are housed in two sanitary blocks. These include free hot showers, washing cabins, good provision for disabled visitors, chemical disposal and a motorcaravan service point. Also on site is a shop (1/6-20/9), bar and restaurant (from 1/5), TV room, minigolf and a play area for children. A security guard patrols in high season and quiet is enforced after 11 pm. Fishing and riding on site, golf 15 km.

Directions: From port of Bastia travel 5 km. on N193 then take D107 towards Lido de la Marana for 4 km. Site is signed on the left.

Charges 2000:
-- Per person Ffr. 32.00; child (under 8 yrs) 16.00; tent 12.00; caravan 16.00; motorcaravan 23.00; car 12.00; m/cycle 6.00; electricity (10A) 18.00.
-- Credit cards accepted.
Open:
1 April - 15 October
Address:
Lido de la Marana, 20620 Biguglia-Bastia.
Tel:
(0)4.95.33.68.02. FAX: (0)4.95.30.84.10.
Reservations:
Possible by phone.

OPEN ALL YEAR

The following sites are understood to accept caravanners and campers all year round, *although the list also includes some sites open for at least 9 months*. For sites marked with a star (★) please check our report for dates and other restrictions. In any case, it is always wise to phone as, for example, facilities available may be reduced.

Brittany

2910	Pen-ar-Steir
2920M	Mun.Bois de Pleuven
4401M	Mun. du Petit Port

Normandy

5004M	Mun. Ste-Mère-Eglise
6101M	Mun. La Campière
7609M	Mun. Etennemare
7610M	Mun. Cany-Barville

Northern France

0200	Vivier aux Carpes ★
5905M	Mun. Mauberge

Paris / Ile de France

7502	Bois de Boulogne
7706	Parc de la Colline
7801	International
7804M	Mun. Etang d'Or

Eastern France

0802M	Dépt. Vieilles-Forges
0803M	Dépt. Lac de Bairon
6702M	Mun. Le Hohwald
6801	Ile du Rhin ★
8802	Belle Hutte ★

8804	Lac de Bouzey
8805	Château d'Epinal

Loire Valley

3605M	Mun. Les Vieux Chênes
4106	Du Dugny
8604	Le Futuriste

Burgundy

2104M	Mun. de Fouché

Jura / Alpes

3807	La Chabannerie
3808	Au Joyeux Réveil ★
7302	Le Versoyen ★
7401	Les Deux Glaciers ★
7407	L'Escale ★
7408	Les Rosières ★

Atlantic Coast

3320	L'Eyre
4009M	Mun. Lou Broustaricq
6404	Les Gaves

Dordogne / Aveyron

2415	Les Deux Vallées
2428	De Barnabé
4607	La Plage

Limousin / Auvergne

6306	Le Clos Auroy

Rhône Valley

6901M	Mun. Porte de Lyon

Provence

8408	La Simioune

Midi-Pyrénées

0903	Le Montagnou
0905M	Mun. Sorgeat
0906	Le Pre Lombard
3105M	Mun. Belvédère
3204N	Naturiste Deveze
6503	Pyrénées
6505M	Mun. St Lary Soulan ★
8101	Entre Deux Lacs

Mediterranean

0605	La Vieille Ferme
0608	Les Cigales
1111	Val d'Aleth
3406	Oliveraie
6613	Eau Vive ★
6616	Europe
8321	Les Tournels ★

NO DOGS !

Following the recent change in legislation, for the benefit of those who want to take their dogs with them to France, we list here the sites which have indicated to us that they do not accept dogs. The sites shown in italics do not accept dogs at certain times. If you are planning to take your dog we do, however, advise that you phone the site first to check – there may be limits on numbers, breeds, or times of the year when they are excluded.

Brittany

2201	Les Capucines

Normandy

1409	Brévedent

Paris / Ile de France

7701	Davy Crockett Ranch

Eastern France

6808	*Clair Vacances (not July/Aug)*

Vendée / Charente

1602	Gorges du Chambon
1701	Bois Soleil
1702	Puits de L'Auture
1704	Bonne Anse Plage
8502	Du Jard
8503	La Loubine
8506	*Le Pas Opton (1 small dog only)*
8515	La Yole
8521	Les Ecureuils

Atlantic Coast

4004	La Paillotte
6406	Le Pavillon Royal

Dordogne / Aveyron

2404	Le Moulin du Roch
4604	Moulin de Laborde

Limousin / Auvergne

2301	*Poinsouze (not in high season)*

Rhône Valley

2603	*La Grand Lierne (not in high season)*
2609	Les Truffières

Provence

8402	Naturiste de Bélézy

Mediterranean

3405N	Naturiste Mas de Lignières
6604	Le Soleil

Corsica

2003	Merendella

BICYCLES & MOUNTAIN BIKES

We understand that the following sites have bicycles to hire **on site**. Where bicycle hire facilities are within easy reach of the site (and we have been given details), we include this information in the individual site reports. However, if this facility is important to you, we would recommend that you contact the site to check as the situation can change.

0101	La Plaine Tonique	2912	Manoir de Kerlut	4902	Chantepie
0200	Vivier aux Carpes	2913	Des Abers	4904	Etang
0301	La Filature	2916	Les Genets d'Or	4907	Vallée des Vignes
0305	La Petite Valette	2920M	Bois de Pleuven	5000	Etang des Haizes
0306	Deneuvre	2925	Bois des Ecureuils	5003	Lez-Eaux
0401	L'Hippocampe	2929	Le Grand Large	5005	Le Cormoran
0402	Du Verdon	3002	La Petite Camargue	5102M	Châlons-sur-Marne
0603	La Bergerie	3005	Eden	5202	Forge de Sainte Marie
0702	L'Ardéchois	3011	Mas de Rey	5601	La Grande Métairie
0703	Soleil Vivarais	3012	Ile des Papes	5605	Kervilor
0704	La Rouveyrolle	3013	Petits Camarguais	5612	Les Iles
0709	Plantas	3014	La Soubeyranne	5613	Mané Guernehué
0802M	Vieilles-Forges	3201	Le Camp de Florence	6104M	Champ Passais
0902	Arize	3204N	Deveze	6201	La Bien-Assise
0906	Le Pre Lombard	3206	Lac des Trois Vallées	6304	La Grange Fort
1001	Du Tertre	3208	Le Talouch	6306	Le Clos Auroy
1101	Eden II	3301	La Dune	6407	Le Ruisseau
1106	Au Pin d'Arnauteille	3302	Fontaine-Vieille	6411	Col d'Ibardin
1107	Les Mimosas	3306	Palace	6601	California
1108	Relais de la Nautique	3308	La Barbanne	6602	Ma Prairie
1111	Val d'Aleth	3320	L'Eyre	6604	Le Soleil
1207	Grange de Monteillac	3403	Le Napoléon	6607	Le Brasilia
1208	Club Les Genêts	3404	Lou Village	6611	Le Dauphin
1403	De Martragny	3406	Oliveraie	6613	L'Eau Vive
1405	Le Colombier	3407	Sérignan-Plage	6807	Les Sources
1407	La Vallée	3408N	Sérignan Plage Nature	7105	Moulin de Collonge
1409	Du Brévedent	3409	La Yole	7107	Epervière
1502N	La Taillade	3500	Le Vieux Chêne	7201M	La Route d'Or
1602	Gorges du Chambon	3502	Des Ormes	7203	Chanteloup
1701	Bois Soleil	3507	Bel Event	7406	La Colombière
1702	Le Puits de L'Auture	3607M	Les Chênes	7408	Les Rosières
1704	Bonne Anse Plage	3701	La Mignardière	7701	Davy Crockett Ranch
1705	Orée du Bois	3703	Le Moulin Fort	7703	Base de Loisirs
1711	Monplaisir	3801	Le Coin Tranquille	7901M	Noron
1714	Sequoia Parc	3805	Le Temps Libre	8001	Drancourt
1717	Les Charmilles	3901	La Plage Blanche	8004	Le Royon
2004N	Riva Bella	3903	De Chalain	8006	Le Val de Trie
2200	Des Vallées	3904	La Pergola	8101	Entre Deux Lacs
2201	Les Capucines	4002	Les Chênes	8302	Esterel
2209	De Galinée	4003	Les Pins du Soleil	8313	Le Beau Vezé
2220M	La Bocage	4004	La Paillotte	8317	La Bergerie
2301	De Poinsouze	4005	Le Col-Vert	8405	La Sorguette
2400	La Tuiliére	4006	Eurosol	8407	Carpe Diem
2401	Le Verdoyer	4007	Lous Seurrots	8502	Du Jard
2406	Le Paradis	4008	St-James Eurolac	8503	La Loubine
2408	Moulin de David	4010	La Rive	8504	La Garangeoire
2410	Le Moulinal	4011	Sen Yan	8505	Les Dunes
2411	Aqua Viva	4012N	Arnaoutchot	8507	Les Biches
2412	La Palombière	4014	Lou P'tit Poun	8508	La Puerta del Sol
2415	Les Deux Vallées	4015	Les Ecureuils	8509	L'Abri des Pins
2417	Le Port de Limeuil	4101	Val de Loire	8513	Pong
2418	Saint Avit Loisirs	4103	Des Alicourts	8514N	Le Colombier
2419N	Le Couderc	4104	Des Marais	8520M	Petite Boulogne
2420M	La Plage	4201M	La Douze	8524M	Jarny-Ocean
2422	Chênes Verts	4401M	Petit Port	8526	La Guyonnière
2423	Moulin de Paulhiac	4404	Sainte-Brigitte	8527	L'Oceano d'Or
2500	Val de Bonnal	4409	Du Deffay	8528	Les Places Dorées
2503	Bois de Reveuge	4410	Le Patisseau	8530	La Grand' Métairie
2505M	Saint Point-Lac	4411	La Roseraie	8531	La Trévillière
2602	De Senaud	4501	Bois du Bardelet	8532	Val de Vie
2603	Le Grand Lierne	4604	Moulin de Laborde	8601	Le Petit Trianon
2604	Le Couspeau	4605	Le Rêve	8603	Le Relais du Miel
2811M	Bonneval	4607	La Plage	8702	Leychoisier
2901	Ty-Nadan	4608	Lacomté	8804	Lac de Bouzey
2905	Orangerie de Lanniron	4610M	Le Soulhol	8805	Château d'Epinal
2908	Le Panoramic	4701	Moulin du Pèrié	8903M	Les Coullemières
2909	Le Raguénèz-Plage	4703	Château de Fonrives		
2911	Grand de la Plage	4901	Etang de la Breche		

FISHING

We are pleased to include details of sites which provide facilities for fishing on the site. Many other sites are near rivers or are in popular fishing areas and have facilities within easy reach. Where we have been given details, we have included this information in the individual site reports. It is always best to contact individual sites to check that they provide for your individual requirements.

0101	La Plaine Tonique	2423	Moulin de Paulhiac	5005	Le Cormoran
0200	Vivier aux Carpes	2500	Val de Bonnal	5006	Le Grand Large
0301	La Filature	2503	Bois de Reveuge	5102M	Châlons-sur-Marne
0305	La Petite Valette	2505M	Saint Point-Lac	5202	Forge de Sainte Marie
0306	Deneuvre	2602	De Senaud	5501	Les Breuils
0401	Hippocampe	2608	Le Gallo Romain	5601	La Grande Métairie
0402	Du Verdon	2811M	Bonneval	5608M	Le Pâtis
0406	Le Haut-Verdon	2900	Les Mouettes	5612	Les Iles
0607N	Club Origan	2901	Ty-Nadan	5613	Mané Guernehué
0608	Les Cigales	2902	Saint-Laurent	5803	Manoir de Bezolle
0702	Ardéchois	2903	Letty	5806M	Les Pres de la Ville
0703	Soleil Vivarais	2905	Orangerie de Lanniron	6101M	La Campière
0704	La Rouveyrolle	2906	Le Pil-Koad	6304	La Grange Fort
0705	Le Ranc Davaine	2909	Le Raguénèz-Plage	6305	La Ribeyre
0706	Mondial	2911	Grand de la Plage	6307	Le Pré Bas
0707	Les Ranchisses	2913	Des Abers	6404	Les Gaves
0708	La Bastide	2927	Des Dunes	6406	Le Pavillon Royal
0709	Des Plantas	3000	Gaujac	6407	Le Ruisseau
0802M	Vieilles-Forges	3006	Fumades	6409	La Chêneraie
0902	Arize	3010N	La Sablière	6506	Pyrenees Natura
0903	Le Montagnou	3012	Ile des Papes	6603	Cala Gogo
0906	Le Pre Lombard	3204N	Deveze	6604	Le Soleil
1101	Eden II	3206	Lac des Trois Vallées	6607	Le Brasilia
1104	Le Martinet Rouge	3302	Fontaine-Vieille	6612N	La Clapère
1111	Val d'Aleth	3308	La Barbanne	6803M	Masevaux
1200	Peyrelade	3309	Le Pressoir	7002M	Lac Vesoul
1202	Les Rivages	3320	Eyre	7104M	Le Val d'Arroux
1204	Les Tours	3500	Le Vieux Chêne	7105	Moulin de Collonge
1205	Les Terrasses du Lac	3502	Des Ormes	7107	Epervière
1208	Les Genêts	3607M	Les Chênes	7201M	La Route d'Or
1209	La Boissiere	3703	Le Moulin Fort	7203	Chanteloup
1210M	Lauradiol	3711M	Au Bord du Cher	7206M	Val de Sarthe
1403	Martragny	3805	Le Temps Libre	7407	Escale
1405	Le Colombier	3806	Les Trois Lacs	7604	La Source
1408	Le Puits	3901	La Plage Blanche	7703	Base de Loisirs
1409	Brévedent	3902	Surchauffant	7901M	Noron
1502N	La Taillade	3903	De Chalain	8001	Drancourt
1601M	Bourgines	3904	La Pergola	8006	Le Val de Trie
1605M	Cognac	3905	Fayolan	8307	Etoile d'Argens
1711	Monplaisir	4004	La Paillotte	8308	Au Paradis
1712	Rex	4005	Le Col-Vert	8310	La Plage
1903	La Plage	4007	Lous Seurrots	8312	Du Domaine
1905	La Riviére	4008	Saint-James Eurolac	8317	La Bergerie
2001	Arinella Bianca	4010	La Rive	8318	Les Rives de l'Agay
2004N	Riva Bella	4012N	Arnaoutchot	8320	Les Pêcheurs
2204	Le Châtelet	4103	Des Alicourts	8403M	Brégoux en Provence
2209	Galinée	4104	Des Marais	8405	La Sorguette
2213	Port l'Epine	4105	Grands Pres	8504	La Garangeoire
2214	Port La Chaine	4201M	La Douze	8506	Le Pas Opton
2220M	La Bocage	4402M	Du Moulin	8513	Pong
2301	Poinsouze	4404	Sainte-Brigitte	8514N	Le Colombier
2400	La Tuiliére	4409	Du Deffay	8519	Le Marais Braud
2401	Le Verdoyer	4501	Les Bois du Bardelet	8526	La Guyonnière
2404	Le Moulin du Roch	4604	Moulin de Laborde	8603	Le Relais du Miel
2406	Le Paradis	4607	La Plage	8604	Le Futuriste
2407	Lestaubière	4610M	Le Soulhol	8701M	Montréal
2409	Soleil Plage	4703	De Fonrives	8702	Leychoisier
2410	Le Moulinal	4705	Moulin de Campech	8801	Les Deux Ballons
2411	Aqua Viva	4901	Etang de la Breche	8802	Belle Hutte
2414	Bel Ombrage	4902	Chantepie	8804	Lac de Bouzey
2415	Les Deux Vallées	4904	Etang	8807	Des Messires
2417	Port de Limeuil	5000	L'Etang des Haizes	8903M	Les Coullemières
2420M	La Plage	5002M	Le Pré de la Rose	9500	Séjours de L'Etang
2421M	Le Repaire	5003	Lez-Eaux		

HORSE RIDING

We understand that the following sites offer horse riding on site for at least part of the year. However, we would recommend that you contact the site to check that the facility meets your requirements. It is worth bearing in mind that French attitudes to safety may differ from your own (for example, take your own hard hat).

0301	La Filature	3406	Oliveraie	6305	La Ribeyre
0402	Du Verdon	3500	Le Vieux Chêne	6604	Le Soleil
0703	Soleil Vivarais	3502	Des Ormes	6807	Les Sources
0902	Arize	4005	Le Col-Vert	7608M	Du Colombier
1106	Au Pin d'Arnauteille	4006	Eurosol	7701	Davy Crockett Ranch
1502N	La Taillade	4008	St-James Eurolac	7703	Base de Loisirs
1714	Sequoia Parc	4409	Du Deffay	8001	Drancourt
2001	Arinella Bianca	5005	Le Cormoran	8302	Esterel
2005N	La Chiappa	5612	Les Iles	8315	La Sainte Baume
2901	Ty-Nadan	5803	Manoir de Bezolle	8504	La Garangeoire
3002	La Petite Camargue	6304	La Grange Fort	8804	Lac de Bouzey

The following sites inform us that there are riding stables within a very short distance (1 km). Where facilities are within easy reach but slighly further away, we have included this information in the individual site reports.

0401	Hippocampe	3000	Domaine de Gaujac	6303	Europe
0706	Mondial	3013	Petits Camarguais	6306	Le Clos Auroy
1107	Les Mimosas	3305	Les Ourmes	6600	Le Pujol
1407	La Vallée	3306	Palace	6601	California
1602	Gorges du Chambon	3403	Le Napoléon	6602	Ma Prairie
1701	Bois Soleil	3506	La Touesse	6701M	Eichelgarten
1702	Le Puits de L'Auture	3806	Les Trois Lacs	8503	La Loubine
1705	L'Orée du Bois	3901	La Plage Blanche	8504	La Garangeoire
2013	San Damiano	4002	Les Chênes	8509	Abri des Pins
2903	Letty	4013	La Côte	9500	Séjours de L'Etang
2926	La Plage	5801	Des Bains		

GOLF

We understand that the following sites have facilities for playing golf. However, we would recommend that you contact the site to check that the facility meets your requirements.

2602	Château de Senaud	4103	Parc des Alicourts
3502	Des Ormes	8001	Château de Drancourt

The following sites inform us that there are golf courses within a short distance (under 4 km). Where facilities are within easy reach but slighly further away, we have included this information in the site reports.

0604	Le Grand Saule	3011	Mas de Rey	6603	Cala Gogo
0605	La Vieille Ferme	3302	Fontaine-Vieille	7401	Les Deux Glaciers
0906	Le Pre Lombard	3506	La Touesse	7407	L'Escale
1602	Gorges du Chambon	3701	La Mignardière	7408	Les Rosières
2102M	Les Cents Vignes	4013	La Côte	7604	La Source
2204	Le Châtelet	4015	Les Ecureuils	8007	Des Aulnes
2209	De Galinée	4302	Bouthezard	8307	Etoile d'Argens
2409	Soleil Plage	4401M	Petit Port	8310	La Plage
2603	Le Grand Lierne	4411	La Roseraie	8313	Le Beau Vezé
2609	Les Truffières	4601	La Paille Basse	8315	La Sainte Baume
2900	Les Mouettes	4902	Chantepie	8317	La Bergerie
2902	Saint-Laurent	5613	Mané Guernehué	8503	La Loubine
2903	Du Letty	6204	Du Château	8509	Abri des Pins
2926	La Plage	6407	Le Ruisseau	8528	Les Places Dorées
3003	Abri de Camargue	6408	Les Tamaris Plage	8802	Belle Hutte

NATURIST SITES

We have had very favourable feedback from readers concerning our choice of naturist sites, which we first introduced in our 1992 edition. Over the last few years we have gradually added a few more, including two in Corsica.

Apart from the need to have a 'Naturist Licence' (see below), there is no need to be a practising naturist before visiting these sites. In fact, at least as far as British visitors are concerned, many are what might be described as 'holiday naturists' as distinct from the practice of naturism at other times. The emphasis in all the sites featured in this guide at least, is on naturism as 'life in harmony with nature', and respect for oneself and others and for the environment, rather than simply on nudity. In fact nudity is really only obligatory in the area of the swimming pools.

There are a number of rules, which amount to sensible and considerate guidelines designed to ensure that no-one invades someone else's privacy, creates any nuisance, or damages the environment. Whether as a result of these rules, the naturist philosophy generally, or the attitude of site owners and campers alike, we have been very impressed by all the naturist sites we have selected. Without exception they had a friendly and welcoming ambience, were all extremely clean and tidy and, in most cases, provided much larger than average pitches, with a wide range of activities both sporting and cultural.

The purpose of our including a number of naturist sites in our guide is to provide an introduction to naturist camping in France for British holidaymakers; we were actually surprised by the number of British campers we met on naturist sites, many of whom had `stumbled across naturism almost by accident' but had found, like us, that these sites were amongst the nicest they had encountered. We mentioned the Naturist Licence – French Law requires all campers over 16 years of age on naturist sites to have a `licence'. These can be obtained in advance from either the British or French national naturist associations, but are also available on arrival at any recognised naturist site (a passport type photograph is required).

The seventeen naturist sites featured in this guide (the site numbers are marked 'N'), together with the number of the page where they may be found, are:

266

SITE BROCHURE SERVICE

The following sites have supplied the Alan Rogers Travel Service with a quantity of their brochures. These leaflets are an interesting supplement to our reports as they contain colour photographs which can be helpful when choosing a site. If you would like any of these simply cut out or copy this page, tick the relevant boxes and send it with an A4 sized stamped addressed envelope. Please allow 40g postage for each brochure requested. Send your brochure requests to:

The Alan Rogers Travel Service, 90-94 High Street, Tunbridge Wells, Kent TN1 1YF.

Brittany

2201	Les Capucines	☐
2209	Château de Galinée	☐
2213	Port L'Epine	☐
2214	Port La Chaîne	☐
2900	Les Mouettes	☐
2901	Castel Ty Nadan	☐
2905	Orangerie de Lanniron	☐
2906	Le Pil Koad	☐
2908	Le Panoramic	☐
2911	Grand de la Plage	☐
2912	Manoir de Kerlut	☐
2913	Des Abers	☐
2916	Les Genets d'Or	☐
2917	La Piscine	☐
2924	De Keranterec	☐
2928	La Pointe	☐
2929	Le Grand Large	☐
3504	Le P'tit Bois	☐
4413	L'Hermitage	☐
5604	De Penboch	☐
5614M	Mun. du Bas de la Lande	☐

Normandy

1403	Castel de Martragny	☐
5005	Le Cormoran	☐
5006	Le Grand Large	☐

Northern France

6203	Château de Gandspette	☐

Paris / Ile de France

7704	Des 4 Vents	☐
7801	International Maisons-Laffitte	☐

Eastern France

5202	Castel Les Forges de Ste Marie	☐

Vendée Charente

1717	Les Charmilles	☐
8520M	Mun. La Petite Boulogne	☐
8521	Les Ecureuils	☐
8524	Jarny Ocean	☐
8526	La Guyonnière	☐
8527	Océano d'Or	☐
8530	La Grand' Métairie	☐

Loire Valley

4104	Château des Marais	☐
4501	Les Bois du Bardelet	☐
7203	Castel Château de Chanteloup	☐
8603	Le Relais du Miel	☐

Burgundy

5801	Les Bains	☐
5803	Castel Manoir de Bezolle	☐
7102M	Le Village des Meuniers	☐

Jura / Alpes

2503	Bois de Reveuge	☐
3801	Le Coin Tranquille	☐
3901	La Plage Blanche	☐
7406	La Colombière	☐
7407	L'Escale	☐

Atlantic Coast

3309	Le Pressoir	☐
4010	Domaine de la Rive	☐
4013	De La Côte	☐
4014	Lou P'tit Poun	☐
6401	Europ	☐

Dordogne / Aveyron

1208	Les Genêts	☐
2408	Le Moulin de David	☐
2422	Domaine des Chênes Verts	☐
4601	Castel de la Paille Basse	☐
4604	Moulin de Laborde	☐
4608	Château de Lacomté	☐
4703	Castel Château de Fonrives	☐

Rhône Valley

0101	La Plaine Tonique	☐
0707	Les Ranchisses	☐
2603	Le Grand Lierne	☐

Provence

0401	L'Hippocampe	☐

Midi-Pyrénées

0902	L'Arize	☐
3201	Le Camp de Florence	☐
8101	Relais de l'Entre Deux Lacs	☐

Mediterranean

0605	La Vieille Ferme	☐
1108	Le Relais de la Nautique	☐
3002	La Petite Camargue	☐
3013	Les Petits Camarguais	☐
3014	Soubeyranne	☐
3409	La Yole	☐
6607	Le Brasilia	☐
8302	Esterel Caravaning	☐

France 4 Naturism

N2004	Naturiste de Riva Bella	☐

FIRST TIME ABROAD

Anyone who has never taken their caravan, motorcaravan or tent abroad before will probably view the prospect with some trepidation. It's all very well experienced campers saying 'it's easy' but you know it can't be. To start with they drive on the 'wrong' side of the road and they speak a foreign language. And what happens if something goes wrong? How do you tell a Gauloise smoking mechanic, who can't speak a word of English beyond Bobby Charlton and Margaret Thatcher, that there was a strange sound from your engine and then it started vibrating.

Well the truth is camping abroad really is easy. After your first trip you will return with the smile of a seasoned Continental traveller. And you can impress your friends by telling them how easy it all was.

Because many campers - if you'll forgive the use of the generic term - are worried about that first trip abroad, we realised that we had to introduce articles to help the newcomer. At the same time they could serve as an aide memoire to more experienced caravanners. And because most first timers pick France, the obvious place to put those articles was in our France Guide.

So where do we start? Well let's start by asking Why France? Because it is the easiest European country to get to. Because they've got nearly two and a half times the land mass of the UK, but no more people than us. Because they are the world's greatest camping nation with more touring sites than any other country. Because they like campers and go out of their way to make us feel welcome. Or because their climate varies - in the north - from the best you'll get in the southeast of England to semi-tropical on the Mediterranean coast.

No, there's no shortage of reasons why, and very few reasons why not.

So France it is. But where in France? We would suggest that 300-400 miles from a Channel Port is about right for a newcomer. With ports in Nord/Pas de Calais, Brittany, Normandy and right on the France - Spain border, that still means that most of France is open to you.

We would suggest that you could do with a bit of experience before heading for the more remote parts of the Pyrénées or Alpes, but with France's excellent motorway network even the mountains aren't really a no-go area for the first timer.

When? Anytime. Even in the depths of a British winter nothing feels better than a few days of Mediterranean sun. Pick the right part of France and you can almost guarantee sunbathing weather from early spring through to late autumn.

If there is a time to avoid travelling it is from mid-July to around 20 August when the French pour out of the cities to enjoy le weekend. And if there is a road to be avoided, it is the A13 motorway out of Paris. We now know why the French are so good at long distance motorcycle racing. They practise on the A13 on a Friday evening.

And that just leaves the question of How?

Well, why not try one of the escorted holidays operated by Four Seasons Touring on behalf of our Alan Rogers Travel Service – these escorted holidays, ideal for first-timers, are fully escorted throughout by well-known caravan journalists, Dave and Liz King – not only will you have the advantage of being met in the UK and escorted on the ferry crossings and at the campsite, but Dave and Liz will also take care of most of the formalities for you and even arrange optional excursions and visits to various attractions in France during your stay. Contact the Alan Rogers' Travel Service for details (01892 559898).

Of course there's no reason why you can't make all the arrangements yourself. Book your ferry and site and arrange your own insurance. However, a lot of first timers like the feeling of security which comes from using one of the excellent booking services which specialise in looking after the camper. Besides the services run by the Caravan Club and the Camping and Caravanning Club for their members, there is Eurocamp Independent, Select Sites and the Camping & Caravanning Service and our own Alan Rogers' Travel Service. See opposite page 64 for details. This service is designed to incorporate everything we've learnt in decades of continental travel with tent, caravan and motorcaravan.

You will read more about the logistics of camping in France later in this guide, so let's use the space left to us to kill some of the myths associated with camping in France. Starting with that old one about the difficulty of driving on the 'wrong' side of the road.

It really isn't a problem, there are even advantages. Because the driver is sitting on the nearside it is easier to keep clear of oncoming traffic. It does help to have a navigator to keep an eye on the road ahead when you want to overtake. But the French understand motorcaravans and cars towing caravans and trailers and instinctively give us more room.

Caravanners, in particular, will be pleased to note there is no French equivalent to our

First Time Abroad

Jeremy Clarkson with his irrational dislike - or is that fear - of caravans. Perhaps that is why Mr Clarkson doesn't like France much either.

Road signs aren't a problem. Most of our road signs are international and you will see, for example, the same stop sign as we use in Britain. They even use the English word Stop. The few additional signs are really self explanatory. A sign showing a caravan going down a hill and the lettering underneath 50 kph, obviously means that caravans should stick to 50 kph (30 mph) whilst going down the hill which lies ahead.

Language isn't a problem either. In most French schools English is the second language of choice and many younger people have a surprisingly good command of our language. But just as we appreciate it if foreign visitors to our country make some efforts to speak a few words of our language, so they appreciate it if we try speaking a few words of theirs. If you have school aged children who are learning French, why not give them the responsibility of acting as the family's translators. Two weeks in France, speaking the language, will do wonders for their school marks. Whether you give them the translation duties or not, they will still return home with increased vocabularies. On French sites children socialise together with none of the competitiveness or aggression which seems to mar our society.

And that naturally brings us to the question of security. Just as in every other country there are parts of the cities which should be avoided. But our natural domain is the countryside, and social crime is almost unknown amongst the French rural communities. There is crime, but they seem to take the view that ignoring European Laws originating in Brussels, brewing a bit of calvados (apple brandy) on the side or fiddling their tax returns is not really a crime.

Let's close by laying to rest that old fear about breaking down whilst abroad. One of our readers had a car breakdown whilst in France. And to make matters worse it happened on a French public holiday. One brief phone call to the French contact number of his holiday insurance company put him touch with an English speaking advisor who told him that someone would be with them in an hour.

He was, and he had a Gauloise cigarette stuck to his top lip and didn't speak a word of English. But he knew what the problem was and soon had the car loaded on the transporter and caravan hooked to the back. Back at his garage he set to work. The evening was creakingly hot, and after twenty minutes he came back in to the office and went in to a back room. Minutes later he emerged clutching bottles of ice cold beer for the adults, and chilled pop for the children. The French love children.

Within the hour the car was fixed. Our family weren't out of the woods yet though. They still had to find their site. They pointed to the site address on their booking form and went into a mime of looking lost. The mechanic stared intently at the booking form for a few minutes, and then went across to the telephone. There then followed a completely unintelligible telephone conversation in machine gun. rapid, heavily Provençal accented French, before the mechanic beckoned the husband across to the phone.

On the line was the site owner. The mechanic had explained their problems, and of course they understood that our family would be late. If they would care to follow the mechanic he would show them a short cut to the site. And he did, driving for three quarters of an hour over roads not shown on any tourist map.

On arrival at the site they asked the mechanic, with the site operator translating, if he would accept a small tip for his help. No he wouldn't. But when they'd pitched they would find him in the bar, and he would be delighted to accept a cold pastis. It was, after all, a very hot night.

That's the real France which you can only discover if you've got a caravan, motorcaravan or tent. With this guide we hope we can help you discover the real France that we know and love.

Mike Cazelet

Public Holidays in France - 2001

1 January	New Year's Day
16 April	Easter Monday
1 May	Labour Day
8 May	VE Day
24 May	Ascension Day
4 June	Whit Monday
14 July	Bastille Day
15 August	Assumption
1 November	All Saints' Day
11 November	Rememberance Day
25 December	Christmas Day

Note: The months of July and August are traditionally when the French take their holidays. For this reason, the less touristic parts of France are quiet during these months, while coastal resorts, especially in the south, are very crowded.

First Time Abroad - Checklist

Before you set off for a holiday abroad it's worth making yourself a checklist of things to do, and what to pack – We've been travelling abroad several times a year for more than thirty years and we still don't rely on our memory for this, so here is a shortlist of essentials to start you off:

- ☐ Passports
- ☐ Tickets
- ☐ Motor Insurance Certificate, including Green Card or Continental Cover clause
- ☐ V5 Registration Document and/or (if not your own vehicle) the owners authority
- ☐ Breakdown Insurance Certificate
- ☐ Driving Licence
- ☐ Form E1-11 (to extend NHS Insurance to European destinations)
- ☐ Foreign Currency and/or Travellers Cheques
- ☐ Credit Card(s)
- ☐ Campsite Guide(s) and Tourist Guide(s)
- ☐ Maps/Road Atlas
- ☐ GB Stickers on car and caravan/trailer

- ☐ Beam deflectors to ensure that your headlights dip towards the right hand side
- ☐ Red Warning Triangle
- ☐ Spare vehicle/caravan driving light bulbs
- ☐ Torch
- ☐ First-Aid Kit, including mosquito repellent
- ☐ Fire extinguisher
- ☐ Basic tool kit (eg screwdriver, pliers, etc)
- ☐ Continental mains connector/adaptor, and a long cable – for continental sites
- ☐ Polarity tester
- ☐ Spare fuses for car and caravan
- ☐ Spare fan/alternator belt

Remember – it is well worth having your car and caravan serviced before you go, and do check that your outfit is properly 'trimmed'.

First Time Abroad – Money

The French unit of currency is the Franc, and there are 100 centimes to the franc. At the time of writing there are 9.5 francs to the £ sterling. The French rarely use the franc symbol on displayed prices, and use a comma between francs and centimes. Hence 74,87 is 74 francs 87 centimes or Ffr. 74.87.

For approximate calculations we usually work on a rate of Ffr. 10 = £1. So a Ffr. 10 coin is worth £1. A Ffr. 1 franc coin is worth 10p and a 10 centime coin is 1p.

With the launch of the Euro in '99, you will find many items 'dual-priced' in both Francs and Euros. However, until Euro notes and coins are introduced, this is mainly of academic interest designed to accustome us to seeing prices in this new currency.

France is one European country where many transactions are still done with cash. We advise all readers to have some cash with them when they land. Major credit cards (Visa and MasterCard) are accepted in most restaurants, cafes and petrol stations, and can also be used to pay for motorway tolls. We tell you in the Site Reports which sites accept them.

In some of the more rural parts of France they may not be familiar with British issue credit cards as French cards incorporate a computer chip rather than just a magnetic strip. If your card is refused by a trader showing the Visa/MasterCard sign you should say :

"Les cartes Britanniques ne sont pas des cartes a puce, mais a pistes magnetiques. Ma carte est valable et je vous serais reconnaissant d'en demander la confirmation aupres de votre banque ou de votre centre de traitement." If you cannot pronounce this don't worry. Just point out this phrase.

Charge cards like American Express and Diners don't seem to be as widely used as they are in the UK.

Eurocheques – these were useful and popular as a means of paying for goods and services, and for obtaining cash. However, they have now been phased out as a result of most European countries having adopted a uniform currency (the Euro).

Travellers cheques are widely accepted but in some places, and small country banks, there is a surcharge for cashing them. We have found that most sites are happy to accept travellers cheques as payment for site fees.

The British Switch card, under the Cirris name, is widely accepted. French cash machines with the Cirris symbol will accept British Switch cards with the Cirris symbol but we suggest not using them if the loss of a card would disrupt your holiday. You can't argue with a machine that just swallowed your card.

Our advice to holidaymakers is to take holiday money in a mixture of cash, travellers cheques and credit card.

First Time Abroad – Insurance

There is probably no subject which causes campers, caravanners and motorcaravanners venturing abroad more worries than insurance. The problem is that there is an overlap, so that sometimes one problem is apparently covered on two insurance policies. To avoid confusion let's cut through the hype and take a clear look at insurance.

If you are planning on camping, caravanning or motorcaravanning abroad, this is what you will need.

Road traffic insurance
Under European Law your ordinary car or motorcaravan road insurance will cover you anywhere in the EU. But many policies only provide minimum cover. So if you have an accident your insurance may only cover the cost of damage to the other person's property.

To maintain the same level of cover abroad as you enjoy at home you need to tell your vehicle insurer. Some will automatically cover you abroad with no extra cost and no extra paperwork. Some will say you need a Green Card – which is neither green or on card – but won't charge for it. Some will charge extra for the green card.

Ideally you should contact your vehicle insurer 3-4 weeks before you set off, and confirm your conversation with them in writing.

A good insurance company will provide a European recognised accident report form. On this you mark details of damage to yours and the other party's property and draw a little diagram showing where the vehicles were in relation to each other. You give a copy of your form to the other motorist, he gives you a copy of his. It prevents all the shouting which often accompanies accidents in this country.

Holiday insurance
This is a multi-part insurance. One part covers your vehicles. If they breakdown or are involved in an accident they can be repaired or returned to this country. The best will even arrange to bring your vehicle home if the driver is unable to proceed.

Many new vehicles come with a free breakdown and recovery insurance which extends into Europe. Some professional motoring journalists have reported that the actual service this provides can be patchy and may not cover the recovery of a caravan or trailer. Our advice is to buy the motoring section of your holiday insurance.

The second section of holiday insurance covers people. It will include the cost of doctor, ambulance and hospital treatment if needed. If needed the better companies will even pay for English language speaking doctors and nurses and will bring a sick or injured holidaymaker home by air ambulance.

The third part of a good holiday insurance policy covers things. If someone breaks in to your motorhome and steals your passports and money, one phone call to the insurance company will have everything sorted out. If you manage to drive over your camera, it's covered.

One part of the insurance which is often ignored is the cancellation section. Few things are as heartbreaking as having to cancel a holiday because a member of the family falls ill. Cancellation insurance cannot take away the disappointment, but it makes sure you don't suffer financially as well.

Ideally you should arrange travel insurance when you book your ferry. If you are using the Alan Rogers' Travel Service they will be able to take care of all your travel insurance requirements.

For those travelling independently, we have arranged special terms with Insure4Europe run in association with Green Flag (and which imposes no restriction on the age of your vehicle). Full details are shown on the colour feature between pages 256/257.

Form E111
By arrangement between the British Government and rest of the European Community Governments, British holidaymakers can enjoy the same health care as that Government offers its own citizens. The form which shows you are entitled to take advantage of this arrangement is called E111.

E111 doesn't replace holiday insurance, but is in addition to. The form is available from all main UK Post Offices. Fill out one for every member of your family. Get it stamped by the counter staff and take it on holiday with you.

In theory one Form E111 lasts you for ever. But we have had reports that in some rural areas in Europe they may not understand that, so our advice is to get a new E111 every year. It is free.

And that is all you need to know about insurance. You know what they say about insurance, don't you? You'll only need it if you haven't got it.

Mike Cazalet

First Time Abroad – On the Road in France

The Law
You must be aged eighteen or over to drive a car in France, but a UK national driving licence is sufficient – only non-EU nationals require an International Driving Permit. You should carry your Registration Document, and your Insurance (which must be valid for use on the Continent) and you must display a GB plate. You must carry a warning triangle, and a spare set of light bulbs and your headlights must be adjusted to dip to the right. A first-aid kit and fire extinguisher are recommended but not compulsory.

Drive on the right-hand-side of the road, and remember to look left when turning onto a another road.

Conditions and Conventions
'A' roads are Autoroutes, usually toll roads

'N' roads are Routes Nationale, the equivalent of our A roads

'D' roads are Routes Departemental, the equivalent of our B roads

'C' roads are Routes Communale, unclassified minor roads

'Prioité a Droite' means 'Give way to traffic coming from your right' (even if you think you are on a more main road and have the right of way – you don't have it, so give way.

On roundabouts (which are rounded anti-clockwise of course) traffic already IN the roundabout has priority, but not all French drivers acknowledge this.

Traffic Lights
Lights in France turn from Red to Green without going through an amber period. Flashing amber means you can proceed with caution

Most traffic lights have small repeater lights at shoulder height adjacent to the line where you must stop – these are very useful as many traffic lights don't have a set of lights on the far side of the junction.

Watch for 'right filters' – a slowly flashing amber light/arrow which allows you to filter right, with care.

Pedestrian Crossings
There are lots of pedestrian crossings, even more than in the UK, but they are more often than not ignored by motorists (except those from abroad). Don't be surprised if you're honked at for stopping for pedestrians!

Autoroutes
Mostly these are toll roads, and you must pay to use them. You will either have to pay at the toll (Péage) where you join, or you must take a ticket from the machine at the Péage and surrender this, with your money or credit card, at the Péage where you leave the Autoroute.

There are service areas (Aires de Service) with full facilities every 40 km. on Autoroutes, and rest areas (Aires de Repos) also at regular intervals. Both have warning signs well in advance, indicating the facilities and even the price of fuel.

Signposting
Is better than in the past but the positioning and angling of signposts is something one just gets used to.

Navigating
Michelin Maps are the most popular, particularly the Michelin 1: 200,000 scale Atlas, but for more detailed maps you can buy IGN Maps, which are the French equivalent of our Ordnance Survey maps, but often even more expensive.

Tips for Navigators: Siitting in the 'hot seat' on the off-side of the car, with a better view ahead, you'll almost certainly be asked to help your driver with advice on when it is safe to overtake – be ultra cautious.

When giving your driver advice at junctions use the word 'OK' if it is safe to go, and 'Wait' if it is not, rather than 'Go, No or Alright', all of which can lead to confusion.

Remember that you go round roundabouts ANTIclockwise so if you use the words 'Second Exit' that's the second one you come to going round anticlockwise!

Breakdowns
You really should have breakdown insurance, towing in France can involve long distances and hefty charges. If you do break down you are required to display your warning triangle 30 m. behind your car (or car and caravan) and it should be visible for at least 100 m. if possible. Don't forget to turn on your hazard lights as well. There are emergency phones every 2 km. on Autoroutes.

Security
Take sensible precautions against theft of, or from, your vehicle and/or caravan – be particularly vigilant in car parks and Aires de Service where thieves are most often active.

Weather Conditions
The French Autoroute System operates its own Radio Station giving forecasts and warnings in both French and English on 107.7 MHhz (FM. Telephone forecasts are available by dialling 08.36.68.02 followed by the two digit number of the departement you require a forecast for.

Introducing the motoring holiday with less motoring.

If you're holidaying with your car in Brittany, Normandy, the Loire or beyond, why drive hundreds of extra miles from the distant, industrial ports of Northern France? Our routes bring your holiday that much closer. So your motoring, via country roads, and ancient villages becomes a pleasure not a chore. To find out more just call us or ask your travel agent.

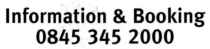

UST RING FOR QUALITY SERVICE

Travelling with
P&O Stena Line means
you can enjoy the most
comprehensive, and stylish
ferry service between
Dover and Calais.

Our spacious ships
feature exciting shopping
opportunities. Langan's
Brasserie, Club Lounges
and themed bars offering
a quality of service that
satisfies time after time.

With a crossing every 30
minutes at peak times –
you know it's a service
that can't be beaten.

reservations
087 0600 0600

P&O Stena
LINE

where time sails by

the hoverspeediest way to france and belgium

dovercalais45mins folkestoneboulogne55mins
doverostend2hrs newhavendieppe2hrs

speed across the channel with hoverspeed for the perfect start to your 2001 holiday. dedicated terminals, with no coaches or hgv's. on board: friendly, airline-style service. why not upgrade to 1st for a touch of extra comfort? at the hoverstores in our continental ports you'll find wines, beers, spirits and tobacco at huge savings over uk high street prices. full details – and online purchasing – at www.hoverstore.co.uk

call **08705 240241** or your travel agent
www.hoverspeed.co.uk
book online and receive a 2% discount

hoverspeed
fastercarferries

Can you cross The Channel in a different style?

Yes you Can Can.

Not only does SeaFrance guarantee you the lowest possible fares between Dover and Calais it also serves up that famous French style. With SeaFrance you can enjoy delicious Gallic cuisine and make great savings on a huge selection of wines, beers, spirits and gifts in our on board shops. Next time you're travelling to France travel in unique style.

08705 711 711
www.seafrance.com

SEE THE DIFFERENCE WITH

SEAFRANCE
DOVER-CALAIS FERRIES

So close,
you can taste it.

08705 35 35 35

Here's a thought to savour: the finest wines, mouthwatering cuisine, and a way of life that is utterly addictive, all just 35 minutes[*] away when you travel with Eurotunnel. So if you have a taste for France, call today and let us whet your appetite.

Or, book on line at www.eurotunnel.com and get £2 off.

[*] platform to platform (45 minutes at night)

www.eurotunnel.com

Folkestone to Calais/Coquelles in 35 minutes, up to 4 times an hour, 24 hours a day

Fabulous

Futuristic Theme Park for all the family

Parc du FUTUROSCOPE

BEAUCOUP PLUS QUE DES IMAGES

Poitiers FRANCE

NEW EVENING LASER SHOW

Step into the world of special effects, aeronautical thrills & spills, soar over the Grand Canyon. Ride a Magic Carpet, go into orbit with astronauts, climb to the top of Everest. Plunge to the depths of 'The Lost City of Alantis', join the Gyrotour for panoramic views from the skies, experience the Heart of a Storm or join our internet "Net Bus". As dusk gathers relax & watch our truly superb festival of light & sound where lasers, music & giant images combine in a whirlwind of music and colour. With spectacular images, action & movement prepare to be amazed. Over 2000 hotel rooms onsite.

Plus much much more...........

Futuroscope is here

Cherbourg • Le Havre • Caen • Roscoff • St Malo • PARIS • Nantes • FUTUROSCOPE • Poitiers • Niort

Situated near Poitiers between Bordeaux, Cognac & The Loire Valley. Only 1½ hours fr Paris & close to the West Coast Holiday Parcs.

FOR BROCHURE & BOOKINGS TELEPHONE

UK: 020 7499 8049

FRANCE: +33 (0)5 4949 3080

www.futuroscope.com

Open your eyes – Expand your mind !

ECONOMY DRIVE.

(P&O DIRECT FROM PORTSMOUTH TO FRANCE OR SPAIN.)

If you're going camping or caravanning this year, why not cut some corners? Avoid the busy Pas de Calais area and a long road journey down through France, by sailing most of the way instead.

Just get onboard at Portsmouth, sit back and relax while we do the driving. You'll not only arrive fully refreshed and nearer your destination, but you'll have saved a fortune in petrol too.

For more information on our routes, sailings, fares and timetables, call our reservations department on 0870 2424 999. For your free brochure, call 0870 9000 212 quoting AR.

www.poportsmouth.com

Caravans not carried on Fastcraft.

Altogether more civilised. **P&O PORTSMOUTH**

PORTSMOUTH TO BILBAO, CHERBOURG & LE HAVRE

First Time Abroad – On the Road in France

The most important and/or requently encountered traffic signs you will be likely to see are:

Absence de Marquage	No white lines	Péage	Toll
Accotements non Stabilisé	Soft verges	Périphique	Ring Road or by-pass
Aire de Repos	Rest area		
Allumez vos Phares	Turn on headlights	Piétons	Pedestrians
		Poids Lourds	Heavy lorries
Attention Ecole	Schoolchildren	Prenez le Ticket	Take a ticket
Attention Travaux	Road Works	Préparez votre Monnaie	Have the right change ready
Bandes des Ralentisse-ment/Transversales	Sleeping Policemen	Priorité Pietons	Pedestrianised area
BIS (Bison Futé)	Alternative route	Prochaine Sortie	Next Exit
Bouchon!	Traffic jam	Ralentissez	Slow down
Brouillard!	Fog!	Rappel	Warning
Carrefour Dangereux	Dangerous junction	Réservé	Reserved
		Risque de.......	Risk of ....
Cédez le Passage	Give Way!	Route Barré a...	Road closed in...
Centre Ville/Bourg	Town or village centre	Roulez au Pas	Drive at walking pace only
Chantier Mobile	Moving road works vehicle	Sauf Caravanes	Except caravans
		Sauf Riverains	Local residents only
Chausée Deformée	Uneven road surface	Section Péage	Toll section
Circulation Alternée	Traffic control ahead	Serrez a Droite	Keep right
		Sortie de Camions	Exit for lorries
Circulation Interdite	No traffic allowed	Stationnement Interdit	No Parking
Convoi Exceptionnel	Slow and or wide load	Travaux	Road Works
Coté de Stationement	Parking on this side of the road	Traversée d'Engins	Diggers etc crossing
Creneau de Depassement	Overtaking lane	Tunnel sous la Manche	Channel Tunnel
Descente Dangereuse	Steep dangerous hill	Utilisez votre frein moteur	Use low gear
		Véhicules Lents	Slow vehicles
Deviation	Diversion	Verglas	Icy road condtions likely
Eteignez vos phares	Switch off headlights		
		Virages	Bends
Feux	Traffic Lights	Voie sans issue	No through road
Gardez votre File	Stay in lane		
Gravillons	Loose chippings		
Halte Péage	Stop at toll booth		
Hauteur Limitée	Height limited		
Inondation	Flood		
Interdit	Forbidden!		
Itinéraire Conseillé	Recommended Route		
Lacet	Hairpin bend		
Par Temps de Pluie	In wet weather		
Passage a Niveau	Level (or not so level!) crossing		
Passage Interdit	No Entry		
Passage Protégé	Priority		

First Time Abroad – On the Road in France - Speed

Most of Europe has a bewildering range of speed limits, but in France it is all very simple and logical. One set of limits covers motorcaravans, solo cars and cars towing trailers or caravans. These are the limits:

In built-up areas 50 kph (31 mph)
Outside built-up areas 90 kph (56 mph)
Motorways 130 kph (81 mph)

There is also a requirement that no vehicle may use a French motorway unless it can cruise at 80 kph (50 mph).

Just as in the UK there will be occasions when these maximum speeds are reduced. When it is raining the maximum speed outside built-up areas is automatically reduced to 80 kph (50 mph) and on motorways to 110 kph (68 mph). The definition of raining is any time you have to put your wipers on, so speeds should be reduced even if it has stopped raining but the roads are wet.

On non-charged sections of motorway, speed limits may be reduced to 110 kph (68 mph) and there may be signs on any road reducing the maximum speed allowed because of the road's condition or some other factor.

Unlike the British the French do not tend to use a sign on the outskirts of a town or village to tell you a speed limit applies. A name post is sufficient to indicate that built-up area limits apply. On the exit from the town you will see the name post again, but with the name crossed out. That means the built-up area speed limits no longer apply.

Unlike Britain speed limits are rigidly enforced. 110 kph means exactly that – not 111 kph. The French have adopted the Gatso automatic speed recording and photographing machine and some holidaymakers have returned home to find a speeding summons waiting on the doormat.

Under French Law the summons for speeding cannot be enforced unless the driver of the vehicle is clearly identifiable in the photograph. However the majority of speeding motorists are caught by a following Police vehicle or Police speed camera. Unlike British Traffic Police, the French Police don't wear reflective jackets and do hide behind hedges.

During the summer months French magistrates have a habit of escaping from their stuffy court rooms and setting up court in a tent by the road. Motorists caught speeding are escorted there and given on-the-spot fines. In some circumstances the Police can themselves impose an on-the-spot fine. On-the-spot means just that. If you can't pay there and then they'll escort you to a cash machine or bank to draw out money. There is a report of a southern French magistrate who accepts all major credit cards. If you really cannot pay, the magistrates have the power to confiscate your vehicle until you do.

So although French speed limits are more generous than ours, it doesn't pay to speed

Passports for Pets

Since the introduction in 2000 of the Passports for Pets scheme many British campers and caravanners have been encouraged to take their pets with them on holiday, but not only are the Pet Travel conditions understandably strict, the procedure is quite lengthy and complicated, and is being modified for 2001 – you can check the current situation via the Passports for Pets web site:

http://freespace.virgin.net/passports.forpets

There is also a help line: 0870 241 1710,

or e-mail: passports.forpets@virgin.net.

In fact we are fairly confident that the main conditions and arrangements will still apply – The main problem still being the need to find a Vet in the country from which you are returning who understands what is required in terms of "tick and tapeworm treatment" neceeary before your pet can re-enter the UK, and who is authorised to issue the necessary certificate.

Last year we advised all the campsites featured in our France Guide to contact their local Vet, alert them to the likely demand for this treatment and the certification requirements, and then for the campsites to make available the details of an appropriate/approved local practice(s). Hopefully this will mean that most of our sites will be able to guide you in the right direction.

CONNECTING UP TO WATER AND DRAINAGE

Dave King offers a few tips to make life easier.

Modern touring caravans are equipped with many of the conveniences of home, enabling us to live a very comfortable life in our home from home. Even so there are still some chores to be done, like filling the water containers and emptying the wastewater. Although they are not major tasks, the benefit of eliminating them is that they never have to be dealt with at an inconvenient moment.

Pitches with electricity, water and drainage are fairly common on sites in Europe (often referred to as "grand confort" in France) and are now available on an increasing number of sites in the UK. They are exactly as described, with a tap and drain to each pitch. The drain is used to discharge your waste (grey) water, and the tap enables you to fill your water containers, or provide continuous supply.

The tap offers two options; the most simple, being a length of hose, from the tap to your water container thereby refilling without moving it. (Only "Food Quality" hose should be used.)

Alternatively you can use a proprietary product such as the Whale Aquasource or the Carver Waterline, both of which incorporates a pressure-reducing valve enabling you to connect the tap directly to the water input used by your pump. Both these systems are effective, provided that the site pressure is not too high or too low. (The valve is absolutely vital as the caravan water system is low pressure, and if mains pressure were applied it would certainly result in a flood!)

Another alternative is to connect the hose to a container, in which the level of water is controlled by a ball-type valve, into which your pump is inserted. There are two benefits to this design; firstly there is no possibility of any pressure build up as you are still using your own pump. Secondly if the water pressure is low, (which can often be the case at peak times on a busy site) you have a "buffer stock" of water. A good example is the 40 litre Aquaroll. By using the mains adapter kit, (available as an accessory) to connect to the tap, you have a continuos source of water, plus a 20 litre buffer supply. However it also is easy to "roll" 40 litres of water, from the water point to the caravan, when your own tap is not available.

So now we have the water supply, how about the drainage.

Most models of caravan have at least two waste drain points, and some have three or more, it is important to identify the source of each outlet. One of the outlets should come from the shower tray, which is at floor level and the other outlets will come from the kitchen sink and the bathroom hand basin, which will probably be around the same height. If they were all joined together you could have the dirty water from the sink, ending up in the shower tray.

In order to prevent this happening join the kitchen sink and hand basin outlets together using two short lengths of hose and a "Y" connector, then attach about a half metre length of hose to the connector and another to the shower outlet. These can then be joined using another "Y" connector. This creates a separated fall, preventing backing up. From this point a single waste hose runs to the drain.

Another alternative is to buy a spare cap for your normal waste container, drill a hole in it, and attach short piece of pipe to which the waste hose can be attached, giving the best of both worlds.

Lastly, a word of warning. On the best sites the tap and drain will be on your pitch. But on some sites you will find although the facilities are advertised, they are located at a central point within a group of pitches with up to six or even eight taps and only one drain. Unless you have remarkably long waste and fresh water hoses it may not be possible to connect at all.

I like connecting up, it releases a few more minutes to sit back and enjoy an extra glass of wine!

Electrical Connections

The Voltage on most campsites in France varies from 220V to 240V AC, which presents no problem for most British appliances. However, the amperage available will vary considerably and may be anything from 2A to 16A, depending on the site, and within the site itself, depending on what supply you wish to pay for. You will probably need a Continental Adapter (rather than the UK CEE 17 one) to plug into the sites' supply.

These can be purchased in the UK, at specialist caravan accessory shops, or in many French hypermarkets, or occasionally they can be borrowed from the site itself. For the sake of safety you should also carry a Polarity Tester, to check that you have connected up correctly.

Gerry and Chris Bullock's Pages

First of all who are Gerry and Chris, and why give them a page in this guide? Chris and Gerry have been motorhome owners for more years than they care to remember but, in the mid seventies Chris suffered a serious back injury which has worsened over the past ten years, taking away her ability to walk any distance more than within the motorhome or around the house, and otherwise she is wheelchair user. They have, therefore, over the years become 'experts' in finding parks with good facilities for the wheelchair user.

We felt that it might be useful for other readers of the guide to learn something of their experiences or indeed be able to tap their experience directly. They are very happy for us to include their address and phone number at the end of this article should you wish to contact them.

As you will be aware, we always include reference to facilities provided by the parks in our Guide but have not felt ourselves qualified to assess these facilities. Below we have listed what Gerry and Chris look at when they assess a site with few examples of what they have found.

Firstly, they look at the access to the sanitary blocks:
* Are they accessible for wheelchair users or walking disabled campers?
* Are door widths adequate for wheelchairs, are there steps for the walking disabled?

Secondly, what does the room offer?
* WC with handrails
* Handrails at the sinks
* Obstructions in the room
* Sink accessible by wheelchair
* Lights with cords
* The shower and its access
* Levers on taps
* Emergency alarm cord
* Handrails in the shower

Thirdly, access checks to other facilities.
* Washing up areas (even less abled persons like to help).
* Reception (Chris likes a chance to pay the bill!)
* Bars and restaurants (why can't we all enjoy ourselves?)
* Games room
* Clubs and other amenities

Fourthly, the pitches
* Where are they in relation to the facilities?
* Conditions of paths - gravel/tarmac/sleeping police men
* Terraced or level?
* Ground - level/sloping?

For example:
One site, recently assessed by Gerry and Chris, came out well with its ramped accesses to all bars, the shop, the takeaway and reception; also for the Radar key system for the sanitary facilities. It did not score so well with some of the paths and roads that connect the facilities - some were unmade and difficult for wheelchair users and their helper (this is an area the site now hopes to address). There were also some problems with the pitches as the park is based on heathland and is consequently somewhat bumpy. Perhaps the site will be able to specially level a pitch close to the facilities. At least their attention has been drawn to some of the problems experienced by wheelchair users and the walking disabled, which they maybe able to improve.

These are the sorts of things which Gerry and Chris look at so, if you have queries concerning sites and the suitability of their facilities or would like suggestions, or have any recommendations, please contact them. They would like to hear from you.

Gerry and Chris Bullock's address is:

97 Stalham Road, Hoveton, Norwich, Norfolk NR12 8EF Telephone. 01603 784152

NOTE. They advise that they are not looking at facilities for persons with special needs. They leave this to the such people as the Sue Ryder Foundation, etc. which cater very well in this field.

Following recent visits in Normandy, France, Gerry and Chris have made the following comments:

Disabled Friendly Sites in Northern France

In the UK we have some excellent campsites with very good and well designed disabled facilities, with sometimes, more than adequate handrails and equipment. However, in Normandy, we found that the standard is not so high. It seems that the site owners do not have as much information available to them as their UK counterparts (we have offered our assistance to the sites we have inspected and they seemed very keen to take our offer. Hopefully, this will improve their situation).

We travelled from Portsmouth to Caen on Brittany Ferries, where loading and positioning of vehicles in the hold of the ships, for disabled persons is excellent, with wheelchair users being as near to the lift as possible. On the Brittany Fleet the following boats are capable of taking wheelchair user passengers M/V BRETAGNE has eight two-berth cabins with wheelchair access, shower and WC. M/V NORMANDIE has two outside two-berth cabins with wheelchair access, shower and WC. M/V QUIBERON has six inside four-berth cabins with wheelchair access, shower and WC and four outside two-berths. M/V VAL DE LOIRE has four outside two-berth cabins with wheelchair access and showers and WC and two inside two-berths with wheelchair access and shower and WC. So if you are a wheelchair user to ensure a pleasant and comfortable trip ensure you are booked on one of the above mentioned boats. The service we received on our trip was excellent.

We toured Normandy and the D-Day Landing Beaches, including museums, along our route as we wanted to see if disabled and ex-Forces persons, who were either involved in the Landings or maybe interested in the historic significance of the battles, that may now be in their later years and would have difficulties with acess. We are pleased to say that most of the museums had excellent access for wheelchairs, with the exception of the original bunkers and blockhouses along the Atlantic Wall.

The sites in Northern France that we inspected had good access, with wide doors, although we do have to say that door handles and catches were small and fiddley. WCs were raised on most occasions with adequate transfer space, but only one angled handrail to assist you! Most washbasins were at the correct height but with no levers on taps. The showers were the most difficult as, although they were level for access for wheelchairs, they only supplied free-standing chairs rather than wall mounted, secure seats and again, maybe only one angled handrail. Access to other areas of the sites was generally very good though.

In conclusion, we found a distinct lack of equipment in French facilities, such as hand-rails, mirrors, soap dishes, levers on taps - even large door handles, etc. Where we did find hand-rails, they consisted of a small angled handle, mounted at WCs only, We did find plastic seats in showers, which is a help if you can leave your wheelchair.

The site owners are very keen to learn more about what the British hope to find when visiting their sites. We have offered our assistance to try to improve this situation.

5006 Camping Le Grand Large
Good disabled en-suite facilities; handrail at WC only. Roadways all tarmac; good level site. Access to main facilities; access to shop and bar; access to pool area via steep ramp; access to beach edge.

Disabled-friendly site, helpful owners. Advice offered on mprovements.

5000 Camping l'Etang des Haizes
Good disabled room; handrail at WC only. Level pitches; slight hill up to facilities; tarmac roads. Access to area around pool; access to bar and reception.

Disabled-friendly site; owner very helpful. Asked for advice.

5005 Camping Le Cormoran
Good disabled facilities; separate shower and WC (unisex blocks); handrails at WC; slight ramp. Tarmac roads. Access to all areas including pool area, bar and shop.

Disabled-friendly site; owners very keen to assist. Any advice was welcome.

1402M Camping Municipal du Bayeux
Separate shower/WC washrooms for wheelchair users; no handrails in shower; free-standing chair in shower. Tarmac roadways; level pitches; hardstanding; level site. Access to washing up area, reception. TV room.

1403 Camping Le Chateau de Martragny
Very good disabled showers and WC; well placed hand-rails; disabled-friendly door catches (large and easy to use); levers on taps. Tarmac roadways; level site. Access to bar, TV room and most areas; access to pool area and fishing lake; disabled facilities in bar. Owner previously worked with disabled persons. Disabled-friendly site.

1407 Camping de la Vallée
Good disabled room; hand-rail in shower and toilet; separate rooms in unisex block; very spacious. Tarmac roadways; concrete paths; some areas hilly; pitches level. Access to reception, shop, games room; no access to bar with wheelchair. Helpful staff.

LE MANS – more than a place, more than a race

The campers and caravanners mini-guide to the Le Mans 24 hour race

Le Mans - another view

The problem with being a freelance journalist is needing an excuse to visit the Le Mans 24 hour race. So how about this? Guy Smith - son of Pete the chairman of caravan manufacturer Swift Group - had a drive alongside Stefan Johansson and Jim Mathews in a Reynard Judd. And **Which Motorcaravan** has just taken delivery of a test Elddis/Peugeot Autostratus which needed a good gallop before I decided to praise it, or otherwise, in print.

Not convinced? Alright I'll come clean. I've wanted to go to Le Mans for years, and this was the first time I had a good excuse. The difference between my story and Phil May's is that he went to watch the racing. For me the racing was just the cream on top of the profiteroles.

It started with early morning coffee in the excellent Club Class lounge in P&O Stena Line's new ferry the Aquitane. For companions I had two Ferraris, two Porsches, two Aston Martins, half a dozen assorted TVRs and a solitary MGB. Actually our coffee companions were the drivers not the cars, but after a while you forget names and start identifying people by what they drive.

We, for obvious reasons, became The Snails. But we still arrived at the lunch stop and the circuit before they did. Score that Snails 2, Ferrari 0.

On paper the route from Calais to Le Mans looks like a long slog. It isn't. It's pure adrenaline entertainment. By leaving the passenger side window open and using her mirror, my wife was able to give me advance warning of the cars about to pass us.

'Ferrari,' screech. 'TVR,' rumble. 'F1 McLaren,' whoosh. 'Cobra,' windscreen shakes. 'Three motorbikes,' growl, growl, growl.' They were all Ducatis. ''Lotai - plural of Lotus' 'Aren't they slow.' If you love exotic cars you can probably get your fix from just driving to Le Mans.

Lunchtime, and we didn't need any guide to decide where to eat. Stop at the first restaurant whose car park overflows with exotic two and four wheelers and you'll get a warm welcome, quick service, fantastic food and a miniscule bill. The good restaurants on the route south know that if they look after race fans, in one weekend every year they'll do more business than they will in a normal month.

To my surprise - I remember what happened at the British GP at Silverstone - getting to the right Le Mans car park for the press office was totally trouble free. All you need to know is which colour parking sign you should be following, and then follow the signs.

Mind you, if you miss the signs you'll just go round in a big circle. "Hey look, it's that Lamborghini again. What do you expect? It's got Belgium plates."

And, surprise, surprise, the press office were friendly, helpful and welcoming. That was something we noticed everywhere we went. The locals, the marshals, the traders and even the police are actually glad to see you.

After the Maserati verses Ferrari demonstration race - some demonstration with half a dozen Ferraris in the kitty litter, but a Ferrari still won - we joined the masses gathered round the goodies stalls.

And here was the next surprise. There were no rip-off merchants. An official tee shirt, colour printed both sides on good quality cotton, costs just Ffr. 40 (£4). Compare that with the shirts on offer at the British Motorcycle GP at Donnington a month later. Pay £8, get the extra large, wash it once and it will fit your grandson. And you can tell his parents that the blodge of colours is really modern art.

With the temperature still soaring we followed the crowds through the tunnel to the bars, restaurants and displays that make up the area called The Village, and our next surprise.

In the days before we left England the television news was full of stories about Euro 2000 soccer fans rioting in Belgium. In The Village and outlying areas there are dozens of bars, some open for 36 consecutive hours. They say there were 50,000 English fans and almost the same number of Germans at Le Mans. Trackside the fight was between the Germans (Audi) and the rest of the World.

And yet there was no violence. Not even a hint of it unless you count a scuffle between two fairground workers over a girl. We heard she eventually dumped both of them in favour of the gendarme who restored peace.

Our new-found friends Mr and Mrs (needs a new engine) 911, or Hans and Frieda to us, put it this way. It isn't drink, sport or national differences which causes violence. Perhaps it's soccer or the type of people soccer attracts.

As the clock ticked round to 4pm so the tem-

Le Mans - another view

perature soared, beaten only by the rising tension in the crowd. Seconds into the hour, released by the pace car, the pack surged through the right-hander at the start of the Dunlop Curves where we were standing.

Like everyone else we took a step back as the wall of sound hit us, and then they were gone. Which left roughly three minutes to join in the breathless multi-lingual "did you see ..." conversations.

Stefan had the first two stints, but much of that time was mucked up with the pack under the control of pace cars. So we did like TVR19, Porsche 43 and Chrysler Viper 4, and retired to a bar within sight of a big television screen.

Two hours in Guy Smith took over car 24, so showing loyalty we went back trackside to watch. Ok, so he was fast, but there were lots of other fast drivers out there. It wasn't until later we found he'd been told to nurse the Reynard. It wasn't until later we found out just how fast he could be.

In early evening we went dinner hunting. "What do fancy, Italian or French? A light supper or a full meal? Under canvas or out in the sun?" Again there was no rip-off. True the prices were a fraction higher than you might pay in a modest French café, but not exorbitant when you consider the logistics of cooking, feeding and washing up for thousands in what is, after all, a temporary structure.

Just as the sun was setting my earphones crackled with an announcement from the English language Radio Le Mans. Guy was back in the Reynard. Unknown to us Guy had been told to catch car 15. Car 15 is a two year old, ex-works BMW run by the well financed Thomas Bscher with experienced co-drivers Geoff Lees and Jean-Marc Gounon. Last year a BMW won Le Mans and car 15 finished fifth.

By comparison the Johansson Mathews Reynard Judd is non-competitor. It doesn't have the power, it certainly isn't as reliable, it

---

Radio Le Mans

Radio Le Mans is the English language radio station which transmits throughout the race weekend. Reception varies between excellent to acceptable in all the public enclosures around the circuit.

Rather than cart a conventional radio around, a small sports radio clipped to a belt and a pair of earphones will keep you in touch with the on-track action and latest pit lane happenings.

A basic sports radio costs around £10-12.

Speeding

Welcoming as everybody is, the police can't resist setting up speed checks on the "N" roads close to the circuit. The traps seem to be restricted to traffic leaving the circuit, and we didn't spot any speed cameras. The police seemed to be restricting their activities to stopping motorists who were obviously driving too fast and irresponsibly.

---

has no winning pedigree and their budget would probably look like the Bscher team's coffee fund. But catch the BMW Guy did, by braking so very impossibly, suicidially, manically late nobody gave him a chance of staying on the road.

I know all you multi-millionaires out there don't like to be identified, but we know who you are. So do something useful with your money or we'll publish your names. Buy Guy Smith a front running drive so he can show what he can do. Please, because I don't think my nerves will stand another year of watching him drive on the limit like that.

Our original plan was to leave the circuit after dark, drive a few miles away and spend the night on a proper camp site. But one thing killed that plan. I fell asleep in the Autostratus before I got as far as the driver's seat.

Of course you aren't allowed to camp in the car parks. Le Mans has proper camp sites around the circuit. But if you've got a self-contained motor caravan, and you don't look like you are really camping, nobody tells you off if you accidentally fall asleep rather than driving away from the circuit.

At 1.39am French time (precisely) my sleep was shattered by my wife's scream. Radio Le Mans had just announced that, with Stefan at the wheel, our Reynard was out with a blown engine.

Dawn broke, the temperature soared, and we joined the throng making their way towards The Village in search of breakfast. We settled for gallons of French wake-up coffee and a croissant. For anglophiles like '1930 Bentley Speed Six' and his wife, the same café served traditional English tea, bacon and eggs.

For mid-morning we'd booked a short coach tour with Just Tickets (see advert between pages 256.257). Just Tickets can make all the arrangements for a Le Mans trip. But many people like to make their own arrangements, but even if you do, at least book a place on one of their coach trips. Despite the side road chaos which is Le Mans, their coach arrived on time, departed on time and dropped us just

Le Mans - another view

where we needed to be to enjoy the Tetre Rouge, Arnage and Mulsanne Corners.

Motoring journalists will recognise that all three corners are duplicated on the Motor Industry Research Association's (MIRA) test track. The Tetre Rouge look-alike is designed to test, and usually break, rear suspension bits. Arnage is the brake breaker, or bonnet bender if the brakes have already broken. And Mulsanne highlights which drivers are still feeling brave. Twenty two hours into the race, plenty still felt brave.

The disappointment, and it was the only one all weekend, was Mario Andretti. At 60 years of age he'd returned to racing in an effort to win the one big race that had always eluded him. The truth was he shouldn't. His Panoz team mates, 34 year old David Brabham and 26 year old Jan Magnussen, were a full five to six seconds a lap faster.

But at least I can say I've seen the great man drive, even if it was in the twilight of his career.

The motoring press were to report that this year's Le Mans 24 Race was predictable and a little boring. True the three works Audis finished in the first three places. But down the field some of the scraps went right to the wire.

As we left the circuit we had the French language circuit radio on and heard an interview with a French driver. "If only," he said, "the race had run for another hour we would have caught him. Still there's always next year."

I know what he means. Next year. We'll be back.

Mike and Christina Cazalet's travel arrangements were handled by Formula-2000.com, a specialist travel service for motor sport competitors, their support crews and motoring journalists. Formula-200.com uses the facilities of the Alan Rogers Travel Service and Mark Hammerton Travel.

Camping at Le Mans

The Le Mans circuit itself offers racegoers several different 'campsites' usually open from the Tuesday prior to the race until the Monday after it, but early booking, or early arrival, is essential if you are not to be disappointed.

These 'sites' include Camping Houx (or Nouveau) with numbered pitches and electrical connections, and a new sanitary block with showers and WCs. This site also has an annexe, Chemin aux Boeufs, with good access to the starting straight.

La Chapelle camping is situated in the woods on the inside of the circuit near the Dunlop Bridge, and is definitely noisy! Tertre Rouge is again close to the track, and to the funfair, whilst Camping Bleu is close to the main entrance/exit for a quick getaway. Camping Expo is also close to the entrance, and to the Museum, while Maison Blanche (also very noisy!) may allow you to get a view of the circuit from the roof of your motorhome or caravan.

Prices for these campsites range from Ffr. 180–450 for the whole period of the practice and the race itself, irrespective of how long you actually stay.

A report by one of our readers, Phil May, who camped at Le Mans follows this article

If you choose not to use the circuit's own camping facilities, and to stay at a 'proper' campsite, there are a fair number to choose from, including quite a few in the département of Sarthe (72) some of which are featured in

this Guide, but bear in mind that all of these are likely to become very heavily booked over the weeks before during and after the race.

Amongst the several sites within about 50 kilometres of the circuit are:

Camping Municipal
Bresse-sur-Braye (about 45 km. SE of Le Mans). Unusual 4-star municipal with around 60 pitches. Tel: 02.43.35.31.13.

Camping Municipal du Lac
St Calais (about 37 km. ESE of Le Mans). Fully described in this Guide (7202M). Tel: 02.43.35.04.81

Camping Les Mollieres
Sille Guillaume (about 35 km. N of Le Mans). A well-shaded 3-star site with 130 pitches. Tel: 02.43.20.16.12

Camping Le Vieux Moulin
Neuville-sur-Sarthe (about 11 km. N of Le Mans). Pleasant 3-star site with about 100 pitches. Tel: 02.43.25.31.82

Camping Municipal La Route d'Or
La Fleche (about 40 km. SW of Le Mans). Fully described in this Guide (7201M). Tel: 02.43.94.55.90

Castel Camping Chateau de Chanteloup
Savigne l'Eveque (15 km. NE of Le Mans). Fully described in this Guide (7203). Tel: 02.43.27.51.07.

LE MANS 2000 - THE AMERICAN CHALLENGE

By Phil May at Le Mans

This year we arrived at the Le Mans circuit at 12 p.m. after catching the 6 a.m. ferry from Dover to Calais. On arrival at our campsite, Bleu Annexe, we pitched our tents and investigated the washing facilities. Unfortunately, shower blocks seemed to be lacking in close proximity, although there were five-star toilet and washing facilities at close hand. The campsite seemed to consist of mainly British people (always a fairly large percentage of race-goers) so there were no problems with the language barrier.

The Le Mans 24 Hours this year was a complete contrast to the previous with only two factory teams - Audi and Panoz entering three and two cars respectively. The pre-race favourite this year was Audi's No.9 car which was driven by Allan McNish, Stephane Ortelli and Laurent Aiello (previous victors in 1998) who all have solid reputations as topline sportscar drivers. McNish had previously put the car on pole closely followed by the two sister Audis and the first Panoz. This car was to be driven in the race by David Brabham, Jan Magnussen and Mario Andretti. The American legend was returning to try and win the only race victory which had deluded him several times in the past. After setting up camp, we went for a stroll along the pit lane and spotted Mario having an interview with French television. After this incident, the media scrum then moved onto the Hawaiian Tropic girls where they were suitably entertained (along with the token PR crowd of course). We spent the rest of the afternoon soaking up the atmosphere (and beers) before returning to the campsite to finish off the red wine bought earlier in the day.

I woke up on Saturday morning to be greeted by both a glorious temperature (32 degrees) and hangover - the two didn't mix very well! After completing a shopping trip to a close supermarket, we went to our hospitality tent near the Ford Chicane. Here Johnny Mowlem (driving a Porsche 911 GT3-R) was interviewed and embarrassed by Perry McCarthy (this year a spectator) to the amusement of the assembled crowd. We made it to the start/ finish straight a little late, but still managed to get through the crowd to obtain a good vantage point. After the parade lap, the cars were off with a roar at 2 p.m. Unsurprisingly, the three Audis (led by Allan McNish) stormed into the lead followed by Brabham's Panoz. Things didn't go according to plan for last year's winner Yannick Dalmas, who retired his ORECA Reynard-Mopar on lap 2. Christophe Tinseau's DAMS Cadillac also exploded into flames on Mulsanne straight to bring out the safety car. While the lead of the race seemed clear, the competition for the loudest car was being contested by the Panoz and the Chevrolet Corvette - it was a close call.

At around 5 p.m. we moved round to Tetre Rouge just in time to witness a Porsche 911 two car pile-up. This incident nearly caused another accident as the prototypes came haring round the corner. The McNish Audi was now leading chased by Tom Kristensen's Audi and Brabham's Panoz. We decided to take a ride in the famous ferris wheel to gain a bird's eye view of the race. Mario Andretti had recently taken over in the Panoz from Brabham and seemed to be struggling to keep up with the blistering pace previously set by the Australian (understandable considering his general lack of time in the car).

We finished off Saturday by visiting Mulsanne Corner at about 11 p.m. where we had a barbecue. A couple of us actually slept next to the track - not for the faint hearted as we were woken up by the scream of a Courage-Judd C60 attempting to shed one of it's rear wheels at six in the morning!

After returning from Mulsanne, we breakfasted and then walked to the Porsche Curves (about a five minute walk from Bleu Annexe). This is always a good place for watching the prototypes pass the GTS/GT2 cars. By this time, (12 o'clock) the Tom Kristensen/Frank Biela/Emmanuele Pirro Audi had established quite a commanding lead over the two sister cars during the night. There was also bad news for the DAMS Cadillac Northstar team when Eric Bernard's suspension snapped while running competitively inside the top ten. The three works cars run by GM Racing were faring worse and were running too far down the field to even challenge a few of the Chrysler Vipers.

The 'American Challenge' had not only suffered at the hands of the three leading Audis, but also from Henry Pescarolo's team. The diminutive Frenchman was running his own team this year using a Courage-Peugeot C52. His three drivers had managed to gain fourth place in front of two Panoz LMP roadsters. We walked back to the circuit to watch the remainder of the race from the Ford Chicane. The three Audis took the first 1-2-3 finish since Peugeot in '93. They couldn't have wished for a better result at La Sarthe. Once again, the Chrysler Viper GTS-R of Olivier Beretta/Karl Wendlinger/Dominic Dupuy took the GTS class win with 8th overall after shaking off the Corvettes. Apparently, this would be the last time we would see the current Viper model in action at Le Mans. To finish off, we returned to the campsite to enjoy the rest of the day in the baking heat as life returned back to some normality after witnessing the monster of a race that is Le Mans!

CAMPING WITH A MOTORCYCLE

A Biker's View by Colin Walker

Over the last ten years motorcycle ownership in Great Britain has been growing. Purchasers are, in the main, within the age range of mid 20's to 50+ and a lot of these bikes are bought as 'toys' maybe only clocking up 500 miles per year. So how are today's 'bikers' perceived and received? Last summer I decided to tour Europe on a Yamaha Virago XV535S and during this trip gauge the attitude of people both in campsites and in general to motorcyclists. Although I have travelled and camped extensively in Europe before this was my first touring trip by motorcycle and also my first solo trip. My route took me from my home in Scotland via Hull/Zeebrugge through Belgium, Germany, Czech Republic, Austria, Slovenia, Italy, France, back to Belgium returning home via Zeebrugge/Hull a distance of nearly 4,000 miles.

My first concern arose on the ferry. On boarding a crew member handed me some rope and it was my responsibility to secure my bike for the crossing. Speaking to other bikers I found out that this was standard practice. I wondered what the legal position would be if a bike was damaged in transit during a rough crossing. Would the shipping company deny liability because their employees had not secured the bike? Fortunately my concerns were not tested as both crossings were dead flat calm.

I entered France from Italy at the Colle di Tenda having travelled into the mountains from Ventimiglia. My destination was Annecy via Brianon and Albertville. This route is an excellent motorcycle run. Stunning views and hairpin bends in the Alps with some long straight sections of 'N' road at the end of the run. At Annecy I stayed at Camping Belevedere (Ffr. 45 per night) which is a very good municipal site within walking distance of the town. Pitches are marked and of reasonable size and I was free to choose my own pitch. My only criticism is that the small camp shop and snack bar is only open from 08.30 to 12.00. I stayed there for a few days and then continued my journey north. Travelling via Besanon and Nancy I arrived at Corny sur Moselle where I chose Le Paquis Camping (Ffr. 36 per night) which was situated on the banks of the river. Again I was free to choose my pitch but this time they were not marked. The site was not overly busy so I had plenty of space. This is a good overnight stop just off the RN57. The snack bar on this site was open until 21.00. Once again I enjoyed to the full good French N-roads with long straight section and sweeping bends. In the morning my destination was Zeebrugge. I decided to drive through Metz then pick up the autoroute to the north of the city which took me all the way through Luxembourg and Belgium.

My experiences over the whole trip was that as a 'biker' I was treated no differently that anyone else but as somebody travelling with a small tent, where pitches were allocated, I was frequently given a very small pitch. Also many campsite shops do not carry stock suitable for the single traveller who does not have fridge or freezer. Prepacked goods, especially frozen or chilled, are in quantities for families therefore the available choice is very limited.

I would certainly recommend biking in France but stay off the autoroutes as much as possible and enjoy the excellent French byways. Car drivers are more biker aware than in Britain and will always, where possible, move over to allow for overtaking, even in the cities.

Colin Walker

REQUESTS FOR INFORMATION

For your convenience, we have printed below some slips which you may cut out and fill in your name and address to obtain further information from any of the sites in the guide in which you are interested. Send the slip to the site concerned at the address given in the site report, not to us.

ALAN ROGERS' GOOD CAMPS GUIDE - 2001

ENQUIRY FORM

To (name of site): . . . .

Please send me a copy of your brochure and details of your conditions for making reservations.

We have our own trailer caravan / motor caravan / tent / trailer tent (delete as appropriate).

Name: . . . .

Address: . . . .

. . . .

ALAN ROGERS' GOOD CAMPS GUIDE - 2001

ENQUIRY FORM

To (name of site): . . . .

Please send me a copy of your brochure and details of your conditions for making reservations.

We have our own trailer caravan / motor caravan / tent / trailer tent (delete as appropriate).

Name: . . . .

Address: . . . .

. . . .

ALAN ROGERS' GOOD CAMPS GUIDE - 2001

ENQUIRY FORM

To (name of site): . . . .

Please send me a copy of your brochure and details of your conditions for making reservations.

We have our own trailer caravan / motor caravan / tent / trailer tent (delete as appropriate).

Name: . . . .

Address: . . . .

. . . .

REPORTS BY READERS

We always welcome reports from readers concerning sites which they have visited. Reports provide us with invaluable feedback on sites already featured in the Guide or, in the case of those not featured, they provide information which we can follow up with a view to adding them in future editions.

However, if you have a complaint about a site, this should be addressed to the campsite owner, preferably in person before you leave.

Please make your comments either on this form or on plain paper. It would be appreciated if you would indicate the approximate dates when you visited the site and, in the case of potential new sites, provide the correct name and address and, if possible, include a site brochure. We cannot always respond as quickly as we would wish, particularly during the summer and autumn months when we are working on the following year's guides. Please accept our apologies if your letter is not answered immediately - it does not mean we haven't followed up your comments. Send your reports to:

Deneway Guides & Travel Ltd, Chesil Lodge, West Bexington, Dorchester DT2 9DG

Name of Site and Ref. No. (or address for new recommendations):

. . . .

. . . .

Dates of Visit: . . . .

Comments:

Reader's Name and Address: . . . .

. . . .

. . . .

. . . .

CAR FERRY SERVICES

The number of different services from the UK to France provides a wide choice of sailings to meet most needs. The actual choice is a matter of personal preference, influenced by factors such as where you live, your actual destination in France, cost and whether you see the channel crossing as a potentially enjoyable part of your holiday or, (if you are prone to sea-sickness) as something to be endured!

You will find a summary of the services likely to be operating in the year 2001, based on information available at the time of going to press (Oct 2000), together with a number of reports on those services which we have used ourselves during the last two years.

Detailed, up-to-date information and bookings for any of these services, and for campsite pitch reservations, travel insurance etc. can be made through the Alan Rogers Travel Service, telephone 01892 559898.

Route	Frequency	Crossing Time
Brittany Ferries (Tel: 08705 360360)		
Portsmouth - Caen	Up to 3 daily	6 hours
Portsmouth - St. Malo	Daily	8.75 hours
Poole - Cherbourg (jointly with Condor)	Daily	2.25 hours
Poole - Cherbourg (conventional ferry)	Up to 2 daily	4.25 hours
Plymouth - Roscoff	Up to 3 daily	6 hours
Condor Ferries (Tel 01305 761551)		
Poole - St. Malo	Daily	4.5 hours
Eurotunnel (Tel 08705 353535)		
Folkestone - Calais	Up to 4 hourly	35 minutes
Hoverspeed (Tel 0990 240241)		
Dover - Calais	Up to 13 daily	45 minutes
Newhaven - Dieppe	Up to 3 daily In peak periods	2 hours
P&O Portsmouth (Tel 0870 2424999)		
Portsmouth - Cherbourg (ferry)	Up to 4 daily	5 hours
Portsmouth - Cherbourg (Fast Craft)	Up to 3 daily	2.75 hours
Portsmouth - Le Havre	3 daily	5.5 hours
P&O Stena Line (Tel 0870 6000600)		
Dover - Calais	Up to 2 hourly	1.25 hours
Sea France (Tel 0870 5711711)		
Dover - Calais	15 daily	1.5 hours

FERRY REPORTS

Even though we travel to France frequently in respect of our extensive Site Inspection Programme and use a variety of services, we do not use all of them every year. Our reports cover those services which we have used over the past two years.

Truckline Service - Poole / Cherbourg

One of our favourite services, partly because we live less than an hour's drive from Poole, which is a small and easily accessible port with facilities that are adequate and friendly. Since it started some years ago this service has offered good value for money, comfortable onboard facilities and good restaurants, and the

Ferry Reports

introduction of the new 'Barfleur' onto the route a few years ago has introduced a degree of luxury to rival any cross channel service. The main restaurant, for example, provides a variety of set menus in very pleasant surroundings and a standard of food and service which we have found to be consistently excellent and which represents very good value – not cheap, but value for money. The self-service cafeteria is also good, with reasonable prices, but tends to become more crowded. The ships, the good facilities and service, the interesting voyage along the Dorset coast for some miles and the competitive fare structure combine to make this service well worth serious consideration. Cherbourg itself is worth a visit (the old town in particular) and there is a huge hypermarket on the outskirts for stocking up with wine, etc. but be prepared for long (I mean half an hour) queues at the checkouts at busy times. The port facilities at Cherbourg were moved to a new terminal a few years ago which includes the offices of the various operators, waiting room, toilets, restaurant, boutiques, bureau de change, phones, cashpoint machines, tourist information office, etc.

Condor Fast Ferries - Weymouth / St Malo

Introduced in 1998, this service has the potential to save a lot of time for those holidaying in Normandy or Brittany, especially if like us they live in the south or southwest. To be honest I am a little wary of super-fast ferry services, whether they be hovercraft, hydrofoils or catamarans as in the past they have so often been heavily 'weather dependent', but I must say that the Weymouth/St Malo service operated by Condor 10 was a real eye-opener. With a capacity for over 700 passengers and around 200 cars and with a cruising speed of around 40 knots, the journey from Weymouth (or Poole) to St Malo takes around five hours, even allowing for stopping in St Peter Port (Guernsey) and or Jersey en-route – impressive stuff! The onboard facilities include aircraft-style seats for all, a bar, cafeteria and duty-free shop, and loading/unloading at Weymouth or Poole and St Malo is fast and efficient. Congratulations to Condor on introducing genuinely innovative services.

We used this service again in 2000, taking advantage of the Club Class seating which certainly enhanced our experience. The service is being transferred to Poole for 2001 and provisional details are shown on pages 285 and 288. CE/LB

P&O Stena Line - Dover / Calais

With 20 sailings each way from October to March and 25 each way from April to September, fares at a reasonable level, the use of 'super ferries' which make the crossing in 75 minutes and a check-in time of 20 minutes, P&O are taking on the Channel Tunnel head on to ensure a competitive alternative to the latest method of reaching mainland Europe. Although prior booking is advisable, the space on each vessel means that, except perhaps at peak times, one can just turn up and cross on the next sailing. The A20 extension to the M20 Folkestone to the Eastern Dock entrance at Dover and the direct access to the French Autoroute system at Calais with the pleasant 'cruise' across the channel in between, now make for a hassle free beginning to the holiday and a smooth start on the continental journey. This also helps the transition to driving on the right as, by the time one needs to use 'ordinary' roads, one has become used to overtaking on the left. Apart from these advantages, the ferries have been modernised to the highest standards with waiter and self-service restaurants, shops selling a wide range of duty-free and other goods, comfortable bars and lounges and Club Class at a small supplement for those who want peace and quiet away from the bustle on the decks below. Boarding and leaving the ships has been made simple by the use of double width ramps on two levels.

P&O European Ferries - Portsmouth / Le Havre or Portsmouth / Cherbourg

The ferries which operate these services are most impressive and provide comfortable crossings. Travellers from the north will find Portsmouth a very easy port to use. There is little difference in mileage between Dover and Portsmouth, the motorway takes you directly into the port, and an added bonus is no M25 to give you hassle. We always find the P&O Ferries clean, with friendly and efficient staff. The meals we have had have always been excellent, and even on busy crossings the staff cope very efficiently. For a small extra charge Club Class allocates reclining seats, drinks and newspapers in a quiet comfortable lounge. Night services offer good cabins, ensuring that you arrive fresh for your journey into France (cabins are also available on day crossings) Embarkation and disembarkation are managed with little fuss. The drive out of Cherbourg is easy, and well signposted. For hypermarket visits, our advice would be to use the large store on the outskirts of the town, before you descend the hill! Arrival and departure via Le Havre are also pretty straightforward, but beware of the height restrictions on the 'fast lane' into town which uses several tunnels under road junctions. JM

Ferry Reports

Brittany Ferries - Portsmouth / St Malo or Portsmouth / Caen

Our directors have used these two services on several occasions this year, usually travelling by night to save time. Both services are very comfortable and the choice of which to use will normally be determined by your onward destination, St Malo being ideal for Brittany, of course, whereas Caen is probably more convenient for those travelling south or east on arrival in France. The timing of the night sailings on these two services are somewhat different – for comfort and relaxation we prefer the St Malo service, which provides the opportunity to dine in some style (but at a reasonable cost) in the 'Bretagnes' very attractive on-board restaurant before getting a good night's sleep in the comfortable cabins, followed by a fairly leisurely breakfast prior to disembarkation around 08.00. The Caen night service, operated by the luxury super-ferry the 'Normandie' and the older (but nevertheless very comfortable 'Duc de Normandie' is arguably more convenient in terms of timing (it leaves later and arrives earlier) than the St Malo service. If you want to dine on board it does involve eating very late and breakfasting very early indeed, but of course this has the advantage of giving a very early start for your onward journey. In terms of on-board facilities, these modern ferries are all very well equipped, with a choice of restaurants, well-stocked duty-free shops, boutiques, cinemas for insomniacs or those who don't want to make use of the choice of comfortable cabins, and an excellent standard of service throughout. (See pages 276/277 for facilities on board this service for travellers with disabilities).

SeaFrance - Dover / Calais

Sea France operates up to thirty departures per day, using three ferries - The 'Cezanne' (550 cars), the 'Manet' and the 'Renoir', each 330 cars. We used the service in the peak season (mid August) and found the staff efficient and friendly. The vessels were clean, with modern decor, and quite comfortable, although not quite full, so movement around shops bars and restaurants was comparatively easy. With a distinctively French feel about them, each ship has a Relais Gourmet self-service restaurant, a Brasserie with waiter service, a Parisien Café and 'Le Pub' bars. The Cezanne and the Renoir both have private lounges (small supplement payable) and all have a bureau de change. One point worth noting was the fact that we had to park our motorhome on a sloping ramp/deck area, and although I was confident that my own vehicle wouldn't move, with the hand-brake on and in first gear, and with a chock provided by Sea France behind one wheel, some drivers still seemed nervous. We found Sea France to be quite flexible about bookings – on our outward journey we simply made a 'phone call (as it was peak season) and picked up the tickets on checking-in at Dover, and on returning to Calais earlier than expected we were offered a place on the very next crossing. We thoroughly enjoyed our crossings with Sea France, and look forward to using them again.
                                                                                                GP

'Le Shuttle' – The Channel Tunnel

The shops (no longer duty free) at both terminals had been enlarged with an increase in the number of check-out points. After shopping, we had a clear run right through to the train after the gas bottle on our motorcaravan had been checked and left on time. The whole operation was smooth and efficient and, being able to drive straight off at the French end without immigration controls, we soon joined the autoroute system and proceeded on our way. The return, six weeks later, mirrored the outward journey and, although we missed the on-board services of a conventional ferry, it was a slick operation. Having a slight disability at the time, the fact that no stairs had to be climbed was a great advantage. There will always be a place for the conventional ferries but it is nice to have this alternative, particularly for those who do not like sea travel and on the rare occasions when bad weather prevents boats from sailing.   GO

Apart from using this service in connection with our Site Inspections, we have also used it on occasion during the winter, to attend the Association of British Tour Operators to France Conference for instance, and (more excitingly) on our way to Reims for the start of the Monte Carle Rallye Historique in which my navigator and I competed in my 1971 Lancia Fulvia. For reliability in bad weather the tunnel is un-beatable!
                                                                                                CE/MB

Eurostar (Channel Tunnel rail link) - London / Paris

Eurostar may not be of immediate interest to those towing caravans or trailer tents, but is good news for passengers on foot, those with limited holiday time or for those who suffer from sea-sickness and do not relish the thought of travelling the unpredictable seas. It is particularly useful for students who wish to link up with their family holiday in France without having to take too much time out from a job or study. For information contact:

    Rail Europe 08705 848 848 (for times and fares in Europe) or
    Eurostar Information 08705 186 186 or www.eurostar.com

BRITTANY FERRIES GOES FASTEST ON WESTERN CHANNEL

Brittany Ferries will be operating the fastest Western Channel ferry crossing yet in 2001. An alliance with Guernsey based Condor Ferries will lead to a new, daily two hours and 15 minutes summer service between Poole and Cherbourg, starting next May (2001).

The new 42 knots (75m/h) catamaran service will be Brittany Ferries' first move into fast ferries and will increase the number of sailings on the Poole - Cherbourg crossing to up to three returns a day, one fast and up to two by cruise ferry. It will thus complement the popular conventional service operated by M.V. Barfleur.

The Condor owned vessel, featuring joint Brittany Ferries branding and on-board service crew will carry 750 passengers and 185 cars. Customers will benefit from interline tickets combining the new Poole Cherbourg fast craft service with Brittany Ferries' Portsmouth - St Malo and other routes as well as Condor's Poole - St Malo service. All the additional services will be bookable through Brittany Ferries, and details will feature in our new brochures, planned for mid-November.

The chance to enter a commercial alliance with the most experienced fast craft operator in the UK is particularly attractive to Brittany Ferries who have been carrying out lengthy and detailed assessments of potential fast craft services for some time.

The introduction of the new high-speed service enable Brittany Ferries and Condor to offer passengers greater choice and flexibility and at the same time increase capacity on the expanding Poole Cherbourg route. Nearly 450,000 passengers have been carried this year.

Ian Carruthers, Brittany Ferries Managing Director for the UK and Ireland, announcing the new service, said: "As the number one ferry operator on the Western Channel we wanted to ally ourselves with the best, most experienced fast craft operator in the UK. We have achieved that aim with our proposed new 'code share' arrangement with Condor.

"They have had a 100% reliability record on their Channel Islands services this summer so I believe our customers who go for speed rather than classic cruise ferry crossings, can look forward to an exciting new era in Brittany Ferries' services", he concluded.

Brittany Ferries is to build the largest cruise ferry specifically designed for Channel crossings. The giant ferry, capable of carrying 2,200 passengers and nearly 800 cars, will be built in Rotterdam and enter service in the spring of 2002.

The sailing schedule for the fast craft service will be:

Departs Poole:	07.30 hrs	Arrive Cherbourg:	10.45 hrs
Departs Cherbourg:	11.30 hrs	Arrive Poole:	12.45 hrs

The service is due to commence on 22 May 2001 and will run until 30 September 2001.

The shape of things to come:

NOTES

This page is for your own notes

TOWN and VILLAGE INDEX

Town and Village Index

Town and Village Index

CAMPSITE INDEX - by Number

Campsite Index - by Number

Campsite Index - by Number

Campsite Index - by Number

CAMPSITE INDEX by REGION

Index by Region

Index by Region

Index by Region

Index by Region

There are three indexes in this guide:

On pages 290-292 you will find an index of towns where the campsites are situated.

On pages 293-296 you will find each campsite indexed by its Number.

On pages 297-301 you will find each campsite indexed by its Region.

Sites that are new to the guide this year are highlighted in bold text in the index.

Municipal sites are marked 'M'
Naturist sites are marked 'N'

The Départements of France - Index

Map of the Départements

ALSACE 67 Bas Rhin, 68 Haut-Rhin

AQUITAINE 24 Dordogne, 33 Gironde, 47 Lot-et-Garonne, 40 Landes, 64 Pyrénées-Atlantiques

AUVERGNE 03 Allier, 63 Puys de Dôme, 15 Cantal, 43 Haute-Loire

BRITTANY 35 Ille-et-Vilaine, 22 Côtes d'Armor, 29 Finistère, 56 Morbihan

BURGUNDY 21 Côte d'Or, 71 Sâone-et-Loire, 58 Nièvre. 89 Yonne

CHAMPAGNE-ARDENNE 08 Ardennes, 51 Marne, 10 Aube, 52 Haute-Marne

COTE D'AZUR 06 Alpes-Maritime

FRANCHE-COMTE 90 Tre. de Belfort, 79 Haute-Saône, 25 Doubs, 39 Jura

LANGUEDOC-ROUSSILLON   48 Lozère, 30 Gard, 34 Hérault, 11 Aude, 66 Pyrénées-Orientales

LIMOUSIN 23 Creuse, 19 Corrèze, 87 Haute-Vienne

LOIRE VALLEY 28 Eure-et Loir, 45 Loiret, 18 Cher, 36 Indre, 37 Indre-et-Loire, 41 Loir-et-Cher

LORRAINE VOSGES 57 Moselle, 54 Meurthe-et-Moselle, 88 Vosges, 55 Meuse

MIDI-PYRENEES 46 Lot, 12 Aveyron, 81 Tarn, 31 Haute-Garonne, 32 Gers, 09 Ariège, 65 Hautes-Pyrénées, 82 Tarn-et-Garonne

NORD / PAS-DE-CALAIS 59 Nord, 62 Pas-de-Calais

NORMANDY 76 Seine Maritime, 27 Eure, 61 Orme, 14 Calvados, 50 Manche

PARIS 75 Paris, 77 Seine-et-Marne, 78 Yvelines, 91 Essone

ILE-DE-FRANCE 92 Hauts-de-Seine, 93 Seine-St-Denis, 94 Val de Marne, 95 Val d'Oise

PICARDY 80 Somme, 02 Aisne, 60 Oise

POITOU-CHARENTES 79 Deux Sèvres, 86 Vienne, 16 Charente,17 Charente-Maritime

PROVENCE 05 Hautes-Alpes, 04 Alpes-de-Haute-Provence, 83 Var, 84 Vaucluse, 13 Bouches-du-Rhône

RHONE VALLEY 01 Ain, 69 Rhône, 26 Drôme, 07 Ardèche, 42 Loire

SAVOY-DAUPHINY ALPES 38 Isère, 74 Haute-Savoie, 73 Savoie

WESTERN LOIRE 53 Mayenne, 72 Sarthe, 49 Maine-et-Loire, 85 Vendée, 44 Loire-Atlantique

Map of the Tourist Regions

Regular readers will see that this year our Site Reports are grouped into sixteen 'tourist regions' and then by the various départements in each of these regions in numerical order.

Regions and départements

For administrative purposes France is actually divided into 23 official Regions, but these do not always coincide with the needs of tourists (for example the area we think of as 'The Dordogne' is split between two of the official Regions. We have, therefore, opted to feature our campsites within unofficial 'tourist regions' although we have of course subdivided these into the official French 'départements', each of which has an official number. For example, the département of Manche is number 50. We have used these département numbers as the first two digits of our campsite numbers, so any campsite in the Manche département will start with the number 50.

On page 302 you will find an index of the official départements and on page 303 a map showing the official regions and départements, with the number of each département marked.

Campsite Maps

The maps that appear on pages 306-320 relate to the Tourist Regions that we have used. The approximate position of each campsite is indicated on the map by a circle, next to which is the site number. The maps are intended to help you find the approximate location of campsites, not to navigate by. Each Site Report includes succinct directions for finding the site, based on the assumption that you will be using a proper road map, such as a Michelin or Collins atlas. All distances are shown in kilometres and metres.

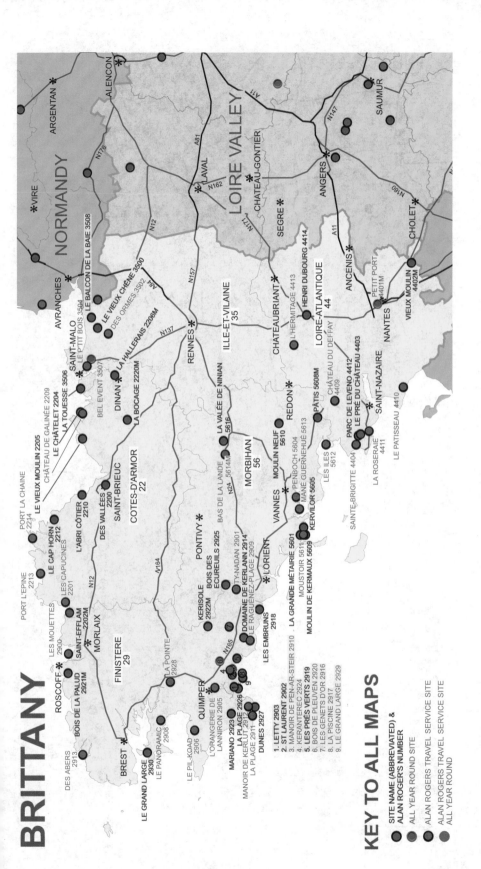

BRITTANY

NORMANDY

LOIRE VALLEY

*VIRE

*ARGENTAN

*ALENCON

*AVRANCHES

*SAUMUR

LAVAL

CHATEAU-GONTIER

*ANGERS

*SEGRE

*CHOLET

*ANCENIS

NANTES

VIEUX MOULIN 4402M

PETIT PORT 4401M

LE PRÉ DU CHÂTEAU 4403

PARC DE LEVENO 4412

HENRI DUBOURG 4414

L'HERMITAGE 4413

*CHATEAUBRIANT

ILLE-ET-VILAINE 35

*RENNES

LE BALCON DE LA BAIE 3508

LE VIEUX CHÊNE 3500

DES ORMES 3502

LE P'TIT BOIS 3504

CHÂTEAU DE GALINÉE 2209

SAINT-MALO

LA TOUESSE 3506

*DINAN

BEL EVENT 3507

LA HALLERAIS 2206M

LA BOCAGE 2220M

*LE VIEUX MOULIN 2205

LE CHÂTELET 2204

PORT LA CHAINE 2214

PORT L'EPINE 2213

LE CAP HORN 2212

LES CAPUCINES

L'ABRI CÔTIER 2210

DES VALLÉES 2200

SAINT-BRIEUC

COTES-D'ARMOR 22

*PONTIVY

KERISOLE 2922M

BOIS DES ECUREUILS 2925

LA VALÉE DE NINIAN 5616

BAS DE LA LANDE

N24 5614M

TY-NADAN 2901

LE RAGUENEZ-PLAGE 2909

DOMAINE DE KERLANN 2914

MORBIHAN 56

MOULIN NEUF 5610

*VANNES

PENBOCH 5604

MANÉ GUERNEHUÉ 5613

LES ILES 5612

CHÂTEAU DU DEFFAY 4409

LOIRE-ATLANTIQUE 44

PÂTIS 5608M

*REDON

LA ROSERAIE 4411

SAINTE-BRIGITTE 4404

LE PATISSEAU 4410

SAINT-NAZAIRE

LA GRANDE MÉTAIRIE 5601

MOUSTOIR 5611

MOULIN DE KERMAUX 5609

KERVILOR 5605

MANOIR DE PEN-AR-STEIR 2910

LES EMBRUNS 2918

*LORIENT

N165

LE PLAGE 2911

MANOIR DE KERLUT 2912

L'ORANGERIE DE LANNIRON 2905

*QUIMPER

MARIANO 2923

LA PLAGE 2926

DUNES 2927

LE PIL-KOAD 2906

LE PANORAMIC 2908

LE GRAND LARGE 2930

*BREST

DES ABERS 2913

BOIS DE LA PALUD 2921M

*ROSCOFF

LES MOUETTES 2900

SAINT-EFFLAM 2202M

MORLAIX

LES CAPUCINES 2001

FINISTERE 29

LA POINTE 2928

N164

N12

1. LETTY 2903
2. ST LAURENT 2902
3. MANOIR DE PEN-AR-STEIR 2910
4. KERANTEREC 2924
5. LES PRÉS VERTS 2919
6. BOIS DE PLEUVEN 2920
7. LES GENETS D'OR 2916
8. LA PISCINE 2917
9. LE GRAND LARGE 2929

KEY TO ALL MAPS

SITE NAME (ABBREVIATED) & ALAN ROGER'S NUMBER

ALL YEAR ROUND SITE

ALAN ROGERS TRAVEL SERVICE SITE

ALAN ROGERS TRAVEL SERVICE SITE ALL YEAR ROUND

305

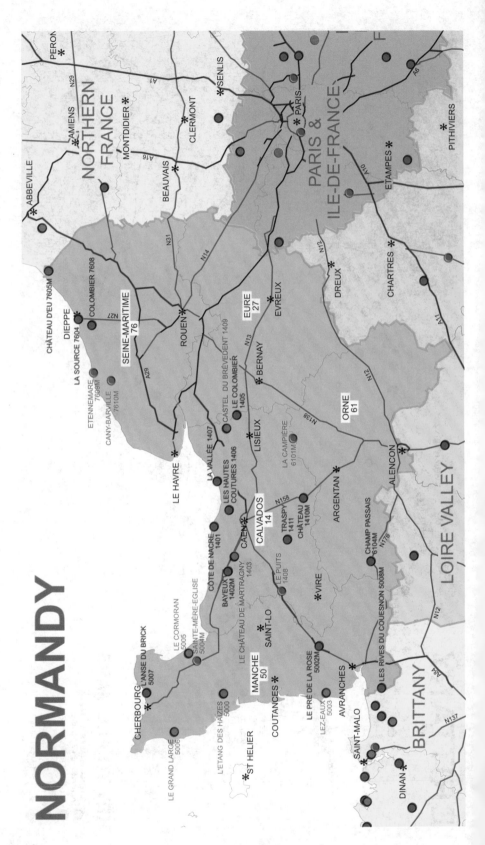

NORMANDY

NORTHERN FRANCE

PARIS & ILE-DE-FRANCE

LOIRE VALLEY

BRITTANY

PERON *

ABBEVILLE *

AMIENS *

MONTDIDIER *

CLERMONT

SENLIS *

BEAUVAIS

PARIS *

ETAMPES *

PITHIVIERS

CHARTRES *

DREUX *

CHÂTEAU D'EU 7605M

DIEPPE
LA SOURCE 7604 *
COLOMBIER 7608 *

| SEINE-MARITIME 76 |

ROUEN

EVREUX *

| EURE 27 |

ETENNEMARE 7609M *

CANY-BARVILLE 7610M

CASTEL DU BRÉVEDENT 1409
LE COLOMBIER 1405 *

BERNAY *

LA VALLÉE 1407 *

LE HAVRE *

LISIEUX *

LA CAMPIÈRE 6101M *

| ORNE 61 |

LES HAUTES COUTURES 1406 *

CÔTE DE NACRE 1401 *

MARTRAGNY 1403

CAEN *

| CALVADOS 14 |

TRASPY 1411 *
CHÂTEAU 1410M *

ARGENTAN *

ALENCON *

BAYEUX 1402M *

LE CORMORAN 5005

SAINTE-MÈRE-EGLISE 5004M *

LE CHÂTEAU DE MARTRAGNY

SAINT-LO *

LE PUITS 1408 *

VIRE *

CHAMP PASSAIS 6104M *

CHERBOURG *
L'ANSE DU BRICK 5007 *

| MANCHE 50 | *

LE PRÉ DE LA ROSE 5002M *

LES RIVES DU COUESNON 5008M *

L'ETANG DES HAIZES 5000

COUTANCES *

LEZ-EAUX 5003

AVRANCHES *

LE GRAND LARGE 5006

* ST HELIER

SAINT-MALO *

DINAN *

306

NORTHERN FRANCE & PARIS/ILE DE FRANCE

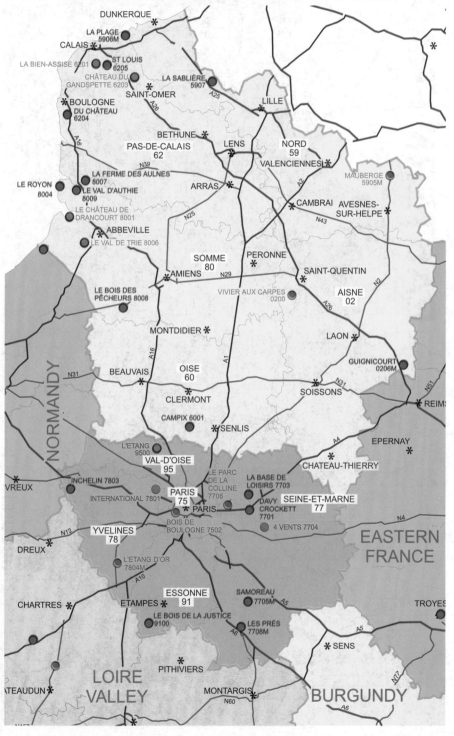

DUNKERQUE

LA PLAGE
5906M
CALAIS

LA BIEN-ASSISE 6201

ST LOUIS
6205

CHÂTEAU DU
GANDSPETTE 6203
SAINT-OMER

LA SABLIÈRE
5907

LILLE

BOULOGNE
DU CHÂTEAU
6204

A26

A16

BETHUNE

PAS-DE-CALAIS
62

LENS

NORD
59

VALENCIENNES

N39

MAUBERGE
5905M

LA FERME DES AULNES
8007
LE ROYON
8004
LE VAL D'AUTHIE
8009

ARRAS

CAMBRAI

AVESNES-
SUR-HELPE

LE CHÂTEAU DE
DRANCOURT 8001

ABBEVILLE

LE VAL DE TRIE 8006

N25

N43

SOMME
80
AMIENS

PERONNE

SAINT-QUENTIN

N29

N2

LE BOIS DES
PÊCHEURS 8008

VIVIER AUX CARPES
0200

AISNE
02

A26

MONTDIDIER

LAON

GUIGNICOURT
0206M

A16

A1

N51

BEAUVAIS

OISE
60

SOISSONS

N31

REIMS

NORMANDY

N31

CLERMONT

CAMPIX 6001

SENLIS

A4

EPERNAY

L'ETANG
9500

VAL-D'OISE
95

CHATEAU-THIERRY

VREUX

INCHELIN 7803

LE PARC
DE LA
COLLINE
7706

LA BASE DE
LOISIRS 7703

INTERNATIONAL 7801

PARIS
75

DAVY
CROCKETT
7701

SEINE-ET-MARNE
77

PARIS

N4

N12

YVELINES
78

BOIS DE
BOULOGNE 7502

4 VENTS 7704

EASTERN
FRANCE

DREUX

L'ETANG D'OR
7804M

A10

ESSONNE
91

SAMOREAU
7705M

A5

CHARTRES

ETAMPES

TROYES

LE BOIS DE LA JUSTICE
9100

LES PRÉS
7708M

A5

A6

SENS

PITHIVIERS

LOIRE
VALLEY

ATEAUDUN

MONTARGIS

BURGUNDY

N60

A6

N157

307

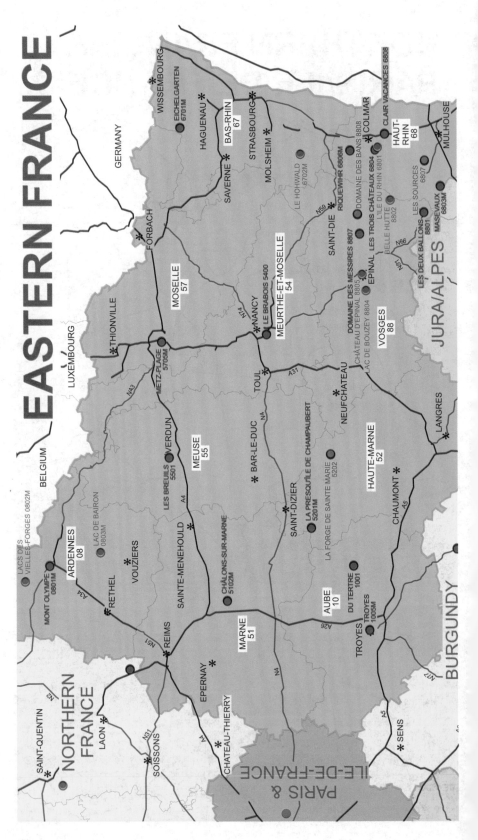

EASTERN FRANCE

GERMANY

LUXEMBOURG

BELGIUM

NORTHERN
FRANCE

PARIS &
ILE-DE-FRANCE

BURGUNDY

JURA/ALPES

SAINT-QUENTIN ✱

LAON ✱

SOISSONS

CHATEAU-THIERRY

EPERNAY ✱

REIMS ✱

RETHEL

VOUZIERS ✱

ARDENNES
08

MONT OLYMPE
0801M

LACS DES
VIELLES-FORGES 0802M

LAC DE BAIRON
0803M

SAINTE-MENEHOULD

CHÂLONS-SUR-MARNE
5102M

MARNE
51

BAR-LE-DUC ✱

MEUSE
55

LES BREUILS
5501

VERDUN

THIONVILLE ✱

FORBACH ✱

METZ-PLAGE
5705M

MOSELLE
57

SAINT-DIZIER

LA PRESQU'ILE DE CHAMPAUBERT
5201M

LA FORGE DE SAINTE MARIE
5202

HAUTE-MARNE
52

CHAUMONT ✱

AUBE
10

DU TERTRE
1001

TROYES
1005M

TROYES

SENS ✱

LANGRES

NEUFCHATEAU ✱

TOUL

NANCY ✱
LE BRABOIS 5400

MEURTHE-ET-MOSELLE
54

SAINT-DIE

LE HOHWALD
6702M

MOLSHEIM ✱

STRASBOURG ✱

SAVERNE

BAS-RHIN
67

HAGUENAU ✱

EICHELGARTEN
6701M

WISSEMBOURG ✱

RIQUEWIHR 6606M

DOMAINE DES BANS 6808

COLMAR ✱

LES TROIS CHATEAUX 6804

L'ILE DU RHIN 6801

CLAR VACANCES 6808

HAUT-
RHIN
68

MULHOUSE

LES SOURCES
6807

MASEVAUX
6803M

LES DEUX BALLONS
6801

BELLE HUTTE
6802

DOMAINE DE MESSIRES 6807

DOMAINE D'EPINAL 8805

EPINAL

CHÂTEAU D'EPINAL 8804

LAC DE BOUZEY 8804

VOSGES
88

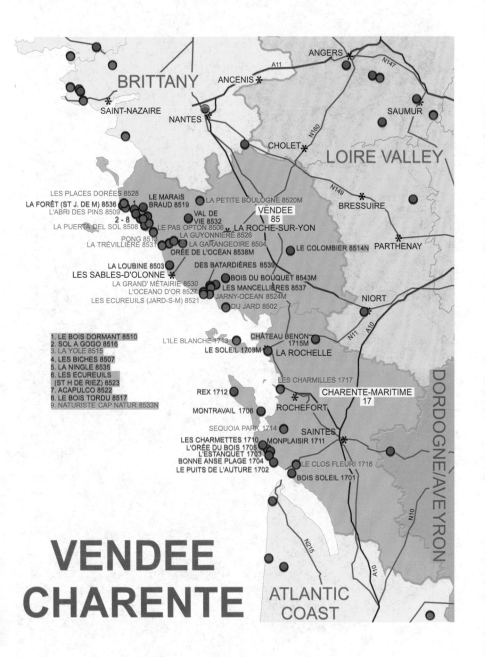

LES PLACES DORÉES 8528
LA FORÊT (ST J. DE M) 8536
L'ABRI DES PINS 8509
LA PUERTA DEL SOL 8508
PONG 8513
LA TRÉVILLIÈRE 8531
LA LOUBINE 8503
LES SABLES-D'OLONNE
LA GRAND' MÉTAIRIE 8530
L'OCEANO D'OR 8527
LES ECUREUILS (JARD-S-M) 8521

LE MARAIS
BRAUD 8519
VAL DE
VIE 8532
LE PAS OPTON 8506
LA GUYONNIÈRE 8526
LA GARANGEOIRE 8504
ORÉE DE L'OCÉAN 8538M

DES BATARDIÈRES 8539
BOIS DU BOUQUET 8543M
LES MANCELLIÈRES 8537
JARNY-OCEAN 8524M
DU JARD 8502

ANGERS
ANCENIS ✳
SAINT-NAZAIRE ✳
NANTES
CHOLET ✳

BRITTANY

SAUMUR

LOIRE VALLEY

LA PETITE BOULOGNE 8520M
VENDÉE
85
LA ROCHE-SUR-YON
LE COLOMBIER 8514N

BRESSUIRE
PARTHENAY

NIORT

1. LE BOIS DORMANT 8510
2. SOL A GOGO 8516
3. LA YOLE 8515
4. LES BICHES 8507
5. LA NINGLE 8535
6. LES ECUREUILS
   (ST H DE RIEZ) 8523
7. ACAPULCO 8522
8. LE BOIS TORDU 8517
9. NATURISTE CAP NATUR 8533N

L'ILE BLANCHE 4713
LE SOLEIL 1709M

REX 1712

MONTRAVAIL 1706

SEQUOIA PARK 1714

LES CHARMETTES 1710
L'ORÉE DU BOIS 1705
L'ESTANQUET 1703
BONNE ANSE PLAGE 1704
LE PUITS DE L'AUTURE 1702

CHÂTEAU BENON
1715M
LA ROCHELLE

LES CHARMILLES 1717

CHARENTE-MARITIME
17
ROCHEFORT

SAINTES

MONPLAISIR 1711

LE CLOS FLEURI 1716
BOIS SOLEIL 1701

DORDOGNE/AVEYRON

VENDEE
CHARENTE

ATLANTIC
COAST

KEY TO ALL MAPS

SITE NAME (ABBREVIATED) &
ALAN ROGER'S NUMBER

ALL YEAR ROUND SITE

ALAN ROGERS TRAVEL SERVICE SITE

ALAN ROGERS TRAVEL SERVICE SITE
ALL YEAR ROUND

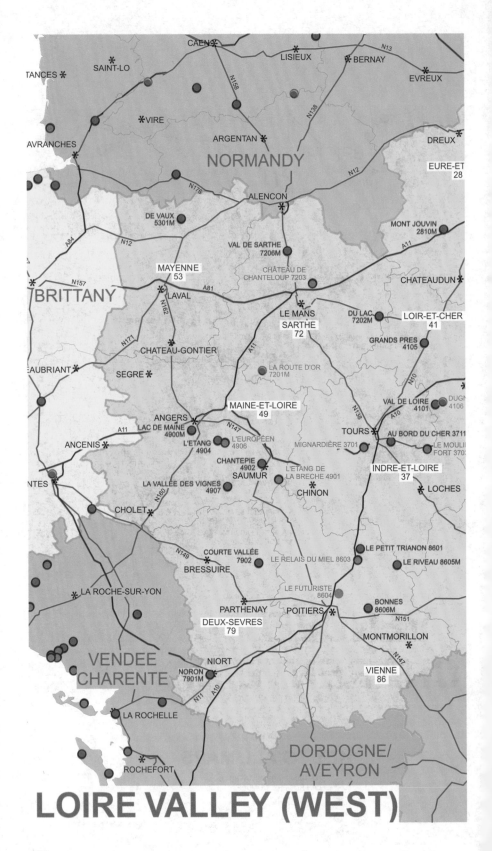

LISIEUX

CAEN

BERNAY

SAINT-LO

TANCES

EVREUX

VIRE

DREUX

ARGENTAN

NORMANDY

EURE-ET
28

AVRANCHES

ALENCON

DE VAUX
5301M

MONT JOUVIN
2810M

VAL DE SARTHE
7206M

CHATEAUDUN

MAYENNE
53

CHÂTEAU DE
CHANTELOUP 7203

BRITTANY

LAVAL

LE MANS
SARTHE
72

DU LAC
7202M

LOIR-ET-CHER
41

GRANDS PRES
4105

CHATEAU-GONTIER

LA ROUTE D'OR
7201M

EAUBRIANT

SEGRE

MAINE-ET-LOIRE
49

VAL DE LOIRE
4101

DUGN
4106

ANGERS

L'EUROPÉEN
4906

TOURS

AU BORD DU CHER 3711

LE MOULI
FORT 370

LAC DE MAINE
4900M

MIGNARDIÈRE 3701

ANCENIS

L'ETANG
4904

CHANTEPIE
4902

INDRE-ET-LOIRE
37

SAUMUR

L'ETANG DE
LA BRECHE 4901

NTES

LA VALLÉE DES VIGNES
4907

CHINON

LOCHES

CHOLET

COURTE VALLÉE
7902

LE PETIT TRIANON 8601

LE RELAIS DU MIEL 8603

LE RIVEAU 8605M

BRESSUIRE

LE FUTURISTE
8604

LA ROCHE-SUR-YON

BONNES
8606M

PARTHENAY

POITIERS

DEUX-SEVRES
79

MONTMORILLON

NIORT

VENDEE
CHARENTE

NORON
7901M

VIENNE
86

LA ROCHELLE

DORDOGNE/
AVEYRON

ROCHEFORT

LOIRE VALLEY (WEST)

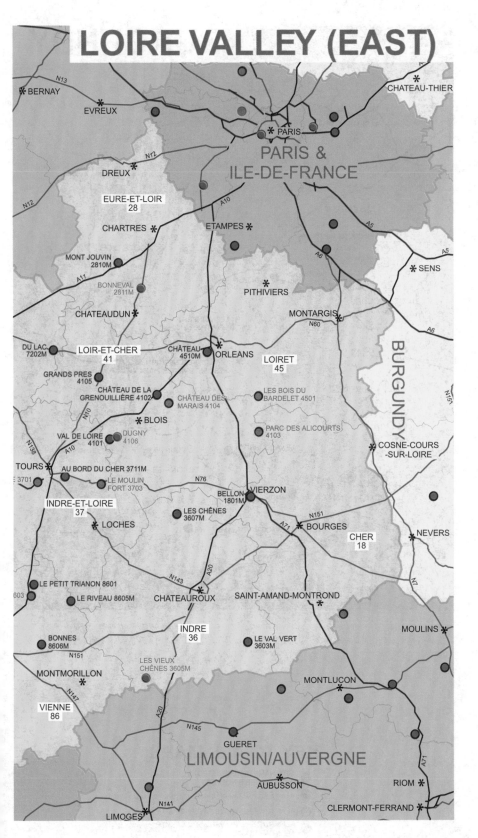

LOIRE VALLEY (EAST)

BERNAY

EVREUX

CHATEAU-THIER

DREUX

PARIS

PARIS &
ILE-DE-FRANCE

EURE-ET-LOIR
28

CHARTRES

ETAMPES

SENS

MONT JOUVIN
2810M

BONNEVAL
2811M

PITHIVIERS

CHATEAUDUN

MONTARGIS

N60

A6

DU LAC
7202M

LOIR-ET-CHER
41

CHÂTEAU
4510M

ORLEANS

LOIRET
45

BURGUNDY

GRANDS PRES
4105

CHÂTEAU DE LA
GRENOUILLIÈRE 4102

CHÂTEAU DES
MARAIS 4104

LES BOIS DU
BARDELET 4501

N151

BLOIS

VAL DE LOIRE
4101

DUGNY
4106

PARC DES ALICOURTS
4103

COSNE-COURS
-SUR-LOIRE

TOURS

E 3701

AU BORD DU CHER 3711M

LE MOULIN
FORT 3703

N76

BELLON-
1801M

VIERZON

INDRE-ET-LOIRE
37

LES CHÊNES
3607M

N151

BOURGES

NEVERS

LOCHES

CHER
18

LE PETIT TRIANON 8601

N143

A20

603

LE RIVEAU 8605M

CHATEAUROUX

SAINT-AMAND-MONTROND

MOULINS

BONNES
8606M

N151

INDRE
36

LE VAL VERT
3603M

MONTMORILLON

LES VIEUX
CHÊNES 3605M

MONTLUCON

VIENNE
86

N147

A20

N145

GUERET

LIMOUSIN/AUVERGNE

RIOM

AUBUSSON

LIMOGES

N141

CLERMONT-FERRAND

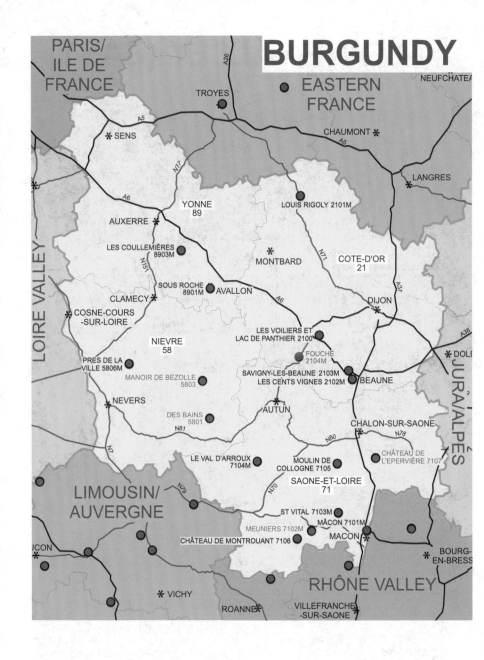

BURGUNDY

PARIS/
ILE DE
FRANCE

EASTERN
FRANCE

NEUFCHATEA

TROYES

CHAUMONT *

* SENS

LANGRES *

LOUIS RIGOLY 2101M

YONNE
89

AUXERRE *

LES COULLEMIÈRES
8903M

MONTBARD

COTE-D'OR
21

SOUS ROCHE
8901M ● AVALLON

CLAMECY *

* COSNE-COURS
-SUR-LOIRE

DIJON
*

LOIRE VALLEY

NIEVRE
58

LES VOILIERS ET
LAC DE PANTHIER 2100

FOUCHÉ
2104M

* DOLE

JURA/ALPES

PRES DE LA
VILLE 5806M

SAVIGNY-LES-BEAUNE 2103M
LES CENTS VIGNES 2102M ● BEAUNE

MANOIR DE BEZOLLE
5803

NEVERS

DES BAINS
5801
N81

AUTUN

CHALON-SUR-SAONE
*

CHÂTEAU DE
L'EPERVIÈRE 7107

LE VAL D'ARROUX
7104M

MOULIN DE
COLLOGNE 7105

SAONE-ET-LOIRE
71

LIMOUSIN/
AUVERGNE

ST VITAL 7103M

MACON 7101M

MEUNIERS 7102M

CHÂTEAU DE MONTROUANT 7106

MACON
*

BOURG-
EN-BRESS

UCON
*

RHÔNE VALLEY

* VICHY

ROANNE *

VILLEFRANCHE
-SUR-SAONE

KEY TO ALL MAPS

● SITE NAME (ABBREVIATED) &
  ALAN ROGER'S NUMBER
● ALL YEAR ROUND SITE
● ALAN ROGERS TRAVEL SERVICE SITE
● ALAN ROGERS TRAVEL SERVICE SITE
  ALL YEAR ROUND

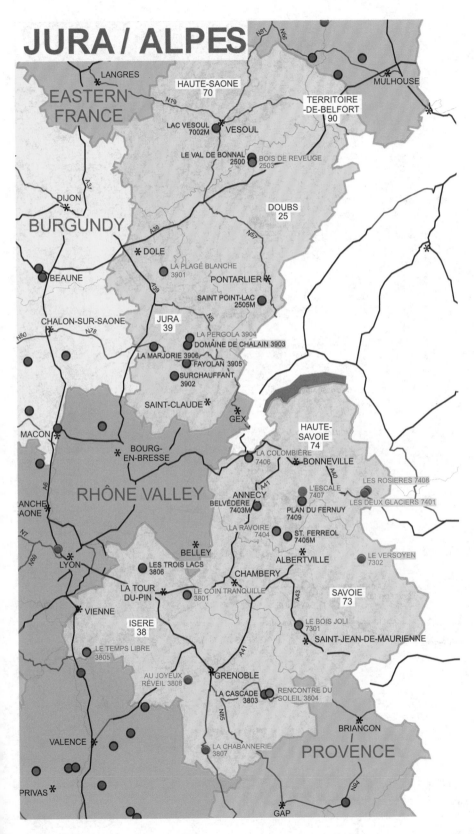

JURA / ALPES

EASTERN FRANCE

LANGRES

HAUTE-SAONE
70

N51 N66

MULHOUSE

TERRITOIRE
-DE-BELFORT
90

N19

LAC VESOUL
7002M   VESOUL

LE VAL DE BONNAL
2500   BOIS DE REVEUGE
2503

DIJON

BURGUNDY

A31   A36

DOUBS
25

N57

DOLE

LA PLAGÉ BLANCHE
3901

PONTARLIER

BEAUNE

A39

SAINT POINT-LAC
2505M

CHALON-SUR-SAONE

N78   N80

JURA
39

N5

LA PERGOLA 3904
DOMAINE DE CHALAIN 3903

LA MARJORIE 3906
FAYOLAN 3905
SURCHAUFFANT
3902

SAINT-CLAUDE

GEX

HAUTE-
SAVOIE
74

MACON

N7   A6

BOURG-
EN-BRESSE

RHÔNE VALLEY

LA COLOMBIÈRE
7406

BONNEVILLE

A40

L'ESCALE
7407   LES ROSIERES 7408

A41

ANNECY
BELVÉDÈRE
7403M

LES DEUX GLACIERS 7401

PLAN DU FERNUY
7409

LA RAVOIRE
7404

ST. FERREOL
7405M

BLANCHE
SAONE

N7

N83

BELLEY

LES TROIS LACS
3806

CHAMBERY

ALBERTVILLE

LE VERSOYEN
7302

LYON

LA TOUR
DU-PIN

LE COIN TRANQUILLE
3801

SAVOIE
73

A43

VIENNE

ISERE
38

LE BOIS JOLI
7301

SAINT-JEAN-DE-MAURIENNE

LE TEMPS LIBRE
3805

AU JOYEUX
RÉVEIL 3808

A41

GRENOBLE

LA CASCADE
3803

RENCONTRE DU
SOLEIL 3804

N85

BRIANCON

VALENCE

LA CHABANNERIE
3807

PROVENCE

PRIVAS

N94

GAP

313

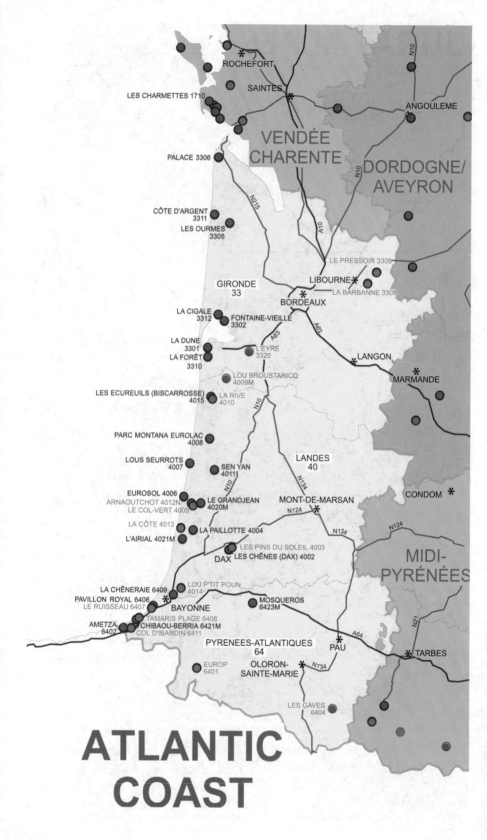

ROCHEFORT

SAINTES

LES CHARMETTES 1710

ANGOULEME

VENDÉE
CHARENTE

DORDOGNE/
AVEYRON

PALACE 3306

N215

CÔTE D'ARGENT
3311

LES OURMES
3305

LE PRESSOIR 3309

GIRONDE
33

LIBOURNE

LA BARBANNE 3308

A10

BORDEAUX

LA CIGALE
3312

FONTAINE-VIEILLE
3302

LA DUNE
3301

L'EYRE
3320

LA FORÊT
3310

A63

A62

LANGON

MARMANDE

LOU BROUSTARICQ
4009M

LES ECUREUILS (BISCARROSSE)
4015

LA RIVE
4010

PARC MONTANA EUROLAC
4008

N10

LANDES
40

LOUS SEURROTS
4007

SEN YAN
4011

EUROSOL 4006

N10

N134

CONDOM

ARNAOUTCHOT 4012N
LE COL-VERT 4005

LE GRANDJEAN
4020M

MONT-DE-MARSAN

N124

LA CÔTE 4013

N124

N124

L'AIRIAL 4021M

LA PAILLOTTE 4004

LES PINS DU SOLEIL 4003

DAX

LES CHÊNES (DAX) 4002

MIDI-
PYRÉNÉES

LA CHÊNERAIE 6409

LOU P'TIT POUN
4014

PAVILLON ROYAL 6406

LE RUISSEAU 6407

BAYONNE

MOSQUEROS
6423M

N21

TAMARIS PLAGE 6408

AMETZA
6402

CHIBAOU-BERRIA 6421M

COL D'IBARDIN 6411

PYRENEES-ATLANTIQUES
64

A64

PAU

TARBES

EUROP
6401

OLORON-
SAINTE-MARIE

N134

LES GAVES
6404

ATLANTIC
COAST

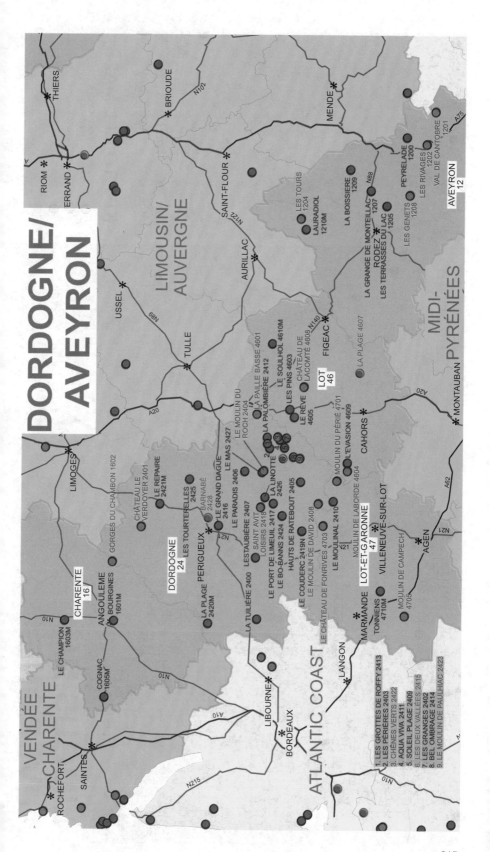

DORDOGNE/AVEYRON

VENDÉE
CHARENTE

ROCHEFORT *
SAINTES *

COGNAC
1605M

LE CHAMPION 1603M

ANGOULEME
1601M

BOURGINES

CHARENTE
16

GORGES DU CHAMBON 1602

CHÂTEAU LE
VERDOYER 2401

LE REPAIRE
2421M

LES TOURTERELLES
2425

BARNABÉ
2428

LE GRAND DAGUE

LA PLAGE 2420M

PERIGUEUX *

LA TUILIÈRE 2400

LESTAUBIÈRE 2407

LE PARADIS 2406

LE MAS 2427

LE MOULIN DU
ROCH 2404

SAINT AVIT
LOISIRS 2418

LA LINOTTE 2426

LE PORT DE LIMEUIL 2417

LE BO-BANNS 2424

HAUTS DE RATEBOUT 2405

LE COUDERC 2419N

LE MOULIN DE DAVID 2408

DORDOGNE
24

LIBOURNE *

BORDEAUX *

LE CHÂTEAU DE FONRIVES 4703

LE MOULINAL 2410

MOULIN DE LABORDE 4604

MOULIN DE CAMPECH
4705

LOT-ET-GARONNE
47

VILLENEUVE-SUR-LOT

MARMANDE *

TONNIENS

MOULIN DE PAULHIAC 2428 4710M

LANGON *

ATLANTIC COAST

1. LES GROTTES DE ROFFY 2413
2. LES PERRIÈRES 2403
3. CHÈNES VERTS 2422
4. AQUA VIVA 2411
5. SOLEIL PLAGE 2409
6. LES DEUX VALLÉES 2415
7. LES GRANGES 2402
8. BEL OMBRAGE 2414
9. LE MOULIN DE PAULHIAC 2423

LIMOGES *

USSEL

TULLE *

A20

LA PAILLE BASSE 4601

LE SOULHOL 4610M

LES PINS 4603

LA PALOMBIÈRE 2412

LE RÊVE
4605

CHÂTEAU DE
LACOMTÉ 4608

MOULIN DU PÉRIÉ 4701

L'EVASION 4609

LOT
46

FIGEAC *

LA PLAGE 4607

CAHORS *

AGEN *

MONTAUBAN *

LIMOUSIN/
AUVERGNE

THIERS *

RIOM *
ERRAND *

BRIOUDE *

SAINT-FLOUR *

AURILLAC *

MENDE *

LES TOURS
1204

LAURADIOL
1210M

LA BOISSIÈRE
1209

LA GRANGE DE MONTEILLAC

RODEZ *
1207

LES TERRASSES DU LAC
1205

PEYRELADE
1200

VAL DE CANTOBRE
1201

LES RIVAGES
1202

LES GENETS
1208

AVEYRON
12

MIDI-
PYRÉNÉES

315

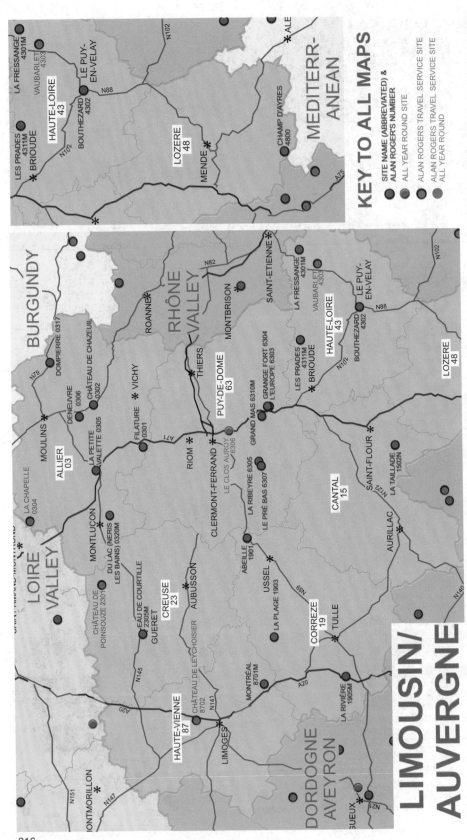

LIMOUSIN/ AUVERGNE

KEY TO ALL MAPS

- SITE NAME (ABBREVIATED) &
  ALAN ROGER'S NUMBER
- ● ALL YEAR ROUND SITE
- ● ALAN ROGERS TRAVEL SERVICE SITE
- ● ALAN ROGERS TRAVEL SERVICE SITE
  ALL YEAR ROUND

Map regions and labels

BURGUNDY

LOIRE VALLEY

RHÔNE VALLEY

MEDITERR- ANEAN

DORDOGNE AVEYRON

ALLIER 03
CREUSE 23
HAUTE-VIENNE 87
CORREZE 19
CANTAL 15
PUY-DE-DOME 63
HAUTE-LOIRE 43
LOZERE 48

Sites and towns

LA CHAPELLE 0304
DOMPIERRE 0317
DENEUVRE 0306
CHÂTEAU DE CHAZEUIL 0302
LA PETITE VALETTE 0305
FILATURE 0301
VICHY
MOULINS
MONTLUÇON
DU LAC (NERIS LES BAINS) 0320M
CHÂTEAU DE POINSOUZE 2301
EAU DE COURTILLE 2305M
GUERET
AUBUSSON
CHÂTEAU DE LEYCHOISIER 8702
MONTRÉAL 8701M
LIMOGES
MONTMORILLON
LA RIVIÈRE 1905M
ABEILLE 1901
USSEL
LA PLAGE 1903
TULLE
LE CLOS AUROY 6306
GRAND MAS 6310M
LA RIBEYRE 6305
LE PRÉ BAS 6307
RIOM
CLERMONT-FERRAND
THIERS
ROANNE
MONTBRISON
SAINT-ETIENNE
GRANGE FORT 6304
L'EUROPE 6303
LES PRADES 4311M
BRIOUDE
LA FRESSANGE 4311M
VAUBARLET 4303
BOUTHEZARD 4302
LE PUY-EN-VELAY
SAINT-FLOUR
LA TAILLADE 1502N
AURILLAC
MENDE
CHAMP D'AYRES 4800
ALE...

Roads

N79, N7, N102, A71, N82, A76, N88, N122, N145, N141, A20, N151, N147, N2..., 68N, N140

316

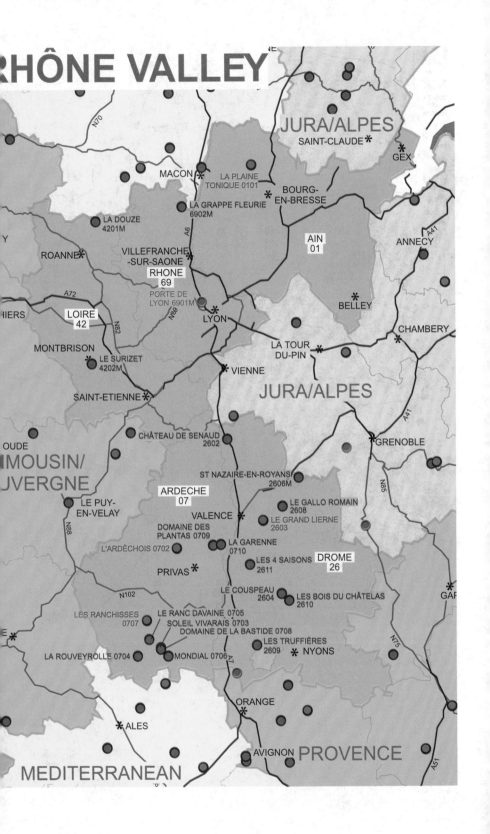

RHÔNE VALLEY

JURA/ALPES
SAINT-CLAUDE ✳
GEX ✳

MACON ✳
LA PLAINE
TONIQUE 0101 ✳
BOURG-
EN-BRESSE
LA GRAPPE FLEURIE
6902M

LA DOUZE
4201M

ROANNE ✳

VILLEFRANCHE
-SUR-SAONE
RHONE
69

AIN
01

ANNECY

PORTE DE
LYON 6901M

LYON ✳

BELLEY ✳

LOIRE
42

HIERS

MONTBRISON

LE SURIZET
4202M

LA TOUR
DU-PIN ✳

CHAMBERY ✳

SAINT-ETIENNE ✳

VIENNE ✳

JURA/ALPES

CHÂTEAU DE SENAUD
2602

GRENOBLE ✳

OUDE

MOUSIN/
UVERGNE

ST NAZAIRE-EN-ROYANS
2606M

ARDECHE
07

LE PUY-
EN-VELAY

VALENCE ✳

LE GALLO ROMAIN
2608

LE GRAND LIERNE
2603

DOMAINE DES
PLANTAS 0709

L'ARDÈCHOIS 0702

LA GARENNE
0710

LES 4 SAISONS
2611

DROME
26

PRIVAS ✳

LE COUSPEAU
2604

LES BOIS DU CHÂTELAS
2610

GAR

N102

LES RANCHISSES
0707

LE RANC DAVAINE 0705
SOLEIL VIVARAIS 0703
DOMAINE DE LA BASTIDE 0708

LES TRUFFIÈRES
2609   ✳ NYONS

LA ROUVEYROLLE 0704

MONDIAL 0706

ORANGE ✳

✳ ALES

AVIGNON   PROVENCE

MEDITERRANEAN

317

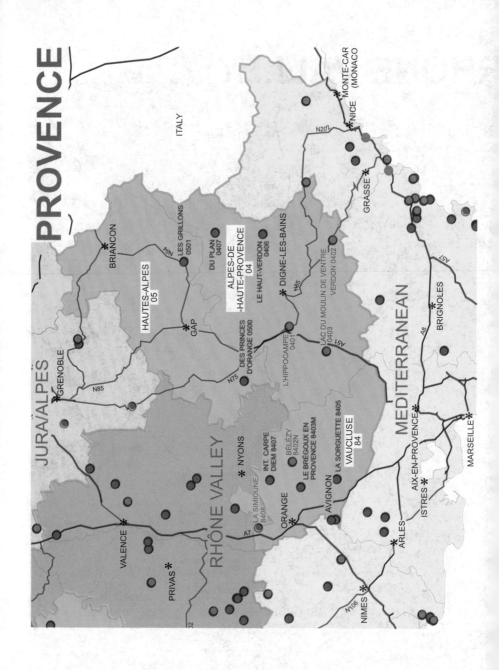

PROVENCE

ITALY

MONTE-CAR
(MONACO
NICE

GRASSE

N201

BRIANÇON

LES GRILLONS
0501

N94

HAUTES-ALPES
05

DU PLAN
0407

ALPES-DE
-HAUTE-PROVENCE
04

LE HAUT-VERDON
0406

DIGNE-LES-BAINS

N85

MEDITERRANEAN

GAP

DES PRINCES
D'ORANGE 0500

N75

L'HIPPOCAMPE
0401

LAC DU MOULIN DE VENTRE
VERDON 0402

A51

LAC DU MOULIN DE VENTRE
0403

A57

BRIGNOLES

A8

GRENOBLE

N85

JURA/ALPES

RHÔNE VALLEY

NYONS

INT. CARPE
DIEM 8407

BÉLÉZY
8402N

LE BRÉGOUX EN
PROVENCE 8403M

LA SORGUETTE 8405

VAUCLUSE
84

AIX-EN-PROVENCE

MARSEILLE

LA SIMIOUNE
8408

ORANGE

AVIGNON

ISTRES

VALENCE

A7

ARLES

PRIVAS

2

N106

NIMES

318

CORSICA

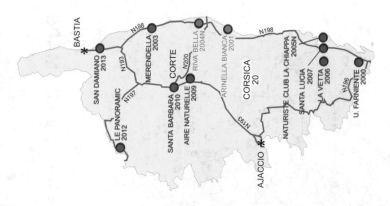

- SAN DAMIANO 2013 ✳
- BASTIA ✳
- MERENDELLA 2003
- LE PANORAMIC 2012
- N197
- N193
- N198
- SANTA BARBARA 2010
- AIRE NATURELLE 2009
- CORTE
- N200
- RIVA BELLA 2004N
- ARINELLA BIANCA 2001
- CORSICA 20
- N198
- NATURIST CLUB LA CHIAPPA 2005N
- SANTA LUCIA 2007
- LA VETTA 2006
- U. FARNIENTE 2000
- N196
- AJACCIO ✳
- N193

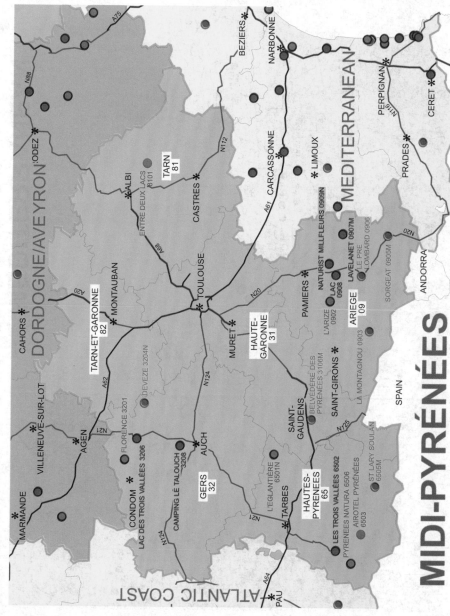

MIDI-PYRÉNÉES

- CAHORS ✳
- DORDOGNE/AVEYRON ✳ RODEZ ✳
- A75
- N88
- BEZIERS ✳
- NARBONNE ✳
- ALBI ✳
- ENTRE DEUX LACS 8101
- TARN 81
- N112
- CARCASSONNE ✳
- CASTRES ✳
- LIMOUX ✳
- PERPIGNAN ✳
- N116
- CERET ✳
- PRADES ✳
- MEDITERRANEAN
- TARN-ET-GARONNE 82
- MONTAUBAN
- A20
- A68
- A61
- NATURIST MILLFLEURS 0909N
- TOULOUSE
- N20
- PAMIERS ✳
- LAC 0908
- LAVELANET 0907M
- LE PRE LOMBARD 0906
- MURET ✳
- HAUTE-GARONNE 31
- L'ARIZE 0902
- ARIEGE 09
- SORGEAT 0905M
- N20
- ANDORRA
- VILLENEUVE-SUR-LOT ✳
- AGEN ✳
- A62
- A20
- DEVEZE 3204N
- N124
- BELVEDERE DES PYRÉNÉES 3106M
- SAINT-GIRONS ✳
- LA MONTAGNOU 0903
- SPAIN
- MARMANDE ✳
- N21
- FLORENCE 3201
- CONDOM ✳
- LAC DES TROIS VALLÉES 3206
- CAMPING LÉ TALOUCH 3208
- AUCH
- GERS 32
- L'EGLANTIÈRE 6501N
- SAINT-GAUDENS
- N125
- ST LARY SOULAN 6505M
- N124
- TARBES
- HAUTES-PYRÉNÉES 65
- LES TROIS VALLÉES 6502
- PYRÉNÉES NATURA 6506
- AIROTEL PYRÉNÉES 6503
- N21
- A64
- PAU
- ATLANTIC COAST

319

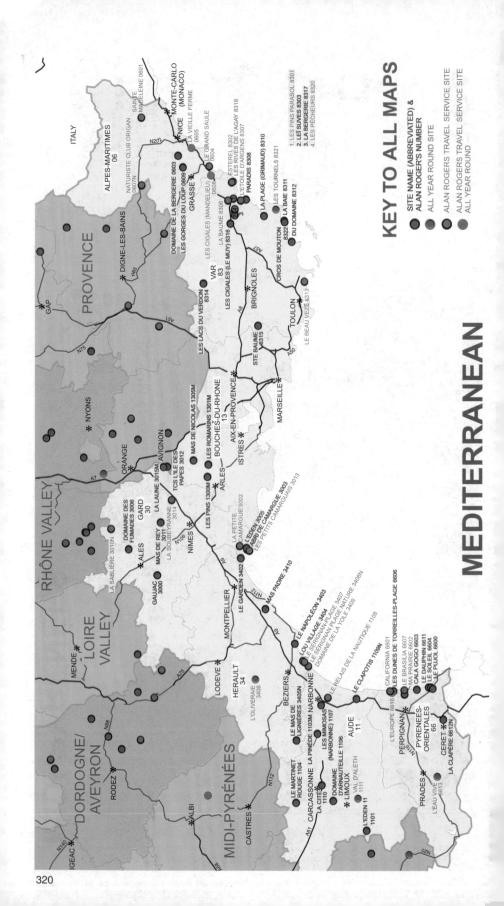

MEDITERRANEAN

KEY TO ALL MAPS

● SITE NAME (ABBREVIATED) &
  ALAN ROGER'S NUMBER

● ALL YEAR ROUND SITE

● ALAN ROGERS TRAVEL SERVICE SITE

● ALAN ROGERS TRAVEL SERVICE SITE
  ALL YEAR ROUND

1. LES PINS PARASOL 8301
2. LEI SUVES 8303
3. LA BERGERIE 8317
4. LES PÊCHEURS 8320

ITALY

ALPES-MARITIMES
06

NATURISTE CLUB ORIGAN 0607N

PROVENCE

DIGNE-LES-BAINS

SAINTE MADELEINE 0601
MONTE-CARLO (MONACO)
NICE
LA VIEILLE FERME 0605
DOMAINE DE LA BERGERIE 0603
LES GORGES DU LOUP 0609
GRASSE
LE GRAND SAULE 0604
LE GRAND SAULE 0608

GAP

NYONS

ORANGE

RHÔNE VALLEY

AVIGNON
TCS L'ILE DES PAPES 3012
LA LAUNE 3015M
LA SOUBEYRANNE 3014
MAS DE NICOLAS 1305M
LES ROMARINS 1301M

ESTEREL 8302
L'ETOILE D'ARGENS 8307
LES RIVES DE L'AGAY 8318
LA PLAGE (GRIMAUD) 8310
LES TOURNELS 8321
LA BAIE 8311
DU DOMAINE 8312
CROS DE MOUTON 8322

PARADIS 8308
LA BAUME 8306
LES CIGALES (MANDELIEU)
LES CIGALES (LE MUY) 8316

VAR
83

LES LACS DU VERDON 8314

BRIGNOLES

TOULON

LE BEAU VEZE 8313

STE BAUME 3315

AIX-EN-PROVENCE

MARSEILLE

BOUCHES-DU-RHONE
13

MAS DE REY 3011
GALLAC 3000
DOMAINE DES FUMADES 3006
LA SABLIÈRE 3010N

GARD
30

ALES

NÎMES

LES PINS 1300M
ARLES
ISTRES

LA PETITE CAMARGUE 3002
L'EDEN 3005
ABRI DE CAMARGUE 2003
LES PETITS CAMARGUAIS 3013

LE GARDEN 3402

MAS PADRE 3410

MONTPELLIER

LE NAPOLEON 3463
LOU VILLAGE 3404
LE SERIGNAN-PLAGE 3407
DOMAINE DE LA YOLE 3409
LE SERIGNAN-PLAGE NATURE 3408N
LE RELAIS DE LA NAUTIQUE 1108

LE CLAPOTIS 1109N

LES DUNES DE TORREILLES-PLAGE 6606

MENDE

LOIRE VALLEY

LODEVE

HERAULT
34

L'OLIVERAIE

BEZIERS

LE MAS DE LIGNIÈRES 3406N
LA PINÈDE 1103M
NARBONNE
LES MIMOSAS 1107
LES MIMOSAS (NARBONNE) 1106

AUDE
11

LE MARTINET ROUGE 1104
CARCASSONNE
LA CITÉ 1110
DOMAINE D'ARNAUTEILLE 1106
VAL D'ALETH 1111
L'EDEN 11 1101

CALIFORNIA 6601
L'EUROPE 6616
LE BRASILIA 6607
MA PRAIRIE 6602
CALA GOGO 6603
LE DAUPHIN 6611
LE SOLEIL 6604
LE PUJOL 6600

PERPIGNAN

PYRÉNÉES-ORIENTALES
66

CERET
LA CLAPERE 6612N

PRADES
L'EAU VIVE 6613

DORDOGNE/ AVEYRON

RODEZ

ALBI

MIDI-PYRÉNÉES

CASTRES

FIGEAC

320